WAGE-PRODUCTIVITY RELATIONSHIP

THEORETICAL ISSUES • INTER-INDUSTRY
AND INTER-STATE ANALYSIS

WAGE-PRODUCTIVITY RELATIONSHIP

THEORETICAL ISSUES • INTER-INDUSTRY AND INTER-STATE ANALYSIS

SANJAY SABHARWAL
Lecturer, S.M.D.R.S.D. College
Pathankot

Foreword by

DR. R.S. BAWA
Registrar,
Guru Nanak Dev University, Amritsar

DEEP & DEEP PUBLICATIONS PVT. LTD.
F-159, Rajouri Garden, New Delhi - 110 027

WAGE-PRODUCTIVITY RELATIONSHIP

ISBN 978-81-8450-029-5

Printed in India at NEW ELEGANT PRINTERS
A-49/1, Mayapuri, Phase-I, New Delhi - 110 064

Published by DEEP & DEEP PUBLICATIONS PVT. LTD.,
F-159, Rajouri Garden, New Delhi - 110 027 • Phone : 25435369, 25440916
E-mail : deep98@del3.vsnl.net.in • ddpbooks@yahoo.co.in
Showroom :
2/13, Ansari Road, Daryaganj, New Delhi - 110 002 • Telefax : 23245122

Dedicated to

My Father

&

Teachers

Contents

Foreword

Not much work has been done in examining the wage-productivity relationship in Indian industry in post-reform era. This is an innovative study on the two-way relationship between wages and productivity in India and the variations across industries and across the States. What is unique is that the study focuses on inter-state variations to add a regional dimension to the analysis that was long over-due.

Though there is two-way relationship between wages and productivity yet the lagged effect of wages on labour productivity has been more pronounced. It has been found that the relationship between labour productivity and wage rate during post-reform era has strengthened in many prosperous states. After liberalisation when market forces have more important role to play, the labour productivity has become more responsive to wage rate.

The analysis is comprehensive, competently designed and uses modern econometric techniques to arrive at meaningful economic propositions that contribute to the ongoing debate in the literature on economic liberalization and wage-productivity turn-around during the last decade or so in India.

The study has brought out a number of conclusions with dynamic policy implications on wage-productivity relationship. Some of the important policy implications are need for giving more incentives to workers, efforts for raising productivity by positive involvement and commitment of workers, need for enhancing technical efficiency and encouragement of gain sharing in the form of bonus, etc. The study also establishes the need for active participation of Government in education and training for enhancing productivity and generation of more employment opportunities. It has also stressed the need of realisation on part of employees that only increased productivity is the panacea for getting higher wages and sustaining a better standard of life which can go a long way in improving both productivity and wages.

The conclusions and recommendations of this study demonstrate the maturity of an economic analyst. I am impressed by the originality of approach, clarity of exposition and the analytical rigor of the study.

I am sure that book will be very useful to the teachers, researchers, students and policy-makers who want to see a resurgent India.

DR. R.S. BAWA
Registrar
Guru Nanak Dev University, Amritsar

Preface

The central objective of planning in India in the present era of liberalization and globalization is to initiate a process of development which will raise living standards and open up to the people new opportunities for a richer and more varied life.

India, as a welfare state, is committed to secure for its working population social and economic justice, which can be achieved through the formulation of an appropriate wage policy. The determination of wages and incentives on some rational basis is essential to achieve the goal of higher productivity and sound industrial relations.

The book is aimed at answering the following queries:

(a) Does two-way relationships between wage rate and productivity exist?
(b) Does the wage-productivity relationship vary in different industries?
(c) Does the wage-productivity relationship vary in different states?
(d) In which direction the wage-productivity relationship has moved after liberalisation?
(e) How was the inter-temporal wage-productivity relationship in different states of India?
(f) How was the trend in different economic parameters and productivity indices in major industries at all India level and in all industries of different states and all-India?

Efforts have been made to highlight different problems relating to wage and salary administration and to suggest suitable remedial measures with regard to wage-productivity relationship in Indian industries.

SANJAY SABHARWAL

Acknowledgements

I express my gratitude to a galaxy of intelligentsia who helped me in diverse ways in accomplishing this study. First, I whole-heartedly thank my honourable, learned and renowned teacher, Professor R.S. Bawa (presently Registrar, G.N.D. University, Amritsar), who not only introduced me to this problem but also ungrudgingly spent lot of his invaluable time in critically going through the whole manuscript. Indeed, as to what I owe to him is difficult to put in words. Without his keen interest, untiring involvement and continuous motivation, the study would not have seen light of the day.

I express my deepest gratitude to my esteemed and illustrious teacher Professor P.S. Raikhy (Ex-Head of Punjab School of Economics, G.N.D. University, Amritsar), for his guidance, encouragement, commitment and his patience in accomplishment of this work.

I also place on record my gratitude to my distinguished teacher Professor J.R. Sabharwal who has been closely associated with this study throughout. I, indeed, gained a lot from his technical expertise for which I shall always remain indebted to him.

At various stages of work, Professor A.S. Sethi (Punjab School of Economics, G.N.D. University, Amritsar), has very gracefully extended his kind help and cooperation, and offered concrete suggestions. I remain highly obliged to him also.

Further, I am grateful to Professor Paramjeet Kaur Dhindsa (Head, Punjab School of Economics) for her motivation and guidance which added to the quality of the book.

I am also thankful to Suleyman Ozmucar (Department of Economics, University of Pennsylvania) for his fruitful suggestions.

During the course of the study, I visited a number of institutions/organisations mainly at New Delhi such as Central Statistical Organisation, Delhi School of Economics, National Council of Applied Economic Research, National Productivity Council, Planning Commission of India, Labour Bureau, Delhi & Chandigarh, Punjab University, Chandigarh, Guru Nanak Dev University, Amritsar. I gratefully acknowledged the help rendered by the Librarians and Staff of these institutions/ organisations for extending me access to the research materials available in these libraries.

I am also thankful to S. Sukhdev Singh of Department of Computer Science, G.N.D. University, Mr. Lovejot (Computer Lecturer, MDK Sn. Sec. School, Pathankot) and Mr. Naveen Gupta (Technical Head, Surya Infonet Ltd.) for their computer assistance.

Last, but certainly not the least, I shall remain highly indebted to my respected parents for their blessings and to my wife and daughter for the sacrifices they made and the patience they showed during my study.

SANJAY SABHARWAL

Introduction

The central objective of planning in India in the present era of liberalization and globalization is to initiate a process of development which will raise living standards and open up to the people new opportunities for a richer and more varied life. The urge for economic and social change comes from the fact of poverty and inequalities in income, wealth and opportunities. The elimination of poverty cannot, obviously, be achieved merely by redistributing existing wealth, nor can a programme aiming only at raising production remove existing inequalities. The two have to be considered together; only a simultaneous advance, involving redistribution with growth will create the conditions in which the community can put forth its best efforts for promoting development.

India, as a welfare state, is committed to secure for its working population social and economic justice, which can be achieved through the formulation of an appropriate wage policy. In India, the wage policy has endeavored to strike a balance between the welfare and protection of the working class on the one hand and achievement of over-riding macro-level objectives like higher rate of capital formation, etc. on the other [Shram Bureau (1992)].

Wages are not only of prime consideration for an individual but also to the society as well. "One seeks a fair wage both to fulfil one's basic needs and to feel reassured that one receives a fair portion of the wealth that one works to generate for society. Society, in its turn, feels that it has a duty to ensure a fair wage to every worker, to ward off starvation and poverty, to promote the growth of human resources, and to ensure social justice without which continuous threats to law and order may undermine economic progress" [National Commission on Labour (2002)].

The promotion of economic growth and development and maintenance of sound industrial relations are closely linked to the pattern and level of wages in various sectors of the economy. Rate of employment, productivity and prices undergo change as a result of variations in wages [Bester and Petrakis (2002)]. In the changing system of consumption, production and distribution, the economic environment is, by and large, considered to be the guiding factor for the practioners in determining wages. The various elements of the internal and external character of society and institutional interests play very important role and affect the level of wages [Mohanty (1993)].

In India, concepts of wages have been influenced by the State policy as well as the various judgements of the Supreme Court. The first principle is that there is a minimum wage which, in any event, must be paid irrespective of the extent of profits, the financial conditions of the establishments or the availability of the workmen on lower wages. The minimum wage is independent of the kind of industry and it applies to all alike. It sets the lowest limit below which wages cannot be allowed to fall. The second principle is that wages must be fair, that is, these should be sufficient to provide a standard family with food, shelter, clothing, medical care and education of the children appropriate to the workman but not at exceeding his wage-earning capacity in the class of establishment to which he belongs. A fair wage is thus related to the earning capacity and workload. It must, however, be realized that 'fair wage' is not 'living wage' by which is meant a wage sufficient to provide not only the essentials mentioned above but a fair measure of frugal comfort with an ability to provide for old age and evil days. 'Fair wage' lies between the minimum wage, which must be paid in any event, and the 'living wage' which is the goal [Verma (1987)]. The Central Government set-up Wage Boards to work out a wage structure for the industry concerned keeping in view considerations relating to the need to guarantee a decent minimum wage, the need to facilitate growth of the industry concerned and the need to provide incentive to workers to upgrade skills.

The determination of wages and incentives on some rational basis is essential to achieve the goal of higher productivity and sound industrial relations. On the side of labour, there should be a keen realization of the fact that, in an underdeveloped economy, it cannot build for itself and the community a better life except on the foundations of a higher level of productivity to which it has itself to make a substantial contribution [Sinha and Sawhney (1970)]. Similarly, the Fair Wage Committee, appointed by the Government of India to go into the whole question of wage fixation observed that, "the objective is not merely to determine wages which are fair in abstract, but to see that employment at existing level is not only maintained but, if possible, increased. From this view point it will be clear that the level of wages should enable the industry to maintain production with efficiency" [Sinha and Sawhney (1970)].

International Labour Office (1954) remarked that, "each individual group of workers will feel much more confident of receiving an adequate share of the benefit of higher productivity and will probably feel much disposed to co-operate in efforts to raise productivity if the policy is one of raising money wages as productivity increases." Peterson (1994), who favoured the increase in minimum wages and other forms of government intervention in the labour market, supports the view that in the long-run, "productivity gains are the ultimate source of . . . increases in real living standards."

So there is two-way link between wages and productivity. In one way increase in productivity facilitates increase in wage, on the other way rise in wage induces increase in productivity. The wage productivity relationship can assume the form of a circular self-generating mechanism where increases in productivity lead to increasing wage and an increase in wages motivates the worker to further increase productivity [Bhatnagar (1982)].

In emphasizing the productivity criterion in the domain of wages, the Fair Wage Committee (1948) pointed out that, "the productivity of labour is one of the important factors in determining actual wages." The First Plan while recommending wage increases stressed for the restoration of the pre-war levels of real wages as the first step towards the 'Living Wage' through increased productivity. The Second Plan, in this connection, emphasized that improvement in wages should result mainly from increased productivity. The Third Plan, while highlighting the role of productivity in improving the living standards of worker, observed that neither the exercise of their organized strength in industrial conflict nor laws and the intervention of the state can help the worker much in realizing their aspirations. Their gains can arise only out of the strength and dynamism of the economy, the only enduring basis of which is a rising level of productivity. The Fourth Plan stressed the need for raising the productivity for higher production, more income and for savings and investment. The Fifth Plan remarked that increase in wages should be closely correlated with increase in productivity [Mohanty (1993)]. The Sixth Plan stressed that criteria would have to be evolved by means of tripartite consultations for allowing increases in wages on the basis of productivity [Government of India (1981)]. The thrust of the Seventh Plan was on improvement in capacity utilisation, efficiency and productivity. Labour enters the production process from the supply side as well as from the demand side. The focal point for both aspects is higher productivity because it is through higher productivity that higher real wages can be ensured [Government of India (1987)]. The Eighth Plan strategy stressed that improvement in the productivity of work-force assumes particular significance in our economy where low productivity and low incomes of a large mass of employed persons constitute a problem of much higher dimension than unemployment [Government of India (1992)]. The Ninth Plan stressed that productive work is not merely a means to the ultimate end of economic well-being. It should be seen as an end in itself. It is a basic source of human dignity and self-respect [Government of India (1997)]. The Tenth Plan pointed out that productivity of labour is an essential condition for the prosperity of enterprises and the well-being of the workers and their families. The production facilities at work place, remunerations and attitudes towards work are important in influencing the productivity of labour [Government of India (2002)]. Committee on Sharing Gains of Productivity (1967) also recommended that the productivity norms should bear some 'optimum' relationship with payments. The general consensus of labour economists also favours the close positive relationship between productivity and wages [Mohapatra (1982)]. The Indian National Trade Union Congress, the largest labour front in India, advocated for rise in wages with increasing industrial productivity [Fonesca (1964)]. Even if rise in productivity is not associated with a corresponding increase in wages in the short-run, workers may not be put to disadvantage as prices, in such cases, have the tendency to decline, which will eventually increase their purchasing power. The resultant increase in the national output, on the other hand, can prove an additional advantage to workmen as in a rapidly growing economy, "labour's income can be raised faster and farther through growth of national output than through redistribution of national output" [Reynolds (1959)]. All these views clearly suggest that productivity analysis should occupy a central place in the study of wage problems and policies.

An effort to fill the gap between the existing and the minimum efficiency wage may lead to direct increase in productivity. Here, it may be emphasized that it is the employers who have to play the most vital role in augmenting labour's productivity. It has been said that "average Indian employers have never been serious enough to create the necessary conditions in their enterprises under which productivity of workers will improve" [Sarkar (1961). The single most important factor affecting labour's productivity is the amount and type of technology needed in production in respect of which the employers alone can play the most decisive role [Greenberg (1962)]. Besides, the nature of contributions made by such factors as quality of raw materials, state of operation, capacity utilization, continuity of operation and supervision and managerial skills which so profoundly affect productivity is essentially conditioned by the efforts put in by employers [Singh

(1961)]. Hence the desired effect of introducing minimum efficiency wage may, therefore, fail to be realized so long as the other aspects of the industry are not set in order.

As a criterion for fixing wages, productivity has not so far been taken into account by wage fixing authorities and boards. Inspite of a specific directive in the terms of reference of several wage boards that consideration relating to a fair wages should also take into account the need for linking wage to productivity and the desirability of extending the system of payment by results, most of them have refrained from doing so on account of the practical difficulties involved. Though it is very difficult to establish a workable link between changes in productivity and changes in wage, it was found that there is a fairly close relationship between productivity in the economy as a whole and the rate of change in real wage levels, but that relationship is valid only over a long period of years and not on a short-term basis [Mohanty (1993)]. Sinha and Sawhney (1970) found that a significant rise in wage rate can be secured without jeopardizing the needs of capital formation and harmonious capital-labour relations only if there is adequate advance in productivity.

However, apart from the efforts of labour, the increase in output is also due to other inputs. Papola (1970) remarked that "the connection between productivity and wages is not so close and direct as to act as a stimulus in determining wages." Increase in output may be due to larger inputs of other resources or their improved efficiency or both. Supplies of other inputs have also a strong claim to higher earnings as workers to higher wages. The employers in India, in this regard put more emphasis on linking wages to productivity with the aim of reducing labour cost so as to raise profitability to a higher level. But the employees argue in favour of labour productivity from the point of view of their low wages. Employees have strongly asserted that productivity of labour in India has constantly been on the increase, but the gains were not shared by the workers [Kumar (1964)].

In the absence of any principle governing the distribution of productivity gains among labour, capital and consumer, it is interesting to examine the share of labour in the overall productivity gains in different industries and states in India.

ISSUES AND PROBLEMS IN WAGE POLICY

ILO (1996) analysed three basic problem areas. The first relates to statutory minimum wages. Lack of proper indexation, irregular revisions and weak enforcement rendered statutory minimum wages largely ineffective; a clear basis for fixing minimum wages has been missing; and the practice of setting different minimum wages for the organized and the unorganized sectors legitimized and institutionalized labour market dualism.

The second problem area relates to wage flexibility. While wage flexibility exists in Indian industries, it is of a wrong type. It is linked to inflationary processes and not to changes in productivity and profitability of enterprises.

The third problem area relates to wage-productivity linkage. Wage growth in Indian industries tends to be exogenously determined. Thus, wage-productivity linkage is sustained through adjustments in productivity to autonomous changes in wages. This imparts a labour saving bias to the growth process.

Given this diagnosis of the problems, the interval between wage revisions should be long enough for productivity trends to be discernible; an interval of 5 years is suggested [National Commission on Labour (2002)]. Wage revisions can then be based on the observed productivity trends over the last 5 years. This means that attention will need to be focused on product-wages in times of revision. Productivity in this context should be interpreted to mean productivity in a particular branch of industry. In an individual enterprise, negative productivity trends can be deliberately generated by reducing capacity utilization. For this reason, productivity trends in individual enterprises do not provide a reliable basis for wage adjustments. This does not mean that wage adjustments in all enterprises in a particular branch of industry must be the same. Deviations from the norm can always occur so long as these are determined through collective bargaining.

NEED OF THE STUDY

Following questions, *inter alia,* need to be answered for laying down the objectives of rational wage policy :

(a) Does two-way relationships between wage rate and productivity exist?
(b) Does the wage-productivity relationship vary in different industries?
(c) Does the wage-productivity relationship vary in different states?
(d) Does wages in labour intensive industries are lower than those in capital intensive industries?
(e) In which direction the wage-productivity relationship has moved after liberalisation.
(f) Whether the share of labour in Gross Value Added has increased or decreased?

Present study aims at answering these questions and examines wage-productivity relationship in Indian industry.

OBJECTIVES

The major objectives of the study are :

1. To analyse the trends in different economic parameters and productivity indices in major industries at all-India level.
2. To analyse the trends in different economic parameters and productivity indices in all industries of different states and all-India level.
3. To compare the share of labour in GVA at constant prices in different industries at all-India level.
4. To compare the share of labour in GVA at constant prices in industries of major states and at all-India level.
5. To compare wage rate as well as labour productivity in different industries at all-India level and all-industries at state level.
6. To examine the extent of dependence of wage rate on labour productivity, capital intensity and total factor productivity in major industries at all-India level and all-industries at state level.

7. To analyse the dependence of labour productivity on wage rate and capital intensity in major industries at all-India level and all-industries at state level.
8. To examine the inter-temporal wage-productivity relationship in different states of the country.
9. To analyse the effect of liberalisation on relationship between wage rate and labour productivity in major industries at all-India level and all-industries at state level.

PLAN OF THE STUDY

The study consists of eleven chapters including the present one. Chapter-II examines the theoretical issues concerning wage-productivity relationship. Chapter-III reviews the empirical literature related to the study. Chapter-IV is devoted to the data base and methodology. Trends in economic parameters in Indian industries have been examined in Chapter-V. Partial and total factor productivities in Indian industries have been worked out in Chapter-VI. Trends in economic parameters in Indian states have been carried out in Chapter-VII. Partial and total factor productivities in Indian states have been analysed in Chapter-VIII. Chapter-IX reports the empirical analysis of wage-productivity relationship in Indian industries. In Chapter-X the empirical wage-productivity relationship in Indian states has been carried out. And, finally, Chapter XI presents main findings of the study and the derives policy implications.

2

Wage-Productivity Relationship—Theoretical Issues

While analyzing the relationship between wage and productivity either theoretically or empirically, there should be clarity on the concept of wage as well as productivity.

"Wages are the remuneration for the expenditure of effort on production of goods and services. The effort of wage earner may be physical, mental or a combination of the two; it may be under another's direction or may be of a managerial and decision-making character. But whatever his specific occupation, the wage-earner supplies some form of human contribution to production and wages are reward for his contribution" [Encyclopedia Britannica]. In precise economic terms, wages are the price of labour, and in the absence of control, they are determined like all prices, by supply and demand [Gupta (1985)]. Wages represent the major if not the sole source of money for a large portion of wage-earners and constitute an important element in the cost of production; more often it becomes a source of industrial conflict also. Wage behaviour, therefore, concerns the workers, managers and the policy-makers [Chamber's Encyclopedia].

Wages are also a means of providing income for employees and as cost of doing business to the employer. 'Wages', in the widest sense, also mean any economic compensation paid to the working people by the employer, under some contract for the services rendered by them. Wages thus include family allowances, relief pay, financial support and other benefits. But in narrower sense, wages are the price paid for the services of labour in the process of production and include only the 'performance wages', i.e. 'wage proper.'

The wages of the working class are of great importance to the workers and also to the society as a whole. Wages determine the standards of living of the wage-earner and his family. Higher rates of wages in the economy are indicative of the level of advancement and prosperity in the society while lower wage rates are prevalent in regions which are economically backward and socially depressed. Standard of living of the workers is influenced by the wage rate and their status and position is also determined in the society. In India, progressive and decent rates of wages are very necessary because indirect benefits in the form of social services are either limited or non-existent. Wages also act as an instrument for achieving increased production through higher efficiency and greater satisfaction. It also relieves individuals from financial worries and thus enables them to put forward the best efforts on their jobs. Individuals are likely to work effectively if the prevailing reward system provides equitable remuneration for their efforts. In other words, wages constitute a major factor in attracting, stimulating and retaining employees at all levels. Wages are the source of, as well as key to the solution of most of the labour problems.

There may generally a direct relation between real wages and money wages. The labourer's demand is more for real wage and not money wage because real wage measures the purchasing power of his income. A wage policy will have to aim at a progressive rise in real wages. As a result of increase in prices, there is an erosion in the wage levels in real terms, and in order to prevent such an erosion, dearness allowance is paid and it is linked to the consumer price index. There are various methods of linking the consumer price index with the dearness allowance and determining the extent of neutralisation of price rise through payment of D.A. Some enterprises may pay a fixed dearness allowance and also a variable dearness allowance linked to the consumer price index. Some pay dearness allowance only linked to the consumer price index [National Commission on Labour (2002)].

ISSUES REGARDING WAGE DIFFERENTIALS

The wage differentials that build up a wage structure may be of different kinds, like occupational differentials, inter-plant wage differentials, inter-industry wage differentials and differentials based on age and sex, etc.

1. Since different occupations require different qualifications, different degree of skills and responsibility, so wages may be fixed on the basis of the differences in occupations and various degrees of skills.
2. There are considerable disparities in inter-firm wage rates which may be due to differences in technological advance, financial capacity, age and size of the firm, managerial efficiency, relative advantages and disadvantages of supply of raw materials, power and availability of transport facilities. According to Reynolds, "the differences in the efficiency of equipment, supervision and other non-labour factors are responsible for inter-firm wage differentials."
3. Inter-area or regional differences may arise when workers in the same industry and in the same occupation group, living in different geographical areas, are paid different wages. The industry mix varies from one area to another, and for this reason alone, the general average of wages would be expected to vary [Clark (1957)].
4. The inter-industry differentials reflect skill differentials. The industry paying higher wages have mostly been industries with a large number of skilled workers while those industries paying less have been industries with a large proportion of unskilled and semi-skilled workers [Dunlop (1957)]. Other factors influencing inter-industry differentials are the extent of

unionization, the structure of product markets, the ability to pay, labour-capital ratio and the stage of development of the industry [Sinha (1971)].

5. Wage differentials based on sex and age may occur due to the differences in the personal characteristics (age or sex) of workers who work in the same plant and the same occupation.

METHODS OF WAGE DETERMINATION

Many theories have been advanced to explain the nature of wages. The first of them was the subsistence theory of wages, also called the "iron law of wages," of which David Ricardo was one of the main exponents. The theory maintains that wages cluster around the bare subsistence level of workers. A wage rate much above the subsistence level causes an increase in the number of workers; competition will then lead to a depression of wages back toward the cost of subsistence. Wages that are below subsistence reduce the size of the working population; in that case competition will raise wages, but only up to the subsistence level again. In the surplus-value theory as propounded by Karl Marx, the value produced by the worker in excess of what is paid in wages is called surplus value. The surplus value, exacted from the worker, constitutes the capitalist's profit. The wage-fund theory is that wages are advanced out of a fixed fund of capital, from which an excess withdrawal, either through legislation or through union pressure, will ultimately reduce the amount available for other workers. Any increase in wages would also have to be taken out of profits, and their reduction would cause a decline in savings, which provide the capital from which the wage fund is derived. The marginal-productivity theory maintains that employers will only pay a wage that is, at most, equal to the amount of extra value-added to the total product by one additional worker. The bargaining theory modifies the marginal-productivity theory by taking into consideration other factors (e.g., laws and social and political changes) that might affect the determination of wage levels and by acknowledging that certain basic assumptions (equal bargaining power of employer and employee, free competition between the two, and mobility of labour) that characterize the marginal-productivity theory do not hold in present economic system [Stonier and Hague (1957)].

After First World War, due to growth of unionism, collective bargaining has become an important method of wage fixation, even though state intervention, adjudication machinery and wage boards retain their importance in the wage system.

(1) Compulsory Adjudication

Adjudication machinery is to regulate wage lever in the course of settlement of disputes which occur when the workers are organized. This machinery may not be efficient for wage regulation in unorganized sector. Moreover, diversities in the approach of different adjudicators may lead to diversity in their awards. Also their decisions are enforced by the state and may not depend upon the parties goodwill and cooperation.

(2) Wage Boards

The basic task of the Wage Boards is to work out a wage structure for the industry concerned keeping in view considerations relating to the need to guarantee a reasonable minimum wage, the need to facilitate growth of the industry concerned and the need to provide incentive to workers to upgrade skills. The wage boards may follow the following principles during the wage fixation : (1) productivity of labour; (2) prevailing rates of wages; (3) level of national income and its distribution; (4) place of industry in the economy of the country; (5) needs of the industry in developing economy; (6) requirement of social justice; and (7) desirability of extending the system of payment by results.

(3) Collective Bargaining

Generally there is very little clear thinking as to what portion of the total wage should be left to be determined by the employer beyond the minimum wage and how much would be determined by collective bargaining. However, under collective bargaining, efforts can be made to settle industrial disputes pertaining to wages without recourse to legal procedures and prolonged and avoidable litigations which perpetrate ill-will and tensions. The cooperation that will emerge out of such combined efforts of management and employees are bound to have a healthy effect on productivity. Thus, collective bargaining may play a major and a decisive role in maintaining industrial harmony and setting of individual disputes, and can prove be an effective determinant of wages [Employer's Federation of India (1971)].

ISSUES AND CRITERIA FOR WAGE FIXATION

Though the collective bargaining was accepted as the normal method for wage fixation, the following criteria may broadly be taken into consideration at the bargaining table during wage fixation.

(1) The Needs of the Workers

The needs of the worker and his family are the main consideration in fixing wages. The needs are considered in terms of an adequate diet, clothing, bedding, footwear requirements, fuel and lighting and miscellaneous requirements. The needs should be reckoned in terms of three equivalent adult consumption units, i.e. in terms of a family containing of husband, wife and two children below twelve years of age [Fair Wage Committee (1948)].

(2) Capacity of Industry to Pay

In fixing a minimum wage for the worker, the capacity to pay is not a prime consideration. This criterion has been applied as indirect test rather than as a positive determining factor of the minimum wage [Sinha (1971)]. In fixing wages higher than the minimum level, the capacity to pay may be an important consideration [Fair Wage Committee (1948), I.L.O. (1956) and Subramanian (1970)].

(3) Prevailing Rates of Wages

The prevailing rates of wages in the locality or neighbouring localities may be considered in the fixation of minimum rates of wages as otherwise in low wage pockets there will be no hope for the workers to raise to a standard of living above the poverty line or subsistence standard. On the other hand, in arriving at a fair wage this is an important consideration. If in an industry or locality wage is fixed in total disregard of the rates prevailing in the same or neighbouring localities, it would cause disruption in employment, workers striving to move from one industry to another, from one unit of an industry to another and from one locality to another, causing tensions and disequilibrium.

(4) Level of National Income

The problem of wages of the industrial workers can not be considered in isolation. The prosperity of the industrial workers and the community would have to advance simultaneously. Care must be taken to ensure that in adopting measures for the betterment of industry or of industrial workers, the interests of the community as a whole are not overlooked [Royal Commission of Labour (1969)].

(5) Cost of Living

The justification of this criterion is that the real wages of workers may not be allowed to fall by price increase. Adjustments in wage levels become necessary due to increase in the cost of living. The trade unions also claim that wages must be flexible enough to adjust themselves to increase and decrease in the cost of living [Fonesca (1964)]. The Fair Wage Committee (1948) emphasized that it is clearly necessary to continue to pay dearness allowance to neutralize wholly or at least substantially, the increase in the cost of living. The criterion of 'cost of living' as such has become the most important factor while there is bargaining for an increase in wages. Practically, every wage claim that has been made has stressed this factor [Dunlop (1957)]. The cost of living becomes an inescapable criterion during the time of rising prices. It should be used not automatically but with a measure of restraint, discretion and discernment [Mohanty (1993)].

(5) Productivity

The word 'productivity' has become a catch word especially in the industrial field. The term has become so popular that the users do not bother for its precise definition. The elusive concept of productivity is surrounded by enormous confusions. Inspite of volume of literature on the subject, people use the same term differently. The different schools of thoughts have given different tilts to the concept according to their needs, purposes and conventions.

Too often the term 'productivity' is viewed as the ratio between output and input both measured in value and volume and at times it is referred to as multipronged attack on waste, optimum use of the tools of production to keep the total operating cost at the minimum and to allow the volume of production to swell up [Bhaduri (1971)].

For all practical purposes it is sufficient to understand 'productivity' in terms of the rate of efficiency with which resources at hand are converted into the production of goods and services which satisfy human wants in the society. If a given set of inputs brings out a significant change in the volume of output without quality deterioration, productivity may be said to have gone up. Further, if same output could be produced at lesser amount of inputs, productivity is said to have risen. In common parlance the term 'productivity' is used to refer to the ratio between input and output and to measure the economic soundness of means. Technically, it can be understood as 'production per factor unit'. According to Dictionary of Management, 'productivity' is "output per unit of input" [Singh and Kitchlu (1991)]. In the International Dictionary of Management, 'productivity' is "relationship between input and output of an individual unit input being measured in men, machines, materials and output in products and services" [Singh and Kitchlu (1991)]. Dictionary of Economics defines 'productivity' as "relationship between output of goods and services and the inputs of resources (Factors of Production) used to produce them" [Singh and Kitchlu (1991)]. Productivity is primarily an attitude of mind, an attitude welcoming a change for the better, an attitude of looking at things afresh so as to explore the scope for improvement; an effort to make the optimum use of available resources towards the achievement of targets [Shah (1981)].

Thus, 'productivity' is the ratio between input in the form of manpower, machine, material and management and output in the form of goods and services produced. 'Productivity' is different from 'production' because it concerns not how much is produced but rather how efficiently the production is carried on. The increase in production can be achieved at any cost by employing more men, materials or money with no increase in productivity, but increase in productivity involves production at a lower cost by saving time, eliminating waste and utilizing the same quantities of the factors efficiently and effectively.

The term productivity is sometimes considered as synonymous with efficiency. The word 'efficiency' does embrace the idea of productivity, but it goes beyond it in the sense that it expresses an aptitude or capacity or the quality of the input, the productivity of which is under consideration, while productivity induces the idea of the relationship between output and input (factors) [National Productivity Council (1955)].

Productivity is understood either in terms of partial productivity or total factor productivity. In partial productivity, output is related to a single input, ignoring other factors, where as in total factor productivity output is related to all inputs combined. There is a lot of controversy centering on the nature of definition of 'productivity'. The trickiest question is : should productivity be taken in the sense of total factor productivity or partial productivity? In the industrial context, goods and services are produced by combinations of many factors or inputs which mean that the output of these goods and services can not be used as a measure of productivity of any one of the inputs. "The output is only a measure of the joint power of inputs to achieve results" [Smith (1973)]. Neither input data nor output data can provide an analyst with conclusive evidence on the productivity of any one of the inputs. Though total factor productivity, i.e., change in effectiveness of production attributable to all factors is more sensible, partial productivity, i.e. productivity in terms of a single factor is more meaningful for policy purpose. But it is extremely difficult to ascertain the role of a single factor in productivity change. There have been, therefore, attempts to measure both total and partial productivities.

The exponents of the theory of "Productivity of Labour" regard labour productivity as one of the basic indicators of economic development, as one of the determinants of the national income and as an important tool for the analysis of economic and social problems. According to European Productivity Council, "Productivity is an attitude of mind. It is the mentality of progress of the constant improvement of that which exists. It is the certainty of being able to do better today than yesterday. It is the constant adoption of economic and social life to changing conditions. It is the continual effort to apply new techniques and new methods. It is the faith in human progress" [Srivastav (1982)].

However, productivity is not merely labour productivity. Labour productivity can be improved without economizing on the use of labour as an input. By seeking the co-operation and commitment of workers and by sharpening their skills and attitudes, employers can raise productivity through better use of other resources. The common interpretations of productivity in recent years include the following :

1. Waste reduction in all forms.
2. Working intelligently, not merely putting in hard work.
3. People will take action for productivity improvement only when they are convinced about the rationale and usefulness of the action.
4. Positive involvement and commitment of workers and unions.
5. Change as a continuous process in terms of technology, materials, products, processes, etc.
6. Productivity is a multi-dimensional concept. It depends on quantity, quality and features of products and the efficiency and effectiveness with which they are produced.

Productivity in any establishment does not depend wholly on the efficiency of the worker. The level of productivity or rate of productivity growth also depends upon organizational and technical factors like, proper supervision, type of equipment, layout of the factory and system of assigning functions, etc. The paradox between fact and custom in the use of term 'productivity' has been nicely put by the German statisticians in the following words : "it is customary to call productivity the result of dividing output by input of the factor labour, it should be continually emphasized that . . . output results from a combination of all the factors of production, it would be equally interesting to relate its output to any of the other factors" [Frust, Raabe and Sperling (1962)].

"Productivity isn't everything, but in the long-run it is almost everything. A country's ability to improve its standard of living over time depends almost entirely on its ability to raise its output per worker" [Krugman (1996)]. The economic performance of any country, the competitiveness of its businesses, and the standard of living of its people depend primarily on productivity. Over time, the higher the rate of productivity growth, the greater will be the competitiveness of business, and the higher will be the standard of living of the people it employs. As a source of growth, it has moved to center stage in the analysis of growth of developing economies in recent years. Earlier the focus was mainly on the growth of capital through greater mobilization of resources. As investment levels have increased substantially in most developing countries and the scope for further increases becomes limited, attention has naturally turned to productivity improvements, which offer a complimentary route to growth by getting more out of limited resources.

Profitability is also not synonymous with productivity, though as an index of productivity, profitability is regarded both as a measure of economic efficiency and as management guide to greater economic efficiency. The change in physical productivity is one of the many indicators of profitability. In the competitive environment, the most sustainable source of profitability is constant productivity improvement. In other words, profitability is the fleeting reward of productivity improvement. When firms increase their profits, there are dual benefits to workers : (1) more and better products and services are sold to consumers, and (2) more funds are made available from retained earnings to pay workers and to improve tools, equipment, and training. When firms are successful, company owners aren't the only ones who benefit. Workers also receive higher wages and more services, including training, better equipment, and fringe benefits. However, a wage increase which occurs because of government regulation or union intervention may not be productivity induced.

In the situation of inflation, linking wage to productivity is highly desirable, because the main cause of inflation is high cost of production. Thus, only through increased productivity can there be sustained increases in real income and rising levels of economic well-being. The implication of this basic insight is that productivity should become the organizing principle of economic policy. Indeed, the bottom line for economic policy-makers should become productivity. This means that all aspects of economic policy, at both the macro and micro-levels, should be analyzed from the perspective of productivity growth. While policies which have negative effects on productivity should not be *a priori* excluded if they have important equity implications, they should be closely scrutinized and their cost in terms of foregone productivity gains made explicit. A pro-economic growth approach which is pro-technology, pro-investment, and pro-education is the best avenue to productivity improvement. Without strong economic growth, potential or trend productivity growth cannot be realized. Without technical progress, trend productivity growth will fall off. Without new investment in plant and equipment, advances in technology cannot be used in the production process. Without more education, the workforce will not be able to either advance the state of technology or use new equipment. In the context of an economy with widespread unemployment and under-employment and also with the simultaneous phenomenon of capital deepening and slow rate of growth of employment in the organized manufacturing sector, the importance of knowledge of trends in wages and productivity can not be over-emphasized.

Productivity and wages can be discussed meaningfully only when they are studied together. Where increases in productivity outstrip increases in wages or compensation, the excess benefits of higher productivity go to the employer. But where wages do not grow in correspondence with productivity but overtake increases in productivity, there is every possibility of a wage-push inflation being triggered off, first, in the initial stages, in an endemic form, but soon in a pandemic form. How soon such wage-push inflation as in the case of other cost-push inflation spreads, of course, depends on by what measure productivity lags behind wages on account of the wage rise and also on the strength of the forward and backward linkages such an industry has with other industries and sectors [Mahindra (1972)]. In a situation where increases in wages exceed that of productivity, not only will there be deterioration in economic competitiveness but there will also be an increasing likelihood of a wage-price inflation spiral. In such an event, the price increases are likely to leapfrog wage increases, leading to an erosion in the purchasing power of workers' wages [Wong and Heng (2001)].

Wages in the organized sector are supposed to be higher than in the unorganized sector because productivity in the former is also higher. Conversely, for giving a sense of direction to wage policy, it is extremely crucial that the movements in productivity are marked and kept account of. It can not be said that a given wage increase would lead to wage-push inflation unless simultaneously it is examined whether a corresponding increase in productivity has more or less compensated the increase in wages, and whether productivity of management, capital, fuel and so forth have remained the same [Mahindra (1972)].

It has already been observed that wages in the organized sector are decided mostly by collective bargaining, and much depends upon the bargaining strength of the management and trade unions. Generally, the practice has been to relate the revision in wages, allowances of all types and other facilities given to workers with time. So far wage rises have not been linked to productivity and profitability conditions. In developing countries like India, due to liberalisation, increase in competition puts a downward pressure on prices and profits. So firms may try to increase their technical efficiency, reduce their costs, and have higher productivity of labour and better capacity utilization. But the ability to put new ideas and technology into productive activities requires resources, skills and right kind of incentives in the form of productivity linked wages.

Another way of linking wages to productivity is to introduce a "share contract" system for giving compensation to workers. The share contract wage moves down with poor earnings so that labour costs adjust quickly without resort to lay-offs. But this system will introduce a lot of uncertainty about the incomes of workers. Moreover, workers and their unions may not believe the employers and the truthfulness and transparency of their book-keeping practices. This will lead to disputes about the profitability of the company. Therefore, this practice of share contract does not seem practicable in a country like India today.

If a productivity linked wage system is to succeed, it would need the involvement and commitment of all the parties, particularly the employers and the unions in coming up with a productivity linked wage system acceptable to all. The productivity emerges from an integrated approach and hence all, from the top management to the bottom rung of workers, should share the gains from increased productivity. Wages for various jobs reflect differences in skills and provide necessary incentives for skill up-gradation. The variable wage element can be determined with the participation of employees at the individual, group, company, or national level.

In a productivity linked wage system, the wage structure will consist of a basic wage and a variable component. The former reflects the value of the job within the market, while the variable component provides the flexible linkage with a measure of performance based on either the performance of the economy, the company or the individual. The wage structure will then be :

Total Wage = basic wage + variable component (depending upon productivity)

The key elements of fixed and variable components include :

Basic wage

1. Annual increment (wherever mentioned in the agreement).
2. Contractual bonus (where applicable).

Variable component, i.e. wage increases based on the productivity/profit sharing formula.

Basic principles of wage-productivity reform should include the following :

1. Wages should aim at providing an adequate standard of living to workers. Adam Smith opined that where

wages are high, accordingly we shall always find the workmen more active, diligent and expeditious than where they are low [Gitlow (1957)].

2. Wage increase must take into account the company's ability to pay and the performance of the employees. If employees are working efficiently and enterprise is in a position to pay, then workers have every right to ask for higher wages in proportion to their performance.
3. Wage must reflect the value of the job, i.e. wage must act as a mirror of the value of job.
4. There must be variable components to accommodate business cycles. The methodology to be applied for deciding the variable part has to be negotiated and decided by mutual agreement by unions and management, and will involve technical time and motion studies.
5. Wage increase must be commensurate with productivity growth. In the absence of linkage between wage and productivity, inflationary pressure may be generated over an economy, which may tend to disturb the relation of wage and cost of living index.

While linking wages with productivity, the possible solutions are as under :

(i) Wage reform at the macro-level may be a tripartite effort among the Government, the Unions and Employers.
(ii) Real built-in wage increases may be tuned to productivity growth.
(iii) At the micro-level, there may be satisfactory labour-management relations with mutual trust and understanding.
(iv) There can be sharing of relevant information.

The productivity linked wage system may be applied company-wise. The typical characteristics of the system may be :

1. Employee involvement.

2. Linkage of a portion of wages with performance at individual, group and company level.
3. Improvement of work culture.
4. Recognition of job differentials and skill development.

Linkages between wages and productivity can at best be partial. If the objective of the linkage is to limit inflationary pressures then wage increases should be restricted to improvements in labour productivity, making the unit cost constant. The linkages can be used for making wages more flexible in tandem with the market conditions. Wage-productivity linkage can also improve the economic performance through paying higher wages or bonus for making extra efforts to achieve the performance goals.

Wage-productivity linkages may vary depending on the objective viz., labour cost containment, wage flexibility, or worker motivation, etc. When wage cost containment is of paramount concern, a conventional measure of labour productivity is generally used, i.e., output divided by a measure of labour input. When the objective is worker motivation, wages linked with productivity can take a number of forms.

Man works if paid enough and works harder if paid more. The motivation in the form of incentives may be used as a key to productivity, i.e. incentive payment system may be regarded as one of the way to link wages to productivity. Workers do not only have to be compensated for increased productivity with publicly announced pay rises, which usually leads to volatile gyrations in prices. They may be rewarded with other productivity incentives like unannounced cash benefits, provision for free food at work, free transportation, etc. Concept of incentive scheme has been devised by many managements with a view to increase productivity, thereby offering suitable rewards to the workers. Higher productivity increases can be achieved only with the workers' participation and workers' involvement proves effective only when they are adequately compensated and rewarded. Thus, incentives serve as lubricants as they gear up the entire economic machinery. Besides, improved earning capacity of the workers helps in maintaining industrial peace, which ensures an increased standard of living for the nation at large [Gupta (1992)]. The most common method used involves worker incentive schemes, the traditional payment-by-results schemes (piece-work, etc.) rating or performance appraisal systems. Motivation may also be enhanced through a variety of bonus schemes based on measures of collective performance. Other performance measures used for calculating collective bonus incentives are based on quality, machine utilization, or savings in raw materials, energy, or other costs. Increases may also be granted in anticipation of productivity improvements linked with changes agreed upon in work methods, as specified in so-called productivity bargaining. The feasibility of identifying suitable performance measures may obviously vary with the circumstances of individual enterprises and groups of workers.

It may be asked as to whether it is necessary that increases in productivity are a precondition for increases in wages and also whether labour can claim all the credit for increase in productivity. In such circumstances the significance of productivity bargaining in face to face negotiations becomes important. The bargaining may be much more on the basis of what the management wants to achieve during the period of settlement, what the management expects from the employees and in return what improvement in wages and other conditions of service the management is prepared to give. This approach can not only lead to harmonious industrial relations but also to a satisfactory settlement both for the employer and the employees in the industry. Thus, collective bargaining may be more and more in the nature of 'productivity bargaining'.

3

Wage-Productivity Relationship : Review of Important Studies

Recently, the theme of improvement in productivity of manufacturing sector as a source of high level of growth and for raising the standard of living of workers, have been applauded by the policy-makers. In productivity linked wage system, success depends upon the involvement and commitment of all the participants. In this chapter some of the important studies regarding wages, productivity and wage-productivity relationship have been reviewed.

Mukherjee (1966) conducted a study of Jute Textile Industry in India, covering the period 1939-50. He examined the trends in wages and compared it with trends in productivity, prices and profit during the same period. He observed that between 1939-50 money wages increased by almost two and half times but real wages remained almost at the same level in 1950 as in 1939. During the study period, labour productivity measured in terms of value-added per worker increased at a higher rate during 1949-58 than the increase in real wage. In fact, real wage in 1958 was less than that in 1949. During the same period, productivity as adjusted by capital changes, also revealed similar reverse trend with wage.

Guha and Marwaha (1968) made a study of productivity in India Coal & Mines in terms of output per man shift and made a comparison with other countries. The output per man shift (OMS) in India Coal Mines was 0.58 tonne in 1966 as compared to 1.6 tonnes in Poland, 2.1 tonnes in West Germany and 9.0 tonnes in Australia. They found that this period faced a challenge of quickly rising cost but relatively low productivity. It has been suggested that if financial encouragement was given in the shape of incentive allowance linked with productivity, it would not only increase production and wage packets of the workers but would also reduce the costs of production.

Shivamaggi, Rajagopalan, and Venkatachalam (1968) examined the trends in wages in seven important industries in India during 1951-61 and compared these with the trends in labour productivity and costs of production during the same period. The seven industries covered were : cotton textiles, jute textiles, iron and steel, cement, paper and paper-boards, chemicals and chemical products and sugar. The broad conclusions which emerged from their exploratory exercise were :

1. Rise in real wages, overall and industry-wise, lagged behind the improvement in labour productivity.
2. In case of money wages, although the overall trend was similar to that in real wages, the rise in money wages outpaced the productivity in cotton textiles, sugar and iron and steel.
3. The larger rise in labour productivity over the period may be partly associated with the increase in fixed capital per unit of labour and improvement in management techniques.
4. The wage component of total industrial costs was relatively small (less than one-fifth of total costs) and the wage-cost ratio declined somewhat over the years except in cotton and jute textiles.
5. This falling trend in the wage-cost ratio holds good even if the overall share of labour cost (i.e. salaries and wages) is taken as a percentage of total costs of industrial output.

Sinha and Sawhney (1970) examined the wage-productivity relationship in five major industries of India for the period 1950-63 using CMI and ASI data for large enterprises. They found an inverse relationship between the share of labour in productivity gain and rate of increase in total productivity. They also considered the rate of unionization, share of labour in non-material input and the rate of growth of industry in influencing wage-productivity relationship. The result implied that significant rise in wage rate can be secured without jeopardizing the needs of capital formation and harmonious capital-labour relations only if there is adequate advance in productivity.

Papola (1970) attempted a statistical analysis of the productivity-wage relationship in cotton textile industry in India as well as in some important centers during the period 1939-62. He concluded that in the long-run wages were found to be moving in line with the value of production per worker, although during one or two years, the two had also moved in opposite directions. For all-India level as well as in the three important centers, namely, Ahmedabad, Bombay and Kanpur, a high correlation was found between the movements in wages and productivity. He also found that the regional differentials in productivity had not been important factor in explaining wage differentials in the case of cotton textile industry. The consistency between different centers in productivity and wage differentials was generally lacking except in limited cases.

Kaiser (1971) considered the evolution of labour productivity in all forest products sectors in the United States. His study provided estimates of the rate of change in output per unit of labour for the period of 1947 to 1967. He found that labour productivity rose in all forest products sectors at an average annual rate of 3.4 percent. The author explained that the rise in labour productivity in the saw milling and lumber sectors (particularly in plywood mills) was due to the automation of the production process. Similarly, the trend in labour productivity in pulp and paper industry was due to increased research and development which led to better automated processing. In most forest products sectors, the average wage rates went up as the number of skilled workers employed increased.

Labour Bureau (1971) worked out productivity indices of 38 industries in India for the period 1947-63. The data were collected from CSO up to 1958 and thereafter from ASI. The Bureau used the concept of net output for productivity measures. The study considered that productivity is the cumulative result of the operation of a large number of factors such as technical improvement, rate of operation, degree of efficiency achieved in different processes, availability of raw materials and components, labour relations, skills and efforts of workers and efficiency of management. On the other hand, partial productivity ratios such as labour productivity or capital productivity were not correct indicators for measuring changes in efficiency of particular factors and also for factor substitution.

Mahindra (1972) found that labour productivity kept pace with capital productivity, though fuel and material productivity had shown a declining trend during the period 1950-64 in cement industry in India. To be more exact, productivity of labour went up by 118 percent, whereas, productivity of capital increased by 132 percent. It was seen that money wages per man-hour had also gone up by 161 percent, though the real wages per man-hour were higher by only 73 percent. Taking total productivity into account, it was found that the increases in money wages were higher than in total productivity.

Dadi (1974) concluded that over the period 1946-65, the workers' share increased by about 5.5 percentage points while employees' share increased by about 8.7 percentage points. However, during the period 1953-65 (the period of planned effort), there has been a fall both in workers' share and employees' share. The fall being more in case of workers' share as compared to that of employees' share. To examine the proposition of constancy or otherwise of workers' share and employees' share more objectively, the trend coefficients were calculated for the period 1946-65 and 1953-65. The regression coefficient had negative signs for workers share during 1946-65 and both workers' share and employee's share for the period 1953-65. However, for 1953-65, workers' share coefficient was found to be significant. He also tried to find the relative role played by industry-mix in making the workers' share decline over time. On isolating the effects of shifts in industry-mix on the overall wage share, it was found that change in industry-mix has been largely responsible for the fall in overall wage share during the period.

Tiwari and Trivedi (1975) studied the impact of the technique of production on the labour productivity in Indian cotton textile industry. The index chosen for production technique was the capital intensity (K/L). The index of capital intensity for the industry during 1956-65 remained more or less static, whereas the indices of productivity increased to 126 over the base year 1956. It was observed that the role of technology during the period had been almost passive and the increase in labour productivity might have taken place due to other factors.

Mukherjee (1975) attempted to make a comparative study of the productivity trends in the large scale manufacturing sector of Bihar relative to the productivity trends at all-India level. The basic data for the study were obtained from Census of Manufacturing Industries (CMI) for the period 1950-58 and from census sector of ASI for the period 1959-67. Partial productivities of labour and capital were calculated. TFP was calculated by using Kendrick method. It has been observed that the index of total factor productivity was considerably influenced by the trend in capital productivity at both the State and all-India levels because of its greater weightage in the total factor productivity mix. Increasing capital intensity had not been associated with productive use of capital. The consequent decline in capital productivity had led to a decline in TFP index at both the State and all-India levels. In Bihar converse relation was found between capital productivity index and capital intensity. The capital productivity in Bihar continued to be significantly lower as compared to the all-India level. Thus, emphasis on fuller utilization on existing capital assets was called for before further capital deepening was permitted.

Devaramani (1980) attempted to present changes in labour productivity in Indian organized industries. The labour productivity per worker and per man-hour was measured in money terms deflated by the general index of wholesale prices. The data were collected from ASI for 1964 to 1975-76 period. It was observed that the index number of workers employed in industries increased from 100.0 in 1964 to 126.0 in 1975-76 and the index of man hours increased from 100.0 in 1964 to 116.3 in 1975-76 whereas the index of gross output increased to 170.0 in 1975-76. The author concluded that the difference between employment index and output index was due to the rise in the level of productivity.

CSO (1981) presented the trends in wages, productivity and share of wages in value-added, during 1960-77 for 20 major groups of industries in registered factory sector in India. The major findings were :

1. The wages at current prices increased two to three-folds in the basic, capital goods and intermediate goods industries. The wages paid to workers in the petroleum refineries was far ahead than in other industries. The real wages also reported increasing trend in the selected industries. In general, basic and capital goods industries reported higher increase than intermediate and consumer goods industries. The real emoluments also behaved in a manner similar to real wages.
2. An increasing trend in labour productivity at current prices was observed in all industries except electric, light and power, miscellaneous foods, tobacco products and sugar. In real terms, the performance of capital goods industries was the best.
3. The increase in real wages lagged behind the labour productivity in chemicals and chemical products, electric, light and power, machinery except electricals, electrical machinery, ship building, structural clay products, spinning, weaving and finishing of textiles, pulp, paper and paper products. On the other hand, in rubber products and petroleum refineries, the rate of increase in real wages was faster than labour productivity.
4. The share of wages in value-added remained static or declined for all industries except electric, light and power, motor vehicles, repair of motor vehicles, rubber products and sugar.

A study of rank correlation coefficient between wages and productivity during various sub-periods indicated concordance between wages and productivity, while that based on labour productivity and share of wages in value-added revealed the two to be discordant indicating that labour was not being rewarded commensurately in some industries, whereas in others was paid more than what their productivity would permit.

Osoba (1982) attempted to highlight how productivity was related to the issue of wage determination in Nigeria and how the particular process adopted for the determination of wages, in turn, affected the productivity of individual worker and that of the nation as a whole. Using figures of value-added and employment for 1963-74, he found that the growth in productivity over the years was on the average due to sharp rise in total value-added rather than decrease in the level of employment. The decline in growth of employment, though not wholly responsible for the growth in productivity, is nonetheless significant. There was justification therefore for rewarding labour for its increased efficiency over the years under review.

Ghosh (1984) examined some efficiency parameters of steel, cement and sugar industries in order to focus attention on the problem of efficiency in Indian manufacturing industry. This micro approach rather than an overall macro-approach is useful in two ways : first, in highlighting the reasons for the low productivity observed in a few key or important industries, and second, in bringing out the absence of any direct link between investment and efficiency. The author concluded that the role of management in improving productivity was overwhelmingly important. Worker efficiency and productivity depended to a large extent on management practices. Finally, worker participation, worker discipline, the work ethos, were also important. They depended partly on work environment and partly on political intervention.

Sahoo (1985) in an excellent work on wages, price, productivity and industrial planning in some leading industries found that in jute industry, labour productivity in the sense of value-added per worker increased at a greater rate during 1949-58 than the increase in real wage. In fact, real wage in 1958 was less than in 1949. Productivity adjusted by capital changes, also revealed similar reverse trend with wage. Up to 1962, money wage was moving perceptibly below the rising labour productivity. In later years, indices of money wage and productivity were almost close to each other. But all through the period 1951-64, real wage was lagging much behind the increase in productivity. During the period 1961-70, the increase in money wage, real wage and productivity were divergent and the latter often falling behind the former two. In cement industry, changes in money wage and productivity seemed to have no consistent correlation. In paper industry, increase in money wage as well as real wage was less than the increase in productivity in the period 1951-64.

Goldar's (1986) analysis of productivity growth in industry covered the period 1951-79. He gave two sets of estimates, the first set was related to the period 1951-65 covering the industries in CMI and the second set was related to 1959-79 where the main data source was ASI. The growth of TFP during 1951-65 was about 1.3 percent per annum, its contribution to growth in value-added being 2.4 percent. However, the productivity performance during 1956-65 was far inferior to that during 1951-65, showing that as industrialization proceeded, productive efficiency suffered a setback. The study confirmed that there emerged a wide variation in the productivity growth of the different industry groups during 1951-65. Two of the five industry groups namely, 'Metals' and 'Chemicals' with a combined value-added share of nearly 40.0 percent experienced productivity decline, this decline being very pronounced in case of 'Metals'. Goldar's estimates of productivity growth for the period 1959-79 as a whole and for three sub-periods indicated that productivity performance in the 70's was better than that in the 60's. Also an improvement was observed in productivity performance in the post-1965 period over the pre-1965 period, TFP growth being positive (even when growth of capital productivity was negative) in both the sub-periods.

Singh (1987) attempted to examine the productivity trends using partial and total factor productivity methods and factor substitutability in the industrial sector in Punjab from 1967-68 to 1981-82. During this period, labour productivity registered a modest increase but capital productivity actually declined. Capital intensity showed an upward trend. The notable finding was that the growth in labour productivity was mainly due to an increase in wage rate. The elasticity of substitution was less than unity. A rise in capital intensity with falling capital productivity indicated an increasing application of capital unaccompanied by technological advances. TFP showed a decreasing trend, i.e. performance of manufacturing industry was sluggish and overall efficiency of factors was declining.

Bhatnagar (1988) attempted to study the relationship between wages and productivity in case of seven engineering industries in India for the period 1960-80. The data were collected from Annual Survey of Industries at two digit level. No significant relationship was seen between wage trends and productivity trends during the study period. Some directional relationship over the long-run between wages and labour productivity was found. Both had shown an increase over the years except in the case of non-ferrous and basic metals. The relationship between productivity and real wages was even less if capital productivity was taken as an index of productivity. Capital productivity had fallen in all except electrical machinery. Capital intensity had been seen to influence productivity to large extent, and in so far as wage level can affect capital intensity, it could indirectly affect productivity. Capital intensity was positively correlated with both wage rate and labour productivity and it was negatively correlated with productivity of capital. Wages neither influenced by nor influenced productivity directly and did not act as a motivating force for increasing productivity. It was concluded that this needed to be corrected by linking changes in wage rate, above a certain minimum with changes in productivity.

Gupta (1990) studied the productivity trends in automobile industry from 1973-74 to 1983-84. He found that the capital intensity had fallen at an annual average rate of 2.7 percent in case of manufacture of motor vehicles and parts (374), whereas the capital intensity in case of manufacture of motor-cycles and scooters and parts (375) registered an annual average increase of 5.3 percent during 1973-74 to 1983-84. The capital intensity of both the groups taken together, however suffered a decline at an annual average rate of 2.4 percent. He found that the partial productivity of capital for manufacture of motor vehicles and parts registered an annual average increase of 4.4 percent whereas the group of motor-cycles and scooters and parts witnessed a higher annual average rate of 6.7 percent during the study period. The capital productivity in both the groups, taken together, increased at an annual average rate of 4.0 percent. TFP index as per Kendrick method increased at an annual average rate of 0.6 percent and 7.9 percent respectively, in case of two groups. The TFP index of both the groups taken together increased at an annual average rate of 1.3 percent. For examining the relationship between the partial productivity of labour, man-hours by all employees and wage rate, regressions were estimated. There was a positive and significant relationship between the wage rate and partial productivity of labour for all the three groups viz. : manufacture of motor vehicles and parts (374), manufacture of motor cycles and scooters and parts (375) and for both the groups taken together.

Rao and Madhvilatta (1990) found that the labour productivity in public enterprises in India widely fluctuated and the capital productivity declined during the period 1975-76 to 1985-86. The total factor productivity indices also showed a growth rate of about 5.0 percent per annum in public enterprises. The productivity indices showed two different phases in the performance of these enterprises in India. While the first phase of decline in factor productivity (1975-76 to 1979-80) stood as an explanation for the poor profitability performance of these enterprises, the second phase (1982-85) indicated that productive use of resources was pre-requisite for better operating performance.

Irland and Maxcy (1991) in their study of Maine's wood industry in America used value-added per worker as a measure of labour productivity. Labour productivity was calculated for each wood product industry (lumber, logging, saw mills, flooring mills, millwork, furniture and fixtures). For the 1982-87 period, the logging industry had the highest labour productivity level while the furniture industry had the lowest. The authors found that higher wage rates were associated with higher levels of labour productivity. Their calculations also showed an inverse relationship between labour productivity and labour intensity (the ratio of wages divided by value- added).

Dowrick (1993) examined OECD data from 18 different countries over the period 1960 through 1990 and revealed a weak inverted hump-shaped relationship between the degree of centralisation and total factor productivity, i.e. fully decentralised and fully centralised wage setting systems performed better in terms of productivity growth than partially centralised systems. The relationship, however, was found to be asymmetric, with the performance of fully decentralized systems somewhat better than fully centralised systems.

Erenburg (1993) examined the relationship between real wages and productivity in United States during 1948-90. The measure of productivity included the impact of public capital as well as private capital. Using Cobb-Douglas production function estimates, the impact of public capital on productivity and real wage was incorporated. The result indicated that when capital stock was controlled for, real wage was counter-cyclical, and validated diminishing returns to labour, positive returns to public capital and a pro-cyclical effect of capacity utilization on real wage. Estimates from the productivity equation established a long-run relationship between productivity, measured as output per unit of capital, and employment to capital ratio, and the public capital to private capital ratio. Estimates from the real wage equation indicated that a long-run relationship existed between real wage and labour productivity and the public to private capital ratio.

Coelli, Fahrer and Lindsay (1994) examined wage dispersion and labour market institutions during 1975-90 in fourteen OECD countries. The analysis of relative wage data suggested that the Australian labour market might have been relatively more flexible over the 1970s and 1980s than the popular perception. In so far as cross-country comparisons of wage flexibility (as measured by wage dispersion across ten sectors) can be made, they observed that Australian wage flexibility was on the scale of that in the United States—a country which is considered to have a flexible labour market. Moreover, Australian wages appeared to have been relatively strongly correlated with factors influencing labour demand, a desirable property when labour was heterogeneous. In fact, the relationship between Australian sectoral wages, productivity and relative prices was among the strongest in the OECD countries for which data were available. International experience showed that wage dispersion might be affected by changes to wage setting institutions within some countries. However, a strong relationship was not found between the degree of centralisation of wage setting institutions and wage dispersion across countries. Countries with similar levels of wage dispersion displayed a diversity of labour market institutions. While they found positive correlation between wages, productivity and prices in the majority of countries, the cross-country evidence was insufficient to draw general conclusions. Overall, the sensitivity of wages to demand conditions did not appear to be systematically related to the degree of centralisation of the wage setting system.

Singh and Ajit (1995) focused on the changing structure of industries in the manufacturing sector in India during 1974-90. Agro-based industries like food products, tobacco products, wool products and jute textiles lost their shares not only in manufacturing output but also in fixed capital and employment. Similar trends were evident in engineering industries. However, the shares of chemical industries in manufacturing output, fixed capital and employment showed improvements. Also there had been an increase in the use of capital relative to that of labour in most of the industries in the manufacturing sector in India during 1974-90. Capital productivity recorded marginal improvements in the 70s followed by the gradual decline in 80s. The labour productivity showed steady improvements during 1974-90, with the signs of significant improvement in the 80s. They also found that the CD and Bairam production functions performed better than the CES and Translog production functions (because of the problem of multicollinearity and limited degrees of freedom). The returns to scale and elasticities of output with respect to capital and labour derived from Bairam production functions were, more or less, similar to those derived from the CD production function. The study invalidated the proposition of constant returns to scale and confirmed the validity of decreasing returns to scale for most of the industries in the manufacturing sector in India.

Hellerstein, Neumark and Troske (1996) estimated plant-level production functions and wage equations, and compared the relative marginal products and relative wages for various groups of workers. The data and empirical framework led to new evidence on numerous questions regarding the determination of wages and the relationship between wages and marginal products of workers in different demographic groups. These included race and sex discrimination in wages, the causes of rising wages over the life cycle, and the returns to marriage.

First; workers who had ever been married were more productive than never-married workers and were paid accordingly. Second, prime aged-workers (aged 35-54) were equally as productive as younger workers, and in some specifications were estimated to receive higher wages. However, older workers (aged 55 +) were less productive than younger workers but were paid more. Third, the data indicated no difference between the relative wage and relative productivity of black workers. Finally, with the exception of managerial and professional occupations, women were paid about 25-35 percent less than men, but estimated productivity differentials for women were generally no larger than 15.0 percent, significantly smaller than the pay differential.

Hostland (1996) explored that during 1988-92, growth in real wages in excess of the rate "warranted" by average labour productivity acted to amplify fluctuations in employment and unemployment rates in Canada. The results supported the neoclassical view of a long-run equilibrium relationship between the real producer wage rate and average labour productivity. Deviations between the real producer wage rate and average labour productivity were large and persistent but were not found to be permanent. However, there did appear to be a stable short-term relationship between growth rates of the real producer wage and average labour productivity and changes in the employment rate. Regression analysis indicated that changes in the employment rate were determined predominantly by real output growth. Further analysis revealed that about two-thirds of these net job losses have been regained over the past three years as a result of growth in the real producer wage lagging behind that in average labour productivity.

Upendra (1996) examined elasticity of labour productivity in India during the period 1973-74 to 1989-90. The results indicated that elasticity of output (gross value-added) with respect to capital was very high, implying that gross value added was more responsive to capital employed during 1973-90. The exercise also revealed that the Indian manufacturing (factory) sector was capital intensive and was characterized by decreasing returns to scale. On the other hand, the main reason for linking labour productivity with wage rate was to find the possibilities of substitution of labour for capital so as to absorb sufficient number of surplus labour. The elasticity of labour productivity with respect to wage rate was significantly more than unity. This indicated that substitution possibilities were quite high in favour of labour because labour productivity was found to be an increasing function of wage rate. In other words, the marginal labour productivity in relation to wage rate was very high than that of average labour productivity. Therefore, there was a need to re-direct the Indian manufacturing sector towards greater use of labour intensive technology until marginal productivity of labour was equal to wage rate.

Kumar (1996) analysed the estimates of TFP in private sector steel industry in India during 1981-82 to 1993-94. The results showed a rising trend till the end of 80s in all the four measures of TFP (Direct, Kendrick, Solow and Divisia methods) and then it started falling by the beginning of 90s. Labour productivity and capital productivity also showed a rising trend till the end of 80s. But in the beginning of 90s, while labour productivity showed a rising trend, capital productivity showed a falling trend. Estimates of CD and CES production functions revealed constant returns to scale for the public sector steel industry. The elasticity of substitution of the steel industry came out to be negative. Annual growth rate of TFP, labour productivity and capital productivity showed a rising trend during the period of study. Annual variations in factor productivity revealed a significant positive relationship with value-added. On the other hand, with time, a significant negative relationship was observed for this industry. It seemed that growth in factor productivities would have been much higher if labour-management relations were better.

Calvet and Jusmet (1997) analysed the Spanish labour market and industrial relations during 1980-95. They concluded that for decades, analysts of the Spanish labour market have referred to excessive wage growth, which was presented as one of the main causes of high unemployment in Spain. The paper provided evidence on wage trends since the early 1980s which suggested that this view was unfounded. Wage costs have in general grown far less than productivity, despite the fact that in some periods and sectors firms have found it difficult to transfer these higher costs into prices. The analysis showed that pay restraint has been even greater if we take into consideration take-home pay, excluding social contributions and income tax, and that the workers who have suffered most have been those on the lowest incomes and those in the public sector.

Centre for the Study of Living Standards (1998) found that growth in real consumer wages significantly lagged productivity growth in Canada in the 1980s and 1990s. But this finding reflected a growing divergence between rates of increase in consumer and producer prices and not any fundamental breakdown in the relationship between wages and productivity. Indeed, the real producer wage, the wage which theory suggests should closely reflect productivity trends, in fact rose at about the same rate as labour productivity. This explained why labour's share of GDP only decreased slightly between 1981 and 1989, and had been stable in the 1990s despite the increasing gap between productivity and real consumer wage growth. Trends in labour's share of GDP were more closely associated with the producer wage-productivity relationship than with the consumer wage-productivity relationship. Indeed, there was no one-to-one relationship between changes in real consumer wages and profits.

Lane (1998) examined profits and wages in Ireland during 1987-96. He found that Ireland's economic resurgence since 1987 was accompanied by a major factor income shift away from labour towards capital, during which wage share in Ireland declined substantially from 74.9 percent in 1987 to 65.2 percent in 1996. He explained how Ireland's national strategy of wage moderation brought about this favourable outcome and cited several benefits of a high profitability environment. He further argued that these benefits, which included increased capital inflows, improved financial positions for firms and faster output growth, were magnified for smaller and more open economies such as Ireland.

Neogi and Ghosh (1998) analysed the impact of liberalisation on the performance of selected Indian industries with the firm level data for 1989-94. They concluded that substantial investment had been made in five major industrial groups, namely; chemical, textile, processed food, non-metallic mineral products and electrical machinery. Capital intensities had been growing at fast rates during the whole period, particularly during the post-reform period. But the annual average growth rates of value-added were much lower in the post-reform period relative to pre-reform period across board. Similar feature was observed regarding labour productivity growth in all these industries. Total factor productivity growth had fallen very sharply during the period of reforms with the exception of chemical industry. The relationship between labour productivity and capital intensity showed that there was downward shift of the scatter points during the later year which indicates a general downfall of efficiency of firms during this period. It was found that the level of technical efficiencies for all the industries was very low and there was no significant improvement of this level during the post-reform period.

Pardhan and Barik (1998) examined the growth path followed by total factor productivity (TFP) during 1963-64 to 1992-93 in the Indian manufacturing sector. They found that TFPG increased at a rate of 0.61 percent per annum over the entire period. TFPG showed a negative rate of growth of –2.09 percent per annum during the sub-period 1963-71, 3.06 percent per annum rate of growth during the sub-period 1972-81 and again a negative –1.23 percent per annum growth rate during the sub-period 1982-92. They suggested an evaluation of TFP by incorporating the idea of fluctuating growth which was often pointed out to be a feature of the Indian economy as a whole.

Trivedi *et. al.* (1999) estimated productivity growth of the manufacturing sector (organised factory sector) and some selected industries during 1973-74 to 1994-95 in terms of total factor productivity [single deflation (TFPSD) and double deflation (TFPDD)] and total productivity (TP). The rate of growth of productivity, as measured by both TFPSD and TFPDD, was found to be higher at 2.7 percent and 4.5 percent respectively, than the rate of growth of 1.0 percent for TP during the study period. Some of the industries which contributed to this trend were textiles and textile products, machinery and transport equipments, chemical and chemical products and leather. A rising trend was noticed both in TFPSD and TFPDD in the 1990s, "thereby providing evidence on the productivity impact of residual factors like technology, better capacity utilization, learning by doing, etc. on the manufacturing sector's growth."

Zavodny (1999) explored the trends in productivity, pay and the unionization rate in manufacturing sector of United States over the period 1974-94. The results indicated that the difference between productivity gains and wage or compensation increases was smaller in industries with higher initial unionization rates. The estimated coefficients implied that if the unionization rate at the beginning of a five year period were to fall by one percentage point, the difference between productivity growth and wage growth over the next five years would increase by 0.23 percentage points, holding other factors constant. Similarly, a one percentage decline in the initial unionization rate was associated with a 0.21 percentage point increase in the difference between productivity growth and compensation growth over the next five years. The results suggested that the industries that experienced larger percentage declines in unionization also experienced larger increases in the wage-productivity gap, but the estimated coefficients on the variable measuring the change in unionization were not statistically significant. These results were consistent with the hypothesis that compensation increases more closely match productivity gains in more highly unionized industries but provide less support for the hypothesis that the decline of unions has contributed to the rise in the wage-productivity gap. The difference between growth in productivity and in compensation was negatively associated with the change in employment, indicating that the wage-productivity gap increased as industries declined. An increase in industry exports was associated with a decline in the wage-productivity gap while a change in import penetration did not affect the wage-productivity gap. Surprisingly, increases in capital were negatively associated with the wage-productivity gap. Productivity was expected to rise more quickly than compensation as capital increased because the increase in capital would raise output per hour, but the data suggested that workers benefit in industries with larger increases in capital stock.

Bande, Fernandez & Montuenga (2000) provided new evidence on the relationship between real wages and productivity in a panel of 89 manufacturing branches for each of the 17 Spanish regions during 1977-98. They observed that the real wage may be seen as the outcome of two countervailing forces, the workers bargaining power (proxied as the degree of indexation of real wage to productivity, reflecting the inside-sector conditions) and the alternative payment measures, reflecting that workers' also take care of wage differential between industries and/or regions. The empirical evidence had shown that the degree of heterogeneity regarding the weight of productivity and the alternative wage in the different regions was high, reflecting that workers bargaining power was not geographically equally distributed. They observed that the distinction among dynamic branches (i.e. those branches where productivity was growing above the national average) and lagging branches (i.e. those branches where productivity grew below the national average) was important in order to explain the regional wage behaviour. It was found that generally, dynamic branches set their real wage with respect to both factors, while lagging branches gave higher importance to alternative payment considerations. Moreover, lagging branches gave more importance to the national alternative wage than to the regional measure. This implied that these sectors were linking their wage performance to outside conditions, instead to their own regional labour market conditions. This might be an important factor behind employment patterns. First, the lagging branches were more likely to destroy employment, because productivity was growing below the average and the real wage was not related to their specific conditions. This may be related to the wage bargain process, which many times was taken at the national level. Second, the dynamic branches (that were the sole candidates to absorb these expelled workers) cannot create enough employment, because they were fixing their real wage giving a high share to productivity. Hence, this behaviour might be one of the leading forces behind the heterogeneous performance of employment and unemployment in the Spanish regions.

Verner (2000) took data from 1994 Regional Program on Enterprise Development (RPED) Survey on Ghana, which covered 215 manufacturing enterprises and interviewed about 1200 of their employees. He compared relative productivities and relative wages for various groups of workers and jointly estimated wages and output functions. The analysis found that wage differentials matched productivity differentials for certain group of workers, while for others did not. Analysis revealed productivity differences for five levels of completed education : middle; secondary; vocational; technical; and university. Only in case of university graduates, the productivity differentials were in line with the wage premium. The results indicated that the workforce employed in the manufacturing sector in Ghana added more to firm-level productivity than the costs it involved. Thus, wages were out of line with productivity, possibly due to externalities or spillover effects, for example, in skills. Hence, the level of wages was not too high to compete internationally. Furthermore, the analysis provided evidence that human capital levels should be increased, through training or education, as it benefited both productivity and wages. It was concluded that economic policies aiming at increasing productivity in Ghanaian enterprises and, hence, long-run economic growth, should emphasize the training and education of the employees.

Dunne, Foster, Haltwanger and Troske (2001) took data for 1975-92 from Centre of Economic Studies, U.S. Census Bureau and analysed changes in the dispersion in wages and productivity for the manufacturing sector. The main findings were; (1) between—plant component of wage dispersion was an important and growing part of total wage dispersion; (2) much of the between—plant increase in dispersion was within industries; (3) the between—plant measures of wage and productivity dispersion increased substantially over the last few decades; and (4) a substantial fraction of the rising dispersion in wages and productivity was accounted for by changes in the distribution of computer investment and capital intensities across plants. The results were consistent with the hypothesis that the factors leading to rising wage dispersion act through between—plant rather than within—plant effects.

Saget (2001) presented the effects of minimum wage legislation on the level on employment and poverty at several points of time (from 1970s to the late 1990s) for approximately 30 developing countries. The paper showed evidence of a high instability of the minimum wage in real terms in many developing countries. Yet some countries have been able to protect the purchasing power of minimum wage earners better than others. The ratio of minimum wage to the average wage in manufacturing varied considerably between countries and within countries across time. In some countries, the minimum wage appeared to be relatively stable over time with respect to the average wage. The results also suggested that other things being equal, the level of the minimum wage had an insignificant effect on the level of employment. The data analysis gave strong support to the idea that the minimum wage might bring positive results in poverty alleviation by improving the living conditions of workers and their families while having no negative results in terms of employment. Raising the minimum wage might have an effect on incentives to provide training and productivity, as well as on working conditions and prices. The idea that a decent minimum wage might force firms of other countries to use more efficiently their labour force has yet been little explored.

Schreiber (2001) took data for 1980-94 for West Germany and found that it was the formulation of the wage policy rule in terms of growth rates instead of levels which was responsible for the failure to achieve a stable labour share. Even starting from a desired value there would be an unforeseeable cumulation of implementation errors and inflation target deviations producing a stochastic trend in the labour share. The theoretically important exception is the special case of a Cobb-Douglas production function, where the labour share is always stationary. As this case is omnipresent in economic policy debate, it is important to stress the fact that this assumption was not adequate at least for the given West Germany data set, which displayed a clearly non-stationary labour share. Another finding was that wage setting in West Germany in the study period is well described as productivity-oriented.

Wong and Heng (2001) took National Income Accounting data from 1980-2000 and concluded that while Singapore's wage share was lower than many OECD countries, it was much higher than Third World developing countries such as Thailand and comparable to the NIEs. The analysis showed that it was high labour productivity increases that allowed for high wage increases without undermining economic competitiveness. The relative stability of Singapore's wage share was simply a reflection that labour productivity increases in Singapore had kept pace with wage increases. In fact, the relationship between changes in wage share, wage adjustment and labour productivity suggested that attempts to artificially move wage share up by raising wages above productivity would be counter-productive leading not only to a deterioration in economic competitiveness but also to an increasing likelihood of a wage-price spiral. In such an event, the price increases were likely to leapfrog wage increases resulting in the erosion of the purchasing power of worker's wages.

Bruce (2002) examined the theory and evidence behind the assertion that wage growth among workers in a specific industry can be linked to the productivity growth of those workers in case of 46 Canadian industries during 1961-95. He found that there were sound theoretical reasons for predicting that there would be very little correlation between an industry's productivity growth and its wage rate. He also found empirical evidence supporting virtually no correlation at all between an industry's relative productivity growth and its growth in relative wages.

Chang (2002) in his paper employed an error correction model, which can perform tests in both the short and long-run, to examine the effects of international trade, productivity growth and education investment on Taiwan's wage differential from 1978-99. There was no convincing evidence of a growing wage differential in Taiwan over the past two decades. The empirical analysis showed smaller decreases in the wage differential in the short-run than in the long-run. In the long-run, if government education investment increased by one percent of GDP, the wage ratio dropped by about 2.34 percent due to more skilled labour being available in the economy. Productivity growth had a significant influence on the wage differential in the short-run, but might have only a minor effect in the long-run. If total factor productivity growth had increased by one percentage point, the wage ratio dropped by about 0.15 percent in the short-run.

Haskel and Pereira (2002) studied the relationship between workers' skills and business productivity using matched employer-employee data for the UK. Workers' wages were decomposed into observed and unobserved fixed firm and worker components. When the firm components were identified, unobserved workers' wage effects were interpreted as a measure of the workers' skill. Results indicated that labour productivity in business in the top quintile of the productivity distribution have on an average 4.374 times higher productivity than business in the bottom quintile and between 30 and 70 percent higher measure of market value human capital. It was found that mean and median wages increased with the labour productivity quintile, suggesting that on an average wages were higher in more productive business. However, the wage gap between the top and bottom productivity quintiles was remarkably lower than the corresponding productivity gap. It was also concluded that the experience part of human capital was less important in determining productivity than the education and other unobservable parts of human capital.

Ohanian (2002) assessed five common explanations for the large decline in U.S. total factor productivity (TFP) during Great Depression : changes in capacity utilization, factor input quality, production composition, labour hoarding and increasing returns to scale. The study found that these factors explained less than one-third of the 18.0 percent TFP decline between 1929 and 1933. The rest of the decline remained unexplained. The analysis suggested two alternative interpretations of productivity puzzle. One interpretation was that some forms of measurement error were responsible for the productivity decreases. Measurement error hypotheses tended to raise two possibilities : either output fell significantly less than measured, which would imply that the Depression was less severe than previously thought, or inputs fell more than measured, which would deepen the puzzle of why employment fell so much during the Depression. The other interpretation of the productivity puzzle was that lower production efficiency contributed to the productivity decreases. A version of this lower efficiency view was that the Depression reduced firm-specific organization capital by disrupting normal production, distribution, marketing, and inventory plans. These different interpretations of the productivity puzzle suggested very different views about the nature of the Great Depression. A major challenge was to explain not only why measured productivity fell, but also why productivity change varied so much across sectors.

Rogers and Vernon (2002) used panel data technique to analyse whether wage dispersion has an influence on manufacturing productivity growth in 9 OECD countries over the period 1970-95. The central findings of the paper were that the higher wage dispersion above the median (90/50 ratio) was associated with higher rates of productivity growth whilst, in contrast, higher wage dispersion below the median (50/10) was associated with lower rates of productivity growth. Wage inequality in the top half of the distribution promoted productivity, apparently not only by encouraging better paid, or more ambitious, employees and potential employees, to invest in vocational education and training, but also by encouraging them to meet the more immediate demands of their employees. In contrast, lower wage inequality in the bottom half of the distribution nurtured productivity growth, apparently not only by encouraging investment in vocational education and training within this range of ambition, but through its implications of upgrading in the organization of work, and its facilitation of structural change.

Skeffington (2002) opined that Australia has been able to achieve the ultimate sweet spot for an economy—high productivity, a downward trend in unemployment and healthy wage increase. During the past three economic cycles, the relationship between productivity and employment has been changing due to the economic reform. In 1992, unemployment peaked at 10.9 percent and there were annualized productivity gains of 3.0 percent. In the next cycle, unemployment peaked at 8.4 percent and the productivity gain was 4.0 percent. The differential was still narrowing : in 2002, Australia had 6.6 percent unemployment and a 5.0 percent productivity gain. A more efficient economy and better management increased productivity and company profits, which benefited people. Due to increased productivity, workers benefited from these wage rises without the harsh effects of high inflation. Instead of unemployment acting as a spur to productivity, it was reductions in productivity that make unemployment increase. Management that did not improve efficiency was not doing its workforce any favours. Economic reforms and deregulation created positive results for labour and capital.

Ozmucur (2003) took 9 two digit manufacturing sub-sectors in Turkey covering the period from 1950-98 and concluded that labour productivity was higher in private sector. On the other hand, average wage rate in the public sector was higher compared to private sector. A very close relationship was also found between wages and productivity in the private sector but no significant relationship between the real wage rate and labour productivity was found in the public sector.

WAGE-PRODUCTIVITY RELATIONSHIP IN DIFFERENT COUNTRIES

The growth of Soviet economy was mainly based on the rising level of productivity and the workers sharing the gains of productivity through rising level of real wage, i.e. living standard [Mohanty (1993)].

A comparison of wage ratios in Poland, during 1955-60 is interesting because a substantial increase in wages and labour productivity occurred at that time. The changes in wage ratios were decisively affected by wage controls [Diatchenko and Dunlop (1964)].

In United States, collective bargaining being a successful method for wage fixation, the workers' productivity and wage rate were accomplished by evaluating each occupation by means of a system agreed to, by the union.

In France and Germany, the real income of the workers generally followed the growth of labour productivity during 1950-60. In these countries, wages moved more in relation with production or labour market conditions than with productivity conditions in strict sense. The relation between wage movements and productivity was clear in the long-run, but obscured in the short-run [Mohanty (1993)].

However, so far as the relationship of wage and productivity was concerned, the only valid relationship between wage movement and productivity movement, observed in advanced countries, was that real average hourly earnings in the economy as a whole changed in line with changes in output per man-hour for all workers in the economy reckoned on a truly long-term basis. Even for the economy as a whole, this relationship ceased to hold well, when calculations were made on a short-term basis" [Subramànian (1970)].

The studies reviewed above, though not exhaustive, mainly analyzed the productivity aspects and changes in wage rate of manufacturing sector. However, not much work has been done, especially after liberalisation, towards examining the wage-productivity relationship, inter-industry and inter-state examination of the share of the labour in Indian industry. The present study aims at filling this gap.

Methodology for Measurement

The present chapter discusses the sources of data, concepts and measurement of relevant variables used in the study. The chapter has been divided into three broad sections. Section I discusses the sources of data that have been used to measure productivity in Indian manufacturing sector. Section II concentrates on the measurement of variables. In section III, the methodology adopted for the present study has been discussed.

Section I

The present study is based on the secondary data compiled primarily from various issues of the Annual Survey of Industries (ASI). The ASI is the prime source of industrial statistics in India. The ASI covers all the factories registered under sections 2m(i) and 2m(ii) of the Indian Factories Act of 1948 which refer to the factories using power and employing 10 or more workers; and those not using power but employing 20 or more workers on any day of processing 12 months respectively.

The factories covered in the ASI framework are classified into two sectors, viz., the 'Census Sector' and 'Sample Sector'. The Census Sector covers all factories employing 50 or more and using power and 100 or more workers but not using power. The information about factories belonging to Census Sector is collected on complete enumeration basis. The Sample Sector constitutes remaining factories and covered through sample survey. The Census Sector and Sample Sector together constitute what is called the 'Factory Sector'. The present study is based on the Factory Sector data and covers the period 1973-74 to 2000-01. The NIC-1970 was followed to classify factories from 1973-74 to ASI 1988-89. NIC-1987 had then been introduced and followed till ASI 1997-98. From ASI 1998-99, the new series of classification, i.e. NIC-1998 had been introduced. The data have been taken at two digit level of industry and for two years, i.e. 1999-00 to 2000-01, the data of 3 and 4 digit level has been merged at two digit level of industry.

Following publications have been used for data collection, compilation and presentation:

1. Annual Survey of Industries, Central Statistical Organisation (CSO), Ministry of Planning, Government of India, New Delhi.
2. Handbook of Statistics, Reserve Bank of India.
3. Handbook of Industrial Policy and Statistics, 2001, Office of the Economic Adviser, Ministry of Commerce and Industry.
4. Handbooks of Indian Labour Statistics.
5. Reports of Centre for Monitoring Indian Economy.

The present study examines the wage-productivity relationship in registered manufacturing sector. For inter-industry comparison, fourteen major industry groups of manufacturing sector have been taken and for inter-state comparison, all industries in sixteen states along with all-India have been selected. However, due to certain conceptual problems (because of changed industrial classification from 1998), the study for inter-industry comparison for three industries, namely, (i) cotton textiles; (ii) jute, hemp and mesta textiles, and (iii) textile products, has been restricted to 1973-74 to 1998-99 period.

The inter-industry analysis has been done for :

(i) (20-21) Food Products Industry (FPI).
(ii) (22) Beverages, Tobacco & Tobacco Products Industry (BTTPI).
(iii) (23) Cotton Textiles Industry (CTI).
(iv) (25) Jute, Hemp & Mesta Textiles (JHMTI).
(v) (26) Textile Products Industry (TPI).
(vi) (28) Paper & Paper Products Industry (PPPI).
(vii) (29) Leather, Leather & Fur Products Industry (LFPI).
(viii) (30) Chemical & Chemical Products Industry (CCPI).
(ix) (31) Rubber, Plastic, Petroleum and Coal Products Industry (RPCPI).
(x) (32) Non-Metallic Mineral Products Industry (NMMPI).
(xi) (33) Basic Metals & Alloys Industry (BMAI).
(xii) (34) Metal Products Industry (MPI).
(xiii) (35-36) Machinery other than Transport Industry (MOTI).
(xiv) (37) Manufacture of Transport Equipment & Parts (TEPI).

The inter-state analysis has been done on for sixteen states, namely, (i) Andhra Pradesh (AP); (ii) Assam (ASM); (iii) Bihar (BIH); (iv) Gujarat (GUJ); (v) Haryana (HAR); (vi) Himachal Pradesh (HP); (vii) Karnataka (KAR); (viii) Kerala (KER); (ix) Madhya Pradesh (MP); (x) Maharashtra (MAH); (xi) Orissa (ORI); (xii) Punjab (PB); (xiii) Rajasthan (RAJ); (xiv) Tamil Nadu (TN); (xv) Uttar Pradesh (UP); and (xvi) West Bengal (WB).

SECTION II

In empirical estimation of different measures of productivity, the major problem encountered was that of specification and measurement of output and inputs. This section is devoted to the analysis of these conceptual problems and issues related to the specification and measurement of output and inputs.

ISSUE-RELATED WITH MEASUREMENT OF OUTPUT

In empirical literature, the choice between gross output

and value-added poses the problem for finding the most appropriate measure of output. A well established argument against of use of gross output as a measure of output is that the use of gross output is that it is sensitive to differences in the material intensities of different industries and even within the same industry it will be biased because it is not able to capture the differences in vertical integration. Therefore, it is difficult to add outputs across industries in the process of aggregation [Griliches and Ringsted (1971); Bruno (1978)].

The literature spells out two distinct approaches to get the figures of real value-added : (i) single deflation method, and (ii) double deflation method. In the single deflation method, both components of value-added—the value of output and value of intermediate inputs (e.g. materials)—are deflated by a single price index e.g. index of manufacturing prices. In case of double deflation method, the value of output is deflated by a price index of output (e.g. price index of manufacturing products); and the value of intermediate inputs by price index of intermediate inputs (e.g. price index of materials input). The method of single deflation is valid only if the price of materials relative to the price of output is more or less constant for the period of analysis [Balakrishnan and Pushpangadan (1994)]. On the other hand, the basic problem in estimating real value-added by double deflation method is the estimation of an appropriate price index of materials input. The price index of materials is difficult to construct because : (i) input groups are difficult to identify properly, and (ii) correct weights attached to each input group are difficult to compute. Most of researchers use single deflation method to arrive at the real value-added figures due to two reasons : (i) it is commonly used method to get the real value of an aggregate defined in terms of the difference between two other aggregates, and (ii) the double deflation method is not necessarily superior to the single deflation method [Dholakia and Dholakia (1994)].

ISSUE-RELATED WITH MEASUREMENT OF CAPITAL INPUT

Capital is an important input variable in productivity analysis. The problems of specifying and measuring capital arise in empirical analysis because of following reasons :

(a) The stock of capital existing at any point of time consists of a variety of physical objects which have been produced by the economic system and which are being used for the production of other commodities at specified point of time. The measurement and comparison of the stock of real capital existing at two different points of time would pose considerable problems, first, because of the intricate problem of greater heterogeneity of capital goods, and second, because of the serious problem of valuation arising out of the more or less continuously changing physical specification and form of capital goods largely on account of the changing technology [Dholakia (1977)].

(b) The future productivity of capital is not exactly assessable because a capital asset is productive over a considerable period of time and future is highly uncertain. The existing capital stock at any time has no association with current market valuation. Further, the productivity of capital asset might not remain the same over its lifetime and this makes it difficult to measure capital with reference to its original cost.

(c) There exists inadequate statistical response about capital. In practice, it is very difficult to find out real value of capital as long as time moves. In this context, Lutz (1961) stated that, "So long as the economy is undergoing any sort of change, and capital goods are altering their form, we cannot know exactly to what extent capital is increasing or decreasing."

In theory, there are two approaches to the measurement of capital. One is the forward looking concept of capital and other is backward looking concept of capital. In the forward looking concept, the value of capital is defined as the discounted future income stream to be derived from it. This implies that the significance of a stock of capital goods lies in its earning power. In reality, future can not be forecasted with confidence and hence the earning power of a given capital stock can not be accurately determined. Consequently, there is not a unique capital stock [Robinson (1970)]. In the backward looking approach, the capital stock of a particular year is measured by the amount of resources that would have been required in the base year to produce capital goods of possibly different vintage. Similarly, gross additions to the capital stock and capital consumption are valued in terms of base year costs for particular capital goods added or consumed. "In a state of perfect tranquility, the two concepts must give the same value, and the rate of discount which makes the two equal must be the rate of interest or the rate of return" [Robinson (1970)]. Denison (1957) strongly favours the backward looking concept (or so called cost approach) of measurement of capital. However, there may be objections to the backward looking approach of measurement of capital on the ground that the cost might correspond to the value of assets when it was new—what about the value of an old asset when the productive capacity has declined? If the productivity of an asset really declines, then the only way to measure it is to know the remaining capacity of the asset and this throws us back to the forward looking concept of value of capital which is based on all sorts of expectations. Any accounting practice of measuring the decline in productivity (i.e. depreciation) would be simply arbitrary and misleading [Hashim and Dadi (1973)].

Of late, a related concept, i.e. 'replacement cost' is very often used as a reference to the value of capital. "The 'replacement cost' valuation of assets is realistic in the sense that it is a suitable measure for the purpose of evaluating the contribution which capital makes to production" [Barna (1961)]. Replacement cost has two variations :

(1) replacement cost new; and
(2) replacement cost written-down.

The first amounts to the cost of new equipments of similar type, while the second is based on the vague notion of decline in productive capacity and its measurement. Barna (1961) holds, "The second concept corresponds to the value of capital in economic theory but the first may be equally important in a study of productivity relationships. The value of assets declines with age partly because of falling efficiency (in an economic or in technical sense). It logically follows that value declines faster than efficiency, and indeed for important classes of assets efficiency does not decline at all. For this reason the relationship between replacement cost new and output may be more stable than between written-down replacement cost and output, and the first concept is more relevant in forecasting incremental requirements of capital." Further, it is a fact that a large amount of expenditure is incurred by business firms on repairs and maintenance, whose main object is to keep the asset in more or less a similar productive capacity. Based on a study of large number of firms, Barna (1961) concludes, "It seems that most assets which are in use are maintained by considerable expenditure; the data collected indicate maintenance expenditures which are of the same magnitude as annual expenditure. Even though some repairs are capitalized, it is almost unavoidable that maintenance expenditure should improve the efficiency of plants." "By convention a large part of such maintenance expenditure is treated as current cost (i.e. current flow) and is deducted from gross value of output for the purpose of finding out gross value-added. Now, since the main object of these expenses is to keep the productive capacity of capital equipment more or less intact, there is no reason why it would not be treated as reinvestment. If so, then the so-called 'gross value-added' is infact net value-added and there is no need for subtracting depreciation from the gross value of capital stock to find out the net value of capital stock. We may conclude from the above discussion that 'gross value' or 'purchase price' (suitably adjusted for price variations) is the most useful concept and is also the closest to the concept of capital in theory" [Hashim and Dadi (1973)].

While making an estimate of capital, important choice arises concerning net capital stock and gross capital stock. It is desirable to have an estimate of net capital stock for economic analysis if a fairly reasonable measure of true economic depreciation can be found. In fact, the available estimates of depreciation either are tax-based accounting concepts or based on certain rules of thumb. Therefore, the use of gross capital stock becomes indispensable in empirical research. Further, most analysts have favoured the gross capital stock over the net capital stock on the ground that the net value typically declines much more rapidly than does the ability of a capital good to contribute to production [Goldar (1986)]. On this issue, Kennedy and Thirlwall (1972) in their survey article have justified the use of gross capital stock. According to them, "The flow of capital services does not decline with age at the rate frequently suggested by allowances for depreciation. Net measure of capital tends to assume that the services derived from capital deteriorate with age much more than they actually do." Ideally, one would like to have a measure of net capital which makes allowances for physical depreciation but not obsolescence. However, lack of evidence renders this rarely practicable. In the absence of such a measure, there would seem to be strong case for measuring capital in gross term. Dholakia (1974), quotes Leontief in this respect, "Use of depreciated capital coefficients implies that capital stock declines in efficiency in exact relation to depreciation charges, where most available evidence indicates that this is not reliable assumption." Banerji (1975) has also used gross capital stock suitably adjusted with variations. He warns against the depreciation allowances which are used generally as a proxy for capital services. He puts that "The use of variables like depreciation rate to represent capital services is not safe and can vary often lead to absurd results." Hashim and Dadi (1973) quote Domar who justifies gross capital figures on the ground that "working with net investment and net stock of capital in the conventional sense one loses sight of gross investment as a major vehicle of technological progress. Hence gross figures may be more meaningful, with some unknown deduction of a smaller magnitude than conventional depreciation of existing capital." Thus, gross capital stock is more consistent concept of capital for empirical investigation.

MEASUREMENT OF VARIABLES

(1) Measurement of Labour Input

The ASI provides three distinct measures of labour input :

(a) Man-hours worked;
(b) Number of workers; and
(c) Number of employees (which include both workers and persons other than workers such as supervisors, technicians, managers, clerks, etc.). Employees relate to all persons engaged by the factory in work connected

> directly or indirectly with the manufacturing process and include all administrative, technical and clerical staff, as also labour engaged in production of capital assets for factory's own use. It includes employees in the so-called sales department, as also those engaged in purchase of raw materials etc. and fixed assets for the factory. They also include proprietors and partners and their unpaid family members who work in or outside the factory. Persons in the head office connected with the manufacturing activity of the factory are also included in this.

Goldar (1986), Ahluwalia (1991), and Balakrishan and Pushpangadan (1991) used number of employees as a measure of labour input in their studies on productivity in Indian manufacturing sector. The present study also used 'number of employees' as a measure of labour input. The main reason for disfavouring the first two measures is that these measures do not take into account the services of persons other than workers who are as much important for getting the work done as the workers who operate the machines. The main drawbacks of 'man-hours' series provided in ASI are : (1) the 'man-hours' series do not actually measure man-hours worked because the computation of 'man-worked' series in ASI has been done by multiplying the number of workers in a shift by eight and not the actual duration of the shift [Sinha and Sawhney (1970)]; (2) 'man-hours' series cover only workers and leave out persons other than workers [Goldar (1986)].

(2) Measurement of Output

The ASI publishes the series on net value-added (NVA) by using following relation :

$$NVA = XO - XI - D$$

where XO and XI represent output and input respectively and D stands for depreciation. The main drawbacks with NVA series are : (i) figures on XO, XI and D are at current prices, and (ii) the value of depreciation, D, is taken as book value which seldom represents true capital consumption because the figures on depreciation, that are presented in ASI are at the rates allowed by income tax authorities. In the present study, gross value-added figures are used as a measure of output. Following Jayadevan (1995) and Goldar (1986), present study preferred gross value-added as a measure of output in place of net value added because depreciation charges in the Indian industries are known to be highly arbitrary, fixed by income tax authorities and seldom represent actual capital consumption. In order to get the gross value-added figures at constant prices, we added real net value and depreciation figures at constant prices. The time series relating to value-added are deflated by the wholesale price indices of different industry groups of manufacturing sector for different industries and by the wholesale price index of all commodities for different states and all-India with 1993-94 as base year. It may be mentioned that WPI with 1993-94 as base was taken by shifting the base from 1970-71 to 1980-81 and then to 1993-94. The time series relating to depreciation are deflated by the wholesale price index of machinery & machine tools for fourteen industry groups of manufacturing sector and for all industries in sixteen states and all-India with 1993-94 as base year. The indices are shifted from 1970-71 to 1980-81 and then to 1993-94 as base year.

(3) Measurement of Capital Input

In the present study, gross fixed capital stock is used as a measure of capital input. The fixed capital represents the depreciated value of all fixed assets of the factory as on the closing day of the accounting year. It covers all goods new or used that have a normal economic life of one/or more years (e.g. land, buildings including those under construction, plant and machinery, transport equipment, etc.). The time series relating to fixed capital are deflated by the wholesale price index of machinery & machine tools for fourteen industry groups of manufacturing sector and for all industries in sixteen states and all-India with 1993-94 as base year. The indices are shifted from 1970-71 to 1980-81 and then to 1993-94 as base year.

(4) Wage Rate

In the present study, the wage rate (WR) is determined as a ratio of real value of emoluments to number of employees. A high ratio would indicate high return to each employee and *vice versa*. Emoluments include the salaries and wages paid during the year to persons in employment. It includes profit sharing, festival and other bonuses and *ex-gratia* payments paid at less frequent intervals (i.e. other than bonuses paid more or less regularly for each pay period). Benefits in kind in respect of supplies made or services rendered such as housing, medical, education and recreational facilities are included in this item. It excludes factory expenses in the shape of employer's contribution to provident fund, pension, gratuity or similar other charges. In case of industries, the time series relating to emoluments have been deflated by the consumer price index (general) for industrial workers (CPI-IW) for different industries with 1993-94 as base. In case of the states, the consumer price indices of the different centres from respective states are used. The different centres relating to different states are :

1. All-India—Assam
2. Hyderabad—Andhra Pradesh
3. Jamshedpur—Bihar
4. Ahmedabad—Gujarat
5. Bhopal—Madhya Pradesh
6. Mumbai—Maharashtra
7. Bangalore—Karnataka
8. Alwaye—Kerala
9. Yamunanagar—Haryana
10. All-India—Himachal Pradesh
11. All-India—Orissa
12. Amritsar—Punjab
13. Ajmer—Rajasthan
14. Chennai—Tamil Nadu
15. Kanpur—Uttar Pradesh
16. Kolkata—West Bengal

Due to non-availability of CPI-IW for three States of Assam, Himachal Pradesh & Orissa, CPI-IW general index of all-India has been used for them.

Since different variables have different units of measurement, so for bringing uniformity and for better interpretation, the data at constant prices were converted into indices form by taking 1973-74 as the base year.

Section III

Factor Shares

The measurement of total factor productivity (TFP) requires knowledge of shares of labour and capital inputs in the value-added. The share of labour (S_L) has been obtained by a ratio of total real emoluments to gross real value-added. Assuming constant returns to scale, the share of capital input has been worked out as the difference between unity and share of labour, i.e. $S_K = 1 - S_L$

Capital Intensity

Fixed asset per employee or capital-labour (K/L) ratio reflects the amount of fixed assets allocated to an employee. A higher K/L ratio is an index of an improved mechanisation while a lower ratio refers to a lower level of technological inputs used and dependence on labour intensive methods of production.

Growth Rate

The annual growth rate (r) which is worked out as follows :

$$Y = a\, b^t e^u$$

where a and b are the unknown parameters, e is the base of natural logarithm, and u is the disturbance term. Rate of growth, r (in percentage) was then obtained from $\hat{b}$, the estimator for b, as

$$r = (\hat{b} - 1) \cdot 100$$

Coefficient of variation is worked out for analyzing the inter-state variations by the following formula:

$$C.V. = (\sigma/\tilde{X})\ 100$$

where, C.V. is the coefficient of variation.
σ is the standard deviation and is calculated as follows :

$$\sigma = \sqrt{1/n \sum (X - \tilde{X})^2}$$

and $\tilde{X}$ is the arithmetic mean, calculated as below:

$$\tilde{X} = \sum X/n$$

where, n is the total number of observations.

Measurement of Partial Factor Productivities

We have calculated partial productivities of major factors of production, i.e. labour and capital. The ratio of output to an input is known as partial productivity. Similarly, we can have partial productivities of materials and fuels as well. But there is obvious limitation to this approach as well, i.e. the effects of other inputs on output are ignored. However, most important and most often used one's are the partial productivity indices of labour and capital. These ratios of productivity can better be represented by :

V/L = Value Added/Labour

which is the average product of labour or labour productivity, and

V/K = Value Added/Capital

which is the average product of capital or capital productivity.

The ratios show the amount of output per unit of labour and capital and if they rise then there is an increase in the productivity of that factor. The inverse of these productivity ratios implies requirement of that factor per unit of output. Increase in any of the above partial productivity ratios means that over a period of time more output is possible with optimum utilisation of that input and there is saving in the use of that particular input over time. Sometimes different partial productivity indices have opposite trends and in such cases no judgement is possible about overall industrial efficiency. It will be possible to draw inference about overall efficiency when these indices have similar trends.

MEASUREMENT OF TOTAL FACTOR PRODUCTIVITY

Total factor productivity and technical progress are concepts which are often synonymously used in the production literature. Goldar (1986) made a distinction between the two. Technical progress implies advancement in knowledge of the art of production. This can take many forms such as new products, new techniques of manufacture and new methods of organizations. All these result in productivity improvement. But, productivity improvement can also result from other factors such as improvement in the quality of inputs and of labour, better utilization of plant and equipments and economies of scale in addition to technical progress. Thus, total factor productivity is much broader concept than technical progress. In empirical work, the concept of total factor productivity is the one which is commonly used.

The important measures of total factor productivity used in this study are due to Kendrick, Solow and Translog.

(1) Kendrick Index

Kendrick Index (1961) states that abstracting from changes in economies of scale and elasticity of substitution, increases in total factor productivity can be measured by subtracting the increases in output due to increases in inputs from the actual increase in output [Nadiri (1972)]. This approach assumes that direct application of complete production function is either unnecessary or inappropriate. The Kendrick's method of measurement of total factor productivity is actually based on a production function which ensures linearity, constant returns to scale, infinite labour-capital substitutability and Hicks-neutral technical change.

Let us assume that there is one homogeneous output denoted by V and there are two factors of production : Capital denoted by K and Labour denoted by L. Further, let w_0 and r_0

denote the factors rewards of labour and capital in the base year of the study. Then the Kendrick index for the year 't' may be written as :

$$K(t) = \frac{V_t}{W_o L_t + r_o K_t} \qquad \ldots (1)$$

This formula may be adjusted suitably to take into account more than two factors of production. Under the assumptions of constant returns to scale, perfect competition and payment to factors according to their marginal product, the total earnings of labour and capital in the base year exactly equal output of that year; so that K(o) is equal to unity by definition. Kendrick index may be interpreted as the ratio of actual output to the inputs which would have resulted from increased inputs in the absence of technological change.

Kendrick makes the following assumptions : (a) other factors than labour and capital change in like manner or do not contribute to productivity; (b) the units are uniform and remunerations in base period are proportionate to their marginal productivities; (c) quality is not changed and marginal productivities do not change over period.

These assumptions may not hold good. Index of productivity may reflect "costless advance in technology and managerial efficiency." Though the Kendrick index is easy to calculate and understand yet it suffers from a serious drawback that it involves a linear production function and, thus fails to allow for the possible diminishing marginal productivity of factors. This index has been extensively used by Schmokler, Abramovitz and Kendrick and hence it is also called SAK index.

(2) Solow Index

This alternative index due to Solow (1957)—also called geometric index—is a refinement over Kendrick's arithmetic index. Rather than a practically unrealistic linear production function used in Kendrick index, the Solow index is based on a more general Cobb-Douglas type of production function, expressed as

$$V_t = A(t) \cdot F(K_t, L_t) \qquad \ldots (2)$$

Where F(K, L) is a homogeneous function of degree one, so that due allowances may be made for the possible diminishing marginal productivity of factors. This index, too, makes the assumptions of constant returns to scale, existence of perfect competition in factor markets and payment to factors according to their marginal products.

A (t) in (2) measures the cumulated effect of technical change. Since it varies independently of K and L, technical change is assumed to be both disembodied and Hicks neutral in the sense that it changes the output obtained from inputs, leaving the marginal rate of substitution between inputs unaltered [Krishna (1970), Yotopolous and Nugent (1976)].

If equation (2) is differentiated totally with respect to time and divided by value-added, V, we would have :

$$\frac{\dot{V}}{V} = \frac{\dot{A}}{A} + A\frac{\partial F}{\partial K}\frac{\dot{K}}{V} + A\frac{\partial F}{\partial L}\frac{\dot{L}}{V} \qquad \ldots (3)$$

where, dots indicate time derivatives. The marginal productivity conditions for capital and labour imply

$$\left(\frac{\partial V}{\partial K}\frac{K}{V}\right) = \frac{rK}{V} = s_k, \text{ and}$$

$$\left(\frac{\partial V}{\partial L}\frac{L}{V}\right) = \frac{wL}{V} = s_L,$$

where s_L and s_k are the relative shares of labour and capital respectively.

Thus equation (3) becomes

$$\frac{\dot{V}}{V} = \frac{\dot{A}}{A} + \frac{\dot{K}}{K}\left(\frac{K}{V}A\frac{\partial F}{\partial K}\right) + \frac{\dot{L}}{L}\left(\frac{L}{V}A\frac{\partial F}{\partial L}\right)$$

or

$$\frac{\dot{V}}{V} = \frac{\dot{A}}{A} + \frac{\dot{K}}{K} s_k + \frac{\dot{L}}{L} s_L \qquad \ldots (4)$$

Equation (4) can therefore be used to measure disembodied technical progress as :

$$\frac{\dot{A}}{A} = \frac{\dot{V}}{V} - \frac{\dot{K}}{K} s_k - \frac{\dot{L}}{L} s_L \qquad \ldots (4^*)$$

If $\dot{A}/A$ is constant over time, say equal to 'a' then A (t) has the exponential form e^{at}, so we have exponential growth over time. A discrete approximation to e^{at} is $(1+a)^t$. To fit data to (4*), we must put (4*) into discrete time form, i.e. change d/dt into year-to-year differences, so (4*) becomes

$$\frac{\Delta A}{A} = \frac{\Delta V}{V} + \frac{\Delta K}{K} s_k - \frac{\Delta L}{L} s_L \qquad \ldots (5)$$

Solow has simplified this basic equation further. Let q = V/L and k = K/L and $s_L = 1 - s_K$ and equation (5) can be written as :

$$\frac{\Delta A}{A} = \frac{\Delta q}{q} - \frac{\Delta k}{k} s_k \qquad \ldots (6)$$

In order to estimate ($\Delta A/A$), all we need is time series of value-added per worker, capital per worker and share of capital in value-added. A whole series of technical change can be derived from the identity :

$$A(t+1) = A\ (t) \left(1 + \frac{\Delta A\ (t)}{A\ (t)}\right) \qquad \ldots (7)$$

assuming that A(0) = 1 as an index base. The restrictive assumptions underlying the measure are competitive equilibrium, constant returns to scale and neutral technical progress. The Solow measure uses changing weights.

(3) Translog Index

The Divisia index of technical change was introduced by Solow (1957) and discussed by Jorgenson and Grilliches (1967). The properties of the Divisia index which make its application highly desirable have been noted by Christensen and Jorgenson (1970), and Ringstad and Griliches (1971).

It has been pointed out that the rates of growth of the Divisia indices of prices and quantities add up to the rate of growth of the value (factor reversal test) and that such indices are symmetric in different directions of time (time reversal test). Divisia indices also have the reproductive property that "a Divisia index of Divisia indices is a Divisia index of the components."

Divisia index is based on the production function F, chracterised by constant returns to scale :

$$V = F\,(K, L, t) \qquad \ldots (8)$$

where V is value-added, K is capital input, L is labour input and t is time. Denoting the price of value-added by q_v, the price of capital input by P_K and the price of labour input by P_L, we can define the shares of capital and labour input in the value-added, say s_k and s_L, by

$$s_k = \frac{P_K\,K}{q_v\,V};$$

$$s_L = \frac{P_L\,L}{q_v\,V} \qquad \ldots (9)$$

Necessary conditions for producer equilibrium are given by equalities between each value share and the elasticity of output with respect to the corresponding input :

$$s_k = \frac{\partial \ln V}{\partial \ln K} (K, L, t)$$

$$s_L = \frac{\partial \ln V}{\partial \ln L} (K, L, t) \qquad \ldots (10)$$

Under the constant returns to scale the elasticities and the value shares sum to unity. The rate of technical change, say P(t), can be obtained by partially differentiating the production function with respect to time, holding capital and labour input constant :

$$P(t) = \frac{\partial \ln V}{\partial t} (K, L, t) \qquad \ldots (11)$$

Under constant returns to scale, the rate of technical change can be expressed as the rate of growth of output less a weighted average of the rates of growth of capital and labour, where the weights are given by the corresponding value shares.

$$P(t) = \frac{d \ln V}{d t} - \frac{\partial \ln V}{\partial \ln K} \frac{d \ln K}{d t} - \frac{\partial \ln V}{\partial \ln L} \frac{d \ln L}{d t}$$

or

$$= \frac{d \ln V}{d t} - s_k \frac{d \ln K}{d t} - s_L \frac{d \ln L}{d t}$$

or

$$= \frac{\dot{V}}{V} - \frac{\dot{K}}{K} s_k - \frac{\dot{L}}{L} s_L \qquad \ldots (12)$$

where P (t) is Divisia quantity index of technical change.

For application to the data at discrete points of time, an approximation to the continuous Divisia index is required. The Translog index is a discrete version (developed by Tranquist) of the continuous Divisia index. Translog index numbers are symmetric in data of different time periods and also satisfy the factoral reversal test approximately. But, they do not have reproductive property.

The Translog index of technical change is based on a Translog Production Function, characterized by constant returns to scale. It allows the variable elasticity of substitution and does not require the assumption of Hicks neutrality. Also, in this framework technical change does not remain entirely exogenous, but becomes a function of the factors of production and time. The Transcendental Logarithmic Production Function or, more simply, the Translog Production Function is given as follows :

$$V = \exp.\,[\,\alpha_o + \alpha_k \ln K + \alpha_L \ln L + \alpha_t t + 1/2\, \beta_{kk} (\ln K)^2 + \beta_{kL} (\ln K)(\ln L) + 1/2\, \beta_{LL} (\ln L)^2 + \beta_{kt} (\ln K)\, t + \beta_{Lt} (\ln L)\, t + 1/2\, \beta_{tt} t^2\,] \quad \ldots (13)$$

The Translog Production Function is characterized by constant returns to scale if and only if the parameters satisfy the conditions.

$$\alpha_k + \alpha_L = 1$$
$$\beta_{kk} + \beta_{kL} = 0$$
$$\beta_{kL} + \beta_{LL} = 0 \quad \ldots (14)$$

The value shares of capital and labour input can be expressed as :

$$s_k = \alpha_k + \beta_{kk} \ln K + \beta_{kL} \ln L + \beta_{kt}\, t$$
$$s_L = \alpha_L + \beta_{kL} \ln K + \beta_{LL} \ln L + \beta_{Lt}\, t \quad \ldots (15)$$

If we consider data at any two discrete points of time, say 't' and 't–1', the average rate of technical change can be expressed as the difference between successive logarithms of output less a weighted average of the difference between successive logarithms of capital and labour input with weights given by average value shares.

$$\overline{P}(t) = [\ln V(t) - \ln V(t\text{-}1)] - \overline{s}_k\ [\ln K(t) - \ln K(t-1)] -$$
$$\overline{s}_L\ [\ln L(t) - \ln L(t-1)] \qquad \ldots (16)$$

where

$$\overline{s}_k = 1/2\ [s_k\ (t) + s_k\ (t-1)]$$
$$\overline{s}_L = 1/2\ [s_L\ (t) + s_L\ (t-1)]$$
$$\overline{P}_t = 1/2\ [P_t\ (t) + P_t\ (t-1)]$$

The expression for the average rate of technical change P(t) as the Translog index of total factor productivity. The total factor productivity index (t+1) is derived from the following relationship[1].

$$P\ (t+1) = P(t) \left(1 + \frac{\Delta P\ (t)}{P\ (t)}\right); \text{ where } P\ (0) = 1 \qquad \ldots (17)$$

Productivity studies applying the Translog index of technical change have generally extended this framework to the components of outputs and inputs [Gollop and Jorgenson (1980)]. Aggregate value-added (v) (or more precisely output), aggregate labour (L) and aggregate capital (K) are considered as functions of their components :

$$V = V\ (V_1, V_2, \ldots\ldots\ldots, V_m)$$
$$L = L\ (L_1, L_2, \ldots\ldots\ldots, L_n)$$
$$K = K\ (K_1, K_2, \ldots\ldots\ldots, K_p)$$

The functional form is assumed to be translog and linear homogeneous. Under the assumption of competitive equilibrium, the shares of individual outputs in the value of aggregate value-added (V_i), the shares of individual labour inputs in the value of aggregate labour input (a_j) and the shares of individual capital inputs in the value of aggregate capital input (b_s) are equal to the elasticities of the corresponding aggregate to their individual components. Considering data at two discrete points of time t and t–1, the translog indices of value added, labour input and capital input may be expressed as :

$$\ln V(t) - \ln V(t-1) = \Sigma\ \bar{v}_i\ [\ \ln V_i\ (t) - \ln V_i\ (t-1)\ ]$$

$$\ln L(t) - \ln L(t-1) = \Sigma\ \bar{a}_j\ [\ \ln Lj\ (t) - \ln L_j\ (t-1)\ ]$$

$$\ln K(t) - \ln K(t-1) = \Sigma\ \bar{b}_s\ [\ \ln K_s\ (t) - \ln K_s\ (t-1)\ ]$$

where,

$$\bar{v}_i = 1/2\ [\ v_i\ (t) + v_i\ (t-1)\ ];\ i = 1, 2, \ldots\ldots, m;$$

$$\bar{a}_j = 1/2\ [\ a_j\ (t) + a_j\ (t-1)\ ];\ j = 1, 2, \ldots\ldots, n;$$

$$\bar{b}_s = 1/2\ [\ b_s\ (t) + b_s\ (t-1)\ ];\ s = 1, 2, \ldots\ldots, p;$$

REGRESSION ANALYSIS

Various log linear regression equations between wages and productivity have been estimated. By introducing dummy variable and by taking data in indices form, the relation between wages and productivity for pre and post-liberalisation era and total study period was examined. Different linear regression equations using data in indices form were also tried but results were not encouraging. Moreover, the log linear regression equations are better in the sense that the slope coefficient reveals the elasticity of regressand with respect to regressor. To introduce stationarity in the time series, the first difference form using data in indices form was also tried, but the results were found difficult to interpret for long-term policy measures. Finally, time series in level form were obtained by introducing trend as additional explanatory variable in different regressions. The various estimated regression equations were derived from the following functions :

1. $\ln WR_t = f\ (\ \ln t, \ln LP_t, \ln LP_{t-1,} \ln LP_{t-2,} \ln LP_{t-3,} \ln LP_{t-4,}$ $\ln LP_{t-5,} \ln LP_{t-6,} \ln K/L_{t,} \ln K/L_{t-1},$ $\ln K/L_{t-2,} \ln K/L_{t-3,} \ln K/L_{t-4,} \ln TFPK_t, \ln TFPS_t, \ln TFPT_t)$

2. $\ln LP_t = f(\ln t, \ln WR_{t,} \ln WR_{t-1,} \ln WR_{t-2,} \ln WR_{t-3,} \ln WR_{t-4} \ln WR_{t-5,} \ln WR_{t-6,} \ln WR_{t-7,} \ln WR_{t-8,} \ln K/L_{t,} \ln K/L_{t-1,} \ln K/L_{t-2,} \ln K/L_{t-3,} \ln K/L_{t-4,} \ln K/L_{t-5,} \ln K/L_{t-6,} \ln K/L_{t-7})$
3. $WR_t = f(t, D, LP_{t,}\ D\ .\ LP_t)$
4. $LP_t = f(t, D, WR_{t,}\ D\ .\ WR_t)$

$\ln WR_t$ is the natural log of indices of real wage rate in time period 't'.

$\ln WR_{t-1}$ is the natural log of indices of real wage rate in time period 't–1'.

$\ln WR_{t-2}$ is the natural log of indices of real wage rate in time period 't–2'.

$\ln WR_{t-3}$ is the natural log of indices of real wage rate in time period 't–3'.

$\ln WR_{t-4}$ is the natural log of indices of real wage rate in time period 't–4'.

$\ln WR_{t-5}$ is the natural log of indices of real wage rate in time period 't–5'.

$\ln WR_{t-6}$ is the natural log of indices of real wage rate in time period 't–6'.

$\ln WR_{t-7}$ is the natural log of indices of real wage rate in time period 't–7'.

$\ln WR_{t-8}$ is the natural log of indices of real wage rate in time period 't–8'.

$\ln LP_t$ is the natural log of indices of partial labour productivity in time period 't'.

$\ln LP_{t-1}$ is the natural log of indices of partial labour productivity in time period 't–1'.

$\ln LP_{t-2}$ is the natural log of indices of partial labour productivity in time period 't–2'.

$\ln LP_{t-3}$ is the natural log of indices of partial labour productivity in. time period 't–3'.

$\ln LP_{t-4}$ is the natural log of indices of partial labour productivity in time period 't–4'.

$\ln LP_{t-5}$ is the natural log of indices of partial labour productivity in time period 't-5'.

$\ln LP_{t-6}$ is the natural log of indices of partial labour productivity in time period 't-6'.

$\ln (K/L)_t$ is the natural log of indices of capital intensity in time period 't'.

$\ln (K/L)_{t-1}$ is the natural log of indices of capital intensity in time period 't–1'.

$\ln (K/L)_{t-2}$ is the natural log of indices of capital intensity in time period 't–2'.

$\ln (K/L)_{t-3}$ is the natural log of indices of capital intensity in time period 't–3'.

$\ln (K/L)_{t-4}$ is the natural log of indices of capital intensity in time period 't–4'.

$\ln (K/L)_{t-5}$ is the natural log of indices of capital intensity in time period 't–5'.

$\ln (K/L)_{t-6}$ is the natural log of indices of capital intensity in time period 't–6'.

$\ln (K/L)_{t-7}$ is the natural log of indices of capital intensity in time period 't–7'.

$\ln TFPK_t$ is the natural log of indices of total factor productivity of Kendrick in time period 't'.

$\ln TFPS_t$ is the natural log of indices of total factor productivity of Solow in time period 't'.

$\ln TFPT_t$ is the natural log of indices of total factor productivity of Translog in time period 't'.

ln t is the natural log of time period.
WR_t is the index of real wage rate.
LP_t is the index of partial labour productivity.
t is time period.
D is the dummy variable.

Equations with different combinations of variables were tried, keeping in view the problem of multicollinearity. The results are presented in Tables given in Appendix. However, the results of only best fit equations were interpreted.

Notes and References

1. The Translog index can also be explained as :

   $\Delta P(t)/P(t) = \Delta V_t/V_t - (s_L \Delta L_t/L_t + s_k \Delta K_t/K_t)$
   Where, $\Delta V_t/V_t$, $\Delta L_t/L_t$, $\Delta K_t/K_t$ are the log of real value-added, labour and capital respectively and

   $\overline{s_k} = 1/2 [s_k (t+1) + s_k (t)]$

   $\overline{s_L} = 1/2 [s_L (t+1) + s_L (t)]$

   The total factor productivity index P(t+1) is derived by the following relation :

   $P(t+1) = P(t) \{ 1 + [\Delta P(t)/P(t)]\}$; where $P(t) = 0$

Trends in Economic Parameters in Industries

In this chapter growth rates, trends and coefficient of variation of various economic parameters like real GVA, real GFC, real emoluments, real wage rate, share of labour in GVA, etc. are analysed for 14 major industries of manufacturing sector at all-India level from 1973-74 to 2000-01.

INTER-INDUSTRY COMPARISON OF REAL WAGE RATE

An inter-industry comparison of real wage rate from 1973-74 to 2000-01 (Table 5.1) revealed that the maximum average annual growth rate and variability were observed in Food Products Industry followed by Machinery Other Than Transport Industry and minimum growth in Leather and Fur Products Industry and least variability in Cotton Textiles Industry. In 1973-74 maximum real wage rate was observed in Chemicals & Chemical Products Industry followed by Basic Metals & Alloys Industry. In 1983-84 maximum real wage rate was found in same industry followed by Transport Equipment and Parts Industry. Similar result was observed in 1993-94. In 2000-01, the maximum real wage rate was observed in Machinery Other Than Transport

TABLE 5.1
Profile of Real Wage Rate in Industries

Year	*FPI*	*BTTPI*	*CTI*	*JHMTI*	*TPI*	*PPPI*	*LFPI*	*CCPI*	*RPCPI*	*NMMPI*	*BMAI*	*MPI*	*MOTI*	*TEPI*
(1)	(2)	(3)	(4)	(5)	(6)	(7)	(8)	(9)	(10)	(11)	(12)	(13)	(14)	(15)
1973-74	0.113	0.088	0.208	0.198	0.154	0.220	0.197	0.320	0.279	0.152	0.318	0.202	0.281	0.282
1974-75	0.078	0.074	0.202	0.181	0.132	0.216	0.185	0.294	0.260	0.144	0.323	0.198	0.218	0.265
1975-76	0.089	0.094	0.212	0.200	0.149	0.230	0.168	0.326	0.301	0.161	0.325	0.209	0.298	0.307
1976-77	0.078	0.087	0.214	0.216	0.162	0.248	0.215	0.346	0.317	0.175	0.361	0.230	0.327	0.333
1977-78	0.088	0.087	0.228	0.217	0.162	0.248	0.217	0.334	0.295	0.172	0.338	0.226	0.325	0.329
1978-79	0.102	0.091	0.233	0.212	0.174	0.259	0.189	0.373	0.326	0.174	0.340	0.231	0.337	0.351
1979-80	0.102	0.095	0.238	0.240	0.167	0.264	0.224	0.349	0.278	0.179	0.366	0.252	0.331	0.338
1980-81	0.093	0.085	0.241	0.247	0.181	0.265	0.223	0.364	0.322	0.195	0.349	0.255	0.341	0.350
1981-82	0.093	0.080	0.224	0.232	0.172	0.282	0.201	0.368	0.285	0.179	0.348	0.250	0.332	0.364
1982-83	0.118	0.121	0.227	0.223	0.178	0.269	0.203	0.377	0.314	0.199	0.366	0.239	0.357	0.377
1983-84	0.145	0.100	0.248	0.218	0.177	0.276	0.218	0.398	0.332	0.186	0.372	0.277	0.372	0.383
1984-85	0.154	0.109	0.260	0.245	0.179	0.295	0.221	0.420	0.358	0.200	0.420	0.298	0.397	0.401
1985-86	0.157	0.126	0.259	0.274	0.183	0.299	0.219	0.419	0.364	0.202	0.392	0.287	0.405	0.422
1986-87	0.163	0.108	0.265	0.286	0.189	0.307	0.217	0.441	0.380	0.209	0.391	0.294	0.384	0.436
1987-88	0.169	0.107	0.263	0.263	0.187	0.326	0.228	0.444	0.366	0.207	0.396	0.299	0.414	0.442

1988-89	0.174	0.113	0.263	0.281	0.192	0.312	0.191	0.424	0.364	0.209	0.412	0.314	0.414	0.439
1989-90	0.190	0.114	0.271	0.286	0.195	0.352	0.210	0.455	0.385	0.227	0.442	0.286	0.454	0.475
1990-91	0.194	0.114	0.273	0.302	0.204	0.347	0.215	0.475	0.370	0.219	0.424	0.300	0.443	0.460
1991-92	0.197	0.112	0.268	0.276	0.194	0.341	0.211	0.443	0.352	0.218	0.335	0.287	0.437	0.457
1992-93	0.198	0.113	0.265	0.300	0.202	0.345	0.223	0.493	0.367	0.231	0.434	0.310	0.445	0.454
1993-94	0.198	0.123	0.265	0.305	0.191	0.355	0.213	0.465	0.370	0.241	0.447	0.316	0.453	0.456
1994-95	0.204	0.120	0.274	0.297	0.193	0.414	0.201	0.487	0.370	0.254	0.468	0.334	0.459	0.472
1995-96	0.211	0.119	0.265	0.305	0.204	0.390	0.214	0.490	0.422	0.251	0.503	0.345	0.498	0.522
1996-97	0.221	0.123	0.258	0.298	0.205	0.390	0.198	0.480	0.381	0.293	0.503	0.324	0.494	0.508
1997-98	0.204	0.123	0.255	0.334	0.212	0.382	0.226	0.490	0.409	0.271	0.509	0.344	0.508	0.540
1998-99	0.246	0.143				0.424	0.256	0.600	0.468	0.294	0.619	0.416	0.475	0.517
1999-00	0.271	0.157				0.448	0.288	0.660	0.521	0.348	0.601	0.445	0.690	0.691
2000-01	0.273	0.182				0.501	0.272	0.641	0.616	0.366	0.711	0.459	0.718	0.698
Growth Rate	4.624* (15.827)	2.173* (9.165)	1.11* (8.112)	2.164* (13.591)	1.405* (10.579)	2.682* (26.330)	0.811* (3.872)	2.393* (16.882)	2.06* (9.562)	2.731* (16.882)	2.308* (10.340)	2.555* (15.565)	2.895* (13.264)	2.783* (17.606)
Linear Slope	0.006* (18.690)	0.002* (8.238)	0.002* (8.176)	0.005* (14.284)	0.002* (12.043)	0.008* (18.810)	0.001* (3.870)	0.01* (13.265)	0.007* (7.916)	0.006* (12.081)	0.01* (8.749)	0.007* (12.367)	0.011* (10.765)	0.011* (13.246)
CV	0.363	0.212	0.091	0.163	0.107	0.226	0.114	0.211	0.209	0.249	0.231	0.227	0.262	0.243

Notes : 1. Figures in brackets are the respective ' t' values.

2. Indicates significant at one percent level.

Industry followed by Basic Metals & Alloys Industry. However, in the above four different years, the least real wage rate was throughout found in Beverages, Tobacco & Tobacco Products Industry.

INTER-INDUSTRY COMPARISON OF SHARE OF LABOUR

An inter-industry comparison of share of labour in real GVA (Table 5.2) showed a declining trend in all industries but minimum decline was found in Chemicals & Chemical Products Industry followed by Paper & Paper Products Industry and maximum in Jute, Hemp & Mesta Textiles Industry. The highest variability was observed in Textile Products Industry followed by Beverages, Tobacco & Tobacco Products Industry and minimum was in Paper & Paper Products Industry. In 1973-74 maximum share of labour was observed in Jute, Hemp & Mesta Textiles Industry followed by Textile Products Industry and least was in Chemicals & Chemical Products Industry. Similar result was observed in 1983-84. In 1993-94 maximum share of labour was again found in Jute, Hemp & Mesta Textiles Industry followed by Cotton Textiles Industry and least in Rubber, Petroleum & Coal Products Industry. In 2000-01, the highest value was observed in Machinery Other Than Transport Industry followed by Transport Equipment & Parts Industry and minimum in Rubber, Petroleum & Coal Products Industry.

In JHMTI, share of labour in GVA at constant prices was greater than one during 1973-74 to 1990-91 because first, CPI-IW increased steadily from 19.93 in 1973-74 to 141.86 in 1997-98, while Wholesale Price Index (WPI) increased in a fluctuating manner from 59.4 in 1973-74 to 100.87 in 1997-98. Second, in initial years WPI was quite high as compared to CPI-IW, due to which real emoluments were greater than real NVA. Similar was the case in BTTPI, CTI, TPI and MPI. However, share of labour in GVA at current prices (Table 5.17 on end of the chapter) was less than one in all industries except in JHMTI in 1985-86 and 1992-93.

ANALYSIS OF VARIABLES IN DIFFERENT INDUSTRIES

The trends in economic parameters in different industries have been discussed on page 83.

TABLE 5.2
Share of Labour in GVA at Constant Prices in Different Industries

Year	FPI	BTTPI	CTI	JHMTI	TPI	PPPI	LFPI	CCPI	RPCPI	NMMPI	BMAI	MPI	MOTI	TEPI
(1)	(2)	(3)	(4)	(5)	(6)	(7)	(8)	(9)	(10)	(11)	(12)	(13)	(14)	(15)
1973-74	0.708	0.767	0.986	2.328	1.742	0.555	0.717	0.265	0.420	0.534	0.608	0.887	0.657	0.712
1974-75	0.544	0.410	1.094	1.986	1.643	0.499	0.534	0.256	0.344	0.545	0.515	0.917	0.630	0.682
1975-76	0.639	0.719	1.282	1.905	1.482	0.543	0.541	0.314	0.455	0.590	0.588	1.007	0.700	0.771
1976-77	0.535	0.638	1.257	2.159	1.746	0.600	0.640	0.307	0.354	0.593	0.581	1.012	0.681	0.679
1977-78	0.526	0.964	1.272	2.317	1.748	0.587	0.646	0.292	0.332	0.503	0.622	1.031	0.678	0.678
1978-79	0.517	0.828	1.091	2.397	1.526	0.629	0.694	0.266	0.417	0.589	0.569	0.999	0.694	0.662
1979-80	0.618	1.007	1.080	2.305	1.803	0.652	0.772	0.306	0.436	0.631	0.677	1.023	0.737	0.795
1980-81	0.870	0.982	1.091	2.010	1.716	0.650	0.838	0.350	0.505	0.659	0.604	1.038	0.687	0.815
1981-82	0.766	0.955	1.045	2.184	1.339	0.659	0.919	0.345	0.481	0.586	0.465	0.878	0.663	0.743
1982-83	0.826	1.476	1.012	2.116	1.206	0.681	0.664	0.322	0.386	0.466	0.503	0.782	0.619	0.686
1983-84	0.576	0.567	0.923	1.572	1.122	0.605	0.619	0.297	0.554	0.451	0.419	0.707	0.612	0.708
1984-85	0.603	0.620	0.986	1.739	0.832	0.568	0.665	0.338	0.444	0.435	0.584	0.861	0.559	0.737
1985-86	0.559	0.713	0.912	2.043	1.147	0.677	0.845	0.338	0.260	0.441	0.425	0.804	0.589	0.734
1986-87	0.549	0.470	0.863	1.735	0.777	0.604	0.857	0.370	0.272	0.491	0.516	0.818	0.601	0.678
1987-88	0.542	0.389	0.811	1.463	0.706	0.606	0.695	0.355	0.248	0.413	0.457	0.706	0.523	0.688
1988-89	0.475	0.337	0.686	1.388	0.787	0.525	0.584	0.347	0.240	0.432	0.333	0.625	0.529	0.675

(Contd.)

TABLE 5.2 (Contd.)

(1)	(2)	(3)	(4)	(5)	(6)	(7)	(8)	(9)	(10)	(11)	(12)	(13)	(14)	(15)
1989-90	0.422	0.395	0.554	1.284	0.776	0.470	0.562	0.320	0.252	0.393	0.327	0.607	0.490	0.605
1990-91	0.485	0.307	0.533	1.182	0.496	0.437	0.425	0.292	0.210	0.294	0.280	0.606	0.469	0.491
1991-92	0.452	0.262	0.568	0.883	0.361	0.396	0.334	0.252	0.222	0.232	0.275	0.447	0.386	0.477
1992-93	0.443	0.263	0.557	0.916	0.294	0.383	0.343	0.221	0.165	0.288	0.262	0.462	0.343	0.448
1993-94	0.305	0.279	0.506	0.872	0.192	0.329	0.228	0.190	0.147	0.283	0.287	0.349	0.344	0.419
1994-95	0.278	0.240	0.370	0.655	0.203	0.390	0.293	0.193	0.144	0.264	0.239	0.381	0.296	0.406
1995-96	0.332	0.262	0.473	0.741	0.242	0.374	0.321	0.169	0.152	0.218	0.226	0.362	0.344	0.381
1996-97	0.348	0.231	0.354	0.567	0.254	0.355	0.312	0.146	0.108	0.184	0.216	0.305	0.308	0.413
1997-98	0.272	0.242	0.411	0.602	0.272	0.445	0.246	0.192	0.187	0.247	0.202	0.371	0.340	0.398
1998-99	0.266	0.295				0.433	0.294	0.180	0.190	0.324	0.261	0.380	0.379	0.517
1999-00	0.304	0.233				0.413	0.315	0.196	0.190	0.339	0.250	0.387	0.479	0.433
2000-01	0.330	0.317				0.343	0.424	0.245	0.216	0.350	0.350	0.464	0.505	0.504
Growth	-3.374*	-5.381*	-5.06*	-5.728*	-9.503*	-2.138*	-3.803*	-2.022*	-4.392*	-3.583*	-4.107*	-4.487*	-2.878*	-2.466*
Rate	(-7.552)	(-7.073)	(-12.720)	(-11.185)	(-13.031)	(-6.059)	(-5.906)	(-4.235)	(-7.446)	(-7.783)	(-9.923)	(-11.825)	(-7.651)	(-7.514)
Linear	-0.015*	-0.027*	-0.038*	-0.078*	-0.076*	-0.01*	-0.018*	-0.004*	-0.012*	-0.014*	-0.016*	-0.029*	-0.014*	-0.014*
Slope	(-6.501)	(-5.149)	(-13.708)	(-12.152)	(-15.896)	(-5.813)	(-5.347)	(-3.935)	(-6.762)	(-8.601)	(-9.964)	(-12.864)	(-8.631)	(-7.629)
CV	0.330	0.594	0.363	0.395	0.602	0.222	0.382	0.240	0.428	0.33	0.366	0.374	0.265	0.232

Notes : 1. Figures in brackets are the respective 't' values.

2*. Indicates significant at one percent level.

The *Food Products Industry* at two-digit level includes, (i) Slaughtering, preparation and preservation of meat; (ii) Manufacture of dairy products; (iii) Canning and preservation of fruits and vegetables; (iv) Canning, preserving and processing of fish, crustancean and similar foods; (v) Grain mill products; (vi) Manufacture of bakery products; (vii) Production of indigenous sugar, *boora, khandsari, gur,* etc. from sugarcane and palm juice; (viii) Production of common salt; (ix) Manufacture of cocoa, choclate and sugar confectionary; (x) Manufacture of hydrogenated oils, vanaspati ghee, etc; (xi) Manufacture of other edible oils & fats; (xii) Tea processing; (xiii) Coffee curing, roasting & grinding; (xiv) Cashew nut processing; (xv) Manufacture of ice; (xvi) Manufacture of prepared animal feeds; (xvii) Manufacture of starch; (xviii) Manufacture of remaining food products.

Table 5.3 shows the indices of various economic parameters along with their growth rate, trend and coefficient of variation in case of food products industry from 1973-74 to 2000-01.

Index of real GVA increased from 100.00 in 1973-74 to 933.64 in 2000-01. It increased at an average rate of 9.26 percent. The overall trend rate of real GVA was found to be 34.705 per annum. The average annual growth rate and trend rate were found statistically significant at one percent level of significance. Coefficient of variation was found to be 0.742.

Index of real emoluments increased from 100.00 in 1973-74 to 434.83 in 2000-01. The real emoluments increased at an average rate of 5.57 percent per annum. The overall trend rate was 12.125 per annum. The average annual growth rate and trend rate were found statistically significant at one percent level of significance. Coefficient of variation was found to be 0.432.

Index of real GFC rose from 100.00 in 1973-74 to 790.98 in 2000-01. The real GFC increased at an average rate of 9.573 percent per annum. The overall trend rate was 30.205 per annum. The average annual growth rate and trend rate were found statistically significant at one percent level of significance. Coefficient of variation was found to be 0.759.

Index of employees increased from 100.00 in 1973-74 to 179.7 in 2000-01. It increased at an average rate of 0.904 percent per annum. The overall trend rate was 1.347 per annum. The average annual growth rate and trend rate were statistically

TABLE 5.3
Economic Parameters of Food Products Industry in India (Code—20-21)

Year	*Index of Real GVA*	*Index of Real Emoluments*	*Index of Real GFC*	*Index of Employees*	*Index of Real Wage Rate*	*Index of CPI-IW*
1973-74	100.00	100.00	100.00	100.00	100.00	100.00
1974-75	119.35	91.75	91.353	132.94	69.01	126.84
1975-76	130.65	118.09	95.109	150.25	78.59	125.23
1976-77	148.19	112.09	108.83	162.44	69.00	120.42
1977-78	181.40	134.77	130.67	171.71	78.49	129.65
1978-79	202.49	147.86	144.10	162.79	90.82	132.46
1979-80	174.87	152.78	139.32	169.12	90.33	144.05
1980-81	124.31	152.89	135.30	185.44	82.44	160.46
1981-82	142.43	154.12	134.19	187.21	82.32	180.48
1982-83	158.91	185.45	150.33	177.54	104.45	194.48
1983-84	229.79	187.21	181.07	145.47	128.69	215.85
1984-85	230.10	196.17	179.85	143.28	136.91	229.45
1985-86	242.25	191.37	191.98	137.57	139.10	245.00
1986-87	249.90	194.04	201.91	134.10	144.69	266.43
1987-88	281.08	215.31	236.65	143.44	150.09	289.76
1988-89	328.65	220.51	235.60	142.97	154.23	317.01
1989-90	442.05	263.36	310.07	155.90	168.92	336.42
1990-91	394.77	270.86	338.17	157.41	172.06	375.31
1991-92	429.67	274.70	394.95	157.59	174.30	425.89
1992-93	479.39	300.15	495.43	171.07	175.45	466.73
1993-94	697.99	300.82	569.26	170.98	175.93	501.75
1994-95	800.41	314.14	634.27	173.40	181.16	552.33
1995-96	737.17	345.94	672.57	184.92	187.07	608.68
1996-97	717.80	353.29	674.03	179.85	196.43	665.12
1997-98	905.30	347.57	807.21	191.81	181.19	711.79
1998-99	1042.19	391.29	851.97	179.46	218.02	805.16
1999-00	1026.13	441.10	858.39	183.37	240.55	832.36
2000-01	933.64	434.83	790.98	179.70	241.97	863.47
Growth Rate	9.260* (20,605)	5.570* (37.691)	9.573* (26.214)	0.904* (3.080)	4.620* (15.825)	8.600* (57.220)
Linear Slope	34.705* (12.324)	12.125* (24.823)	30.205* (12.910)	1.347* (3.101)	6.104* (18.687)	27.986* (15.853)
CV	0.742	0.432	0.759	0.132	0.363	0.669

Notes : 1. Figures in parentheses are the respective 't' values.
2* Indicates one percent level of significance.

significant at one percent level of significance. Coefficient of variation was found to be 0.132.

Consumer price index for industrial workers increased at an average rate of 8.6 percent per annum. The overall trend rate was 27.986 per annum. Both the average annual growth rate and trend rate were found statistically significant at one percent level of significance.

Index of real wage rate increased at an average rate of 4.62 percent per annum. The overall trend rate was 6.104 per annum. Both the average annual growth rate and trend rate were found statistically significant at one percent level of significance.

An inter-variable comparison in this industry revealed that the maximum growth rate and variability have been observed in GFC followed by GVA and minimum in case of employees. It has been found that the growth rates and variability of both the emoluments as well as the wage rate were higher than that of employees. The Index of GVA increased at much higher rate than of real emoluments and real wage rate.

Table 5.4 shows the indices of various economic parameters of *Beverages, Tobacco & Tobacco Products Industry* from 1973-74 to 2000-01 which includes; (i) distilling, rectifying and blending of spirits; (ii) wine industries; (iii) malt liquors and malt; (iv) production of country liquor and toddy; (v) soft drinks and carbonated water industries; (vi) tobacco stemming, redrying and all other operations which are connected with preparing raw leaf tobacco for manufacture; (vii) manufacture of *bidi*; (viii) manufacture of cigars, cigarettes, cheroot and cigarettes tobacco; (ix) manufacturing of chewing tobacco, *zarda* and snuff; (x) manufacture of tobacco and tobacco products not elsewhere classified.

Index of real GVA increased from 100.00 in 1973-74 to 1271.43 in 2000-01. It rose at an average rate of 11.290 percent. The overall trend rate of real GVA was found to be 50.296 per annum. The average annual growth rate and trend rate were found statistically significant at one percent level of significance. Coefficient of variation was found to be 0.780.

Index of real emoluments increased from 100.00 in 1973-74 to 526.20 in 2000-01. The real emoluments increased at an average rate of 5.302 percent per annum. The over all trend rate was found to be 12.244 per annum. The average annual growth

TABLE 5.4

Economic Parameters of Beverages, Tobacco and Tobacco Products Industry in India (Code—22)

Year	*Index of Real GVA*	*Index of Real Emoluments*	*Index of Real GFC*	*Index of Employees*	*Index of Real Wage Rate*
1973-74	100.00	100.00	100.00	100.00	100.00
1974-75	156.46	83.66	94.85	99.41	84.16
1975-76	114.46	107.32	108.95	100.97	106.29
1976-77	171.25	142.44	119.18	144.68	98.45
1977-78	128.70	161.79	121.14	164.24	98.51
1978-79	168.19	181.54	124.65	176.87	102.64
1979-80	149.32	195.97	119.21	182.08	107.63
1980-81	135.74	173.81	122.21	181.88	95.56
1981-82	141.63	176.37	122.32	194.55	90.66
1982-83	142.51	274.17	117.26	199.94	137.13
1983-84	301.53	222.83	184.63	197.86	112.62
1984-85	242.45	196.11	160.36	159.08	123.28
1985-86	241.75	224.82	248.54	157.63	142.63
1986-87	350.47	214.81	258.00	175.54	122.37
1987-88	470.94	238.67	331.61	196.92	121.20
1988-89	566.22	248.48	391.79	193.83	128.20
1989-90	584.82	301.01	349.63	233.69	128.81
1990-91	705.52	282.78	396.55	219.82	128.64
1991-92	860.82	293.85	460.37	232.27	126.51
1992-93	920.81	315.44	654.88	247.96	127.21
1993-94	882.48	321.34	693.99	230.88	139.18
1994-95	1138.30	355.93	883.18	262.07	135.82
1995-96	963.88	329.63	898.77	244.17	135.00
1996-97	1173.33	353.33	1077.75	253.66	139.30
1997-98	1186.80	374.56	1235.92	270.42	138.51
1998-99	991.22	381.13	1186.79	235.05	162.15
1999-00	1439.53	437.34	1536.17	245.79	177.94
2000-01	1271.43	526.20	1676.00	255.47	205.97
Growth Rate	11.290* (18.354)	5.302* (15.334)	12.154* (23.434)	3.062* (8.973)	2.173* (9.163)
Linear Slope	50.296* (14.927)	12.244* (16.342)	51.706* (10.375)	5.417* (10.883)	2.750* (8.236)
CV	0.780	0.409	0.963	0.248	0.212

Notes : 1. Figures in parentheses are the respective 't' values.
2*. Indicates one percent level of significance.

rate and trend rate were found statistically significant at one percent level of significance. Coefficient of variation was found to be 0.409.

Index of real GFC rose from 100.00 in 1973-74 to 1675.99 in 2000-01. The real GFC increased at an average rate of 12.154 percent per annum. The overall trend rate was 51.706 per annum. The average annual growth rate and trend rate were found statistically significant at one percent level of significance. Coefficient of variation was found to be 0.963.

Index of employees increased from 100.00 in 1973-74 to 255.47 in 2000-01. The increase in average rate was 3.062 percent per annum. The overall trend rate was 5.417 per annum. The average annual growth rate and trend rate were statistically significant at one percent level of significance. Coefficient of variation was found to be 0.248.

Index of real wage rate indicated an increase of 2.173 percent per annum. The overall trend rate was 2.75 per annum. Both the average annual growth rate and trend rate were found statistically significant at one percent level of significance. Coefficient of variation was found to be 0.212

An inter-variable comparison in this industry revealed that the maximum growth rate and variability have been observed in GFC followed by GVA and minimum in case of wage rate. It has been found that the growth rate and variability of employees were lesser than emoluments but greater than the wage rate. Index of real emoluments and real wage rate increased at much slower rate than of GVA.

Table 5.5 shows the indices of various economic parameters of *Cotton Textiles Industry* from 1973-74 to 1997-98 which includes, (i) cotton ginning, cleaning and bailing; (ii) cotton spinning, weaving, shrinking, safranizing, mercerizing and finishing of cotton textiles in mills; (iii) printing, dyeing and bleaching of cotton textiles; (iv) cotton spinning other than in mills (*charkha*); (v) production of *khadi*; (vi) weaving and finishing of cotton textiles in handlooms other than *khadi*; (vii) weaving and finishing of cotton textiles in power looms; (viii) cotton textiles not elsewhere classified.

Index of real GVA increased from 100.00 in 1973-74 to 260.68 in 1997-98. It increased at an average rate of 4.956 percent per annum. The overall trend rate of real GVA was found to be

TABLE 5.5
Economic Parameters of Cotton Textiles Industry in India (Code—23)

Year	*Index of Real GVA*	*Index of Real Emoluments*	*Index of Real GFC*	*Index of Employees*	*Index of Real Wage Rate*
1973-74	100.00	100.00	100.00	100.00	100.00
1974-75	95.50	105.97	90.48	109.05	97.17
1975-76	86.66	112.66	88.63	110.26	102.17
1976-77	87.45	111.50	96.88	108.48	102.77
1977-78	93.35	120.38	107.00	109.98	109.45
1978-79	116.85	129.27	114.40	115.13	112.28
1979-80	121.72	133.26	112.52	116.59	114.29
1980-81	115.62	127.88	121.99	110.28	115.95
1981-82	106.07	112.45	119.82	104.53	107.57
1982-83	115.22	118.27	149.69	108.47	109.03
1983-84	135.45	126.84	171.85	106.25	119.38
1984-85	122.55	122.50	175.53	97.95	125.06
1985-86	123.08	113.77	190.36	91.19	124.76
1986-87	133.95	117.29	183.12	92.03	127.45
1987-88	132.35	108.79	188.80	85.98	126.53
1988-89	150.74	104.82	186.93	82.92	126.41
1989-90	204.57	114.95	194.62	88.24	130.26
1990-91	206.39	111.48	207.50	84.95	131.23
1991-92	180.26	103.85	232.94	80.53	128.95
1992-93	187.38	105.77	313.78	83.09	127.30
1993-94	207.62	106.61	378.98	83.55	127.60
1994-95	284.91	107.01	457.82	81.14	131.87
1995-96	235.29	112.92	522.06	88.65	127.37
1996-97	293.42	105.22	575.94	84.83	124.03
1997-98	260.68	108.54	703.57	88.63	122.45
Growth Rate	4.956* (14.025)	-0.355*** (-1.755)	8.205* (15.491)	-1.449* (-7.846)	1.110* (8.110)
Linear Slope	7.759* (10.598)	-0.421*** (-1.799)	19.492* (7.978)	-1.409* (-7.738)	1.271* (8.174)
CV	0.402	0.078	0.723	0.126	0.091

Notes : 1. Figures in parentheses are the respective 't' values.
2. * indicates one percent level of significance.
3. *** indicate 10 percent level of significance.

7.759 per annum. The average annual growth rate and trend rate were found statistically significant at one percent level of significance. Coefficient of variation was found to be 0.402.

Index of real emoluments indicated a mild increase from 100.00 in 1973-74 to 108.54 in 1997-98. The real emoluments decreased at an average rate of 0.355 percent per annum. The overall trend rate was found to be –0.421 per annum. The average annual growth rate and trend rate were statistically significant at ten percent level of significance. Coefficient of variation was found to be 0.078.

Index of real GFC rose from 100.00 in 1973-74 to 703.57 in 1997-98. The real GFC increased at an average rate of 8.205 percent per annum. The overall trend rate was found to be 19.492 per annum. The average annual growth rate and trend rate were found statistically significant at one percent level of significance. Coefficient of variation was found to be 0.723.

Index of employees decreased from 100.00 in 1973-74 to 88.63 in 1997-98, which worked out to decrease of 1.449 percent per annum. The overall trend rate was –1.409 per annum. The average annual growth rate and trend rate were statistically significant at one percent level of significance. Coefficient of variation was found to be 0.126.

Index of real wage rate rose from 100.00 in 1973-74 to 122.45 in 1997-98. It indicated an average growth rate of 1.11 percent per annum. The overall trend rate was 1.271 per annum. Both the average annual growth rate and trend rate were found statistically significant at one percent level of significance. Coefficient of variation was found to be 0.091.

An inter-variable comparison in this industry revealed that the maximum growth rate and variability have been observed in GFC followed by GVA and negative growth rate was in case of employees and least variability in case of emoluments. It has been found that the growth rates of both the emoluments as well as the wage rate were higher than that of employees. While real emoluments experienced negative growth rate, real wages experienced very low growth rate as compared to growth rate of GVA.

Table 5.6 shows the indices of various economic parameters of *Jute, Hemp and Mesta Textiles Industry* which includes, (i) jute and mesta pressing and bailing; (ii) jute and mesta spinning and

TABLE 5.6
Economic Parameters of Jute, Hemp & Mesta Textiles Industry in India (Code—25)

Year	*Index of Real GVA*	*Index of Real Emoluments*	*Index of Real GFC*	*Index of Employees*	*Index of Real Wage Rate*
1973-74	100.00	100.00	100.00	100.00	100.00
1974-75	97.21	82.92	78.87	90.59	91.53
1975-76	120.81	98.84	74.15	97.94	100.92
1976-77	107.39	99.60	69.94	91.32	109.07
1977-78	107.59	107.06	74.72	97.69	109.60
1978-79	102.46	105.50	81.06	98.43	107.18
1979-80	131.59	130.31	76.43	107.54	121.18
1980-81	146.46	126.43	81.21	101.58	124.46
1981-82	111.99	105.05	75.11	89.68	117.14
1982-83	119.30	108.42	87.21	96.44	112.43
1983-84	134.95	91.14	86.58	82.82	110.05
1984-85	180.18	134.60	119.23	109.02	123.47
1985-86	125.22	109.90	108.16	79.46	138.32
1986-87	152.84	113.89	87.06	78.87	144.40
1987-88	154.30	96.96	115.11	73.08	132.68
1988-89	185.32	110.50	193.49	77.82	142.00
1989-90	206.93	114.12	170.24	79.02	144.43
1990-91	224.34	113.94	189.71	74.83	152.26
1991-92	274.97	104.35	219.16	74.88	139.35
1992-93	293.91	115.70	187.57	76.52	151.21
1993-94	267.18	100.04	193.87	64.93	154.07
1994-95	370.04	104.17	192.03	69.59	149.70
1995-96	471.98	150.24	284.73	97.68	153.80
1996-97	467.72	114.00	251.64	75.82	150.36
1997-98	525.37	135.78	205.90	80.53	168.60
Growth Rate	6.924* (12.501)	0.799** (2.374)	5.853* (10.077)	-1.335* (-4.515)	2.164* (13.598)
Linear Slope	15.008* (8.380)	0.889** (2.312)	7.844* (9.083)	-1.144* (-4.387)	2.723* (14.287)
CV	0.614	0.136	0.480	0.144	0.163

Notes : 1. Figures in parentheses are the respective 't' values.
2. * Indicates one percent level of significance.
3. ** Indicate 5 percent level of significance.

weaving; (iii) dyeing, printing and bleaching of jute textiles; (iv) preparing, spinning, weaving and finishing of hemp and other coarse fibres; (v) manufacture of jute bags and other jute textiles not elsewhere classified.

Index of real GVA increased from 100.00 in 1973-74 to 525.36 in 1997-98. It increased at an average rate of 6.924 percent per annum. The overall trend rate of real GVA was found to be 15.008 per annum. The average annual growth rate and trend rate were found statistically significant at one percent level of significance. Coefficient of variation was found to be 0.614.

Index of real emoluments increased from 100.00 in 1973-74 to 135.78 in 1997-98. The real emoluments increased at an average rate of 0.799 percent per annum. The overall trend rate was found to be 0.889 per annum. The average annual growth rate and trend rate were found statistically significant at five percent level of significance. Coefficient of variation was found to be 0.136.

Index of real GFC rose from 100.00 in 1973-74 to 205.90 in 1997-98. The index of real GFC increased at an average rate of 5.853 percent per annum. The overall trend rate was 7.844 per annum. Both the average annual growth rate and trend rate were found statistically significant at one percent level of significance. Coefficient of variation was estimated to be 0.480.

Index of employees decreased from 100.00 in 1973-74 to 80.53 in 1997-98, which worked out to decrease of 1.335 percent per annum. The overall trend rate was –1.144 per annum. The average annual growth rate and trend rate were statistically significant at one percent level of significance. Coefficient of variation was found to be 0.144.

Index of real wage rate rose from 100.00 in 1973-74 to 168.60 in 1997-98. It worked out to growth rate of 2.164 percent per annum. The overall trend rate was 2.723 per annum. Both the average annual growth rate and trend rate were found statistically significant at one percent level of significance. Coefficient of variation was found to be 0.163.

An inter-variable comparison in this industry revealed that the maximum growth rate and variability have been observed in GVA followed by GFC and negative growth rate was in case of employees and least variability in case of emoluments. It has been found that the growth rates of both the emoluments as well as the wage rate were higher than that of employees. In this industry also growth of GVA was much higher as compared to of real emoluments and real wages.

Table 5.7 shows the indices of various economic parameters in *Textiles Products Industry* which includes, (i) knitting mills; (ii) manufacture of all types of threads, cordage, ropes, twines, nets, etc.; (iii) embroidery and making of crepes, laces and fringes; (iv) weaving carpets, rugs and other similar textile products; (v) manufacture of all types of textiles garments including wearing apparel; (vi) manufacture of raincoats, hats, etc.; (vii) manufacture of made up textiles goods (except garments) such as curtains, mosquito nets, etc; (viii) manufacture of water proof textiles such as oil cloth, tarpaulin, etc; (ix) manufacture of coir and coir products; and (x) manufacture of textiles not elsewhere classified like linoleum, padding, wadding, up holstering filling, etc.

Index of real GVA increased from 100.00 in 1973-74 to 4891.96 in 1997-98. A tremendous increase was observed especially after 1989-90. The index of GVA increased at an average annual rate of 19.734 percent. The overall trend rate of real GVA was found to be 206.416 per annum. The average annual growth rate and trend rate were found statistically significant at one percent level of significance. Coefficient of variation was found to be 1.35.

Index of real emoluments increased from 100.00 in 1973-74 to 762.57 in 1997-98. The real emoluments increased at an average rate of 8.352 percent per annum. The overall trend rate was found to be 24.098 per annum. The average annual growth rate and trend rate were found statistically significant at one percent level of significance. Coefficient of variation was found to be 0.678.

Index of real GFC rose from 100.00 in 1973-74 to 2828.45 in 1997-98. The index of real GFC increased at an average rate of 15.792 percent per annum. The overall trend rate was 96.106 per annum. Both the average annual growth rate and trend rate were found statistically significant at one percent level of significance. Coefficient of variation was found to be 1.198.

Index of employees increased from 100.00 in 1973-74 to 555.08 in 1997-98, which worked out to average annual rate of 6.85 percent. The overall trend rate was 16.858 per annum. The

Table 5.7
Economic Parameters of Textile Products Industry in India (Code—26)

Year	*Index of Real GVA*	*Index of Real Emoluments*	*Index of Real GFC*	*Index of Employees*	*Index of Real Wage Rate*
1973-74	100.00	100.00	100.00	100.00	100.00
1974-75	98.31	92.71	86.01	108.67	85.31
1975-76	131.83	112.20	100.49	115.73	96.95
1976-77	142.44	142.79	117.48	135.82	105.13
1977-78	154.03	154.56	138.52	147.17	105.02
1978-79	189.57	166.04	174.75	147.17	112.82
1979-80	165.34	171.14	174.30	158.42	108.03
1980-81	176.89	174.32	164.00	148.19	117.64
1981-82	216.66	166.55	164.35	149.56	111.36
1982-83	247.77	171.55	196.80	148.95	115.17
1983-84	286.07	184.34	224.44	160.35	114.96
1984-85	401.42	191.82	245.52	165.19	116.12
1985-86	305.62	201.26	279.23	169.90	118.46
1986-87	432.50	192.98	278.57	157.83	122.27
1987-88	579.90	235.10	534.48	193.44	121.53
1988-89	553.93	250.37	459.79	201.03	124.55
1989-90	690.92	307.79	552.34	243.34	126.49
1990-91	1195.40	340.59	609.30	257.47	132.28
1991-92	1627.29	337.09	786.25	267.79	125.88
1992-93	2333.78	394.58	943.12	301.40	130.91
1993-94	4641.98	512.87	1581.53	414.88	123.62
1994-95	5200.42	605.08	2177.63	482.67	125.36
1995-96	4857.71	674.83	2371.51	510.64	132.16
1996-97	4629.68	673.83	2370.62	505.99	133.17
1997-98	4891.96	762.57	2828.46	555.09	137.38
Growth Rate	19.734* (17.784)	8.352* (18.006)	15.792* (20.028)	6.850* (13.844)	1.405* (10.582)
Linear Slope	206.416* (6.908)	24.098* (9.557)	96.106* (7.310)	16.858* (8.902)	1.594* (12.042)
CV	1.350	0.678	1.198	0.593	0.107

Notes : 1. Figures in parentheses are the respective 't' values.
2. * Indicates one percent level of significance.

average annual growth rate and trend rate were statistically significant at one percent level of significance. Coefficient of variation was found to be 0.593.

Index of real wage rate rose from 100.00 in 1973-74 to 137.37 in 1997-98. It worked out to increase of 1.405 percent per annum. The overall trend rate was 1.594 per annum. Both the average annual growth rate and trend rate were found statistically significant at one percent level of significance. Coefficient of variation was found to be 0.107.

An inter-variable comparison in this industry revealed that the maximum growth rate and variability have been observed in GVA followed by GFC and minimum in case of wage rate. It has been found that the growth rate and variability of employees were lesser than emoluments but greater than the wage rate. In this industry also growth of GVA was much higher as compared to of real emoluments and real wages.

Table 5.8 shows the indices of various economic parameters of *Paper & Paper Products Industry* which includes, (i) manufacture of pulp, paper and paper board including newsprint; (ii) manufacture of container and boxes of paper and paper board; (iii) manufacture of pulp products not elsewhere classified like dolls; (iv) manufacture of paper and paper board articles not elsewhere classified; (v) printing and publishing of newspapers; (vi) printing and publishing of periodicals, books, journals, atlases, maps and sheet music directories, etc.; (vii) printing of bank notes, currency notes, postage stamps, security presses, etc; (viii) engraving, block making, etc.; (ix) book binding; and (x) printing, publishing and allied activities not elsewhere classified like envelope printing, picture post card printing, embossing etc.

Index of real GVA of this industry increased from 100.00 in 1973-74 to 436.47 in 2000-01. The Index increased at an average annual rate of 5.896 percent. The overall trend rate of real GVA was found to be 11.557 per annum. The average annual growth rate and trend rate were found statistically significant at one percent level of significance. Coefficient of variation was found to be 0.516.

Index of real emoluments increased from 100.00 in 1973-74 to 269.75 in 2000-01, which worked out to an average rate of 3.631 percent per annum. The overall trend rate was found to be

TABLE 5.8
Economic Parameters of Paper and Paper Products Industry in India (Code 28)

Year	*Index of Real GVA*	*Index of Real Emoluments*	*Index of Real GFC*	*Index of Employees*	*Index of Real Wage Rate*
1973-74	100.00	100.00	100.00	100.00	100.00
1974-75	105.89	95.10	92.60	98.18	96.87
1975-76	100.19	98.04	93.65	104.81	93.54
1976-77	101.99	110.26	108.25	112.91	97.65
1977-78	110.36	116.62	119.45	112.86	103.33
1978-79	107.40	121.71	117.55	117.79	103.33
1979-80	111.99	131.41	125.18	120.05	109.46
1980-81	112.30	131.50	154.41	120.76	108.90
1981-82	124.65	147.91	168.27	128.14	115.43
1982-83	120.68	148.02	207.84	122.38	120.95
1983-84	137.36	149.69	251.11	125.58	119.20
1984-85	152.19	155.56	290.14	134.16	115.95
1985-86	123.52	150.53	222.49	136.28	110.46
1986-87	139.29	151.44	276.12	139.69	108.41
1987-88	157.44	171.94	304.21	148.40	115.86
1988-89	162.22	153.27	316.56	141.96	107.97
1989-90	205.48	174.07	278.12	159.95	108.82
1990-91	227.99	179.24	329.75	157.84	113.56
1991-92	251.15	178.96	363.94	155.33	115.21
1992-93	273.59	188.79	428.50	156.92	120.31
1993-94	327.38	194.07	504.46	161.52	120.15
1994-95	342.33	240.23	829.14	188.56	127.41
1995-96	373.52	251.82	574.08	177.35	141.99
1996-97	391.23	249.79	811.51	177.52	140.72
1997-98	291.50	233.33	747.13	173.73	134.31
1998-99	276.67	215.92	820.20	192.74	112.02
1999-00	311.78	232.08	870.05	204.01	113.76
2000-01	436.48	269.76	770.71	227.93	118.35
Growth Rate	5.896* (15.458)	3.631* (21.256)	9.359* (26.136)	2.682* (26.301)	0.923* (5.580)
Linear Slope	11.557* (11.061)	5.897* (17.337)	29.764* (12.518)	3.883* (18.798)	1.046* (5.325)
CV	0.516	0.299	0.720	0.226	0.104

Notes : 1. Figures in parentheses are the respective 't' values.
2. * Indicates one percent level of significance.

5.897 per annum. The average annual growth rate and trend rate were found statistically significant at one percent level of significance. Coefficient of variation was found to be 0.299.

Index of real GFC rose from 100.00 in 1973-74 to 770.70 in 2000-01. The index of real GFC increased at an average rate of 9.359 percent per annum. The overall trend rate was 29.764 per annum. Both the average annual growth rate and trend rate were found statistically significant at one percent level of significance. Coefficient of variation was found to be 0.72.

Index of employees increased from 100.00 in 1973-74 to 227.93 in 2000-01, which worked out to average rate of 2.682 percent per annum. The overall trend rate was 3.883 per annum. The average annual growth rate and trend rate were statistically significant at one percent level of significance. Coefficient of variation was found to be 0.226.

Index of real wage rate rose from 100.00 in 1973-74 to 118.35 in 2000-01. It indicated 0.923 percent per annum increase. The overall trend rate was 1.046 per annum. Both the average annual growth rate and trend rate were found statistically significant at one percent level of significance. Coefficient of variation was found to be 0.104.

An inter-variable comparison in this industry revealed that the maximum growth rate and variability have been observed in GFC followed by GVA and minimum in case of wage rate. It has been found that the growth rate and variability of employees were lesser than emoluments but greater than the wage rate. In this industry also growth of GVA was higher as compared to of real emoluments and real wages.

Table 5.9 shows the indices of various economic parameters in *Leather & Fur Products Industry* which includes, (i) tanning, curing, finishing, embossing and japanning of leather; (ii) manufacture of footwear (excluding repair) except vulcanized or moulded rubber or plastic footwear; (iii) manufacture of wearing apparel coats, like gloves, etc. of leather and substitutes of leather; (iv) manufacture of leather consumer goods (other than apparel and footwear); (v) scrapping, currying, tanning, bleaching and dyeing of fur and other pelts for the trade; (vi) manufacture of wearing apparel of fur and pelts; (vii) manufacture of fur and skin rugs and other articles; and (viii) manufacture of leather and fur products not elsewhere classified.

TABLE 5.9

Economic Parameters of Leather and Fur Products Industry in India (Code 29)

Year	*Index of Real GVA*	*Index of Real Emoluments*	*Index of Real GFC*	*Index of Employees*	*Index of Real Wage Rate*
1973-74	100.00	100.00	100.00	100.00	100.00
1974-75	126.50	94.18	113.25	93.68	100.54
1975-76	77.66	58.61	99.50	85.27	68.74
1976-77	133.38	119.02	175.45	109.02	109.17
1977-78	136.81	123.26	218.62	109.99	112.06
1978-79	142.40	137.89	265.66	96.13	143.44
1979-80	143.84	154.84	291.82	113.70	136.19
1980-81	126.60	147.90	282.46	113.33	130.50
1981-82	108.51	139.02	280.48	101.81	136.56
1982-83	155.76	144.19	344.53	103.03	139.95
1983-84	180.30	155.67	372.54	110.78	140.52
1984-85	187.07	173.56	377.10	111.95	155.03
1985-86	152.49	179.78	449.31	111.37	161.43
1986-87	146.23	174.75	406.46	110.22	158.55
1987-88	204.01	197.81	492.18	115.53	171.21
1988-89	242.65	197.55	567.22	96.86	203.96
1989-90	313.20	245.48	626.78	106.44	230.63
1990-91	428.08	253.76	887.72	108.98	232.85
1991-92	560.69	261.24	980.74	107.13	243.85
1992-93	595.43	285.17	1252.73	113.37	251.55
1993-94	891.23	283.66	1469.60	108.17	262.25
1994-95	735.61	300.28	1785.78	101.81	294.96
1995-96	731.00	327.65	1822.35	108.57	301.80
1996-97	644.46	280.53	2064.75	100.65	278.71
1997-98	913.49	313.84	1664.14	114.76	273.47
1998-99	840.90	344.83	2138.76	129.70	265.86
1999-00	908.63	399.68	1940.49	146.35	273.10
2000-01	724.05	428.01	2237.77	138.15	309.81
Growth Rate	9.921* (14.182)	5.743* (17.573)	12.554* (28.126)	0.811* (3.873)	4.892* (16.721)
Linear Slope	32.978* (10.568)	11.251* (18.948)	82.830* (13.066)	0.920* (3.871)	8.560* (18.546)
CV	0.792	0.446	0.864	0.114	0.380

Notes : 1. Figures in parentheses are the respective 't' values.
2. * Indicates one percent level of significance.

Index of real GVA of this industry increased from 100.00 in 1973-74 to 724.04 in 2000-01. The index increased at an average rate of 9.921 percent per annum. The overall trend rate of real GVA was found to be 32.978 per annum. The average annual growth rate and trend rate were found statistically significant at one percent level of significance. Coefficient of variation was found to be 0.792.

Index of real emoluments indicated an increase from 100.00 in 1973-74 to 428.00 in 2000-01. The index increased at an average rate of 5.743 percent per annum. The overall trend rate was found to be 11.251 per annum. The average annual growth rate and trend rate were found statistically significant at one percent level of significance. Coefficient of variation was found to be 0.446.

Index of real GFC rose from 100.00 in 1973-74 to 2237.76 in 2000-01. The index increased at an average rate of 12.554 percent per annum. The overall trend rate was 82.83 per annum. Both the average annual growth rate and trend rate were found statistically significant at one percent level of significance. Coefficient of variation was found to be 0.864.

Index of employees increased from 100.00 in 1973-74 to 138.15 in 2000-01, which worked to an average rate of 0.811 percent per annum. The overall trend rate was 0.92 per annum. The average annual growth rate and trend rate were statistically significant at one percent level of significance. Coefficient of variation was found to be 0.114.

Index of real wage rate rose from 100.00 in 1973-74 to 309.80 in 2000-01. It indicated 4.892 percent per annum increase. The overall trend rate was 8.56 per annum. Both the average annual growth rate and trend rate were found statistically significant at one percent level of significance. Coefficient of variation was found to be 0.38.

An inter-variable comparison in this industry revealed that the maximum growth rate and variability have been observed in GFC followed by GVA and minimum in case of employees. It has been found that the growth rates and variability of both the emoluments as well as the wage rate were higher than that of employees. However, the growth rates of real emoluments and real wage rate were commensurate with growth rate of GVA in this industry.

TABLE 5.10
Economic Parameters of Chemicals and Chemical Products Industry in India (Code 30)

Year	*Index of Real GVA*	*Index of Real Emoluments*	*Index of Real GFC*	*Index of Employees*	*Index of Real Wage Rate*
1973-74	100.00	100.00	100.00	100.00	100.00
1974-75	97.12	93.92	93.09	91.64	102.49
1975-76	95.28	113.19	106.99	101.75	111.25
1976-77	108.11	125.34	110.46	107.85	116.21
1977-78	121.75	134.25	125.79	104.17	128.88
1978-79	153.21	154.22	134.90	116.30	132.61
1979-80	143.94	166.27	155.21	108.87	152.72
1980-81	129.85	172.00	160.25	113.58	151.44
1981-82	132.15	172.11	155.92	114.89	149.81
1982-83	148.74	181.19	155.72	117.65	154.00
1983-84	,173.93	194.94	183.78	124.20	156.95
1984-85	163.75	209.10	179.75	131.14	159.44
1985-86	170.47	217.98	211.37	130.66	166.83
1986-87	158.89	222.28	219.03	137.76	161.35
1987-88	176.94	237.29	248.32	138.67	171.12
1988-89	178.21	233.87	250.79	132.33	176.73
1989-90	205.43	248.61	323.39	142.06	175.01
1990-91	228.33	252.23	369.78	148.13	170.28
1991-92	259.63	247.80	408.82	138.23	179.26
1992-93	365.46	304.72	529.20	154.04	197.82
1993-94	401.75	288.70	596.87	145.13	198.93
1994-95	435.42	318.06	674.49	152.01	209.24
1995-96	565.37	361.23	821.35	152.99	236.12
1996-97	630.99	349.20	817.86	149.92	232.93
1997-98	515.16	373.82	950.30	152.87	244.54
1998-99	642.51	437.45	957.50	187.20	233.69
1999-00	706.61	524.01	996.45	205.95	254.44
2000-01	536.62	497.94	971.46	200.11	248.84
Growth Rate	7.842* (16.611)	5.669* (29.086)	10.120* (27.362)	2.394* (16.885)	3.198* (22.272)
Linear Slope	21.057* (10.090)	13.215* (5.706)	35.617* (12.101)	3.247* (13.269)	5.335* (22.398)
CV	0.702	0.462	0.809	0.211	0.259

Notes : 1. Figures in parentheses are the respective 't' values.
2. * Indicates one percent level of significance.

Table 5.10 shows the indices of various economic parameters in *Chemicals & Chemical Products Industry* which includes, (i) manufacture of basic and industrial organic and inorganic chemicals and gases such as acids, alkalies and their salts, gases like acetylene, oxygen, nitrogen etc.; (ii) manufacture of fertilizers and pesticides; (iii) manufacture of paints, varnishes and lacquers; (iv) manufacture of drugs and medicines; (v) manufacture of perfumes, cosmetics, lotions, hair dressings, tooth pastes, soap in any form, synthetic detergents, shampoos, shaving products, cleaners, washing and scouring products and other toilet preparations; (vi) manufacture of inedible oils; (vii) manufacture of turpentine, synthetic resins, plastic materials and synthetic fibres like nylone, terylene except glass; (viii) manufacture of matches; (ix) manufacture of explosives and ammunition and fire works; and (x) manufacture of chemical products not elsewhere classified (including photo-chemicals, sensitized films and paper).

Index of real GVA increased from 100.00 in 1973-74 to 536.61 in 2000-01. The index increased at an average rate of 7.842 percent per annum. The overall trend rate of real GVA was found to be 21.057 per annum. The average annual growth rate and trend rate were found statistically significant at one percent level of significance. Coefficient of variation was found to be 0.702.

Index of real emoluments increased from 100.00 in 1973-74 to 497.94 in 2000-01. It increased at an average rate of 5.669 percent per annum. The overall trend rate was found to be 13.215 per annum. The average annual growth rate and trend rate were found statistically significant at one percent level of significance. Coefficient of variation was found to be 0.462.

Index of real GFC rose from 100.00 in 1973-74 to 971.46 in 2000-01. The index increased at an average rate of 10.12 percent per annum. The overall trend rate was 35.617 per annum. Both the average annual growth rate and trend rate were found statistically significant at one percent level of significance. Coefficient of variation was found to be 0.809.

Index of employees increased from 100.00 in 1973-74 to 200.10 in 2000-01. The increase worked out to average annual rate of 2.394 percent. The overall trend rate was 3.247 per annum. The average annual growth rate and trend rate were statistically significant at one percent level of significance. Coefficient of variation was found to be 0.211.

Index of real wage rate rose from 100.00 in 1973-74 to 248.83 in 2000-01. It worked out to 3.198 percent per annum increase. The overall trend rate was 5.335 per annum. Both the average annual growth rate and trend rate were found statistically significant at one percent level of significance. Coefficient of variation was found to be 0.259.

An inter-variable comparison in this industry revealed that the maximum growth rate and variability have been observed in GFC followed by GVA and minimum in case of employees. It has been found that the growth rates and variability of both the emoluments as well as the wage rate were higher than that of employees. The growth rates of real emoluments and real wage rate were commensurate with growth rate in GVA in this industry.

Table 5.11 shows the indices of various economic parameters in *Rubber, Petroleum & Coal Products Industry* which includes, (i) tyre and tube industries; (ii) manufacture of footwear made primarily of vulcanized or moulded rubber; (iii) manufacture of rubber products not elsewhere classified; (iv) manufacture of plastic products not elsewhere classified (except house furnishing); (v) petroleum refineries; (vi) manufacture of products of petroleum not elsewhere classified; (vii) products of coal tar on coke ovens; and (vii) manufacture of other coal and coal tar products not elsewhere classified.

Index of real GVA in this industry increased from 100.00 in 1973-74 to 1212.82 in 2000-01. The index increased at an average rate of 11.28 percent per annum. The overall trend rate of real GVA was found to be 50.491 per annum. The average annual growth rate was found statistically significant at one percent level of significance but the trend rate was statistically non-significant. Coefficient of variation was found to be 0.835.

Index of real emoluments indicated an increase from 100.00 in 1973-74 to 624.52 in 2000-01. The real emoluments increased at an average rate of 6.395 percent per annum. The overall trend rate was found to be 16.552 per annum. The average annual growth rate and trend rate were found statistically significant at one percent level of significance. Coefficient of variation was found to be 0.521.

Index of real GFC rose from 100.00 in 1973-74 to 1918.74 in 2000-01. The index increased at an average rate of 12.644 percent

TABLE 5.11
Economic Parameters of Rubber, Petroleum and Coal Products Industry in India (Code 31)

Year	*Index of Real GVA*	*Index of Real Emoluments*	*Index of Real GFC*	*Index of Employees*	*Index of Real Wage Rate*
1973-74	100.00	100.00	100.00	100.00	100.00
1974-75	116.80	95.74	89.81	92.95	103.00
1975-76	120.11	130.19	101.57	107.77	120.80
1976-77	159.57	134.68	165.00	113.48	118.69
1977-78	179.95	142.08	184.03	105.77	134.34
1978-79	149.57	148.66	208.70	116.81	127.27
1979-80	154.35	160.26	193.23	99.44	161.16
1980-81	146.40	176.16	124.52	115.30	152.79
1981-82	139.98	160.22	165.94	102.22	156.75
1982-83	213.91	196.44	213.94	112.57	174.51
1983-84	144.85	191.00	279.22	118.90	160.65
1984-85	199.22	210.81	289.14	128.32	164.28
1985-86	348.07	215.83	355.09	130.52	165.36
1986-87	361.77	234.65	311.19	136.11	172.39
1987-88	411.05	242.49	416.49	130.97	185.14
1988-89	451.13	258.32	510.46	130.48	197.97
1989-90	476.90	286.55	468.55	137.80	207.95
1990-91	581.39	291.41	568.27	132.45	220.01
1991-92	535.12	282.74	638.79	125.98	224.44
1992-93	824.66	324.69	838.42	131.52	246.88
1993-94	978.53	342.29	1071.11	132.41	258.51
1994-95	1039.11	356.80	979.86	132.47	269.34
1995-96	1213.04	440.18	1116.99	151.30	290.94
1996-97	1625.07	417.94	1672.17	136.60	305.96
1997-98	1012.00	450.31	1422.67	146.50	307.38
1998-99	1133.18	512.03	2768.92	167.55	305.59
1999-00	1252.64	567.91	1791.51	186.70	304.18
2000-01	1212.83	624.52	1918.74	220.69	282.98
Growth Rate	11.280* (19.121)	6.395* (38.819)	12.644* (24.423)	2.060* (9.563)	4.246* (26.026)
Linear Slope	50.491 NS (1.312)	16.552* (15.653)	71.686* (8.692)	2.775* (7.917)	8.048* (22.251)
CV	0.835	0.521	1.009	0.209	0.338

Notes : 1. Figures in parentheses are the respective 't' values.
2. * Indicates one percent level of significance.
3. NS indicates not significant.

per annum. The overall trend rate was 71.686 per annum. Both the average annual growth rate and trend rate were found statistically significant at one percent level of significance. Coefficient of variation was found to be 1.009.

Index of employees increased from 100.00 in 1973-74 to 220.69 in 2000-01. The increase worked out to a rate of 2.060 percent per annum. The overall trend rate was 2.775 per annum. The average annual growth rate and trend rate were statistically significant at one percent level of significance. Coefficient of variation was found to be 0.209.

Index of real wage rate rose from 100.00 in 1973-74 to 282.98 in 2000-01. It indicated 4.246 percent per annum increase. The overall trend rate was 8.048 per annum. Both the average annual growth rate and trend rate were found statistically significant at one percent level of significance. Coefficient of variation was found to be 0.338.

An inter-variable comparison in this industry revealed that the maximum growth rate and variability have been observed in GFC followed by GVA and minimum in case of employees. It has been found that the growth rates and variability of both the emoluments as well as the wage rate were higher than that of employees. Real emoluments and real wage rate in this industry also increased at reasonable rates as compared to GVA.

Table 5.12 shows the indices of various economic parameters in *Non-Metallic Mineral Products Industry* which includes, (i) manufacture of structural clay products; (ii) manufacture of glass & glass products; (iii) manufacture of earthen ware & earthen pottery; (iv) manufacture of China ware & porcelain ware; (v) manufacture of cement, lime & plaster; (vi) manufacture of mica products; (vii) manufacture of structural stone goods, stone dressing and stone crushing and stone ware; (viii) manufacture of earthen and plaster statues and other products; (ix) manufacture of asbestos, cement and other cement products; and (x) manufacture of miscellaneous non-metallic mineral products such as slate products, abrasives, graphite products, mineral wool, silica products and other non-metallic mineral products not elsewhere classified.

Index of real GVA in this industry increased from 100.00 in 1973-74 to 575.16 in 2000-01. The index increased at an average rate of 8.481 percent per annum. The overall trend rate of real GVA was found to be 23.603 per annum. Both the average annual

TABLE 5.12

Economic Parameters of Non-Metallic Mineral Products Industry in India (Code 32)

Year	*Index of Real GVA*	*Index of Real Emoluments*	*Index of Real GFC*	*Index of Employees*	*Index of Real Wage Rate*
1973-74	100.00	100.00	100.00	100.00	100.00
1974-75	92.26	94.06	83.35	94.71	99.31
1975-76	98.05	108.39	86.04	105.63	102.61
1976-77	107.25	119.14	94.88	115.10	103.51
1977-78	128.41	120.88	97.51	113.09	106.89
1978-79	123.24	135.84	109.44	114.27	118.88
1979-80	118.81	140.34	105.63	117.44	119.50
1980-81	124.46	153.62	123.07	128.19	119.84
1981-82	138.65	152.13	143.67	117.62	129.34
1982-83	214.18	186.80	186.76	130.51	143.14
1983-84	217.78	183.75	250.46	121.94	150.69
1984-85	234.15	190.51	257.76	131.25	145.16
1985-86	241.60	199.56	362.08	132.63	150.46
1986-87	219.09	201.35	412.18	137.16	146.79
1987-88	261.49	202.33	496.63	135.68	149.12
1988-89	255.99	206.82	524.04	136.99	150.98
1989-90	310.91	228.67	545.61	149.08	153.39
1990-91	396.67	218.22	539.58	143.53	152.04
1991-92	528.65	229.38	675.74	143.21	160.17
1992-93	451.93	243.92	776.97	151.66	160.84
1993-94	465.45	246.26	906.96	158.37	155.49
1994-95	526.88	260.78	977.68	166.35	156.76
1995-96	687.38	280.03	1034.01	164.94	169.77
1996-97	888.10	306.55	1249.38	192.47	159.27
1997-98	599.61	277.65	1277.90	177.76	156.20
1998-99	467.46	283.20	1727.25	193.08	146.67
1999-00	572.48	363.11	1846.15	228.20	159.12
2000-01	575.16	376.36	1372.05	240.37	156.58
Growth Rate	8.481* (18.301)	4.593* (25.194)	13.362* (30.868)	2.731* (16.884)	1.811* (9.274)
Linear Slope	23.603* (10.659)	8.86* (21.170)	59.464* (12.766)	4.02* (12.083)	2.348* (9.078)
CV	0.659	0.361	0.901	0.249	0.156

Notes : 1. Figures in parentheses are the respective 't' values.
2. * Indicates one percent level of significance.

growth rate and trend rate were found statistically significant at one percent level of significance. Coefficient of variation was found to be 0.659.

Index of real emoluments increased from 100.00 in 1973-74 to 376.36 in 2000-01. The index increased at an average rate of 4.593 percent per annum. The overall trend rate was found to be 8.86 per annum. The average annual growth rate and trend rate were found statistically significant at one percent level of significance. Coefficient of variation was found to be 0.361.

Index of real GFC rose from 100.00 in 1973-74 to 1372.05 in 2000-01. The index increased at an average rate of 13.362 percent per annum. The overall trend rate was 59.464 per annum. Both the average annual growth rate and trend rate were found statistically significant at one percent level of significance. Coefficient of variation was found to be 0.901.

Index of employees increased from 100.00 in 1973-74 to 240.36 in 2000-01. The increase worked out to a rate of 2.731 percent per annum. The overall trend rate was 4.02 per annum. The average annual growth rate and trend rate were statistically significant at one percent level of significance. Coefficient of variation was found to be 0.249.

Index of real wage rate rose from 100.00 in 1973-74 to 156.57 in 2000-01. It indicated 1.811 percent per annum increase. The overall trend rate was 2.348 per annum. Both the average annual growth rate and trend rate were found statistically significant at one percent level of significance. Coefficient of variation was found to be 0.156.

An inter-variable comparison in this industry revealed that the maximum growth rate and variability have been observed in GFC followed by GVA and minimum in case of wage rate. It has been found that the growth rate and variability of employees were lesser than emoluments but greater than the wage rate. In this industry the increase in real wage rate was not consistent with increase in GVA.

Table 5.13 shows the indices of various economic parameters in *Basic Metals & Alloys Industry* which includes, (i) iron and steel industries; (ii) foundries for casting and forging iron and steel; (iii) manufacture of ferro-alloys; (iv) copper manufacturing; (v) brass manufacturing; (vi) aluminium manufacturing; (vii) zinc manufacturing; and (viii) other non-ferrous metal products.

TABLE 5.13
Economic Parameters of Basic Metals and Alloys Industry in India (Code 33)

Year	Index of Real GVA	Index of Real Emoluments	Index of Real GFC	Index of Employees	Index of Real Wage Rate
1973-74	100.00	100.00	100.00	100.00	100.00
1974-75	110.46	93.51	75.13	101.47	92.16
1975-76	114.20	110.42	118.09	102.31	107.93
1976-77	125.26	119.55	133.57	113.33	105.49
1977-78	113.80	116.43	143.10	106.34	109.48
1978-79	137.16	128.27	148.47	106.92	119.97
1979-80	125.65	139.76	156.67	114.91	121.62
1980-81	139.58	138.56	165.27	109.70	126.31
1981-82	184.71	141.05	177.14	109.46	128.86
1982-83	183.72	151.91	204.31	115.09	131.99
1983-84	229.13	157.93	223.92	116.91	135.08
1984-85	201.16	193.03	246.89	131.96	146.28
1985-86	229.61	160.47	248.40	123.19	130.26
1986-87	194.85	165.16	237.34	122.96	134.33
1987-88	223.64	168.01	286.16	124.55	134.89
1988-89	319.34	174.71	283.11	129.51	134.90
1989-90	333.78	179.22	291.97	138.89	129.03
1990-91	394.28	181.26	445.95	133.27	136.01
1991-92	302.80	137.03	542.89	105.25	130.20
1992-93	458.19	197.40	704.56	136.47	144.64
1993-94	407.22	192.08	738.90	140.55	136.66
1994-95	517.17	203.15	760.75	147.25	137.96
1995-96	684.61	254.50	865.90	158.13	160.94
1996-97	610.60	216.95	731.36	158.04	137.28
1997-98	700.49	232.95	805.17	159.92	145.67
1998-99	614.87	263.88	1104.50	194.66	135.56
1999-00	632.68	260.25	811.68	189.00	137.70
2000-01	478.88	275.44	726.49	223.59	123.19
Growth Rate	7.879* (20.596)	3.45* (14.480)	9.648* (21.597)	2.308* (10.339)	1.116* (5.637)
Linear Slope	22.215* (12.380)	5.786* (13.388)	33.605* (11.921)	3.214* (8.747)	1.352* (5.592)
CV	0.624	0.294	0.733	0.231	0.117

Notes : 1. Figures in parentheses are the respective 't' values.
2. * Indicates one percent level of significance.

Index of real GVA of this industry increased from 100.00 in 1973-74 to 478.87 in 2000-01. The index increased at an average rate of 7.879 percent per annum. The overall trend rate of real GVA was found to be 22.215 per annum. Both the average annual growth rate and trend rate were found statistically significant at one percent level of significance. Coefficient of variation was found to be 0.624.

Index of real emoluments increased from 100.00 in 1973-74 to 275.44 in 2000-01. The real emoluments increased at an average rate of 3.45 percent per annum. The overall trend rate was found to be 5.786 per annum. The average annual growth rate and trend rate were found statistically significant at one percent level of significance. Coefficient of variation was found to be 0.294.

Index of real GFC rose from 100.00 in 1973-74 to 726.48 in 2000-01. The index increased at an average rate of 9.648 percent per annum. The overall trend rate was 33.605 per annum. Both the average annual growth rate and trend rate were found statistically significant at one percent level of significance. Coefficient of variation was found to be 0.733.

Index of employees increased from 100.00 in 1973-74 to 223.58 in 2000-01. The increase worked out to a rate of 2.308 percent per annum. The overall trend rate was 3.214 per annum. The average annual growth rate and trend rate were statistically significant at one percent level of significance. Coefficient of variation was found to be 0.231.

Index of real wage rate rose from 100.00 in 1973-74 to 123.19 in 2000-01. It indicated 1.116 percent per annum increase. The overall trend rate was 1.352 per annum. Both the average annual growth rate and trend rate were found statistically significant at one percent level of significance. Coefficient of variation was found to be 0.117.

An inter-variable comparison in this industry revealed that the maximum growth rate and variability have been observed in GFC followed by GVA and minimum in case of wage rate. It has been found that the growth rate and variability of employees were lesser than emoluments but greater than the wage rate. The increase in wage rate was not commensurate with increase in GVA in this industry.

Table 5.14 shows the indices of various economic parameters in *Metal Products Industry* which includes,

(i) manufacture of fabricated metal products such as metal cans from tin-plate, terne plate or enameled sheet metal, metal shipping containers, barrels, drums, kegs, pails, safe vaults, enameled sanitary and all other fabricated metal products not elsewhere classified; (ii) manufacture of structural metal products; (iii) manufacture of furniture and fixtures, primarily of metal; (iv) manufacture of hand tools and general hardware; (v) enamelling, japanning, lacquering, galvanizing, plating and polishing of metal products; (vi) manufacture of metal utensils, cutlery and kitchenware; and (vii) manufacture of metal products except machinery and transport equipment not elsewhere classified like type founding.

Index of real GVA in this industry increased from 100.00 in 1973-74 to 730.61 in 2000-01. The index increased at an average rate of 9.444 percent per annum. The overall trend rate of real GVA was found to be 27.402 per annum. Both the average annual growth rate and trend rate were found statistically significant at one percent level of significance. Coefficient of variation was found to be 0.766.

Index of real emoluments indicated an increase from 100.00 in 1973-74 to 382.13 in 2000-01. The real emoluments increased at an average rate of 4.534 percent per annum. The overall trend rate was found to be 8.488 per annum. The average annual growth rate and trend rate were found statistically significant at one percent level of significance. Coefficient of variation was found to be 0.407.

Index of real GFC rose from 100.00 in 1973-74 to 741.03 in 2000-01. The index increased at an average rate of 10.513 percent per annum. The overall trend rate was 32.95 per annum. Both the average annual growth rate and trend rate were found statistically significant at one percent level of significance. Coefficient of variation was found to be 0.831.

Index of employees increased from 100.00 in 1973-74 to 227.75 in 2000-01. The increase worked out to a rate of 2.555 percent per annum. The overall trend rate was 3.72 per annum. The average annual growth rate and trend rate were statistically significant at one percent level of significance. Coefficient of variation was found to be 0.227.

Index of real wage rate rose from 100.00 in 1973-74 to 167.78 in 2000-01. It indicated 1.929 percent per annum increase. The

TABLE 5.14

Economic Parameters of Metal Products Industry in India (Code 34)

Year	*Index of Real GVA*	*Index of Real Emoluments*	*Index of Real GFC*	*Index of Employees*	*Index of Real Wage Rate*
1973-74	100.00	100.00	100.00	100.00	100.00
1974-75	92.93	96.08	86.52	98.03	98.01
1975-76	90.76	103.12	87.79	103.45	99.68
1976-77	102.78	117.26	105.15	113.97	102.89
1977-78	107.08	124.54	108.82	112.19	111.01
1978-79	106.29	119.76	102.26	114.33	104.75
1979-80	124.48	143.64	111.62	124.84	115.06
1980-81	117.80	137.86	123.56	126.46	109.02
1981-82	136.23	134.92	117.81	124.21	108.62
1982-83	149.72	132.10	134.95	118.40	111.57
1983-84	181.86	145.09	167.62	137.54	105.49
1984-85	170.23	165.20	161.13	147.65	111.89
1985-86	166.78	151.19	169.44	142.19	106.33
1986-87	154.21	142.18	163.64	145.84	97.49
1987-88	213.48	169.93	234.90	148.35	114.55
1988-89	268.97	189.59	274.98	155.51	121.91
1989-90	255.46	174.76	249.33	141.89	123.17
1990-91	278.44	190.25	342.26	148.66	127.98
1991-92	358.05	180.53	373.26	142.21	126.95
1992-93	393.30	204.94	504.73	153.86	133.20
1993-94	524.19	206.51	666.94	156.93	131.60
1994-95	535.64	230.33	682.71	165.73	138.98
1995-96	660.70	270.04	795.69	170.85	158.06
1996-97	745.31	256.54	818.36	160.88	159.46
1997-98	646.91	270.62	956.49	170.52	158.70
1998-99	728.71	312.55	871.67	206.21	151.57
1999-00	806.06	351.85	799.87	220.76	159.38
2000-01	730.61	382.13	741.03	227.75	167.78
Growth Rate	9.444* (23.256)	4.534* (20.472)	10.513* (19.977)	2.555* (15.562)	1.929* (11.845)
Linear Slope	27.402* (12.095)	8.488* (12.244)	32.95* (11.124)	3.72* (12.366)	2.434* (11.246)
CV	0.766	0.407	0.831	0.227	0.178

Notes : 1. Figures in parentheses are the respective 't' values.
2. * Indicates one percent level of significance.

overall trend rate was 2.434 per annum. Both the average annual growth rate and trend rate were found statistically significant at one percent level of significance. Coefficient of variation was found to be 0.178.

An inter-variable comparison in this industry revealed that the maximum growth rate and variability have been observed in GFC followed by GVA and minimum in case of wage rate. It has been found that the growth rate and variability of employees were lesser than emoluments but greater than the wage rate. Increase in wage rate was somewhat on lower side as compared to increase in GVA in this industry.

Table 5.15 shows the indices of various economic parameters in *Machinery Other Than Transport Industry* which includes, (i) manufacture of agricultural machinery and equipment and parts; (ii) manufacture and repair of drills, coal cutting machines, earth moving, lifting and hoisting machinery cranes, conveyors and road rollers and other heavy machinery and equipment used by construction and mining industries; (iii) manufacture of prime movers, boilers and steam generating plants such as diesel engines and parts; (iv) industrial machinery for food and textile industries; (v) industrial machinery for other than food and textile industries; (vi) manufacture of refrigerators, air conditioners and fire fighting equipment and other parts, components and accessories; (vii) manufacture, alteration and repair of general items of non-electrical machinery, components, equipment and accessories not elsewhere classified; (viii) manufacture of machine tools, their parts and accessories; (ix) manufacture of office computing and accounting machinery and their accessories; (x) manufacture of repair and non-electrical machinery, equipment, components and accessories not elsewhere classified (such as sewing machines, automatic merchandising machines, washing, laundry, dry cleaning and pressing machines, cooking rangers and ovens, other service industry machines, arms and armament, etc.; (xi) manufacture of electrical industrial machinery and apparatus and parts (such as electrical motors, generators, transformers, electromagnetic clutches and brakes, etc.; (xii) manufacture of insulated wires and cables; (xiii) manufacture of dry and wet batteries; (xiv) manufacture of electrical apparatus, appliances and other parts such as lamps, bulbs, tubes, sockets, switches, fans, insulators (except porcelain), conductors, irons, heaters, shavers,

TABLE 5.15

Economic Parameters of Machinery Other Than Transport Industry in India (Code 35-36)

Year	*Index of Real GVA*	*Index of Real Emoluments*	*Index of Real GFC*	*Index of Employees*	*Index of Real Wage Rate*
1973-74	100.00	100.00	100.00	100.00	100.00
1974-75	102.21	98.03	99.77	77.35	126.73
1975-76	103.84	110.76	100.07	105.99	104.51
1976-77	119.52	123.90	110.13	116.10	106.71
1977-78	127.83	131.95	120.02	115.61	114.13
1978-79	131.71	139.19	118.23	119.95	116.04
1979-80	133.75	150.09	120.37	117.82	127.38
1980-81	144.30	151.04	120.15	121.21	124.60
1981-82	147.17	148.61	124.97	117.98	125.97
1982-83	179.56	169.35	151.88	127.00	133.35
1983-84	192.76	179.53	176.41	132.10	135.90
1984-85	225.17	191.68	182.78	141.18	135.77
1985-86	220.29	197.45	215.68	144.10	137.02
1986-87	205.20	187.78	193.00	136.47	137.60
1987-88	259.29	206.67	246.35	147.01	140.58
1988-89	257.81	207.70	265.32	147.19	141.11
1989-90	306.50	228.90	286.15	161.28	141.93
1990-91	323.98	231.29	317.64	157.50	146.85
1991-92	389.75	228.87	370.10	155.20	147.46
1992-93	467.30	243.84	490.06	158.05	154.28
1993-94	460.53	241.56	498.40	161.06	149.98
1994-95	555.23	250.03	547.38	162.99	153.40
1995-96	574.88	300.90	578.43	177.07	169.93
1996-97	590.53	277.41	597.04	175.73	157.86
1997-98	544.34	281.59	625.97	180.49	156.02
1998-99	562.24	324.51	760.94	168.90	192.14
1999-00	483.04	352.62	717.58	245.14	143.85
2000-01	455.01	349.60	638.99	255.27	136.95
Growth Rate	7.567* (22.314)	4.47* (30.725)	8.899* (28.177)	2.896* (13.266)	1.53* (8.535)
Linear Slope	19.768* (14.106)	8.675* (25.531)	25.158* (14.557)	4.238* (10.765)	2.053* (8.125)
CV	0.579	0.351	0.692	0.262	0.145

Notes : 1. Figures in parentheses are the respective 't' values.
2. * Indicates one percent level of significance.

cleaners, etc. excluding repairing; (xv) manufacture of radio and television, transmitting and receiving sets, sound reproducing and recording equipment, gramophone record and pre recorded magnetic tapes, etc; (xvi) manufacture and repair of radiographic X-ray apparatus and tubes and parts; (xvii) manufacture of electronic computers control instrument and other equipment; (xviii) manufacture of electronic components and accessories not elsewhere classified; and (xix) manufacture of electrical machinery, apparatus, appliances and supplies and parts not elsewhere classified.

Index of real GVA of this industry increased from 100.00 in 1973-74 to 455.01 in 2000-01. The index increased at an average rate of 7.567 percent per annum. The overall trend rate of real GVA was found to be 19.768 per annum. Both the average annual growth rate and trend rate were found statistically significant at one percent level of significance. Coefficient of variation was found to be 0.579.

Index of real emoluments increased from 100.00 in 1973-74 to 349.60 in 2000-01. The real emoluments increased at an average rate of 4.47 percent per annum. The overall trend rate was found to be 8.675 per annum. The average annual growth rate and trend rate were found statistically significant at one percent level of significance. Coefficient of variation was found to be 0.351.

Index of real GFC rose from 100.00 in 1973-74 to 638.99 in 2000-01. The index increased at an average rate of 8.899 percent per annum. The overall trend rate was 25.158 per annum. Both the average annual growth rate and trend rate were found statistically significant at one percent level of significance. Coefficient of variation was found to be 0.692.

Index of employees increased from 100.00 in 1973-74 to 255.27 in 2000-01. The increase worked out to a rate of 2.896 percent per annum. The overall trend rate was 4.238 per annum. The average annual growth rate and trend rate were statistically significant at one percent level of significance. Coefficient of variation was found to be 0.262.

Index of real wage rate rose from 100.00 in 1973-74 to 136.95 in 2000-01. It indicated 1.53 percent per annum increase. The overall trend rate was 2.053 per annum. Both the average annual growth rate and trend rate were found statistically significant at one percent level of significance. Coefficient of variation was found to be 0.145.

An inter-variable comparison in this industry revealed that the maximum growth rate and variability have been observed in GFC followed by GVA and minimum in case of wage rate. It has been found that the growth rate and variability of employees were lesser than emoluments but greater than the wage rate. In this industry also increase in wage rate was somewhat on lower side as compared to increase in GVA.

Table 5.16 shows the indices of various economic parameters in *Transport Equipment and Parts Industry* which includes, (i) ship building and repairing; (ii) manufacture of locomotives and parts; (iii) manufacture of railway wagons and coaches and parts; (iv) manufacture of other rail road equipment; (v) manufacture of motor vehicles and parts; (vi) manufacture of motor-cycles and scooters and parts; (vii) manufacture of bicycles and cycle-rickshaws and parts; (viii) manufacture of aircraft and its parts; (ix) bullock-carts, push-carts, hand-carts, etc.; and (x) manufacture of transport equipment and parts not elsewhere classified.

Index of real GVA of this industry increased from 100.00 in 1973-74 to 393.95 in 2000-01. The index increased at an average rate of 6.74 percent per annum. The overall trend rate of real GVA was found to be 15.479 per annum. Both the average annual growth rate and trend rate were found statistically significant at one percent level of significance. Coefficient of variation was found to be 0.548.

Index of real emoluments increased from 100.00 in 1973-74 to 278.94 in 2000-01. The real emoluments increased at an average rate of 4.108 percent per annum. The overall trend rate was found to be 7.126 per annum. The average annual growth rate and trend rate were found statistically significant at one percent level of significance. Coefficient of variation was found to be 0.320.

Index of real GFC rose from 100.00 in 1973-74 to 1189.71 in 2000-01. The index increased at an average rate of 9.809 percent per annum. The overall trend rate was 36.719 per annum. Both the average annual growth rate and trend rate were found statistically significant at one percent level of significance. Coefficient of variation was found to be 0.789.

Index of employees increased from 100.00 in 1973-74 to 247.20 in 2000-01. The increase worked out to a rate of 2.783 percent per annum. The overall trend rate was 4.207 per annum. The average annual growth rate and trend rate were statistically

TABLE 5.16
Economic Parameters of Transport Equipment and Parts Industry in India (Code 37)

Year	*Index of Real GVA*	*Index of Real Emoluments*	*Index of Real GFC*	*Index of Employees*	*Index of Real Wage Rate*
1973-74	100.00	100.00	100.00	100.00	100.00
1974-75	99.14	94.90	86.09	93.96	101.00
1975-76	91.50	99.00	82.69	108.87	90.93
1976-77	107.67	102.56	100.25	118.03	86.90
1977-78	111.50	106.16	106.05	116.69	90.98
1978-79	133.91	124.49	232.39	124.26	100.18
1979-80	132.21	147.48	217.16	119.72	123.18
1980-81	134.28	153.61	204.75	124.06	123.82
1981-82	157.25	164.11	203.72	129.04	127.18
1982-83	179.43	172.80	226.43	133.66	129.28
1983-84	174.51	173.49	229.51	135.75	127.80
1984-85	183.01	189.42	266.18	142.16	133.25
1985-86	175.44	180.86	279.85	149.47	121.01
1986-87	200.08	190.46	289.59	154.29	123.45
1987-88	199.39	192.47	341.30	156.41	123.05
1988-89	213.13	201.81	336.29	155.49	129.79
1989-90	239.24	203.24	340.49	168.18	120.85
1990-91	287.00	197.76	332.65	162.88	121.41
1991-92	302.92	202.96	406.81	161.77	125.47
1992-93	328.98	207.03	516.54	160.81	128.74
1993-94	354.29	208.42	561.35	161.58	128.99
1994-95	404.58	230.80	571.71	167.37	137.90
1995-96	547.17	292.62	693.73	184.87	158.29
1996-97	478.32	277.11	896.12	179.87	154.07
1997-98	482.22	269.65	794.37	191.25	141.00
1998-99	348.57	252.94	986.24	183.33	137.97
1999-00	488.09	296.60	1294.30	244.91	121.11
2000-01	393.95	278.94	1189.71	247.20	112.84
Growth Rate	6.74* (20.941)	4.108* (17.029)	9.809* (22.728)	2.783* (17.610)	1.288* (5.048)
Linear Slope	15.479* (12.298)	7.126* (19.112)	36.719* (10.628)	4.207* (13.248)	1.489* (4.997)
CV	0.548	0.32	0.789	0.243	0.143

Notes : 1. Figures in parentheses are the respective 't' values.
2. * Indicates one percent level of significance.

significant at one percent level of significance. Coefficient of variation was found to be 0.243.

Index of real wage rate rose from 100.00 in 1973-74 to 112.83 in 2000-01. It indicated 1.288 percent per annum increase. The overall trend rate was 1.489 per annum. Both the average annual growth rate and trend rate were found statistically significant at one percent level of significance. Coefficient of variation was found to be 0.143.

An inter-variable comparison in this industry revealed that the maximum growth rate and variability have been observed in GFC followed by GVA and minimum in case of wage rate. It has been found that the growth rate and variability of employees were lesser than emoluments but greater than the wage rate. In this industry also increase in wage rate was somewhat on lower side as compared to increase in GVA.

Inter-Industry Comparison

The maximum growth rate and variability in the index of real GVA and real emoluments have been found in Textile Products Industry and minimum in the Cotton Textiles Industry.

The highest growth rate and variability in the index of real GFC have been observed in Textile Products Industry and least in Jute, Hemp & Mesta Textiles Industry.

The maximum growth rate and variability in the index of real wage rate have been found in the Leather and Fur Products Industry and least growth rate has been found in the Paper & Paper Products Industry and the minimum variability in the Cotton Textiles Industry.

The maximum growth rate and variability in the index of employees have been found in the Textile Products Industry and most negative growth rate was found in the Cotton Textiles Industry and the minimum variability in the Leather & Fur Products Industry.

It may be concluded from this chapter that the real wage rate in all industries showed rising trend. The maximum average annual growth rate of real wage rate was in FPI and least in LFPI. In FPI, BTTPI, CTI, JHMTI, TPI, PPPI, NMMPI, BMAI, MPI, MOTI and TEPI, the index of GVA increased at much higher rate than the wage rate. However, in LFPI, CCPI, and RPCPI, the growth rates of real wage rate were commensurate with growth rate of GVA. The trend in share of labour was declining in all industries, but minimum decline was found in CCPI followed by PPPI and maximum in JHMTI.

TABLE 6.17

Share of Labour in GVA at Current Prices in Different Industries

Year	FPI	BTTPI	CTI	JHMTI	TPI	PPPI	LFPI	CCPI	RPCPI	NMMPI	BMAI	MPI	MOTI	TEPI
1973-74	0.421	0.376	0.511	0.839	0.459	0.491	0.644	0.301	0.339	0.502	0.509	0.472	0.469	0.622
1974-75	0.366	0.207	0.601	0.682	0.453	0.398	0.560	0.261	0.269	0.494	0.444	0.466	0.447	0.598
1975-76	0.431	0.327	0.755	0.760	0.429	0.425	0.492	0.300	0.313	0.463	0.467	0.485	0.442	0.612
1976-77	0.335	0.270	0.665	0.867	0.465	0.459	0.513	0.288	0.235	0.442	0.432	0.455	0.419	0.526
1977-78	0.362	0.435	0.649	0.883	0.456	0.472	0.555	0.293	0.237	0.397	0.486	0.473	0.444	0.555
1978-79	0.414	0.364	0.553	0.825	0.388	0.487	0.527	0.275	0.266	0.431	0.420	0.480	0.439	0.502
1979-80	0.402	0.458	0.542	0.603	0.444	0.455	0.495	0.294	0.256	0.433	0.457	0.427	0.439	0.539
1980-81	0.458	0.443	0.568	0.686	0.447	0.457	0.543	0.308	0.288	0.452	0.420	0.436	0.416	0.542
1981-82	0.399	0.462	0.609	0.874	0.394	0.482	0.531	0.295	0.261	0.422	0.362	0.432	0.406	0.514
1982-83	0.414	0.746	0.699	0.939	0.386	0.545	0.515	0.290	0.225	0.371	0.406	0.434	0.406	0.498
1983-84	0.336	0.326	0.635	0.907	0.420	0.510	0.463	0.273	0.324	0.339	0.401	0.442	0.416	0.516
1984-85	0.373	0.355	0.702	0.849	0.311	0.432	0.445	0.303	0.252	0.310	0.517	0.486	0.380	0.535
1985-86	0.355	0.435	0.647	1.089	0.407	0.496	0.511	0.303	0.152	0.302	0.376	0.447	0.418	0.553
1986-87	0.356	0.348	0.648	0.956	0.366	0.439	0.530	0.319	0.174	0.354	0.459	0.456	0.426	0.520
1987-88	0.372	0.359	0.668	0.968	0.356	0.474	0.457	0.299	0.167	0.328	0.418	0.419	0.411	0.551
1988-89	0.327	0.312	0.621	0.900	0.303	0.424	0.426	0.276	0.162	0.322	0.309	0.384	0.393	0.519
1989-90	0.301	0.349	0.512	0.914	0.282	0.382	0.410	0.255	0.174	0.300	0.321	0.371	0.362	0.469
1990-91	0.346	0.299	0.483	0.897	0.273	0.362	0.333	0.248	0.160	0.243	0.277	0.408	0.355	0.399
1991-92	0.352	0.282	0.547	0.846	0.237	0.367	0.317	0.239	0.193	0.208	0.291	0.364	0.338	0.444
1992-93	0.384	0.293	0.551	1.003	0.267	0.379	0.346	0.220	0.156	0.280	0.306	0.438	0.333	0.439
1993-94	0.305	0.279	0.506	0.872	0.192	0.329	0.228	0.190	0.147	0.283	0.287	0.349	0.344	0.419
1994-95	0.269	0.267	0.408	0.802	0.207	0.373	0.307	0.193	0.152	0.266	0.270	0.358	0.281	0.394
1995-96	0.309	0.269	0.509	0.971	0.238	0.315	0.343	0.169	0.162	0.214	0.258	0.320	0.303	0.328
1996-97	0.342	0.227	0.380	0.792	0.256	0.337	0.353	0.155	0.120	0.184	0.210	0.288	0.283	0.333
1997-98	0.289	0.242	0.442	0.843	0.310	0.421	0.300	0.199	0.212	0.237	0.201	0.368	0.316	0.363
1998-99	0.311	0.269				0.419	0.382	0.192	0.215	0.307	0.294	0.432	0.392	0.465
1999-00	0.348	0.202				0.379	0.374	0.210	0.220	0.268	0.271	0.450	0.436	0.375
2000-01	0.355	0.355				0.350	0.467	0.235	0.232	0.283	0.378	0.489	0.443	0.453

6

Profile of Partial and Total Factor Productivities in Industries

In this chapter growth rates, trends and coefficient of variation of partial labour and capital productivities, total factor productivity (Kendrick, Solow & Translog) (TFPK, TFPS, TFPT) and capital intensity have been examined for 14 major industries of manufacturing sector at all-India level during 1973-74 to 2000-01.

Table 6.1 presents the trends in productivity (both partial and total) and capital intensity in case of *Food Products Industry* at all-India level. Index of partial labour productivity increased from 100.00 in 1973-74 to 519.55 in 2000-01. The labour productivity increased at an average rate of 8.828 percent per annum. The overall trend rate was 18.555 per annum. The average annual growth rate and trend rate were found statistically significant at one percent level of significance. Coefficient of variation was found to be 0.66.

Index of partial capital productivity declined at an average annual rate of 0.285 percent. The overall trend rate was 0.385 per annum. The average annual growth rate and trend rate of partial capital productivity were non-significant. The coefficient of variation was found to be 0.115.

TABLE 6.1
Productivity Indices in Food Products Industry in India (Code 20-21)

Year	*Index of Partial Labour Productivity*	*Index of Partial Capital Productivity*	*Index of Real Capital Intensity*	*Index of TFPK*	*Index of TFPS*	*Index of TFPT*
1973-74	100.00	100.00	100.00	100.00	100.00	100.00
1974-75	89.78	130.65	68.71	102.18	105.38	103.39
1975-76	86.95	137.37	63.29	101.53	105.02	103.52
1976-77	91.22	136.16	66.99	104.66	107.51	105.94
1977-78	105.64	138.81	76.10	116.24	118.14	116.35
1978-79	124.38	140.52	88.51	129.62	129.18	128.14
1979-80	103.39	125.51	82.37	110.64	110.09	108.04
1980-81	67.03	91.87	72.96	74.81	69.43	68.84
1981-82	76.08	106.13	71.68	85.41	79.18	78.47
1982-83	89.50	105.70	84.67	94.82	90.05	87.57
1983-84	157.96	126.90	124.47	142.73	131.80	128.61
1984-85	160.60	127.93	125.52	144.55	133.53	130.28
1985-86	176.09	126.18	139.55	150.71	139.58	136.11
1986-87	186.34	123.76	150.56	153.57	142.66	139.08
1987-88	195.94	118.77	164.97	154.00	143.84	139.75
1988-89	229.87	139.49	164.79	180.77	168.74	163.95
1989-90	283.54	142.56	198.88	200.93	189.68	185.48
1990-91	250.78	116.73	214.83	169.87	159.66	155.87
1991-92	272.64	108.79	250.60	168.02	159.01	155.11
1992-93	280.21	96.76	289.59	157.23	148.85	143.39
1993-94	408.21	122.61	332.93	208.33	201.33	193.66
1994-95	461.59	126.19	365.78	220.45	213.47	205.87
1995-96	398.63	109.60	363.70	191.16	183.29	176.75
1996-97	399.11	106.49	374.77	187.32	179.96	173.34
1997-98	471.96	112.15	420.82	203.52	197.82	190.29
1998-99	580.71	122.32	474.72	228.67	222.68	214.83
1999-00	559.59	119.54	468.11	222.73	216.61	208.93
2000-01	519.55	118.03	440.16	216.65	209.92	196.29
Growth Rate	8.828* (15.552)	(0.285)NS (1.038)	8.591* (19.293)	3.553* (9.607)	3.383* (8.483)	3.239* (8.158)
Linear Slope	18.555* (13.371)	0.385NS (1.198)	16.153* (14.464)	5.187* (11.225)	4.833* (10.101)	4.499* (9.633)
CV	0.660	0.115	0.676	0.304	0.300	0.290

Notes : 1. Figures in parentheses are the respective 't' values.
2. * Indicates one percent level of significance.
3. NS Indicates non-significant.

Index of capital intensity inclined from 100.00 in 1973-74 to 440.16 in 2000-01. The index increased at an average rate of 8.591 percent per annum. The overall trend rate was 16.153 per annum. The average annual growth rate and trend rate were found statistically significant at one percent level of significance. Coefficient of variation was found to be 0.676.

Index of TFPK increased from 100.00 in 1973-74 to 216.65 in 2000-01. It increased at an average rate of 3.553 percent per annum. The overall trend rate for Kendrick index was 5.187 per annum. Both the average annual growth rate and trend rate were found statistically significant at one percent level of significance. Coefficient of variation was found to be 0.304.

Index of TFPS increased from 100.00 in 1973-74 to 209.92 in 2000-01. It increased at an average rate of 3.383 percent per annum. The overall trend rate for Solow index was 4.833 per annum. Both the average annual growth rate and trend rate were found statistically significant at one percent level of significance. Coefficient of variation was found to be 0.300.

Index of TFPT increased from 100.00 in 1973-74 to 196.29 in 2000-01. It increased at an average rate of 3.239 percent per annum. The overall trend rate for Translog index was 4.499 per annum. Both the average annual growth rate and trend rate were found statistically significant at one percent level of significance. Coefficient of variation was found to be 0.290.

An inter-variable comparison in this industry revealed that the maximum growth rate was observed in labour productivity followed by capital intensity and minimum in capital productivity. It has been found that the maximum variability was found in capital intensity and minimum in capital productivity.

RELATIONSHIP OF TOTAL FACTOR PRODUCTIVITY WITH PARTIAL PRODUCTIVITIES OF CAPITAL AND LABOUR

Regression models in which total factor productivity (Kendrick, Solow & Translog) depended upon trend, labour and capital productivity were estimated. The estimated equations are :

$$\ln TFPK_t = -0.142 + 0.021 \ln t + 0.44 \ln LP_t + 0.576 \ln CP_t$$
$$(-0.408)\ (1.207)\qquad (20.836)\qquad (7.972);$$
$$R^2 = 0.984; \quad \tilde{R}^2 = 0.982; \quad S = 0.044$$
$$F \text{ ratio} = 494.22; \quad D\text{–}W = 0.420; \quad \tilde{p} = 0.712$$

$$\ln TFPS_t = -0.569 - 0.027 \ln t + 0.477 \ln LP_t + 0.64 \ln CP_t$$
$$(-2.488)\ (-2.402)\qquad (34.418)\qquad (13.482);$$
$$R^2 = 0.993; \quad \tilde{R}^2 = 0.992; \quad S = 0.029$$
$$F \text{ ratio} = 1113.15; \quad D\text{–}W = 0.665; \quad \tilde{p} = 0.622$$

$$\ln TFPT_t = -0.531 - 0.032 \ln t + 0.466 \ln LP_t + 0.641 \ln CP_t$$
$$(-2.152)\ (-2.633)\qquad (31.14)\qquad (12.506);$$
$$R^2 = 0.991; \quad \tilde{R}^2 = 0.990; \quad S = 0.031$$
$$F \text{ ratio} = 893.27; \quad D\text{-}W = 0.558; \quad \tilde{p} = 0.622$$

Both labour productivity and capital productivity significantly affected the total factor productivity, indicating consistency and robustness in the relationship between labour productivity, capital productivity and total factor productivity as measured through Kendrick, Solow and Translog indices.

Table 6.2 presents the empirical results productivity and capital intensity in case of *Beverages, Tobacco & Tobacco Products Industry* at all-India level during 1973-74 to 2000-01. Index of partial labour productivity increased from 100.00 in 1973-74 to 497.67 in 2000-01. The labour productivity increased at an average rate of 7.983 percent per annum and was significant. The overall trend rate of labour productivity was 17.801 per annum, which was significant. Coefficient of variation was found to be 0.621.

Index of partial capital productivity declined at an average annual rate of 0.769 percent. The overall trend rate was -0.791 per annum. The average annual growth rate of partial capital productivity was mildly significant at twenty percent level of significance while the trend rate was non-significant. The coefficient of variation was found to be 0.227.

Index of capital intensity increased from 100.00 in 1973-74 to 656.03 in 2000-01. The index increased at an average rate of 8.821 percent per annum. The overall trend rate was 18.765 per

TABLE 6.2
Productivity Indices in Beverages, Tobacco and Tobacco Products Industry in India (Code 22)

Year	Index of Partial Labour Productivity	Index of Partial Capital Productivity	Index of Real Capital Intensity	Index of TFPK	Index of TFPS	Index of TFPT
1973-74	100.00	100.00	100.00	100.00	100.00	100.00
1974-75	157.39	164.95	95.42	162.09	159.74	159.03
1975-76	113.36	105.06	107.90	110.25	108.39	107.05
1976-77	118.37	143.69	82.37	129.90	128.54	121.04
1977-78	78.36	106.24	73.76	89.89	79.77	76.10
1978-79	95.09	134.94	70.47	111.00	98.78	93.90
1979-80	82.00	125.25	65.47	98.35	84.73	80.63
1980-81	74.63	111.06	67.19	88.67	77.08	73.32
1981-82	72.80	115.79	62.87	88.58	75.30	70.31
1982-83	71.28	121.54	58.65	88.82	71.20	68.70
1983-84	152.39	163.32	93.31	158.52	133.35	129.73
1984-85	152.41	151.19	100.81	153.06	130.09	126.95
1985-86	153.37	97.27	157.67	122.08	110.06	98.77
1986-87	199.65	135.84	146.97	165.38	151.46	136.23
1987-88	239.15	142.02	168.40	183.20	169.93	152.26
1988-89	292.13	144.52	202.13	200.09	184.75	166.42
1989-90	250.26	167.27	149.61	205.24	187.85	171.48
1990-91	320.96	177.92	180.40	235.93	212.59	193.31
1991-92	370.61	186.99	198.20	257.01	230.98	210.04
1992-93	371.35	140.61	264.11	212.94	171.03	156.14
1993-94	382.22	127.16	300.58	200.00	159.84	145.53
1994-95	434.35	128.89	337.01	209.02	167.87	153.07
1995-96	394.76	107.24	368.09	177.78	142.97	130.16
1996-97	462.57	108.87	424.89	186.47	150.86	137.46
1997-98	438.86	96.03	457.03	167.00	133.40	121.84
1998-99	421.71	83.52	504.92	148.10	120.30	109.53
1999-00	585.68	93.71	625.00	172.38	146.27	134.32
2000-01	497.68	75.86	656.04	140.59	118.27	113.63
Growth Rate	7.983* (10.788)	-0.769^{NS} (-1.462)	8.821* (11.736)	2.538* (4.199)	1.934* (2.879)	1.655** (2.527)
Linear Slope	17.801* (13.114)	-0.791^{NS} (-1.18)	18.765* (9.464)	3.562* (3.926)	2.335** (2.644)	1.843** (2.311)
CV	0.621	0.227	0.802	0.308	0.307	0.291

Notes : 1. Figures in parentheses are the respective 't' values.
2. * Indicates one percent level of significance.
3. ** Indicate 5 percent level of significance.
4. ^{NS} Indicates non-significant.

annum. The average annual growth rate and trend rate were found statistically significant at one percent level of significance. Coefficient of variation was found to be 0.802.

Index of TFPK increased from 100.00 in 1973-74 to 140.59 in 2000-01. It increased at an average rate of 2.538 percent per annum. The overall trend rate for Kendrick index was 3.562 per annum. Both the average annual growth rate and trend rate were found statistically significant at one percent level of significance. Coefficient of variation was found to be 0.308.

Index of TFPS increased from 100.00 in 1973-74 to 118.26 in 2000-01. It increased at an average rate of 1.934 percent per annum. The overall trend rate for Solow index was 2.335 per annum. The average annual growth rate was found statistically significant at one percent level of significance and trend rate at five percent level of significance. Coefficient of variation was found to be 0.307.

Index of TFPT increased from 100.00 in 1973-74 to 113.62 in 2000-01. It increased at an average annual rate of 1.655 percent. The overall trend rate for Translog index was 1.843 per annum. Both the average annual growth rate and trend rate were found statistically significant at five percent level of significance. Coefficient of variation was found to be 0.291.

An inter-variable comparison in this industry revealed that the maximum growth rate and variability were observed in capital intensity followed by labour productivity and negative growth rate and least variability in capital productivity.

RELATIONSHIP OF TOTAL FACTOR PRODUCTIVITY WITH PARTIAL PRODUCTIVITIES OF CAPITAL AND LABOUR

The regression models in which total factor productivity (Kendrick, Solow & Translog) depended upon trend, labour and capital productivity were estimated. The estimated equations are :

$$\ln TFPK_t = -0.891 - 0.02 \ln t + 0.431 \ln LP_t + 0.757 \ln CP_t$$

$$(-4.717) \quad (-1.386) \quad (24.763) \quad (21.486)$$

$$R^2 = 0.985; \quad \tilde{R}^2 = 0.983; \quad S = 0.042$$

$$\text{F ratio} = 530.25; \quad \text{D-W} = 1.355; \quad \tilde{p} = 0.285$$

$$\ln TFPS_t = -1.344 - 0.101 \ln t + 0.465 \ln LP_t + 0.826 \ln CP_t$$
$$(-4.1) \quad (-4.026) \quad (15.373) \quad (13.518)$$
$$R^2 = 0.954; \quad \tilde{R}^2 = 0.948; \quad S = 0.073$$
$$F \text{ ratio} = 166.45; \quad D\text{–}W = 0.974; \quad \tilde{p} = 0.513$$

$$\ln TFPT_t = -1.227 - 0.129 \ln t + 0.461 \ln LP_t + 0.806 \ln CP_t$$
$$(-4.403) \quad (-6.087) \quad (17.935) \quad (15.521)$$
$$R^2 = 0.963; \quad \tilde{R}^2 = 0.959; \quad S = 0.062$$
$$F \text{ ratio} = 209.49; \quad D\text{–}W = 1.032; \quad \tilde{p} = 0.476$$

Both labour productivity and capital productivity significantly affected the total factor productivity, indicating consistency and robustness in the relationship between labour productivity, capital productivity and total factor productivity as measured through Kendrick, Solow and Translog indices.

Table 6.3 presents the empirical results in case of *Cotton Textiles Industry* at all-India level from 1973-74 to 1997-98. Index of partial labour productivity increased from 100.00 in 1973-74 to 294.10 in 1997-98. The labour productivity increased at an average rate of 6.500 percent per annum and was significant. The overall trend rate was 10.675 per annum which was significant. Coefficient of variation was found to be 0.499.

The index of partial capital productivity declined from 100.00 in 1973-74 to 37.05 in 1997-98. It declined at an average annual rate of 3.002 percent. The overall trend rate was –2.146 per annum. Both the average annual growth rate and the trend rate were significant at one percent level of significance. The coefficient of variation was found to be 0.256.

The index of capital intensity increased from 100.00 in 1973-74 to 793.78 in 1997-98. It increased at an average rate of 9.796 percent per annum. The overall trend rate was 24.371 per annum. The average annual growth rate and trend rate were found statistically significant at one percent level of significance. Coefficient of variation was found to be 0.794.

Index of TFPK increased from 100.00 in 1973-74 to 132.88 in 1997-98. It increased at an average rate of 3.225 percent per annum. The overall trend rate for Kendrick index was 3.990 per

TABLE 6.3
Productivity Indices in Cotton Textiles Industry in India (Code 23)

Year	*Index of Partial Labour Productivity*	*Index of Partial Capital Productivity*	*Index of Real Capital Intensity*	*Index of TFPK*	*Index of TFPS*	*Index of TFPT*
1973-74	100.00	100.00	100.00	100.00	100.00	100.00
1974-75	87.57	105.55	82.97	90.87	84.70	82.96
1975-76	78.60	97.78	80.38	81.94	75.17	73.65
1976-77	80.61	90.27	89.30	82.69	79.17	77.64
1977-78	84.88	87.24	97.29	85.83	85.38	83.08
1978-79	101.49	102.14	99.36	102.26	103.04	100.26
1979-80	104.40	108.17	96.51	105.72	105.79	102.92
1980-81	104.84	94.77	110.61	103.56	107.54	104.30
1981-82	101.47	88.52	114.62	99.54	104.43	101.23
1982-83	106.22	76.97	138.00	100.16	109.77	105.45
1983-84	127.48	78.82	161.74	115.66	129.88	125.32
1984-85	125.10	69.82	179.18	110.43	127.46	122.53
1985-86	134.97	64.65	208.74	113.91	135.08	129.40
1986-87	145.55	73.15	198.97	124.65	146.64	140.64
1987-88	153.93	70.10	219.58	127.87	151.85	144.78
1988-89	181.79	80.64	225.43	149.73	177.12	168.63
1989-90	231.81	105.11	220.54	192.29	230.82	219.79
1990-91	242.95	99.46	244.26	194.79	230.32	219.72
1991-92	223.83	77.38	289.24	168.76	195.77	186.54
1992-93	225.51	59.71	377.64	152.20	169.92	160.43
1993-94	248.48	54.78	453.56	153.84	170.37	158.65
1994-95	351.10	62.23	564.18	194.01	213.28	200.55
1995-96	265.40	45.07	588.86	143.22	151.04	141.44
1996-97	345.86	50.94	678.88	171.96	180.58	169.70
1997-98	294.10	37.05	793.78	132.88	133.52	138.12
Growth Rate	6.500* (16.822)	-3.002* (-6.089)	9.796* (19.398)	3.225* (8.029)	3.863* (7.391)	3.722* (7.450)
Linear Slope	10.675* (11.749)	-2.146* (-5.957)	24.371* (8.912)	3.990* (6.916)	4.996* (6.231)	4.631* (6.273)
CV	0.499	0.256	0.794	0.279	0.332	0.319

Notes : 1. Figures in parentheses are the respective 't' values.
2. * Indicates one percent level of significance.

annum. Both the average annual growth rate and trend rate were found statistically significant at one percent level of significance. Coefficient of variation was found to be 0.279.

Index of TFPS increased from 100.00 in 1973-74 to 133.52 in 1997-98. It increased at an average rate of 3.863 percent per annum. The overall trend rate for Solow index was 4.996 per annum. Both the average annual growth rate and trend rate were found statistically significant at one percent level of significance. Coefficient of variation was found to be 0.332.

Index of TFPT increased from 100.00 in 1973-74 to 138.12 in 1997-98. It increased at an average annual rate of 3.722 percent. The overall trend rate for Translog index was 4.631 per annum. Both the average annual growth rate and trend rate were found statistically significant at one percent level of significance. Coefficient of variation was found to be 0.319.

An inter-variable comparison in this industry revealed that the maximum growth rate and variability were observed in capital intensity followed by labour productivity and negative growth rate and least variability in capital productivity.

RELATIONSHIP OF TOTAL FACTOR PRODUCTIVITY WITH PARTIAL PRODUCTIVITIES OF CAPITAL AND LABOUR

The regression models in which total factor productivity (Kendrick, Solow & Translog) depended upon trend, labour and capital productivity were estimated. The estimated equations are :

$$\ln TFPK_t = -0.468 + 0.06 \ln t + 0.626 \ln LP_t + 0.461 \ln CP_t$$
$$(-1.816) \quad (3.501) \quad (20.511) \quad (11.708)$$
$$R^2 = 0.982; \quad \tilde{R}^2 = 0.980; \quad S = 0.039$$
$$F \text{ ratio} = 383.64; \quad D\text{-}W = 0.540; \quad \tilde{p} = 0.602$$

$$\ln TFPS_t = -1.212 + 0.153 \ln t + 0.633 \ln LP_t + 0.592 \ln CP_t$$
$$(-1.921) \quad (3.629) \quad (8.466) \quad (6.14)$$
$$R^2 = 0.928; \quad \tilde{R}^2 = 0.918; \quad S = 0.095$$
$$F \text{ ratio} = 90.31; \quad D\text{-}W = 0.514; \quad \tilde{p} = 0.623$$

$$\ln TFPT_t = -1.023 + 0.136 \ln t + 0.624 \ln LP_t + 0.56 \ln CP_t$$

$$(-1.681) \quad (3.335) \quad (8.657) \quad (6.017)$$

$$R^2 = 0.928; \quad \tilde{R}^2 = 0.917; \quad S = 0.092$$

$$\text{F ratio} = 89.81; \quad D\text{–}W = 0.537; \quad \tilde{p} = 0.634$$

Both labour productivity and capital productivity significantly affected the total factor productivity, indicating consistent and strong relationship between labour productivity, capital productivity and total factor productivity as measured through Kendrick, Solow and Translog indices.

Table 6.4 shows productivity indices in case of *Jute, Hemp & Mesta Textiles Industry* at all-India level from 1973-74 to 1997-98. The index of partial labour productivity increased from 100.00 in 1973-74 to 652.37 in 1997-98. It increased at an average rate of 8.372 percent per annum and was significant. The overali trend rate was 20.918 per annum, which was significant. Coefficient of variation was found to be 0.674.

The index of partial capital productivity increased from 100.00 in 1973-74 to 255.15 in 1997-98. It indicated an increase at the average annual rate of 1.011 percent. The overall trend rate was 1.731 per annum. The average annual growth rate and the trend rate were mildly significant at ten percent level of significance. The coefficient of variation was found to be 0.227.

The index of capital intensity increased from 100.00 in 1973-74 to 255.68 in 1997-98. It increased at an average rate of 7.286 percent per annum. The overall trend rate was 11.334 per annum. The average annual growth rate and trend rate were found statistically significant at one percent level of significance. Coefficient of variation was found to be 0.552.

Index of TFPK increased from 100.00 in 1973-74 to 598.23 in 1997-98. It increased at an average rate of 7.801 percent per annum. The overall trend rate for Kendrick index was 18.387 per annum. Both the average annual growth rate and trend rate were found statistically significant at one percent level of significance. Coefficient of variation was found to be 0.634.

Index of TFPS increased from 100.00 in 1973-74 to 972.85 in 1997-98. It increased at an average rate of 11.993 percent per annum. The overall trend rate for Solow index was 35.701 per annum. Both the average annual growth rate and trend rate were

TABLE 6.4

Productivity Indices in Jute, Hemp & Mesta Textiles Industry in India (Code 25)

Year	*Index of Partial Labour Productivity*	*Index of Partial Capital Productivity*	*Index of Real Capital Intensity*	*Index of TFPK*	*Index of TFPS*	*Index of TFPT*
1973-74	100.00	100.00	100.00	100.00	100.00	100.00
1974-75	107.31	123.25	87.07	106.25	95.08	95.55
1975-76	123.35	162.92	75.71	122.79	98.31	97.08
1976-77	117.59	153.55	76.58	117.01	95.25	94.15
1977-78	110.14	144.00	76.49	109.60	88.63	87.60
1978-79	104.09	126.39	82.35	103.29	93.29	91.89
1979-80	122.37	172.16	71.08	122.08	92.97	93.61
1980-81	144.18	180.34	79.95	143.24	119.69	121.48
1981-82	124.88	149.11	83.75	123.84	111.49	112.98
1982-83	123.71	136.79	90.43	122.29	121.04	120.02
1983-84	162.94	155.86	104.54	160.01	163.29	163.26
1984-85	165.28	151.12	109.36	161.94	173.71	175.18
1985-86	157.59	115.77	136.12	152.49	200.13	197.01
1986-87	193.77	175.56	110.38	189.77	218.15	219.77
1987-88	211.14	134.05	157.51	202.31	276.21	275.02
1988-89	238.14	95.78	248.64	219.05	379.88	369.41
1989-90	261.88	121.55	215.45	244.46	403.72	394.04
1990-91	299.80	118.25	253.53	275.18	474.34	451.67
1991-92	367.19	125.46	292.67	331.35	572.50	546.30
1992-93	384.09	156.69	245.12	353.85	607.37	581.60
1993-94	411.47	137.81	298.58	370.37	629.68	591.33
1994-95	531.77	192.70	275.96	483.35	844.59	791.09
1995-96	483.17	165.76	291.48	436.23	718.97	668.00
1996-97	616.88	185.87	331.90	547.42	839.93	781.62
1997-98	652.37	255.15	255.68	598.23	972.86	891.64
Growth Rate	8.372* (17.335)	1.011*** (1.737)	7.286* (11.400)	7.801* (17.093)	11.993* (19.175)	11.610* (19.520)
Linear Slope	20.918* (10.183)	1.731*** (1.942)	11.334* (10.495)	18.387* (10.189)	35.701* (11.425)	33.072* (11.903)
CV	0.674	0.227	0.552	0.634	0.839	0.809

Notes : 1. Figures in parentheses are the respective 't' values.
2. * Indicates one percent level of significance.
3. ***Indicate 10 percent level of significance.

found statistically significant at one percent level of significance. Coefficient of variation was found to be 0.839.

Index of TFPT increased from 100.00 in 1973-74 to 891.63 in 1997-98. It increased at an average annual rate of 11.61 percent. The overall trend rate for Translog index was 33.072 per annum. Both the average annual growth rate and trend rate were found statistically significant at one percent level of significance. Coefficient of variation was found to be 0.809.

An inter-variable comparison in this industry revealed that the maximum growth rate and variability were observed in TFPS followed by TFPT and minimum in capital productivity.

RELATIONSHIP OF TOTAL FACTOR PRODUCTIVITY WITH PARTIAL PRODUCTIVITIES OF CAPITAL AND LABOUR

The regression models in which total factor productivity (Kendrick, Solow & Translog) depended upon trend, labour and capital productivity were estimated. The estimated equation is :

$$\ln TFPK_t = 0.048 - 0.001 \ln t + 0.927 \ln LP_t + 0.06 \ln CP_t$$

(1.492) (–0.277) (242.92) (8.984)

$R^2 = 1.00$; $\tilde{R}^2 = 1.00$; $S = 0.006$

F ratio = 63084.51; D–W = 1.473; $\tilde{p} = 0.130$

$$\ln TFPS_t = 0.959 + 0.062 \ln t + 1.402 \ln LP_t - 0.624 \ln CP_t$$

(2.886) (2.196) (35.234) (–9.006)

$R^2 = 0.995$; $\tilde{R}^2 = 0.994$; $S = 0.067$

F ratio = 1294.03; D–W = 2.014; $\tilde{p} = -0.077$

$$\ln TFPT_t = 1.175 + 0.074 \ln t + 1.343 \ln LP_t - 0.614 \ln CP_t$$

(3.313) (2.439) (31.623) (–8.305)

$R^2 = 0.993$; $\tilde{R}^2 = 0.993$; $S = 0.072$

F ratio = 1064.91; D–W = 1.832; $\tilde{p} = 0.026$

Both labour productivity and capital productivity significantly affected the total factor productivity, indicating consistency and strength in the relationship between labour productivity, capital productivity and total factor productivity as measured through Kendrick, Solow and Translog indices.

Table 6.5 shows the empirical results in case of *Textile Products Industry* at all-India level from 1973-74 to 1997-98. The index of partial labour productivity increased from 100.00 in 1973-74 to 881.29 in 1997-98. It increased at an average rate of 12.057 percent per annum and was significant. The overall trend rate was 41.62 per annum which was highly significant. Coefficient of variation was found to be 0.902.

The index of partial capital productivity increased from 100.00 in 1973-74 to 172.95 in 1997-98. It increased at an average annual rate of 3.404 percent. The overall trend rate was 5.397 per annum. Both the average annual growth rate and the trend rate were highly significant at one percent level of significance. The coefficient of variation was found to be 0.35.

The index of capital intensity increased from 100.00 in 1973-74 to 509.55 in 1997-98. It increased at an average rate of 8.368 percent per annum. The overall trend rate of capital intensity was 17.462 per annum. The average annual growth rate and trend rate were found statistically significant at one percent level of significance. Coefficient of variation was found to be 0.628.

Index of TFPK increased from 100.00 in 1973-74 to 281.49 in 1997-98. It increased at an average rate of 6.133 percent per annum. The overall trend rate for Kendrick index was 12.091 per annum. Both the average annual growth rate and trend rate were found statistically significant at one percent level of significance. Coefficient of variation was found to be 0.519.

Index of TFPS increased from 100.00 in 1973-74 to 489.17 in 1997-98. It increased at an average rate of 8.524 percent per annum. The overall trend rate for Solow index was 21.054 per annum. Both the average annual growth rate and trend rate were found statistically significant at one percent level of significance. Coefficient of variation was found to be 1.021.

Index of TFPT increased from 100.00 in 1973-74 to 447.81 in 1997-98. It increased at an average annual rate of 7.892 percent. The overall trend rate for Translog index was 17.922 per annum. Both the average annual growth rate and trend rate were found statistically significant at one percent level of significance. Coefficient of variation was found to be 0.998.

TABLE 6.5
Productivity Indices in Textile Products Industry in India (Code 26)

Year	*Index of Partial Labour Productivity*	*Index of Partial Capital Productivity*	*Index of Real Capital Intensity*	*Index of TFPK*	*Index of TFPS*	*Index of TFPT*
1973-74	100.00	100.00	100.00	100.00	100.00	100.00
1974-75	90.47	114.30	79.15	102.06	117.61	116.95
1975-76	113.91	131.19	86.83	122.95	122.85	118.06
1976-77	104.87	121.25	86.49	113.41	112.76	108.36
1977-78	104.66	111.20	94.12	108.51	86.72	85.49
1978-79	128.81	108.48	118.74	117.86	66.33	60.78
1979-80	104.37	94.86	110.02	99.64	67.84	61.68
1980-81	119.37	107.86	110.67	113.60	77.13	69.99
1981-82	144.87	131.82	109.89	138.40	88.50	81.34
1982-83	166.35	125.90	132.13	143.07	78.33	73.00
1983-84	178.41	127.46	139.97	148.23	77.42	74.38
1984-85	243.00	163.50	148.63	194.60	105.95	97.66
1985-86	179.88	109.45	164.35	135.18	69.87	60.06
1986-87	274.03	155.26	176.50	196.57	104.03	90.10
1987-88	299.78	108.50	276.30	156.58	74.79	61.09
1988-89	275.55	120.48	228.72	165.36	77.84	63.49
1989-90	283.93	125.09	226.98	171.32	85.19	71.39
1990-91	464.28	196.19	236.65	271.87	158.49	135.07
1991-92	607.68	206.97	293.61	303.12	226.80	195.81
1992-93	774.30	247.45	312.91	367.77	341.35	298.54
1993-94	1118.88	293.51	381.20	454.55	730.01	636.90
1994-95	1077.43	238.81	451.16	381.21	731.16	633.84
1995-96	951.30	204.84	464.42	328.55	559.73	485.61
1996-97	914.97	195.29	468.51	313.69	513.58	445.78
1997-98	881.29	172.95	509.55	281.49	489.17	447.82
Growth Rate	12.057* (16.391)	3.404* (5.861)	8.368* (21.476)	6.133* (10.589)	8.524* (5.213)	7.892* (4.611)
Linear Slope	41.620* (8.683)	5.397* (5.353)	17.462* (12.104)	12.091* (7.840)	21.054* (4.989)	17.922* (4.794)
CV	0.902	0.350	0.628	0.519	1.021	0.998

Notes : 1. Figures in parentheses are the respective 't' values.
2. * Indicates one percent level of significance.

An inter-variable comparison in this industry revealed that the maximum growth rate was observed in labour productivity followed by TFPS and minimum in capital productivity. It has been found that the maximum variability was found in TFPS and minimum in capital productivity.

RELATIONSHIP OF TOTAL FACTOR PRODUCTIVITY WITH PARTIAL PRODUCTIVITIES OF CAPITAL AND LABOUR

The regression models in which total factor productivity (Kendrick, Solow & Translog) depended upon trend, labour and capital productivity were estimated in following equations :

$$\ln TFPK_t = \underset{(0.567)}{0.067} + \underset{(3.759)}{0.043} \ln t + \underset{(15.151)}{0.279} \ln LP_t + \underset{(18.473)}{0.696} \ln CP_t$$

$$R^2 = 0.998; \quad \tilde{R}^2 = 0.997; \quad S = 0.025$$

$$F \text{ ratio} = 2943.97; \quad D\text{–}W = 0.721; \quad \tilde{p} = 0.479$$

$$\ln TFPS_t = \underset{(-2.449)}{-3.108} - \underset{(-4.573)}{0.563} \ln t + \underset{(5.135)}{1.015} \ln LP_t + \underset{(1.845)}{0.747} \ln CP_t$$

$$R^2 = 0.905; \quad \tilde{R}^2 = 0.892; \quad S = 0.269$$

$$F \text{ ratio} = 67.02; \quad D\text{-}W = 0.701; \quad \tilde{p} = 0.549$$

$$\ln TFPT_t = \underset{(-2.495)}{-3.415} - \underset{(-4.637)}{0.615} \ln t + \underset{(4.603)}{0.981} \ln LP_t + \underset{(1.948)}{0.85} \ln CP_t$$

$$R^2 = 0.887; \quad \tilde{R}^2 = 0.871; \quad S = 0.290$$

$$F \text{ ratio} = 54.90; \quad D\text{–}W = 0.661; \quad \tilde{p} = 0.559$$

Both labour productivity and capital productivity significantly affected the total factor productivity, indicating consistency and strength in the relationship between labour productivity, capital productivity and total factor productivity as measured through Kendrick, Solow and Translog indices.

Table 6.6 shows productivity indices in case of *Paper & Paper Products Industry* at all-India level from 1973-74 to 2000-01. The index of partial labour productivity increased from 100.00 in

TABLE 6.6

Productivity Indices in Paper & Paper Products Industry in India (Code 28)

Year	Index of Partial Labour Productivity	Index of Partial Capital Productivity	Index of Real Capital Intensity	Index of TFPK	Index of TFPS	Index of TFPT
1973-74	100.00	100.00	100.00	100.00	100.00	100.00
1974-75	109.32	114.36	95.59	111.00	111.16	111.07
1975-76	107.11	106.99	100.12	107.16	106.68	106.73
1976-77	104.45	94.22	110.86	100.95	99.14	99.11
1977-78	106.81	92.39	115.61	101.71	99.65	99.72
1978-79	103.94	91.36	113.77	99.54	97.56	97.61
1979-80	102.31	89.46	114.37	97.80	95.75	95.80
1980-81	103.12	72.73	141.80	90.80	88.52	88.66
1981-82	107.99	74.08	145.78	94.02	92.05	92.22
1982-83	99.78	58.06	171.85	80.87	79.21	78.71
1983-84	115.24	54.70	210.67	84.70	84.34	83.48
1984-85	131.26	52.46	250.23	88.11	89.09	89.01
1985-86	111.83	55.52	201.42	84.06	81.88	82.40
1986-87	128.48	50.45	254.69	85.41	85.43	86.00
1987-88	135.89	51.75	262.57	160.12	89.57	90.06
1988-89	150.25	51.24	293.20	92.18	93.77	94.01
1989-90	188.82	73.88	255.57	125.28	124.46	124.99
1990-91	200.77	69.14	290.39	123.87	122.71	122.87
1991-92	218.00	69.01	315.89	127.93	126.78	126.88
1992-93	227.40	63.85	356.16	123.89	122.09	121.73
1993-94	272.46	64.90	419.84	133.33	131.62	131.89
1994-95	268.69	41.29	650.78	96.05	82.84	82.42
1995-96	263.06	65.06	404.30	132.01	102.78	102.60
1996-97	278.03	48.21	576.70	108.79	80.54	82.35
1997-98	217.03	39.02	556.27	87.20	65.19	66.67
1998-99	246.98	33.73	732.17	80.63	62.94	64.20
1999-00	274.06	35.84	764.79	86.46	68.28	69.54
2000-01	368.80	56.63	651.20	131.77	99.77	99.48
Growth Rate	4.926* (13.267)	-3.166* (-6.93)	8.358* (26.039)	0.407^{NS} (0.946)	-0.580^{NS} (-1.307)	-0.533^{NS} (-1.224)
Linear Slope	8.483* (10.970)	-2.163* (-7.167)	23.355* (12.248)	0.511^{NS} (1.084)	-0.400^{NS} (-0.935)	-0.367^{NS} (-0.868)
CV	0.445	0.327	0.673	0.193	0.190	0.187

Notes : 1. Figures in parentheses are the respective 't' values.
2. * Indicates one percent level of significance.
3. ^{NS} indicates non-significant.

1973-74 to 368.80 in 2000-01. It increased at an average rate of 4.926 percent per annum and was significant. The overall trend rate was 8.483 per annum which was significant. Coefficient of variation was found to be 0.445.

The index of partial capital productivity decreased from 100.00 in 1973-74 to 56.63 in 2000-01. It declined at an average annual rate of 3.166 percent. The overall trend rate was –2.163 per annum. But both the average annual growth rate and the trend rate were significant at one percent level of significance. The coefficient of variation was found to be 0.327.

The index of capital intensity indicated an incline from 100.00 in 1973-74 to 651.20 in 2000-01. It increased at an average rate of 8.358 percent per annum. The overall trend rate was 23.355 per annum. The average annual growth rate and trend rate were found statistically significant at one percent level of significance. Coefficient of variation was found to be 0.673.

Index of TFPK increased from 100.00 in 1973-74 to 131.77 in 2000-01. It increased at an average rate of 0.407 percent per annum. The overall trend rate of TFPK was 0.511 per annum. Both the average annual growth rate and trend rate were found statistically non-significant. Coefficient of variation was found to be 0.193.

Index of TFPS decreased from 100.00 in 1973-74 to 99.76 in 2000-01. It declined at an average annual rate of 0.58 percent. The overall trend rate for Solow index was –0.40 per annum. Both the average annual growth rate and trend rate were found statistically non-significant. Coefficient of variation was found to be 0.19.

Index of TFPT decreased from 100.00 in 1973-74 to 99.48 in 2000-01. It declined at an average annual rate of 0.533 percent. The overall trend rate for Translog index was –0.367 per annum. Both the average annual growth rate and trend rate were found statistically non-significant. Coefficient of variation was found to be 0.187.

An inter-variable comparison in this industry revealed that the maximum growth rate and variability were observed in capital intensity followed by labour productivity and most negative growth rate was in capital productivity and least variability was in TFPT.

RELATIONSHIP OF TOTAL FACTOR PRODUCTIVITY WITH PARTIAL PRODUCTIVITIES OF CAPITAL AND LABOUR

The estimated regression models in which total factor productivity (Kendrick, Solow & Translog) depended upon trend, labour and capital productivity are given as under :

$$\ln TFPK_t = \underset{(0.936)}{0.649} + \underset{(1.659)}{0.104} \ln t + \underset{(2.897)}{0.266} \ln LP_t + \underset{(4.607)}{0.576} \ln CP_t$$

$R^2 = 0.581$; $\tilde{R}^2 = 0.529$; $S = 0.126$

F ratio = 11.09; D–W = 1.883; $\tilde{p} = 0.05$

$$\ln TFPS_t = \underset{(0.35)}{0.192} + \underset{(2.907)}{0.144} \ln t + \underset{(1.911)}{0.139} \ln LP_t + \underset{(8.044)}{0.796} \ln CP_t$$

$R^2 = 0.762$; $\tilde{R}^2 = 0.733$; $S = 0.10$

F ratio = 25.64; D-W = 0.410; $\tilde{p} = 0.749$

$$\ln TFPT_t = \underset{(0.466)}{0.248} + \underset{(2.915)}{0.14} \ln t + \underset{(2.045)}{0.144} \ln LP_t + \underset{(8.114)}{0.779} \ln CP_t$$

$R^2 = 0.766$; $\tilde{R}^2 = 0.736$; $S = 0.097$

F ratio = 26.15; D–W = 0.414; $\tilde{p} = 0.741$

Both labour productivity and capital productivity significantly affected the total factor productivity, indicating consistency and robustness in the relationship between labour productivity, capital productivity and total factor productivity as measured through Kendrick, Solow and Translog indices.

Table 6.7 shows the empirical results in case of *Leather & Fur Products Industry* at all-India level from 1973-74 to 2000-01. The index of partial labour productivity increased from 100.00 in 1973-74 to 233.71 in 2000-01. The index increased at an average rate of 4.794 percent per annum and was significant. The overall trend rate was 8.507 per annum which was significant. Coefficient of variation was found to be 0.493.

The index of partial capital productivity decreased from 100.00 in 1973-74 to 32.35 in 2000-01. It declined at an average annual rate of 2.339 percent. The overall trend rate was –1.446

TABLE 6.7

Productivity Indices in Leather & Fur Products Industry in India (Code 29)

Year	*Index of Partial Labour Productivity*	*Index of Partial Capital Productivity*	*Index of Real Capital Intensity*	*Index of TFPK*	*Index of TFPS*	*Index of TFPT*
1973-74	100.00	100.00	100.00	100.00	100.00	100.00
1974-75	125.82	111.70	112.64	120.73	120.03	119.38
1975-76	112.98	78.05	144.75	97.20	100.92	81.84
1976-77	122.17	76.02	160.71	99.97	107.60	100.41
1977-78	122.08	62.58	195.09	90.37	99.15	86.43
1978-79	99.27	53.60	185.21	75.56	77.41	76.33
1979-80	105.62	49.29	214.27	74.24	79.47	71.06
1980-81	97.01	44.82	216.44	67.80	73.14	64.54
1981-82	79.46	38.69	205.40	57.19	59.61	55.68
1982-83	111.29	45.21	246.17	72.17	80.01	71.77
1983-84	128.31	48.40	265.13	79.54	89.94	79.33
1984-85	120.67	49.61	243.25	78.81	86.77	81.57
1985-86	94.46	33.94	278.34	56.82	65.13	53.20
1986-87	92.23	35.98	256.36	58.36	64.34	54.96
1987-88	119.16	41.45	287.47	70.22	82.05	69.26
1988-89	118.97	42.78	278.10	71.59	83.23	76.33
1989-90	135.80	49.97	271.76	82.91	97.48	94.57
1990-91	183.84	48.22	381.24	89.77	109.50	114.31
1991-92	229.93	57.17	402.19	108.13	134.05	145.67
1992-93	236.70	47.53	498.01	95.25	116.49	143.15
1993-94	339.84	60.64	560.39	125.00	157.67	207.81
1994-95	249.40	41.19	605.44	86.37	100.39	157.80
1995-96	242.21	40.11	603.83	84.06	97.62	155.78
1996-97	231.23	31.21	740.82	68.12	79.46	131.56
1997-98	334.04	54.89	608.52	115.22	124.62	193.37
1998-99	316.29	39.32	804.47	87.07	90.64	161.20
1999-00	332.71	46.82	710.55	101.40	102.91	179.71
2000-01	233.71	32.36	722.31	70.29	67.06	137.37
Growth Rate	4.794* (7.715)	-2.339* (-4.124)	7.304* (22.303)	0.122^{NS} (0.237)	0.388^{NS} (0.705)	3.247^{NS} (4.380)
Linear Slope	8.507* (7.451)	-1.446* (-4.1032)	24.565* (13.987)	0.093^{NS} (0.210)	0.427^{NS} (0.803)	3.745* (4.867)
CV	0.493	0.364	0.585	0.218	0.239	0.408

Notes : 1. Figures in parentheses are the respective 't' values.
2. * Indicates one percent level of significance.
3. ^{NS} Indicates non-significant.

per annum. But both the average annual rate and the trend rate were significant at one percent level of significance. The coefficient of variation was found to be 0.364.

The index of capital intensity indicated a rise from 100.00 in 1973-74 to 722.31 in 2000-01. It increased at an average rate of 7.304 percent per annum. The overall trend rate was 24.565 per annum. The average annual growth rate and trend rate were found statistically significant at one percent level of significance. Coefficient of variation was found to be 0.585.

Index of TFPK decreased from 100.00 in 1973-74 to 70.28 in 2000-01. It increased at an average rate of 0.122 percent per annum. The overall trend rate for Kendrick index was 0.093 per annum. Both the average annual growth rate and trend rate were found statistically non-significant. Coefficient of variation was found to be 0.218.

Index of TFPS decreased from 100.00 in 1973-74 to 67.06 in 2000-01. It increased at an average rate of 0.388 percent per annum. The overall trend rate for Solow index was 0.427 per annum. Both the average annual growth rate and trend rate were found statistically non-significant. Coefficient of variation was found to be 0.239.

Index of TFPT increased from 100.00 in 1973-74 to 137.36 in 2000-01. It increased at average annual rate of 3.247 percent. The overall trend rate was 3.745 per annum. Both the average annual growth rate and trend rate were found statistically significant at one percent level of significance. Coefficient of variation was found to be 0.408.

An inter-variable comparison in this industry revealed that the maximum growth rate and variability were observed in capital intensity followed by labour productivity and negative growth in capital productivity and least variability in TFPK.

RELATIONSHIP OF TOTAL FACTOR PRODUCTIVITY WITH PARTIAL PRODUCTIVITIES OF CAPITAL AND LABOUR

The estimated regression models in which total factor productivity (Kendrick, Solow & Translog) depended upon trend, labour and capital productivity are given as on next page.

$$\ln TFPK_t = 0.036 + 0.105 \ln t + 0.215 \ln LP_t + 0.781 \ln CP_t$$
$$(0.419) \quad (8.394) \quad (14.82) \quad (29.784)$$
$$R^2 = 0.994; \quad \tilde{R}^2 = 0.994; \quad S = 0.017$$
$$F \text{ ratio} = 1387.63; \quad D\text{–}W = 1.283; \quad \tilde{p} = 0.315$$

$$\ln TFPS_t = -0.514 + 0.244 \ln t + 0.11 \ln LP_t + 0.996 \ln CP_t$$
$$(-1.463) \quad (4.757) \quad (1.855) \quad (9.278)$$
$$R^2 = 0.917; \quad \tilde{R}^2 = 0.906; \quad S = 0.071$$
$$F \text{ ratio} = 88.08; \quad D\text{–}W = 1.067; \quad \tilde{p} = 0.361$$

$$\ln TFPT_t = -0.73 - 0.093 \ln t + 0.959 \ln LP_t + 0.19 \ln CP_t$$
$$(-2.258) \quad (-1.974) \quad (17.534) \quad (1.923)$$
$$R^2 = 0.977; \quad \tilde{R}^2 = 0.974; \quad S = 0.066$$
$$F \text{ ratio} = 332.86; \quad D\text{–}W = 1.907; \quad \tilde{p} = 0.009$$

Both labour productivity and capital productivity significantly affected the total factor productivity, indicating consistency and strength in the relationship between labour productivity, capital productivity and total factor productivity as measured through Kendrick, Solow and Translog indices.

Table 6.8 shows the productivity indices in case of *Chemicals & Chemical Products Industry* at all-India level from 1973-74 to 2000-01. The index of partial labour productivity increased from 100.00 in 1973-74 to 215.64 in 2000-01. The index increased at an average rate of 4.499 percent per annum and was significant. The overall trend rate was 6.822 per annum which was significant. Coefficient of variation was found to be 0.451.

The index of partial capital productivity decreased from 100.00 in 1973-74 to 55.23 in 2000-01. It declined at an average annual rate of 2.068 percent. The overall trend rate was—1.658 per annum. But both the average annual growth rate and the trend rate were significant at one percent level of significance. The coefficient of variation was found to be 0.20.

The index of capital intensity increased from 100.00 in 1973-74 to 390.40 in 2000-01. It increased at an average rate of 6.707 percent per annum. The overall trend rate was 13.034. The average annual growth rate and trend rate were found statistically significant at one percent level of significance. Coefficient of variation was found to be 0.580.

TABLE 6.8

Productivity Indices in Chemicals & Chemical Products Industry in India (Code 30)

Year	*Index of Partial Labour Productivity*	*Index of Partial Capital Productivity*	*Index of Real Capital Intensity*	*Index of TFPK*	*Index of TFPS*	*Index of TFPT*
1973-74	100.00	100.00	100.00	100.00	100.00	100.00
1974-75	94.76	104.32	90.83	99.81	101.62	101.35
1975-76	85.65	89.06	96.17	87.32	86.57	86.31
1976-77	93.03	97.87	95.05	95.48	95.09	94.81
1977-78	94.47	96.78	97.61	95.49	94.71	94.40
1978-79	115.54	113.58	101.73	113.99	113.43	113.14
1979-80	94.25	92.74	101.63	93.04	89.45	89.22
1980-81	85.74	81.03	105.82	82.63	79.07	78.85
1981-82	88.21	84.76	104.08	85.86	82.17	81.96
1982-83	96.58	95.52	101.11	95.63	91.81	91.61
1983-84	110.82	94.64	117.09	100.37	95.20	95.29
1984-85	102.71	91.10	112.74	95.24	90.50	90.59
1985-86	102.18	80.65	126.70	88.04	82.26	82.53
1986-87	98.48	72.54	135.75	81.13	75.79	76.00
1987-88	103.40	71.25	145.12	81.48	76.23	76.42
1988-89	100.84	71.06	141.91	80.66	75.42	75.62
1989-90	117.39	63.53	184.78	78.12	72.33	72.21
1990-91	134.09	61.75	217.16	79.19	73.62	73.26
1991-92	144.83	63.51	228.06	82.42	76.92	76.48
1992-93	184.75	69.06	267.52	92.85	88.87	88.13
1993-94	201.96	67.31	300.04	92.59	88.40	87.68
1994-95	208.10	64.56	322.36	89.99	85.64	84.87
1995-96	239.44	68.83	347.86	97.23	93.85	92.91
1996-97	270.89	77.15	351.11	109.15	105.27	104.24
1997-98	210.66	54.21	388.60	77.95	71.16	72.85
1998-99	274.94	67.10	409.73	97.26	90.43	92.69
1999-00	277.72	70.91	391.63	102.09	92.91	95.26
2000-01	215.65	55.24	390.40	79.48	72.70	73.45
Growth Rate	4.499* (9.745)	-2.068* (-8.623)	6.707* (17.081)	-0.272NS (-1.126)	-0.552*** (-2.023)	-0.509*** (-1.874)
Linear Slope	6.822* (8.630)	-1.658* (-8.526)	13.034* (12.784)	-0.239NS (-1.069)	-0.481*** (-1.996)	-0.444*** (-1.854)
CV	0.451	0.200	0.580	0.105	0.125	0.123

Notes :
1. Figures in parentheses are the respective 't' values.
2. * indicates one percent level of significance.
3. *** indicates 10 percent level of significance.
4. NS Indicates non-significant.

Index of TFPK decreased from 100.00 in 1973-74 to 79.48 in 2000-01. It decreased at an average annual rate of 0.272 percent. The overall trend rate for Kendrick index was –0.239 per annum. Both the average annual growth rate and trend rate were found statistically non-significant. Coefficient of variation was found to be 0.105.

Index of TFPS decreased from 100.00 in 1973-74 to 72.70 in 2000-01. It decreased at an average annual rate of 0.552 percent. The overall trend rate for Solow index was –0.481 per annum. Both the average annual growth rate and trend rate were found mildly statistically significant at ten percent level of significance. Coefficient of variation was found to be 0.125.

Index of TFPT decreased from 100.00 in 1973-74 to 73.44 in 2000-01. It decreased at an average annual rate of 0.509 percent. The overall trend rate for Translog index was –0.444 per annum. Both the average annual growth rate and trend rate were found mildly statistically significant at ten percent level of significance. Coefficient of variation was found to be 0.123.

An inter-variable comparison in this industry revealed that the maximum growth rate and variability were observed in capital intensity followed by labour productivity and most negative growth rate was in capital productivity and least variability in TFPK.

RELATIONSHIP OF TOTAL FACTOR PRODUCTIVITY WITH PARTIAL PRODUCTIVITIES OF CAPITAL AND LABOUR

The regression models in which total factor productivity (Kendrick, Solow & Translog) depended upon trend, labour and capital productivity are given as under :

$$\ln TFPK_t = \underset{(2.589)}{0.303} + \underset{(2.173)}{0.012} \ln t + \underset{(26.775)}{0.24} \ln LP_t + \underset{(31.8)}{0.69} \ln CP_t$$

$R^2 = 0.985$; $\tilde{R}^2 = 0.984$; $S = 0.013$

F ratio $= 538.13$; D–W $= 0.852$; $\tilde{p} = 0.457$

$$\ln TFPS_t = \underset{(-0.597)}{-0.109} - \underset{(-1.375)}{0.012} \ln t + \underset{(18.889)}{0.264} \ln LP_t + \underset{(22.496)}{0.76} \ln CP_t$$

$R^2 = 0.975$; $\tilde{R}^2 = 0.972$; $S = 0.021$

F ratio $= 308.71$; D–W $= 0.522$; $\tilde{p} = 0.691$

$$\ln TFPT_t = -0.095 - 0.013 \ln t + 0.27 \ln LP_t + 0.751 \ln CP_t$$
$$(-0.82) \quad (-2.3) \quad (30.224) \quad (34.794)$$
$$R^2 = 0.989; \quad \tilde{R}^2 = 0.988; \quad S = 0.013$$
$$F \text{ ratio} = 745.12; \quad D\text{–}W = 0.629; \quad \tilde{p} = 0.598$$

Both labour productivity and capital productivity significantly affected the total factor productivity, indicating consistency and robustness in the relationship between labour productivity, capital productivity and total factor productivity as measured through Kendrick, Solow and Translog indices.

Table 6.9 presents the empirical results in case of *Rubber, Petroleum & Coal Products Industry* at all-India level from 1973-74 to 2000-01. The index of partial labour productivity increased from 100.00 in 1973-74 to 428.59 in 2000-01. It increased at an average rate of 6.747 percent per annum and was significant. The overall trend rate was 14.473 per annum, which was significant. Coefficient of variation was found to be 0.565.

Index of partial capital productivity decreased from 100.00 in 1973-74 to 63.21 in 2000-01. It declined at an average annual rate of 1.21 percent. The overall trend rate was –1.003 per annum. Both the average annual growth rate and the trend rate were significant at five percent level of significance. The coefficient of variation was found to be 0.227.

The index of capital intensity increased from 100.00 in 1973-74 to 678.04 in 2000-01. It increased at an average rate of 8.055 percent per annum. The overall trend rate was 21.457 per annum. The average annual growth rate and trend rate were found statistically significant at one percent level of significance. Coefficient of variation was found to be 0.727.

Index of TFPK decreased from 100.00 in 1973-74 to 97.84 in 2000-01. It increased marginally at an average annual rate of 0.649 percent. The overall trend rate for Kendrick index was 0.835 per annum. The average annual growth rate was found statistically non-significant but the trend rate was found mildly statistically significant at 20 percent level of significance. Coefficient of variation was found to be 0.218.

Index of TFPS decreased from 100.00 in 1973-74 to 38.49 in 2000-01. It decreased at the average annual rate of 1.46 percent. The overall trend rate for Solow index was –0.782 per annum.

TABLE 6.9

Productivity Indices in Rubber, Petroleum & Coal Products Industry in India (Code 31)

Year	*Index of Partial Labour Productivity*	*Index of Partial Capital Productivity*	*Index of Real Capital Intensity*	*Index of TFPK*	*Index of TFPS*	*Index of TFPT*
1973-74	100.00	100.00	100.00	100.00	100.00	100.00
1974-75	113.40	130.05	87.20	122.37	122.45	121.72
1975-76	99.43	118.25	84.08	109.44	107.55	107.17
1976-77	134.44	96.71	139.02	109.34	100.19	99.05
1977-78	133.95	97.78	136.99	110.00	100.88	99.66
1978-79	117.52	71.67	163.99	85.44	78.19	77.41
1979-80	95.78	79.88	119.90	85.68	74.88	73.23
1980-81	95.82	117.57	81.50	107.25	86.16	84.53
1981-82	89.31	84.36	105.86	86.22	66.43	63.94
1982-83	122.58	99.99	122.60	108.13	86.80	84.49
1983-84	90.17	51.88	173.81	62.92	50.77	47.65
1984-85	121.26	68.90	176.00	83.87	68.32	64.05
1985-86	210.49	98.02	214.74	125.88	107.72	101.08
1986-87	209.86	116.25	180.52	142.55	120.41	113.19
1987-88	222.02	98.69	224.96	128.19	103.95	97.61
1988-89	227.88	88.38	257.85	118.43	94.54	88.87
1989-90	229.34	101.78	225.32	132.25	104.54	98.52
1990-91	264.25	102.31	258.29	137.15	108.60	102.43
1991-92	238.42	83.77	284.61	114.59	88.99	83.63
1992-93	334.03	98.36	339.60	139.06	112.45	105.52
1993-94	378.53	91.36	414.35	133.33	106.03	99.46
1994-95	385.80	106.05	363.80	151.68	119.69	112.22
1995-96	416.94	108.60	383.93	156.67	124.06	116.17
1996-97	531.14	97.18	546.54	147.06	110.51	102.48
1997-98	329.24	71.13	462.84	105.44	84.12	77.06
1998-99	370.82	40.93	906.09	64.90	29.81	27.32
1999-00	411.80	69.92	588.96	106.69	41.50	37.91
2000-01	428.59	63.21	678.05	97.84	38.49	35.94
Growth Rate	6.747* (11.836)	-1.21** (-2.137)	8.055* (15.282)	0.649NS (1.186)	-1.46*** (-1.765)	-1.77** (-2.132)
Linear Slope	14.473* (11.049)	-1.003** (-2.215)	21.457* (8.938)	0.835NS (1.476)	-0.782NS (-1.293)	-1.01*** (-1.767)
CV	0.565	0.227	0.727	0.218	0.289	0.292

Notes : 1. Figures in parentheses are the respective 't' values.
2. * Indicates one percent level of significance.
3. ** Indicate 5 percent level of significance.
4. *** Indicate 10 percent level of significance.
5. NS Indicates non-significant.

The average annual growth rate was mildly statistically significant at ten percent level of significance but the trend rate was found statistically non-significant. Coefficient of variation was found to be 0.289.

Index of TFPT decreased from 100.00 in 1973-74 to 35.93 in 2000-01. It decreased at an average annual rate of 1.77 percent. The overall trend rate for Translog index was –1.01 per annum. The average annual growth rate was found statistically significant at five percent level and trend rate mildly at ten percent level of significance. Coefficient of variation was found to be 0.292.

An inter-variable comparison in this industry revealed that the maximum growth rate and variability were observed in capital intensity followed by labour productivity and most negative growth rate was in TFPT and least variability in TFPK.

RELATIONSHIP OF TOTAL FACTOR PRODUCTIVITY WITH PARTIAL PRODUCTIVITIES OF CAPITAL AND LABOUR

The regression models in which total factor productivity (Kendrick) depended upon trend, labour and capital productivity are given as under :

$$\ln TFPK_t = \underset{(-0.818)}{-0.122} + \underset{(2.157)}{0.033} \ln t + \underset{(10.187)}{0.209} \ln LP_t + \underset{(26.415)}{0.812} \ln CP_t$$

$$R^2 = 0.978; \quad \tilde{R}^2 = 0.975; \quad S = 0.037$$

$$F \text{ ratio} = 349.68; \quad D\text{-}W = 1.143; \quad \tilde{p} = 0.397$$

$$\ln TFPS_t = \underset{(-2.039)}{-1.488} + \underset{(0.026)}{0.002} \ln t + \underset{(0.395)}{0.04} \ln LP_t + \underset{(8.514)}{1.277} \ln CP_t$$

$$R^2 = 0.785; \quad \tilde{R}^2 = 0.759; \quad S = 0.182$$

$$F \text{ ratio} = 29.29; \quad D\text{-}W = 0.83; \quad \tilde{p} = 0.482$$

$$\ln TFPT_t = \underset{(-2.085)}{-1.511} - \underset{(-0.267)}{0.02} \ln t + \underset{(0.279)}{0.028} \ln LP_t + \underset{(8.708)}{1.297} \ln CP_t$$

$$R^2 = 0.8; \quad \tilde{R}^2 = 0.775; \quad S = 0.18$$

$$F \text{ ratio} = 31.92; \quad D\text{-}W = 0.834; \quad \tilde{p} = 0.487$$

Both labour productivity and capital productivity significantly affected the total factor productivity as measured through Kendrick index.

Table 6.10 presents the empirical results in case of *Non-Metallic Mineral Products Industry* at all-India level from 1973-74 to 2000-01. The index of partial labour productivity increased from 100.00 in 1973-74 to 367.33 in 2000-01. The index increased at an average rate of 6.551 percent per annum and was significant. The overall trend rate was 13.421 per annum which was significant. Coefficient of variation was found to be 0.565.

The index of partial capital productivity decreased from 100.00 in 1973-74 to 41.92 in 2000-01. It declined at an average rate of 4.305 percent per annum. The overall trend rate was –3.14 per annum. Both the average annual growth rate and the trend rate were significant at one percent level of significance. The coefficient of variation was found to be 0.381.

The index of capital intensity increased from 100.00 in 1973-74 to 876.27 in 2000-01. It increased at an average rate of 11.345 percent per annum. The overall trend rate was 36.621 per annum. The average annual growth rate and trend rate were found statistically significant at one percent level of significance. Coefficient of variation was found to be 0.857.

Index of TFPK increased from 100.00 in 1973-74 to 110.00 in 2000-01. It increased marginally at an average annual rate of 0.534 percent. The overall trend rate for Kendrick index was 0.807 per annum. The average annual growth rate was found statistically non-significant but the trend rate was found mildly statistically significant at 20 percent level of significance. Coefficient of variation was found to be 0.208.

Index of TFPS decreased from 100.00 in 1973-74 to 71.292 in 2000-01. It decreased at an average annual rate of 1.03 percent. The overall trend rate for Solow index was –0.785 per annum. The average annual growth rate was found mildly statistically significant at ten percent level of significance and the trend rate at 20 percent level of significance. Coefficient of variation was found to be 0.212.

Index of TFPT decreased from 100.00 in 1973-74 to 65.86 in 2000-01. It decreased at an average annual rate of 1.096 percent. The overall trend rate for Translog index was –0.832 per annum. The average annual growth rate was found statistically

TABLE 6.10
Productivity Indices in Non-Metallic Mineral Products Industry in India (Code 32)

Year	*Index of Partial Labour Productivity*	*Index of Partial Capital Productivity*	*Index of Real Capital Intensity*	*Index of TFPK*	*Index of TFPS*	*Index of TFPT*
1973-74	100.00	100.00	100.00	100.00	100.00	100.00
1974-75	92.89	110.68	83.93	98.09	100.21	99.85
1975-76	95.56	113.96	83.85	100.92	103.22	102.84
1976-77	103.61	113.04	91.66	106.77	108.06	107.22
1977-78	120.14	131.70	91.22	123.97	126.12	125.12
1978-79	103.67	112.61	92.06	106.70	106.36	105.54
1979-80	99.42	112.47	88.40	103.50	103.55	102.70
1980-81	103.86	101.13	102.70	103.47	102.45	101.00
1981-82	107.19	96.50	111.08	104.17	102.27	100.29
1982-83	149.63	114.68	130.47	137.58	136.53	133.73
1983-84	144.52	86.95	166.20	120.89	109.99	107.43
1984-85	161.31	90.84	177.57	131.17	118.20	115.47
1985-86	160.58	66.73	240.65	113.07	93.33	92.23
1986-87	149.25	53.15	280.79	96.83	79.17	77.66
1987-88	175.36	52.65	333.04	103.20	84.46	82.98
1988-89	169.56	48.85	347.10	97.36	79.58	78.12
1989-90	202.69	56.98	355.71	114.67	94.16	92.33
1990-91	260.90	73.52	354.89	147.81	121.12	118.77
1991-92	330.06	78.23	421.89	167.77	136.44	134.46
1992-93	280.99	58.17	483.08	130.56	101.93	100.39
1993-94	299.35	51.32	583.29	121.95	93.70	92.11
1994-95	336.10	53.89	623.66	130.45	100.49	98.63
1995-96	404.89	66.48	609.07	159.88	124.75	122.49
1996-97	557.61	71.08	784.45	182.11	141.41	139.89
1997-98	383.88	46.92	818.13	121.34	93.72	92.94
1998-99	318.71	27.06	1177.61	75.01	52.64	52.48
1999-00	359.78	31.01	1160.23	85.73	60.56	60.37
2000-01	367.33	41.92	876.27	110.01	71.29	65.86
Growth Rate	6.551* (15.546)	-4.305* (-8.615)	11.345* (25.609)	0.534^{NS} (1.153)	-1.03*** (-2.03)	-1.096** (-2.162)
Linear Slope	13.421* (10.005)	-3.14* (-9.309)	36.621* (11.500)	0.807^{NS} (1.440)	-0.785^{NS} (-1.605)	-0.832*** (-1.726)
CV	0.565	0.381	0.857	0.208	0.212	0.213

Notes :
1. Figures in parentheses are the respective 't' values.
2. * Indicates one percent level of significance.
3. ** Indicates 5 percent level of significance.
4. *** Indicates 10 percent level of significance.
5. ^{NS} Indicates non-significant.

significant at 5 percent level and trend rate was mildly significant at ten percent level of significance. Coefficient of variation was found to be 0.213.

An inter-variable comparison in this industry revealed that the maximum growth rate and variability were observed in capital intensity followed by labour productivity and most negative growth rate was in capital productivity and least variability in TFPK.

RELATIONSHIP OF TOTAL FACTOR PRODUCTIVITY WITH PARTIAL PRODUCTIVITIES OF CAPITAL AND LABOUR

The estimated regression models in which total factor productivity (Kendrick, Solow & Translog) depended upon trend, labour and capital productivity are given as under :

$$\ln TFPK_t = -0.111 + 0.074 \ln t + 0.4 \ln LP_t + 0.605 \ln CP_t$$
$$(-0.326) \quad (2.47) \quad (8.987) \quad (12.632)$$
$$R^2 = 0.898; \quad \tilde{R}^2 = 0.886; \ S = 0.067$$
$$F \text{ ratio} = 70.79; \quad D\text{–}W = 0.278; \ \tilde{p} = 0.809$$

$$\ln TFPS_t = -0.473 + 0.059 \ln t + 0.302 \ln LP_t + 0.784 \ln CP_t$$
$$(-1.401) \quad (1.979) \quad (6.848) \quad (16.539)$$
$$R^2 = 0.926; \quad \tilde{R}^2 = 0.917; \ S = 0.066$$
$$F \text{ ratio} = 100.00; \quad D\text{–}W = 0.334; \ \tilde{p} = 0.672$$

$$\ln TFPT_t = -0.465 + 0.048 \ln t + 0.306 \ln LP_t + 0.78 \ln CP_t$$
$$(-1.286) \quad (1.517) \quad (6.483) \quad (15.376)$$
$$R^2 = 0.917; \quad \tilde{R}^2 = 0.906; \ S = 0.071$$
$$F \text{ ratio} = 87.94; \quad D\text{-}W = 0.412; \ \tilde{p} = 0.562$$

Both labour productivity and capital productivity significantly affected the total factor productivity, indicating consistent and strong relationship between labour productivity, capital productivity and total factor productivity as measured through Kendrick, Solow and Translog indices.

Table 6.11 presents the empirical results in case of *Basic Metals & Alloys Industry* at all-India level from 1973-74 to 2000-01.

TABLE 6.11
Productivity Indices in Basic Metals & Alloys Industry in India (Code 33)

Year	*Index of Partial Labour Productivity*	*Index of Partial Capital Productivity*	*Index of Real Capital Intensity*	*Index of TFPK*	*Index of TFPS*	*Index of TFPT*
1973-74	100.00	100.00	100.00	100.00	100.00	100.00
1974-75	119.86	147.02	81.53	127.47	126.56	125.94
1975-76	105.81	96.71	109.41	102.93	88.31	87.68
1976-77	118.74	93.78	126.62	109.74	93.16	92.78
1977-78	103.94	79.53	130.70	94.93	79.93	79.52
1978-79	114.32	92.38	123.75	106.54	90.69	89.98
1979-80	103.32	80.20	128.82	94.87	80.62	79.85
1980-81	110.50	84.46	130.84	100.89	85.92	85.01
1981-82	143.34	104.28	137.46	128.43	109.60	108.52
1982-83	139.19	89.92	154.79	118.90	99.31	97.75
1983-84	169.62	102.33	165.77	140.75	117.35	116.09
1984-85	137.52	81.48	168.78	113.22	92.34	91.16
1985-86	176.27	92.43	190.69	137.33	109.37	108.45
1986-87	145.05	82.10	176.69	117.03	93.41	92.87
1987-88	165.79	78.15	212.13	122.73	96.60	94.88
1988-89	236.72	112.80	209.87	176.16	138.62	136.16
1989-90	258.68	114.32	226.27	185.39	143.94	141.14
1990-91	289.90	88.41	327.88	169.05	113.17	110.82
1991-92	232.56	55.78	416.96	116.58	70.41	68.76
1992-93	316.77	65.03	487.10	142.99	89.03	87.10
1993-94	297.98	55.11	540.69	125.00	77.44	75.55
1994-95	374.87	67.98	551.43	155.06	96.43	94.06
1995-96	425.38	79.06	538.03	179.07	113.70	110.93
1996-97	444.78	83.49	532.75	188.56	118.87	115.97
1997-98	480.87	87.00	552.73	198.57	125.33	122.41
1998-99	453.58	55.67	814.77	139.76	77.85	75.75
1999-00	459.47	77.95	589.47	181.09	95.28	91.64
2000-01	388.72	65.92	589.72	153.16	82.19	74.18
Growth Rate	6.688* (17.501)	-1.612* (-3.753)	8.437* (19.403)	2.139* (6.096)	0.026^{NS} (0.060)	-0.134^{NS} (-0.301)
Linear Slope	14.931* (12.980)	-1.385* (-3.595)	23.306* (11.713)	2.883* (5.789)	0.071^{NS} (0.158)	-0.072^{NS} (-0.162)
CV	0.559	0.23	0.688	0.231	0.189	0.192

Notes : 1. Figures in parentheses are the respective 't' values.
2. * Indicates one percent level of significance.
3. ^{NS} Indicates non-significant.

The index of partial labour productivity increased from 100.00 in 1973-74 to 388.72 in 2000-01. The index increased at an average rate of 6.688 per cent per annum and was significant. The overall trend rate was 14.931 per annum which was significant. Coefficient of variation was found to be 0.559.

The index of partial capital productivity decreased from 100.00 in 1973-74 to 65.91 in 2000-01. It declined at an average annual rate of 1.612 per cent. The overall trend rate was –1.385 per annum. Both the average annual growth rate and the trend rate were significant at one percent level of significance. The coefficient of variation was found to be 0.23.

The index of capital intensity increased from 100.00 in 1973-74 to 589.71 in 2000-01. The index increased at an average rate of 8.437 per cent per annum. The overall trend rate was 23.306 per annum. The average annual growth rate and trend rate were found statistically significant at one percent level of significance. Coefficient of variation was found to be 0.688.

Index of TFPK increased from 100.00 in 1973-74 to 153.16 in 2000-01. It increased at an average rate of 2.139 percent per annum. The overall trend rate was 2.883 per annum. The average annual growth rate and trend rate were found statistically significant at one percent level of significance. Coefficient of variation was found to be 0.231.

Index of TFPS decreased from 100.00 in 1973-74 to 82.12 with fluctuations in 2000-01. It increased marginally at an average annual rate of 0.026 percent. The overall trend rate was 0.071 per annum. Both the average annual growth rate and the trend rate were found statistically non-significant. Coefficient of variation was found to be 0.189.

Index of TFPT decreased from 100.00 in 1973-74 to 74.17 in 2000-01. It decreased at an average annual rate of 0.134 percent. The overall trend rate for Translog index was –0.072 per annum. Both the average annual growth rate and the trend rate were found statistically non-significant. Coefficient of variation was found to be 0.192.

An inter-variable comparison in this industry revealed that the maximum growth rate and variability were observed in capital intensity followed by labour productivity and most negative growth rate was in capital productivity and least variability in TFPS.

RELATIONSHIP OF TOTAL FACTOR PRODUCTIVITY WITH PARTIAL PRODUCTIVITIES OF CAPITAL AND LABOUR

The regression models in which total factor productivity (Kendrick, Solow & Translog) depended upon trend, labour and capital productivity were estimated. The estimated equations are :

$$\ln TFPK_t = \underset{(0.234)}{0.035} + \underset{(6.012)}{0.072} \ln t + \underset{(22.294)}{0.376} \ln LP_t + \underset{(21.682)}{0.606} \ln CP_t$$

$R^2 = 0.987$; $\tilde{R}^2 = 0.986$; $S = 0.027$

F ratio = 628.77; D-W = 1.418; $\tilde{p} = 0.212$

$$\ln TFPS_t = \underset{(-1.244)}{-0.388} + \underset{(2.26)}{0.056} \ln t + \underset{(4.398)}{0.154} \ln LP_t + \underset{(15.58)}{0.908} \ln CP_t$$

$R^2 = 0.917$; $\tilde{R}^2 = 0.906$; $S = 0.056$

F ratio = 88.24; D–W = 0.836; $\tilde{p} = 0.429$

$$\ln TFPT_t = \underset{(-1.045)}{-0.379} + \underset{(1.866)}{0.054} \ln t + \underset{(3.395)}{0.139} \ln LP_t + \underset{(13.599)}{0.922} \ln CP_t$$

$R^2 = 0.892$; $\tilde{R}^2 = 0.879$; $S = 0.065$

F ratio = 66.23; D–W = 0.680; $\tilde{p} = 0.452$

Both labour productivity and capital productivity significantly affected the total factor productivity, indicating consistency and robustness in the relationship between labour productivity, capital productivity and total factor productivity as measured through Kendrick, Solow and Translog indices.

Table 6.12 presents productivity indices in case of *Metal Products Industry* at all-India level from 1973-74 to 2000-01. The index of partial labour productivity increased from 100.00 in 1973-74 to 435.45 in 2000-01. It increased at an average rate of 7.372 percent per annum and was significant. The overall trend rate was 16.181 per annum which was significant. Coefficient of variation was found to be 0.60.

The index of partial capital productivity decreased from 100.00 in 1973-74 to 98.59 in 2000-01. It decreased at an average rate of 0.968 percent per annum. The overall trend rate was

TABLE 6.12
Productivity Indices in Metal Products Industry in India (Code 34)

Year	Index of Partial Labour Productivity	Index of Partial Capital Productivity	Index of Real Capital Intensity	Index of TFPK	Index of TFPS	Index of TFPT
1973-74	100.00	100.00	100.00	100.00	100.00	100.00
1974-75	94.81	107.41	88.28	97.07	95.87	95.35
1975-76	91.06	103.39	88.07	93.28	92.01	91.51
1976-77	99.90	97.74	102.20	98.47	101.40	101.00
1977-78	96.46	98.40	98.03	96.16	97.50	97.19
1978-79	101.47	103.94	97.63	101.27	102.28	101.95
1979-80	108.18	111.52	97.01	108.14	109.70	109.33
1980-81	108.06	95.34	113.34	103.44	110.24	108.48
1981-82	125.42	115.64	108.46	121.60	128.46	126.63
1982-83	134.20	110.95	120.95	125.97	134.38	131.91
1983-84	172.40	108.50	158.90	147.58	158.89	158.97
1984-85	152.14	105.65	144.01	134.90	141.29	141.80
1985-86	156.86	98.43	159.36	134.13	142.64	143.26
1986-87	158.18	94.24	167.85	132.65	142.47	142.70
1987-88	186.37	90.88	205.07	144.11	161.39	160.15
1988-89	220.63	97.81	225.56	163.57	186.52	184.93
1989-90	207.41	102.46	202.43	161.26	182.84	181.28
1990-91	217.57	81.35	267.44	148.78	168.10	161.87
1991-92	282.05	95.93	294.02	183.81	208.35	200.74
1992-93	295.28	77.92	378.94	167.34	184.64	174.47
1993-94	398.33	78.60	506.80	188.68	208.25	197.71
1994-95	385.40	78.46	491.22	186.28	205.30	194.96
1995-96	418.00	83.04	503.41	198.87	221.36	210.06
1996-97	467.40	91.07	513.22	219.59	244.72	232.37
1997-98	407.62	67.63	602.69	171.92	186.86	177.61
1998-99	480.78	83.60	575.10	209.38	223.95	212.85
1999-00	505.74	100.77	501.86	241.09	254.56	240.84
2000-01	435.45	98.59	441.66	225.09	234.55	220.11
Growth Rate	7.372* (23.536)	-0.968* (-3.993)	8.421* (18.707)	3.526* (20.212)	3.893* (19.179)	3.638* (17.222)
Linear Slope	16.181* (14.098)	-0.892* (-4.031)	19.954* (11.791)	5.128* (17.115)	5.929* (17.954)	5.373* (16.736)
CV	0.6	0.124	0.681	0.293	0.313	0.294

Notes : 1. Figures in parentheses are the respective 't' values.
2. * Indicates one percent level of significance.

–0.892 per annum. Both the average annual growth rate and the trend rate were significant at one percent level of significance. The coefficient of variation was found to be 0.124.

The index of capital intensity increased from 100.00 in 1973-74 to 441.66 in 2000-01. The index increased at an average rate of 8.421 percent per annum. The overall trend rate was 19.954 per annum. The average annual growth rate and trend rate were found statistically significant at one percent level of significance. Coefficient of variation was found to be 0.681.

Index of TFPK increased from 100.00 in 1973-74 to 225.09 in 2000-01. It increased at an average rate of 3.526 percent per annum. The overall trend rate for Kendrick index was 5.128 per annum. The average annual growth rate and trend were found statistically significant at one percent level of significance. Coefficient of variation was found to be 0.293.

Index of TFPS increased from 100.00 in 1973-74 to 234.55 in 2000-01. It increased at an average rate of 3.893 percent per annum. The overall trend rate for Solow index was 5.929 per annum. The average annual growth rate and trend rate were found statistically significant at one percent level of significance. Coefficient of variation was found to be 0.313.

Index of TFPT increased from 100.00 in 1973-74 to 220.11 in 2000-01. It increased at an average rate of 3.638 percent per annum. The overall trend rate for Translog index was 5.373 per annum. The average annual growth rate and trend rate were found statistically significant at one percent level of significance. Coefficient of variation was found to be 0.294.

An inter-variable comparison in this industry revealed that the maximum growth rate and variability were observed in capital intensity followed by labour productivity and negative growth and least variability in capital productivity.

RELATIONSHIP OF TOTAL FACTOR PRODUCTIVITY WITH PARTIAL PRODUCTIVITIES OF CAPITAL AND LABOUR

The estimated regression models in which total factor productivity (Kendrick, Solow & Translog) depended upon trend, labour and capital productivity are given as on next page.

$$\ln TFPK_t = -0.016 + 0.046 \ln t + 0.494 \ln LP_t + 0.497 \ln CP_t$$
$$(-0.045)\ (3.232)\quad (21.92)\quad (7.852)$$
$$R^2 = 0.989; \quad \tilde{R}^2 = 0.988; \quad S = 0.033$$
$$F\ ratio = 727.14;\ D\text{-}W = 0.534; \quad \tilde{p} = 0.664$$

$$\ln TFPS_t = 0.368 + 0.091 \ln t + 0.476 \ln LP_t + 0.424 \ln CP_t$$
$$(0.602)\ (3.635)\quad (12.053)\quad (3.821)$$
$$R^2 = 0.973; \quad \tilde{R}^2 = 0.969; \quad S = 0.057$$
$$F\ ratio = 284.42;\ D\text{-}W = 0.578; \quad \tilde{p} = 0.639$$

$$\ln TFPT_t = 0.403 + 0.097 \ln t + 0.437 \ln LP_t + 0.453 \ln CP_t$$
$$(0.604)\ (3.559)\quad (10.137)\quad (3.733)$$
$$R^2 = 0.963; \quad \tilde{R}^2 = 0.959; \quad S = 0.062$$
$$F\ ratio = 209.93;\ D\text{-}W = 0.578; \quad \tilde{p} = 0.629$$

Both labour productivity and capital productivity significantly affected the total factor productivity, indicating consistency and strength in the relationship between labour productivity, capital productivity and total factor productivity as measured through Kendrick, Solow and Translog indices.

Table 6.13 presents the empirical results in case of *Machinery Other Than Transport Industry* at all-India level from 1973-74 to 2000-01. The index of partial labour productivity increased from 100.00 in 1973-74 to 332.24 in 2000-01. It increased at an average rate of 5.946 percent per annum and was significant. The overall trend rate was 11.31 per annum which was significant. Coefficient of variation was found to be 0.478.

The index of partial capital productivity decreased from 100.00 in 1973-74 to 71.21 in 2000-01. It decreased at an average rate of 1.222 percent per annum. The overall trend rate was -1.138 per annum. But both the average annual growth rate and the trend rate were significant at one percent level of significance. The coefficient of variation was found to be 0.134.

The index of capital intensity increased from 100.00 in 1973-74 to 466.57 in 2000-01. It increased at an average rate of 7.257 percent per annum. The overall trend rate was 14.918 per annum. The average annual growth rate and trend rate were found statistically significant at one percent level of significance. Coefficient of variation was found to be 0.602.

TABLE 6.13

Productivity Indices in Machinery Other Than Transport Industry in India (Code 35-36)

Year	Index of Partial Labour Productivity	Index of Partial Capital Productivity	Index of Real Capital Intensity	Index of TFPK	Index of TFPS	Index of TFPT
1973-74	100.00	100.00	100.00	100.00	100.00	100.00
1974-75	80.65	102.45	78.72	87.59	85.46	84.51
1975-76	99.36	103.77	95.75	101.12	97.24	96.01
1976-77	112.00	108.53	103.20	110.93	107.41	106.04
1977-78	112.00	106.50	105.16	110.15	106.71	105.36
1978-79	113.50	111.40	101.89	112.95	109.19	107.74
1979-80	105.00	111.11	94.50	107.36	102.50	101.35
1980-81	115.80	120.10	96.42	117.56	112.18	110.90
1981-82	116.84	117.76	99.21	117.40	112.09	110.73
1982-83	134.66	118.22	113.90	128.42	123.49	121.94
1983-84	141.83	109.27	129.81	128.19	123.38	121.37
1984-85	165.84	123.20	134.62	147.56	142.23	139.98
1985-86	160.77	102.14	157.40	133.23	127.84	125.97
1986-87	149.13	106.32	140.26	130.31	124.13	122.84
1987-88	184.45	105.25	175.24	145.06	139.09	137.73
1988-89	182.70	97.17	188.02	138.62	132.97	131.48
1989-90	215.96	107.11	201.62	157.93	152.39	150.58
1990-91	220.63	101.99	216.31	155.28	149.69	147.44
1991-92	264.30	105.31	250.98	170.87	164.65	161.67
1992-93	302.89	95.36	317.64	169.30	159.73	156.87
1993-94	307.07	92.40	332.32	166.67	157.16	154.18
1994-95	361.95	101.43	356.83	187.39	177.54	174.46
1995-96	338.30	99.39	340.38	180.74	170.64	167.83
1996-97	374.08	98.91	378.20	186.19	175.23	172.61
1997-98	348.89	86.96	401.22	166.71	156.61	154.48
1998-99	292.62	73.89	396.04	141.09	127.05	125.19
1999-00	335.81	67.32	498.85	137.19	128.23	126.66
2000-01	332.24	71.21	466.57	142.57	130.85	124.28
Growth Rate	5.946* (19.791)	-1.222* (-4.856)	7.257* (21.387)	2.112* (7.978)	1.92* (6.822)	1.869* (6.531)
Linear Slope	11.31* (14.646)	-1.138* (-4.846)	14.918* (14.078)	2.775* (7.437)	2.418* (6.395)	2.323* (6.142)
CV	0.478	0.134	0.602	0.2	0.193	0.191

Notes : 1. Figures in parentheses are the respective 't' values.
2. *Indicates one percent level of significance.

Index of TFPK increased from 100.00 in 1973-74 to 142.57 in 2000-01. It increased at an average rate of 2.112 percent per annum. The overall trend rate for Kendrick index was 2.775 per annum. The average annual growth rate and trend rate were found statistically significant at one percent level of significance. Coefficient of variation was found to be 0.20.

Index of TFPS increased from 100.00 in 1973-74 to 130.85 in 2000-01. It increased at an average rate of 1.92 percent per annum. The overall trend rate for Solow index was 2.418 per annum. The average annual growth rate and trend rate were found statistically significant at one percent level of significance. Coefficient of variation was found to be 0.193.

Index of TFPT increased from 100.00 in 1973-74 to 124.28 in 2000-01. It increased at an average rate of 1.869 percent per annum. The overall trend rate for Translog index was 2.323 per annum. The average annual growth rate and trend rate were found statistically significant at one percent level of significance. Coefficient of variation was found to be 0.191.

An inter-variable comparison in this industry revealed that the maximum growth rate and variability were observed in capital intensity followed by labour productivity and negative growth and least variability in capital productivity.

RELATIONSHIP OF TOTAL FACTOR PRODUCTIVITY WITH PARTIAL PRODUCTIVITIES OF CAPITAL AND LABOUR

The estimated regression models in which total factor productivity (Kendrick, Solow & Translog) depended upon trend, labour and capital productivity are given as under :

$$\ln TFPK_t = \underset{(-2.923)}{-0.739} + \underset{(1.472)}{0.017} \ln t + \underset{(21.516)}{0.479} \ln LP_t + \underset{(16.702)}{0.675} \ln CP_t$$

$R^2 = 0.988$; $\tilde{R}^2 = 0.987$; $S = 0.023$

F ratio $= 675.28$; D–W $= 0.844$; $\tilde{p} = 0.532$

$$\ln TFPS_t = \underset{(-3.561)}{-1.165} - \underset{(-0.203)}{0.003} \ln t + \underset{(17.19)}{0.495} \ln LP_t + \underset{(14.338)}{0.749} \ln CP_t$$

$R^2 = 0.979$; $\tilde{R}^2 = 0.976$; $S = 0.03$

F ratio $= 366.6$; D–W $= 0.692$; $\tilde{p} = 0.608$

$$\ln TFPT_t = -1.268 - 0.008 \ln t + 0.498 \ln LP_t + 0.768 \ln CP_t$$
$$(-3.575)\ (-0.475)\quad (15.938)\quad (13.547)$$
$$R^2 = 0.974; \quad \tilde{R}^2 = 0.971; \quad S = 0.033$$
$$F \text{ ratio} = 303.57; \quad D\text{-}W = 0.772; \quad \tilde{p} = 0.527$$

Both labour productivity and capital productivity significantly affected the total factor productivity, indicating consistency and robustness in the relationship between labour productivity, capital productivity and total factor productivity as measured through Kendrick, Solow and Translog indices.

Table 6.14 presents the empirical results in case of *Transport Equipment & Parts Industry* at all-India level from 1973-74 to 2000-01. The index of partial labour productivity increased from 100.00 in 1973-74 to 349.13 in 2000-01. It increased at an average rate of 5.382 percent per annum and was significant. The overall trend rate was found to be 10.395 per annum which was significant. Coefficient of variation was found to be 0.463.

The index of partial capital productivity decreased from 100.00 in 1973-74 to 33.11 in 2000-01. It declined at an average annual rate of 2.795 percent per annum. The overall trend rate was –1.938 per annum. Both the average annual growth rate and the trend rate were significant at one percent level of significance. The coefficient of variation was found to be 0.297.

The index of capital intensity increased from 100.00 in 1973-74 to 1054.36 in 2000-01. It increased at an average rate of 8.412 percent per annum. The overall trend rate was 27.019. The average annual growth rate and trend rate were found statistically significant at one percent level of significance. Coefficient of variation was found to be 0.777.

Index of TFPK increased from 100.00 in 1973-74 to 105.44 in 2000-01. It increased at an average rate of 1.419 percent per annum. The overall trend rate for Kendrick index was 1.822 per annum. The average annual growth rate and trend rate were found statistically significant at one percent level of significance. Coefficient of variation was found to be 0.208.

Index of TFPS decreased from 100.00 in 1973-74 to 82.02 in 2000-01. It increased marginally at an average annual rate of 0.49 percent. The overall trend rate for Solow index was 0.545 per annum. The average annual growth rate and trend rate were found statistically non-significant. Coefficient of variation was found to be 0.194.

TABLE 6.14
Productivity Indices in Transport Equipment and Parts Industry in India (Code 37)

Year	*Index of Partial Labour Productivity*	*Index of Partial Capital Productivity*	*Index of Real Capital Intensity*	*Index of TFPK*	*Index of TFPS*	*Index of TFPT*
1973-74	100.00	100.00	100.00	100.00	100.00	100.00
1974-75	98.16	115.16	85.24	101.62	102.89	102.22
1975-76	100.63	110.65	90.94	102.71	103.80	102.84
1976-77	123.90	107.40	115.36	119.26	118.17	117.08
1977-78	122.56	105.15	116.56	117.64	116.42	115.34
1978-79	133.67	57.62	231.97	101.18	85.18	92.71
1979-80	107.33	60.88	176.29	90.47	69.70	75.59
1980-81	108.45	65.58	165.37	93.50	71.24	77.42
1981-82	123.65	77.19	160.18	107.77	82.08	89.27
1982-83	138.79	79.24	175.14	117.27	89.85	97.82
1983-84	136.55	76.04	179.59	114.34	87.76	95.58
1984-85	137.34	68.75	199.76	110.48	85.59	93.21
1985-86	144.99	62.69	231.27	109.89	86.66	93.99
1986-87	162.08	69.09	234.59	122.10	96.67	104.86
1987-88	162.04	58.42	277.36	113.24	91.16	98.76
1988-89	164.21	63.37	259.10	118.41	94.51	102.62
1989-90	197.96	70.26	281.75	137.33	109.56	118.49
1990-91	236.38	86.28	273.99	166.15	132.47	143.29
1991-92	241.43	74.46	324.23	156.34	122.27	131.86
1992-93	255.53	63.69	401.22	147.66	113.17	121.57
1993-94	274.67	63.11	435.19	151.52	116.08	124.64
1994-95	293.40	70.77	414.59	166.42	128.03	137.55
1995-96	345.68	78.87	438.27	189.91	149.02	160.24
1996-97	310.47	53.38	581.65	143.26	106.38	114.02
1997-98	342.01	60.70	563.39	161.09	118.11	126.40
1998-99	252.64	35.34	714.81	101.49	72.91	76.63
1999-00	403.02	37.71	1068.71	120.46	93.03	98.97
2000-01	349.13	33.11	1054.36	105.44	82.02	83.57
Growth Rate	5.382* (17.758)	-2.795* (-5.675)	8.412* (18.932)	1.419* (3.697)	0.49^{NS} (1.085)	0.652^{NS} (1.497)
Linear Slope	10.395* (12.891)	-1.938* (-5.762)	27.019* (8.468)	1.822* (3.612)	0.545^{NS} (1.198)	0.787^{NS} (1.674)
CV	0.463	0.297	0.777	0.208	0.194	0.194

Notes : 1. Figures in parentheses are the respective 't' values.
2. *Indicates one percent level of significance.
3. ^{NS} Indicates non-significant.

Index of TFPT decreased from 100.00 in 1973-74 to 83.57 in 2000-01. It increased at marginal rate of 0.652 percent per annum. The overall trend rate for Translog index was 0.787 per annum. The average annual growth rate and trend rate were found mildly statistically significant at twenty percent level of significance. Coefficient of variation was found to be 0.194.

An inter-variable comparison in this industry revealed that the maximum growth rate and variability were observed in capital intensity followed by labour productivity and negative growth in capital productivity and least variability in TFPS and TFPT.

RELATIONSHIP OF TOTAL FACTOR PRODUCTIVITY WITH PARTIAL PRODUCTIVITIES OF CAPITAL AND LABOUR

The regression models in which total factor productivity (Kendrick, Solow & Translog) depended upon trend, labour and capital productivity were estimated. The estimated equations are :

$$\ln TFPK_t = 0.0 + 0.116 \ln t + 0.386 \ln LP_t + 0.597 \ln CP_t$$
$$(-0.002)\ (5.449)\quad (10.71)\quad (15.266)$$
$$R^2 = 0.954; \quad \tilde{R}^2 = 0.948; \quad S = 0.045$$
$$F \text{ ratio} = 165.07; \quad D\text{-}W = 1.234; \quad \tilde{p} = 0.259$$

$$\ln TFPS_t = -0.803 - 0.015 \ln t + 0.493 \ln LP_t + 0.68 \ln CP_t$$
$$(-3.035)\ (-0.685)\quad (12.902)\quad (16.39)$$
$$R^2 = 0.946; \quad \tilde{R}^2 = 0.939; \quad S = 0.048$$
$$F \text{ ratio} = 139.09; \quad D\text{–}W = 0.771; \quad \tilde{p} = 0.614$$

$$\ln TFPT_t = -0.545 + 0.04 \ln t + 0.427 \ln LP_t + 0.682 \ln CP_t$$
$$(-1.906)\ (1.641)\quad (10.342)\quad (15.225)$$
$$R^2 = 0.934; \quad \tilde{R}^2 = 0.926; \quad S = 0.052$$
$$F \text{ ratio} = 113.61; \quad D\text{–}W = 1.089; \quad \tilde{p} = 0.421$$

Both labour productivity and capital productivity significantly affected the total factor productivity, indicating consistency and robustness in the relationship between labour productivity, capital productivity and total factor productivity as measured through Kendrick, Solow and Translog indices.

Inter-Industry Comparison

The maximum growth rate and variability in the index of partial labour productivity was found in the Textile Products Industry, but the minimum growth rate was observed in Chemicals and Chemical Products Industry and least variability in the Paper & Paper Products Industry.

The highest growth rate in the index of partial capital productivity has been found in the Textile Products Industry and minimum in Non-Metallic Mineral Products Industry. The maximum variability has been seen in Non-Metallic Mineral Products Industry and the least in Food Products Industry.

The highest growth rate and variability in the index of real capital intensity have been found in Non-Metallic Mineral Products Industry, but the least growth rate was in Chemicals and Chemical Products Industry and minimum variability in Jute, Hemp & Mesta Textiles Industry.

In case of total factor productivity index of Kendrick, the maximum growth rate and variability have been found in the Jute, Hemp & Mesta Textiles Industry and minimum in the Chemicals and Chemical Products Industry.

In case of both total factor productivity indices of Solow and Translog, the maximum growth rate has been found in the Jute, Hemp & Mesta Textiles Industry and minimum in the Rubber, Petroleum and Coal Products Industry. The highest variability has been seen in Textile Products Industry and least in Chemicals and Chemical Products Industry.

Both labour productivity and capital productivity significantly affected the total factor productivity as measured through Kendrick, Solow and Translog indices in all industries except in Rubber, Petroleum and Coal Products Industry where labour productivity and capital productivity significantly affected the total factor productivity as measured through Kendrick index only.

Inter-Industry Comparison of Partial Labour Productivity

An inter-industry comparison of partial labour productivity from 1973-74 to 2000-01 (Table 6.15) revealed that it showed

TABLE 6.15
Partial Labour Productivity in Industries

Year	*FPI*	*BTTPI*	*CTI*	*JHMTI*	*TPI*	*PPPI*	*LFPI*	*CCPI*	*RPCPI*	*NMMPI*	*BMAI*	*MPI*	*MOTI*	*TEPI*
1973-74	0.159	0.115	0.211	0.085	0.089	0.396	0.275	1.211	0.665	0.285	0.523	0.227	0.428	0.396
1974-75	0.143	0.182	0.185	0.091	0.080	0.433	0.346	1.147	0.754	0.265	0.627	0.216	0.346	0.389
1975-76	0.139	0.131	0.166	0.105	0.101	0.424	0.311	1.037	0.661	0.273	0.553	0.207	0.426	0.399
1976-77	0.145	0.137	0.170	0.100	0.093	0.413	0.336	1.126	0.894	0.296	0.621	0.227	0.480	0.491
1977-78	0.168	0.090	0.179	0.094	0.093	0.423	0.336	1.144	0.891	0.343	0.544	0.219	0.480	0.486
1978-79	0.198	0.110	0.214	0.089	0.114	0.411	0.273	1.399	0.782	0.296	0.598	0.231	0.486	0.530
1979-80	0.165	0.095	0.220	0.104	0.092	0.405	0.290	1.141	0.637	0.284	0.540	0.246	0.450	0.425
1980-81	0.107	0.086	0.221	0.123	0.106	0.408	0.267	1.038	0.637	0.296	0.578	0.246	0.496	0.430
1981-82	0.121	0.084	0.214	0.106	0.128	0.427	0.218	1.068	0.594	0.306	0.750	0.285	0.501	0.490
1982-83	0.143	0.082	0.224	0.105	0.147	0.395	0.306	1.170	0.815	0.427	0.728	0.305	0.577	0.550
1983-84	0.252	0.176	0.269	0.139	0.158	0.456	0.353	1.342	0.600	0.413	0.887	0.392	0.608	0.541
1984-85	0.256	0.176	0.264	0.141	0.215	0.519	0.332	1.244	0.806	0.460	0.719	0.346	0.710	0.544
1985-86	0.281	0.177	0.285	0.134	0.159	0.443	0.260	1.237	1.400	0.458	0.922	0.357	0.689	0.574
1986-87	0.297	0.230	0.307	0.165	0.243	0.508	0.253	1.193	1.396	0.426	0.759	0.360	0.639	0.642
1987-88	0.312	0.276	0.325	0.180	0.265	0.538	0.327	1.252	1.476	0.501	0.867	0.424	0.790	0.642
1988-89	0.366	0.337	0.383	0.203	0.244	0.595	0.327	1.221	1.515	0.484	1.238	0.502	0.783	0.651
1989-90	0.452	0.289	0.489	0.223	0.251	0.747	0.373	1.421	1.525	0.579	1.353	0.472	0.925	0.784

1990-91	0.400	0.370	0.512	0.255	0.411	0.795	0.505	1.624	1.757	0.745	1.516	0.495	0.945	0.937
1991-92	0.434	0.428	0.472	0.312	0.538	0.863	0.632	1.754	1.586	0.942	1.216	0.641	1.132	0.957
1992-93	0.446	0.428	0.475	0.327	0.685	0.900	0.651	2.237	2.221	0.802	1.657	0.672	1.298	1.012
1993-94	0.650	0.441	0.524	0.350	0.990	1.078	0.934	2.446	2.517	0.854	1.558	0.906	1.315	1.088
1994-95	0.735	0.501	0.740	0.453	0.954	1.063	0.685	2.520	2.566	0.959	1.961	0.877	1.551	1.163
1995-96	0.635	0.455	0.560	0.411	0.842	1.041	0.666	2.900	2.773	1.156	2.225	0.951	1.449	1.370
1996-97	0.636	0.534	0.729	0.525	0.810	1.100	0.635	3.280	3.532	1.592	2.326	1.063	1.603	1.230
1997-98	0.752	0.506	0.620	0.555	0.780	0.859	0.918	2.551	2.189	1.096	2.515	0.927	1.495	1.355
1998-99	0.925	0.487				0.977	0.869	3.329	2.466	0.910	2.372	1.093	1.254	1.001
1999-00	0.892	0.676				1.085	0.914	3.363	2.738	1.027	2.403	1.150	1.439	1.597
2000-01	0.828	0.574				1.460	0.642	2.611	2.850	1.048	2.033	0.990	1.423	1.383
Growth Rate	8.282* (15.563)	7.985* (10.793)	6.499* (16.816)	8.373* (17.349)	12.051* (16.360)	4.926* (13.263)	4.793* (7.714)	4.499* (9.744)	6.747* (11.836)	6.552* (15.554)	6.688* (17.501)	7.373* (23.572)	5.947* (19.803)	5.382* (17.763)
Linear Slope	0.029* (13.375)	0.02* (13.118)	0.022* (11.749)	0.017* (10.186)	0.036* (8.681)	0.033* (10.969)	0.023* (7.450)	0.082* (8.630)	0.096* (11.049)	0.038* (10.007)	0.078* (12.980)	0.036* (14.104)	0.048* (14.650)	0.041* (12.892)
CV	0.660	0.621	0.499	0.673	0.902	0.445	0.493	0.451	0.565	0.565	0.559	0.600	0.478	0.463

Notes : 1. Figures in parentheses are the respective 't' values.
2. *Indicates significant at one percent level.

rising trend in all industries. The maximum average annual growth rate and variability were observed in Textile Products Industry followed by Jute, Hemp & Mesta Textiles Industry and minimum growth in Chemicals & Chemical Products Industry and least variability in Paper & Paper Products Industry. In 1973-74 maximum value of partial labour productivity was observed in Chemicals & Chemical Products Industry followed by Rubber, Petroleum & Coal Products Industry and least in Jute, Hemp & Mesta Textiles Industry. In 1983-84 similar results for maximum and minimum values were found in respective industries. In 1993-94 maximum partial labour productivity was found in Rubber, Petroleum & Coal Products Industry followed by Chemicals & Chemical Products Industry and least in Jute, Hemp & Mesta Textiles industry. Similar results for highest and second highest were found in 2000-01.

It was found that the average annual growth rates of labour productivity in all industries were higher than that of wage rate in respective industries (Table 5.16). In TPI the difference between average annual growth rates of labour productivity and wage rate was maximum, i.e. the average annual growth rate of labour productivity was 8.57 times higher than wage rate, indicating that workers were not getting due reward in the form of higher wages as a result of increased productivity. In CCPI, the difference between average annual growth rates of labour productivity and wage rate was minimum, i.e. average annual growth rate in labour productivity was 1.88 times higher than wage rate and this indicated that the growth rate of wage rate was commensurate with labour productivity in this industry. Even in industries like BTTPI, CTI, JHMTI, LFTI, RPCPI, NMMPI, BMAI, MPI and MOTI the difference between average annual growth rates of labour productivity and wage rate were themselves greater than the average annual growth rates of wage rate in respective industries. It was also observed that the growth rates of both capital intensity and labour productivity were positive and highly significant and the growth rates of capital intensity were higher than that of labour productivity in all industries except in JHMTI and TPI where growth rates of labour productivity were higher than that of capital intensity.

It may be concluded from the discussion in this chapter that the labour productivity showed rising trend in all industries.

Except in JHMTI and TPI, growth rates of capital intensity were higher than that of labour productivity in all industries. It was also observed that average annual growth rates of labour productivity in all industries were higher than that of wage rate in respective industries. This might be because when industries were growing, they went in for more technological innovation which led to increase in labour productivity and therefore higher wages as well. However, in comparison to their labour productivity, workers in TPI received the least reward in the form of higher wages and workers in CCPI received the highest reward followed by workers in PPPI. It was also observed that except in RPCPI, both labour productivity and capital productivity significantly affected the total factor productivity as measured through Kendrick, Solow and Translog indices in all industries.

Trends in Economic Parameters in (All) Industries in Indian States

This chapter deals with the analysis of growth rates, trends, t-values and coefficient of variation of various economic indicators in index form like real GVA, real GFC, real emoluments, real wage rate, share of labour in GVA, etc. in all industries for sixteen major states and all-India during 1973-74 to 2000-01.

INTER-STATE COMPARISON OF REAL WAGE RATE

An inter-state comparison of real wage rate during 1973-74 to 2000-01 (Table 7.1) indicated a rising trend in all states. The maximum average annual growth rate in real wage rate was observed in Uttar Pradesh followed by Haryana and minimum growth was in Tamil Nadu. The maximum variability was observed in Uttar Pradesh followed by Bihar and minimum was in Tamil Nadu. In 1973-74 maximum real wage rate was observed in Maharashtra followed by Orissa and least was in Andhra Pradesh. In 1983-84 maximum real wage rate remained in Maharashtra followed by Bihar and Madhya Pradesh jointly and least was in Assam. In 1993-94, the maximum real wage

TABLE 7.1
Profile of Real Wage Rate in States and All-India

Year	*AP*	*ASM*	*BIH*	*GUJ*	*HAR*	*HP*	*KAR*	*KER*	*MP*
(1)	*(2)*	*(3)*	*(4)*	*(5)*	*(6)*	*(7)*	*(8)*	*(9)*	*(10)*
1973-74	0.119	0.124	0.235	0.188	0.169	0.184	0.193	0.136	0.250
1974-75	0.111	0.087	0.201	0.175	0.197	0.165	0.222	0.124	0.246
1975-76	0.118	0.100	0.236	0.200	0.189	0.210	0.200	0.135	0.258
1976-77	0.117	0.121	0.246	0.209	0.200	0.230	0.210	0.145	0.277
1977-78	0.115	0.116	0.250	0.218	0.193	0.221	0.216	0.154	0.275
1978-79	0.124	0.124	0.260	0.219	0.211	0.213	0.247	0.175	0.270
1979-80	0.121	0.122	0.301	0.221	0.210	0.195	0.263	0.175	0.282
1980-81	0.144	0.116	0.279	0.242	0.207	0.218	0.231	0.180	0.263
1981-82	0.118	0.108	0.300	0.217	0.227	0.223	0.219	0.172	0.251
1982-83	0.157	0.106	0.332	0.230	0.242	0.275	0.252	0.195	0.254
1983-84	0.158	0.130	0.324	0.238	0.246	0.264	0.277	0.185	0.324
1984-85	0.188	0.140	0.374	0.270	0.259	0.265	0.284	0.197	0.327
1985-86	0.187	0.153	0.365	0.276	0.249	0.274	0.297	0.224	0.296

(*Contd.*)

TABLE 7.1 (Contd.)

(1)	(2)	(3)	(4)	(5)	(6)	(7)	(8)	(9)	(10)
1986-87	0.177	0.140	0.352	0.277	0.257	0.290	0.301	0.233	0.302
1987-88	0.172	0.139	0.350	0.281	0.275	0.329	0.317	0.239	0.313
1988-89	0.178	0.142	0.395	0.287	0.291	0.290	0.320	0.267	0.322
1989-90	0.182	0.154	0.429	0.283	0.309	0.305	0.380	0.268	0.354
1990-91	0.197	0.145	0.463	0.306	0.332	0.326	0.384	0.271	0.357
1991-92	0.185	0.151	0.319	0.264	0.286	0.319	0.314	0.292	0.311
1992-93	0.202	0.170	0.484	0.329	0.339	0.310	0.374	0.254	0.333
1993-94	0.221	0.166	0.496	0.334	0.348	0.318	0.323	0.236	0.353
1994-95	0.230	0.187	0.507	0.319	0.352	0.313	0.379	0.237	0.377
1995-96	0.239	0.182	0.548	0.358	0.368	0.337	0.393	0.278	0.429
1996-97	0.239	0.179	0.553	0.341	0.395	0.357	0.388	0.293	0.400
1997-98	0.200	0.237	0.531	0.358	0.425	0.378	0.352	0.270	0.408
1998-99	0.245	0.211	0.517	0.345	0.403	0.410	0.435	0.294	0.321
1999-00	0.222	0.200	0.300	0.356	0.408	0.298	0.364	0.255	0.362
2000-01	0.227	0.225	0.295	0.366	0.409	0.329	0.385	0.258	0.402
Growth Rate	3.104* (14.554)	2.869* (12.450)	2.821* (6.258)	2.607* (20.660)	3.402* (31.093)	2.57* (11.181)	2.788* (13.500)	2.974* (11.467)	1.8* (9.653)
Linear Slope	0.005* (15.053)	0.004* (11.666)	0.009* (5.929)	0.006* (21.672)	0.009* (24.036)	0.006* (11.236)	0.006* (13.168)	0.005* (11.453)	0.005* (9.170)
CV	0.254	0.257	0.295	0.212	0.278	0.219	0.233	0.245	0.168

TABLE 7.1 (Contd.)

Year	MAH	ORI	PB	RAJ	TN	UP	WB	All India
(1)	(11)	(12)	(13)	(14)	(15)	(16)	(17)	(18)
1973-74	0.320	0.303	0.142	0.255	0.245	0.147	0.259	0.215
1974-75	0.304	0.227	0.129	0.186	0.188	0.163	0.238	0.199
1975-76	0.317	0.259	0.141	0.220	0.201	0.177	0.261	0.217
1976-77	0.326	0.264	0.143	0.229	0.217	0.174	0.268	0.228
1977-78	0.334	0.259	0.150	0.220	0.216	0.166	0.259	0.229
1978-79	0.360	0.275	0.158	0.245	0.231	0.176	0.261	0.241
1979-80	0.357	0.297	0.154	0.233	0.219	0.185	0.282	0.244
1980-81	0.354	0.286	0.182	0.260	0.231	0.181	0.296	0.247
1981-82	0.356	0.277	0.174	0.234	0.223	0.185	0.299	0.242
1982-83	0.369	0.303	0.194	0.258	0.234	0.215	0.291	0.259
1983-84	0.405	0.313	0.195	0.265	0.235	0.235	0.295	0.274
1984-85	0.429	0.323	0.205	0.280	0.238	0.255	0.302	0.296
1985-86	0.442	0.320	0.209	0.313	0.253	0.251	0.309	0.304
1986-87	0.453	0.338	0.214	0.312	0.266	0.256	0.325	0.311
1987-88	0.453	0.337	0.206	0.304	0.264	0.257	0.331	0.313

(Contd.)

TABLE 7.1 (Contd.)

(1)	(11)	(12)	(13)	(14)	(15)	(16)	(17)	(18)
1988-89	0.469	0.340	0.223	0.305	0.275	0.296	0.323	0.321
1989-90	0.515	0.355	0.251	0.318	0.294	0.305	0.329	0.337
1990-91	0.519	0.348	0.268	0.334	0.308	0.310	0.359	0.337
1991-92	0.466	0.334	0.214	0.331	0.296	0.251	0.339	0.302
1992-93	0.492	0.340	0.275	0.336	0.254	0.325	0.364	0.336
1993-94	0.494	0.334	0.203	0.361	0.248	0.276	0.366	0.329
1994-95	0.512	0.337	0.281	0.361	0.296	0.372	0.368	0.353
1995-96	0.532	0.366	0.334	0.373	0.292	0.359	0.361	0.370
1996-97	0.522	0.418	0.306	0.370	0.292	0.383	0.389	0.370
1997-98	0.510	0.428	0.317	0.370	0.301	0.403	0.371	0.366
1998-99	0.521	0.416	0.310	0.374	0.317	0.405	0.419	0.324
1999-00	0.492	0.384	0.289	0.340	0.270	0.333	0.377	0.353
2000-01	0.489	0.435	0.285	0.339	0.278	0.346	0.386	0.369
Growth Rate	2.147* (13.469)	1.829* (11.777)	3.334* (15.382)	2.253* (12.505)	1.429* (8.009)	3.695* (16.599)	1.808* (21.128)	2.237* (15.366)
Linear Slope	0.008* (13.663)	0.005* (11.672)	0.007* (13.633)	0.006* (13.570)	0.003* (7.907)	0.009* (14.752)	0.005* (20.913)	0.006* (16.092)
CV	0.179	0.162	0.280	0.188	0.136	0.305	0.150	0.184

Notes : 1. Figures in brackets are the respective ' t' values.
2. *Indicates significant at one percent level.

rate was in Bihar followed by Maharashtra and minimum was in Assam. In 2000-01, the highest real wage rate again was in Maharashtra followed by Bihar and least was in Assam.

INTER-STATE COMPARISON OF SHARE OF LABOUR

An inter-state comparison of share of labour in real GVA (Table 7.2) reported a declining trend in all states, however, minimum decline was found in Assam, Haryana and Punjab followed by Kerala and maximum in Madhya Pradesh. The maximum variability was perceived in Himachal Pradesh followed by Orissa and minimum in West Bengal. In 1973-74 maximum value of share of labour was observed in Himachal Pradesh followed by West Bengal and least was in Assam. In 1983-84, maximum value was in West Bengal followed by Orissa and least was in Himachal Pradesh. In 1993-94, the maximum value of share of labour was in West Bengal followed by Haryana and minimum was in Assam. In 2000-01, the highest value was again in West Bengal followed by Bihar and least was in Himachal Pradesh.

ANALYSIS OF VARIABLES IN ALL INDUSTRIES IN DIFFERENT STATES

Table 7.3 shows the indices of various economic parameters in case of Andhra Pradesh for all industries. Index of real GVA increased at an average rate of 8.029 percent per annum. The overall trend rate was 22.761 per annum. Coefficient of variation was found to be 0.632.

Index of real emoluments increased at an average rate of 6.171 percent per annum. The overall trend rate was 16.352 per annum. Coefficient of variation was found to be 0.459.

Index of real GFC increased at an average rate of 10.496 percent per annum. The overall trend rate was 36.626 per annum. Coefficient of variation was found to be 0.761.

Consumer price index for industrial workers (CPI-IW) increased at an average annual rate of 8.087 percent. The overall trend rate was 25.098 per annum. Coefficient of variation was found to be 0.629.

Index of real wage rate increased at an average annual rate

TABLE 7.2
Share of Labour in Gross Value Added at Constant Prices in Different States and All-India

Year	AP	ASM	BIH	GUJ	HAR	HP	KAR	KER	MP
(1)	(2)	(3)	(4)	(5)	(6)	(7)	(8)	(9)	(10)
1973-74	0.353	0.320	0.486	0.408	0.457	0.752	0.447	0.450	0.463
1974-75	0.418	0.213	0.400	0.407	0.450	0.988	0.593	0.446	0.548
1975-76	0.382	0.252	0.414	0.511	0.362	0.520	0.504	0.505	0.628
1976-77	0.408	0.248	0.551	0.459	0.340	0.372	0.514	0.508	0.546
1977-78	0.405	0.220	0.627	0.444	0.333	0.306	0.526	0.490	0.615
1978-79	0.409	0.265	0.520	0.433	0.306	0.248	0.389	0.461	0.598
1979-80	0.441	0.323	0.612	0.478	0.338	0.214	0.541	0.446	0.614
1980-81	0.535	0.459	0.783	0.550	0.373	0.289	0.560	0.476	0.523
1981-82	0.440	0.374	0.485	0.472	0.411	0.237	0.474	0.467	0.433
1982-83	0.455	0.334	0.466	0.484	0.432	0.225	0.519	0.452	0.406
1983-84	0.357	0.285	0.333	0.360	0.339	0.198	0.437	0.406	0.513
1984-85	0.384	0.224	0.554	0.420	0.480	0.286	0.519	0.346	0.586
1985-86	0.421	0.198	0.507	0.432	0.436	0.286	0.482	0.392	0.379
1986-87	0.402	0.170	0.467	0.386	0.417	0.322	0.485	0.413	0.525
1987-88	0.454	0.178	0.410	0.382	0.467	0.511	0.530	0.392	0.435

1988-89	0.372	0.273	0.364	0.352	0.409	0.320	0.492	0.411	0.371
1989-90	0.384	0.168	0.396	0.361	0.425	0.417	0.482	0.326	0.393
1990-91	0.336	0.159	0.473	0.341	0.379	0.341	0.428	0.444	0.365
1991-92	0.315	0.204	0.293	0.373	0.363	0.353	0.328	0.412	0.373
1992-93	0.316	0.250	0.474	0.274	0.518	0.380	0.367	0.416	0.357
1993-94	0.314	0.219	0.252	0.269	0.471	0.234	0.351	0.392	0.297
1994-95	0.297	0.264	0.443	0.225	0.396	0.292	0.337	0.411	0.307
1995-96	0.299	0.251	0.424	0.236	0.320	0.318	0.362	0.360	0.287
1996-97	0.254	0.232	0.382	0.182	0.333	0.231	0.321	0.363	0.222
1997-98	0.268	0.342	0.229	0.217	0.348	0.292	0.317	0.369	0.258
1998-99	0.307	0.219	0.277	0.210	0.390	0.222	0.368	0.286	0.306
1999-00	0.273	0.195	0.272	0.221	0.272	0.155	0.312	0.309	0.250
2000-01	0.302	0.307	0.396	0.254	0.344	0.154	0.342	0.354	0.256
Growth Rate	-1.719 (-6.086)*	-0.702 (-1.178)NS	-2.168 (-4.107)*	-3.288 (-9.207)*	-0.295 (-0.808)NS	-2.626 (-3.156)*	-1.944 (-6.771)*	-1.38 (-6.457)*	-3.363 (-10.427)*
Linear Slope	-0.006 (-5.581)*	-0.001 (-1.204)NS	-0.009 (-3.895)*	-0.011 (-9.210)*	-0.001 (-0.728)	-0.011 (-3.067)*	-0.008 (-6.609)*	-0.005 (-6.766)*	-0.013 (-9.731)*
CV	0.185	0.271	0.281	0.287	0.154	0.525	0.196	0.140	0.300

(*Contd.*)

TABLE 7.2 (Contd.)

Year	*MAH*	*ORI*	*PB*	*RAJ*	*TN*	*UP*	*WB*	*All India*
(1)	(11)	(12)	(13)	(14)	(15)	(16)	(17)	(18)
1973-74	0.527	0.523	0.412	0.440	0.479	0.381	0.696	0.484
1974-75	0.559	0.486	0.391	0.489	0.595	0.524	0.666	0.498
1975-76	0.584	0.684	0.368	0.505	0.588	0.576	0.695	0.539
1976-77	0.561	0.460	0.357	0.518	0.533	0.483	0.679	0.525
1977-78	0.545	0.562	0.368	0.478	0.503	0.585	0.689	0.533
1978-79	0.510	0.454	0.351	0.448	0.464	0.537	0.608	0.487
1979-80	0.552	0.479	0.350	0.433	0.503	0.605	0.716	0.538
1980-81	0.586	0.711	0.408	0.550	0.551	0.686	0.758	0.590
1981-82	0.559	0.670	0.427	0.503	0.518	0.389	0.773	0.524
1982-83	0.559	0.774	0.472	0.595	0.477	0.496	0.714	0.527
1983-84	0.527	0.651	0.449	0.431	0.478	0.637	0.737	0.484
1984-85	0.548	0.951	0.497	0.545	0.313	0.671	0.733	0.541
1985-86	0.446	0.729	0.443	0.540	0.457	0.625	0.646	0.509
1986-87	0.479	0.627	0.446	0.414	0.453	0.409	0.670	0.485
1987-88	0.513	0.667	0.445	0.588	0.480	0.435	0.558	0.498
1988-89	0.432	0.372	0.487	0.495	0.408	0.467	0.700	0.447

1989-90	0.423	0.333	0.313	0.475	0.391	0.389	0.703	0.430
1990-91	0.395	0.341	0.427	0.382	0.377	0.390	0.613	0.394
1991-92	0.429	0.381	0.334	0.409	0.404	0.267	0.583	0.259
1992-93	0.359	0.398	0.534	0.348	0.343	0.364	0.611	0.379
1993-94	0.301	0.366	0.298	0.383	0.278	0.372	0.504	0.324
1994-95	0.318	0.355	0.401	0.311	0.328	0.298	0.569	0.333
1995-96	0.298	0.338	0.479	0.318	0.308	0.298	0.558	0.324
1996-97	0.270	0.282	0.391	0.244	0.288	0.305	0.475	0.283
1997-98	0.285	0.267	0.394	0.233	0.353	0.273	0.455	0.294
1998-99	0.327	0.400	0.282	0.350	0.367	0.338	0.597	0.269
1999-00	0.251	0.275	0.254	0.218	0.293	0.270	0.563	0.270
2000-01	0.286	0.370	0.370	0.233	0.298	0.304	0.599	0.320
Growth Rate	-3.073 (-11.876)*	-2.764 (-4.494)*	-0.447 (-1.081)NS	-2.691 (-6.165)*	-2.426 (-8.873)*	-2.73 (-5.916)*	-1.177 (-5.015)*	-2.739 (-8.828)*
Linear Slope	-0.012 (-12.675)*	-0.012 (-3.712)*	-0.001 (-0.827)NS	-0.01 (-5.814)*	-0.01 (-9.237)*	-0.011 (-5.289)*	-0.007 (-5.057)*	-0.011 (-9.138)*
CV	0.256	0.358	0.17	0.258	0.227	0.299	0.133	0.242

Notes :
1. Figures in parentheses are the respective 't' values.
2. * Indicates one percent level of significance.
3. NS Indicates non-significant.

TABLE 7.3
Different Economic Parameters of Industries in Andhra Pradesh

Year	*Index of Real GVA*	*Index of Real Emoluments*	*Index of Real GFC*	*Index of CPI-IW*	*Index of Real Wage Rate*	*Index of Employees*
1973-74	100.00	100.00	100.00	100.00	100.00	100.00
1974-75	89.12	105.26	88.05	121.11	93.25	112.87
1975-76	109.42	118.33	90.75	125.90	98.96	119.58
1976-77	123.01	142.14	104.57	122.67	98.64	144.10
1977-78	127.82	146.49	124.15	134.24	96.86	151.23
1978-79	148.59	172.08	135.85	135.85	104.07	165.36
1979-80	147.24	183.50	151.75	146.59	101.92	180.05
1980-81	136.87	207.08	162.65	161.75	121.16	170.91
1981-82	148.43	184.92	156.59	185.25	98.91	186.97
1982-83	200.21	257.74	187.01	194.42	132.30	194.81
1983-84	245.89	248.56	219.22	217.14	132.77	187.21
1984-85	254.43	276.59	225.12	234.24	157.77	175.31
1985-86	224.18	267.05	253.19	248.62	157.59	169.46
1986-87	228.00	259.11	265.07	274.88	149.05	173.84
1987-88	206.45	264.99	297.49	299.59	144.89	182.90
1988-89	264.61	278.44	341.24	325.12	149.77	185.91
1989-90	295.77	321.40	398.09	333.64	153.40	209.52
1990-91	371.82	353.01	746.57	342.21	165.35	213.49
1991-92	378.56	337.74	837.74	394.70	155.32	217.45
1992-93	455.75	406.82	985.75	441.38	169.66	239.78
1993-94	468.22	415.71	1043.32	460.83	185.60	223.98
1994-95	619.13	520.94	1018.38	501.66	193.51	269.20
1995-96	725.34	613.96	852.14	550.23	201.14	305.24
1996-97	719.52	517.79	821.21	598.85	200.94	257.68
1997-98	680.79	517.10	941.96	643.59	168.05	307.70
1998-99	527.69	458.20	794.83	733.04	206.17	222.24
1999-00	564.28	436.40	710.67	768.06	186.84	233.57
2000-01	520.42	443.93	647.71	814.75	190.76	232.72
Growth Rate	8.029* (18.970)	6.171* (17.115)	10.496* (14.912)	8.087* (74.830)	3.104* (14.560)	2.975* (9.847)
Linear Slope	22.761* (11.432)	16.352* (13.766)	36.626* (9.128)	25.098* (16.720)	4.301* (15.058)	5.479* (9.361)
CV	0.632	0.459	0.761	0.629	0.254	0.260

Notes : 1. Figures in parentheses are the respective 't' values.
2. *Indicates one percent level of significance.

of 3.104 percent. The overall trend rate was 4.301 per annum. Coefficient of variation was found to be 0.254.

Index of employees increased at an average rate of 2.975 percent per annum. The overall trend rate was 5.479 per annum. Coefficient of variation was found to be 0.260.

An inter-variable comparison in this State revealed that the maximum growth rate and variability were in GFC and minimum growth rate in case of employees and least variability in the real wage rate. It was found that the growth rates of both the emoluments as well as the wage rate were higher than that of employees. The Index of GVA increased at a much higher rate than real emoluments and real wage rate.

Table 7.4 shows the indices of various economic parameters in case of Assam for all industries. Index of real GVA rose at an average rate of 4.367 percent per annum. The overall trend rate was 9.732 per annum. Coefficient of variation was found to be 0.367.

Index of real emoluments increased at an average rate of 3.272 percent per annum. The overall trend rate was found to be 5.526 per annum. Coefficient of variation was found to be 0.324.

Index of real GFC rose at an average rate of 6.192 percent per annum. The overall trend rate was 14.954 per annum. Coefficient of variation was found to be 0.576.

Consumer price index for industrial workers increased at an average annual rate of 8.60 percent. The overall trend rate was 27.986 per annum. Coefficient of variation was found to be 0.669.

Index of real wage rate increased at an average annual rate of 2.868 percent. The overall trend rate was 3.452 per annum. Coefficient of variation was found to be 0.257.

Index of employees increased at an average rate of 0.392 percent per annum. The overall trend rate was 0.537 per annum. Coefficient of variation was found to be 0.111.

An inter-variable comparison in this state revealed that the maximum growth rate and variability were in CPI-IW and minimum in case of employees. It was found that the growth rates and variability of both the emoluments as well as the wage rate were higher than that of employees. The Index of GVA increased at a higher rate than of real emoluments and real wage rate.

TABLE 7.4

Different Economic Parameters of Industries in Assam

Year	Index of Real GVA	Index of Real Emoluments	Index of Real GFC	Index of CPI-IW	Index of Real Wage Rate	Index of Employees
1973-74	100.00	100.00	100.00	100.00	100.00	100.00
1974-75	138.85	87.20	79.35	126.84	70.35	123.94
1975-76	146.88	112.43	153.22	125.24	80.57	139.55
1976-77	190.79	137.28	168.49	120.42	97.72	140.48
1977-78	229.80	143.53	178.77	129.65	93.77	153.07
1978-79	198.85	147.96	172.41	132.46	100.56	147.14
1979-80	165.72	150.38	138.42	144.05	99.14	151.70
1980-81	109.22	135.33	124.74	160.46	93.73	144.38
1981-82	115.99	121.76	104.97	180.48	87.35	139.39
1982-83	120.98	113.48	101.10	194.48	85.57	132.61
1983-84	177.23	146.16	112.73	215.86	105.51	138.53
1984-85	232.72	149.07	164.01	229.45	113.32	131.55
1985-86	297.22	168.74	165.31	245.01	123.99	136.09
1986-87	294.50	142.37	227.14	266.43	113.42	125.53
1987-88	266.90	133.88	197.92	289.76	112.32	119.20
1988-89	226.18	155.49	315.83	317.01	115.14	135.04
1989-90	375.12	176.92	252.04	336.43	124.90	141.64
1990-91	335.50	148.63	244.82	375.31	117.56	126.43
1991-92	318.34	172.90	321.85	425.89	122.30	141.38
1992-93	324.68	210.87	388.86	466.73	137.74	153.10
1993-94	296.61	176.68	345.67	501.76	134.08	131.78
1994-95	304.50	217.38	379.80	552.33	150.96	144.00
1995-96	371.51	252.19	447.74	608.68	147.06	171.49
1996-97	343.70	221.77	333.33	665.13	144.78	153.18
1997-98	372.15	344.06	618.06	711.79	191.93	179.26
1998-99	363.56	223.20	333.69	805.17	170.91	130.60
1999-00	386.34	213.92	309.51	832.36	161.83	132.19
2000-01	296.80	237.48	629.24	863.47	181.85	130.59
Growth Rate	4.367* (7.520)	3.272* (9.090)	6.192* (9.364)	8.600* (57.219)	2.868* (12.445)	0.392^{NS} (1.542)
Linear Slope	9.732* (8.567)	5.526* (7.554)	14.954* (7.941)	27.986* (15.853)	3.452* (11.659)	0.537^{NS} (1.526)
CV	0.367	0.324	0.576	0.669	0.257	0.111

Notes :
1. Figures in parentheses are the respective 't' values.
2. *Indicates one percent level of significance.
3. ^{NS} indicates non-significant.

TABLE 7.5

Different Economic Parameters of Industries in Bihar

Year	Index of Real GVA	Index of Real Emoluments	Index of Real GFC	Index of CPI-IW	Index of Real Wage Rate	Index of Employees
1973-74	100.00	100.00	100.00	100.00	100.00	100.00
1974-75	126.64	94.48	84.27	125.74	85.56	110.43
1975-76	166.97	129.27	166.33	117.67	100.50	128.62
1976-77	136.97	133.55	191.28	115.69	104.90	127.31
1977-78	135.28	145.30	276.40	126.93	106.51	136.43
1978-79	184.04	157.66	291.77	129.35	110.52	142.65
1979-80	165.02	165.66	299.53	140.19	128.28	129.14
1980-81	134.53	165.76	244.45	153.86	118.59	139.77
1981-82	201.63	172.82	244.78	171.13	127.82	135.20
1982-83	232.18	192.46	282.14	184.40	141.29	136.22
1983-84	298.39	182.23	285.83	206.08	137.96	132.09
1984-85	220.16	203.51	289.85	212.08	159.03	127.97
1985-86	229.46	195.26	292.06	233.01	155.37	125.68
1986-87	229.63	193.12	283.94	256.68	149.94	128.80
1987-88	290.51	210.79	306.69	273.16	148.97	141.49
1988-89	350.52	234.78	269.35	298.06	168.06	139.70
1989-90	335.83	243.11	279.25	314.98	182.56	133.16
1990-91	310.76	259.89	269.42	331.91	197.07	131.88
1991-92	344.96	178.32	321.30	376.16	135.93	131.19
1992-93	339.65	274.68	371.10	416.75	206.08	133.29
1993-94	554.35	263.70	427.20	440.72	211.34	124.77
1994-95	340.64	270.89	465.58	479.42	215.90	125.47
1995-96	388.80	286.90	441.34	516.31	233.10	123.08
1996-97	413.56	279.95	446.13	591.89	235.24	119.00
1997-98	611.02	259.61	401.71	626.93	225.85	114.95
1998-99	173.24	96.40	139.12	709.92	220.24	43.77
1999-00	61.23	31.69	29.65	732.04	127.82	24.79
2000-01	41.94	28.88	30.78	746.80	125.44	23.02
Growth Rate	1.851^NS (1.294)	-0.25^NS (-0.182)	-0.313^NS (-0.187)	8.034* (56.981)	2.821* (6.257)	-2.988* (-3.087)
Linear Slope	7.492** (2.578)	2.156^NS (1.298)	3.481^NS (1.283)	23.876* (16.247)	4.233* (5.928)	-2.006* (-3.011)
CV	0.537	0.391	0.436	0.631	0.295	0.275

Notes : 1. Figures in parentheses are the respective 't' values.
2. * Indicates one percent level of significance.
3. ** Indicates 5 percent level of significance.
4. NS Indicates non-significant.

Table 7.5 shows the indices of various economic parameters in case of industries in Bihar. Index of real GVA rose at an average rate of 1.851 percent per annum. The overall trend rate was 7.492 per annum. Coefficient of variation was found to be 0.537.

Index of real emoluments decreased at an average rate of 0.25 percent per annum. The overall trend rate was found to be 2.156 per annum. Coefficient of variation was found to be 0.391.

Index of real GFC declined at an average rate of 0.313 percent per annum. The overall trend rate was 3.481 per annum. Coefficient of variation was found to be 0.436.

Consumer price index for industrial workers increased at an average annual rate of 8.034 percent. The overall trend rate was 23.876 per annum. Coefficient of variation was found to be 0.631.

Index of real wage rate increased at an average annual rate of 2.821 percent. The overall trend rate was 4.233 per annum. The average annual growth rate and trend rate were statistically significant at one percent level of significance. Coefficient of variation was found to be 0.295.

Index of employees increased from 100.00 in 1973-74 to 114.95 in 1997-98 and then fell to 23.02 in 2000-01. The decrease in average annual rate was 2.988 percent. Coefficient of variation was found to be 0.275.

An inter-variable comparison in this State revealed that the maximum growth rate and variability were perceived in CPI-IW and negative growth and least variability in case of employees. It was found that the growth rates and variability of both the emoluments as well as the wage rate were higher than that of employees. Index of real wage rate increased at a higher rate than of GVA, emoluments and of employees.

Table 7.6 shows the indices of various economic parameters in case of industries in Gujarat. Index of real GVA rose at an average rate of 8.07 percent per annum. The overall trend rate of real GVA was 23.955 per annum. Coefficient of variation was found to be 0.678.

Index of real emoluments increased at an average rate of 3.933 percent per annum. The overall trend rate was found to be 7.436 per annum. Coefficient of variation was found to be 0.325.

Index of real GFC rose at an average rate of 11.306 percent

TABLE 7.6

Different Economic Parameters of Industries in Gujarat

Year	*Index of Real GVA*	*Index of Real Emoluments*	*Index of Real GFC*	*Index of CPI-IW*	*Index of Real Wage Rate*	*Index of Employees*
1973-74	100.00	100.00	100.00	100.00	100.00	100.00
1974-75	108.28	98.98	97.43	124.45	93.42	105.95
1975-76	103.77	117.81	111.00	119.58	106.63	110.49
1976-77	121.40	124.64	127.06	114.71	111.55	111.74
1977-78	139.65	138.76	143.24	126.54	115.97	119.65
1978-79	151.12	145.14	170.54	131.81	116.57	124.51
1979-80	149.38	157.60	162.83	142.05	117.48	134.15
1980-81	142.77	169.71	170.94	153.48	129.14	131.42
1981-82	143.62	147.49	163.42	180.02	115.83	127.33
1982-83	166.63	174.53	204.03	198.81	122.44	142.54
1983-84	237.14	185.23	253.35	222.07	127.01	145.84
1984-85	206.40	185.09	247.89	232.65	143.80	128.71
1985-86	203.69	184.13	263.12	244.48	147.19	125.09
1986-87	227.09	187.30	287.48	268.19	147.33	127.13
1987-88	241.12	188.63	357.12	295.53	149.46	126.21
1988-89	259.99	191.90	329.89	311.43	152.74	125.64
1989-90	265.83	200.06	356.52	339.96	150.56	132.87
1990-91	288.24	206.66	443.71	371.77	162.83	126.92
1991-92	246.04	182.05	467.21	433.40	140.40	129.66
1992-93	430.66	238.83	689.25	479.13	175.04	136.44
1993-94	454.29	254.22	798.83	497.02	177.92	142.88
1994-95	523.50	247.09	807.54	554.67	170.20	145.18
1995-96	700.58	342.78	1368.08	602.39	190.70	179.75
1996-97	740.09	280.12	1179.51	662.03	181.91	153.99
1997-98	711.35	315.14	1412.18	709.74	190.98	165.01
1998-99	670.84	281.70	1489.09	793.24	183.73	153.32
1999-00	679.16	293.48	1241.06	838.97	189.81	154.62
2000-01	570.70	275.22	1244.51	876.74	194.77	141.30
Growth Rate	8.070* (19.689)	3.933* (16.167)	11.306* (26.524)	8.711* (59.082)	2.607* (20.667)	1.292* (6.954)
Linear Slope	23.955* (10.900)	7.436* (13.847)	51.000* (10.361)	28.152* (16.122)	3.684* (21.674)	1.700* (6.618)
CV	0.678	0.325	0.891	0.672	0.212	0.132

Notes : 1. Figures in parentheses are the respective 't' values.
2. *Indicates one percent level of significance.

per annum. The overall trend rate was 51.00 per annum. Coefficient of variation was found to be 0.891.

Consumer price index for industrial workers increased at an average annual rate of 8.711 percent. The overall trend rate was 28.152 per annum. Coefficient of variation was found to be 0.672.

Index of real wage rate increased at an average annual rate of 2.607 percent. The overall trend rate was 3.684 per annum. Coefficient of variation was found to be 0.212.

Index of employees increased at an average rate of 1.292 percent per annum. The overall trend rate was 1.70 per annum. Coefficient of variation was found to be 0.132.

An inter-variable comparison in this State revealed that the maximum growth rate and variability were in the index of real GFC and minimum in case of employees. It has been found that the growth rates and variability of both the emoluments as well as the wage rate were higher than that of employees. Index of real emoluments and real wage rate increased at much slower rate than of GVA.

Table 7.7 shows the indices of various economic parameters in case of industries in Haryana. Index of real GVA increased at an average rate of 8.377 percent per annum. The overall trend rate of real GVA was 31.629 per annum. Coefficient of variation was found to be 0.656.

Index of real emoluments increased at an average rate of 7.585 percent per annum. The overall trend rate was 19.691 per annum. Coefficient of variation was found to be 0.555.

Index of real GFC rose at an average rate of 8.451 percent per annum. The overall trend rate was 24.809 per annum. Coefficient of variation was found to be 0.622.

Consumer price index for industrial workers increased at an average annual rate of 8.153 percent. The overall trend rate was 25.953 per annum. Coefficient of variation was found to be 0.640.

Index of real wage rate increased at an average annual rate of 3.402 percent per annum. The overall trend rate was 5.572 per annum. Coefficient of variation was found to be 0.278.

Index of employees worked out to increase at an average rate of 4.044 percent per annum. The overall trend rate was 6.097 per annum. Coefficient of variation was found to be 0.316.

TABLE 7.7
Different Economic Parameters of Industries in Haryana

Year	*Index of Real GVA*	*Index of Real Emoluments*	*Index of Real GFC*	*Index of CPI-IW*	*Index of Real Wage Rate*	*Index of Employees*
1973-74	100.00	100.00	100.00	100.00	100.00	100.00
1974-75	112.19	100.17	92.88	128.50	116.36	86.09
1975-76	128.14	92.93	102.47	125.39	111.73	83.17
1976-77	152.32	104.31	115.22	123.83	117.88	88.49
1977-78	166.46	111.15	126.66	136.69	114.03	97.48
1978-79	199.58	122.91	133.83	140.60	124.28	98.90
1979-80	211.94	144.33	170.05	149.60	124.07	116.33
1980-81	203.82	147.63	166.93	169.15	121.91	121.10
1981-82	239.07	192.69	156.60	187.52	134.04	143.76
1982-83	265.40	224.28	177.52	200.42	142.81	157.05
1983-84	348.21	234.56	214.26	215.64	145.45	161.27
1984-85	270.24	246.26	227.49	225.81	152.95	161.00
1985-86	299.49	248.42	261.41	243.76	146.73	169.30
1986-87	310.22	247.83	261.26	260.57	151.93	163.12
1987-88	320.06	274.87	296.98	296.51	162.21	169.45
1988-89	361.92	279.83	308.53	319.59	171.48	163.19
1989-90	390.02	315.77	322.24	336.18	182.36	173.15
1990-91	479.77	355.00	342.22	352.76	196.03	181.09
1991-92	466.31	320.25	402.36	402.87	168.73	189.80
1992-93	411.54	381.19	463.76	436.93	200.27	190.33
1993-94	492.86	421.70	555.58	471.03	205.10	205.61
1994-95	629.10	454.43	549.87	519.12	208.03	218.44
1995-96	868.51	524.79	582.90	585.26	216.90	241.95
1996-97	897.78	564.96	652.90	631.37	233.36	242.10
1997-98	884.36	566.79	668.22	671.46	251.03	225.79
1998-99	876.98	640.83	675.50	757.65	237.72	269.58
1999-00	1001.86	514.91	683.97	785.68	240.97	213.68
2000-01	841.93	520.42	683.41	825.77	241.62	215.39
Growth Rate	8.377* (25.954)	7.585* (26.405)	8.451* (42.889)	8.153* (65.508)	3.402* (31.107)	4.044* (15.161)
Linear Slope	31.629* (13.064)	19.691* (19.251)	24.809* (19.726)	25.953* (16.058)	5.572* (24.039)	6.097* (16.669)
CV	0.656	0.555	0.622	0.640	0.278	0.316

Notes : 1. Figures in parentheses are the respective 't' values.
2. *Indicates one percent level of significance.

An inter-variable comparison in this State revealed that the maximum growth rate was in real GFC and minimum in wage rate. The highest variability was found in GVA and least in wage rate. It was found that the growth rates and variability of both the emoluments as well as of employees were higher than that of wage rate. However, the growth rates of real emoluments and real wage rate were commensurate with growth rate of GVA.

Table 7.8 shows the indices of various economic parameters in case of industries in Himachal Pradesh. Index of real GVA increased at an average rate of 10.537 percent per annum. The overall trend rate was 64.204 per annum. Coefficient of variation was found to be 0.668.

Index of real emoluments increased at an average rate of 7.310 percent per annum. The overall trend rate was 16.530 per annum. Coefficient of variation was found to be 0.580.

Index of real GFC rose at an average rate of 11.635 percent per annum. The overall trend rate was 65.076 per annum. Coefficient of variation was found to be 0.665.

Consumer price index for industrial workers increased at an average annual rate of 8.60 percent. The overall trend rate was 27.986 per annum. Coefficient of variation was found to be 0.669.

Index of real wage rate increased at an average annual rate of 2.571 percent. The overall trend rate was 3.692 per annum. Coefficient of variation was found to be 0.219.

Index of employees worked out to increase at an average rate of 4.620 percent per annum. The overall trend rate was 7.098 per annum. Coefficient of variation was found to be 0.432.

An inter-variable comparison in this State revealed that the maximum growth rate was in real GFC and minimum in wage rate. The highest variability was found in CPI-IW and least in wage rate. It was found that the growth rates and variability of both the emoluments as well as of employees were higher than that of wage rate. Index of real emoluments and real wage rate increased at a slower rate than of GVA.

Table 7.9 shows the indices of various economic parameters in case of industries in Karnataka. Index of real GVA increased at an average rate of 7.216 percent per annum. The overall trend rate was 18.913 per annum. Coefficient of variation was found to be 0.576.

TABLE 7.8
Different Economic Parameters of Industries in Himachal Pradesh

Year	*Index of Real GVA*	*Index of Real Emoluments*	*Index of Real GFC*	*Index of CPI-IW*	*Index of Real Wage Rate*	*Index of Employees*
1973-74	100.00	100.00	100.00	100.00	100.00	100.00
1974-75	69.82	84.92	75.23	126.84	89.51	94.87
1975-76	143.76	92.74	86.18	125.24	114.00	81.35
1976-77	232.28	108.59	160.71	120.42	124.85	86.97
1977-78	265.70	102.39	179.51	129.65	120.21	85.18
1978-79	339.64	98.71	274.12	132.46	115.85	85.21
1979-80	390.13	102.87	293.05	144.05	106.19	96.87
1980-81	336.40	113.12	287.58	160.46	118.59	95.39
1981-82	420.71	125.14	340.49	180.48	121.21	103.24
1982-83	619.92	168.69	617.30	194.48	149.67	112.71
1983-84	726.65	174.15	614.10	215.86	143.58	121.29
1984-85	599.33	199.46	698.46	229.45	143.86	138.65
1985-86	701.81	236.68	794.05	245.01	148.78	159.08
1986-87	710.69	266.64	795.46	266.43	157.86	168.90
1987-88	576.38	341.56	979.45	289.76	178.64	191.19
1988-89	923.55	359.46	872.12	317.01	157.77	227.84
1989-90	731.83	374.04	831.61	336.43	165.97	225.36
1990-91	990.20	407.30	879.39	375.31	177.33	229.69
1991-92	948.57	400.23	1029.25	425.89	173.58	230.58
1992-93	967.62	423.47	1235.31	466.73	168.57	251.21
1993-94	1545.33	442.24	1435.31	501.76	172.80	255.92
1994-95	1320.67	459.76	1493.74	552.33	170.08	270.32
1995-96	1396.66	530.70	1569.87	608.68	183.15	289.76
1996-97	2053.88	571.06	1954.65	665.13	194.29	293.91
1997-98	1863.12	615.20	1745.14	711.79	205.56	299.28
1998-99	1291.25	321.84	1462.22	805.17	223.01	144.31
1999-00	1569.62	278.46	1397.94	832.36	161.77	172.13
2000-01	1686.56	302.33	1382.32	863.47	179.14	168.77
Growth Rate	10.537* (13.443)	7.310* (10.114)	11.635* (13.369)	8.600* (57.219)	2.571* (11.180)	4.620* (7.615)
Linear Slope	64.204* (14.130)	16.530* (7.931)	65.076* (16.457)	27.986* (15.853)	3.692* (11.233)	7.098* (6.598)
CV	0.668	0.580	0.665	0.669	0.219	0.432

Notes : 1. Figures in parentheses are the respective 't' values.
2. *Indicates one percent level of significance.

TABLE 7.9

Different Economic Parameters of Industries in Karnataka

Year	Index of Real GVA	Index of Real Emoluments	Index of Real GFC	Index of CPI-IW	Index of Real Wage Rate	Index of Employees
1973-74	100.00	100.00	100.00	100.00	100.00	100.00
1974-75	92.92	111.58	88.13	119.98	114.99	97.03
1975-76	110.10	113.24	101.92	125.29	103.92	108.96
1976-77	121.04	124.87	115.28	121.13	108.96	114.60
1977-78	127.67	134.04	126.96	129.04	112.23	119.43
1978-79	196.57	152.81	159.01	127.89	127.95	119.43
1979-80	154.00	168.78	141.28	141.86	136.75	123.43
1980-81	141.61	157.41	147.49	163.75	119.88	131.31
1981-82	142.77	135.97	143.27	190.94	113.44	119.85
1982-83	164.53	171.47	170.13	201.90	130.81	131.08
1983-84	211.37	187.09	185.37	228.29	143.74	130.15
1984-85	188.65	193.31	186.77	244.17	147.36	131.18
1985-86	199.52	192.04	199.98	257.34	154.04	124.67
1986-87	208.20	200.75	205.45	277.77	156.40	128.36
1987-88	208.75	211.47	254.31	305.31	164.48	128.57
1988-89	232.28	221.23	266.47	328.69	166.32	133.02
1989-90	286.97	270.94	271.26	316.98	196.98	137.55
1990-91	328.69	276.37	300.39	355.33	199.07	138.83
1991-92	358.05	230.09	306.01	411.87	162.81	141.33
1992-93	394.81	282.06	428.64	464.40	194.13	145.30
1993-94	370.87	249.77	449.07	500.75	167.54	149.08
1994-95	458.37	304.27	521.91	549.17	196.50	154.85
1995-96	487.69	345.69	551.21	615.82	203.73	169.69
1996-97	565.30	352.52	672.11	668.30	201.14	175.26
1997-98	599.22	362.93	951.59	728.89	182.86	198.47
1998-99	609.52	418.18	1378.15	789.48	225.66	185.31
1999-00	510.69	308.28	871.69	817.73	189.16	162.97
2000-01	485.27	313.88	799.77	858.14	199.77	157.13
Growth Rate	7.216* (21.645)	4.802* (19.332)	9.397* (20.199)	8.564* (56.748)	2.788* (13.504)	1.959* (12.433)
Linear Slope	18.913* (13.908)	10.020* (15.138)	32.263* (7.882)	27.744* (16.184)	4.173* (13.171)	2.686* (10.885)
CV	0.576	0.387	0.877	0.661	0.233	0.177

Notes : 1. Figures in parentheses are the respective 't' values.
2. *Indicates one percent level of significance.

Index of real emoluments increased at an average rate of 4.802 percent per annum. The overall trend rate was 10.02 per annum. Coefficient of variation was found to be 0.387.

Index of real GFC rose at an average rate of 9.397 percent per annum. The overall trend rate was 32.263 per annum. Coefficient of variation was found to be 0.877.

Consumer price index for industrial workers increased at an average annual rate of 8.564 percent. The overall trend rate was 27.744 per annum. Coefficient of variation was found to be 0.661.

Index of real wage rate increased at an average annual rate of 2.788 percent. The overall trend rate was 4.173 per annum. Coefficient of variation was found to be 0.233.

Index of employees worked out to increase at an average rate of 1.959 percent per annum. The overall trend rate was 2.686 per annum. Coefficient of variation was found to be 0.177.

An inter-variable comparison in this State revealed that the maximum growth rate and variability were in real GFC and minimum in case of employees. It was found that the growth rates and variability of both the emoluments as well as of wage rate were higher than that of employees. Index of real emoluments and real wage rate increased at a slower rate than of GVA.

Table 7.10 shows the indices of various economic parameters in case of industries in Kerala. Index of real GVA rose at an average rate of 5.606 percent per annum. The overall trend rate of real GVA was 12.289 per annum. Coefficient of variation was found to be 0.432.

Index of real emoluments increased at an average rate of 3.975 percent per annum. The overall trend rate was found to be 6.957 per annum. Coefficient of variation was found to be 0.319.

Index of real GFC rose at an average rate of 5.203 percent per annum. The overall trend rate was 8.935 per annum. Coefficient of variation was found to be 0.441.

Consumer price index for industrial workers increased at an average annual rate of 8.27 percent. The overall trend rate was 25.95 per annum. Coefficient of variation was found to be 0.661.

TABLE 7.10
Different Economic Parameters of Industries in Kerala

Year	*Index of Real GVA*	*Index of Real Emoluments*	*Index of Real GFC*	*Index of CPI-IW*	*Index of Real Wage Rate*	*Index of Employees*
1973-74	100.00	100.00	100.00	100.00	100.00	100.00
1974-75	103.73	92.46	88.87	129.59	90.66	101.99
1975-76	99.86	100.94	83.33	134.12	98.88	102.08
1976-77	112.53	114.11	97.41	120.23	106.34	107.31
1977-78	134.23	133.40	105.01	119.50	112.81	118.25
1978-79	150.96	142.18	112.69	125.48	128.26	110.86
1979-80	165.69	152.69	115.49	137.47	127.97	119.32
1980-81	160.12	154.76	107.11	152.49	132.11	117.14
1981-82	163.64	155.99	108.98	172.67	125.90	123.90
1982-83	172.14	158.60	127.28	186.20	142.61	111.21
1983-84	175.05	142.35	138.07	220.63	135.41	105.13
1984-85	212.86	149.77	134.22	237.51	144.30	103.79
1985-86	204.91	160.60	160.87	248.73	164.49	97.63
1986-87	202.12	162.76	157.86	273.48	170.86	95.26
1987-88	237.14	180.22	178.61	287.33	174.79	103.11
1988-89	237.25	192.80	171.43	301.22	195.46	98.64
1989-90	321.15	213.62	179.97	310.72	196.73	108.58
1990-91	251.43	226.13	189.31	320.27	198.51	113.91
1991-92	308.59	249.37	230.32	363.08	213.63	116.73
1992-93	308.41	250.93	261.45	409.64	186.34	134.66
1993-94	280.31	218.56	268.71	452.49	172.65	126.59
1994-95	311.51	256.74	261.07	508.33	173.82	147.71
1995-96	385.22	276.42	327.58	579.10	203.41	135.90
1996-97	390.34	282.02	251.86	647.96	214.62	131.40
1997-98	408.75	296.56	386.19	690.81	197.80	149.93
1998-99	450.14	257.17	280.03	752.26	215.53	119.32
1999-00	383.80	237.22	247.95	787.65	186.74	127.04
2000-01	359.23	248.22	252.28	823.03	189.11	131.25
Growth Rate	5.606* (22.728)	3.975* (15.331)	5.203* (16.344)	8.270* (38.271)	2.293* (11.468)	0.972 (4.192)
Linear Slope	12.289* (18.437)	6.957* (14.786)	8.935* (11.244)	25.950* (4.474)	4.363* (11.454)	1.630* (4.252)
CV	0.432	0.319	0.441	0.661	0.244	0.128

Notes : 1. Figures in parentheses are the respective 't' values.
2. *Indicates one percent level of significance.

Index of real wage rate increased at an average annual rate of 2.293 percent. The overall trend rate was 4.363 per annum. Coefficient of variation was found to be 0.244.

Index of employees increased at an average rate of 0.972 percent per annum. The overall trend rate was 1.63 per annum. Coefficient of variation was found to be 0.128.

An inter-variable comparison in this State revealed that the maximum growth rate and variability were in CPI-IW and minimum in case of employees. It was found that the growth rates and variability of both the emoluments as well as of wage rate were higher than that of employees. Real emoluments and real wage rate increased at reasonable rates as compared to GVA.

Table 7.11 shows the indices of various economic parameters in case of industries in Madhya Pradesh. Index of real GVA rose at an average rate of 7.219 percent per annum. The overall trend rate was 18.488 per annum. Coefficient of variation was found to be 0.642.

Index of real emoluments increased at an average rate of 3.197 percent per annum. The overall trend rate was 5.929 per annum. Coefficient of variation was found to be 0.363.

Index of real GFC rose at an average rate of 7.777 percent per annum. The overall trend rate was 21.395 per annum. Coefficient of variation was found to be 0.616.

Consumer price index for industrial workers increased at an average annual rate of 9.057 percent. The overall trend rate was 30.939 per annum. Coefficient of variation was found to be 0.689.

Index of real wage rate increased at an average annual rate of 1.80 percent. The overall trend rate was 2.273 per annum. Coefficient of variation was found to be 0.168.

Index of employees increased at an average rate of 1.372 percent per annum. The overall trend rate was 2.09 per annum. Coefficient of variation was found to be 0.218.

An inter-variable comparison in this State revealed that the maximum growth rate and variability were perceived in CPI-IW and minimum growth rate in case of employees and least variability in wage rate. It was found that the growth rates of both the emoluments as well as of wage rate were higher than

TABLE 7.11
Different Economic Parameters of Industries in Madhya Pradesh

Year	Index of Real GVA	Index of Real Emoluments	Index of Real GFC	Index of CPI-IW	Index of Real Wage Rate	Index of Employees
1973-74	100.00	100.00	100.00	100.00	100.00	100.00
1974-75	98.13	103.90	79.97	125.91	98.27	105.72
1975-76	95.42	116.28	89.43	121.51	103.01	112.88
1976-77	116.20	124.67	107.54	117.93	110.83	112.49
1977-78	113.73	134.63	124.90	131.08	110.11	122.26
1978-79	116.82	134.03	134.66	134.65	107.90	124.22
1979-80	126.98	146.94	135.24	143.01	112.64	130.46
1980-81	140.08	141.38	163.02	160.95	104.98	134.66
1981-82	165.28	140.69	185.50	190.04	100.30	140.27
1982-83	188.82	152.10	227.84	205.23	101.38	150.03
1983-84	194.60	192.06	267.78	192.85	129.61	148.19
1984-85	199.69	213.27	308.82	245.87	130.90	162.92
1985-86	242.60	169.59	327.63	274.97	118.36	143.29
1986-87	195.31	178.65	334.58	307.65	120.93	147.73
1987-88	258.57	194.60	392.40	328.49	125.00	155.68
1988-89	254.98	169.68	234.05	344.28	128.65	131.90
1989-90	337.26	242.96	398.84	367.11	141.44	171.77
1990-91	371.79	246.94	437.37	389.93	142.76	172.98
1991-92	304.54	204.84	426.19	447.41	124.37	164.69
1992-93	420.60	250.90	667.14	508.97	132.99	188.67
1993-94	479.38	264.75	663.69	550.06	141.31	187.36
1994-95	504.57	278.99	744.25	597.25	150.94	184.84
1995-96	698.71	372.98	762.91	640.32	171.40	217.60
1996-97	743.68	313.36	697.72	720.41	160.04	195.80
1997-98	671.19	319.57	605.69	773.76	163.29	195.70
1998-99	304.42	160.25	472.47	894.83	128.19	125.01
1999-00	355.44	160.63	386.90	911.28	144.69	111.01
2000-01	353.68	169.14	304.76	925.63	160.92	105.11
Growth Rate	7.219* (11.616)	3.197* (5.749)	7.777* (9.741)	9.057* (54.259)	1.800* (9.655)	1.372* (3.066)
Linear Slope	18.488* (7.147)	5.929* (4.966)	21.395* (7.232)	30.939* (16.102)	2.273* (9.172)	2.090* (3.212)
CV	0.642	0.363	0.616	0.689	0.168	0.218

Notes : 1. Figures in parentheses are the respective 't' values.
2. *Indicates one percent level of significance.

Table 7.12
Different Economic Parameters of Industries in Maharashtra

Year	*Index of Real GVA*	*Index of Real Emoluments*	*Index of Real GFC*	*Index of CPI-IW*	*Index of Real Wage Rate*	*Index of Employees*
1973-74	100.00	100.00	100.00	100.00	100.00	100.00
1974-75	100.98	99.34	85.35	124.00	94.93	104.64
1975-76	100.86	103.61	85.42	128.76	99.09	104.56
1976-77	112.23	110.59	104.18	127.88	101.83	108.60
1977-78	121.00	116.28	117.49	136.47	104.26	111.52
1978-79	142.50	129.27	126.75	139.47	112.50	114.90
1979-80	136.83	133.86	129.25	154.06	111.34	120.22
1980-81	128.95	132.85	138.97	171.65	110.65	120.06
1981-82	133.94	131.39	150.84	197.41	111.24	118.12
1982-83	136.54	133.32	164.56	215.47	115.04	115.89
1983-84	156.59	142.68	189.56	242.06	126.43	112.85
1984-85	163.03	150.85	204.27	261.35	133.86	112.69
1985-86	192.15	148.73	211.86	280.65	138.12	107.68
1986-87	184.63	152.20	222.52	307.71	141.27	107.74
1987-88	181.97	155.09	259.76	339.47	141.49	109.61
1988-89	217.83	159.66	270.83	367.35	146.52	108.97
1989-90	247.72	176.63	325.09	385.65	160.77	109.86
1990-91	270.52	180.06	351.22	420.12	161.91	111.21
1991-92	222.41	155.86	396.04	486.94	145.61	107.04
1992-93	302.43	176.57	521.05	549.41	153.49	115.04
1993-94	359.89	182.21	599.05	588.24	154.30	118.09
1994-95	364.90	189.41	588.26	659.29	159.97	118.40
1995-96	451.17	226.32	660.10	730.41	166.12	136.24
1996-97	461.23	206.31	763.30	782.12	162.99	126.58
1997-98	457.52	214.43	774.52	861.88	159.29	134.62
1998-99	376.41	203.56	573.09	976.06	162.74	125.08
1999-00	403.85	167.72	604.86	1008.35	153.52	109.25
2000-01	345.20	160.83	542.60	1088.12	152.80	105.25
Growth Rate	6.223* (19.426)	2.560* (11.311)	9.001* (22.791)	9.390* (74.210)	2.147* (31.464)	0.404** (2.563)
Linear Slope	13.639* (12.428)	3.774* (10.316)	25.325* (12.389)	34.885* (15.208)	2.745* (13.657)	0.475** (2.568)
CV	0.517	0.223	0.681	0.716	0.178	0.076

Notes : 1. Figures in parentheses are the respective 't' values.
2. * Indicates one percent level of significance.
3. ** Indicates 5 percent level of significance.

that of employees. The growth of real GVA was much higher as compared to real emoluments and real wages.

Table 7.12 shows the indices of various economic parameters in case of industries in Maharashtra. Index of real GVA rose at an average rate of 6.223 percent per annum. The overall trend rate was 13.639 per annum. Coefficient of variation was found to be 0.517.

Index of real emoluments increased at an average rate of 2.56 percent per annum. The overall trend rate was 3.774 per annum. Coefficient of variation was found to be 0.223.

Index of real GFC rose at an average rate of 9.001 percent per annum. The overall trend rate was 25.325 per annum. Coefficient of variation was found to be 0.681.

Consumer price index for industrial workers increased at an average annual rate was 9.39 percent. The overall trend rate was 34.885 per annum. Coefficient of variation was found to be 0.716.

Index of real wage rate increased at an average annual rate of 2.147 percent. The overall trend rate was 2.745 per annum. Coefficient of variation was found to be 0.178.

Index of employees increased at an average rate of 0.404 percent per annum. The overall trend rate was 0.475 per annum. Coefficient of variation was found to be 0.076.

An inter-variable comparison in this State revealed that the maximum growth rate and variability were in CPI-IW and minimum in case of employees. It was observed that the growth rates and variability of both the emoluments as well as of wage rate were higher than that of employees. In this State also growth of GVA was much higher as compared to of real emoluments and real wages.

Table 7.13 shows the indices of various economic parameters in case of industries in Orissa. Index of real GVA rose at an average rate of 7.181 percent per annum. The overall trend rate was 15.659 per annum. Coefficient of variation was found to be 0.612.

Index of real emoluments increased at an average rate of 5.647 percent per annum. The overall trend rate was found to be 5.248 per annum. Coefficient of variation was found to be 0.304.

TABLE 7.13
Different Economic Parameters of Industries in Orissa

Year	*Index of Real GVA*	*Index of Real Emoluments*	*Index of Real GFC*	*Index of CPI-IW*	*Index of Real Wage Rate*	*Index of Employees*
1973-74	100.00	100.00	100.00	100.00	100.00	100.00
1974-75	92.64	72.39	77.50	126.84	74.71	96.90
1975-76	76.70	90.69	69.91	125.24	85.28	106.34
1976-77	120.60	93.95	82.55	120.42	87.06	107.91
1977-78	111.18	103.98	89.01	129.65	85.41	121.74
1978-79	130.22	101.93	90.56	132.46	90.49	112.63
1979-80	139.15	114.38	89.70	144.05	98.05	116.66
1980-81	112.48	123.78	94.89	160.46	94.41	131.11
1981-82	109.46	124.49	95.82	180.48	91.19	136.52
1982-83	105.24	137.16	113.46	194.48	99.92	137.27
1983-84	128.83	140.94	129.89	215.86	103.06	136.74
1984-85	99.55	148.05	139.57	229.45	106.42	139.12
1985-86	139.44	157.75	152.43	245.01	105.43	149.62
1986-87	161.67	159.16	174.67	266.43	111.38	142.90
1987-88	182.84	176.74	332.07	289.76	111.06	159.13
1988-89	305.43	171.35	363.09	317.01	112.09	152.87
1989-90	347.28	183.31	361.44	336.43	116.91	156.79
1990-91	321.17	172.82	314.86	375.31	114.58	150.83
1991-92	328.04	184.35	416.06	425.89	110.09	167.45
1992-93	349.53	197.45	517.72	466.73	112.09	176.15
1993-94	357.75	199.78	564.53	501.76	110.10	181.45
1994-95	386.59	211.44	684.38	552.33	110.93	190.60
1995-96	445.09	232.80	693.92	608.68	120.60	193.04
1996-97	543.60	245.43	858.31	665.13	137.70	178.23
1997-98	602.89	252.02	652.12	711.79	141.20	178.48
1998-99	336.91	191.63	462.64	805.17	137.04	139.84
1999-00	371.14	164.36	342.96	832.36	126.43	130.00
2000-01	319.39	181.41	382.33	863.47	143.23	126.65
Growth Rate	7.181* (11.100)	5.647* (11.028)	9.633* (11.629)	8.600* (57.219)	1.829* (11.774)	1.784* (5.708)
Linear Slope	15.659* (8.752)	5.248* (10.395)	23.456* (7.695)	27.986* (15.853)	1.960* (11.669)	2.442* (5.452)
CV	0.612	0.304	0.767	0.669	0.162	0.192

Notes : 1. Figures in parentheses are the respective 't' values.
2. *Indicates one percent level of significance.

Index of real GFC rose at an average rate of 9.633 percent per annum. The overall trend rate was 23.456 per annum. Coefficient of variation was found to be 0.767.

Consumer price index for industrial workers increased at an average annual rate of 8.60 percent. The overall trend rate was 27.986 per annum. Coefficient of variation was found to be 0.669.

Index of real wage rate increased at an average annual rate of 1.829 percent. The overall trend rate was 1.96 per annum. Coefficient of variation was found to be 0.162.

Index of employees increased at an average rate of 1.784 percent per annum. The overall trend rate was 2.442 per annum. Coefficient of variation was found to be 0.192.

An inter-variable comparison in this State revealed that the maximum growth rate and variability were in GFC and minimum growth rate in case of employees and least variability in wage rate. It was perceived that the growth rate of both the emoluments as well as of wage rate was higher than that of employees. Index of real emoluments and real wage rate increased at a slower rate than of GVA.

Table 7.14 shows the indices of various economic parameters in case of industries in Punjab. Index of real GVA increased at an average rate of 7.968 percent per annum. The overall trend rate of real GVA was 27.629 per annum. Coefficient of variation was found to be 0.576.

Index of real emoluments increased at an average rate of 7.026 percent per annum. The overall trend rate was found to be 19.31 per annum. Coefficient of variation was found to be 0.527.

Index of real GFC rose at an average rate of 6.974 percent per annum. The overall trend rate was 19.877 per annum. Coefficient of variation was found to be 0.587.

Consumer price index for industrial workers increased at an average annual rate of 7.864 percent. The overall trend rate was 24.267 per annum. Coefficient of variation was found to be 0.608.

Index of real wage rate increased at an average annual rate of 3.333 percent. The overall trend rate was 4.932 per annum. Coefficient of variation was found to be 0.28.

TABLE 7.14
Different Economic Parameters of Industries in Punjab

Year	*Index of Real GVA*	*Index of Real Emoluments*	*Index of Real GFC*	*Index of CPI-IW*	*Index of Real Wage Rate*	*Index of Employees*
1973-74	100.00	100.00	100.00	100.00	100.00	100.00
1974-75	106.51	93.30	96.93	130.04	91.07	102.44
1975-76	132.52	110.34	109.89	129.62	98.96	111.50
1976-77	154.84	124.59	133.20	127.60	101.04	123.31
1977-78	167.41	138.58	150.32	135.61	105.54	131.31
1978-79	208.41	162.74	158.21	139.64	110.97	146.66
1979-80	231.27	175.07	183.02	149.63	108.46	161.42
1980-81	217.92	187.65	170.98	166.82	127.83	146.80
1981-82	221.86	200.01	175.34	186.83	122.42	163.38
1982-83	226.94	224.29	206.78	196.86	136.41	164.42
1983-84	254.36	236.25	235.37	215.28	137.40	171.95
1984-85	270.41	278.55	247.16	231.26	144.46	192.83
1985-86	313.55	287.75	267.88	246.86	147.48	195.11
1986-87	308.74	290.13	269.47	263.68	150.91	192.25
1987-88	391.48	345.92	356.70	301.73	145.34	238.01
1988-89	373.74	367.97	336.48	322.91	157.00	234.37
1989-90	653.34	442.62	374.92	343.58	176.53	250.74
1990-91	529.05	473.18	386.87	364.25	189.03	250.32
1991-92	525.64	361.26	535.78	401.64	150.62	239.85
1992-93	491.17	509.99	608.31	433.13	193.31	263.82
1993-94	639.97	390.64	653.64	468.60	143.02	273.14
1994-95	681.62	543.68	629.14	513.87	197.72	274.98
1995-96	705.99	693.83	660.58	547.33	235.06	295.17
1996-97	800.70	642.90	693.65	586.74	215.18	298.77
1997-98	807.30	646.01	712.47	618.23	223.37	289.21
1998-99	739.87	439.20	376.78	726.52	218.29	201.20
1999-00	811.20	430.06	387.80	746.20	203.41	211.42
2000-01	588.40	449.35	304.18	763.92	200.74	223.85
Growth Rate	7.968* (19.575)	7.026* (13.977)	6.974* (10.117)	7.864* (68.235)	3.333* (15.374)	3.573* (9.510)
Linear Slope	27.629* (15.229)	19.310* (10.747)	19.877* (7.273)	24.267* (18.033)	4.932* (13.628)	6.418* (8.824)
CV	0.576	0.527	0.587	0.608	0.280	0.302

Notes : 1. Figures in parentheses are the respective 't' values.
2. *Indicates one percent level of significance.

Table 7.15
Different Economic Parameters of Industries in Rajasthan

Year	Index of Real GVA	Index of Real Emoluments	Index of Real GFC	Index of CPI-IW	Index of Real Wage Rate	Index of Employees
1973-74	100.00	100.00	100.00	100.00	100.00	100.00
1974-75	101.67	96.06	93.14	127.25	72.79	131.98
1975-76	133.75	134.21	130.71	118.68	86.10	155.89
1976-77	143.82	148.03	132.22	117.89	89.56	165.28
1977-78	158.01	152.18	148.49	130.34	86.21	176.52
1978-79	188.71	170.50	161.26	132.69	95.81	177.95
1979-80	215.75	191.44	168.86	142.00	91.32	209.65
1980-81	190.89	210.66	194.92	149.63	102.07	206.39
1981-82	194.54	195.05	201.81	185.25	91.64	212.84
1982-83	200.80	234.99	230.07	196.91	100.95	232.77
1983-84	295.00	253.78	162.74	209.77	103.82	244.43
1984-85	250.79	261.63	282.06	222.97	109.89	238.08
1985-86	277.57	287.05	322.30	244.00	122.67	234.01
1986-87	334.97	279.22	321.99	264.62	122.30	228.32
1987-88	288.42	301.16	345.82	294.62	119.00	253.08
1988-89	321.33	297.66	363.10	316.39	119.41	249.29
1989-90	384.79	350.32	353.03	345.29	124.78	280.74
1990-91	460.41	340.87	405.43	374.14	130.80	260.60
1991-92	461.00	348.36	404.42	427.35	129.79	268.39
1992-93	559.97	370.62	619.31	478.53	131.65	281.53
1993-94	546.85	385.23	489.71	498.26	141.58	272.08
1994-95	719.49	416.68	761.48	551.42	141.30	294.88
1995-96	758.17	463.60	704.22	600.65	146.08	317.35
1996-97	979.68	466.92	739.45	653.81	144.99	322.04
1997-98	1008.66	460.35	779.60	703.04	145.13	317.19
1998-99	586.88	375.98	586.52	772.00	146.58	256.49
1999-00	834.03	337.42	862.74	809.42	133.16	253.39
2000-01	743.80	333.53	558.05	852.72	133.03	250.72
Growth Rate	8.450* (21.836)	5.152* (12.105)	8.240* (19.705)	8.601* (56.768)	2.253* (12.501)	2.835* (8.037)
Linear Slope	30.110* (11.529)	12.350* (12.607)	26.608* (12.705)	27.525* (16.710)	2.502* (13.567)	5.842* (8.995)
CV	0.663	0.385	0.622	0.662	0.189	0.235

Notes : 1. Figures in parentheses are the respective 't' values.
2. *Indicates one percent level of significance.

Index of employees increased at an average rate of 3.573 percent per annum. The overall trend rate was 6.418 per annum. Coefficient of variation was found to be 0.302.

An inter-variable comparison in this State revealed that the maximum growth rate was in GVA and minimum in wage rate. The highest variability was found in CPI-IW and least in the wage rate. It was perceived that the growth rates and variability of both the emoluments as well as of employees were higher than that of wage rate. The growth rates of real emoluments and real wage rate were commensurate with growth rate in GVA.

Table 7.15 shows the indices of various economic parameters in case of industries in Rajasthan. Index of real GVA increased at an average rate of 8.45 percent per annum. The overall trend rate was 30.11 per annum. Coefficient of variation was found to be 0.663.

Index of real emoluments increased at the average annual rate of 5.152 percent per annum. The overall trend rate was found to be 12.35 per annum. Coefficient of variation was found to be 0.385.

Index of real GFC rose at an average rate of 8.24 percent per annum. The overall trend rate was 26.608 per annum. Coefficient of variation was found to be 0.622.

Consumer price index for industrial workers increased at an average annual rate of 8.601 percent. The overall trend rate was 27.525 per annum. Coefficient of variation was found to be 0.662.

Index of real wage rate increased at an average annual rate of 2.253 percent. The overall trend rate was 2.502 per annum. Coefficient of variation was found to be 0.189.

Index of employees increased at an average rate of 2.835 percent per annum. The overall trend rate was 5.842 per annum. Coefficient of variation was found to be 0.235.

An inter-variable comparison in this State revealed that the maximum growth rate was in CPI-IW and minimum in wage rate. The highest variability was found in GVA and least in the wage rate. It was perceived that the growth rates and variability of both the emoluments as well as of employees were higher than that of wage rate. Increase in wage rate was somewhat on lower side as compared to increase in GVA.

TABLE 7.16
Different Economic Parameters of Industries in Tamil Nadu

Year	Index of Real GVA	Index of Real Emoluments	Index of Real GFC	Index of CPI-IW	Index of Real Wage Rate	Index of Employees
1973-74	100.00	100.00	100.00	100.00	100.00	100.00
1974-75	88.26	96.80	80.57	131.42	76.72	126.16
1975-76	99.75	110.14	80.78	137.15	82.19	134.02
1976-77	122.06	124.14	89.71	125.80	88.81	139.78
1977-78	136.70	130.07	103.54	135.81	88.41	147.12
1978-79	160.17	142.71	108.10	138.87	94.32	151.30
1979-80	153.82	147.71	106.69	152.84	89.31	165.39
1980-81	149.87	156.79	109.15	169.43	94.28	166.31
1981-82	158.88	156.85	121.53	194.81	91.10	172.17
1982-83	179.29	162.96	132.63	207.44	95.51	170.62
1983-84	184.09	163.18	151.82	240.20	95.93	170.10
1984-85	296.29	179.79	165.82	251.61	97.20	184.97
1985-86	220.86	185.28	211.92	275.16	103.44	179.12
1986-87	230.03	192.91	213.89	297.43	108.63	177.59
1987-88	234.97	199.98	253.46	330.62	107.91	185.31
1988-89	282.62	210.61	283.04	350.32	112.20	187.71
1989-90	329.96	235.87	295.85	364.99	120.08	196.43
1990-91	363.10	253.14	326.29	379.71	125.71	201.37
1991-92	346.67	251.74	375.85	431.58	121.16	207.78
1992-93	380.92	231.76	459.09	493.79	103.73	223.41
1993-94	461.06	235.13	552.53	535.33	101.46	231.75
1994-95	497.35	291.27	669.72	595.50	120.98	240.76
1995-96	542.17	308.69	615.42	684.69	119.25	258.86
1996-97	585.33	306.76	660.98	738.65	119.51	256.69
1997-98	540.23	334.38	653.92	792.61	123.05	271.75
1998-99	474.41	304.33	642.17	881.80	129.39	235.21
1999-00	494.65	255.17	584.53	925.37	110.49	230.94
2000-01	512.91	270.56	547.39	985.55	113.82	237.70
Growth Rate	7.272* (22.344)	4.282* (18.448)	9.497* (22.447)	8.836* (54.998)	1.429* (8.013)	2.812* (15.239)
Linear Slope	18.742* (16.919)	8.049* (16.648)	24.874* (13.550)	31.233* (15.051)	1.456* (7.912)	5.072* (16.491)
CV	0.541	0.338	0.704	0.687	0.136	0.229

Notes : 1. Figures in parentheses are the respective 't' values.
2. *Indicates one percent level of significance.

Table 7.16 shows the indices of various economic parameters in case of industries in Tamil Nadu. Index of real GVA rose at an average rate of 7.272 percent per annum. The overall trend rate was 18.742 per annum. Coefficient of variation was found to be 0.541.

Index of real emoluments increased at an average rate of 4.282 percent per annum. The overall trend rate was found to be 8.049 per annum. Coefficient of variation was found to be 0.338.

Index of real GFC rose at an average rate of 9.497 percent per annum. The overall trend rate was 24.874 per annum. Coefficient of variation was found to be 0.704.

Consumer price index for industrial workers increased at an average annual rate of 8.836 percent. The overall trend rate was 31.233. Coefficient of variation was found to be 0.687.

Index of real wage rate increased at an average annual rate of 1.429 percent. The overall trend rate was 1.456 per annum. Coefficient of variation was found to be 0.136.

Index of employees increased at an average rate of 2.812 percent per annum. The overall trend rate was 5.072 per annum. Coefficient of variation was found to be 0.229.

An inter-variable comparison in this State revealed that the maximum growth rate and variability were in GFC and minimum in wage rate. It was found that the growth rates and variability of both the emoluments as well as of employees were higher than that of wage rate. Increase in wage rate was somewhat on lower side as compared to increase in GVA.

Table 7.17 shows the indices of various economic parameters in case of industries in Uttar Pradesh. Index of real GVA increased at an average rate of 7.924 percent per annum.

The overall trend rate was 23.134 per annum. Coefficient of variation was found to be 0.608.

Index of real emoluments increased at an average rate of 4.409 percent per annum. The overall trend rate was found to be 11.044 per annum. Coefficient of variation was found to be 0.365.

Index of real GFC rose at an average rate of 9.097 percent per annum. The overall trend rate was 22.462 per annum. Coefficient of variation was found to be 0.666.

TABLE 7.17
Different Economic Parameters of Industries in Uttar Pradesh

Year	*Index of Real GVA*	*Index of Real Emoluments*	*Index of Real GFC*	*Index of CPI-IW*	*Index of Real Wage Rate*	*Index of Employees*
1973-74	100.00	100.00	100.00	100.00	100.00	100.00
1974-75	104.47	127.60	90.46	106.96	111.06	114.89
1975-76	110.32	148.88	43.66	98.72	121.00	123.04
1976-77	138.55	158.73	58.94	97.04	118.36	134.11
1977-78	130.14	175.79	125.90	108.96	113.30	155.15
1978-79	148.25	185.21	132.81	111.24	120.21	154.07
1979-80	144.25	203.51	124.83	117.87	126.29	161.14
1980-81	130.12	215.13	125.93	130.75	123.25	174.55
1981-82	234.86	221.07	143.36	144.94	126.48	174.79
1982-83	231.47	270.37	177.68	156.18	146.86	184.10
1983-84	189.98	263.20	188.70	174.65	160.38	164.11
1984-85	198.11	294.73	201.10	182.57	173.63	169.75
1985-86	192.87	264.51	192.44	203.40	171.02	154.67
1986-87	288.52	275.34	224.91	221.87	174.84	157.48
1987-88	306.06	298.72	259.03	241.02	175.23	170.48
1988-89	326.70	345.14	255.36	257.22	201.77	171.06
1989-90	433.41	376.13	293.60	280.09	208.33	180.55
1990-91	433.25	377.81	332.68	303.00	211.40	178.71
1991-92	494.05	292.38	423.14	346.70	171.28	170.71
1992-93	506.58	394.99	494.76	379.53	221.82	178.07
1993-94	574.31	331.46	575.99	399.84	188.14	176.17
1994-95	645.72	437.16	589.28	434.19	253.80	172.25
1995-96	645.63	441.79	526.81	479.49	244.64	180.59
1996-97	719.01	480.72	614.52	512.28	261.36	183.93
1997-98	798.38	483.95	649.60	548.18	275.06	175.94
1998-99	537.04	388.41	726.95	641.90	276.07	140.69
1999-00	500.66	294.05	461.64	668.45	227.07	129.50
2000-01	446.91	288.82	400.44	668.45	236.25	122.25
Growth Rate	7.924* (15.014)	4.409* (9.098)	9.097* (14.013)	8.242* (45.936)	3.695* (16.599)	0.688*** (1.896)
Linear Slope	23.134* (10.699)	11.044* (8.511)	22.462* (11.167)	21.724* (16.059)	6.297* (14.752)	0.976*** (1.870)
CV	0.608	0.365	0.666	0.647	0.305	0.147

Notes : 1. Figures in parentheses are the respective 't' values.
2. * indicates one percent level of significance.
3. *** indicates 10 percent level of significance.

TABLE 7.18

Different Economic Parameters of Industries in West Bengal

Year	*Index of Real GVA*	*Index of Real Emoluments*	*Index of Real GFC*	*Index of CPI-IW*	*Index of Real Wage Rate*	*Index of Employees*
1973-74	100.00	100.00	100.00	100.00	100.00	100.00
1974-75	100.18	89.61	84.65	126.31	91.86	97.54
1975-76	109.08	102.52	86.09	125.91	100.87	101.63
1976-77	111.10	101.64	95.94	130.29	103.63	98.08
1977-78	112.23	103.94	102.16	140.37	100.00	103.94
1978-79	127.06	104.69	104.05	145.16	100.95	103.70
1979-80	121.27	117.46	103.38	153.98	108.88	107.89
1980-81	118.75	121.26	115.15	167.54	114.55	105.85
1981-82	114.51	118.65	126.44	181.60	115.56	102.67
1982-83	123.72	118.34	145.35	196.12	112.49	105.20
1983-84	117.97	113.38	153.00	224.14	113.95	99.50
1984-85	124.02	119.01	161.43	252.67	116.62	102.05
1985-86	126.47	106.90	194.90	267.59	119.22	89.66
1986-87	119.53	106.50	148.30	294.35	125.59	84.81
1987-88	142.16	104.54	197.70	307.51	127.99	81.68
1988-89	118.70	106.02	213.13	343.50	124.96	84.85
1989-90	117.09	104.33	232.14	363.96	127.14	82.06
1990-91	142.89	114.29	244.80	384.38	138.72	82.39
1991-92	149.20	111.47	337.13	427.52	131.04	85.06
1992-93	154.55	118.71	463.01	466.73	140.68	84.38
1993-94	177.92	116.12	551.51	504.03	141.41	82.12
1994-95	166.80	118.05	524.52	549.09	142.13	83.06
1995-96	181.39	128.01	480.71	611.90	139.53	91.74
1996-97	206.41	123.02	517.61	666.78	150.41	81.79
1997-98	233.36	134.65	492.09	704.03	143.26	93.99
1998-99	159.77	123.43	197.50	815.83	162.03	76.17
1999-00	138.95	95.43	277.51	857.01	145.73	65.48
2000-01	131.43	94.40	258.54	884.48	149.00	63.36
Growth Rate	2.034* (6.515)	0.415*** (1.907)	6.725* (8.926)	8.448* (77.523)	1.808* (21.126)	-1.368* (-7.102)
Linear Slope	2.880* (5.644)	0.475*** (1.992)	14.449* (6.102)	28.117* (16.427)	2.205* (20.921)	-1.200* (-7.293)
CV	0.232	0.096	0.646	0.652	0.150	0.133

Notes : 1. Figures in parentheses are the respective 't' values.

2. *Indicates one percent level of significance.

3. **Indicates 10 percent level of significance.

Consumer price index for industrial workers increased at an average annual rate of 8.242 percent per annum. The overall trend rate was 21.724 per annum. Coefficient of variation was found to be 0.647.

Index of real wage rate increased at an average annual rate of 3.695 percent. The overall trend rate was 6.297 per annum. Coefficient of variation was found to be 0.305.

Index of employees increased at an average rate of 0.688 percent per annum. The overall trend rate was 0.976 per annum. Coefficient of variation was found to be 0.147.

An inter-variable comparison in this state revealed that the maximum growth rate and variability were in GFC and minimum in case of employees. It was found that the growth rates and variability of both the emoluments as well as of wage rate were higher than that of employees. Real emoluments and real wage rate in this State increased at reasonable rates as compared to GVA.

Table 7.18 shows the indices of various economic parameters in case of industries in West Bengal. Index of real GVA rose at an average rate of 2.034 percent per annum. The overall trend rate was 2.88 per annum. Coefficient of variation was found to be 0.232.

Index of real emoluments increased marginally at an average rate of 0.415 percent per annum. The overall trend rate was found to be 0.475 per annum. Coefficient of variation was found to be 0.096.

Index of real GFC increased at an average rate of 6.725 percent per annum. The overall trend rate was 14.449 per annum. Coefficient of variation was found to be 0.646.

Consumer price index for industrial workers increased at an average annual rate of 8.448 percent. The overall trend rate was 28.117 per annum. Coefficient of variation was found to be 0.652.

Index of real wage rate increased at an average annual rate of 1.808 percent. The overall trend rate was 2.205 per annum. Coefficient of variation was found to be 0.150.

Index of employees decreased at an average rate of 1.368 percent per annum. The overall trend rate was—1.20 per

TABLE 7.19

Different Economic Parameters of Industries in All India

Year	*Index of Real GVA*	*Index of Real Emoluments*	*Index of Real GFC*	*Index of CPI-IW*	*Index of Real Wage Rate*	*Index of Employees*
1973-74	100.00	100.00	100.00	100.00	100.00	100.00
1974-75	102.71	96.28	86.57	126.84	92.58	104.00
1975-76	108.77	110.66	91.69	125.24	100.93	109.63
1976-77	122.14	120.86	106.99	120.42	105.79	114.25
1977-78	129.72	129.52	126.83	129.65	106.27	121.87
1978-79	152.21	139.34	141.16	132.46	111.89	124.54
1979-80	147.91	149.24	142.92	144.05	113.12	131.93
1980-81	138.91	152.05	145.60	160.46	114.71	132.55
1981-82	153.23	150.29	151.86	180.48	112.46	133.64
1982-83	168.32	165.57	177.63	194.48	120.31	137.63
1983-84	191.63	170.91	198.91	215.86	127.13	134.43
1984-85	189.76	185.93	211.21	229.45	137.47	135.25
1985-86	197.07	181.00	226.65	245.01	140.99	128.38
1986-87	208.35	184.74	231.96	266.43	144.48	127.87
1987-88	221.91	194.48	278.52	289.76	145.38	133.77
1988-89	247.45	198.56	276.34	317.01	149.24	133.05
1989-90	283.39	218.99	307.68	336.43	156.52	139.91
1990-91	309.34	219.51	351.67	375.31	156.52	140.25
1991-92	413.80	197.06	407.43	425.89	139.97	140.78
1992-93	356.56	233.45	523.81	466.73	156.08	149.57
1993-94	405.33	228.43	582.53	501.76	152.67	149.62
1994-95	435.07	256.07	618.86	552.33	163.73	156.40
1995-96	509.44	296.63	654.95	608.68	171.87	172.59
1996-97	552.09	279.10	683.07	665.13	171.91	162.35
1997-98	564.79	293.70	720.49	711.79	169.74	173.03
1998-99	469.98	221.81	654.42	805.17	150.31	147.57
1999-00	483.31	230.03	577.07	832.36	163.81	140.43
2000-01	425.00	235.07	536.48	863.47	171.28	137.25
Growth Rate	6.942* (23.364)	3.611* (13.738)	8.671* (23.948)	8.600* (57.219)	2.236* (15.364)	1.344* (7.761)
Linear Slope	17.423* (14.233)	6.309* (12.823)	24.603* (13.668)	27.286* (15.853)	2.924* (16.088)	1.774* (7.562)
CV	0.547	0.293	0.649	0.669	0.184	0.130

Notes : 1. Figures in parentheses are the respective 't' values.
2. *Indicates one percent level of significance.

annum. Coefficient of variation was found to be 0.133.

An inter-variable comparison in this State revealed that the maximum growth rate and variability were in CPI-IW and negative growth rate in case of employees and least variability in emoluments. The growth rate of wage rate was higher than that of employees as well as emoluments, but lesser than the GVA.

Table 7.19 shows the indices of various economic parameters in case of industries at All-India level. Index of real GVA rose at an average rate of 6.942 percent per annum. The overall trend rate of real GVA was 17.423 per annum. Coefficient of variation was found to be 0.547.

Index of real emoluments increased at an average rate of 3.611 percent per annum. The overall trend rate was found to be 6.309 per annum. Coefficient of variation was found to be 0.293.

Index of real GFC rose at an average rate of 8.671 percent per annum. The overall trend rate was 24.603 per annum. Coefficient of variation was found to be 0.649.

Consumer price index for industrial workers increased at an average annual rate of 8.60 percent. The overall trend rate was 27.286 per annum. Coefficient of variation was found to be 0.669.

Index of real wage rate increased at an average annual rate of 2.236 percent. The overall trend rate was 2.924 per annum. Coefficient of variation was found to be 0.184.

Index of employees increased at an average rate of 1.344 percent per annum. The overall trend rate was 1.774 per annum. Coefficient of variation was found to be 0.130.

An inter-variable comparison at all-India level revealed that the maximum growth rate was in GFC and minimum in case of employees. The highest variability was found in CPI-IW and least in case of employees. It was perceived that the growth rates and variability of both the emoluments as well as of wage rate were higher than that of employees. Index of real emoluments and real wage rate increased at a slower rate than of GVA.

Inter-State Comparison

The maximum growth rate in the index of real GVA and

real GFC were found in Himachal Pradesh and minimum growth in real GVA and negative growth in real GFC was in Bihar. The highest variability for these variables was seen in Gujarat, but the least for real GVA was found in West Bengal and for real GFC was in Bihar.

The highest growth rate in real emoluments was seen in Haryana and least in Bihar, while the maximum variability was observed in Himachal Pradesh and minimum in West Bengal.

The maximum growth rate and variability in real wage rate were found in Uttar Pradesh and minimum in Tamil Nadu.

The maximum growth rate in case of employees was perceived in Himachal Pradesh and minimum was in Bihar. The highest variability was in Himachal Pradesh and least was in Maharashtra.

It may be concluded from the discussion in this chapter that the trend in share of labour was declining in all states, but minimum decline was found in Assam, Haryana and Punjab followed by Kerala and maximum was in Madhya Pradesh. Generally at different points of time, the value of share of labour in real GVA was highest in West Bengal and this perhaps indicates the policy emphasis at state level. The real wage rate in all the states showed rising trend. The maximum average annual growth rate in real wage rate was observed in Uttar Pradesh followed by Haryana and minimum growth was in Tamil Nadu. The index of GVA increased at a higher rate as compared to real wage rate in all states except Bihar. The comparative profile of different economic parameters in States like Andhra Pradesh, Gujarat, Haryana, Himachal Pradesh, Karnataka, Orissa, Punjab, Rajasthan, Tamil Nadu, and Uttar Pradesh with All-India showed that these States were performing better than All-India average, while States like Assam, Bihar, Kerala, Maharashtra, and West Bengal were on lower side as compared to All-India average.

Profile of Partial and Total Factor Productivities of Industries in States

In this chapter empirical results regarding the trends in partial productivity (both labour and capital), total factor productivity (Kendrick, Solow and Translog) and capital intensity in case of industries in sixteen States and All-India are estimated for all industries.

Table 8.1 presents the empirical results in case of industries in Andhra Pradesh. Index of partial labour productivity increased at an average annual rate of 4.908 percent. The overall trend rate was 7.081 per annum. Coefficient of variation was found to be 0.415.

The index of partial capital productivity declined at an average annual rate of 2.232 percent. The overall trend rate of capital productivity was –1.861 per annum. The coefficient of variation was found to be 0.264.

The index of capital intensity increased at an average annual rate of 7.304 percent. The overall trend rate was 12.912 per annum. Coefficient of variation was found to be 0.611.

Index of TFPK increased at an average annual rate of 1.678

TABLE 8.1

Productivity Indices of Industries in Andhra Pradesh

Year	*Index of Partial Labour Productivity*	*Index of Partial Capital Productivity*	*Index of Real Capital Intensity*	*Index of TFPK*	*Index of TFPS*	*Index of TFPT*
1973-74	100.00	100.00	100.00	100.00	100.00	100.00
1974-75	78.95	101.21	78.01	84.70	90.70	91.14
1975-76	91.51	120.58	75.89	98.89	107.60	108.08
1976-77	85.36	117.63	72.57	93.32	102.24	102.71
1977-78	84.52	102.95	82.09	89.42	92.80	93.26
1978-79	89.86	109.38	82.15	95.05	99.17	99.66
1979-80	81.78	97.03	84.28	85.88	87.90	88.46
1980-81	80.08	84.15	95.16	81.13	81.16	81.17
1981-82	79.39	94.79	83.75	83.52	86.34	86.28
1982-83	102.77	107.06	96.00	103.84	105.67	104.95
1983-84	131.34	112.17	117.09	124.23	119.56	119.04
1984-85	145.13	113.02	128.41	132.71	124.65	124.31
1985-86	132.30	88.55	149.41	113.97	102.59	102.12
1986-87	131.15	86.01	152.48	112.04	100.39	99.98
1987-88	112.88	69.40	162.65	93.81	81.82	81.20
1988-89	142.33	77.54	183.55	112.06	96.81	96.15
1989-90	141.17	74.30	190.00	109.36	93.56	92.82
1990-91	174.16	49.80	349.69	96.64	62.60	61.31
1991-92	174.09	45.19	385.25	90.86	58.14	56.93
1992-93	190.07	46.23	411.11	95.09	61.08	59.81
1993-94	209.04	44.88	465.80	96.15	61.57	60.23
1994-95	229.99	60.80	378.30	121.44	78.75	77.02
1995-96	237.63	85.12	279.17	150.75	98.11	96.47
1996-97	279.23	87.62	318.69	163.97	103.86	102.21
1997-98	221.25	72.27	306.13	133.07	81.69	80.30
1998-99	237.44	66.39	357.64	129.91	79.13	77.61
1999-00	241.59	79.40	304.27	145.82	89.60	87.71
2000-01	223.63	80.35	278.32	142.11	88.28	83.66
Growth Rate	4.908* (13.994)	-2.232* (-4.174)	7.304* (11.109)	1.678* (4.921)	-0.933** (-2.197)	-1.071* (-2.948)
Linear Slope	7.081* (12.916)	-1.861* (-4.792)	12.912* (8.018)	1.910* (4.913)	-0.800** (-2.204)	-0.916** (-2.529)
CV	0.415	0.264	0.611	0.206	0.183	0.189

Notes : 1. Figures in parentheses are the respective 't' values.

2. * Indicates one percent level of significance.

3. ** Indicates 5 percent level of significance.

percent. The overall trend rate for Kendrick index was 1.910 per annum. Coefficient of variation was found to be 0.206.

Index of TFPS decreased at an average annual rate of 0.933 percent. The overall trend rate for Solow index was –0.80 per annum. Coefficient of variation was found to be 0.183.

Index of TFPT declined at an average annual rate of 1.071 percent. The overall trend rate for Translog index was –0.916 per annum. Coefficient of variation was found to be 0.189.

An inter-variable comparison in this State revealed that the maximum growth rate and variability were observed in capital intensity followed by labour productivity and negative growth was in capital productivity and least variability in TFPS.

RELATIONSHIP OF TOTAL FACTOR PRODUCTIVITY WITH PARTIAL PRODUCTIVITIES OF CAPITAL AND LABOUR

The regression models in which total factor productivity (Kendrick, Solow & Translog) depended upon trend, labour and capital productivity were estimated. The estimated equations are :

$$\ln TFPK_t = -0.32 + 0.023 \ln t + 0.544 \ln LP_t + 0.514 \ln CP_t$$

(-1.899) (1.968) (23.479) (20.859)

$R^2 = 0.980$; $\tilde{R}^2 = 0.978$; $S = 0.029$

F ratio = 401.61; D–W = 0.615; $\tilde{p} = 0.623$

$$\ln TFPS_t = 0.475 + 0.022 \ln t + 0.131 \ln LP_t + 0.753 \ln CP_t$$

(1.315) (0.872) (2.637) (14.234)

$R^2 = 0.908$; $\tilde{R}^2 = 0.896$; $S = 0.063$

F ratio = 78.87; D-W = 0.507; $\tilde{p} = 0.695$

$$\ln TFPT_t = 0.526 + 0.02 \ln t + 0.112 \ln LP_t + 0.762 \ln CP_t$$

(1.391) (0.757) (2.154) (13.759)

$R^2 = 0.906$; $\tilde{R}^2 = 0.894$; $S = 0.066$

F ratio = 76.67; D–W = 0.513; $\tilde{p} = 0.668$

Both labour productivity and capital productivity significantly affected the total factor productivity, indicating consistency and strength of the relationship between labour productivity, capital productivity and total factor productivity as measured through Kendrick, Solow and Translog indices.

Table 8.2 shows the productivity indices in case of industries in Assam. Index of partial labour productivity increased at an average annual rate of 3.595 percent per annum. The overall trend rate was 5.283 per annum. Coefficient of variation was found to be 0.347.

The index of partial capital productivity declined at an average annual rate of 1.966 percent. The overall trend rate of capital productivity was –1.821 per annum. The coefficient of variation was found to be 0.316.

The index of capital intensity increased at an average annual rate of 5.736 percent. The overall trend rate was 10.033 per annum. Coefficient of variation was found to be 0.545.

Index of TFPK decreased at an average annual rate of 0.161 percent. The overall trend rate for Kendrick index was –0.404 per annum. Coefficient of variation was found to be 0.248.

Index of TFPS decreased at an average annual rate of 8.080 percent. The overall trend rate for Solow index was –3.008 per annum. Coefficient of variation was found to be 0.636.

Index of TFPT decreased at an average annual rate of 7.356 percent. The overall trend rate for Translog index was –3.042 per annum. Coefficient of variation was found to be 0.660.

An inter-variable comparison in this State revealed that the maximum growth rate was in capital intensity followed by labour productivity and negative was in TFPS. The highest variability was found in TFPT and minimum was in TFPK.

RELATIONSHIP OF TOTAL FACTOR PRODUCTIVITY WITH PARTIAL PRODUCTIVITIES OF CAPITAL AND LABOUR

The estimated regression model in which total factor productivity (Kendrick) depended upon trend, labour and capital productivity are given as under :

Table 8.2
Productivity Indices of Industries in Assam

Year	*Index of Partial Labour Productivity*	*Index of Partial Capital Productivity*	*Index of Real Capital Intensity*	*Index of TFPK*	*Index of TFPS*	*Index of TFPT*
1973-74	100.00	100.00	100.00	100.00	100.00	100.00
1974-75	105.60	177.38	64.56	144.11	150.00	149.12
1975-76	102.13	94.90	116.71	99.26	49.50	48.95
1976-77	125.99	111.43	122.63	120.93	60.50	59.78
1977-78	136.47	127.25	116.31	136.03	68.80	67.93
1978-79	121.23	112.83	116.53	122.20	62.04	61.27
1979-80	98.19	117.56	90.58	115.52	59.37	57.67
1980-81	65.25	82.46	85.82	82.62	43.62	42.49
1981-82	74.69	107.70	75.21	98.23	51.21	50.00
1982-83	82.00	117.50	75.69	106.97	55.50	54.18
1983-84	118.48	158.46	81.09	144.62	76.03	74.10
1984-85	161.76	141.79	123.72	153.53	73.86	71.50
1985-86	200.00	184.14	117.79	192.84	93.36	90.40
1986-87	213.45	128.46	180.20	156.38	64.75	62.86
1987-88	201.97	134.01	163.44	159.02	66.11	63.95
1988-89	134.94	63.91	228.97	91.65	24.98	22.62
1989-90	237.48	149.52	172.25	178.74	45.43	41.15
1990-91	236.32	136.33	187.99	168.09	42.50	38.57
1991-92	191.94	93.89	221.70	125.86	28.66	26.18
1992-93	176.42	77.02	248.43	108.65	24.16	22.02
1993-94	195.91	80.98	262.36	112.36	24.90	22.71
1994-95	182.85	75.01	264.36	105.09	23.14	21.11
1995-96	187.37	77.86	260.96	108.55	24.03	21.92
1996-97	199.11	99.58	216.84	129.93	27.54	24.94
1997-98	179.34	55.18	352.49	82.61	12.74	10.49
1998-99	249.11	105.98	254.91	141.94	17.78	14.66
1999-00	265.45	123.23	233.61	159.78	19.89	16.33
2000-01	189.60	41.62	493.99	67.63	1.11	6.73
Growth Rate	3.595* (5.828)	-1.966** (-2.744)	5.736* (9.198)	-0.161NS (-0.265)	-8.080* (-5.984)	-7.356* (-8.83)
Linear Slope	5.283* (6.219)	-1.821** (-2.435)	10.033* (8.008)	-0.404NS (-0.054)	-3.008* (-6.423)	-3.042* (-6.584)
CV	0.347	0.316	0.545	0.248	0.636	0.66

Notes :
1. Figures in parentheses are the respective 't' values.
2. * Indicates one percent level of significance.
3. ** Indicate 5 percent level of significance.
4. NS Indicates non-significant.

$$\ln TFPK_t = 0.202 + 0.016 \ln t + 0.298 \ln LP_t + 0.66 \ln CP_t$$
$$(1.967) \quad (1.618) \qquad (14.993) \qquad (37.762)$$
$$R^2 = 0.989; \quad \tilde{R}^2 = 0.988; \quad S = 0.028$$
$$F \text{ ratio} = 739.01; \quad D\text{–}W = 1.084; \quad \tilde{p} = 0.349$$

$$\ln TFPS_t = -2.248 - 0.275 \ln t - 0.459 \ln LP_t + 1.908 \ln CP_t$$
$$(-1.506) \quad (-1.95) \qquad (-1.585) \qquad (7.497)$$
$$R^2 = 0.822; \quad \tilde{R}^2 = 0.8; \quad S = 0.407$$
$$F \text{ ratio} = 37.03; \quad D\text{–}W = 0.79; \quad \tilde{p} = 0.341$$

$$\ln TFPT_t = -0.105 - 0.038 \ln t - 0.369 \ln LP_t + 1.383 \ln CP_t$$
$$(-0.125) \quad (-4.239) \qquad (-2.254) \qquad (9.611)$$
$$R^2 = 0.911; \quad \tilde{R}^2 = 0.899; \quad S = 0.23$$
$$F \text{ ratio} = 81.43; \quad D\text{-}W = 0.674; \quad \tilde{p} = 0.66$$

Both labour productivity and capital productivity significantly affected the total factor productivity as measured through Kendrick index only.

Table 8.3 presents the empirical results in case of industries in Bihar. Index of partial labour productivity increased at an average rate of 5.102 percent per annum. The overall trend rate was 9.426 per annum. Coefficient of variation was found to be 0.524.

The index of partial capital productivity declined at an average annual rate of 1.966 percent. The overall trend rate was –1.821 per annum. The coefficient of variation was found to be 0.316.

The index of capital intensity increased at an average annual rate of 2.707 percent. The overall trend rate was 5.968 per annum. Coefficient of variation was found to be 0.371.

Index of TFPK increased at an average annual rate of 3.209 percent. The overall trend rate for Kendrick index was 4.279 per annum. Coefficient of variation was found to be 0.339.

Index of TFPS increased at an average annual rate of 2.445 percent. The overall trend rate for Solow index was 2.452 per annum. Coefficient of variation was found to be 0.313.

TABLE 8.3
Productivity Indices of Industries in Bihar

Year	Index of Partial Labour Productivity	Index of Partial Capital Productivity	Index of Real Capital Intensity	Index of TFPK	Index of TFPS	Index of TFPT
1973-74	100.00	100.00	100.00	100.00	100.00	100.00
1974-75	103.95	145.82	76.27	130.86	131.91	131.73
1975-76	117.94	95.30	132.40	114.33	89.67	96.81
1976-77	92.60	64.65	153.24	86.92	68.02	74.03
1977-78	82.60	42.39	208.46	66.39	52.83	56.02
1978-79	103.33	53.68	205.96	85.83	69.21	73.41
1979-80	101.93	46.37	235.20	78.05	65.35	70.09
1980-81	73.58	44.79	175.76	70.86	51.66	58.19
1981-82	128.01	74.79	183.12	107.42	78.21	88.07
1982-83	147.52	75.11	210.11	112.45	83.41	93.08
1983-84	201.58	98.33	219.33	144.70	107.31	120.19
1984-85	139.45	66.01	226.01	106.82	80.36	89.88
1985-86	149.10	68.80	231.85	111.38	84.18	94.11
1986-87	156.10	74.31	224.74	112.77	84.51	94.62
1987-88	176.41	86.81	217.42	131.37	99.51	111.44
1988-89	224.50	124.42	193.05	173.54	128.23	143.41
1989-90	224.00	113.99	210.24	165.00	122.39	137.34
1990-91	202.37	107.23	201.91	156.88	116.08	130.58
1991-92	225.85	99.25	243.45	154.63	113.22	129.70
1992-93	211.43	81.92	276.15	136.68	101.38	114.14
1993-94	408.41	125.44	348.34	204.08	155.63	177.55
1994-95	237.11	66.80	379.78	117.16	87.45	99.63
1995-96	267.48	79.63	359.39	140.02	103.15	117.58
1996-97	299.21	84.94	376.89	148.78	110.33	125.38
1997-98	478.38	147.39	347.25	240.35	172.34	195.64
1998-99	386.77	123.33	335.52	217.54	168.45	191.15
1999-00	228.60	205.97	118.74	226.99	152.72	163.13
2000-01	154.07	127.80	128.98	157.45	105.40	112.16
Growth Rate	5.102* (7.700)	2.382* (2.993)	2.707* (3.334)	3.209* (6.130)	2.445* (4.110)	2.705* (4.693)
Linear Slope	9.426* (6.034)	2.194* (2.886)	5.968* (3.689)	4.279* (6.066)	2.452* (4.084)	3.008* (4.661)
CV	0.524	0.391	0.371	0.339	0.313	0.322

Notes : 1. Figures in parentheses are the respective 't' values.
2. * Indicates one percent level of significance.

Index of TFPT increased at an average annual rate of 2.705 percent. The overall trend rate for Translog index was 3.008 per annum. Coefficient of variation was found to be 0.322.

An inter-variable comparison in this State revealed that the maximum growth rate was labour productivity followed by TFPK and minimum in capital productivity. The maximum variability was found in labour productivity and least in TFPS.

RELATIONSHIP OF TOTAL FACTOR PRODUCTIVITY WITH PARTIAL PRODUCTIVITIES OF CAPITAL AND LABOUR

The regression models in which total factor productivity (Kendrick, Solow & Translog) depended upon trend, labour and capital productivity were estimated. The estimated equations are :

$$\ln TFPK_t = 0.884 + 0.058 \ln t + 0.279 \ln LP_t + 0.535 \ln CP_t$$
$$(11.484) \quad (5.373) \quad (12.398) \quad (27.195)$$
$$R^2 = 0.993; \quad \tilde{R}^2 = 0.993; \quad S = 0.029$$
$$F \text{ ratio} = 1208.90; \quad D\text{-}W = 1.503; \quad \tilde{p} = 0.214$$

$$\ln TFPS_t = 0.511 - 0.071 \ln t + 0.38 \ln LP_t + 0.513 \ln CP_t$$
$$(3.817) \quad (-3.788) \quad (9.693) \quad (14.985)$$
$$R^2 = 0.977; \quad \tilde{R}^2 \; 0.975; \quad S = 0.051$$
$$F \text{ ratio} = 345.04; \quad D\text{–}W = 2.126; \quad \tilde{p} = -0.068$$

$$\ln TFPT_t = 0.573 - 0.05 \ln t + 0.423 \ln LP_t + 0.46 \ln CP_t$$
$$(4.471) \quad (-2.776) \quad (11.288) \quad (14.029)$$
$$R^2 = 0.980; \quad \tilde{R}^2 = 0.978; \quad S = 0.048$$
$$F \text{ ratio} = 396.48; \quad D\text{–}W = 1.997; \quad \tilde{p} = -0.029$$

Both labour productivity and capital productivity significantly affected the total factor productivity, indicating consistency and strength in the relationship between labour productivity, capital productivity and total factor productivity as measured through Kendrick, Solow and Translog indices.

Table 8.4 presents the empirical results in case of industries in Gujarat. Index of partial labour productivity increased from 100.00 in 1973-74 to 313.22 in 2000-01. The index increased at an average annual rate of 6.098 percent per annum. The overall trend rate was 11.387 per annum. Coefficient of variation was found to be 0.533.

The index of partial capital productivity declined from 100.00 in 1973-74 to 38.59 in 2000-01. It decreased at an average annual rate of 3.379 percent. The overall trend rate of capital productivity was –2.314 per annum. The average annual growth rate and the trend rate were found statistically significant at one percent level of significance. The coefficient of variation was found to be 0.283.

The index of capital intensity increased from 100.00 in 1973-74 to 879.40 in 2000-01. The index increased at an average annual rate of 9.874 percent. The overall trend rate of capital intensity was 32.307 per annum. Coefficient of variation was found to be 0.793.

Index of TFPK increased marginally at an average annual rate of 0.565 percent. The overall trend rate for Kendrick index was 0.635 per annum. Coefficient of variation was found to be 0.104.

Index of TFPS declined at an average annual rate of 0.295 percent. The overall trend rate for Solow index was –0.242 per annum. Coefficient of variation was found to be 0.114.

Index of TFPT decreased at an average annual rate of 0.439 percent. The overall trend rate for Translog index was –0.371 per annum. Coefficient of variation was found to be 0.118.

An inter-variable comparison in this State revealed that the maximum growth rate and variability were in capital intensity followed by labour productivity and negative growth was in capital productivity and least variability in TFPK.

RELATIONSHIP OF TOTAL FACTOR PRODUCTIVITY WITH PARTIAL PRODUCTIVITIES OF CAPITAL AND LABOUR

The estimated regression models in which total factor productivity (Kendrick, Solow & Translog) depended upon trend, labour and capital productivity are given as under :

TABLE 8.4

Productivity Indices of Industries in Gujarat

Year	*Index of Partial Labour Productivity*	*Index of Partial Capital Productivity*	*Index of Real Capital Intensity*	*Index of TFPK*	*Index of TFPS*	*Index of TFPT*
1973-74	100.00	100.00	100.00	100.00	100.00	100.00
1974-75	93.69	109.61	92.61	105.16	107.38	106.93
1975-76	85.14	90.80	101.60	93.56	93.25	92.60
1976-77	99.30	93.16	115.48	103.09	101.31	100.50
1977-78	106.62	95.18	121.37	108.41	106.18	105.30
1978-79	109.87	85.69	138.91	106.31	101.56	101.08
1979-80	100.38	88.82	122.45	102.84	99.03	98.12
1980-81	95.97	79.70	130.47	97.38	93.53	92.40
1981-82	100.15	84.37	128.62	101.69	97.63	96.45
1982-83	103.29	77.80	143.85	100.35	95.12	93.19
1983-84	143.97	90.25	172.83	127.00	119.86	118.05
1984-85	139.68	78.99	191.59	118.65	111.74	110.12
1985-86	139.01	72.33	208.23	114.79	107.74	105.94
1986-87	155.78	74.64	226.15	120.85	113.31	111.41
1987-88	159.91	61.69	280.88	112.88	103.65	101.50
1988-89	177.25	73.87	259.98	128.09	117.05	114.59
1989-90	170.33	69.34	266.17	122.19	111.21	108.84
1990-91	195.21	60.01	352.46	116.83	104.35	102.63
1991-92	153.86	46.21	360.77	95.62	84.77	83.21
1992-93	260.97	56.30	502.19	124.72	117.91	115.66
1993-94	269.67	51.63	565.88	116.28	109.18	106.81
1994-95	309.35	59.81	560.37	132.39	124.50	121.80
1995-96	329.57	46.08	774.95	111.47	93.61	90.08
1996-97	407.35	57.36	769.43	136.73	111.88	107.67
1997-98	358.86	44.81	867.62	111.86	88.52	85.14
1998-99	358.10	39.32	986.70	102.01	80.98	77.95
1999-00	350.76	47.71	796.60	120.23	92.35	88.66
2000-01	313.22	38.59	879.40	102.30	79.43	75.38
Growth Rate	6.098* (15.898)	-3.379* (-14.932)	9.874* (25.617)	0.565** (2.565)	-0.295NS (-1.091)	-0.439NS (-1.586)
Linear Slope	11.387* (11.481)	-2.314* (-16.585)	32.307* (11.800)	0.635** (2.554)	-0.242NS (-0.886)	-0.371NS (-1.361)
CV	0.533	0.283	0.793	0.104	0.114	0.118

Notes :
1. Figures in parentheses are the respective 't' values.
2. * Indicates one percent level of significance.
3. ** Indicate 5 percent level of significance.
4. NS Indicates non-significant.

$$\ln TFPK_t = 0.416 + 0.104 \ln t + 0.284 \ln LP_t + 0.614 \ln CP_t$$
$$(1.187) \quad (6.51) \qquad (9.646) \qquad (11.33)$$
$$R^2 = 0.891; \quad \tilde{R}^2 = 0.877; \quad S = 0.036$$
$$F \text{ ratio} = 65.29; \quad D\text{-}W = 0.518; \quad \tilde{p} = 0.693$$

$$\ln TFPS_t = -0.07 + 0.106 \ln t + 0.23 \ln LP_t + 0.772 \ln CP_t$$
$$(-0.114) \quad (3.798) \qquad (4.484) \qquad (8.164)$$
$$R^2 = 0.738; \quad \tilde{R}^2 = 0.705; \quad S = 0.063$$
$$F \text{ ratio} = 22.49; \quad D\text{-}W = 0.358; \quad \tilde{p} = 0.788$$

$$\ln TFPT_t = -0.11 + 0.104 \ln t + 0.22 \ln LP_t + 0.791 \ln CP_t$$
$$(-0.169) \quad (3.496) \qquad (4.013) \qquad (7.829)$$
$$R^2 = 0.728; \quad \tilde{R}^2 = 0.694; \quad S = 0.067$$
$$F \text{ ratio} = 21.43; \quad D\text{-}W = 0.357; \quad \tilde{p} = 0.783$$

Both labour productivity and capital productivity significantly affected the total factor productivity, indicating consistency and strength in the relationship between labour productivity, capital productivity and total factor productivity as measured through Kendrick, Solow and Translog indices.

Table 8.5 shows the productivity indices in case of industries in Haryana. Index of partial labour productivity increased at an average rate of 3.707 percent per annum. The overall trend rate of labour productivity was 7.747 per annum. Coefficient of variation was found to be 0.365.

The index of partial capital productivity decreased at an average annual rate of 0.288 percent. The overall trend rate of capital productivity was –0.306 per annum. The coefficient of variation was found to be 0.161.

The index of capital intensity increased at an average annual rate of 4.048 percent. The overall trend rate of capital intensity was 7.278 per annum. Coefficient of variation was found to be 0.350.

Index of TFPK increased at an average annual rate of 1.976 percent. The overall trend rate for Kendrick index was 3.425 per annum. Coefficient of variation was found to be 0.213.

TABLE 8.5
Productivity Indices of Industries in Haryana

Year	*Index of Partial Labour Productivity*	*Index of Partial Capital Productivity*	*Index of Real Capital Intensity*	*Index of TFPK*	*Index of TFPS*	*Index of TFPT*
1973-74	100.00	100.00	100.00	100.00	100.00	100.00
1974-75	118.19	115.34	108.10	126.08	122.37	122.07
1975-76	140.90	120.10	123.77	141.36	133.20	132.69
1976-77	158.22	127.61	130.80	154.30	144.51	143.94
1977-78	156.24	126.56	130.23	153.21	143.47	142.90
1978-79	185.86	144.98	135.23	177.89	165.74	165.17
1979-80	167.82	120.07	147.44	155.14	136.42	136.24
1980-81	149.29	115.42	136.45	147.16	130.68	130.35
1981-82	148.92	147.20	106.73	160.30	147.99	147.27
1982-83	150.89	143.78	110.71	160.56	147.15	146.15
1983-84	195.80	158.07	130.67	191.87	171.61	172.30
1984-85	145.53	110.82	138.54	145.15	127.80	128.08
1985-86	153.84	106.76	152.02	146.86	128.01	128.17
1986-87	166.49	111.31	157.80	155.16	134.59	134.87
1987-88	158.62	98.07	170.62	147.43	126.62	126.50
1988-89	191.41	109.07	185.13	166.52	142.18	142.12
1989-90	196.03	113.28	182.55	170.51	145.90	145.89
1990-91	236.54	134.18	185.97	198.97	171.32	171.29
1991-92	212.08	107.67	207.79	173.49	144.36	146.02
1992-93	176.80	78.22	238.45	141.10	116.56	117.40
1993-94	198.82	78.92	265.78	147.06	122.99	123.35
1994-95	240.02	104.22	242.94	184.37	154.71	155.50
1995-96	309.44	141.43	230.80	235.79	201.93	202.92
1996-97	319.76	129.53	260.42	227.77	192.53	193.65
1997-98	329.98	122.95	283.13	227.11	191.22	192.70
1998-99	278.32	121.23	242.18	208.82	173.88	177.30
1999-00	404.20	138.81	307.19	258.57	206.87	212.35
2000-01	320.63	112.15	301.60	216.80	173.39	178.22
Growth Rate	3.707* (9.834)	-0.288^{NS} (-0.729)	4.048* (14.902)	1.976* (6.080)	1.326* (3.946)	1.409* (4.181)
Linear Slope	7.747* (8.460)	-0.306^{NS} (-0.676)	7.278* (13.715)	3.425* (6.124)	4.048* (4.077)	2.191* (4.315)
CV	0.365	0.161	0.350	0.213	0.180	0.185

Notes : 1. Figures in parentheses are the respective 't' values.
2. * Indicates one percent level of significance.
3. ^{NS} Indicates non-significant.

Index of TFPS increased at an average annual rate of 1.326 percent. The overall trend rate for Solow index was 4.048 per annum. Coefficient of variation was found to be 0.180.

Index of TFPT increased at an average annual rate of 1.409 percent. The overall trend rate for Translog index was 2.191 per annum. Coefficient of variation was found to be 0.185.

An inter-variable comparison in this state revealed that the maximum growth rate was observed in capital intensity followed by labour productivity and negative in capital productivity. The highest variability was found in labour productivity followed by capital intensity and least was in capital productivity.

RELATIONSHIP OF TOTAL FACTOR PRODUCTIVITY WITH PARTIAL PRODUCTIVITIES OF CAPITAL AND LABOUR

The regression models in which total factor productivity (Kendrick, Solow & Translog) depended upon trend, labour and capital productivity were estimated. The estimated equations are :

$$\ln TFPK_t = \underset{(7.613)}{0.634} + \underset{(8.141)}{0.049} \ln t + \underset{(29.275)}{0.449} \ln LP_t + \underset{(22.962)}{0.442} \ln CP_t$$

$R^2 = 0.996$; $\tilde{R}^2 = 0.995$; $S = 0.014$

F ratio $= 1978.29$; D–W $= 1.532$; $\tilde{p} = 0.062$

$$\ln TFPS_t = \underset{(3.84)}{0.445} + \underset{(0.504)}{0.004} \ln t + \underset{(18.11)}{0.395} \ln LP_t + \underset{(19.648)}{0.514} \ln CP_t$$

$R^2 = 0.989$; $\tilde{R}^2 = 0.987$; $S = 0.02$

F ratio $= 688.88$; D–W $= 1.279$; $\tilde{p} = 0.27$

$$\ln TFPT_t = \underset{(4.001)}{0.406} + \underset{(0.225)}{0.002} \ln t + \underset{(22.547)}{0.421} \ln LP_t + \underset{(22.196)}{0.497} \ln CP_t$$

$R^2 = 0.992$; $\tilde{R}^2 = 0.991$; $S = 0.017$

F ratio $= 989.86$; D–W $= 1.626$; $\tilde{p} = 0.111$

Both labour productivity and capital productivity significantly affected the total factor productivity, indicating consistency and strength in the relationship between labour productivity, capital productivity and total factor productivity as measured through Kendrick, Solow and Translog indices.

Table 8.6 presents the empirical results in case of industries in Himachal Pradesh. Index of partial labour productivity increased at an average annual rate of 5.336 percent per annum. The overall trend rate was 18.271 per annum. Coefficient of variation was found to be 0.459.

The index of partial capital productivity decreased at an average annual rate of 1.196 percent. The trend rate was –1.348 per annum. The coefficient of variation was found to be 0.238.

The index of capital intensity increased at an average annual rate of 6.640 percent. The overall trend rate was 22.824 per annum. Coefficient of variation was found to be 0.481.

Index of TFPK increased at an average annual rate of 1.244 percent. The overall trend rate for Kendrick index was 1.855 per annum. Coefficient of variation was found to be 0.217.

Index of TFPS decreased at an average annual rate of 0.519 percent. The overall trend rate for Solow index was –0.798 per annum. Coefficient of variation was found to be 0.240.

Index of TFPT decreased at an average annual rate of 0.834 percent. The overall trend rate for Translog index was –1.188 per annum. Coefficient of variation was found to be 0.254.

An inter-variable comparison in this State revealed that the maximum growth rate and variability were in capital intensity followed by labour productivity and negative growth was in capital productivity and least variability in TFPK.

RELATIONSHIP OF TOTAL FACTOR PRODUCTIVITY WITH PARTIAL PRODUCTIVITIES OF CAPITAL AND LABOUR

The regression models in which total factor productivity (Kendrick, Solow & Translog) depended upon trend, labour and capital productivity were estimated. The estimated equations are :

TABLE 8.6

Productivity Indices of Industries in Himachal Pradesh

Year	*Index of Partial Labour Productivity*	*Index of Partial Capital Productivity*	*Index of Real Capital Intensity*	*Index of TFPK*	*Index of TFPS*	*Index of TFPT*
1973-74	100.00	100.00	100.00	100.00	100.00	100.00
1974-75	68.10	88.49	79.88	79.52	75.18	79.78
1975-76	164.83	163.36	104.72	171.35	155.11	162.90
1976-77	252.02	141.26	185.16	198.64	162.44	166.32
1977-78	295.09	144.93	211.32	215.49	173.66	177.13
1978-79	351.38	116.47	313.12	211.09	153.13	154.62
1979-80	372.94	128.65	300.87	222.25	163.10	164.29
1980-81	308.62	109.12	293.53	195.06	143.53	144.59
1981-82	384.64	120.16	332.23	212.20	156.55	157.62
1982-83	500.14	94.98	546.51	197.44	128.81	128.13
1983-84	546.06	112.86	502.15	228.54	149.58	148.33
1984-85	377.59	78.57	498.79	165.53	102.58	101.72
1985-86	391.35	81.87	496.15	170.14	105.77	104.87
1986-87	368.70	82.13	465.89	169.59	104.88	103.39
1987-88	262.98	53.02	514.75	113.97	66.12	64.21
1988-89	370.18	100.63	381.80	190.23	106.81	102.78
1989-90	299.24	83.54	371.77	156.41	88.01	84.84
1990-91	390.70	106.82	379.59	202.29	115.18	111.04
1991-92	369.44	86.20	444.83	172.60	97.48	94.23
1992-93	333.79	71.02	487.77	150.25	84.02	80.46
1993-94	554.78	102.73	560.51	212.77	123.40	118.50
1994-95	437.23	82.37	550.94	174.16	99.88	95.88
1995-96	433.41	83.16	540.93	174.49	99.87	95.96
1996-97	632.64	99.31	661.14	214.90	127.71	123.39
1997-98	529.28	97.36	564.19	212.73	124.86	121.18
1998-99	754.32	79.09	989.85	193.06	116.65	111.75
1999-00	785.75	103.56	787.44	237.71	142.65	136.67
2000-01	872.31	113.99	794.23	258.66	155.05	147.70
Growth Rate	5.336* (6.158)	-1.196** (-2.348)	6.640* (8.368)	1.244** (2.170)	-0.519NS (-0.878)	-0.834NS (-1.392)
Linear Slope	18.271* (6.734)	-1.348** (-2.658)	22.824* (9.352)	1.855* (2.084)	-0.798NS (-1.169)	-1.188*** (-1.715)
CV	0.459	0.238	0.481	0.217	0.240	0.254

Notes :
1. Figures in parentheses are the respective 't' values.
2. * Indicates one percent level of significance.
3. ** Indicates 5 percent level of significance.
4. *** Indicates 10 percent level of significance.
5. NS Indicates non-significant.

$$\ln TFPK_t = 0.103 + 0.032 \ln t + 0.36 \ln LP_t + 0.631 \ln CP_t$$
$$(0.456)\ (1.033)\qquad (8.293)\qquad (10.706)$$
$$R^2 = 0.966; \quad \tilde{R}^2 = 0.962; \quad S = 0.051$$
$$F\ ratio = 226.33; \quad D\text{-}W = 0.68; \quad \tilde{p} = 0.583$$

$$\ln TFPS_t = -0.508 - 0.169 \ln t + 0.396 \ln LP_t + 0.733 \ln CP_t$$
$$(-2.447)\ (-5.839)\qquad (9.893)\qquad (13.491)$$
$$R^2 = 0.969; \quad \tilde{R}^2 = 0.965; \quad S = 0.047$$
$$F\ ratio = 251.82; \quad D\text{–}W = 1.266; \quad \tilde{p} = 0.29$$

$$\ln TFPT_t = -0.559 - 0.188 \ln t + 0.384 \ln LP_t + 0.766 \ln CP_t$$
$$(-2.22)\ (-5.36)\qquad (7.918)\qquad (11.632)$$
$$R^2 = 0.958; \quad \tilde{R}^2 = 0.953; \quad S = 0.057$$
$$F\ ratio = 182.21; \quad D\text{–}W = 1.2; \quad \tilde{p} = 0.276$$

Both labour productivity and capital productivity significantly affected the total factor productivity, indicating consistency and robustness in the relationship between labour productivity, capital productivity and total factor productivity as measured through Kendrick, Solow and Translog indices.

Table 8.7 shows the empirical results in case of industries in Karnataka. Index of partial labour productivity increased at an average rate of 4,827 percent per annum. The overall trend rate was 7.868 per annum. Coefficient of variation was found to be 0.396.

The index of partial capital productivity declined at an average annual rate of 2.261 percent. The overall trend rate was –1.758 per annum. The coefficient of variation was found to be 0.219.

The index of capital intensity increased at an average annual rate of 7.309 percent. The overall trend rate was 17.317 per annum. Coefficient of variation was found to be 0.704.

Index of TFPK increased at an average annual rate of 0.661 percent. The overall trend rate for Kendrick index was 0.847 per annum. Coefficient of variation was found to be 0.166.

Index of TFPS increased at an average annual rate of 0.220 percent. The overall trend rate for Solow index was 0.392 per annum. Coefficient of variation was found to be 0.186.

Table 8.7
Productivity Indices of Industries in Karnataka

Year	*Index of Partial Labour Productivity*	*Index of Partial Capital Productivity*	*Index of Real Capital Intensity*	*Index of TFPK*	*Index of TFPS*	*Index of TFPT*
1973-74	100.00	100.00	100.00	100.00	100.00	100.00
1974-75	86.79	102.88	90.63	100.25	99.51	99.90
1975-76	92.17	105.77	93.62	104.49	104.02	104.45
1976-77	94.81	102.17	99.70	105.89	104.97	105.45
1977-78	95.44	97.34	105.33	104.58	103.35	103.40
1978-79	146.96	122.03	129.39	144.58	143.20	145.24
1979-80	113.05	106.64	113.90	117.98	116.92	118.39
1980-81	95.73	92.41	111.29	102.88	101.07	102.44
1981-82	107.16	96.62	119.16	110.35	107.60	109.19
1982-83	112.86	93.52	129.64	111.68	109.05	110.25
1983-84	147.02	111.94	141.11	137.80	134.94	136.86
1984-85	126.94	97.48	139.90	122.05	119.40	121.10
1985-86	142.91	96.52	159.07	127.39	124.77	126.56
1986-87	144.35	98.07	158.13	129.26	126.64	128.45
1987-88	138.80	76.76	194.26	114.48	112.71	113.75
1988-89	151.14	82.41	197.04	122.19	120.76	121.87
1989-90	182.69	102.34	191.78	147.38	146.09	147.48
1990-91	208.13	106.33	210.29	157.99	157.77	158.55
1991-92	222.11	114.48	208.43	168.98	168.95	169.78
1992-93	236.49	87.71	289.65	147.77	141.71	141.90
1993-94	213.48	77.41	296.30	133.33	127.44	127.59
1994-95	260.84	83.69	334.87	146.48	142.14	142.51
1995-96	251.67	84.15	321.31	146.04	141.21	141.69
1996-97	280.15	79.38	379.17	145.17	141.17	141.60
1997-98	257.85	57.60	480.97	114.49	103.63	104.95
1998-99	274.69	38.98	756.98	87.00	78.55	78.06
1999-00	271.21	53.76	542.00	108.92	88.63	87.78
2000-01	261.07	55.01	509.85	111.70	90.12	86.33
Growth Rate	4.827* (16.546)	-2.261* (-5.293)	7.309* (17.885)	0.661*** (1.775)	0.220^{NS} (0.497)	0.157^{NS} (0.344)
Linear Slope	7.868* (15.402)	-1.758* (-5.496)	17.317* (8.537)	0.847*** (1.833)	0.392^{NS} (0.747)	0.332^{NS} (0.617)
CV	0.396	0.219	0.704	0.166	0.186	0.189

Notes :
1. Figures in parentheses are the respective 't' values.
2. * Indicates one percent level of significance.
3. *** Indicate 10 percent level of significance.
4. ^{NS} Indicates non-significant.

Index of TFPT increased at an average annual rate of 0.157 percent. The overall trend rate for Translog index was 0.332 per annum. Coefficient of variation was found to be 0.189.

An inter-variable comparison in this State revealed that the maximum growth rate and variability were observed in capital intensity followed by labour productivity and negative growth in capital productivity and least variability in TFPK.

RELATIONSHIP OF TOTAL FACTOR PRODUCTIVITY WITH PARTIAL PRODUCTIVITIES OF CAPITAL AND LABOUR

The regression models in which total factor productivity (Kendrick, Solow & Translog) depended upon trend, labour and capital productivity were estimated. The estimated equations are :

$$\ln TFPK_t = -0.211 + 0.061 \ln t + 0.351 \ln LP_t + 0.691 \ln CP_t$$
$$(-1.597) \quad (7.288) \quad (19.124) \quad (38.628)$$
$$R^2 = 0.988; \quad \tilde{R}^2 = 0.986; \quad S = 0.019$$
$$F \text{ ratio} = 648.83; \quad D\text{–}W = 1.196; \quad \tilde{p} = 0.385$$

$$\ln TFPS_t = -0.844 + 0.063 \ln t + 0.332 \ln LP_t + 0.845 \ln CP_t$$
$$(-2.802) \quad (3.29) \quad (7.953) \quad (20.749)$$
$$R^2 = 0.951; \quad \tilde{R}^2 = 0.945; \quad S = 0.044$$
$$F \text{ ratio} = 154.75; \quad D\text{–}W = 0.983; \quad \tilde{p} = 0.396$$

$$\ln TFPT_t = -0.88 + 0.07 \ln t + 0.316 \ln LP_t + 0.868 \ln CP_t$$
$$(-2.616) \quad (3.297) \quad (6.776) \quad (19.081)$$
$$R^2 = 0.942; \quad \tilde{R}^2 = 0.934; \quad S = 0.049$$
$$F \text{ ratio} = 129.16; \quad D\text{–}W = 0.853; \quad \tilde{p} = 0.410$$

Both labour productivity and capital productivity significantly affected the total factor productivity, indicating consistency and robustness in the relationship between labour productivity, capital productivity and total factor productivity as measured through Kendrick, Solow and Translog indices.

Table 8.8 presents the productivity indices in case of industries in Kerala. Index of partial labour productivity

TABLE 8.8

Productivity Indices of Industries in Kerala

Year	*Index of Partial Labour Productivity*	*Index of Partial Capital Productivity*	*Index of Real Capital Intensity*	*Index of TFPK*	*Index of TFPS*	*Index of TFPT*
1973-74	100.00	100.00	100.00	100.00	100.00	100.00
1974-75	91.38	111.20	85.86	107.87	109.01	108.63
1975-76	88.05	114.44	80.39	106.65	108.25	107.86
1976-77	94.08	109.92	89.43	109.24	110.18	109.67
1977-78	103.44	123.19	87.74	119.40	121.54	121.01
1978-79	124.97	129.81	100.60	134.72	135.41	134.69
1979-80	128.87	140.09	96.12	140.53	142.13	141.28
1980-81	124.68	145.53	89.52	141.93	143.99	143.16
1981-82	121.26	146.51	86.48	139.51	141.95	141.18
1982-83	141.83	131.04	113.09	144.58	142.83	141.17
1983-84	149.92	121.52	128.91	144.85	141.22	138.99
1984-85	187.50	155.12	126.30	179.88	174.92	172.12
1985-86	188.87	122.10	161.62	160.73	151.33	149.38
1986-87	185.98	121.45	160.01	161.93	152.44	150.47
1987-88	200.38	126.02	166.15	170.95	161.76	159.73
1988-89	213.70	132.80	168.15	178.42	168.53	166.40
1989-90	271.28	176.16	160.91	225.70	216.94	213.69
1990-91	200.80	128.21	163.65	168.17	158.86	156.47
1991-92	233.07	127.86	190.47	181.32	173.12	170.58
1992-93	201.38	111.34	188.99	158.70	148.30	146.15
1993-94	197.85	98.46	209.97	144.93	135.77	133.93
1994-95	190.19	114.01	174.30	154.86	143.85	142.55
1995-96	253.70	111.88	236.94	170.51	158.60	157.22
1996-97	266.01	150.49	184.71	207.50	185.97	184.27
1997-98	241.16	99.46	253.36	156.71	122.46	118.36
1998-99	338.54	156.66	225.80	231.07	166.04	160.38
1999-00	271.38	150.42	188.52	208.65	151.39	145.58
2000-01	239.98	136.34	183.92	190.85	138.21	134.59
Growth Rate	4.413* (12.943)	0.334^{NS} (0.966)	4.098* (12.220)	2.256* (7.152)	1.202* (3.486)	1.109* (3.189)
Linear Slope	7.346* (11.536)	0.464^{NS} (1.036)	5.688* (11.509)	3.383* (6.923)	1.629* (3.159)	1.489* (2.900)
CV	0.359	0.149	0.341	0.218	0.174	0.171

Notes :
1. Figures in parentheses are the respective 't' values.
2. * Indicates one percent level of significance.
3. ^{NS} Indicates non-significant.

increased at an average rate of 4.413 percent per annum. The overall trend rate was 7.346 per annum. Coefficient of variation was found to be 0.359.

The index of partial capital productivity inclined at an average annual rate of 0.334 percent. The overall trend rate was 0.464 per annum. The coefficient of variation was found to be 0.149.

The index of capital intensity increased at an average annual rate of 4.098 percent. The overall trend rate of capital intensity was 5.688 per annum. Coefficient of variation was found to be 0.341.

Index of TFPK increased at an average annual rate of 2.256 percent. The overall trend rate for Kendrick index was 3.383 per annum. Coefficient of variation was found to be 0.218.

Index of TFPS increased at an average annual rate of 1.202 percent. The overall trend rate for Solow index was 1.629 per annum. Coefficient of variation was found to be 0.174.

Index of TFPT increased at an average annual rate of 1.109 percent. The overall trend rate for Translog index was 1.489 per annum. Coefficient of variation was found to be 0.171.

An inter-variable comparison in this State revealed that the maximum growth rate and variability were in labour productivity followed by capital intensity and minimum in capital productivity.

RELATIONSHIP OF TOTAL FACTOR PRODUCTIVITY WITH PARTIAL PRODUCTIVITIES OF CAPITAL AND LABOUR

The estimated regression models in which total factor productivity (Kendrick, Solow & Translog) depended upon trend, labour and capital productivity are given as under :

$$\ln TFPK_t = \underset{(2.367)}{0.287} + \underset{(3.289)}{0.028} \ln t + \underset{(21.822)}{0.419} \ln LP_t + \underset{(23.044)}{0.522} \ln CP_t$$

$$R^2 = 0.995; \quad \tilde{R}^2 = 0.995; \quad S = 0.016$$

$$F \text{ ratio} = 1676.25; \; D\text{–}W = 1.046; \; \tilde{p} = 0.449$$

$$\ln TFPS_t = 1.092 + 0.041 \ln t + 0.187 \ln LP_t + 0.582 \ln CP_t$$
$$(1.788)\ (0.955)\qquad (1.937)\qquad (5.102)$$
$$R^2 = 0.805; \quad \tilde{R}^2 = 0.781; \quad S = 0.082$$
$$F \text{ ratio} = 33.02; \quad D\text{–}W = 0.315; \quad \tilde{p} = 0.732$$

$$\ln TFPT_t = 1.162 + 0.04 \ln t + 0.171 \ln LP_t + 0.583 \ln CP_t$$
$$(1.781)\ (0.866)\qquad (1.653)\qquad (4.785)$$
$$R^2 = 0.77; \quad \tilde{R}^2 = 0.741; \quad S = 0.087$$
$$F \text{ ratio} = 26.71; \quad D\text{–}W = 0.336; \quad \tilde{p} = 0.729$$

Both labour productivity and capital productivity significantly affected the total factor productivity total factor productivity as measured through Kendrick and Solow indices only.

Table 8.9 presents the empirical results in case of industries in Madhya Pradesh. Index of partial labour productivity increased at an average rate of 5.345 percent per annum. The overall trend rate was 8.337 per annum. Coefficient of variation was found to be 0.479.

The index of partial capital productivity decreased at an average annual rate of 0.776 percent. The overall trend rate was –0.594 per annum. The coefficient of variation was found to be 0.236.

The index of capital intensity increased at an average annual rate of 6.228 percent. The overall trend rate was 11.917 per annum. Coefficient of variation was found to be 0.471.

Index of TFPK increased at an average annual rate of 1.976 percent. The overall trend rate for Kendrick index was 2.459 per annum. Coefficient of variation was found to be 0.242.

Index of TFPS increased at an average annual rate of 1.093 percent. The overall trend rate for Solow index was 1.283 per annum. Coefficient of variation was found to be 0.188.

Index of TFPT decreased at an average annual rate of 1.47 percent. The overall trend rate for Translog index was –0.661 per annum. Coefficient of variation was found to be 0.424.

An inter-variable comparison in this State revealed that the maximum growth rate was observed in capital intensity followed by labour productivity and negative was in TFPT. The highest variability was found in labour productivity and least in TFPS.

TABLE 8.9
Productivity Indices of Industries in Madhya Pradesh

Year	*Index of Partial Labour Productivity*	*Index of Partial Capital Productivity*	*Index of Real Capital Intensity*	*Index of TFPK*	*Index of TFPS*	*Index of TFPT*
1973-74	100.00	100.00	100.00	100.00	100.00	100.00
1974-75	83.05	117.51	76.14	104.14	104.05	104.05
1975-76	76.03	101.50	80.70	93.15	92.17	95.90
1976-77	93.95	103.41	97.88	105.25	103.95	99.68
1977-78	82.99	85.50	104.56	92.01	89.72	89.44
1978-79	83.61	81.10	111.08	90.50	88.48	79.14
1979-80	84.97	87.25	104.92	95.63	93.30	73.83
1980-81	93.04	80.57	124.41	94.88	92.20	68.07
1981-82	107.30	84.56	136.70	102.74	99.92	68.02
1982-83	115.64	78.84	158.02	101.87	97.78	66.51
1983-84	116.91	67.43	186.79	96.16	93.05	61.89
1984-85	103.41	57.51	193.72	87.20	84.16	52.08
1985-86	144.46	66.87	232.73	107.01	102.91	53.60
1986-87	106.75	49.99	230.05	84.08	80.14	42.95
1987-88	133.16	56.59	253.52	98.40	96.39	41.40
1988-89	160.53	99.84	173.23	143.09	124.98	51.74
1989-90	166.84	76.81	233.99	122.86	97.03	50.21
1990-91	181.07	76.84	253.86	127.07	100.77	50.59
1991-92	154.41	63.47	262.10	107.62	85.95	43.49
1992-93	172.35	52.56	353.26	103.86	83.01	36.10
1993-94	220.21	65.51	362.12	119.05	95.09	34.33
1994-95	227.46	59.93	408.87	115.29	92.48	31.75
1995-96	276.69	84.35	353.41	150.55	121.71	38.64
1996-97	334.63	100.37	359.16	175.94	140.34	54.22
1997-98	293.63	103.23	306.42	176.13	140.42	76.14
1998-99	193.88	54.97	379.99	107.93	100.65	76.63
1999-00	268.41	83.30	347.13	150.78	134.01	102.69
2000-01	291.37	109.12	287.67	181.01	156.34	160.55
Growth Rate	5.345* (14.029)	-0.776^NS (-1.395)	6.228* (14.305)	1.976* (5.468)	1.093* (3.110)	-1.470^NS (-1.63)
Linear Slope	8.337* (10.422)	-0.594^NS (-1.361)	11.917* (12.840)	2.459* (5.333)	1.283* (3.317)	-0.661^NS (-0.979)
CV	0.479	0.236	0.471	0.242	0.188	0.424

Notes : 1. Figures in parentheses are the respective 't' values.
2. * Indicates one percent level of significance.
4. NS Indicates non-significant.

RELATIONSHIP OF TOTAL FACTOR PRODUCTIVITY WITH PARTIAL PRODUCTIVITIES OF CAPITAL AND LABOUR

The estimated regression models in which total factor productivity (Kendrick & Solow) depended upon trend, labour and capital productivity are given as under :

$$\ln TFPK_t = \underset{(6.7)}{0.677} + \underset{(4.754)}{0.059} \ln t + \underset{(16.575)}{0.344} \ln LP_t + \underset{(19.575)}{0.504} \ln CP_t$$

$R^2 = 0.989$; $\tilde{R}^2 = 0.988$; $S = 0.024$

F ratio $= 732.0425$; D–W $= 0.847$; $\tilde{p} = 0.553$

$$\ln TFPS_t = \underset{(4.966)}{1.257} + \underset{(1.489)}{0.046} \ln t + \underset{(3.791)}{0.197} \ln LP_t + \underset{(8.073)}{0.522} \ln CP_t$$

$R^2 = 0.888$; $\tilde{R}^2 = 0.874$; $S = 0.061$

F ratio $= 63.7$; D–W $= 0.606$; $\tilde{p} = 0.658$

$$\ln TFPT_t = \underset{(0.19)}{0.23} + \underset{(0.084)}{0.013} \ln t - \underset{(-0.886)}{0.22} \ln LP_t + \underset{(3.698)}{1.142} \ln CP_t$$

$R^2 = 0.530$; $\tilde{R}^2 = 0.472$; $S = 0.291$

F ratio $= 9.03$; D–W $= 0.484$; $\tilde{p} = 0.633$

Both labour productivity and capital productivity significantly affected the total factor productivity as measured through Kendrick and Solow indices only.

Table 8.10 presents the empirical results in case of industries in Maharashtra. Index of partial labour productivity increased at an average rate of 5.385 percent per annum. The overall trend rate was 9.197 per annum. Coefficient of variation was found to be 0.444.

The index of partial capital productivity declined at an average annual rate of 2.836 percent per annum. The overall trend rate was –2.328 per annum. The coefficient of variation was found to be 0.263.

The index of capital intensity increased at an average annual rate of 8.531 percent. The overall trend rate was 20.815 per annum. Coefficient of variation was found to be 0.634.

TABLE 8.10
Productivity Indices of Industries in Maharashtra

Year	*Index of Partial Labour Productivity*	*Index of Partial Capital Productivity*	*Index of Real Capital Intensity*	*Index of TFPK*	*Index of TFPS*	*Index of TFPT*
1973-74	100.00	100.00	100.00	100.00	100.00	100.00
1974-75	89.61	119.71	81.61	102.84	104.86	104.61
1975-76	89.47	119.46	81.65	102.74	104.74	104.49
1976-77	95.82	108.13	96.61	104.49	104.17	103.78
1977-78	100.90	103.00	106.81	106.14	104.72	104.15
1978-79	116.25	113.13	112.04	119.28	117.67	117.13
1979-80	106.39	106.08	109.35	110.51	108.94	108.38
1980-81	99.58	92.08	117.90	101.44	99.37	98.75
1981-82	104.95	87.83	130.28	102.99	100.36	99.74
1982-83	108.46	81.61	144.89	102.33	99.35	98.56
1983-84	126.55	81.07	170.18	111.65	108.17	107.50
1984-85	128.79	77.66	180.79	112.18	108.92	107.80
1985-86	163.33	89.71	198.48	132.75	128.29	127.11
1986-87	155.57	81.37	208.43	124.30	119.87	118.88
1987-88	145.40	67.02	236.52	111.73	107.31	105.70
1988-89	179.06	78.44	248.88	130.94	126.13	124.21
1989-90	200.39	73.80	296.01	133.15	128.42	126.13
1990-91	216.34	74.69	315.78	137.93	133.37	131.14
1991-92	178.87	52.32	372.74	106.31	102.09	99.62
1992-93	225.62	54.14	454.30	117.02	115.42	111.93
1993-94	270.36	57.06	516.60	125.00	124.35	120.72
1994-95	264.95	58.26	495.83	128.34	127.50	123.80
1995-96	294.15	65.58	489.01	140.45	140.99	136.95
1996-97	317.85	56.98	608.12	131.29	130.76	127.24
1997-98	294.39	55.43	579.06	126.92	125.96	122.45
1998-99	262.83	62.41	459.13	132.86	128.61	125.89
1999-00	322.00	63.47	553.10	142.10	136.74	134.24
2000-01	281.89	59.89	513.19	132.94	128.36	120.38
Growth Rate	5.385* (19.345)	-2.836* (-11.319)	8.531* (24.279)	1.141* (6.910)	1.061* (6.271)	0.918* (5.305)
Linear Slope	9.197* (15.138)	-2.328* (-11.248)	20.815* (15.279)	1.342* (6.831)	1.233* (6.298)	1.052* (5.317)
CV	0.444	0.263	0.634	0.116	0.112	0.105

Notes : 1. Figures in parentheses are the respective 't' values.
2. * Indicates one percent level of significance.

Index of TFPK increased at an average annual rate of 1.141 percent. The overall trend rate for Kendrick index was 1.342 per annum. Coefficient of variation was found to be 0.116.

Index of TFPS increased at an average annual rate of 1.061 percent. The overall trend rate for Solow index was 1.233 per annum. Coefficient of variation was found to be 0.112.

Index of TFPT increased at an average annual rate of 0.918 percent. The overall trend rate for Translog index was 1.052 per annum. Coefficient of variation was found to be 0.105.

An inter-variable comparison in this State revealed that the maximum growth rate and variability were in capital intensity followed by labour productivity and negative growth was in capital productivity and least variability in TFPT.

RELATIONSHIP OF TOTAL FACTOR PRODUCTIVITY WITH PARTIAL PRODUCTIVITIES OF CAPITAL AND LABOUR

The estimated regression models in which total factor productivity (Kendrick, Solow & Translog) depended upon trend, labour and capital productivity are given as under :

$$\ln TFPK_t = \underset{(2.837)}{0.924} + \underset{(4.432)}{0.063} \ln t + \underset{(12.077)}{0.348} \ln LP_t + \underset{(8.873)}{0.442} \ln CP_t$$

$$R^2 = 0.942; \quad \tilde{R}^2 = 0.934; \quad S = 0.03$$

$$F \text{ ratio} = 129.21; \quad D\text{–}W = 0.568; \quad \tilde{p} = 0.665$$

$$\ln TFPS_t = \underset{(2.959)}{0.74} + \underset{(3.492)}{0.038} \ln t + \underset{(17.339)}{0.384} \ln LP_t + \underset{(11.793)}{0.452} \ln CP_t$$

$$R^2 = 0.963; \quad \tilde{R}^2 = 0.958; \quad S = 0.023$$

$$F \text{ ratio} = 207.94; \quad D\text{–}W = 0.603; \quad \tilde{p} = 0.659$$

$$\ln TFPT_t = \underset{(2.514)}{0.714} + \underset{(3.094)}{0.038} \ln t + \underset{(14.683)}{0.369} \ln LP_t + \underset{(10.854)}{0.472} \ln CP_t$$

$$R^2 = 0.945; \quad \tilde{R}^2 = 0.938; \quad S = 0.026$$

$$F \text{ ratio} = 137.99; \quad D\text{–}W = 0.526; \quad \tilde{p} = 0.608$$

Both labour productivity and capital productivity significantly affected the total factor productivity, indicating consistency and robustness in the relationship between labour productivity, capital productivity and total factor productivity as measured through Kendrick, Solow and Translog indices.

Table 8.11 presents the empirical results in case of industries in Orissa. Index of partial labour productivity increased at an average rate of 4.72 percent per annum. The overall trend rate was 6.275 per annum. Coefficient of variation was found to be 0.470.

The index of partial capital productivity decreased at an average rate of 2.734 percent per annum. The overall trend rate was –2.387 per annum. The coefficient of variation was found to be 0.332.

The index of capital intensity increased at an average annual rate of 7.733 percent. The overall trend rate was 13.552 per annum. Coefficient of variation was found to be 0.636.

Index of TFPK increased at an average annual rate of 1.059 percent. The overall trend rate for Kendrick index was 1.236 per annum. Coefficient of variation was found to be 0.209.

Index of TFPS increased at an average annual rate of 0.882 percent. The overall trend rate for Solow index was 0.968 per annum. Coefficient of variation was found to be 0.205.

Index of TFPT decreased at an average annual rate of 0.019 percent. The overall trend rate for Translog index was –0.021 per annum. Coefficient of variation was found to be 0.181.

An inter-variable comparison in this State revealed that the maximum growth rate and variability were in capital intensity followed by labour productivity and negative growth was in capital productivity and least variability in TFPT.

RELATIONSHIP OF TOTAL FACTOR PRODUCTIVITY WITH PARTIAL PRODUCTIVITIES OF CAPITAL AND LABOUR

The regression models in which total factor productivity (Kendrick, Solow & Translog) depended upon trend, labour and capital productivity were estimated. The estimated equations are :

TABLE 8.11
Productivity Indices of Industries in Orissa

Year	Index of Partial Labour Productivity	Index of Partial Capital Productivity	Index of Real Capital Intensity	Index of TFPK	Index of TFPS	Index of TFPT
1973-74	100.00	100.00	100.00	100.00	100.00	100.00
1974-75	80.49	108.03	81.20	104.37	105.72	103.80
1975-76	65.23	103.14	68.92	84.52	83.77	84.51
1976-77	98.94	137.68	78.32	124.08	122.96	124.76
1977-78	79.52	115.51	75.03	103.10	100.29	102.10
1978-79	104.33	136.71	83.17	125.97	119.92	122.20
1979-80	106.97	147.67	78.95	132.18	126.67	128.44
1980-81	69.49	104.52	72.45	97.20	89.12	90.54
1981-82	71.15	106.32	72.93	91.85	83.97	85.16
1982-83	67.50	85.07	86.47	82.64	76.89	77.04
1983-84	82.83	91.15	99.03	95.94	90.43	92.32
1984-85	58.53	61.22	104.20	71.17	68.05	68.89
1985-86	75.63	79.18	104.10	92.07	89.88	90.93
1986-87	92.94	80.87	125.25	102.69	101.85	103.39
1987-88	87.09	43.85	216.46	77.54	76.91	66.07
1988-89	157.49	70.87	242.17	124.21	125.09	107.29
1989-90	183.37	84.61	236.20	140.38	141.54	121.38
1990-91	175.90	90.04	212.91	143.67	144.75	123.92
1991-92	151.16	65.07	253.15	118.25	112.97	96.94
1992-93	147.32	53.49	300.16	106.88	101.42	86.72
1993-94	157.53	53.08	323.45	102.04	96.87	82.81
1994-95	163.37	47.38	375.76	94.65	89.68	76.55
1995-96	186.49	54.29	374.38	107.50	102.04	87.09
1996-97	255.09	55.03	505.16	113.74	109.49	93.24
1997-98	276.32	80.53	373.96	155.61	140.66	118.29
1998-99	179.04	58.04	336.17	119.34	115.30	97.51
1999-00	240.28	97.10	269.69	165.58	150.87	126.72
2000–01	202.37	71.29	309.36	133.32	120.36	105.07
Growth Rate	4.720* (7.311)	–2.734* (–4.747)	7.733* (11.795)	1.059** (2.350)	0.882*** (1.908)	–0.019^NS (–0.043)
Linear Slope	6.275* (7.528)	–2.387* (–4.93)	13.552* (9.556)	1.236** (2.483)	0.968*** (1.988)	–0.021^NS (–0.05)
CV	0.470	0.332	0.636	0.209	0.205	0.181

Notes :
1. Figures in parentheses are the respective 't' values.
2. * Indicates one percent level of significance.
3. ** Indicates 5 percent level of significance.
4. *** Indicates 10 percent level of significance.
5. NS Indicates non-significant.

$$\ln TFPK_t = 0.637 + 0.042 \ln t + 0.414 \ln LP_t + 0.449 \ln CP_t$$
$$(2.97) \quad (2.32) \qquad (15.109) \qquad (11.851)$$
$$R^2 = 0.947; \quad \tilde{R}^2 = 0.941; \quad S = 0.05$$
$$F \text{ ratio} = 144.08; \quad D\text{–}W = 1.064; \quad \tilde{p} = 0.468$$

$$\ln TFPS_t = 0.788 + 0.01 \ln t + 0.426 \ln LP_t + 0.41 \ln CP_t$$
$$(2.598) \quad (0.406) \qquad (10.983) \qquad (7.645)$$
$$R^2 = 0.894; \quad \tilde{R}^2 = 0.880; \quad S = 0.071$$
$$F \text{ ratio} = 67.20; \quad D\text{–}W = 0.760; \quad \tilde{p} = 0.609$$

$$\ln TFPT_t = 0.87 + 0.011 \ln t + 0.294 \ln LP_t + 0.518 \ln CP_t$$
$$(3.233) \quad (0.467) \qquad (8.547) \qquad (10.905)$$
$$R^2 = 0.895; \quad \tilde{R}^2 = 0.882; \quad S = 0.063$$
$$F \text{ ratio} = 68.53; \quad D\text{–}W = 1.061; \quad \tilde{p} = 0.467$$

Both labour productivity and capital productivity significantly affected the total factor productivity, indicating consistency and strength in the relationship between labour productivity, capital productivity and total factor productivity as measured through Kendrick, Solow and Translog indices.

Table 8.12 shows the productivity indices in case of industries in Punjab. Index of partial labour productivity increased at an average rate of 3.797 percent per annum. The overall trend rate was 6.458 per annum. Coefficient of variation was found to be 0.374.

The index of partial capital productivity inclined at an average rate of 0.733 percent per annum. The overall trend rate was 1.274 per annum. The coefficient of variation was found to be 0.274.

The index of capital intensity increased at an average annual rate of 3.065 percent. The overall trend rate was 4.553 per annum. Coefficient of variation was found to be 0.317.

Index of TFPK increased at an average annual rate of 2.075 percent. The overall trend rate for Kendrick index was 3.313 per annum. Coefficient of variation was found to be 0.279.

Index of TFPS increased at an average annual rate of 1.516 percent. The overall trend rate for Solow index was 2.225 per annum. Coefficient of variation was found to be 0.212.

TABLE 8.12
Productivity Indices of Industries in Punjab

Year	*Index of Partial Labour Productivity*	*Index of Partial Capital Productivity*	*Index of Real Capital Intensity*	*Index of TFPK*	*Index of TFPS*	*Index of TFPT*
1973-74	100.00	100.00	100.00	100.00	100.00	100.00
1974-75	95.80	104.39	94.67	106.68	107.43	107.49
1975-76	110.73	115.67	98.75	119.26	121.08	121.12
1976-77	116.64	111.17	108.23	119.67	120.38	120.50
1977-78	117.91	106.09	114.65	117.48	117.51	117.56
1978-79	129.98	125.39	106.93	135.53	137.45	137.52
1979-80	127.56	118.21	111.32	132.77	133.68	133.97
1980-81	128.95	117.57	113.14	135.40	136.11	136.43
1981-82	117.89	116.62	104.28	129.90	130.01	130.06
1982-83	119.07	99.92	122.93	120.22	120.28	120.07
1983-84	125.98	97.47	133.32	122.24	123.17	123.23
1984-85	119.56	98.83	124.79	120.73	120.41	120.70
1985-86	137.13	106.23	133.16	132.55	133.36	133.70
1986-87	139.13	104.85	136.88	130.73	131.74	132.08
1987-88	134.36	96.40	143.78	128.26	129.43	130.00
1988-89	132.72	98.86	138.49	127.85	128.30	129.32
1989-90	231.80	166.16	143.91	203.49	211.41	213.43
1990-91	182.12	126.15	148.93	161.52	167.48	168.75
1991-92	185.42	87.61	218.31	129.52	125.83	133.99
1992-93	148.93	68.44	224.47	107.49	102.93	109.04
1993-94	197.71	87.27	233.72	131.58	127.65	135.44
1994-95	203.10	95.26	219.94	143.94	138.47	146.69
1995-96	202.08	95.83	217.54	141.17	134.95	143.11
1996-97	226.53	104.04	224.60	153.94	148.30	157.28
1997-98	233.10	101.21	237.59	153.38	148.96	157.45
1998-99	318.88	187.29	175.63	246.67	199.69	211.44
1999-00	329.55	200.24	169.77	261.12	212.01	224.22
2000-01	223.32	182.87	125.97	218.22	177.97	175.43
Growth Rate	3.797* (11.068)	0.733[NS] (1.308)	3.065* (7.425)	2.075* (5.138)	1.516* (4.257)	1.751* (5.136)
Linear Slope	6.458* (8.489)	1.274*** (1.802)	4.553* (6.415)	3.313* (4.705)	2.225* (4.049)	2.599* (4.731)
CV	0.374	0.274	0.317	0.279	0.212	0.222

Notes :
1. Figures in parentheses are the respective 't' values.
2. * Indicates one percent level of significance.
3. *** Indicates 10 percent level of significance.
4. NS Indicates non-significant.

Index of TFPT increased at an average annual rate of 1.751 percent. The overall trend rate for Translog index was 2.599 per annum. Coefficient of variation was found to be 0.222.

An inter-variable comparison in this State revealed that the maximum growth rate and variability were in labour productivity followed by capital intensity and minimum growth in capital productivity and least variability in TFPS.

RELATIONSHIP OF TOTAL FACTOR PRODUCTIVITY WITH PARTIAL PRODUCTIVITIES OF CAPITAL AND LABOUR

The estimated regression models in which total factor productivity (Kendrick, Solow & Translog) depended upon trend, labour and capital productivity are given as under :

$$\ln TFPK_t = \underset{(11.615)}{0.549} + \underset{(13.644)}{0.063} \ln t + \underset{(20.427)}{0.27} \ln LP_t + \underset{(53.511)}{0.609} \ln CP_t$$

$R^2 = 0.998$; $\tilde{R}^2 = 0.998$; $S = 0.011$

F ratio = 4259.92; D–W = 2.24; $\tilde{p} = -0.139$

$$\ln TFPS_t = \underset{(7.419)}{1.509} + \underset{(3.4)}{0.068} \ln t + \underset{(2.615)}{0.149} \ln LP_t + \underset{(10.783)}{0.528} \ln CP_t$$

$R^2 = 0.947$; $\tilde{R}^2 = 0.941$; $S = 0.047$

F ratio = 143.99; D–W = 1.105; $\tilde{p} = 0.334$

$$\ln TFPT_t = \underset{(7.183)}{1.398} + \underset{(2.738)}{0.052} \ln t + \underset{(4.965)}{0.27} \ln LP_t + \underset{(9.256)}{0.434} \ln CP_t$$

$R^2 = 0.956$; $\tilde{R}^2 = 0.950$; $S = 0.045$

F ratio = 172.15; D–W = 1.067; $\tilde{p} = 0.295$

Both labour productivity and capital productivity significantly affected the total factor productivity, indicating consistency and robustness in the relationship between labour productivity, capital productivity and total factor productivity as measured through Kendrick, Solow and Translog indices.

Table 8.13 shows the empirical results in case of industries in Rajasthan. Index of partial labour productivity increased at

TABLE 8.13
Productivity Indices of Industries in Rajasthan

Year	*Index of Partial Labour Productivity*	*Index of Partial Capital Productivity*	*Index of Real Capital Intensity*	*Index of TFPK*	*Index of TFPS*	*Index of TFPT*
1973-74	100.00	100.00	100.00	100.00	100.00	100.00
1974-75	65.54	99.25	71.98	91.69	89.55	89.23
1975-76	75.05	94.27	86.76	93.89	91.73	91.53
1976-77	76.14	100.56	82.52	97.50	95.26	95.15
1977-78	79.33	99.03	87.30	97.79	95.45	95.25
1978-79	94.24	109.63	93.69	111.47	109.11	108.83
1979-80	92.84	121.24	83.46	114.92	113.41	112.29
1980-81	81.68	90.57	98.28	95.10	93.44	92.06
1981-82	80.28	88.77	98.55	93.78	92.12	90.77
1982-83	74.67	79.21	102.74	86.53	84.72	83.14
1983-84	106.06	174.41	66.27	147.53	136.75	132.58
1984-85	88.77	79.30	122.00	95.25	72.56	70.10
1985-86	100.02	76.70	142.12	97.81	76.22	72.92
1986-87	129.99	96.69	146.52	119.18	92.79	88.92
1987-88	89.03	70.20	138.21	94.44	71.15	68.32
1988-89	106.11	77.64	148.95	102.57	78.00	74.86
1989-90	115.70	98.62	127.87	119.57	89.87	86.78
1990-91	150.80	103.73	158.44	134.69	101.74	98.52
1991-92	139.58	101.15	150.39	133.71	100.78	97.68
1992-93	166.75	80.44	225.93	119.18	85.76	83.95
1993-94	162.91	98.75	179.80	138.89	95.93	94.44
1994-95	200.00	83.03	262.53	129.71	87.04	85.84
1995-96	201.99	97.41	225.98	142.24	94.07	93.26
1996-97	261.68	122.94	231.97	176.62	117.65	116.63
1997-98	274.69	120.11	249.26	175.49	116.64	116.10
1998-99	184.34	87.31	230.11	133.25	94.46	94.45
1999-00	268.88	84.90	345.17	140.82	99.70	100.04
2000-01	250.89	122.66	222.91	176.23	116.15	102.88
Growth Rate	5.081* (11.516)	-0.016^{NS} (-0.35)	5.165* (12.142)	2.087* (6.606)	0.248^{NS} (0.698)	0.149^{NS} (0.409)
Linear Slope	7.050* (9.542)	-0.008^{NS} (-0.018)	7.719* (10.204)	2.563* (6.396)	0.247^{NS} (0.711)	0.141^{NS} (0.410)
CV	0.482	0.210	0.464	0.225	0.153	0.154

Notes : 1. Figures in parentheses are the respective 't' values.
2. * Indicates one percent level of significance.
3. ^{NS} Indicates non-significant.

an average rate of 5.081 percent per annum. The overall trend rate was 7.05 per annum. Coefficient of variation was found to be 0.482.

The index of partial capital productivity decreased at an average rate of 0.016 percent per annum. The overall trend rate was –0.008 per annum. The coefficient of variation was found to be 0.210.

The index of capital intensity increased at an average annual rate of 5.165 percent. The overall trend rate was 7.719 per annum. Coefficient of variation was found to be 0.464.

Index of TFPK increased at an average annual rate of 2.087 percent. The overall trend rate for Kendrick index was 2.563 per annum. Coefficient of variation was found to be 0.225.

Index of TFPS increased an average annual rate of 0.248 percent. The overall trend rate for Solow index was 0.247 per annum. Coefficient of variation was found to be 0.153.

Index of TFPT increased at an average annual rate of 0.149 percent. The overall trend rate for Translog index was 0.141 per annum. Coefficient of variation was found to be 0.154.

An inter-variable comparison in this State revealed that the maximum growth rate was observed in capital intensity followed by labour productivity and negative was in capital productivity. The highest variability was found in labour productivity and least in TFPS.

RELATIONSHIP OF TOTAL FACTOR PRODUCTIVITY WITH PARTIAL PRODUCTIVITIES OF CAPITAL AND LABOUR

The regression models in which total factor productivity (Kendrick, Solow & Translog) depended upon trend, labour and capital productivity were estimated. The estimated equations are :

$$\ln TFPK_t = \underset{(6.887)}{0.766} + \underset{(5.433)}{0.045} \ln t + \underset{(20.294)}{0.328} \ln LP_t + \underset{(19.842)}{0.505} \ln CP_t$$

$$R^2 = 0.990; \quad \tilde{R}^2 = 0.988; \quad S = 0.023$$

$$F \text{ ratio} = 762.17; \quad D\text{–}W = 1.77; \quad \tilde{p} = -0.108$$

$$\ln TFPS_t = 0.989 - 0.025 \ln t + 0.103 \ln LP_t + 0.684 \ln CP_t$$
$$(4.486) \quad (-1.508) \quad (3.23) \quad (13.555)$$
$$R^2 = 0.917; \quad \tilde{R}^2 = 0.906; \quad S = 0.046$$
$$F \text{ ratio} = 87.95; \quad D\text{–}W = 0.951; \quad \tilde{p} = 0.521$$

$$\ln TFPT_t = 1.02 - 0.044 \ln t + 0.122 \ln LP_t + 0.663 \ln CP_t$$
$$(3.635) \quad (-2.07) \quad (2.993) \quad (10.326)$$
$$R^2 = 0.870; \quad \tilde{R}^2 = 0.854; \quad S = 0.059$$
$$F \text{ ratio} = 53.71; \quad D\text{–}W = 1.003; \quad \tilde{p} = 0.426$$

Both labour productivity and capital productivity significantly affected the total factor productivity, indicating consistent and strong relationship between labour productivity, capital productivity and total factor productivity as measured through Kendrick, Solow and Translog indices.

Table 8.14 presents the productivity indices in case of industries in Tamil Nadu. Index of partial labour productivity increased at an average rate of 3.952 percent per annum. The overall trend rate was 4.716 per annum. Coefficient of variation was found to be 0.327.

The index of partial capital productivity declined at an average rate of 2.335 percent per annum. The overall trend rate was –2.408 per annum. The coefficient of variation was found to be 0.265.

The index of capital intensity increased at an average annual rate of 6.498 percent. The overall trend rate was 8.723. Coefficient of variation was found to be 0.527.

Index of TFPK increased at an average annual rate of 0.314 percent. The overall trend rate for Kendrick index was 0.313 per annum. Coefficient of variation was found to be 0.128.

Index of TFPS decreased at an average annual rate of 0.001 percent. The overall trend rate for Solow index was –0.003 per annum. Coefficient of variation was found to be 0.136.

Index of TFPT decreased at an average annual rate of 0.162 percent. The overall trend rate for Translog index was –0.191 per annum. Coefficient of variation was found to be 0.137.

An inter-variable comparison in this State revealed that the maximum growth rate and variability were observed in capital

TABLE 8.14
Productivity Indices of Industries in Tamil Nadu

Year	*Index of Partial Labour Productivity*	*Index of Partial Capital Productivity*	*Index of Real Capital Intensity*	*Index of TFPK*	*Index of TFPS*	*Index of TFPT*
1973-74	100.00	100.00	100.00	100.00	100.00	100.00
1974-75	61.73	105.30	63.31	87.48	80.56	80.73
1975-76	66.98	120.59	59.98	95.50	88.01	88.33
1976-77	79.76	134.34	64.12	108.95	101.14	101.41
1977-78	84.12	129.85	69.96	111.05	102.85	102.93
1978-79	97.23	147.42	71.23	125.62	116.73	116.85
1979-80	85.09	143.06	64.23	115.76	107.39	107.21
1980-81	81.99	135.60	65.30	111.29	103.19	102.98
1981-82	84.26	128.67	70.72	110.14	101.87	101.50
1982-83	95.84	133.38	77.60	119.62	110.53	110.13
1983-84	96.13	117.86	88.08	114.67	105.30	103.58
1984-85	148.63	180.59	88.88	169.31	159.92	157.35
1985-86	108.48	99.63	117.59	111.20	97.36	95.71
1986-87	114.81	103.36	119.95	115.56	101.29	99.59
1987-88	107.62	86.38	134.53	104.48	91.60	89.56
1988-89	131.80	94.92	149.95	116.44	103.36	100.98
1989-90	147.08	107.10	148.30	130.00	115.95	113.28
1990-91	159.73	107.24	160.85	132.88	119.06	116.43
1991-92	143.71	86.48	179.45	113.97	101.36	98.70
1992-93	145.00	76.61	204.40	106.32	94.00	91.07
1993-94	174.59	78.32	240.74	111.11	99.00	96.28
1994-95	176.78	68.20	279.94	102.46	91.41	88.73
1995-96	185.48	83.36	240.29	117.22	102.66	99.80
1996-97	198.72	83.20	257.95	120.09	105.67	102.99
1997-98	166.96	75.76	238.00	110.25	96.07	93.58
1998-99	168.73	66.94	272.19	101.51	90.20	87.46
1999-00	180.51	77.91	250.20	114.30	100.25	97.19
2000-01	182.92	87.36	226.12	123.70	107.55	102.52
Growth Rate	3.952* (12.342)	-2.335* (-5.863)	6.498* (14.081)	0.314^{NS} (1.132)	-0.001^{NS} (-0.003)	-0.162^{NS} (-0.557)
Linear Slope	4.716* (12.762)	-2.408* (-5.108)	8.723* (12.840)	0.313^{NS} (0.915)	-0.003^{NS} (-0.101)	-0.191^{NS} (-0.582)
CV	0.327	0.265	0.527	0.128	0.136	0.137

Notes :
1. Figures in parentheses are the respective 't' values.
2. * Indicates one percent level of significance.
3. ^{NS} Indicates non-significant.

intensity followed by labour productivity and negative growth in capital productivity and least variability in TFPK.

RELATIONSHIP OF TOTAL FACTOR PRODUCTIVITY WITH PARTIAL PRODUCTIVITIES OF CAPITAL AND LABOUR

The estimated regression models in which total factor productivity (Kendrick, Solow & Translog) depended upon trend, labour and capital productivity are given as under :

$$\ln TFPK_t = 0.44 + 0.027 \ln t + 0.353 \ln LP_t + 0.548 \ln CP_t$$
$$(2.403)\ (2.868)\quad (13.949)\quad (23.961)$$
$$R^2 = 0.967; \quad \tilde{R}^2 = 0.962; \quad S = 0.023$$
$$F \text{ ratio} = 231.71; \text{ D–W} = 0.460; \ \tilde{p} = 0.758$$

$$\ln TFPS_t = -0.059 - 0.013 \ln t + 0.403 \ln LP_t + 0.603 \ln CP_t$$
$$(-0.327)\ (-1.403)\quad (16.056)\quad (26.574)$$
$$R^2 = 0.969; \quad \tilde{R}^2 = 0.965; \quad S = 0.023$$
$$F \text{ ratio} = 249.85; \text{ D–W} = 0.712; \ \tilde{p} = 0.594$$

$$\ln TFPT_t = -0.051 - 0.019 \ln t + 0.387 \ln LP_t + 0.617 \ln CP_t$$
$$(-0.298)\ (-2.238)\quad (16.422)\quad (29.002)$$
$$R^2 = 0.973; \quad \tilde{R}^2 = 0.970; \quad S = 0.021$$
$$F \text{ ratio} = 287.38; \text{ D–W} = 0.748; \ \tilde{p} = 0.543$$

Both labour productivity and capital productivity significantly affected the total factor productivity, indicating consistency and robustness in the relationship between labour productivity, capital productivity and total factor productivity as measured through Kendrick, Solow and Translog indices.

Table 8.15 presents the empirical results in case of industries in Uttar Pradesh. Index of partial labour productivity increased at an average rate of 6.068 percent per annum. The overall trend rate was 11.094 per annum. Coefficient of variation was found to be 0.551.

The index of partial capital productivity declined at an average rate of 1.497 percent per annum. The overall trend rate

TABLE 8.15

Productivity Indices of Industries in Uttar Pradesh

Year	*Index of Partial Labour Productivity*	*Index of Partial Capital Productivity*	*Index of Real Capital Intensity*	*Index of TFPK*	*Index of TFPS*	*Index of TFPT*
1973-74	100.00	100.00	100.00	100.00	100.00	100.00
1974-75	80.70	107.44	78.65	102.09	101.19	101.89
1975-76	80.05	249.55	33.59	134.79	124.93	155.12
1976-77	93.36	230.95	42.32	145.65	128.87	161.15
1977-78	73.77	95.11	81.22	92.87	48.48	100.84
1978-79	85.33	103.63	86.22	103.52	54.17	111.31
1979-80	79.52	107.57	77.40	101.26	52.49	107.60
1980-81	68.44	97.80	73.27	87.06	44.21	91.04
1981-82	123.87	158.20	81.98	148.03	76.03	125.41
1982-83	112.90	122.76	96.29	127.87	63.75	109.47
1983-84	95.97	88.89	113.05	107.24	55.29	92.07
1984-85	98.53	87.95	117.30	106.32	55.19	91.87
1985-86	104.24	88.96	122.68	110.48	57.69	96.01
1986-87	162.78	120.07	141.95	149.62	80.12	119.10
1987-88	153.57	107.58	149.46	141.13	75.24	113.22
1988-89	164.50	117.59	146.47	151.79	80.76	121.13
1989-90	204.11	136.18	156.93	180.80	98.01	138.85
1990-91	206.55	119.09	181.60	167.14	90.40	128.31
1991-92	244.26	105.34	242.78	163.32	86.15	127.22
1992-93	232.45	89.61	271.61	147.53	77.71	116.79
1993-94	192.85	68.93	292.93	149.25	80.39	120.02
1994-95	324.81	100.14	339.62	165.64	89.62	132.21
1995-96	313.14	113.46	288.97	178.71	94.99	141.31
1996-97	326.75	104.94	326.01	175.97	94.25	140.64
1997-98	384.21	111.51	360.76	188.73	101.86	151.30
1998-99	311.16	63.28	514.81	120.30	67.38	78.00
1999-00	319.94	96.12	348.51	165.36	82.21	106.22
2000-01	296.09	97.74	317.18	167.13	82.37	100.05
Growth Rate	6.608* (13.743)	-1.497** (-2.442)	8.265* (13.641)	2.028* (5.236)	0.510^NS (0.776)	0.180^NS (0.421)
Linear Slope	11.094* (11.985)	-2.094** (-2.414)	13.523* (11.078)	2.686* (5.366)	0.135^NS (0.262)	0.209^NS (0.416)
CV	0.551	0.353	0.661	0.220	0.270	0.180

Notes :
1. Figures in parentheses are the respective 't' values.
2. * Indicates one percent level of significance.
3. ** Indicates 5 percent level of significance.
4. ^NS Indicates non-significant.

was –2.094 per annum. The coefficient of variation was found to be 0.353.

The index of capital intensity increased at an average annual rate of 8.265 percent. The overall trend rate was 13.523 per annum. Coefficient of variation was found to be 0.661.

Index of TFPK increased at an average annual rate of 2.028 percent. The overall trend rate for Kendrick index was 2.686 per annum. Coefficient of variation was found to be 0.220.

Index of TFPS increased marginally at an average annual rate of 0.510 percent. The overall trend rate for Solow index was 0.135 per annum. Coefficient of variation was found to be 0.270.

Index of TFPT increased at an average annual rate of 0.180 percent. The overall trend rate for Translog index was 0.209 per annum. Coefficient of variation was found to be 0.180.

An inter-variable comparison in this State revealed that the maximum growth rate and variability were in capital intensity followed by labour productivity and negative growth was in capital productivity and least variability in TFPT.

RELATIONSHIP OF TOTAL FACTOR PRODUCTIVITY WITH PARTIAL PRODUCTIVITIES OF CAPITAL AND LABOUR

The estimated regression models in which total factor productivity (Kendrick, Solow & Translog) depended upon trend, labour and capital productivity are given as under :

$$\ln TFPK_t = \underset{(4.177)}{1.11} + \underset{(2.414)}{0.061} \ln t + \underset{(9.079)}{0.329} \ln LP_t + \underset{(9.096)}{0.425} \ln CP_t$$

$R^2 = 0.931$; $\tilde{R}^2 = 0.923$; $S = 0.064$

F ratio $= 108.17$; D–W $= 1.647$; $\tilde{p} = 0.173$

$$\ln TFPS_t = \underset{(-1.123)}{-0.542} - \underset{(-5.711)}{0.26} \ln t + \underset{(8.952)}{0.588} \ln LP_t + \underset{(6.422)}{0.545} \ln CP_t$$

$R^2 = 0.844$; $\tilde{R}^2 = 0.825$; $S = 0.117$

F ratio $= 43.28$; D–W $= 1.474$; $\tilde{p} = -0.255$

$$\ln TFPT_t = \underset{(3.563)}{1.441} - \underset{(-0.057)}{0.002} \ln t + \underset{(3.035)}{0.167} \ln LP_t + \underset{(7.41)}{0.526} \ln CP_t$$

$R^2 = 0.739$; $\tilde{R}^2 = 0.706$; $S = 0.098$

F ratio $= 22.59$; D–W $= 0.936$; $\tilde{p} = 0.451$

Both labour productivity and capital productivity significantly affected the total factor productivity, indicating consistency and strength in the relationship between labour productivity, capital productivity and total factor productivity as measured through Kendrick, Solow and Translog indices.

Table 8.16 presents the productivity indices in case of industries in West Bengal. Index of partial labour productivity increased at an average rate of 3.023 percent per annum. The overall trend rate of labour productivity indicated an increase at the rate of 4.219 per annum. Coefficient of variation was found to be 0.274.

The index of partial capital productivity decreased at an average rate of 4.791 percent per annum. The overall trend rate was –3.409 per annum. The coefficient of variation was found to be 0.448.

The index of capital intensity increased at an average annual rate of 8.267 percent. The overall trend rate was 19.991 per annum. Coefficient of variation was found to be 0.700.

Index of TFPK increased at an average annual rate of 1.103 percent. The overall trend rate for Kendrick index was 1.392 per annum. Coefficient of variation was found to be 0.135.

Index of TFPS decreased at an average annual rate of 0.327 percent. The overall trend rate for Solow index was –0.317 per annum. Coefficient of variation was found to be 0.095.

Index of TFPT decreased at an average annual rate of 0.220 percent. The overall trend rate for Translog index was –0.205 per annum. Coefficient of variation was found to be 0.093.

An inter-variable comparison in this State revealed that the maximum growth rate was in capital intensity followed by labour productivity and negative was in capital productivity. The highest variability was found in capital intensity and least in TFPT.

RELATIONSHIP OF TOTAL FACTOR PRODUCTIVITY WITH PARTIAL PRODUCTIVITIES OF CAPITAL AND LABOUR

The regression models in which total factor productivity (Kendrick, Solow & Translog) depended upon trend, labour and capital productivity were estimated. The estimated equations are :

TABLE 8.16
Productivity Indices of Industries in West Bengal

Year	*Index of Partial Labour Productivity*	*Index of Partial Capital Productivity*	*Index of Real Capital Intensity*	*Index of TFPK*	*Index of TFPS*	*Index of TFPT*
1973-74	100.00	100.00	100.00	100.00	100.00	100.00
1974-75	96.11	118.93	87.03	104.97	106.94	106.75
1975-76	101.02	127.90	85.06	110.06	112.78	112.60
1976-77	106.25	116.18	98.49	113.85	113.41	113.31
1977-78	101.04	109.83	99.08	108.44	107.61	107.49
1978-79	115.64	122.89	101.35	122.66	121.19	121.18
1979-80	105.84	117.77	96.79	113.31	112.38	112.26
1980-81	105.30	102.68	110.44	110.90	108.56	108.55
1981-82	104.12	89.42	125.40	107.93	104.78	104.36
1982-83	109.80	83.76	141.18	111.36	106.88	106.61
1983-84	107.63	74.81	154.94	109.81	104.70	104.41
1984-85	110.81	74.63	159.90	111.86	106.57	106.14
1985-86	128.57	62.39	221.91	119.94	109.21	109.19
1986-87	130.52	78.90	178.16	126.79	115.79	116.90
1987-88	159.64	69.72	246.61	143.45	123.07	127.30
1988-89	124.38	52.45	255.39	114.01	96.53	99.86
1989-90	125.97	47.05	288.35	111.90	94.90	97.62
1990-91	157.55	55.72	304.50	133.75	113.57	116.76
1991-92	156.55	41.28	408.44	121.23	98.57	101.90
1992-93	160.38	30.37	568.72	109.19	88.27	89.18
1993-94	195.23	29.94	702.39	116.28	94.45	96.06
1994-95	173.86	28.64	653.79	111.40	89.92	91.49
1995-96	174.13	34.65	541.28	120.56	95.86	98.24
1996-97	220.44	36.50	650.41	139.84	110.16	112.72
1997-98	219.19	44.08	535.47	151.46	120.03	121.23
1998-99	189.12	78.61	259.10	169.24	124.73	126.82
1999-00	180.40	45.67	425.37	142.57	96.23	99.09
2000-01	173.31	45.95	406.16	141.65	95.53	96.05
Growth Rate	3.023* (12.401)	-4.791* (-7.919)	8.267* (11.395)	1.103* (5.171)	-0.327^{NS} (-1.511)	-0.220^{N} (-1.017)
Linear Slope	4.219* (10.595)	-3.409* (-8.923)	19.991* (7.344)	1.392* (4.983)	-0.317^{NS} (-1.373)	-0.205^{NS} (-0.875)
CV	0.274	0.448	0.700	0.135	0.095	0.093

Notes :. 1. Figures in parentheses are the respective 't' values.
2. * Indicates one percent level of significance.
3. ^{NS} Indicates non-significant.

$$\ln TFPK_t = \underset{(1.279)}{0.376} + \underset{(5.196)}{0.072} \ln t + \underset{(12.744)}{0.611} \ln LP_t + \underset{(11.962)}{0.297} \ln CP_t$$

$R^2 = 0.937$; $\tilde{R}^2 = 0.929$; $S = 0.034$

F ratio = 119.63; D–W = 0.544; $\tilde{p} = 0.639$

$$\ln TFPS_t = \underset{(4.087)}{1.544} + \underset{(1.688)}{0.03} \ln t + \underset{(5.662)}{0.348} \ln LP_t + \underset{(10.023)}{0.32} \ln CP_t$$

$R^2 = 0.816$; $\tilde{R}^2 = 0.793$; $S = 0.043$

F ratio = 35.53; D–W = 0.707; $\tilde{p} = 0.525$

$$\ln TFPT_t = \underset{(3.818)}{1.512} + \underset{(1.719)}{0.032} \ln t + \underset{(5.634)}{0.363} \ln LP_t + \underset{(9.295)}{0.311} \ln CP_t$$

$R^2 = 0.788$; $\tilde{R}^2 = 0.762$; $S = 0.045$

F ratio = 29.80; D–W = 0.605; $\tilde{p} = 0.557$

Both labour productivity and capital productivity significantly affected the total factor productivity, indicating consistent and strong relationship between labour productivity, capital productivity and total factor productivity as measured through Kendrick, Solow and Translog indices.

Table 8.17 presents the empirical results in case of industries at All-India level. Index of partial labour productivity increased at an average rate of 5.117 percent per annum. The overall trend rate was 8.375 per annum. Coefficient of variation was found to be 0.427.

The index of partial capital productivity declined at an average rate of 1.873 percent per annum. The overall trend rate was –1.637 per annum. The coefficient of variation was found to be 0.182.

The index of capital intensity increased at an average annual rate of 7.179 percent. The overall trend rate was 14.883 per annum. Coefficient of variation was found to be 0.555.

Index of TFPK increased at an average annual rate of 1.395 percent. The overall trend rate for Kendrick index was 1.718 per annum. Coefficient of variation was found to be 0.138.

Index of TFPS increased at an average annual rate of 1.037 percent. The overall trend rate for Solow index was 1.270 per annum. Coefficient of variation was found to be 0.125.

TABLE 8.17
Productivity Indices of Industries in All India

Year	Index of Partial Labour Productivity	Index of Partial Capital Productivity	Index of Real Capital Intensity	Index of TFPK	Index of TFPS	Index of TFPT
1973-74	100.00	100.00	100.00	100.00	100.00	100.00
1974-75	90.06	115.77	83.35	106.35	107.46	107.10
1975-76	90.70	115.82	83.91	106.65	107.73	107.36
1976-77	97.62	111.14	94.12	110.13	110.05	109.73
1977-78	96.68	98.70	104.96	105.09	103.44	102.84
1978-79	111.24	104.47	114.09	116.36	114.27	113.85
1979-80	101.93	99.98	109.25	108.84	106.74	106.21
1980-81	94.22	91.28	110.61	101.13	99.12	98.58
1981-82	103.98	97.22	114.60	109.03	106.89	106.30
1982-83	110.60	90.85	130.45	109.79	107.16	106.26
1983-84	127.16	91.92	148.23	119.74	116.58	116.03
1984-85	123.12	84.67	155.81	114.66	111.75	111.12
1985-86	134.26	81.61	176.27	117.52	114.93	114.12
1986-87	144.21	84.99	181.82	122.90	120.35	119.52
1987-88	141.34	73.29	206.63	115.66	113.29	112.04
1988-89	161.68	83.99	206.25	129.86	127.10	125.69
1989-90	176.22	86.62	217.98	136.71	134.53	132.90
1990-91	192.51	82.56	249.87	137.30	135.06	132.17
1991-92	261.80	97.22	288.56	166.74	164.66	162.37
1992-93	199.46	61.21	349.15	118.67	108.79	106.27
1993-94	228.40	62.97	388.68	125.00	115.41	112.79
1994-95	238.33	64.28	397.27	126.85	117.33	114.66
1995-96	256.67	72.22	380.80	138.75	128.83	126.00
1996-97	294.67	75.11	420.40	148.22	137.81	134.86
1997-98	279.92	72.27	415.00	143.37	132.98	130.15
1998-99	270.73	65.46	443.15	133.47	124.84	122.19
1999-00	293.51	77.39	406.36	152.65	140.77	137.58
2000-01	259.72	72.22	385.35	142.47	131.55	124.77
Growth Rate	5.117* (18.908)	-1.873* (-8.223)	7.179* (24.579)	1.395* (8.235)	1.037* (5.444)	0.946* (4.758)
Linear Slope	8.375* (14.859)	-1.637* (-8.558)	14.883* (16.565)	1.718* (7.552)	1.270* (5.023)	1.116* (4.405)
CV	0.427	0.182	0.555	0.138	0.125	0.119

Notes : 1. Figures in parentheses are the respective 't' values.
2. * Indicates one percent level of significance.

Index of TFPT increased at an average rate of 0.946 percent per annum. The overall trend rate for Translog index was 1.116 per annum. Coefficient of variation was found to be 0.119.

An inter-variable comparison at all-India level revealed that the maximum growth rate and variability were observed in capital intensity followed by labour productivity and negative growth was in capital productivity and least variability in TFPT.

RELATIONSHIP OF TOTAL FACTOR PRODUCTIVITY WITH PARTIAL PRODUCTIVITIES OF CAPITAL AND LABOUR

The estimated regression models in which total factor productivity (Kendrick, Solow & Translog) depended upon trend, labour and capital productivity are given as under :

$$\ln TFPK_t = \underset{(2.781)}{0.645} + \underset{(6.232)}{0.062} \ln t + \underset{(18.607)}{0.352} \ln LP_t + \underset{(12.556)}{0.503} \ln CP_t$$

$$R^2 = 0.977; \quad \tilde{R}^2 = 0.974; \quad S = 0.021$$

$$F \text{ ratio} = 343.38; \quad D\text{–}W = 0.385; \quad \tilde{p} = 0.785$$

$$\ln TFPS_t = \underset{(0.719)}{0.255} + \underset{(4.252)}{0.065} \ln t + \underset{(11.195)}{0.325} \ln LP_t + \underset{(10.0).}{0.613} \ln CP_t$$

$$R^2 = 0.933; \quad \tilde{R}^2 = 0.924; \quad S = 0.033$$

$$F \text{ ratio} = 110.65; \quad D\text{–}W = 0.295; \quad \tilde{p} = 0.825$$

$$\ln TFPT_t = \underset{(0.69)}{0.263} + \underset{(3.944)}{0.064} \ln t + \underset{(9.934)}{0.309} \ln LP_t + \underset{(9.54)}{0.627} \ln CP_t$$

$$R^2 = 0.915; \quad \tilde{R}^2 = 0.904; \quad S = 0.035$$

$$F \text{ ratio} = 85.64; \quad D\text{–}W = 0.316; \quad \tilde{p} = 0.781$$

Both labour productivity and capital productivity significantly affected the total factor productivity, indicating consistency and robustness in the relationship between labour productivity, capital productivity and total factor productivity as measured through Kendrick, Solow and Translog indices.

Inter-State Comparison

The maximum growth rate and variability in the index of partial labour productivity have been found in Uttar Pradesh and minimum in West Bengal.

The highest growth rate in the index of partial capital productivity was found in Bihar and most negative was in West Bengal. The maximum variability was seen in West Bengal and the least in Kerala.

The highest growth rate and variability in the index of real capital intensity were found in Gujarat, but the least growth rate was in Bihar and minimum variability in Punjab.

For TFPK, the maximum growth rate and variability were perceived in Bihar but negative growth rate was in Assam and minimum variability in Gujarat.

For TFPS and TFPT, the maximum growth rates were found in Bihar but the most negative growth rates and highest variability were in Assam and minimum variability in West Bengal.

Both labour productivity and capital productivity significantly affected the total factor productivity in all states and all-India except in case of Assam where labour productivity and capital productivity significantly affected only TFPK and in Kerala and Madhya Pradesh, labour productivity and capital productivity significantly affected only TFPK and TFPS.

Inter-State Comparison of Partial Labour Productivity

An inter-state comparison of partial labour productivity from 1973-74 to 2000-01 (Table 8.18) revealed that the maximum average annual growth rate was observed in Gujarat followed by Maharashtra and minimum was in West Bengal. The highest variability was found in Uttar Pradesh followed by Gujarat and least was in West Bengal. In 1973-74 maximum partial labour productivity was perceived in Maharashtra followed by Orissa and Rajasthan simultaneously and least was in Himachal Pradesh. In 1983-84 maximum value of labour productivity was in Himachal Pradesh followed by Bihar and least was in Uttar Pradesh. In 1993-94 maximum value was in Bihar followed by Maharashtra and least was in Kerala. In 2000-01 maximum labour productivity was in Himachal Pradesh followed by Maharashtra and least was in West Bengal.

TABLE 8.18
Profile of Partial Labour Productivity in States and All-India

Year	*AP*	*ASM*	*BIH*	*GUJ*	*HAR*	*HP*	*KAR*	*KER*	*MP*
(1)	*(2)*	*(3)*	*(4)*	*(5)*	*(6)*	*(7)*	*(8)*	*(9)*	*(10)*
1973-74	0.336	0.386	0.483	0.460	0.371	0.245	0.431	0.304	0.540
1974-75	0.266	0.408	0.502	0.431	0.438	0.167	0.374	0.277	0.448
1975-76	0.308	0.395	0.570	0.391	0.523	0.403	0.397	0.267	0.411
1976-77	0.287	0.487	0.447	0.456	0.587	0.616	0.408	0.286	0.507
1977-78	0.284	0.527	0.399	0.490	0.579	0.722	0.411	0.314	0.448
1978-79	0.302	0.469	0.499	0.505	0.689	0.860	0.633	0.379	0.451
1979-80	0.275	0.379	0.493	0.461	0.622	0.912	0.487	0.391	0.459
1980-81	0.269	0.252	0.356	0.441	0.554	0.755	0.412	0.378	0.502
1981-82	0.267	0.289	0.619	0.460	0.552	0.941	0.462	0.368	0.579
1982-83	0.346	0.317	0.713	0.475	0.560	1.223	0.486	0.430	0.624
1983-84	0.442	0.458	0.974	0.662	0.726	1.336	0.633	0.455	0.631
1984-85	0.488	0.625	0.674	0.642	0.540	0.924	0.547	0.569	0.558
1985-86	0.445	0.773	0.721	0.639	0.571	0.957	0.616	0.573	0.780
1986-87	0.441	0.825	0.754	0.716	0.617	0.902	0.622	0.564	0.576
1987-88	0.380	0.780	0.852	0.735	0.588	0.643	0.598	0.608	0.719

(Contd.)

TABLE 8.18 (Contd.)

(1)	(2)	(3)	(4)	(5)	(6)	(7)	(8)	(9)	(10)
1988-89	0.479	0.521	1.085	0.815	0.710	0.905	0.651	0.649	0.867
1989-90	0.475	0.918	1.082	0.783	0.727	0.732	0.787	0.823	0.901
1990-91	0.586	0.913	0.978	0.897	0.877	0.956	0.896	0.609	0.978
1991-92	0.586	0.742	1.091	0.707	0.787	0.904	0.957	0.707	0.834
1992-93	0.640	0.682	1.022	1.199	0.656	0.816	1.019	0.611	0.931
1993-94	0.703	0.757	1.974	1.239	0.737	1.357	0.920	0.601	1.189
1994-95	0.774	0.707	1.146	1.422	0.890	1.069	1.124	0.577	1.228
1995-96	0.800	0.724	1.293	1.515	1.148	1.060	1.084	0.770	1.494
1996-97	0.940	0.769	1.446	1.872	1.186	1.547	1.207	0.807	1.807
1997-98	0.744	0.693	2.312	1.649	1.224	1.295	1.111	0.732	1.586
1998-99	0.799	0.963	1.869	1.646	1.032	1.845	1.183	1.028	1.047
1999-00	0.813	1.026	1.105	1.612	1.499	1.922	1.168	0.824	1.449
2000-01	0.752	0.733	0.745	1.440	1.189	2.134	1.124	0.728	1.573
Growth Rate	4.909* (14.008)	3.595* (5.829)	5.102* (7.701)	6.097* (15.892)	3.707* (9.834)	5.334* (6.159)	4.827* (16.538)	4.412* (12.938)	5.345* (14.029)
Linear Slope	0.023* (12.923)	0.02* (6.220)	0.045* (6.034)	0.052* (11.479)	0.028* (8.459)	0.044* (6.734)	0.033* (15.397)	0.022* (11.534)	0.045* (10.422)
CV	0.415	0.347	0.524	0.533	0.365	0.459	0.396	0.359	0.479

TABLE 8.18 (Contd.)

Year	MAH	ORI	PB	RAJ	TN	UP	WB	All India
(1)	(11)	(12)	(13)	(14)	(15)	(16)	(17)	(18)
1973-74	0.607	0.580	0.345	0.580	0.511	0.385	0.372	0.445
1974-75	0.544	0.467	0.330	0.380	0.315	0.311	0.357	0.400
1975-76	0.543	0.378	0.382	0.435	0.342	0.308	0.375	0.403
1976-77	0.582	0.574	0.402	0.441	0.408	0.359	0.395	0.434
1977-78	0.613	0.461	0.407	0.460	0.430	0.284	0.375	0.430
1978-79	0.706	0.605	0.448	0.546	0.497	0.328	0.430	0.495
1979-80	0.646	0.621	0.440	0.538	0.435	0.306	0.393	0.453
1980-81	0.605	0.403	0.445	0.474	0.419	0.263	0.391	0.419
1981-82	0.637	0.413	0.407	0.465	0.431	0.477	0.387	0.462
1982-83	0.659	0.392	0.411	0.433	0.490	0.435	0.408	0.492
1983-84	0.769	0.480	0.435	0.615	0.491	0.369	0.400	0.565
1984-85	0.782	0.340	0.412	0.515	0.759	0.379	0.412	0.547
1985-86	0.992	0.439	0.473	0.580	0.554	0.401	0.478	0.597
1986-87	0.945	0.539	0.480	0.754	0.587	0.627	0.485	0.641
1987-88	0.883	0.505	0.463	0.516	0.550	0.591	0.593	0.628
1988-89	1.087	0.914	0.458	0.615	0.673	0.633	0.462	0.719

(Contd.)

TABLE 8.18 (Contd.)

(1)	(11)	(12)	(13)	(14)	(15)	(16)	(17)	(18)
1989-90	1.217	1.064	0.800	0.671	0.752	0.786	0.468	0.784
1990-91	1.314	1.020	0.628	0.874	0.816	0.795	0.585	0.856
1991-92	1.086	0.877	0.640	0.809	0.734	0.940	0.582	1.164
1992-93	1.370	0.855	0.514	0.967	0.741	0.895	0.596	0.887
1993-94	1.642	0.914	0.682	0.944	0.892	0.742	0.725	1.016
1994-95	1.609	0.948	0.701	1.159	0.903	1.250	0.646	1.060
1995-96	1.786	1.082	0.697	1.171	0.948	1.205	0.647	1.141
1996-97	1.930	1.480	0.781	1.517	1.015	1.258	0.819	1.310
1997-98	1.788	1.603	0.804	1.593	0.853	1.479	0.815	1.245
1998-99	1.596	1.039	1.100	1.069	0.862	1.198	0.703	1.204
1999-00	1.956	1.394	1.137	1.559	0.922	1.231	0.670	1.305
2000-01	1.712	1.174	0.770	1.455	0.935	1.140	0.644	1.155
Growth Rate	5.385* (19.354)	4.72* (7.311)	3.797* (11.069)	5.081* (11.513)	3.952* (12.341)	4.608* (13.740)	3.022* (12.394)	5.117* (18.892)
Linear Slope	0.055* (15.141)	0.036* (7.528)	0.022* (8.489)	0.04* (9.541)	0.024* (12.760)	0.042* (11.984)	0.015* (10.591)	0.037* (14.853)
CV	0.444	0.470	0.374	0.482	0.327	0.552	0.274	0.427

Notes : 1. Figures in parentheses are the respective ' t' values.
2. *Indicates significant at one percent level.

It was found that the growth rates of capital intensity and labour productivity were positive and highly significant in all states. Except in three states namely, Bihar, Kerala and Punjab, the growth rates of capital intensity were higher than the labour productivity in all states. It was also observed that the average annual growth rates of labour productivity in all states were higher than that of wage rates in respective states (Table 7.19). This might be because when industries in the states were growing, they went in for more technological innovation which increased the labour productivity and therefore higher wages as well. In Madhya Pradesh, the difference between average annual growth rate of labour productivity and wage rate was maximum, i.e. average annual growth rate of labour productivity was 2.96 times higher than that of wage rate and the second highest difference was in Gujarat. The least difference was in Haryana where average annual growth rate of labour productivity was 1.08 times higher than that of wage rate followed by Punjab. Even in states like Gujarat, Himachal Pradesh, Madhya Pradesh, Maharashtra, Orissa, Rajasthan, Tamil Nadu and All-India, the difference between average annual growth rates of labour productivity and wage rate were greater than average annual growth rates of wage rate in respective states.

It may be concluded from the discussion in this chapter that the labour productivity showed rising trend in all states. However, in states like Bihar, Gujarat, Himachal Pradesh, Madhya Pradesh, Maharashtra, Rajasthan and Uttar Pradesh, the trends in labour productivity were greater that that of All-India and in states like Andhra Pradesh, Assam, Haryana, Karnataka, Kerala, Orissa, Punjab, Tamil Nadu and West Bengal, the trends in labour productivity were lesser than that of All-India. In comparison to the growth in their labour productivity, workers in Madhya Pradesh received the least reward in the form of higher wages and workers in Haryana received the highest reward followed by workers in Punjab. It was also perceived that growth rates of capital intensity and labour productivity were highly significant and except Bihar, Kerala and Punjab, the growth rates of capital intensity were higher than that of labour productivity in all states. The average annual growth rate of capital productivity was positive only in Bihar,

Kerala and Punjab but was found significant in Bihar only. Both labour productivity and capital productivity significantly affected the total factor productivity in all states and all-India except in case of Assam where labour productivity and capital productivity significantly affected only TFPK and in Kerala and Madhya Pradesh, labour productivity and capital productivity significantly affected only TFPK and TFPS.

Wage-Productivity Relationship in Industries

In the present chapter an attempt has been made to analyse the relationship between variables like wage rate, labour productivity, total factor productivity and capital intensity, etc. during the period 1973-74 to 2000-01 in fourteen major industries of manufacturing sector at all-India level. The different log-linear regressions have been derived (discussed in Chapter-IV) and are given in tables in the appendix. The results in each case are discussed below.

1. FOOD PRODUCTS INDUSTRY

Effect of Productivity on Wages

Nine models of effect of productivity and capital intensity on wages have been estimated (Table 9.1.1) and the results of selected models with significant effect on explanatory variables are discussed below :

Consider the regression equation in Model II (Table 9.1.1) in which wage rate depends upon trend and one period lagged partial labour productivity. Coefficient of time is 0.326 and trend is upward and is significant. The coefficient of LP_{t-1} is 0.25 and

TABLE 9.1.1

Regression Function for Wages (Food Products Industry—All India)

Dependent Variable—Real Wage Rate

Explanatory Variables	*Model Numbers*								
	I	*II*	*III*	*IV*	*V*	*VI*	*VII*	*VIII*	*IX*
(1)	*(2)*	*(3)*	*(4)*	*(5)*	*(6)*	*(7)*	*(8)*	*(9)*	*(10)*
Constant	2.377 (11.243)	2.773 (16.379)	3.065 (15.374)	2.425 (13.332)	2.849 (17.138)	3.015 (16.773)	0.656 (1.191)	1.015 (1.848)	0.980 (1.740)
ln Time	0.116** (2.604)	0.326* (7.144)	0.467* (7.314)	0.099** (2.410)	0.323* (6.626)	0.434* (6.816)	0.163* (3.311)	0.207* (4.306)	0.213* (4.473)
ln LP_t	0.423* (7.758)								
ln LP_{t-1}		0.25* (5.209)							
ln LP_{t-2}			0.126** (2.074)						
ln $(K/L)_t$				0.436* (8.801)					
ln $(K/L)_{t-1}$					0.245* (4.854)				

ln $(K/L)_{t-2}$						0.158** (2.652)			
ln TFPK							0.77* (6.008)		
ln TFPS								0.682* (5.377)	
ln TFPT									0.69* (5.308)
R^2	0.922	0.952	0.928	0.935	0.948	0.935	0.891	0.876	0.875
$\tilde{R}^2$	0.915	0.948	0.922	0.930	0.944	0.929	0.882	0.866	0.865
S	0.114	0.090	0.105	0.104	0.094	0.101	0.134	0.143	0.144
F	147.23	235.67	148.95	179.64	218.39	165.00	102.06	88.60	87.22
D-W	1.072	0.912	0.957	0.835	0.910	0.914	1.204	1.112	1.092
$\tilde{\rho}$	0.332	0.520	0.433	0.517	0.535	0.492	0.194	0.228	0.235

Notes : 1. Figures in brackets are the respective 't' values.
2. * ** *** Indicates significant at 1%, 5% and 10% levels respectively.

it shows that 100 percent increase in labour productivity brings about 25.0 percent increase in wage rate in the next year, keeping the effect of time constant. The value of R^2 is 0.952 and of $\tilde{R}^2$ is 0.948 which reveals that about 95.2 percent variations in wage rate were due to trend and one year lagged partial labour productivity. Thus, increase in partial labour productivity has benefited the workers in food products industry. The given model fits the data well.

Graph 9.1 indicates that there are no outliers. The points representing pairs of explanatory and explained variables cluster around the fitted regression line. This can be taken as an indication of good fit of the linear regression line to the given data. The scattered points show upward tendency which is an indication of the positive correlation between two variables and this is indicated by high Pearson's correlation coefficient (0.949). The estimated regression slope is found to be 0.538. The graph indicates that the deviations from the regression are positive in the middle.

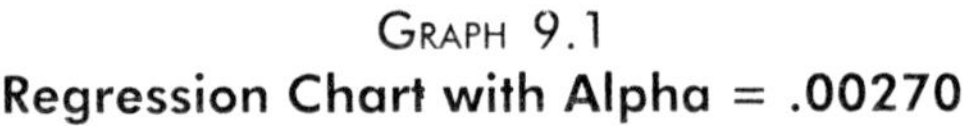

GRAPH 9.1
Regression Chart with Alpha = .00270

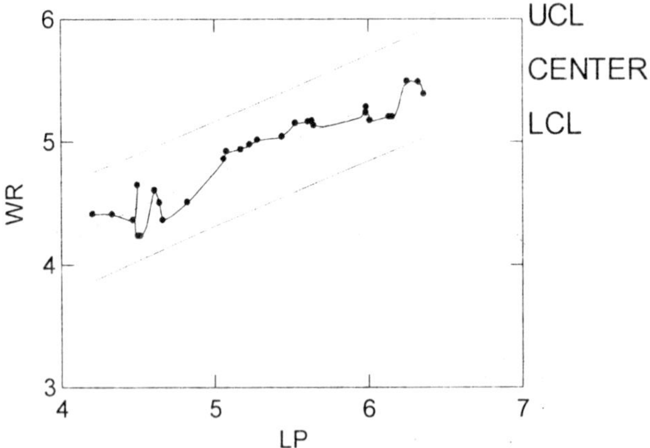

Consider the regression equation in Model V in which real wage rate depends upon trend and one year lagged capital intensity. The coefficient of time is 0.323 and trend is upward and significant. The slope coefficient of $(K/L)_{t-1}$ is 0.254 and this shows that 100 percent increase in capital intensity, keeping the effect of time constant, brings about 25.4 percent increase in wage rate in next year. The value of R^2 is 0.948 and of $\tilde{R}^2$ is 0.944 which reveals that about 94.8 percent variations in wage rate were due to trend and one year lagged capital intensity. The given model fits the data well. Thus capital intensity, is an index of increased and improved mechanisation. Increase in capital-labour ratio has gone in favour of workers in this industry, i.e. workers have benefited in terms of wages due to increase in the capital intensity.

Graph 9.2 indicates that there are no outliers. The points representing pairs of explanatory and explained variables cluster around the fitted regression line. This can be taken as an indication of good fit of the linear regression line to the given data. The scattered points show upward tendency which is an indication of the positive correlation between two variables and this is indicated by high Pearson's correlation coefficient (0.959). The estimated regression slope is found to be 0.534. The graph indicates that at the extreme ends, the deviations from the regression are negative and in the middle they are positive.

GRAPH 9.2
Regression Chart with Alpha = .00270

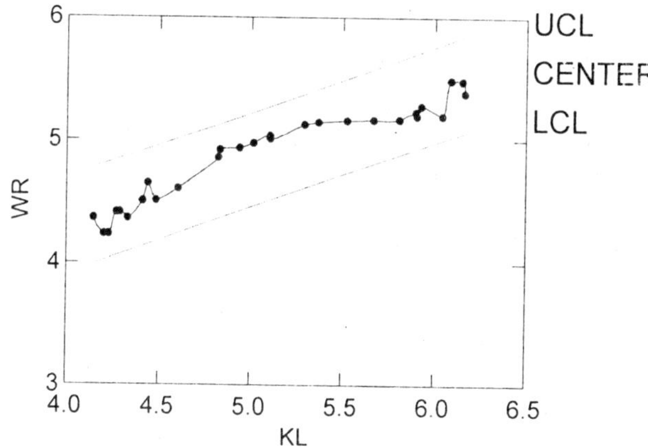

In Model VII real wage rate depends upon trend and total factor productivity index (Kendrick). Coefficient of time is 0.163 and is statistically significant. The slope coefficient of TFPK is

0.77 and this shows that 100 percent increase in TFPK brings about 77.0 percent increase in wage rate, when the effect of time is held constant. The value of R^2 is 0.891 and of $\tilde{R}^2$ is 0.882 which indicates that about 89.1 percent variations in wage rate were due to TFPK and time. The given model fits the data well.

In Model VIII real wage rate depends upon trend and total factor productivity index (Solow). Coefficient of time is 0.207 and is statistically significant. The slope coefficient of TFPS is 0.682 and this shows that 100 percent increase in TFPS brings about 68.2 percent increase in wage rate, when the effect of time is held constant. The value of R^2 is 0.876 and of $\tilde{R}^2$ is 0.866 which indicates that about 87.6 percent variations in wage rate were due to TFPS and time. The given model fits the data well.

In Model IX real wage rate depends upon trend and total factor productivity index (Translog). Coefficient of time is 0.213 and is statistically significant. The slope coefficient of TFPT is 0.69 and this shows that 100 percent increase in TFPT brings about 69.0 percent increase in wage rate, when the effect of time is held constant. The value of R^2 is 0.875 and of $\tilde{R}^2$ is 0.865 which indicates that about 87.5 percent variations in wage rate were due to TFPT and time. The given model fits the data well.

On the whole, the results obtained in case of models VII, VIII and IX are robust and consistent, indicating that total factor productivity has positive and significant effect on wage rate.

Effect of Wages on Productivity

In the above discussion we have considered wage rate as a function of labour productivity. The estimated values show that wage rate is responsive to the changes in the labour productivity. It will be interesting to find that labour productivity is also influenced by wage rate as the workers are human beings and their productivity increases with improvement in working and living conditions, reflected by wages. Taking labour productivity as dependent upon trend and up to seven year lagged wage rate in Table 9.1.2, models X-XVI indicate that though the value of slope parameter of wage rate (from t to t–6) indicate declining trend, but it continued to be significant at 5 percent level. The regression coefficient turned out to be negative and non-significant in the seventh year. This indicated that wage rate affected labour productivity

TABLE 9.1.2

Regression Function for Labour Productivity (Food Products Industry—All India)

Dependent Variable—Partial Labour Productivity

Explanatory Variables	*Model Numbers*										
	X	*XI*	*XII*	*XIII*	*XIV*	*XV*	*XVI*	*XVII*	*XVIII*	*XIX*	*XX*
(1)	*(2)*	*(3)*	*(4)*	*(5)*	*(6)*	*(7)*	*(8)*	*(9)*	*(10)*	*(11)*	*(12)*
Constant	-2.890 (-3.371)	-1.922 (-1.876)	-0.901 (-0.783)	-0.683 (-0.616)	-1.019 (-1.08)	-1.033 (-1.318)	-0.178 (-0.284)	1.417 (2.907)	0.378 (1.792)	0.739 (2.359)	1.073 (2.738)
ln Time	0.001 (0.012)	0.182 (1.243)	0.413** (2.165)	0.539** (2.552)	0.548** (2.599)	0.682* (3.142)	1.148* (6.291)	1.878* (11.668)	0.013 (0.275)	0.167*** (1.822)	0.371** (2.670)
ln WR_t	1.671* (7.758)										
ln WR_{t-1}		1.391* (5.083)									
ln WR_{t-2}			1.068* (3.295)								
ln WR_{t-3}				0.961* (2.930)							
ln WR_{t-4}					1.03* (3.479)						

(Contd.)

TABLE 9.1.2 (CONTD.)

(1)	(2)	(3)	(4)	(5)	(6)	(7)	(8)	(9)	(10)	(11)	(12)
ln WR_{t-5}						0.963* (3.718)					
ln WR_{t-6}							0.515** (2.356)				
ln WR_{t-7}								-0.254 (-1.418)			
ln $(K/L)_t$									0.955* (16.595)		
ln $(K/L)_{t-1}$										0.819* (8.615)	
ln $(K/L)_{t-2}$											0.659* (5.071)
R^2	0.901	0.881	0.863	0.874	0.902	0.929	0.952	0.968	0.972	0.940	0.905
$\tilde{R}^2$	0.893	0.871	0.851	0.862	0.893	0.922	0.947	0.965	0.970	0.934	0.897
S	0.226	0.247	0.263	0.249	0.216	0.183	0.151	0.121	0.120	0.176	0.219
F	113.15	88.66	72.62	76.21	96.73	130.80	188.30	272.86	430.60	186.41	109.52
D-W	0.809	0.955	0.945	0.948	1.147	1.379	1.447	1.728	1.144	1.312	1.080
$\tilde{\rho}$	0.580	0.517	0.527	0.518	0.425	0.280	0.219	0.108	0.387	0.328	0.453

Notes : 1. Figures in brackets are the respective 't' values.
2. * ** *** Indicates significant at 1%, 5% and 10% levels respectively.

significantly even up to six years lag. In Model XVI coefficient of time is 1.148 and this shows that trend is upward and significant. The slope coefficient 0.515 shows that 100 percent increase in wage rate results into 51.5 percent increase in labour productivity in the next sixth year, keeping the effect of time constant. Hence labour productivity is highly responsive to change in wage rate in food products industry. It appears that increase in wage rate is in the interest of this industry. The value of R^2 is 0.952 and of $\tilde{R}^2$ is 0.947 which indicates that 95.2 percent variations in labour productivity were due to trend and sixth year lagged wage rate. Hence, wage rate is a highly significant explanatory variable. The model fits the data well.

Consider the regression equations in models XVIII-XX in which labour productivity depends upon trend and current, one year and two year lagged capital intensity. The regression coefficient of current year capital intensity was the highest and its level of significance as indicated by t value was also the highest. With time lag, the value of regression coefficient and its level of significance decreased but it remained significant at one percent level. This indicated that current capital intensity and also with up to two years lag affected the labour productivity significantly. In case of Model XIX coefficient of time is 0.167 and it is upward and mildly significant. The slope coefficient shows that 100 percent increase in $(K/L)_{t-1}$ brings about 81.9 percent increase in labour productivity in the next year. Thus, capital intensity, is an index of intensity of mechanisation; therefore the results showed that an increase in capital-labour ratio helped in raising the productivity of labour. The value of R^2 is 0.94 and of $\tilde{R}^2$ is 0.934 which reveals that 94.0 percent variations in labour productivity were due to trend and one year lagged capital intensity. The given model fits the data well.

Graph 9.3 indicates that there are no outliers. The points representing pairs of explanatory and explained variables cluster around the fitted regression line. This can be taken as an indication of good fit of the linear regression line to the given data. The scattered points show upward tendency which is an indication of the positive correlation between two variables and this is indicated by high Pearson's correlation coefficient (0.986). The estimated regression slope is found to be 0.968.

Graph 9.3
Regression Chart with Alpha = .00270

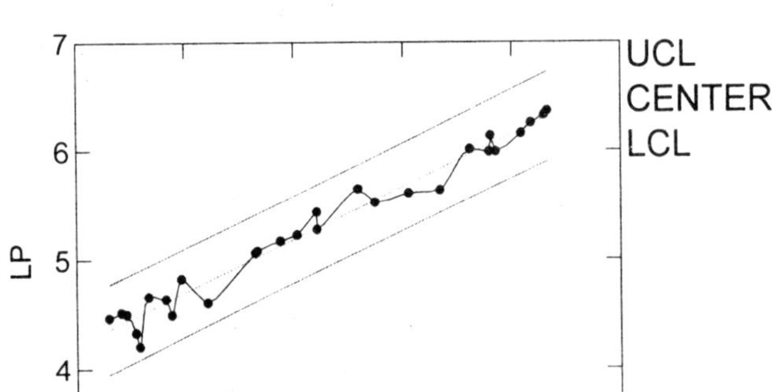

Pre and Post-liberalisation Period

Consider the regression equation in Model XXI, in which wage rate is dependent upon dummy, labour productivity and product of dummy times labour productivity variables in Table 9.1.3. This model is introduced to examine the stability of relationship between wage rate and labour productivity in pre and post-liberalisation period. The estimated equation is :

$$WR_t = 39.583 + 73.515\ D + 0.516\ LP_t - 0.322\ D\ .\ LP_t$$

Pre-liberalisation Era I—1973 to 1990 and D = 0; then

$$WR_t = 39.583 + 0.516\ LP_t$$

Post-liberalisation Era II—1991 to 2000 and D = 1; then

$$WR_t = 113.098 + 0.194\ LP_t$$

The differential intercept and the differential slope parameter are highly significant. The function has shifted from period I to period II due to significant difference in intercept values and in slope parameters. In post-liberalisation period though the intercept has increased but, the slope of regression line has become flatter. Thus relationship between wage and labour productivity during post-reform era has weakened, i.e.

TABLE 9.1.3
Structural Stability of Regression Functions (Food Products Industry—All India)

Dependent Variables	*I*		*II*	
	Real Wage Rate		*Labour Productivity*	
Explanatory Variables	*Model Numbers*			
	XXI	*XXII*	*XXIII*	*XXIV*
Constant	39.583 (4.688)	41.48 (5.906)	-52.502 (-1.432)	-16.971 (-0.371)
Time		3.43* (3.450)		5.846 (1.271)
Dummy	73.515* (3.315)	29.008 (1.291)	-107.031 (-0.901)	-163.95 (-1.305)
LP_t	0.516* (9.554)	0.275* (3.309)		
D. LP_t	-0.322 (-4.548)	-0.169 (-2.286)		
WR_t			1.725* (5.577)	0.922 (1.313)
D.WR_t			1.29*** (1.994)	1.506** (2.277)
R^2	0.931	0.955	0.931	0.936
$\tilde{R}^2$	0.922	0.947	0.923	0.925
S	14.497	12.021	45.425	44.854
F	108.04	120.83	108.39	83.78
D-W	1.055	1.171	1.353	1.268
$\tilde{\rho}$	0.384	0.237	0.294	0.334

Notes : 1. Figures in brackets are the respective 't' values.
2. * ** *** Indicates significant at 1%, 5% and 10% levels respectively.

proportionate gains from productivity increase have not been distributed among the workers.

In Model XXII wage rate depends upon dummy, time, labour productivity and product of dummy times labour productivity variables. The estimated equation is :

$$WR_t = 41.48 + 3.43\ t + 29.008\ D + 0.275\ LP_t - 0.169\ D\ .\ LP_t$$

Pre-liberalisation Era I—1973 to 1990 and D = 0; then

$$WR_t = 41.48 + 3.43\ t + 0.275\ LP_t$$

Post-liberalisation Era II—1991 to 2000 and D = 1; then

$$WR_t = 70.488 + 3.43\ t + 0.106\ LP_t$$

The trend effect in pre and post-reform period remains the same. The differential intercept is non-significant but the differential slope parameter is significant. In post-liberalisation period the slope of regression line has become flatter, i.e. the relationship between wage and labour productivity during post-reform era has weakened. Since the time period of post-reform era is less, so over long period it has to be seen whether this relationship reverts back or further weakens.

Consider the regression equation in Model XXIII, in which labour productivity is dependent upon dummy, wage rate and product of dummy times wage rate variables. The estimated equation is :

$$LP_t = -52.502 - 107.031\ D + 1.725\ WR_t + 1.29\ D\ .\ WR_t$$

Pre-liberalisation Era I—1973 to 1990 and D = 0; then

$$LP_t = -52.502 + 1.725\ WR_t$$

Post-liberalisation Era II—1991 to 2000 and D = 1; then

$$LP_t = -159.533 + 3.015\ WR_t$$

The differential intercept is non-significant but the differential slope parameter is mildly significant. In post-liberalisation period the slope of regression line has become steeper, i.e. the relationship between labour productivity and wage rate during post-reform era has strengthened. After liberalisation when market forces have more important role to play, the labour productivity has become more responsive to wage rate.

Consider the regression equation in Model XXIV, in which labour productivity is dependent upon time, dummy, wage rate and product of dummy times wage rate variables. The estimated equation is :

$$LP_t = -16.971 + 5.846\ t - 163.95\ D + 0.922\ WR_t + 1.506\ D\ .\ WR_t$$

Pre-liberalisation Era I—1973 to 1990 and D = 0; then

$$LP_t = -16.971 + 5.846\ t + 0.922\ WR_t$$

Post-liberalisation Era II—1991 to 2000 and D = 1; then

$$LP_t = -180.921 + 5.846\ t + 2.428\ WR_t$$

The trend effect in pre and post-reform period remains the same. The differential intercept is non-significant but the differential slope parameter is significant. In post-liberalisation period the slope of regression line has become steeper, i.e. the relationship between labour productivity and wage rate during post-reform era has strengthened. After liberalisation when market forces have more important role to play, the labour productivity has become more responsive to wage rate.

2. BEVERAGES, TOBACCO, AND TOBACCO PRODUCTS INDUSTRY

Effect of Productivity on Wages

Eight models of effect of productivity and capital intensity on wages have been estimated (Table 9.2.1) and the results of selected models with significant effect of explanatory variables are discussed below :

Consider the regression equation in Model II in which wage rate depends upon trend and one period lagged partial labour productivity. Coefficient of time is 0.162 and trend is upward and is significant. The coefficient of LP_{t-1} is 0.097 and it shows that 100 percent increase in labour productivity brings about 9.7 percent increase in wage rate in the next year, keeping the effect of time constant. The value of R^2 is 0.727 and of $\tilde{R}^2$ is 0.704 which reveals that about 72.7 percent variations in wage rate were due to trend and one year lagged partial labour productivity. Thus increase in partial labour productivity has benefited the workers in beverages, tobacco, and tobacco products industry. The given model fits the data well.

Consider the regression equation in Model IV in which real wage rate depends upon trend and current period capital intensity. The coefficient of time is 0.092 and trend is upward and significant. The slope coefficient of $(K/L)_t$ is 0.147 and this shows that 100 percent increase in capital intensity, keeping the

TABLE 9.2.1
Regression Function for Wages
(Beverages, Tobacco and Tobacco Products Industry—All India)

Dependent Variable—Real Wage Rate

Explanatory Variables	*Model Numbers*							
	I	*II*	*III*	*IV*	*V*	*VI*	*VII*	*VIII*
(1)	*(2)*	*(3)*	*(4)*	*(5)*	*(6)*	*(7)*	*(8)*	*(9)*
Constant	3.922 (19.558)	3.901 (21.103)	3.993 (20.092)	3.837 (26.243)	3.880 (25.199)	4.486 (10.320)	4.438 (11.177)	4.392 (10.803)
ln Time	0.117* (2.862)	0.162* (3.410)	0.184* (3.087)	0.092** (2.733)	0.151* (3.479)	0.194* (5.251)	0.19* (5.748)	0.188* (5.856)
ln LP_t	0.114** (2.318)							
ln LP_{t-1}		0.097*** (1.974)						
ln LP_{t-2}			0.070 (1.254)					
ln $(K/L)_t$				0.147* (3.916)				
ln $(K/L)_{t-1}$					0.111** (2.606)			

ln TFPK						-0.029 (-0.3)		
ln TFPS							-0.018 (-0.206)	
ln TFPT								-0.008 (-0.084)
R^2	0.681	0.727	0.654	0.759	0.753	0.613	0.613	0.612
$\tilde{R}^2$	0.655	0.704	0.624	0.740	0.732	0.582	0.582	0.581
S	0.119	0.110	0.117	0.103	0.105	0.131	0.131	0.131
F	26.63	31.97	21.75	39.46	36.53	19.82	19.76	19.72
D-W	1.578	1.235	1.151	1.686	1.494	1.058	1.073	1.092
$\tilde{\rho}$	0.043	0.256	0.247	0.045	0.144	0.264	0.255	0.245

Notes : 1. Figures in brackets are the respective 't' values.
2. * ** *** Indicates significant at 1%, 5% and 10% levels respectively.

effect of time constant, brings about 14.7 percent increase in wage rate in the same year. The value of R^2 is 0.759 and of $\tilde{R}^2$ is 0.740 which reveals that about 75.9 percent variations in wage rate were due to trend and current year capital intensity. The given model fits the data well. Thus capital intensity, which is an index of increased and improved mechanisation, showed that workers have benefited in terms of wages due to increase in the capital intensity.

Effect of Wages on Productivity

Taking labour productivity as dependent upon trend and up to five year lagged wage rate in Table 9.2.2, models IX-XIV have been estimated. In Model IX coefficient of time is 0.329 and this shows that trend is upward and significant. The slope coefficient 1.548 shows that 100 percent increase in wage rate results into 154.8 percent increase in labour productivity in the same year, keeping the effect of time constant. Hence labour productivity is highly responsive to change in wage rate in beverages, tobacco, and tobacco products industry. The value of R^2 is 0.637 and of $\tilde{R}^2$ is 0.608 which indicates that 63.7 percent variations in labour productivity were due to trend and wage rate. Hence wage rate is a highly significant explanatory variable. The model fits the data well.

Taking labour productivity as dependent upon trend and up to five year lagged capital intensity in Table 9.2.2, models XV-XX indicate that though the value of slope parameter of capital intensity (from t to t—4) indicate declining trend, but it continued to be significant. The regression coefficient turned out to be non-significant in the fifth year. This indicated that capital intensity affected labour productivity significantly even up to four years lag. In Model XIX coefficient of time is 1.164 and it is upward and significant. The slope coefficient shows that 100 percent increase in $(K/L)_{t-4}$ brings about 21.2 percent increase in labour productivity in the next fourth year. Thus capital intensity, which is an index of intensity of mechanisation, helped in raising the productivity of labour. The value of R^2 is 0.916 and of $\tilde{R}^2$ is 0.908 which reveals that 91.6 percent variations in labour productivity were due to trend and fourth year lagged capital intensity. The given model fits the data well.

TABLE 9.2.2

Regression Function for Labour Productivity (Beverages, Tobacco and Tobacco Products Industry—All India)

Dependent Variable—Partial Labour Productivity

Explanatory Variables	*Model Numbers*											
	IX	*X*	*XI*	*XII*	*XIII*	*XIV*	*XV*	*XVI*	*XVII*	*XVIII*	*XIX*	*XX*
(1)	*(2)*	*(3)*	*(4)*	*(5)*	*(6)*	*(7)*	*(8)*	*(9)*	*(10)*	*(11)*	*(12)*	*(13)*
Constant	-2.931 (-1.003)	-6.995 (-2.286)	-2.553 (-0.785)	-2.290 (-0.777)	-0.408 (-0.18)	-0.786 (-0.388)	1.012 (3.407)	1.074 (2.851)	1.158 (2.943)	1.124 (2.882)	1.228 (3.317)	1.258 (3.257)
ln Time	0.329 (2.053)	0.266 (1.487)	0.707* (3.488)	0.906* (4.607)	1.223* (7.172)	1.313* (7.770)	0.108 (1.566)	0.209*** (1.973)	0.514* (4.113)	0.768* (5.651)	1.164* (8.479)	1.397* (9.463)
ln WR_t	1.548** (2.318)											
ln WR_{t-1}		2.434* (3.413)										
ln WR_{t-2}			-2.553 (-0.785)									
ln WR_{t-3}				1.106 (1.566)								
ln WR_{t-4}					0.528 (0.954)							
ln WR_{t-5}						0.554 (1.103)						

(Contd.)

TABLE 9.2.2 (CONTD.)

(1)	(2)	(3)	(4)	(5)	(6)	(7)	(8)	(9)	(10)	(11)	(12)	(13)
$\ln (K/L)_t$							0.792* (10.357)					
$\ln (K/L)_{t-1}$								0.741* (7.100)				
$\ln (K/L)_{t-2}$									0.574* (5.009)			
$\ln (K/L)_{t-3}$										0.449* (3.834)		
$\ln (K/L)_{t-4}$											0.212*** (1.877)	
$\ln (K/L)_{t-5}$												0.074 (0.628)
R^2	0.637	0.741	0.779	0.841	0.906	0.919	0.917	0.876	0.882	0.894	0.916	0.916
$\tilde{R}^2$	0.608	0.720	0.760	0.827	0.897	0.911	0.910	0.866	0.871	0.885	0.908	0.908
S	0.437	0.370	0.348	0.296	0.230	0.207	0.210	0.256	0.254	0.242	0.218	0.211
F	21.940	34.35	40.49	58.37	100.78	113.99	137.51	84.74	85.65	93.13	114.06	109.18
D-W	0.753	0.528	0.882	0.864	1.014	1.273	1.115	1.102	1.088	0.870	1.053	1.137
$\tilde{\rho}$	0.602	0.656	0.483	0.436	0.430	0.247	0.400	0.356	0.393	0.442	0.417	0.306

Notes : 1. Figures in brackets are the respective 't' values.
2. * ** *** Indicates significant at 1%, 5% and 10% levels respectively.

Pre and Post-liberalisation Period

Consider the regression equation in Model XXI, in which wage rate is dependent upon dummy, labour productivity and product of dummy times labour productivity variables in Table 9.2.3. The estimated equation is :

TABLE 9.2.3
Structural Stability of Regression Functions (Beverages, Tobacco and Tobacco Products Industry— All India)

Dependent Variables	*I*		*II*	
	Real Wage Rate		*Labour Productivity*	
Explanatory Variables	*Model Numbers*			
	XXI	*XXII*	*XXIII*	*XXIV*
Constant	95.48 (11.401)	90.075 (13.165)	-127.486 (-1.246)	104.499 (-1.028)
Time	3.206* (3.817)			12.933* (3.830)
Dummy	-70.17*** (-1.937)	-89.268* (-3.038)	276.957*** (1.733)	-63.927 (-0.411)
LP_t	0.114** (2.305)	-0.052 (-0.882)		
$D. LP_t$	0.169*** (1.801)	0.218* (2.863)		
WR_t			2.474** (2.754)	-0.675 (-0.618)
$D. WR_t$			-0.548 (-0.452)	1.29 (1.194)
R^2	0.677	0.802	0.859	0.914
$\tilde{R}^2$	0.637	0.868	0.841	0.899
S	16.034	12.816	62.574	49.95
F	16.77	23.34	48.74	61.03
D-W	1.853	1.852	1.626	1.196
$\tilde{\rho}$	-0.058	-0.084	0.173	0.372

Notes : 1. Figures in brackets are the respective 't' values.
2. * ** *** Indicates significant at 1%, 5% and 10% levels respectively.

$$WR_t = 95.48 - 70.17\ D + 0.114\ LP_t + 0.169\ D\ .\ LP_t$$

Pre-liberalisation Era I—1973 to 1990 and D = 0; then

$$WR_t = 95.48 + 0.114\ LP_t$$

Post-liberalisation Era II—1991 to 2000 and D = 1; then

$$WR_t = 25.31 + 0.283\ LP_t$$

The differential intercept and the differential slope parameter are mildly significant. The function has shifted from period I to period II due to significant difference in intercept values and in slope parameters. In post-liberalisation period though the intercept has decreased but, the slope of regression line has become steeper, i.e. the relationship between wage and labour productivity during post-reform era has strengthened. Thus workers in this industry have gained in terms of wages from the liberalisation wave.

In Model XXII wage rate depends upon dummy, time, labour productivity and product of dummy times labour productivity variables. The estimated equation is :

$$WR_t = 90.075 + 3.206\ t - 89.268\ D - 0.052\ LP_t + 0.218\ D\ .\ LP_t$$

Pre-liberalisation Era I—1973 to 1990 and D = 0; then

$$WR_t = 90.075 + 3.206\ t - 0.052\ LP_t$$

Post-liberalisation Era II—1991 to 2000 and D = 1; then

$$WR_t = 0.807 + 3.206\ t + 0.166\ LP_t$$

The trend effect in pre and post-reform period remains the same. The differential intercept and the differential slope parameter are highly significant. The function has shifted from period I to period II due to significant difference in intercept values and in slope parameters. In post-liberalisation period though the intercept has decreased but, the slope of regression line has become steeper, i.e. the relationship between wage and labour productivity during post-reform era has strengthened in beverages, tobacco and tobacco products industry. This reveals that workers have benefited from the structural adjustment programme of post-reform era.

In models XXIII and XXIV labour productivity as a function of time, dummy, wage rate and product of dummy times wage rate was found non-significant in this industry, indicating no significant change in relationship between labour productivity and wages during post-liberalisation period.

3. COTTON TEXTILES INDUSTRY

Effect of Productivity on Wages

Thirteen models of effect of productivity and capital intensity on wages have been estimated (Table 9.3.1), and the results of selected models with significant effect of explanatory variables are discussed below :

Consider the regression equation in Model IV in which wage rate depends upon trend and third period lagged partial labour productivity. Coefficient of time is 0.18 and trend is upward and significant. The coefficient of LP_{t-3} is –0.087 and it shows that in cotton textiles industry productivity lagged behind due to lack of renovation of machinery but increase in wages might be due to unionization or some other factors. Hence the negative sign of the coefficient. The value of R^2 is 0.807 and of $\tilde{R}^2$ is 0.787 which reveals that about 80.7 percent variations in wage rate were due to trend and third year lagged partial labour productivity.

Taking wage rate as dependent upon trend and up to three year lagged capital intensity, models VII to X showed non-significant results.

In Model XI real wage rate depends upon trend and total factor productivity index (Kendrick). Coefficient of time is 0.069 and is statistically significant. The slope coefficient of TFPK is 0.133 and this shows that 100 percent increase in TFPK brings about 13.3 percent increase in wage rate, when the effect of time is held constant. The value of R^2 is 0.886 and of $\tilde{R}^2$ is 0.875 which indicates that about 88.6 percent variations in wage rate were due to TFPK and time. The given model fits the data well.

In Model XII real wage rate depends upon trend and total factor productivity index (Solow). Coefficient of time is 0.059 and is statistically significant. The slope coefficient of TFPS is 0.139 and this shows that 100 percent increase in TFPS brings about 13.9 percent increase in wage rate, when the effect of time is held constant. The value of R^2 is 0.913 and of $\tilde{R}^2$ is 0.905 which indicates that about 91.3 percent variations in wage rate were due to TFPS and time. The given model fits the data well.

In Model XIII real wage rate depends upon trend and total factor productivity index (Translog). Coefficient of time is 0.06

TABLE 9.3.1

Regression Function for Wages
(Cotton Textiles Industry—All India)

Dependent Variable—Real Wage Rate

Explanatory Variables	*Model Numbers*												
	I	*II*	*III*	*IV*	*V*	*VI*	*VII*	*VIII*	*IX*	*X*	*XI*	*XII*	*XIII*
(1)	*(2)*	*(3)*	*(4)*	*(5)*	*(6)*	*(7)*	*(8)*	*(9)*	*(10)*	*(11)*	*(12)*	*(13)*	*(14)*
Constant	4.369 (37.521)	4.568 (39.872)	4.675 (38.950)	4.767 (42.337)	4.678 (31.951)	4.633 (29.633)	4.517 (55.973)	4.581 (58.678)	4.592 (53.306)	4.637 (50.266)	3.973 (23.627)	3.960 (31.840)	3.950 (30.637)
ln Time	0.083* (4.929)	0.13* (6.200)	0.152* (6.008)	0.18* (6.483)	0.151* (3.997)	0.145* (3.245)	0.099* (5.580)	0.14* (6.530)	0.148* (5.361)	0.169* (5.090)	0.069* (5.390)	0.059* (4.969)	0.06* (5.080)
ln LP_t	0.042 (1.458)												
ln LP_{t-1}		-0.020 (-0.659)											
ln LP_{t-2}			-0.053 (-1.554)										
ln LP_{t-3}				-0.087** (-2.555)									
ln LP_{t-4}					-0.055 (-1.186)								

ln LP_{t-5}						-0.043 (-0.83)							
ln $(K/L)_t$							0.005 (0.236)						
ln $(K/L)_{t-1}$								-0.026 (-1.169)					
ln $(K/L)_{t-2}$									-0.033 (-1.22)				
ln $(K/L)_{t-3}$										-0.053 (-1.709)			
ln TFPK											0.133* (3.369)		
ln TFPS												0.139* (4.675)	
ln TFPT													0.141* (4.576)
R^2	0.842	0.844	0.814	0.807	0.689	0.622	0.827	0.851	0.806	0.775	0.886	0.913	0.911
$\tilde{R}^2$	0.828	0.829	0.796	0.787	0.655	0.578	0.812	0.836	0.787	0.752	0.875	0.905	0.903
S	0.039	0.037	0.036	0.034	0.038	0.040	0.041	0.036	0.037	0.037	0.033	0.029	0.029
F	58.64	56.86	43.81	39.71	19.95	13.98	52.67	59.79	41.59	32.76	85.27	115.60	112.97
D-W	0.817	0.841	0.867	0.832	0.825	0.848	0.887	0.871	0.902	0.849	1.003	1.233	1.174
$\tilde{\rho}$	0.497	0.514	0.482	0.560	0.518	0.500	0.446	0.510	0.493	0.548	0.460	0.372	0.387

Notes : 1. Figures in brackets are the respective 't' values.
2. * ** *** Indicates s significant at 1%, 5% and 10% levels respectively.

and is statistically significant. The slope coefficient of TFPT is 0.141 and this shows that 100 percent increase in TFPT brings about 14.1 percent increase in wage rate, when the effect of time is held constant. The value of R^2 is 0.911 and of $\tilde{R}^2$ is 0.903 which indicates that about 91.1 percent variations in wage rate were due to TFPT and time. The given model fits the data well.

On the whole, the results obtained in models XI, XII and XIII are robust and consistent, indicating that total factor productivity has positive and significant effect on wage rate.

Effect of Wages on Productivity

Taking labour productivity as dependent upon trend and up to five year lagged wage rate, models XIV-XIX (Table 9.3.2) showed non-significant results.

Taking labour productivity as dependent upon trend and up to three year lagged capital intensity, models XX-XXIII indicate that though the value of slope parameter of capital intensity (from t to t–3) indicate declining trend, but it continued to be significant. In Model XXII coefficient of time is 0.32 and it is upward and significant. The slope coefficient shows that 100 percent increase in $(K/L)_{t-2}$ brings about 46.5 percent increase in labour productivity in the next second year. Thus capital intensity, which is an index of intensity of mechanisation, helped in raising the productivity of labour. The value of R^2 is 0.940 and of $\tilde{R}^2$ is 0.934 which reveals that 94.0 percent variations in labour productivity were due to trend and second year lagged capital intensity. The given model fits the data well.

Pre and Post-liberalisation Period

Consider the regression equation in Model XXIV, in which wage rate is dependent upon dummy, labour productivity and product of dummy times labour productivity variables in Table 9.3.3. The estimated equation is :

$$WR_t = 91.326 + 36.788\ D + 0.191\ LP_t - 0.195\ D\ .\ LP_t$$

Pre-liberalisation Era I—1973-74 to 1990-91 and D = 0;

then $WR_t = 91.326 + 0.191\ LP_t$

Post-liberalisation Era II—1991-92 to 1997-98 and D = 1;

then $WR_t = 128.114 - 0.004\ LP_t$

Table 9.3.2
Regression Function for Labour Productivity (Cotton Textiles Industry—All India)

Dependent Variable—Partial Labour Productivity

Explanatory Variables	*Model Numbers*									
	XIV	*XV*	*XVI*	*XVII*	*XVIII*	*XIX*	*XX*	*XXI*	*XXII*	*XXIII*
(1)	*(2)*	*(3)*	*(4)*	*(5)*	*(6)*	*(7)*	*(8)*	*(9)*	*(10)*	*(11)*
Constant	-5.503 (-0.851)	-0.943 (-0.16)	0.678 (0.127)	-0.566 (-0.113)	-1.652 (-0.355)	-4.159 (-0.945)	1.742 (6.085)	1.837 (6.352)	1.858 (6.468)	1.890 (5.783)
ln Time	0.260 (1.615)	0.494** (2.707)	0.649* (3.287)	0.673* (3.144)	0.682* (3.050)	0.594** (2.471)	0.057 (0.895)	0.196** (2.473)	0.32* (3.485)	0.421* (3.579)
ln WR_t	2.078 (1.458)									
ln WR_{t-1}		1.003 (0.761)								
ln WR_{t-2}			0.580 (0.477)							
ln WR_{t-3}				0.827 (0.714)						

(Contd.)

TABLE 9.3.2 (CONTD.)

(1)	(2)	(3)	(4)	(5)	(6)	(7)	(8)	(9)	(10)	(11)
ln WR_{t-4}					1.050 (0.961)					
ln WR_{t-5}						1.628 (1.549)				
ln $(K/L)_t$							0.595* (7.993)			
ln $(K/L)_{t-1}$								0.521* (6.255)		
ln $(K/L)_{t-2}$									0.465* (5.165)	
ln $(K/L)_{t-3}$										0.416* (3.771)
R^2	0.703	0.805	0.862	0.881	0.889	0.897	0.917	0.930	0.940	0.930
$\tilde{R}^2$	0.676	0.786	0.848	0.868	0.876	0.884	0.909	0.923	0.934	0.923
S	0.274	0.224	0.187	0.169	0.158	0.147	0.145	0.134	0.123	0.130
F	26.020	43.26	62.22	70.09	71.89	73.68	120.80	139.30	156.69	126.01
D-W	0.321	0.553	0.667	0.801	0.989	1.124	1.005	1.287	1.231	1.453
$\tilde{\rho}$	0.714	0.607	0.594	0.555	0.475	0.369	0.433	0.299	0.336	0.214

Notes : 1. Figures in brackets are the respective 't' values.
2. * ** *** Indicates significant at 1%, 5% and 10% levels respectively.

TABLE 9.3.3
Structural Stability of Regression Functions for Cotton Textiles Industry (All India)

Dependent Variables	*I*		*II*	
	Real Wage Rate		*Labour Productivity*	
Explanatory Variables	*Model Numbers*			
	XXIV	*XXV*	*XXVI*	*XXVII*
Constant	91.326 (23.030)	95.712 (29.499)	-289.937 (-3.072)	264.781 (1.462)
Time		1.563* (3.943)		12.871* (3.386)
Dummy	36.788** (2.765)	10.104 (0.824)	708.26 (1.120)	-875.761 (-1.257)
LP_t	0.191* (6.541)	0.04 (0.902)		
D. LP_t	-0.195* (-3.64)	-0.087*** (-1.763)		
WR_t			3.609* (4.441)	-2.245 (-1.212)
D. WR_t			-4.703 (-0.943)	7.021 (1.313)
R^2	0.747	0.858	0.831	0.892
$\tilde{R}^2$	0.711	0.83	0.807	0.871
S	5.828	4.479	37.314	30.485
F	20.72	30.19	34.38	41.49
D-W	0.594	1.234	1.602	1.70
$\tilde{\rho}$	0.612	0.289	0.183	0.09

Notes : 1. Figures in brackets are the respective 't' values.
2. * ** *** Indicates significant at 1%, 5% and 10% levels respectively.

The differential intercept and the differential slope parameter are significant. The function has shifted from period I to period II due to significant difference in intercept values and in slope parameters. In post-liberalisation period though the intercept has increased but, the slope of regression line has become flatter, i.e. the relationship between wage and labour productivity during post-reform era has weakened in cotton textiles industry. This implies that workers have not benefited in terms of higher wages in post-reform era.

In Model XXV wage rate depends upon dummy, time, labour productivity and product of dummy times labour productivity variables. The estimated equation is :

$$WR_t = 95.712 + 1.563\, t + 10.104\, D + 0.04\, LP_t - 0.087\, D\,.\, LP_t$$

Pre-liberalisation Era I—1973-74 to 1990-91 and D = 0;

$$\text{then } WR_t = 95.712 + 1.563\, t + 0.04\, LP_t$$

Post-liberalisation Era II—1991-92 to 1997-98; D = 1;

$$\text{then } WR_t = 105.816 + 1.563\, t - 0.047\, LP_t$$

The trend effect in pre and post-reform period remains the same. The differential intercept is non-significant but the differential slope parameter is mildly significant. In post-liberalisation period the slope of regression line has become flatter i.e. the relationship between wage and labour productivity during post-reform era has weakened in cotton textiles industry.

Taking labour productivity as dependent upon trend, dummy, wage rate and product of dummy times wage rate, models XXVI and XXVII showed non-significant results, indicating no significant change in relationship between labour productivity and wages during post-liberalisation period.

4. JUTE, HEMP AND MESTA TEXTILES INDUSTRY

Effect of Productivity on Wages

Nine models regarding effect of productivity and capital intensity on wages have been estimated (Table 9.4.1) and the results of selected models with significant effect of explanatory variables are discussed below :

Consider the regression equation in Model II in which wage rate depends upon trend and one period lagged partial labour productivity. Coefficient of time is 0.155 and trend is upward and is significant. The coefficient of LP_{t-1} is 0.09 and it shows that 100 percent increase in labour productivity brings about 9.0 percent increase in wage rate in the next year, keeping the effect of time constant. The value of R^2 is 0.901 and of $\tilde{R}^2$ is

TABLE 9.4.1
Regression Function for Wages
Jute, Hemp and Mesta Textiles Industry

Dependent Variable—Real Wage Rate

Explanatory Variables	*Model Numbers*								
	I	*II*	*III*	*IV*	*V*	*VI*	*VII*	*VIII*	*IX*
(1)	*(2)*	*(3)*	*(4)*	*(5)*	*(6)*	*(7)*	*(8)*	*(9)*	*(10)*
Constant	3.953 (28.231)	4.012 (29.728)	4.030 (25.935)	4.003 (29.772)	4.052 (34.720)	4.025 (33.919)	3.914 (26.004)	4.097 (45.308)	4.079 (43.331)
ln Time	0.108* (4.277)	0.155* (5.194)	0.158* (4.031)	0.122* (5.305)	0.164* (6.324)	0.157* (5.014)	0.108* (4.288)	0.1* (4.058)	0.098* (3.975)
ln LP_t	0.122* (3.560)								
ln LP_{t-1}		0.09** (2.523)							
ln LP_{t-2}			0.087*** (1.981)						
ln $(K/L)_t$				0.114* (3.336)					
ln $(K/L)_{t-1}$					0.084** (2.606)				

(*Contd.*)

TABLE 9.4.1 (CONTD.)

(1)	(2)	(3)	(4)	(5)	(6)	(7)	(8)	(9)	(10)
ln $(K/L)_{t-2}$						0.095** (2.718)			
ln TFPK							0.13* (3.561)		
ln TFPS								0.096* (4.026)	
ln TFPT									0.1* (4.049)
R^2	0.882	0.901	0.865	0.877	0.902	0.882	0.882	0.893	0.894
$\tilde{R}^2$	0.872	0.891	0.852	0.866	0.893	0.871	0.872	0.884	0.884
S	0.060	0.054	0.057	0.061	0.053	0.053	0.060	0.057	0.057
F	82.51	95.09	64.21	78.33	96.74	74.96	82.52	92.03	92.53
D-W	1.621	1.42	1.414	1.744	1.500	1.500	1.606	1.712	1.726
$\tilde{\rho}$	0.128	0.277	0.271	0.036	0.210	0.214	0.137	0.096	0.090

Notes : 1. Figures in brackets are the respective 't' values.
2. * ** *** Indicates significant at 1%, 5% and 10% levels respectively.

0.891 which reveals that about 90.1 percent variations in wage rate were due to trend and one year lagged partial labour productivity. Thus increase in partial labour productivity has benefited the workers in jute, hemp and mesta textiles industry. The given model fits the data well.

Consider the regression equation in Model V in which real wage rate depends upon trend and one year lagged capital intensity. The coefficient of time is 0.164 and trend is upward and significant. The slope coefficient of $(K/L)_{t-1}$ is 0.084 and this shows that 100 percent increase in capital intensity, keeping the effect of time constant, brings about 8.4 percent increase in wage rate in next year. The value of R^2 is 0.902 and of $\tilde{R}^2$ is 0.893 which reveals that about 90.2 percent variations in wage rate were due to trend and one year lagged capital intensity. The given model fits the data well. Thus capital intensity, which is an index of increased and improved mechanisation, showed that workers have benefited in terms of wages due to increase in the capital intensity.

In Model VII real wage rate depends upon trend and total factor productivity index (Kendrick). Coefficient of time is 0.108 and is statistically significant. The slope coefficient of TFPK is 0.13 and this shows that 100 percent increase in TFPK brings about 13.0 percent increase in wage rate, when the effect of time is held constant. The value of R^2 is 0.882 and of $\tilde{R}^2$ is 0.872 which indicates that about 88.2 percent variations in wage rate were due to TFPK and time. The given model fits the data well.

In Model VIII real wage rate depends upon trend and total factor productivity index (Solow). Coefficient of time is 0.10 and is statistically significant. The slope coefficient of TFPS is 0.096 and this shows that 100 percent increase in TFPS brings about 9.6 percent increase in wage rate, when the effect of time is held constant. The value of R^2 is 0.893 and of $\tilde{R}^2$ is 0.884 which indicates that about 89.3 percent variations in wage rate were due to TFPS and time. The given model also fits the data well.

In Model IX real wage rate depends upon trend and total factor productivity index (Translog). Coefficient of time is 0.098 and is statistically significant. The slope coefficient of TFPT is 0.10 and this shows that 100 percent increase in TFPT brings about 10.0 percent increase in wage rate, when the effect of time is held constant. The value of R^2 is 0.894 and of $\tilde{R}^2$ is 0.884 which indicates that about 89.4 percent variations in wage rate were due to TFPT and time. The given model also fits the data well.

On the whole, the results obtained in case of models VII, VIII and IX are robust and consistent, indicating that total factor productivity has positive and significant effect on wage rate.

Effect of Wages on Productivity

Taking labour productivity as dependent upon trend and up to five year lagged wage rate (Table 9.4.2), models X-XV indicate that the value of slope parameter of wage rate (from t to t–4) continued to be significant. The regression coefficient turned out to be non-significant in the fifth year. This indicated that wage rate affected labour productivity significantly even up to four years lag. In Model XIV coefficient of time is 0.617 and this shows that trend is upward and significant. The slope coefficient 1.838 shows that 100 percent increase in wage rate results in 183.8 percent increase in labour productivity in the next fourth year, keeping the effect of time constant. Hence labour productivity is highly responsive to change in wage rate in jute, hemp and mesta textiles industry. The value of R^2 is 0.903 and of $\tilde{R}^2$ is 0.893 which indicates that 90.3 percent variations in labour productivity were due to trend and fourth year lagged wage rate. The model fits the data well.

Consider the regression equations in models XVI-XX in which labour productivity depends upon trend and up to four year lagged capital intensity. The regression coefficient of capital intensity was significant even up to four years lag. In Model XIX coefficient of time is 0.445 and it is upward and highly significant. The slope coefficient shows that 100 percent increase in $(K/L)_{t-3}$ brings about 73.8 percent increase in labour productivity in the next third year. The value of R^2 is 0.975 and of $\tilde{R}^2$ is 0.972 which reveals that 97.5 percent variations in labour productivity were due to trend and third year lagged capital intensity. The given model fits the data well.

Pre and Post-liberalisation Period

Consider the regression equation in Model XXI, in which wage rate is dependent upon dummy, labour productivity and product of dummy times labour productivity variables

TABLE 9.4.2

Regression Function for Labour Productivity Jute, Hemp and Mesta Textiles Industry

Dependent Variable—Partial Labour Productivity

Explanatory Variables	*Model Numbers*										
	X	XI	XII	XIII	XIV	XV	XVI	XVII	XVIII	XIX	XX
(1)	(2)	(3)	(4)	(5)	(6)	(7)	(8)	(9)	(10)	(11)	(12)
Constant	-18.643 (-2.499)	-6.750 (-1.565)	-5.694 (-1.379)	-4.660 (-1.286)	-5.007 (-1.69)	-0.872 (-0.292)	0.854 (1.919)	0.756 (2.210)	0.748 (2.321)	0.699 (3.123)	0.840 (3.191)
ln Time	0.057 (0.337)	0.234 (1.016)	0.354 (1.370)	0.533** (2.060)	0.617* (2.577)	1.058* (3.975)	0.179** (2.346)	0.212** (2.786)	0.303* (3.571)	0.445* (6.545)	0.665* (7.393)
ln WR_t	2.998* (3.560)										
ln WR_{t-1}		2.386** (2.398)									
ln WR_{t-2}			2.112** (2.165)								
ln WR_{t-3}				1.808** (2.065)							
ln WR_{t-4}					1.838* (2.509)						

(Contd.)

TABLE 9.4.2 (CONTD.)

(1)	(2)	(3)	(4)	(5)	(6)	(7)	(8)	(9)	(10)	(11)	(12)
ln WR_{t-5}						0.739 (0.980)					
ln $(K/L)_t$							0.82* (7.234)				
ln $(K/L)_{t-1}$								0.831* (8.782)			
ln $(K/L)_{t-2}$									0.796* (8.409)		
ln $(K/L)_{t-3}$										0.738* (10.708)	
ln $(K/L)_{t-4}$											0.597* (7.098)
R^2	0.786	0.779	0.808	0.857	0.903	0.900	0.900	0.940	0.948	0.975	0.966
$\tilde{R}^2$	0.766	0.758	0.789	0.842	0.893	0.888	0.891	0.934	0.943	0.972	0.962
S	0.297	0.299	0.277	0.240	0.196	0.197	0.263	0.156	0.144	0.100	0.117
F	40.32	37.10	42.09	56.88	84.20	76.19	99.02	164.12	181.41	371.960	253.370
D-W	0.708	0.500	0.582	0.633	0.464	0.631	0.912	1.187	1.814	1.559	2.231
$\tilde{\rho}$	0.622	0.659	0.607	0.561	0.680	0.606	0.404	0.357	0.017	0.109	-0.139

Notes : 1. Figures in brackets are the respective 't' values.
2. * ** *** indicates significant at 1%, 5% and 10% levels respectively.

(Table 9.4.3). The estimated equation is :

$$WR_t = 79.409 + 48.334\ D + 0.262\ LP_t - 0.212\ D\ .\ LP_t$$

Pre-liberalisation Era I—1973-74 to 1990-91 and D = 0;

then $WR_t = 79.409 + 0.262\ LP_t$

Post-liberalisation Era II—1991-92 to 1997-98 and D = 1;

then $WR_t = 127.743 + 0.05\ LP_t$

The differential intercept and the differential slope

TABLE 9.4.3
Structural Stability of Regression Functions (Jute, Hemp and Mesta Textiles Industry)

Dependent Variables	*I*		*II*	
	Real Wage Rate		*Labour Productivity*	
Explanatory Variables	*Model Numbers*			
	XXI	*XXII*	*XXIII*	*XXIV*
Constant	79.409 (13.295)	88.123 (16.379)	-191.697 (-2.179)	145.099 (-2.463)
Time		2.51* (3.557)		13.963** (2.805)
Dummy	48.334* (2.894)	6.852 (0.386)	-617.659 (-1.591)	-856.13** (-2.463)
LP_t	0.262* (7.431)	0.058 (0.902)		
D . LP_t	-0.212* (-4.515)	-0.053 (-0.911)		
WR_t			2.897* (4.031)	-0.977 (-0.645)
D . WR_t			5.643** (2.188)	6.857* (3.007)
R^2	0.856	0.912	0.916	0.94
$\tilde{R}^2$	0.835	0.894	0.905	0.928
S	8.579	6.88	52.585	45.64
F	41.59	51.67	76.77	78.38
D-W	1.235	1.626	1.662	1.602
$\tilde{\rho}$	0.351	0.147	0.165	0.175

Notes : 1. Figures in brackets are the respective 't' values.
2. * ** *** indicates significant at 1%, 5% and 10% levels respectively.

parameter are highly significant. The function has shifted from period I to period II due to significant difference in intercept values and in slope parameters. In post-liberalisation period though the intercept has increased but, the slope of regression line has become flatter, i.e. the relationship between wage and labour productivity during post-reform era has weakened. Since the time period of post-reform era is less, so over long period it has to be seen whether this relationship reverts back or further weakens.

Taking wage rate as dependent upon time, dummy, labour productivity and product of dummy times labour productivity, model XXII showed non-significant result.

Consider the regression equation in Model XXIII, in which labour productivity is dependent upon dummy, wage rate and product of dummy times wage rate variables. The estimated equation is :

$$LP_t = -191.697 - 617.659\ D + 2.897\ WR_t + 5.643\ D\ .\ WR_t$$

Pre-liberalisation Era I—1973-74 to 1990-91 and D = 0;

$$\text{then } LP_t = -191.697 + 2.897\ WR_t$$

Post-liberalisation Era II—1991-92 to 1997-98 and D = 1;

$$\text{then } LP_t = -809.356 + 8.54\ WR_t$$

The differential intercept is non-significant but the differential slope parameter is significant. In post-liberalisation period the slope of regression line has become steeper, i.e. the relationship between labour productivity and wage rate during post-reform era has strengthened. Thus after liberalisation when market forces have more important role to play, the labour productivity has become more responsive to wage rate.

Consider the regression equation in Model XXIV, in which labour productivity is dependent upon time, dummy, wage rate and product of dummy times wage rate variables. The estimated equation is :

$$LP_t = 145.099 + 13.963\ t - 856.13\ D - 0.977\ WR_t + 6.857\ D\ .\ WR_t$$

Pre-liberalisation Era I—1973-74 to 1990-91 and D = 0;

$$\text{then } LP_t = 145.099 + 13.963\ t - 0.977\ WR_t$$

Post-liberalisation Era II—1991-92 to 1997-98; D = 1;

$$LP_t = -711.031 + 13.963\ t + 5.88\ WR_t$$

The trend effect in pre and post-reform period remains the same. The differential intercept and the differential slope parameter are significant. In post-liberalisation period though the differential intercept has decreased but the slope of regression line has become steeper, i.e. the relationship between labour productivity and wage rate during post-reform era has strengthened in jute, hemp and mesta textiles industry. Thus after liberalisation when market forces have more important role to play, the labour productivity has become more responsive to wage rate.

5. TEXTILE PRODUCTS INDUSTRY

Effect of Productivity on Wages

Twelve models regarding effect of productivity and capital intensity on wages have been estimated (Table 9.5.1) and the results of selected models with significant effect of explanatory variables are discussed below :

Consider the regression equation in Model VI in which wage rate depends upon trend and fifth period lagged partial labour productivity. Coefficient of time is 0.082 and trend is upward and is significant. The coefficient of LP_{t-5} is 0.045 and it shows that 100 percent increase in labour productivity brings about 4.5 percent increase in wage rate in the next fifth year, keeping the effect of time constant. The value of R^2 is 0.868 and of $\tilde{R}^2$ is 0.853 which reveals that about 86.8 percent variations in wage rate were due to trend and fifth year lagged partial labour productivity. The given model fits the data well.

Consider the regression equation in Model V in which real wage rate depends upon trend and current year capital intensity. The coefficient of time is 0.09 and trend is upward and significant. The slope coefficient of $(K/L)_t$ is 0.056 and this shows that 100 percent increase in capital intensity, keeping the effect of time constant, brings about 5.6 percent increase in wage rate in the same year. The value of R^2 is 0.870 and of $\tilde{R}^2$ is 0.858 which reveals that about 87.0 percent variations in wage rate were due to trend and current year capital intensity.

TABLE 9.5.1

Regression Function for Wages
(Textile Products Industry—All India)

Dependent Variable—Real Wage Rate

Explanatory Variables	*Model Numbers*											
	I	*II*	*III*	*IV*	*V*	*VI*	*VII*	*VIII*	*IX*	*X*	*XI*	*XII*
(1)	*(2)*	*(3)*	*(4)*	*(5)*	*(6)*	*(7)*	*(8)*	*(9)*	*(10)*	*(11)*	*(12)*	*(13)*
Constant	4.385 (61.368)	4.454 (93.744)	4.407 (103.066)	4.400 (103.328)	4.376 (97.151)	4.349 (85.219)	4.339 (70.707)	4.263 (40.744)	4.458 (54.867)	4.368 (32.461)	4.451 (76.448)	4.454 (77.098)
ln Time	0.103* (5.320)	0.172* (10.069)	0.127* (6.747)	0.11* (5.095)	0.106* (4.293)	0.082** (2.837)	0.118* (3.296)	0.09* (4.636)	0.165* (8.670)	0.113* (6.117)	0.121* (9.222)	0.122* (9.566)
ln LP_t	0.025 (1.342)											
ln LP_{t-1}		-0.018 (-1.295)										
ln LP_{t-2}			0.011 (0.804)									
ln LP_{t-3}				0.021 (1.424)								
ln LP_{t-4}					0.027 (1.697)							

$\ln LP_{t-5}$						0.045** (2.308)						
$\ln LP_{t-6}$							0.029 (1.171)					
$\ln (K/L)_t$								0.056** (2.077)				
$\ln (K/L)_{t-1}$									-0.017 (-0.747)			
ln TFPK										0.026 (0.803)		
ln TFPS											0.006 (0.440)	
ln TFPT												0.005 (0.393)
R^2	0.856	0.932	0.912	0.891	0.882	0.868	0.856	0.870	0.928	0.849	0.846	0.845
$\tilde{R}^2$	0.843	0.925	0.904	0.879	0.868	0.853	0.838	0.858	0.922	0.835	0.832	0.831
S	0.045	0.030	0.027	0.027	0.026	0.026	0.026	0.042	0.031	0.046	0.046	0.046
F	65.47	143.82	104.02	77.36	67.01	55.96	47.45	73.55	136.20	61.75	60.30	60.18
D-W	2.106	1.766	2.152	2.335	2.396	2.362	2.116	2.183	1.796	2.077	2.112	2.110
$\tilde{\rho}$	-0.197	0.027	-0.129	-0.193	-0.219	-0.203	-0.090	-0.191	0.010	-0.216	-0.247	-0.247

Notes : 1. Figures in brackets are the respective 't' values.

2. * ** *** Indicates significant at 1%, 5% and 10% levels respectively.

Effect of Wages on Productivity

Taking labour productivity as dependent upon trend and up to five year lagged wage rate, models XIII-XVIII (Table 9.5.2) showed non-significant results.

Consider the regression equations in models XIX–XXVI in which labour productivity depends upon trend and up to seven year lagged capital intensity. The regression coefficient of capital intensity was significant even up to seven years lag. In case of Model XXV coefficient of time is 1.012 and it is upward and highly significant. The slope coefficient shows that 100 percent increase in $(K/L)_{t-6}$ brings about 98.1 percent increase in labour productivity in the next sixth year. The value of R^2 is 0.946 and of $\tilde{R}^2$ is 0.939 which reveals that 94.6 percent variations in labour productivity were due to trend and sixth year lagged capital intensity. The given model fits the data well.

Pre and Post-liberalisation Period

Consider the regression equation in Model XXVII, in which wage rate is dependent upon dummy, labour productivity and product of dummy times labour productivity variables (Table 9.5.3). The estimated equation is :

$$WR_t = 95.419 + 39.794\ D + 0.094\ LP_t - 0.10\ D\ .\ LP_t$$

Pre-liberalisation Era I—1973-74 to 1990-91 and D = 0;

then $WR_t = 95.419 + 0.094\ LP_t$

Post-liberalisation Era II—1991-92 to 1997-98 and D = 1;

then $WR_t = 135.213 - 0.006\ LP_t$

The differential intercept and the differential slope parameter are significant. The function has shifted from period I to period II due to significant difference in intercept values and in slope parameters. In post-liberalisation period though the intercept has increased but, the slope of regression line has become flatter, i.e. the relationship between wage and labour productivity during post-reform era has weakened in textile products industry. Since the time period of post-reform era is less, so over long period it has to be seen whether this relationship is strengthened or weakened.

Taking wage rate as dependent upon time, dummy, labour productivity and product of dummy times labour productivity, model XXVIII showed non-significant results.

TABLE 9.5.2

Regression Function for Labour Productivity (Textile Products Industry—All India)

Dependent Variable—Real Wage Rate

Explanatory Variables	*Model Numbers*													
	XIII	*XIV*	*XV*	*XVI*	*XVII*	*XVIII*	*XIX*	*XX*	*XXI*	*XXII*	*XXIII*	*XXIV*	*XXV*	*XXVI*
(1)	*(2)*	*(3)*	*(4)*	*(5)*	*(6)*	*(7)*	*(8)*	*(9)*	*(10)*	*(11)*	*(12)*	*(13)*	*(14)*	*(15)*
Constant	-10.074 (-0.99)	0.899 (0.089)	-1.512 (-0.161)	0.527 (0.064)	-1.341 (-0.18)	-1.758 (-0.247)	-1.661 (-3.127)	-1.031 (-1.395)	-0.822 (-1.028)	-0.813 (-1.035)	-1.169 (-1.483)	-1.693 (-2.26)	-1.718 (-2.443)	-1.353 (-1.58)
ln Time	0.484 (1.573)	1.015* (2.789)	1.097** (2.808)	1.386* (3.590)	1.478* (3.673)	1.609* (3.647)	0.014 (0.140)	0.222 (1.283)	0.369 (1.651)	0.586** (2.345)	0.697** (2.547)	0.719** (2.552)	1.012* (3.500)	1.334* (3.554)
ln WR_t	3.053 (1.342)													
ln WR_{t-1}		0.478 (0.208)												
ln WR_{t-2}			0.937 (0.432)											
ln WR_{t-3}				0.348 (0.181)										
ln WR_{t-4}					0.686 (0.386)									
ln WR_{t-5}						0.697 (0.403)								

(Contd.)

TABLE 9.5.2 (CONTD.)

(1)	(2)	(3)	(4)	(5)	(6)	(7)	(8)	(9)	(10)	(11)	(12)	(13)	(14)	(15)
$\ln (K/L)_t$							1.383* (10.180)							
$\ln (K/L)_{t-1}$								1.183* (5.700)						
$\ln (K/L)_{t-2}$									1.087* (4.470)					
$\ln (K/L)_{t-3}$										0.99* (3.865)				
$\ln (K/L)_{t-4}$											1.016* (3.73)			
$\ln (K/L)_{t-5}$												1.123* (4.11)		
$\ln (K/L)_{t-6}$													0.981* (3.64)	
$\ln (K/L)_{t-7}$														0.739** (2.18)
R^2	0.704	0.757	0.789	0.835	0.861	0.874	0.944	0.904	0.894	0.907	0.921	0.936	0.946	0.921
$\tilde{R}^2$	0.677	0.734	0.768	0.818	0.846	0.860	0.939	0.895	0.883	0.898	0.912	0.929	0.939	0.910
S	0.496	0.447	0.410	0.362	0.327	0.304	0.216	0.281	0.292	0.271	0.247	0.217	0.197	0.230
F	26.20	32.67	37.42	48.05	55.83	59.21	185.39	99.24	83.93	93.12	104.87	125.24	140.48	87.10
D-W	0.285	0.281	0.328	0.414	0.486	0.617	1.155	1.161	0.935	0.863	1.172	1.543	1.143	1.334
$\tilde{\rho}$	0.815	0.792	0.754	0.717	0.702	0.605	0.392	0.408	0.507	0.523	0.363	0.169	0.329	0.306

Notes : 1. Figures in brackets are the respective 't' values.
2. * ** *** indicates significant at 1%, 5% and 10% levels respectively.

TABLE 9.5.3

Structural Stability of Regression Functions (Textile Products Industry—All India)

Dependent Variables	*I*		*II*	
	Real Wage Rate		*Labour Productivity*	
Explanatory Variables	*Model Numbers*			
	XXVII	*XXVIII*	*XXIX*	*XXX*
Constant	95.419 (28.374)	94.094 (43.818	-610.65 (-2.427)	565.76 (1.303)
Time		2.098* (5.667)		30.258* (3.104)
Dummy	39.794** (2.751)	4.597 (0.415)	2477.72** (2.156)	1889.68*** (1.916)
LP_t	0.094* (5.891)	-0.005 (-0.27)		
$D . LP_t$	-0.1* (-4.515)	-0.011 (-0.534)		
WR_t			7.064* (3.189)	-5.89 (-1.288)
$D . WR_t$			-14.487 (-1.625)	-11.195 (-1.477)
R^2	0.763	0.909	0.921	0.946
$\tilde{R}^2$	0.73	0.891	0.909	0.936
S	6.569	4.17	105.359	88.696
F	22.57	50.05	81.24	88.38
D-W	1.043	2.185	1.769	2.16
$\tilde{\rho}$	0.435	-0.121	0.113	-0.107

Notes : 1. Figures in brackets are the respective 't' values.
2. * ** *** indicates significant at 1%, 5% and 10% levels respectively.

Taking labour productivity as dependent upon trend, dummy, wage rate and product of dummy times wage rate, models XXIX and XXX showed non-significant results.

6. PAPER AND PAPER PRODUCTS INDUSTRY

Effect of Productivity on Wages

Eight models regarding effect of productivity and capital intensity on wages have been estimated (Table 9.6.1) and the

TABLE 9.6.1
Regression Function for Wages
(Paper and Paper Products Industry—All India)

Dependent Variable—Real Wage Rate

Explanatory Variables	*Model Numbers*							
	I	*II*	*III*	*IV*	*V*	*VI*	*VII*	*VIII*
(1)	*(2)*	*(3)*	*(4)*	*(5)*	*(6)*	*(7)*	*(8)*	*(9)*
Constant	3.151 (19.438)	3.323 (16.645)	3.438 (25.668)	3.486 (27.528)	3.476 (25.026)	3.853 (8.246)	4.589 (9.702)	4.573 (9.478)
ln Time	0.12* (6.188)	0.169* (6.054)	0.062** (2.288)	0.083** (2.507)	0.079*** (1.800)	0.234* (10.621)	0.235* (10.246)	0.236* (10.277)
ln LP_t	0.3* (7.767)							
ln LP_{t-1}		0.244* (4.874)						
ln $(K/L)_t$			0.249* (7.299)					
ln $(K/L)_{t-1}$				0.233* (6.486)				
ln $(K/L)_{t-2}$					0.241* (5.565)			

ln TFPK						0.117 (1.150)		
ln TFPS							-0.044 (-0.433)	
ln TFPT								-0.040 (-0.39)
R^2	0.946	0.929	0.942	0.948	0.939	0.826	0.819	0.818
$\tilde{R}^2$	0.942	0.923	0.937	0.944	0.933	0.813	0.804	0.804
S	0.053	0.060	0.056	0.051	0.053	0.096	0.098	0.098
F	220.98	156.07	201.66	220.51	176.11	59.52	56.41	56.32
D-W	1.087	0.972	1.298	1.866	1.720	0.498	0.472	0.470
$\tilde{\rho}$	0.344	0.334	0.158	-0.050	0.057	0.541	0.531	0.533

Notes : 1. Figures in brackets are the respective 't' values.
2. * ** *** Indicates significant at 1%, 5% and 10% levels respectively.

results of selected models with significant effect of explanatory variables are discussed below :

Consider the regression equation in Model I in which wage rate depends upon trend and current year partial labour productivity. Coefficient of time is 0.12 and trend is upward and is significant. The coefficient of LP_t is 0.30 and it shows that 100 percent increase in labour productivity brings about 30.0 percent increase in wage rate in the same year, keeping the effect of time constant. This implies that it is in the interest of workers to increase their productivity. The value of R^2 is 0.946 and of $\tilde{R}^2$ is 0.942 which reveals that about 94.6 percent variations in wage rate were due to trend and current year partial labour productivity. Thus, increase in partial labour productivity has benefited the workers in paper and paper products industry. The given model fits the data well.

Consider the regression equation in Model IV in which real wage rate depends upon trend and one year lagged capital intensity. The coefficient of time is 0.083 and trend is upward and significant. The slope coefficient of $(K/L)_{t-1}$ is 0.233 and this shows that 100 percent increase in capital intensity, keeping the effect of time constant, brings about 23.3 percent increase in wage rate in the next year. The value of R^2 is 0.948 and of $\tilde{R}^2$ is 0.944 which reveals that about 94.8 percent variations in wage rate were due to trend and one year lagged capital intensity. The given model fits the data well.

Effect of Wages on Productivity

In Model IX (Table 9.6.2) coefficient of time is –0.168 and trend is significant. The slope coefficient 2.355 shows that 100 percent increase in wage rate results into 235.5 percent increase in labour productivity in the same year, keeping the effect of time constant. Hence labour productivity is highly responsive to change in wage rate in paper and paper products industry. It appears that increase in wage rate is in the interest of this industry. The value of R^2 is 0.885 and of $\tilde{R}^2$ is 0.876 which indicates that 88.5 percent variations in labour productivity were due to trend and current year wage rate. The model fits the data well.

TABLE 9.6.2
Regression Function for Labour Productivity
(Paper and Paper Products Industry—All India)

Dependent Variable—Partial Labour Productivity

Explanatory Variables	*Model Numbers*					
	IX	*X*	*XI*	*XII*	*XIII*	*XIV*
(1)	(2)	(3)	(4)	(5)	(6)	(7)
Constant	-6.213 (-4.663)	-7.274 (-3.728)	1.582 (3.862)	1.694 (3.924)	1.669 (3.920)	2.029 (4.099)
ln Time	-0.168** (-2.111)	-0.226 (-1.706)	-0.077 (-0.929)	-0.055 (-0.486)	-0.008 (-0.058)	0.202 (1.121)
ln WR_t	2.355* (7.767)					
ln WR_{t-1}		2.613* (5.718)				
ln $(K/L)_t$			0.665* (6.374)			
ln $(K/L)_{t-1}$				0.643* (5.244)		
ln $(K/L)_{t-2}$					0.634* (4.773)	
ln $(K/L)_{t-3}$						0.473* (2.812)
R^2	0.885	0.859	0.850	0.845	0.866	0.841
$\tilde{R}^2$	0.876	0.848	0.838	0.832	0.855	0.827
S	0.149	0.165	0.170	0.173	0.161	0.176
F	96.160	73.270	71.070	65.460	74.450	58.340
D-W	0.853	1.409	0.877	1.133	0.678	0.916
$\tilde{\rho}$	0.564	0.288	0.507	0.417	0.647	0.487

Notes : 1. Figures in brackets are the respective 't' values.
2. * ** *** indicates significant at 1%, 5% and 10% levels respectively.

Taking labour productivity as dependent upon trend and up to three period capital intensity, models XI and XIV showed non-significant results.

Pre and Post-liberalisation Period

Taking wage rate as dependent upon dummy, labour productivity and product of dummy times labour productivity variables (Table 9.6.3), Model XV showed non-significant results.

Consider the regression equation in Model XVI, in which wage rate is dependent upon dummy, time, labour productivity and product of dummy times labour productivity variables in Table 9.6.3. The estimated equation is :

TABLE 9.6.3
Structural Stability of Regression Functions
(Paper and Paper Products Industry—All India)

Dependent Variables	*I*		*II*	
	Real Wage Rate		*Labour Productivity*	
Explanatory Variables	*Model Numbers*			
	XXVII	*XXVIII*	*XXIX*	*XXX*
Constant	64.4 (5.274)	89.767 (13.453)	-49.21 (-1.361)	-191.41 (-2.063)
Time		3.293* (8.728)		-5.329 (-1.654)
Dummy	7.944 (0.294)	-59.344* (-3.86)	30.445 (0.450)	183.245 (1.620)
LP_t	0.509* (5.248)	0.047 (0.654)		
$D . LP_t$	-0.094 (-0.709)	0.233* (3.102)		
WR_t			1.356* (4.798)	2.877* (3.000)
$D . WR_t$			0.199 (0.472)	-0.691 (-1.025)
R^2	0.885	0.973	0.932	0.939
$\tilde{R}^2$	0.871	0.969	0.924	0.929
S	11.906	5.857	21.262	20.532
F	61.57	209.89	109.90	89.07
D-W	0.772	2.17	1.326	1.788
$\tilde{\rho}$	0.579	-0.091	0.277	0.062

Notes : 1. Figures in brackets are the respective 't' values.
2. * ** *** indicates significant at 1%, 5% and 10% levels respectively.

$WR_t = 89.767 + 3.293\ t - 59.344\ D - 0.047\ LP_t + 0.233\ D\ .\ LP_t$

Pre-liberalisation Era I—1973 to 1990 and D = 0;

then $WR_t = 89.767 + 3.293\ t - 0.047\ LP_t$

Post-liberalisation Era II—1991 to 2000 and D = 1;

then $WR_t = 30.423 + 3.293\ t + 0.186\ LP_t$

The trend effect in pre and post-reform period remains the same. The differential intercept and the differential slope parameter are highly significant. The function has shifted from period I to period II due to significant difference in intercept values and in slope parameters. In post-liberalisation period though the intercept has decreased but, the slope of regression line has become steeper, i.e. the relationship between wage and labour productivity during post-reform era has strengthened in paper and paper products industry.

Taking labour productivity as dependent upon trend, dummy, wage rate and product of dummy times wage rate, Models XVII and XVIII showed non-significant results.

7. LEATHER AND FUR PRODUCTS INDUSTRY

Effect of Productivity on Wages

Thirteen models regarding effect of productivity and capital intensity on wages have been estimated (Table 9.7.1) and the results were non-significant.

Effect of Wages on Productivity

Taking labour productivity as dependent upon trend and second year lagged wage rate (Table 9.7.2) in Model XVI, coefficient of time is 0.673 and this shows that trend is upward and significant. The slope coefficient –1.791 shows that labour productivity lagged behind the increase in wage rate in this industry.

Consider the regression equations in Model XX in which labour productivity depends upon trend and current year capital intensity. Coefficient of time is –0.435 and it is highly significant. The slope coefficient shows that 100 percent increase in $(K/L)_t$ brings about 123.0 percent increase in labour productivity in the same year. The value of R^2 is 0.839 and of $\tilde{R}^2$ is 0.826 which reveals that 83.9 percent variations in labour

TABLE 9.7.1
Regression Function for Wages
(Leather and Fur Products Industry—All India)

Dependent Variable—Real Wage Rate

Explanatory Variables	*Model Numbers*												
	I	*II*	*III*	*IV*	*V*	*VI*	*VII*	*VIII*	*IX*	*X*	*XI*	*XII*	*XIII*
(1)	*(2)*	*(3)*	*(4)*	*(5)*	*(6)*	*(7)*	*(8)*	*(9)*	*(10)*	*(11)*	*(12)*	*(13)*	*(14)*
Constant	4.324	4.319	4.212	4.255	4.243	4.032	4.111	4.076	3.954	3.855	4.410	4.693	4.395
	(19.477)	(19.587)	(18.468)	(18.622)	(17.000)	(16.762)	(13.195)	(12.642)	(12.201)	(12.083)	(11.287)	(13.091)	(20.761)
ln Time	0.056***	0.072**	0.059	0.027	0.046	0.039	0.010	0.011	-0.034	-0.126	0.073*	0.072*	0.066*
	(1.975)	(2.076)	(1.445)	(0.615)	(0.915)	(0.733)	(0.189)	(0.155)	(-0.412)	(-1.362)	(3.331)	(3.340)	(2.818)
ln LP_t	0.046												
	(0.888)												
ln LP_{t-1}		0.038											
		(0.712)											
ln LP_{t-2}			0.067										
			(1.182)										
ln LP_{t-3}				0.077									
				(1.330)									
ln LP_{t-4}					0.070								
					(1.095)								

(Contd.)

TABLE 9.7.1 (CONTD.)

(1)	(2)	(3)	(4)	(5)	(6)	(7)	(8)	(9)	(10)	(11)	(12)	(13)	(14)
ln LP_{t-5}						0.117***							
						(1.900)							
ln $(K/L)_t$							0.097						
							(1.317)						
ln $(K/L)_{t-1}$								0.103					
								(1.244)					
ln $(K/L)_{t-2}$									0.147				
									(1.621)				
ln $(K/L)_{t-3}$										0.211**			
										(2.205)			
ln TFPK											0.023		
											(0.272)		
ln TFPS												-0.039	
												(-0.502)	
ln TFPT													0.029
													(0.591)
R^2	0.328	0.343	0.315	0.207	0.213	0.325	0.352	0.369	0.348	0.299	0.309	0.314	0.316
$\tilde{R}^2$	0.274	0.288	0.255	0.135	0.138	0.258	0.300	0.317	0.291	0.235	0.254	0.259	0.262
S	0.094	0.093	0.094	0.090	0.092	0.087	0.092	0.091	0.091	0.085	0.095	0.095	0.094
F	6.10	6.26	5.29	2.88	2.84	4.82	6.78	7.03	6.13	4.68	5.59	5.71	5.78
D-W	1.089	1.199	1.070	1.035	1.058	1.061	1.178	1.221	1.230	1.246	1.100	1.218	1.097
$\tilde{\rho}$	0.380	0.350	0.372	0.427	0.394	0.399	0.354	0.341	0.300	0.308	0.364	0.314	0.375

Notes : 1. Figures in brackets are the respective 't' values.

2. * ** *** Indicates significant at 1%, 5% and 10% levels respectively.

TABLE 9.7.2

Regression Function for Labour Productivity
(Leather and Leather Products Industry—All India)

Dependent Variable—Partial Labour Productivity

Explanatory Variables	*Model Numbers*							
	XIV	*XV*	*XVI*	*XVII*	*XVIII*	*XIX*	*XX*	*XXI*
(1)	*(2)*	*(3)*	*(4)*	*(5)*	*(6)*	*(7)*	*(8)*	*(9)*
Constant	1.156 (0.340)	6.270 (1.734)	11.686 (3.038)	9.938 (2.364)	7.765 (1.949)	8.917 (2.524)	-0.966 (-1.483)	-0.452 (-0.534)
ln Time	0.309* (3.162)	0.479* (4.189)	0.673* (5.949)	0.741* (5.993)	0.843* (6.504)	1.027* (7.932)	-0.435* (-4.015)	-0.441** (-2.468)
ln WR_t	0.668 (0.888)							
ln WR_{t-1}		-0.517 (-0.643)						
ln WR_{t-2}			-1.791** (-2.098)					
ln WR_{t-3}				-1.463 (-1.571)				
ln WR_{t-4}					-1.062 (-1.203)			

$\ln WR_{t-5}$						-1.423*** (-1.801)		
$\ln (K/L)_t$							1.23* (8.004)	
$\ln (K/L)_{t-1}$								1.159* (5.309)
R^2	0.445	0.468	0.613	0.630	0.681	0.771	0.839	0.751
$\tilde{R}^2$	0.401	0.423	0.580	0.597	0.651	0.748	0.826	0.730
S	0.357	0.351	0.304	0.301	0.284	0.245	0.192	0.240
F	10.028	10.54	18.25	18.74	22.40	33.64	65.30	36.17
D-W	0.291	0.372	0.571	0.832	0.842	0.759	1.713	0.862
$\tilde{\rho}$	0.833	0.746	0.631	0.501	0.467	0.537	0.111	0.526

Notes : 1. Figures in brackets are the respective 't' values.
2. * ** *** Indicates significant at 1%, 5% and 10% levels respectively.

productivity were due to trend and current year capital intensity. The given model fits the data well.

Taking wage rate as dependent upon trend, dummy, labour productivity and product of dummy times labour productivity (Table 9.7.3), Models XXII-XXIII showed non-significant results, indicating no significant change in relationship between wages and labour productivity during post-liberalisation period.

TABLE 9.7.3

Structural Stability of Regression Functions (Leather and Leather Products Industry—All India)

Dependent Variables	*I*		*II*	
	Real Wage Rate		*Labour Productivity*	
Explanatory Variables	*Model Numbers*			
	XXII	*XXIII*	*XXIV*	*XXV*
Constant	101.929 (7.195)	102.504 (8.033)	90.637 (0.868)	125.181 (1.144)
Time		1.178** (2.567)		1.69 (1.038)
Dummy	-18.216 (-0.709)	-40.244 (-1.63)	47.667 (0.356)	2.098 (0.015)
LP_t	0.031 (0.253)	-0.072 (-0.618)		
D. LP_t	0.09 (0.628)	0.17 (1.278)		
WR_t			0.231 (0.233)	-0.249 (-0.229)
D. WR_t			0.936 (0.768)	1.17 (0.946)
R^2	0.274	0.436	0.86	0.866
$\tilde{R}^2$	0.183	0.338	0.842	0.843
S	11.314	10.189	33.672	33.618
F	3.02	4.44	49.08	37.2
D-W	0.908	1.221	1.937	1.97
$\tilde{\rho}$	0.43	0.303	-0.051	-0.076

Notes : 1. Figures in brackets are the respective 't' values.
2. * ** *** Indicates significant at 1%, 5% and 10% levels respectively.

Taking labour productivity as dependent upon trend, dummy, wage rate and product of dummy times wage rate, Models XIV and XV showed non-significant results.

8. CHEMICALS AND CHEMICAL PRODUCTS INDUSTRY

Effect of Productivity on Wages

Nine models regarding effect of productivity and capital intensity on wages have been estimated (Table 9.8.1) and the results of selected models with significant effect of explanatory variables are discussed below :

Consider the regression equation in Model II in which wage rate depends upon trend and one period lagged partial labour productivity. Coefficient of time is 0.188 and trend is upward and is significant. The coefficient of LP_{t-1} is 0.162 and it shows that 100 percent increase in labour productivity brings about 16.2 percent increase in wage rate in the next year, keeping the effect of time constant. The value of R^2 is 0.880 and of $\tilde{R}^2$ is 0.870 which reveals that about 88.0 percent variations in wage rate were due to trend and one year lagged partial labour productivity. Thus increase in partial labour productivity has benefited the workers in chemicals and chemical products industry. The given model fits the data well.

Consider the regression equation in Model V in which real wage rate depends upon trend and one year lagged capital intensity. The coefficient of time is 0.155 and trend is upward and significant. The slope coefficient of $(K/L)_{t-1}$ is 0.159 and this shows that 100 percent increase in capital intensity, keeping the effect of time constant, brings about 15.9 percent increase in wage rate in next year. The value of R^2 is 0.888 and of $\tilde{R}^2$ is 0.879 which reveals that about 88.8 percent variations in wage rate were due to trend and one year lagged capital intensity. The given model fits the data well.

Effect of Wages on Productivity

Taking labour productivity as dependent upon trend and up to five year lagged wage rate, Models X-XV (Table 9.8.2) showed non-significant results.

Consider the regression equations in Model XVI which labour productivity depends upon trend and current year

TABLE 9.8.1
Regression Function for Wages
(Chemicals and Chemical Products Industry—All India)

Dependent Variable—Real Wage Rate

Explanatory Variables	*Model Numbers*								
	I	*II*	*III*	*IV*	*V*	*VI*	*VII*	*VIII*	*IX*
(1)	*(2)*	*(3)*	*(4)*	*(5)*	*(6)*	*(7)*	*(8)*	*(9)*	*(10)*
Constant	3.488 (16.663)	3.639 (18.237)	3.553 (17.389)	3.605 (21.479)	3.699 (22.648)	3.673 (22.069)	3.569 (4.024)	3.894 (4.799)	3.692 (4.554)
ln Time	0.137* (5.640)	0.188* (6.586)	0.19* (5.843)	0.106* (3.817)	0.155* (4.589)	0.153* (3.801)	0.218* (9.167)	0.218* (8.512)	0.221* (8.732)
ln LP_t	0.219* (4.351)								
ln LP_{t-1}		0.162* (3.223)							
ln LP_{t-2}			0.18* (3.391)						
ln $(K/L)_t$				0.2* (4.760)					
ln $(K/L)_{t-1}$					0.159* (3.609)				

ln $(K/L)_{t-2}$						0.167* (3.492)			
ln TFPK							0.176 (0.914)		
ln TFPS								0.105 (0.598)	
ln TFPT									0.149 (0.848)
R^2	0.869	0.880	0.872	0.880	0.888	0.875	0.778	0.774	0.777
$\tilde{R}^2$	0.859	0.870	0.861	0.870	0.879	0.864	0.760	0.756	0.759
S	0.076	0.072	0.070	0.073	0.069	0.069	0.100	0.100	0.100
F	83.28	87.92	78.63	91.39	95.58	80.44	43.82	42.78	43.57
D-W	0.756	1.103	0.992	0.877	0.919	1.030	0.585	0.591	0.591
$\tilde{\rho}$	0.472	0.389	0.454	0.458	0.460	0.427	0.494	0.497	0.490

Notes : 1. Figures in brackets are the respective 't' values.
2. * ** *** Indicates significant at 1%, 5% and 10% levels respectively.

TABLE 9.8.2

Regression Function for Labour Productivity (Chemicals and Chemical Products Industry—All India)

Dependent Variable—Partial Labour Productivity

Explanatory Variables	*Model Numbers*							
	X	*XI*	*XII*	*XIII*	*XIV*	*XV*	*XVI*	*XVII*
(1)	*(2)*	*(3)*	*(4)*	*(5)*	*(6)*	*(7)*	*(8)*	*(9)*
Constant	-4.554	-2.616	-1.604	-5.267	-3.880	-5.226	0.923	0.947
	(-2.293)	(-1.004)	(-0.438)	(-1.079)	(-0.795)	(-1.131)	(3.753)	(3.832)
ln Time	-0.078	0.077	0.213	0.033	0.163	0.095	-0.091**	-0.066
	(-0.713)	(0.470)	(0.892)	(0.101)	(0.439)	(0.239)	(-2.229)	(-1.289)
ln WR_t	1.969*							
	(4.351)							
ln WR_{t-1}		1.502**						
		(2.464)						
ln WR_{t-2}			1.228					
			(1.406)					
ln WR_{t-3}				2.087***				
				(1.766)				
ln WR_{t-4}					1.724			
					(1.435)			

ln WR_{t-5}						2.057*** (1.754)		
ln $(K/L)_t$							0.814* (13.220)	
ln $(K/L)_{t-1}$								0.806* (12.074)
R^2	0.709	0.664	0.664	0.695	0.709	0.746	0.936	0.941
$\tilde{R}^2$	0.686	0.636	0.635	0.667	0.681	0.721	0.931	0.936
S	0.229	0.249	0.251	0.238	0.233	0.218	0.107	0.105
F	30.50	23.72	22.74	25.01	25.54	29.39	183.03	189.69
D-W	0.397	0.558	0.555	0.570	0.663	0.875	1.451	1.685
$\tilde{\rho}$	0.775	0.684	0.705	0.707	0.654	0.502	0.247	0.099

Notes : 1. Figures in brackets are the respective 't' values.
2. * ** *** indicates significant at 1%, 5% and 10% levels respectively.

capital intensity. Coefficient of time is –0.091 and it is significant. The slope coefficient shows that 100 percent increase in $(K/L)_t$ brings about 81.4 percent increase in labour productivity in the same year. The value of R^2 is 0.936 and of $\tilde{R}^2$ is 0.931 which reveals that 93.6 percent variations in labour productivity were due to trend and current year capital intensity. The given model fits the data well.

Taking wage rate as dependent upon trend, dummy, labour productivity and product of dummy times labour productivity (Table 9.8.3), Models XVIII-XIX showed non-significant results.

TABLE 9.8.3
Structural Stability of Regression Functions (Chemicals and Chemical Products Industry—All India)

Dependent Variables	*I*		*II*	
	Real Wage Rate		*Labour Productivity*	
Explanatory Variables	*Model Numbers*			
	XVIII	*XIX*	*XX*	*XXI*
Constant	30.866 (0.964)	83.377 (3.734)	41.27 (1.003)	151.802 (1.541)
Time		3.198* (5.958)		3.851 (1.232)
Dummy	59.736 (1.409)	-31.819 (-1.02)	12.238 (0.185)	-121.628 (-0.959)
LP_t	0.883* (2.805)	0.063 (0.257)		
$D . LP_t$	-0.555 (-1.641)	0.104 (0.427)		
WR_t			0.497 (1.465)	-0.728 (-0.693)
$D . WR_t$			0.536 (1.162)	1.352 (1.681)
R^2	0.728	0.893	0.892	0.898
$\tilde{R}^2$	0.693	0.874	0.878	0.881
S	15.844	10.148	22.772	22.53
F	21.35	47.92	65.75	50.75
D-W	0.484	0.751	1.463	1.717
$\tilde{\rho}$	0.604	0.501	0.185	0.034

Notes : 1. Figures in brackets are the respective 't' values.
2. * ** *** Indicates significant at 1%, 5% and 10% levels respectively.

Taking labour productivity as dependent upon trend, dummy, wage rate and product of dummy times wage rate, Models XX and XXI showed non-significant results.

9. RUBBER, PETROLEUM AND COAL PRODUCTS INDUSTRY

Effect of Productivity on Wage

Nine models of effect of productivity and capital intensity on wages have been estimated (Table 9.9.1) and the results of selected models with significant effect of explanatory variables are discussed below :

Consider the regression equation in Model I in which wage rate depends upon trend and current year partial labour productivity. Coefficient of time is 0.091 and trend is upward and is significant. The coefficient of LP_t is 0.157 and it shows that 100 percent increase in labour productivity brings about 15.7 percent increase in wage rate in the same year, keeping the effect of time constant. The value of R^2 is 0.701 and of $\tilde{R}^2$ is 0.677 which reveals that about 70.1 percent variations in wage rate were due to trend and current year partial labour productivity. Thus, increase in partial labour productivity has benefited the workers in rubber, petroleum and coal products industry. The given model fits the data well.

Taking wage rate as dependent upon trend and up to three year lagged capital intensity, models III-VI showed non-significant results.

Effect of Wages on Productivity

In Model XII (Table 9.9.2) coefficient of time is 0.473 and trend is significant. The slope coefficient 1.602 shows that 100 percent increase in wage rate results into 160.2 percent increase in labour productivity in the next second year, keeping the effect of time constant. Hence labour productivity is highly responsive to change in wage rate in rubber, petroleum and coal products industry. It appears that increase in wage rate is in the interest of this industry. The value of R^2 is 0.759 and of $\tilde{R}^2$ is 0.738 which indicates that 75.9 percent variations in labour productivity were due to trend and two period lagged wage rate. The model fits the data well.

TABLE 9.9.1
Regression Function for Wages
(Rubber, Petroleum and Coal Products Industry—All India)

Dependent Variable—Real Wage Rate

Explanatory Variables	*Model Numbers*								
	I	*II*	*III*	*IV*	*V*	*VI*	*VII*	*VIII*	*IX*
(1)	*(2)*	*(3)*	*(4)*	*(5)*	*(6)*	*(7)*	*(8)*	*(9)*	*(10)*
Constant	3.800 (16.042)	3.938 (16.155)	3.659 (19.173)	3.688 (18.476)	3.552 (19.762)	3.844 (14.309)	4.709 (9.978)	5.170 (18.167)	5.178 (18.299)
ln Time	0.091** (2.277)	0.141** (2.727)	0.045 (1.177)	0.067 (1.344)	0.016 (0.292)	0.139 (1.637)	0.18* (6.330)	0.157* (6.141)	0.153* (5.855)
ln LP_t	0.157** (2.725)								
ln LP_{t-1}		0.108 (1.696)							
ln $(K/L)_t$			0.2* (4.183)						
ln $(K/L)_{t-1}$				0.187* (3.421)					
ln $(K/L)_{t-2}$					0.24* (4.543)				

ln $(K/L)_{t-3}$						0.127 (1.514)			
ln TFPK							-0.063 (-0.613)		
ln TFPS								-0.158** (-2.692)	
ln TFPT									-0.158** (-2.737)
R^2	0.701	0.680	0.772	0.759	0.788	0.648	0.618	0.700	0.702
$\tilde{R}^2$	0.677	0.653	0.754	0.739	0.770	0.617	0.588	0.676	0.678
S	0.108	0.110	0.094	0.096	0.086	0.111	0.122	0.108	0.108
F	29.35	25.49	42.36	37.80	42.74	20.29	20.25	29.13	29.44
D-W	0.835	0.784	1.266	1.300	0.875	0.934	0.662	0.933	0.955
$\tilde{\rho}$	0.369	0.410	0.185	0.145	0.489	0.329	0.434	0.358	0.347

Notes : 1. Figures in brackets are the respective 't' values.
2. * ** *** indicates significant at 1%, 5% and 10% levels respectively.

TABLE 9.9.2
Regression Function for Labour Productivity (Rubber, Petroleum and Coal Products Industry—All India)

Dependent Variable—Partial Labour Productivity

Explanatory Variables	*Model Numbers*							
	X	*XI*	*XII*	*XIII*	*XIV*	*XV*	*XVI*	*XVII*
(1)	*(2)*	*(3)*	*(4)*	*(5)*	*(6)*	*(7)*	*(8)*	*(9)*
Constant	-2.489 (-1.047)	-4.702 (-1.567)	-3.601 (-0.973)	0.160 (0.037)	1.102 (2.361)	1.399 (2.609)	1.698 (3.048)	1.421 (2.207)
ln Time	0.288** (2.384)	0.304*** (1.962)	0.473** (2.427)	0.743* (3.124)	0.052 (0.560)	0.163 (1.223)	0.348** (2.109)	0.393*** (1.937)
ln WR_t	1.46** (2.725)							
ln WR_{t-1}		1.915** (2.786)						
ln WR_{t-2}			1.602*** (1.866)					
ln WR_{t-3}				0.675 (0.661)				
ln $(K/L)_t$					0.75* (6.411)			

$\ln (K/L)_{t-1}$						0.652* (4.444)		
$\ln (K/L)_{t-2}$							0.514* (3.135)	
$\ln (K/L)_{t-3}$								0.551** (2.743)
R^2	0.706	0.750	0.759	0.741	0.856	0.818	0.805	0.803
$\tilde{R}^2$	0.683	0.729	0.738	0.717	0.844	0.803	0.788	0.785
S	0.329	0.302	0.297	0.304	0.231	0.257	0.267	0.265
F	30.050	35.95	36.15	31.42	74.26	54.05	47.57	44.83
D-W	0.588	0.693	0.759	0.696	1.125	1.250	0.968	0.835
$\tilde{\rho}$	0.665	0.601	0.595	0.561	0.432	0.360	0.482	0.530

Notes : 1. Figures in brackets are the respective 't' values.
2. * ** *** Indicates significant at 1%, 5% and 10% levels respectively.

In case of Model XVI coefficient of time is 0.348 and it is upward and significant. The slope coefficient shows that 100 percent increase in $(K/L)_{t-2}$ brings about 51.4 percent increase in labour productivity in the next second year. The value of R^2 is 0.805 and of $\tilde{R}^2$ is 0.788 which reveals that 80.5 percent variations in labour productivity were due to trend and second year lagged capital intensity. The given model fits the data well.

Pre and Post-liberalisation Period

Taking wage rate as dependent upon trend, dummy, labour productivity and product of dummy times labour productivity (Table 9.9.3), Models XVIII-XIX showed non-significant results.

TABLE 9.9.3

Structural Stability of Regression Functions
(Rubber, Petroleum and Coal Products Industry—All India)

Dependent Variables	*I*		*II*	
	Real Wage Rate		*Labour Productivity*	
Explanatory Variables	*Model Numbers*			
	XVIII	*XIX*	*XX*	*XXI*
Constant	89.037	93.258	-252.095	-28.105
	(7.249)	(9.417)	(-2.325)	(-0.165)
Time		3.744*		7.555
		(3.793)		(1.673)
Dummy	14.937	-47.703	509.991*	209.227
	(0.434)	(-1.483)	(3.600)	(0.927)
LP_t	0.19**	-0.077		
	(2.472)	(-0.825)		
$D . LP_t$	-0.062	0.129		
	(-0.545)	(1.243)		
WR_t			3.417*	0.896
			(3.722)	(0.513)
$D . WR_t$			-2.603**	-0.74
			(-2.391)	(-0.483)
$\underset{\sim}{R}^2$	0.568	0.734	0.853	0.869
R^2	0.514	0.688	0.835	0.847
S	18.922	15.16	53.259	51.368
F	10.53	15.90	46.55	38.23
D-W	0.676	0.768	1.997	1.69
$\tilde{\rho}$	0.438	0.385	0.000	0.149

Notes : 1. Figures in brackets are the respective 't' values.
2. * ** *** Indicates significant at 1%, 5% and 10% levels respectively.

Consider the regression equation in Model XX, in which labour productivity depends upon dummy, wage rate and product of dummy times wage rate variables. The estimated equation is :

$$LP_t = -252.095 + 509.991\ D + 3.417\ WR_t - 2.603\ D.\ WR_t$$

Pre-liberalisation Era I—1973-74 to 1990-91 and D = 0;

$$\text{then } LP_t = -252.095 + 3.417\ WR_t$$

Post-liberalisation Era II—1991-92 to 2000-01 and D = 1;

$$\text{then } LP_t = 257.896 + 0.814\ WR_t$$

Coefficients of all variables are significant. The results reveal that in post-liberalisation period though the intercept has increased but, the slope of regression line has become flatter, i.e. the relationship between labour productivity and wage rate in post-liberalisation period has weakened in this industry. Thus, after liberalisation the labour productivity has become less responsive to wage rate.

Taking labour productivity as dependent upon trend, dummy, wage rate and product of dummy times wage rate, Model XXI showed non-significant result.

10. NON-METALLIC MINERAL PRODUCTS INDUSTRY

Effect of Productivity on Wages

Nine models regarding effect of productivity and capital intensity on wages have been estimated (Table 9.10.1) and the results of selected models with significant effect of explanatory variables are discussed below :

Consider the regression equation in Model I in which wage rate depends upon trend and current year partial labour productivity. Coefficient of time is 0.102 and trend is upward and is significant. The coefficient of LP_t is 0.245 and it shows that 100 percent increase in labour productivity brings about 24.5 percent increase in wage rate in the same year, keeping the effect of time constant. The value of R^2 is 0.835 and of $\tilde{R}^2$ is 0.822 which reveals that about 83.5 percent variations in wage rate were due to trend and current year partial labour productivity. Thus increase in partial labour productivity has benefited the workers

TABLE 9.10.1
Regression Function for Wages
(Non-Metallic Mineral Products Industry—All India)

Dependent Variable—Real Wage Rate

Explanatory Variables	*Model Numbers*								
	I	*II*	*III*	*IV*	*V*	*VI*	*VII*	*VIII*	*IX*
(1)	*(2)*	*(3)*	*(4)*	*(5)*	*(6)*	*(7)*	*(8)*	*(9)*	*(10)*
Constant	3.416 (13.584)	3.580 (13.906)	3.739 (29.326)	3.740 (31.677)	3.700 (32.772)	3.685 (30.117)	5.095 (9.069)	5.502 (11.886)	5.527 (12.026)
ln Time	0.102** (2.509)	0.154* (2.907)	0.062 (1.649)	0.072 (1.551)	0.031 (0.563)	0.026 (0.370)	0.245* (8.580)	0.219* (8.335)	0.217* (8.252)
ln LP_t	0.245* (3.921)								
ln LP_{t-1}		0.19** (2.734)							
ln $(K/L)_t$			0.189* (5.410)						
ln $(K/L)_{t-1}$				0.187* (4.998)					
ln $(K/L)_{t-2}$					0.218* (5.394)				

ln $(K/L)_{t-3}$						0.228* (4.661)			
ln TFPK							-0.157 (-1.29)		
ln TFPS								-0.237** (-2.458)	
ln TFPT									-0.242** (-2.531)
R^2	0.835	0.824	0.877	0.887	0.889	0.872	0.750	0.785	0.788
$\tilde{R}^2$	0.822	0.810	0.867	0.878	0.879	0.860	0.730	0.768	0.771
S	0.098	0.099	0.084	0.079	0.075	0.078	0.120	0.111	0.111
F	63.25	56.33	89.33	94.32	91.77	74.77	37.53	45.75	46.43
D-W	0.502	0.788	0.704	0.873	0.872	0.775	0.578	0.797	0.808
$\tilde{\rho}$	0.574	0.448	0.465	0.420	0.466	0.485	0.506	0.433	0.439

Notes : 1. Figures in brackets are the respective 't' values.
2. * ** *** Indicates significant at 1%, and 5% levels respectively.

in non-metallic mineral products industry. The given model fits the data well.

Taking wage rate as dependent upon trend and up to three year lagged capital intensity, models III-VI showed non-significant results.

Effect of Wages on Productivity

In Model XII (Table 9.10.2) coefficient of time is 0.383 and trend is significant. The slope coefficient 1.378 shows that 100 percent increase in wage rate results into 137.8 percent increase in labour productivity in the next second year, keeping the effect of time constant. Hence labour productivity is highly responsive to change in wage rate in non-metallic mineral products industry. It appears that increase in wage rate is in the interest of this industry. The value of R^2 is 0.835 and of $\tilde{R}^2$ is 0.820 which indicates that 83.5 percent variations in labour productivity were due to trend and two period lagged wage rate. The model fits the data well.

In case of Model XVI coefficient of time is 0.232 and it is upward and significant. The slope coefficient shows that 100 percent increase in $(K/L)_{t-2}$ brings about 43.8 percent increase in labour productivity in the next second year. The value of R^2 is 0.895 and of $\tilde{R}^2$ is 0.886 which reveals that 89.5 percent variations in labour productivity were due to trend and second year lagged capital intensity. The given model fits the data well.

Pre and Post-liberalisation Period

Taking wage rate as dependent upon dummy, labour productivity and product of dummy times labour productivity (Table 9.10.3), Model XVIII showed non-significant result.

Consider the regression equation in Model XIX, in which wage rate is dependent upon dummy, time, labour productivity and product of dummy times labour productivity variables in Table 9.10.3. The estimated equation is :

$$WR_t = 114.725 + 5.83\ t - 88.811\ D - 0.335\ LP_t + 0.386\ D\ .\ LP_t$$

Pre-liberalisation Era I—1973 to 1990 and D = 0;

$$\text{then } WR_t = 114.725 + 5.83\ t - 0.335\ LP_t$$

Post-liberalisation Era II—1991 to 2000 and D = 1;

$$\text{then } WR_t = 25.914 + 5.83\ t + 0.051\ LP_t$$

TABLE 9.10.2
Regression Function for Labour Productivity (Non-Metallic Mineral Products Industry—All India)

Dependent Variable—Partial Labour Productivity

Explanatory Variables	*Model Numbers*							
	X	*XI*	*XII*	*XIII*	*XIV*	*XV*	*XVI*	*XVII*
(1)	*(2)*	*(3)*	*(4)*	*(5)*	*(6)*	*(7)*	*(8)*	*(9)*
Constant	-2.886 (-1.656)	-1.890 (-0.88)	-2.454 (-0.889)	0.195 (0.061)	2.147 (7.786)	2.341 (8.245)	2.294 (8.416)	2.177 (8.164)
ln Time	0.178 (1.637)	0.335** (2.252)	0.383*** (1.929)	0.645** (2.616)	0.060 (0.741)	0.183 (1.627)	0.232*** (1.744)	0.253 (1.646)
ln WR_t	1.556* (3.921)							
ln WR_{t-1}		1.282** (2.551)						
ln WR_{t-2}			1.378** (2.092)					
ln WR_{t-3}				0.700 (0.903)				

(Contd.)

TABLE 9.10.2 (CONTD.)

(1)	(2)	(3)	(4)	(5)	(6)	(7)	(8)	(9)
ln $(K/L)_t$					0.529* (6.986)			
ln $(K/L)_{t-1}$						0.445* (4.946)		
ln $(K/L)_{t-2}$							0.438* (4.494)	
ln $(K/L)_{t-3}$								0.458* (4.303)
R^2	0.813	0.822	0.835	0.827	0.898	0.888	0.895	0.903
$\tilde{R}^2$	0.799	0.807	0.820	0.812	0.890	0.878	0.886	0.894
S	0.247	0.240	0.227	0.228	0.182	0.190	0.181	0.171
F	54.510	55.30	58.07	52.69	110.00	94.92	98.26	102.10
D-W	0.461	0.733	0.661	0.690	0.956	0.947	0.897	1.070
$\tilde{\rho}$	0.698	0.576	0.632	0.606	0.521	0.506	0.506	0.438

Notes : 1. Figures in brackets are the respective 't' values.
2. * ** *** Indicates significant at 1%, 5% and 10% levels respectively.

TABLE 9.10.3
Structural Stability of Regression Functions (Rubber, Petroleum and Coal Products Industry—All India)

Dependent Variables	*I*		*II*	
	Real Wage Rate		*Labour Productivity*	
Explanatory Variables	*Model Numbers*			
	XVIII	*XIX*	*XX*	*XXI*
Constant	85.033 (5.405)	114.725 (10.459)	-171.41 (-1.696)	93.95 (0.386)
Time		5.83* (6.174)		8.171 (1.197)
Dummy	53.036 1.491	-88.811** (-2.774)	407.64* (2.927)	81.412 (0.267)
LP_t	0.278** (2.571)	-0.335** (-2.788)		
$D . LP_t$	-0.158 (-1.144)	0.386* (3.128)		
WR_t			2.511* (3.092)	-0.264 (-0.108)
$D . WR_t$			-1.808*** (-1.875)	0.245 (0.125)
R^2	0.722	0.895	0.854	0.863
$\tilde{R}^2$	0.687	0.877	0.836	0.839
S	20.089	12.588	50.213	49.766
F	20.73	49.13	46.81	36.1
D-W	0.375	1.04	1.259	1.38
$\tilde{\rho}$	0.629	0.314	0.355	0.296

Notes : 1. Figures in brackets are the respective 't' values.
2. * ** *** Indicates significant at 1%, 5% and 10% levels respeetively.

The trend effect in pre and post-reform period remains the same. The differential intercept and the differential slope parameter are significant. The function has shifted from period I to period II due to significant difference in intercept values and in slope parameters. In post-liberalisation period though the intercept has decreased but, the slope of regression line has become steeper, i.e. the relationship between wage and labour productivity during post-reform era has strengthened in non-metallic mineral products industry.

Consider the regression equation in Model XX, in which labour productivity depends upon dummy, wage rate and product of dummy times wage rate variables. The estimated equation is :

$$LP_t = -171.41 + 407.64\ D + 2.511\ WR_t - 1.808\ D\ .\ WR_t$$

Pre-liberalisation Era I; 1973-74 to 1990-91 and D = 0;

then $LP_t = -171.41 + 2.511\ WR_t$

Post-liberalisation Era II; 1991-92 to 2000-01

and D = 1; then $LP_t = 236.23 + 0.703\ WR_t$

Coefficients of all variables are significant. The results reveal that in post-liberalisation period though the intercept has increased but, the slope of regression line has become flatter, i.e. the relationship between labour productivity and wage rate in post-liberalisation period has weakened in this industry. Thus after liberalisation the labour productivity has become less responsive to wage rate.

Taking labour productivity as dependent upon trend, dummy, wage rate and product of dummy times wage rate, Model XXI showed non-significant result.

11. BASIC METALS AND ALLOYS INDUSTRY

Effect of Productivity on Wages

Thirteen models regarding effect of productivity and capital intensity on wages have been estimated (Table 9.11.1) and the results of selected models with significant effect of explanatory variables are discussed below :

Taking wage rate as dependent upon trend and up to five year lagged labour productivity, models I-VI showed non-significant results.

Taking wage rate as dependent upon trend and up to three year lagged capital intensity, models VII-X showed non-significant results.

In Model XI real wage rate depends upon trend and total factor productivity index (Kendrick). Coefficient of time is 0.136

TABLE 9.11.1

Regression Function for Wages
(Basic Metals and Alloys Industry—All India)

Dependent Variable—Real Wage Rate

Explanatory Variables	*Model Numbers*												
	I	*II*	*III*	*IV*	*V*	*VI*	*VII*	*VIII*	*IX*	*X*	*XI*	*XII*	*XIII*
(1)	*(2)*	*(3)*	*(4)*	*(5)*	*(6)*	*(7)*	*(8)*	*(9)*	*(10)*	*(11)*	*(12)*	*(13)*	*(14)*
Constant	3.280	3.247	3.242	3.151	3.013	2.923	3.556	3.519	3.357	3.320	3.115	4.385	4.565
	(11.964)	(12.230)	(11.993)	(11.977)	(12.034)	(11.148)	(14.792)	(15.271)	(17.355)	(15.605)	(4.556)	(6.469)	(6.861)
ln Time	0.036	0.035	0.043	0.027	0.037	0.040	0.033	0.032	-0.015	-0.021	0.136*	0.189*	0.189*
	(0.808)	(0.652)	(0.650)	(0.375)	(0.485)	(0.464)	(0.672)	(0.516)	(-0.234)	(-0.26)	(3.307)	(5.931)	(5.921)
ln LP_t	0.282*												
	(4.218)												
ln LP_{t-1}		0.291*											
		(4.136)											
ln LP_{t-2}			0.291*										
			(3.806)										
ln LP_{t-3}				0.32*									
				(4.051)									
ln LP_{t-4}					0.345*								
					(4.378)								

(Contd.)

TABLE 9.11.1 (CONTD.)

(1)	(2)	(3)	(4)	(5)	(6)	(7)	(8)	(9)	(10)	(11)	(12)	(13)	(14)
ln LP_{t-5}						0.365* (4.254)							
ln $(K/L)_t$							0.224* (3.676)						
ln $(K/L)_{t-1}$								0.234* (3.612)					
ln $(K/L)_{t-2}$									0.289* (4.858)				
ln $(K/L)_{t-3}$										0.303* (4.308)			
ln TFPK											0.29*** (1.900)		
ln TFPS												0.005 (0.031)	
ln TFPT													-0.035 (-0.241)
R^2	0.757	0.774	0.768	0.781	0.822	0.822	0.730	0.749	0.813	0.793	0.637	0.585	0.586
$\tilde{R}^2$	0.738	0.755	0.748	0.762	0.806	0.804	0.709	0.728	0.797	0.774	0.608	0.551	0.552
S	0.107	0.102	0.103	0.099	0.090	0.089	0.113	0.108	0.092	0.096	0.131	0.140	0.140
F	39.01	41.06	38.09	39.31	48.62	46.19	33.85	35.83	50.14	42.13	21.93	17.59	17.66
D-W	0.897	1.191	1.283	1.450	1.511	1.704	0.787	1.115	1.111	1.187	0.744	0.525	0.536
$\tilde{\rho}$	0.361	0.268	0.236	0.178	0.159	0.083	0.451	0.289	0.369	0.257	0.432	0.555	0.556

Notes : 1. Figures in brackets are the respective 't' values.
2. * ** *** Indicates significant at 1% and 10% levels respectively.

and is statistically significant. The slope coefficient of TFPK is 0.29 and this shows that 100 percent increase in TFPK brings about 29.0 percent increase in wage rate, when the effect of time is held constant. The value of R^2 is 0.637 and of $\tilde{R}^2$ is 0.608 which indicates that about 63.7 percent variations in wage rate were due to TFPK and time. The given model fits the data well.

Effect of Wages on Productivity

In Model XIV (Table 9.11.2) coefficient of time is 0.267 and trend is significant. The slope coefficient 1.474 shows that 100 percent increase in wage rate results into 147.4 percent increase in labour productivity in the same year, keeping the effect of time constant. Hence labour productivity is highly responsive to change in wage rate in basic metals and alloys industry. It appears that increase in wage rate is in the interest of this industry. The value of R^2 is 0.819 and of $\tilde{R}^2$ is 0.805 which indicates that 81.9 percent variations in labour productivity were due to trend and wage rate. The model fits the data well.

In case of Model XX coefficient of time is 0.537 and it is upward and significant. The slope coefficient shows that 100 percent increase in $(K/L)_{t-4}$ brings about 42.9 percent increase in labour productivity in the next fourth year. The value of R^2 is 0.932 and of $\tilde{R}^2$ is 0.925 which reveals that 93.2 percent variations in labour productivity were due to trend and fourth year lagged capital intensity. The given model fits the data well.

Pre and Post-liberalisation Period

Taking wage rate as dependent upon dummy, labour productivity and product of dummy times labour productivity (Table 9.11.3), model XXII showed non-significant result.

Consider the regression equation in Model XXIII, in which wage rate is dependent upon dummy, time, labour productivity and product of dummy times labour productivity variables in Table 9.11.3. The estimated equation is :

$$WR_t = 101.31 + 3.86\ t - 92.061\ D - 0.14\ LP_t + 0.298\ D\ .\ LP_t$$

Pre-liberalisation Era I—1973-74 to 1990-91 and D = 0;

then $WR_t = 101.31 + 3.86\ t - 0.14\ LP_t$

Post-liberalisation Era II—1991-92 to 2000-01 and D = 1;

then $WR_t = 9.249 + 3.86\ t + 0.158\ LP_t$

TABLE 9.11.2

Regression Function for Labour Productivity (Basic Metals and Alloys Industry—All India)

Dependent Variable—Partial Labour Productivity

Explanatory Variables	*Model Numbers*							
	XIV	*XV*	*XVI*	*XVII*	*XVIII*	*XIX*	*XX*	*XXI*
(1)	*(2)*	*(3)*	*(4)*	*(5)*	*(6)*	*(7)*	*(8)*	*(9)*
Constant	-2.503 (-1.619)	-2.048 (-1.058)	1.191 (3.356)	1.364 (3.798)	1.686 (4.691)	1.516 (4.515)	1.682 (5.267)	1.691 (5.415)
ln Time	0.267* (3.078)	0.388* (3.372)	0.031 (0.426)	0.086 (0.896)	0.27** (2.282)	0.32** (2.555)	0.537* (3.913)	0.655* (4.331)
ln WR_t	1.474* (4.218)							
ln WR_{t-1}		1.324* (2.969)						
ln $(K/L)_t$			0.738* (8.212)					
ln $(K/L)_{t-1}$				0.689* (6.829)				
ln $(K/L)_{t-2}$					0.55* (4.974)			

$\ln (K/L)_{t-3}$						0.564* (5.077)		
$\ln (K/L)_{t-4}$							0.429* (3.782)	
$\ln (K/L)_{t-5}$								0.371* (3.612)
R^2	0.819	0.812	0.916	0.913	0.910	0.928	0.932	0.930
$\tilde{R}^2$	0.805	0.797	0.910	0.906	0.902	0.921	0.925	0.923
S	0.245	0.247	0.167	0.168	0.171	0.151	0.146	0.144
F	56.720	51.96	137.01	125.67	115.96	140.83	143.00	133.51
D-W	0.705	0.868	1.615	1.270	1.326	1.354	1.586	1.317
$\tilde{\rho}$	0.561	0.474	0.191	0.333	0.251	0.242	0.145	0.236

Notes : 1. Figures in brackets are the respective 't' values.
2. * ** *** Indicates significant at 1%, and 5% levels respectively.

TABLE 9.11.3
Structural Stability of Regression Functions (Basic Metals and Alloys Industry—All India)

Dependent Variables	*I*		*II*	
	Real Wage Rate		*Labour Productivity*	
Explanatory Variables	*Model Numbers*			
	XVIII	*XIX*	*XX*	*XXI*
Constant	90.757 (7.909)	101.31 (10.508)	-305.689 (-2.717)	129.3 (0.577)
Time		3.86* (3.760)		10.946** (2.192)
Dummy	-34.544 (-1.194)	-92.061* (-3.307)	434.441* (3.203)	-106.637 (-0.385)
LP_t	0.171** (2.404)	-0.14 (-1.394)		
$D . LP_t$	0.101 (1.029)	0.298* (3.154)		
WR_t			3.923* (4.088)	-0.695 (-0.304)
$D . WR_t$			-2.319** (-2.178)	1.362 (0.699)
R^2	0.742	0.84	0.89	0.909
$\tilde{R}^2$	0.71	0.813	0.876	0.893
S	16.484	13.251	46.477	43.179
F	23.02	30.25	64.56	57.3
D-W	0.989	1.126	1.502	1.18
$\tilde{\rho}$	0.206	0.18	0.153	0.306

Notes : 1. Figures in brackets are the respective 't' values.
2. * ** *** Indicates significant at 1% and 5% levels respectively.

The trend effect in pre and post-reform period remains the same. The differential intercept and the differential slope parameter are significant. The function has shifted from period I to period II due to significant difference in intercept values and in slope parameters. In post-liberalisation period though the intercept has decreased but, the slope of regression line has become steeper, i.e. the relationship between wage and labour productivity during post-reform era has strengthened in basic metals and alloys industry.

Consider the regression equation in Model XXV, in which labour productivity depends upon dummy, wage rate and product of dummy times wage rate variables. The estimated equation is :

$$LP_t = -305.68 + 434.441\ D + 3.923\ WR_t - 2.319\ D\ .\ WR_t$$

Pre-liberalisation Era I; 1973-74 to 1990-91 and D = 0;

$$\text{then } LP_t = -305.68 + 3.923\ WR_t$$

Post-liberalisation Era II; 1991-92 to 2000-01 and D = 1;

$$\text{then } LP_t = 128.761 + 1.604\ WR_t$$

Coefficients of all variables are significant. The results reveal that in post-liberalisation period though the intercept has increased but, the slope of regression line has become flatter, i.e. the relationship between labour productivity and wage rate in post-liberalisation period has weakened in this industry. Thus after liberalisation the labour productivity has become less responsive to wage rate.

Taking labour productivity as dependent upon trend, dummy, wage rate and product of dummy times wage rate, Model XXI showed non-significant result.

12. METAL PRODUCTS INDUSTRY

Effect of Productivity on Wages

Nine models regarding effect of productivity and capital intensity on wages have been estimated (Table 9.12.1) and the results of selected models with significant effect of explanatory variables are discussed below :

Consider the regression equation in Model II in which wage rate depends upon trend and one period lagged partial labour productivity. Coefficient of time is 0.131 and trend is upward and is significant. The coefficient of LP_{t-1} is 0.187 and it shows that 100 percent increase in labour productivity brings about 18.7 percent increase in wage rate in the next year, keeping the effect of time constant. This implies that it is in the interest of workers to make efforts for increasing their productivity. The value of R^2 is 0.874 and of $\tilde{R}^2$ is 0.863 which reveals that about 87.4 percent variations in wage rate were due

TABLE 9.12.1
Regression Function for Wages
(Metal Products Industry—All India)

Dependent Variable—Real Wage Rate

Explanatory Variables	*Model Numbers*								
	I	*II*	*III*	*IV*	*V*	*VI*	*VII*	*VIII*	*IX*
(1)	*(2)*	*(3)*	*(4)*	*(5)*	*(6)*	*(7)*	*(8)*	*(9)*	*(10)*
Constant	3.622 (18.108)	3.657 (18.801)	3.615 (18.220)	3.866 (22.024)	3.848 (24.239)	3.814 (25.161)	2.414 (5.194)	2.778 (5.565)	2.717 (5.022)
ln Time	0.105* (2.928)	0.131* (2.920)	0.123** (2.261)	0.129* (3.480)	0.151* (3.411)	0.143** (2.755)	0.085** (2.241)	0.095** (2.094)	0.099** (2.132)
ln LP_t	0.204* (4.026)								
ln LP_{t-1}		0.187* (3.447)							
ln LP_{t-2}			0.201* (3.363)						
ln $(K/L)_t$				0.146* (3.207)					
ln $(K/L)_{t-1}$					0.14* (3.051)				

ln $(K/L)_{t-2}$						0.152* (3.164)			
ln TFPK							0.47* (4.301)		
ln TFPS								0.387* (3.273)	
ln TFPT									0.399* (3.131)
R^2	0.868	0.874	0.863	0.845	0.864	0.858	0.875	0.847	0.843
$\tilde{R}^2$	0.857	0.863	0.851	0.833	0.852	0.846	0.865	0.835	0.831
S	0.083	0.078	0.077	0.089	0.081	0.079	0.080	0.089	0.090
F	81.97	82.89	72.66	68.40	76.09	69.48	87.23	69.37	67.29
D-W	0.670	0.791	0.816	0.560	0.660	0.818	0.963	0.752	0.758
$\tilde{\rho}$	0.525	0.504	0.495	0.559	0.533	0.484	0.412	0.495	0.485

Notes : 1. Figures in brackets are the respective 't' values.
2. * ** Indicates significant at 1% and 5% levels respectively.

to trend and one year lagged partial labour productivity. Thus increase in partial labour productivity has benefited the workers in food products industry. The given model fits the data well.

Consider the regression equation in Model V in which real wage rate depends upon trend and one year lagged capital intensity. The coefficient of time is 0.151 and trend is upward and significant. The slope coefficient of $(K/L)_{t-1}$ is 0.14 and this shows that 100 percent increase in capital intensity, keeping the effect of time constant, brings about 14.0 percent increase in wage rate in next year. The value of R^2 is 0.864 and of $\tilde{R}^2$ is 0.852 which reveals that about 86.4 percent variations in wage rate were due to trend and one year lagged capital intensity. The given model fits the data well. Thus, capital intensity, which is an index of increased and improved mechanisation, showed that an increase in capital-labour ratio has gone in favour of workers in this industry, i.e. workers have benefited in terms of wages due to increase in the capital intensity.

In Model VII real wage rate depends upon trend and total factor productivity index (Kendrick). Coefficient of time is 0.085 and is statistically significant. The slope coefficient of TFPK is 0.47 and this shows that 100 percent increase in TFPK brings about 47.0 percent increase in wage rate, when the effect of time is held constant. The value of R^2 is 0.875 and of $\tilde{R}^2$ is 0.865 which indicates that about 87.5 percent variations in wage rate were due to TFPK and time. The given model fits the data well.

In Model VIII real wage rate depends upon trend and total factor productivity index (Solow). Coefficient of time is 0.095 and is statistically significant. The slope coefficient of TFPS is 0.387 and this shows that 100 percent increase in TFPS brings about 38.7 percent increase in wage rate, when the effect of time is held constant. The value of R^2 is 0.847 and of $\tilde{R}^2$ is 0.835 which indicates that about 84.7 percent variations in wage rate were due to TFPS and time. The given model fits the data well.

In Model IX real wage rate depends upon trend and total factor productivity index (Translog). Coefficient of time is 0.099 and is statistically significant. The slope coefficient of TFPT is 0.399 and this shows that 100 percent increase in TFPT brings about 39.9 percent increase in wage rate, when the effect of time is held constant. The value of R^2 is 0.843 and of $\tilde{R}^2$ is 0.831 which indicates that about 84.3 percent variations in wage rate were due to TFPT and time. The given model fits the data well.

On the whole, the results obtained in case of models VII, VIII and IX are robust and consistent, indicating that total factor productivity has positive and significant effect on wage rate.

Effect of Wages on Productivity

In Model XI (Table 9.12.2) coefficient of time is 0.412 and this shows that trend is upward and significant. The slope coefficient 1.312 shows that 100 percent increase in wage rate results in 131.2 percent increase in labour productivity in the next year, keeping the effect of time constant. It appears that increase in wage rate is in the interest of this industry. The value of R^2 is 0.844 and of $\tilde{R}^2$ is 0.831 which indicates that 84.4 percent variations in labour productivity were due to trend and one year lagged wage rate. The model fits the data well.

Consider the regression equation in Model XIV in which labour productivity depends upon trend and one year lagged capital intensity. Coefficient of time is 0.165 and it is upward and mildly significant. The slope coefficient shows that 100 percent increase in $(K/L)_{t-1}$ brings about 70.6 percent increase in labour productivity in the next year. Thus, capital intensity, which is an index of intensity of mechanisation, showed that an increase in capital-labour ratio helped in raising the productivity of labour. The value of R^2 is 0.982 and of $\tilde{R}^2$ is 0.981 which reveals that 98.2 percent variations in labour productivity were due to trend and one year lagged capital intensity. The given model fits the data well.

Pre and Post-liberalisation Period

Taking wage rate as dependent upon dummy, labour productivity and product of dummy times labour productivity (Table 9.12.3), model XVI showed non-significant result.

In Model XVII wage rate depends upon time, dummy, labour productivity and product of dummy times labour productivity variables. The estimated equation is :

$$WR_t = 111.729 + 5.613\ t - 105.881\ D - 0.264\ LP_t + 0.361\ D \ .\ LP_t$$

Pre-liberalisation Era I—1973-74 to 1990-91 and D = 0;

then $WR_t = 111.729 + 5.613\ t - 0.264\ LP_t$

Post-liberalisation Era II—1991-92 to 2000-01 and D = 1;

then $WR_t = 5.848 + 5.613\ t + 0.097\ LP_t$

TABLE 9.12.2
Regression Function for Labour Productivity (Metal Products Industry—All India)

Dependent Variable—Partial Labour Productivity

Explanatory Variables	*Model Numbers*					
	X	*XI*	*XII*	*XIII*	*XIV*	*XV*
(1)	(2)	(3)	(4)	(5)	(6)	(7)
Constant	-4.652	-2.202	1.102	0.876	1.148	1.445
	(-2.204)	(-0.866)	(0.352)	(5.222)	(7.080)	(6.632)
ln Time	0.164	0.412**	0.74*	0.058	0.165*	0.321*
	(1.324)	(2.457)	(3.384)	(1.629)	(3.662)	(4.292)
ln WR_t	1.925*					
	(4.026)					
ln WR_{t-1}		1.312**				
		(2.217)				
ln WR_{t-2}			0.473			
			(0.638)			
ln $(K/L)_t$				0.8*		
				(18.427)		
ln $(K/L)_{t-1}$					0.706*	
					(15.090)	
ln $(K/L)_{t-2}$						0.582*
						(8.431)
R^2	0.834	0.844	0.862	0.981	0.982	0.966
$\tilde{R}^2$	0.821	0.831	0.850	0.980	0.981	0.963
S	0.254	0.244	0.227	0.085	0.083	0.113
F	62.78	64.98	71.77	653.56	658.08	323.20
D-W	0.432	0.437	0.433	1.779	2.248	1.800
$\tilde{\rho}$	0.714	0.707	0.711	0.055	-0.129	0.068

Notes : 1. Figures in brackets are the respective 't' values.
2. * ** Indicates significant at 1% and 5% levels respectively.

The trend effect in pre and post-reform period remains the same. The differential intercept and the differential slope parameter are highly significant. The function has shifted from period I to period II due to significant difference in intercept values and in slope parameters. In post-liberalisation period

TABLE 9.12.3
Structural Stability of Regression Functions
(Metal Products Industry—All India)

Dependent Variables	*I*		*II*	
	Real Wage Rate		*Labour Productivity*	
Explanatory Variables	*Model Numbers*			
	XVIII	*XIX*	*XX*	*XXI*
Constant	76.651 (6.661)	111.729 (9.872)	-134.592 (-2.235)	180.119 -1.664
Time		5.613* (4.651)		12.378* (3.292)
Dummy	-18.831 (-0.637)	-105.881* (-3.698)	224.798** (2.401)	-175.097 (-1.209)
LP_t	0.365* (4.670)	-0.264*** (-1.796)		
$D . LP_t$	-0.071 (-0.697)	0.361* (3.026)		
WR_t			2.151* (4.614)	-1.228 (-1.117)
$D . WR_t$			-0.363 (-0.592)	1.857** (2.186)
R^2	0.83	0.912	0.944	0.962
$\bar{R}^2$	0.809	0.897	0.937	0.955
S	14.478	10.617	35.572	29.96
F	39.05	59.88	134.50	144.92
D-W	0.856	1.205	1.39	1.726
$\tilde{\rho}$	0.379	0.287	0.236	0.029

Notes : 1. Figures in brackets are the respective 't' values.
2. * ** *** Indicates significant at 1%, 5% and 10% levels respectively.

though the intercept has decreased but, the slope of regression line has become steeper i.e. the relationship between wage and labour productivity during post-reform era has strengthened in metal products industry.

Taking labour productivity as dependent upon dummy, wage rate and product of dummy times wage rate, Model XVIII showed non-significant result.

Consider the regression equation in Model XIX, in which labour productivity is dependent upon time, dummy, wage rate and product of dummy times wage rate variables. The estimated equation is :

$LP_t = 180.119 + 12.378\ t - 175.097\ D - 1.228\ WR_t + 1.857\ D\ .\ WR_t$

Pre-liberalisation Era I—1973 to 1990 and D = 0;

then $LP_t = 180.119 + 12.378\ t - 1.228\ WR_t$

Post-liberalisation Era II—1991 to 2000 and D = 1;

then $LP_t = 5.022 + 12.378\ t + 0.629\ WR_t$

The trend effect in pre and post-reform period remains the same. The differential intercept is non-significant but the differential slope parameter is significant. In post-liberalisation period the slope of regression line has become steeper, i.e. the relationship between labour productivity and wage rate during post-reform era has strengthened. Thus after liberalisation when market forces have more important role to play, the labour productivity has become more responsive to wage rate.

13. MACHINERY OTHER THAN TRANSPORT INDUSTRY

Effect of Productivity on Wages

Seven models regarding effect of productivity and capital intensity on wages have been estimated (Table 9.13.1) and the results of selected models with significant effect of explanatory variables are discussed below :

Consider the regression equation in Model I in which wage rate depends upon trend and current year partial labour productivity. Coefficient of time is 0.121 and trend is upward and is significant. The coefficient of LP_t is 0.277 and it shows that 100 percent increase in labour productivity brings about 27.7 percent increase in wage rate in the same year, keeping the effect of time constant. The value of R^2 is 0.838 and of $\tilde{R}^2$ is 0.825 which reveals that about 83.8 percent variations in wage rate were due to trend and current year partial labour productivity. The given model fits the data well.

Consider the regression equation in Model III in which real wage rate depends upon trend and current year capital

TABLE 9.13.1
Regression Function for Wages
(Machinery Other Than Transport Industry—All India)

Dependent Variable—Real Wage Rate

Explanatory Variables	*Model Numbers*						
	I	*II*	*III*	*IV*	*V*	*VI*	*VII*
(1)	*(2)*	*(3)*	*(4)*	*(5)*	*(6)*	*(7)*	*(8)*
Constant	3.226 (9.399)	3.847 (10.697)	3.384 (15.921)	3.647 (15.737)	4.291 (4.143)	4.412 (4.546)	4.528 (4.751)
ln Time	0.121** (2.452)	0.257* (3.917)	0.116* (3.047)	0.205* (3.949)	0.259* (4.579)	0.265* (5.205)	0.27* (5.452)
ln LP_t	0.277* (3.265)						
ln LP_{t-1}		0.093 (0.964)					
ln $(K/L)_t$			0.249* (4.595)				
ln $(K/L)_{t-1}$				0.157** (2.435)			
ln TFPK					0.009 (0.037)		
ln TFPS						-0.019 (-0.086)	
ln TFPT							-0.045 (-0.21)
R^2	0.838	0.829	0.874	0.858	0.768	0.769	0.769
$\tilde{R}^2$	0.825	0.815	0.864	0.846	0.750	0.750	0.750
S	0.105	0.106	0.093	0.097	0.126	0.126	0.126
F	64.50	58.28	87.06	72.37	41.48	41.50	41.58
D-W	0.948	0.901	1.224	1.143	1.033	1.058	1.087
$\tilde{\rho}$	0.337	0.363	0.239	0.244	0.238	0.225	0.211

Notes : 1. Figures in brackets are the respective 't' values.
2. * ** ** Indicates significant at 1% and 5% levels respectively.

intensity. The coefficient of time is 0.116 and trend is upward and significant. The slope coefficient of $(K/L)_t$ is 0.249 and this shows that 100 percent increase in capital intensity, keeping the effect of time constant, brings about 24.9 percent increase in wage rate in same year. The value of R^2 is 0.874 and of $\tilde{R}^2$ is 0.864 which reveals that about 87.4 percent variations in wage rate were due to trend and current year capital intensity. The given model fits the data well.

Effect of Wages on Productivity

In Model VIII (Table 9.13.2) coefficient of time is 0.225 and this shows that trend is upward and significant. The slope

TABLE 9.13.2

Regression Function for Labour Productivity (Machinery Other Than Transport Industry—All India)

Dependent Variable—Partial Labour Productivity

Explanatory Variables	*Model Numbers*			
	VIII	*IX*	*X*	*XI*
(1)	*(2)*	*(3)*	*(4)*	*(5)*
Constant	-0.691 (-0.481)	1.621 (0.940)	1.390 (7.185)	1.814 (6.707)
ln Time	0.225** (2.285)	0.483* (3.679)	0.108* (3.128)	0.253* (4.166)
ln WR_t	1.08* (3.265)			
ln WR_{t-1}		0.486 (1.189)		
ln $(K/L)_t$			0.684* (13.870)	
ln $(K/L)_{t-1}$				0.539* (7.169)
R^2	0.833	0.852	0.973	0.950
$\tilde{R}^2$	0.820	0.840	0.970	0.946
S	0.208	0.194	0.084	0.113
F	62.53	69.03	444.93	228.42
D-W	0.290	0.457	0.863	1.405
$\tilde{\rho}$	0.781	0.744	0.495	0.223

Notes : 1. Figures in brackets are the respective 't' values.
2. * ** *** Indicates significant at 1% and 5% levels respectively.

coefficient 1.08 shows that 100 percent increase in wage rate results into 108.0 percent increase in labour productivity in the same year, keeping the effect of time constant. The value of R^2 is 0.833 and of $\tilde{R}^2$ is 0.820 which indicates that 83.3 percent variations in labour productivity were due to trend and current year wage rate. The model fits the data well.

Consider the regression equation in Model X in which labour productivity depends upon trend and current year capital intensity. Coefficient of time is 0.165 and it is upward and significant. The slope coefficient shows that 100 percent increase in $(K/L)_t$ brings about 68.4 percent increase in labour productivity in the same year. The value of R^2 is 0.973 and of $\tilde{R}^2$ is 0.970 which reveals that 97.3 percent variations in labour productivity were due to trend and current year capital intensity. The given model fits the data well.

Pre and Post-liberalisation Period

Taking wage rate as dependent upon trend, dummy, labour productivity and product of dummy times labour productivity (Table 9.13.3), Models XII-XIII showed non-significant results.

Consider the regression equation in Model XIV in which labour productivity depends upon dummy, wage rate and product of dummy times wage rate variables. The estimated equation is :

$$LP_t = -92.622 + 370.396\ D + 1.828\ WR_t - 1.567\ D\ .\ WR_t$$

Pre-liberalisation Era I; 1973-74 to 1990-91 and D = 0;

$$\text{then } LP_t = -92.622 + 1.828\ WR_t$$

Post-liberalisation Era II; 1991-92 to 2000-01 and D = 1;

$$\text{then } LP_t = 277.774 + 0.261\ WR_t$$

Coefficients of all variables are significant. The results reveal that in post-liberalisation period though the intercept has increased but, the slope of regression line has become flatter i.e. the relationship between labour productivity and wage rate in post-liberalisation period has weakened in this industry. Thus after liberalisation the labour productivity has become less responsive to wage rate.

Taking labour productivity as dependent upon trend, dummy, wage rate and product of dummy times wage rate, model XV showed non-significant result.

TABLE 9.13.3
Structural Stability of Regression Functions
(Machinery Other Than Transport Industry—All India)

Dependent Variables	*I*		*II*	
	Real Wage Rate		*Labour Productivity*	
Explanatory Variables	*Model Numbers*			
	XII	*XIII*	*XIV*	*XV*
Constant	58.9 (3.131)	107.694 (5.825)	-92.622 (-2.757)**	0.362 (0.006)
Time		6.426* (4.220)		4.517*** (1.887)
Dummy	28.231 (0.384)	-93.151 (-1.472)	370.396* (7.131)	228.376** (2.537)
LP_t	0.488* (3.765)	-0.299 (-1.416)		
D. LP_t	-0.191 (-0.755)	0.356 (1.526)		
WR_t			1.828* (7.001)	0.758 (1.224)
D. WR_t			-1.567* (-4.661)	-0.807 (-1.57)
R^2	0.712	0.838	0.952	0.959
$\tilde{R}^2$	0.676	0.81	0.946	0.951
S	21.953	16.835	22.845	21.716
F	19.79	29.70	159.36	133.16
D-W	0.513	1.306	1.539	1.609
$\tilde{\rho}$	0.533	0.192	0.221	0.173

Notes : 1. Figures in brackets are the respective 't' values.
2. * ** *** Indicates significant at 1%, 5% and 10% levels respectively.

14. TRANSPORT EQUIPMENT AND PARTS INDUSTRY

Effect of Productivity on Wages

Seven models regarding effect of productivity and capital intensity on wages have been estimated (Table 9.14.1) and the results of selected models with significant effect of explanatory variables are discussed on next page.

TABLE 9.14.1
Regression Function for Wages
(Manufacture of Transport Equipment and Parts—All India)

Dependent Variable—Partial Labour Productivity

Explanatory Variables	*Model Numbers*						
	I	*II*	*III*	*IV*	*V*	*VI*	*VII*
(1)	*(2)*	*(3)*	*(4)*	*(5)*	*(6)*	*(7)*	*(8)*
Constant	3.190 (12.955)	3.666 (12.512)	3.447 (25.860)	3.577 (20.096)	4.559 (8.233)	4.271 (8.972)	4.459 (9.012)
ln Time	0.121* (3.857)	0.208* (4.511)	0.078* (2.863)	0.128* (2.870)	0.257* (8.951)	0.251* (10.531)	0.253* (10.366)
ln LP_t	0.292* (4.953)						
ln LP_{t-1}		0.16** (2.142)					
ln $(K/L)_t$			0.245* (7.321)				
ln $(K/L)_{t-1}$				0.202* (4.112)			
ln TFPK					-0.038 (-0.306)		
ln TFPS						0.027 (0.254)	
ln TFPT							-0.015 (-0.139)
R^2	0.908	0.873	0.942	0.911	0.819	0.819	0.819
$\tilde{R}^2$	0.901	0.863	0.938	0.904	0.805	0.805	0.804
S	0.074	0.084	0.059	0.070	0.104	0.104	0.104
F	124.10	82.67	204.28	123.48	56.70	56.62	56.50
D-W	0.526	1.022	1.354	1.420	0.677	0.610	0.653
$\tilde{\rho}$	0.565	0.380	0.262	0.238	0.437	0.460	0.447

Notes : 1. Figures in brackets are the respective 't' values.
2. * ** *** Indicates significant at 1% and 5% levels respectively.

Consider the regression equation in Model I in which wage rate depends upon trend and current year partial labour productivity. Coefficient of time is 0.121 and trend is upward and is significant. The coefficient of LP_t is 0.292 and it shows that 100 percent increase in labour productivity brings about 29.2 percent increase in wage rate in the same year, keeping the effect of time constant. The value of R^2 is 0.908 and of $\tilde{R}^2$ is 0.901 which reveals that about 90.8 percent variations in wage rate were due to trend and current year partial labour productivity. The given model fits the data well.

Consider the regression equation in Model III in which real wage rate depends upon trend and current year capital intensity. The coefficient of time is 0.078 and trend is upward and significant. The slope coefficient of $(K/L)_t$ is 0.245 and this shows that 100 percent increase in capital intensity, keeping the effect of time constant, brings about 24.5 percent increase in wage rate in same year. The value of R^2 is 0.942 and of $\tilde{R}^2$ is 0.938 which reveals that about 94.2 percent variations in wage rate were due to trend and current year capital intensity. The given model fits the data well.

Effect of Wages on Labour Productivity

Taking labour productivity as dependent upon trend and up to five year lagged wage rate, models VIII-XIII (Table 9.14.2) showed non-significant results.

Taking labour productivity as dependent upon trend and up to three year lagged capital intensity, models XIV-XVII showed non-significant results.

Pre and Post-liberalisation Period

Taking wage rate as dependent upon dummy, labour productivity and product of dummy times labour productivity (Table 9.14.3), model XVIII showed non-significant result.

Consider the regression equation in Model XIX, in which wage rate is dependent upon time, dummy, labour productivity and product of dummy times labour productivity variables in Table 9.14.2. The estimated equation is :

$$WR_t = 96.782 + 4.412\ t - 111.071\ D - 0.041\ LP_t + 0.364\ D\ .\ LP_t$$

TABLE 9.14.2

Regression Function for Labour Productivity (Manufacture of Transport Equipment and Parts—All India)

Dependent Variable—Partial Labour Productivity

Explanatory Variables	*Model Numbers*									
	VIII	*IX*	*X*	*XI*	*XII*	*XIII*	*XIV*	*XV*	*XVI*	*XVII*
(1)	*(2)*	*(3)*	*(4)*	*(5)*	*(6)*	*(7)*	*(8)*	*(9)*	*(10)*	*(11)*
Constant	-3.331 (-2.213)	-1.475 (-0.659)	-3.670 (-0.975)	-0.136 (-0.034)	-1.591 (-0.416)	-3.207 (-0.99)	2.034 (5.442)	2.365 (5.033)	2.355 (4.061)	1.945 (3.354)
ln Time	0.021 (0.223)	0.186 (1.164)	0.080 (0.285)	0.372 (1.093)	0.325 (0.913)	0.229 (0.686)	0.066 (0.862)	0.194 (1.653)	0.260 (1.589)	0.186 (0.998)
ln WR_t	1.694* (4.953)									
ln WR_{t-1}		1.249** (2.386)								
ln WR_{t-2}			1.754*** (1.948)							
ln WR_{t-3}				0.892 (0.902)						
ln WR_{t-4}					1.214 (1.262)					

(Contd.)

TABLE 9.1.2 (CONTD.)

(1)	(2)	(3)	(4)	(5)	(6)	(7)	(8)	(9)	(10)	(11)
ln WR_{t-5}						1.599*** (1.908)				
ln $(K/L)_t$							0.538* (5.739)			
ln $(K/L)_{t-1}$								0.428* (3.293)		
ln $(K/L)_{t-2}$									0.405* (2.330)	
ln $(K/L)_{t-3}$										0.522* (2.783)
R^2	0.854	0.810	0.814	0.796	0.843	0.886	0.875	0.838	0.825	0.844
$\tilde{R}^2$	0.843	0.794	0.798	0.778	0.828	0.874	0.866	0.825	0.810	0.830
S	0.178	0.200	0.194	0.199	0.174	0.148	0.165	0.185	0.188	0.174
F	73.31	51.22	50.47	42.98	56.38	77.40	87.88	62.19	54.25	59.38
D-W	0.330	1.003	0.748	0.811	0.927	1.335	0.874	1.004	1.016	0.890
$\tilde{\rho}$	0.793	0.468	0.610	0.528	0.470	0.207	0.541	0.478	0.485	0.521

Notes : 1. Figures in brackets are the respective 't' values.
2. * ** *** Indicates significant at 1%, 5% and 10% levels respectively.

TABLE 9.14.3

Structural Stability of Regression Functions (Manufacture of Transport Equipment and Parts—All India)

Dependent Variables	*I*		*II*	
	Real Wage Rate		*Labour Productivity*	
Explanatory Variables	*Model Numbers*			
	XVIII	*XIX*	*XX*	*XXI*
Constant	58.943 (4.258)	96.782 (8.777)	-55.779 (-1.58)	-41.733 (-0.433)
Time		4.412* (5.871)		0.622 (0.157)
Dummy	-24.055 (-0.763)	-111.071* (-4.409)	113.603*** (1.952)	94.487 (0.698)
LP_t	0.533* (5.513)	-0.041 (-0.357)		
$D \cdot LP_t$	-0.033 (-0.249)	0.364* (3.330)		
WR_t			1.464* (5.580)	1.314 (1.324)
$D \cdot WR_t$			-0.142 (-0.396)	-0.042 (-0.058)
R^2	0.867	0.947	0.942	0.942
$\tilde{R}^2$	0.850	0.937	0.935	0.932
S	14.363	9.282	23.515	24.008
F	52.00	102.00	129.63	93.28
D-W	0.954	0.891	2.078	2.09
$\tilde{\rho}$	0.364	0.39	-0.09	-0.095

Notes : 1. Figures in brackets are the respective 't' values.
2. * ** *** Indicates significant at 1%, 5% and 10% levels respectively.

Pre-liberalisation Era I—1973-74 to 1990-91 and D = 0;
then $WR_t = 96.782 + 4.412\ t - 0.041\ LP_t$
Post-liberalisation Era II—1991-92 to 2000-01 and D = 1;
then $WR_t = -14.289 + 4.412\ t + 0.323\ LP_t$

The trend effect in pre and post-reform period remains the same. The differential intercept and the differential slope parameter are highly significant. The function has shifted from period I to period II due to significant difference in intercept values and in slope parameters. In post-liberalisation period though the intercept has decreased but, the slope of regression line has become steeper, i.e. the relationship between wage and labour productivity during post-reform era has strengthened in manufacture of transport equipment and parts industry. Thus workers in this industry has benefited from the liberalisation wave.

Taking labour productivity as dependent upon trend, dummy, wage rate and product of dummy times wage rate, models XX-XXI showed non-significant result.

It may be concluded from the discussion that labour productivity has significantly affected the wage rate in all-industries except in two industries namely, LFPI, and BMAI. Capital intensity has positively and significantly affected the wage rate in all-industries except in five industries namely, CTI, LFPI, RPCPI, NMMPI and BMAI. Total factor productivity (Kendrick, Solow and Translog) has positively and significantly affected the wage rate in FPI, CTI, JHMTI and MPI only.

Wage rate has also significantly affected labour productivity in all industries except CTI, TPI, CCPI, and TEPI. Capital intensity has significantly affected labour productivity in all industries except PPPI.

It was found that the relationship between wages and labour productivity during post-reform era has strengthened in BTTPT, PPPI, NMMPI, BMAI, MPI and TEPI. But the relationship between wages and labour productivity during post-reform era has weakened in FPI, CTI, JHMTI and TPI. This indicates that proportionate gains from productivity increase were not passed on to the workers in these industries.

The relationship between labour productivity and wage rate during post-reform era has strengthened in FPI, JHMTI and MPI. After liberalisation when market forces have more important role to play, the labour productivity has become more responsive to wage rate in these industries. It is found that the relationship between labour productivity and wage rate during post-reform era has weakened in RPCPI, NMMPI, BMAI and MOTI.

10

Wage-Productivity Relationship in Industry—State-wise Analysis

In the present chapter an attempt has been made to analyse the relationship between variables like wage rate, labour productivity, total factor productivity and capital intensity, etc. during the period 1973-74 to 2000-01 in industry in sixteen states and at all-India level. The different log-linear regressions (discussed in Chapter-IV) have been derived and results of selected models have been interpreted.

1. ANDHRA PRADESH

Effect of Productivity on Wages

Ten models regarding effect of productivity and capital intensity on wages have been estimated (Table 10.1.1) and the results of selected models with significant effect of explanatory variables are discussed below:

Consider the regression equation in Model I in which wage rate depends upon trend and current period partial labour productivity. Coefficient of time is 0.11 and trend is upward and is significant. The coefficient of LP_t is 0.426 and it shows that 100 percent increase in labour productivity brings about 42.6

Table 10.1.1
Regression Function for Wages
(Andhra Pradesh—All Industries)

Dependent Variable—Partial Labour Productivity

Explanatory Variables	*Model Numbers*									
	I	*II*	*III*	*IV*	*V*	*VI*	*VII*	*VIII*	*IX*	*X*
(1)	*(2)*	*(3)*	*(4)*	*(5)*	*(6)*	*(7)*	*(8)*	*(9)*	*(10)*	*(11)*
Constant	2.590 (12.891)	3.161 (12.300)	3.444 (19.376)	3.650 (21.881)	3.619 (24.752)	3.729 (25.532)	2.280 (4.302)	4.154 (6.512)	4.234 (6.716)	0.629 (1.424)
ln Time	0.11* (4.438)	0.217* (5.466)	0.141* (4.039)	0.235* (5.414)	0.259* (5.461)	0.345* (6.129)	0.219* (7.764)	0.282* (9.046)	0.281* (8.855)	0.098* (4.383)
ln LP_t	0.426* (8.556)									
ln LP_{t-1}		0.257* (3.784)								
ln $(K/L)_t$			0.228* (4.920)							0.374* (10.403)
ln $(K/L)_{t-1}$				0.142* (2.965)						
ln $(K/L)_{t-2}$					0.137* (2.980)					

ln $(K/L)_{t-3}$						0.071 (1.445)				
ln TFPK							0.459* (3.796)			
ln TFPS								0.026 (0.196)		
ln TFPT									0.009 (0.071)	0.484* (6.572)
R^2	0.946	0.914	0.892	0.899	0.911	0.901	0.865	0.787	0.787	0.961
$\tilde{R}^2$	0.941	0.907	0.883	0.891	0.904	0.891	0.854	0.770	0.770	0.957
S	0.064	0.080	0.091	0.087	0.078	0.080	0.102	0.128	0.128	0.056
F	218.04	127.22	103.00	107.13	118.05	99.58	80.02	46.27	46.20	198.95
D-W	2.037	2.347	1.310	1.924	1.835	2.076	1.173	0.903	0.909	2.634
$\tilde{\rho}$	-0.033	-0.185	0.308	0.180	0.065	-0.054	0.323	0.414	0.412	-0.335

Notes : 1. Figures in brackets are the respective 't' values.
2. * ** *** Indicates significant at 1% level.

percent increase in wage rate in the same year, keeping the effect of time constant. The value of R^2 is 0.946 and of $\tilde{R}^2$ is 0.941 which reveals that about 94.6 percent variations in wage rate were due to trend and current period partial labour productivity. Thus increase in partial labour productivity has benefited the workers in Andhra Pradesh. The given model fits the data well.

Consider the regression equation in Model V in which real wage rate depends upon trend and two period lagged capital intensity. The coefficient of time is 0.259 and trend is upward and is significant. The slope coefficient of $(K/L)_{t-2}$ is 0.137 and this shows that 100 percent increase in capital intensity, keeping the effect of time constant, brings about 13.7 percent increase in wage rate in the next second year. The value of R^2 is 0.911 and of $\tilde{R}^2$ is 0.904 which reveals that about 91.1 percent variations in wage rate were due to trend and two period lagged capital intensity. The given model fits the data well. Thus, capital intensity, which is an index of increased and improved mechanisation, showed that workers have benefited in terms of wages due to increase in the capital intensity.

In Model VII real wage rate depends upon trend and total factor productivity index (Kendrick). Coefficient of time is 0.219 and is statistically highly significant. The slope coefficient of TFPK is 0.459 and this shows that 100 percent increase in TFPK brings about 45.9 percent increase in wage rate, when the effect of time is held constant. The value of R^2 is 0.865 and of $\tilde{R}^2$ is 0.854 which indicates that about 86.5 percent variations in wage rate were due to TFPK and time. The given model fits the data well.

Effect of Wages on Productivity

In Model XIII (Table 10.1.2) labour productivity depends upon trend and two period lagged wage rate. Coefficient of time is 0.25 and this shows that trend is upward and mildly significant. The slope coeffiecient 0.889 shows that 100 percent increase in wage rate results into 88.9 percent increase in labour productivity in the next second year, keeping the effect of time constant. Hence, labour productivity is highly responsive to change in wage rate in Andhra Pradesh. The value of R^2 is 0.851 and of $\tilde{R}^2$ is 0.839 which indicates that 85.1 percent variations in labour productivity were due to trend and second year lagged wage rate. The model fits the data well.

TABLE 10.1.2

Regression Function for Labour Productivity (Andhra Pradesh—All Industries)

Dependent Variable—Partial Labour Productivity

Explanatory Variables	*Model Numbers*								
	XI	*XII*	*XIII*	*XIV*	*XV*	*XVI*	*XVII*	*XVIII*	*XIX*
(1)	*(2)*	*(3)*	*(4)*	*(5)*	*(6)*	*(7)*	*(8)*	*(9)*	*(10)*
Constant	-3.524 (-4.011)	-1.321 (-1.167)	-0.065 (-0.052)	1.320 (1.079)	2.041 (6.694)	2.309 (8.261)	2.296 (9.442)	2.336 (11.040)	2.423 (11.531)
ln Time	-0.090 (-1.4)	0.113 (1.100)	0.25*** (1.868)	0.477* (3.235)	0.080 (1.334)	0.212* (2.916)	0.244* (3.088)	0.356* (4.355)	0.481* (5.032)
ln WR_t	1.75* (8.556)								
ln WR_{t-1}		1.21* (4.396)							
ln WR_{t-2}			0.889* (2.819)						
ln WR_{t-3}				0.489 (1.530)					

(Contd.)

TABLE 10.1.2 (CONTD.)

(1)	(2)	(3)	(4)	(5)	(6)	(7)	(8)	(9)	(10)
$\ln (K/L)_t$					0.525* (6.614)				
$\ln (K/L)_{t-1}$						0.411* (5.106)			
$\ln (K/L)_{t-2}$							0.401* (5.244)		
$\ln (K/L)_{t-3}$								0.338* (4.734)	
$\ln (K/L)_{t-4}$									0.256* (3.386)
R^2	0.910	0.874	0.851	0.866	0.872	0.891	0.909	0.927	0.921
$\tilde{R}^2$	0.903	0.864	0.839	0.854	0.861	0.882	0.901	0.920	0.913
S	0.131	0.156	0.167	0.157	0.156	0.145	0.130	0.117	0.120
F	126.56	83.27	65.93	71.30	84.83	98.10	114.85	139.17	121.64
D-W	1.525	1.489	1.000	0.858	0.643	1.140	1.126	1.186	1.351
$\tilde{\rho}$	0.230	0.253	0.458	0.528	0.644	0.427	0.418	0.397	0.305

Notes : 1. Figures in brackets are the respective 't' values.
2. * *** Indicates significant at 1% and 10% levels respectively.

Consider the regression equations in Models XV–XIX in which labour productivity depends upon trend and up to four year lagged capital intensity. The regression coefficient of current year capital intensity was the highest and its level of significance as indicated by t value was also the highest. With time lag, the value of regression coefficient and its level of significance decreased but it remained significant at one percent level. This indicated that capital intensity up to four years lag affected the labour productivity significantly. In case of Model XVIII coefficient of time is 0.356 and it is upward and highly significant. The slope coefficient shows that 100 percent increase in $(K/L)_{t-3}$ brings about 33.8 percent increase in labour productivity in the next third year. Thus capital intensity, which is an index of intensity of mechanisation, showed that an increase in capital-labour ratio helped in raising the productivity of labour. The value of R^2 is 0.927 and of $\tilde{R}^2$ is 0.92 which reveals that 92.7 percent variations in labour productivity were due to trend and third year lagged capital intensity. The given model fits the data well.

Pre and Post-liberalisation Period

Consider the regression equation in Model XX, in which wage rate is dependent upon dummy, labour productivity and product of dummy times labour productivity variables in Table 10.1.3. The estimated equation is :

$$WR_t = 35.024 + 47.828\ D + 0.819\ LP_t - 0.361\ D\ .\ LP_t$$

Pre-liberalisation Era I—1973 to 1990 and D = 0;

$$\text{then } WR_t = 35.024 + 0.819\ LP_t$$

Post-liberalisation Era II—1991 to 2000 and D = 1;

$$\text{then } WR_t = 113.098 + 0.458\ LP_t$$

The differential intercept is non-significant but the differential slope parameter is significant. In post-liberalisation period the slope of regression line has become flatter, i.e. the relationship between wage and labour productivity during post-reform era has weakened. Since the time period of post-reform era is less, so over long period it has to be seen whether this relationship is strengthened or weakened.

TABLE 10.1.3
Structural Stability of Regression Functions
(Andhra Pradesh—All Industries)

Dependent Variables	*I*		*II*	
	Real Wage Rate		*Labour Productivity*	
Explanatory Variables	*Model Numbers*			
	XX	XXI	XXII	XXIII
Constant	35.024 (3.405)	48.946 (4.881)	-16.891 (-0.979)	-5.017 (-0.203)
Time		1.966* (3.012)		0.856 (0.679)
Dummy	47.828 (1.595)	15.554 (0.554)	-22.26 (-0.387)	-39.258 (-0.62)
LP_t	0.819* (9.070)	0.524* (4.174)		
$D . LP_t$	-0.361** (-2.343)	-0.189 (-1.306)		
WR_t			1.014* (7.522)	0.855* (3.146)
$D . WR_t$			0.404 (1.250)	0.483 (1.392)
R^2	0.924	0.946	0.952	0.953
$\tilde{R}^2$	0.915	0.936	0.946	0.944
S	10.887	9.419	14.606	14.773
F	97.95	100.43	157.46	115.56
D-W	1.755	2.123	1.892	1.794
$\tilde{\rho}$	0.067	-0.068	0.025	0.056

Notes : 1. Figures in brackets are the respective 't' values.
2. * ** Indicates significant at 1% and 5% levels respectively.

Taking wage rate as dependent upon time, dummy, labour productivity and product of dummy times labour productivity, model XXI showed non-significant result.

Taking labour productivity as dependent upon trend, dummy, wage rate and product of dummy times wage rate, models XXII-XXIII showed non-significant results, indicating no significant change in relationship between labour productivity and wages during post-liberalisation period.

2. ASSAM

Effect of Productivity on Wages

Nine models regarding effect of productivity and capital intensity on wages have been estimated (Table 10.2.1) and the results of selected models with significant effect of explanatory variables are discussed below :

Consider the regression equation in Model II in which wage rate depends upon trend and one period lagged partial labour productivity. Coefficient of time is 0.251 and trend is upward and is highly significant. The coefficient of LP_{t-1} is 0.175 and it shows that 100 percent increase in labour productivity brings about 17.5 percent increase in wage rate in the next year, keeping the effect of time constant. The value of R^2 is 0.829 and of $\tilde{R}^2$ is 0.814 which reveals that about 82.9 percent variations in wage rate were due to trend and one year lagged partial labour productivity. Thus, increase in partial labour productivity has benefited the workers in Assam. The given model fits the data well.

Consider the regression equation in Model V in which real wage rate depends upon trend and one period lagged capital intensity. The coefficient of time is 0.211 and trend is upward and is highly significant. The slope coefficient of $(K/L)_{t-1}$ is 0.206 and this shows that 100 percent increase in capital intensity, keeping the effect of time constant, brings about 20.6 percent increase in wage rate in the next year. The value of R^2 is 0.855 and of $\tilde{R}^2$ is 0.843 which reveals that about 85.5 percent variations in wage rate were due to trend and one year lagged capital intensity. The given model fits the data well. Thus capital intensity, which is an index of increased and improved mechanisation, showed that workers have benefited in terms of wages due to increase in the capital intensity.

Effect of Wages on Productivity

Taking labour productivity as dependent upon trend and up to five year lagged wage rate, Models X-XV (Table 10.2.2) showed non-significant results.

Taking labour productivity as dependent upon trend and up to three period lagged capital intensity, Models XVI-XIX showed non-significant results.

TABLE 10.2.1
Regression Function for Wages
(Assam—All Industries)

Dependent Variable—Partial Labour Productivity

Explanatory Variables	*Model Numbers*								
	I	*II*	*III*	*IV*	*V*	*VI*	*VII*	*VIII*	*IX*
(1)	*(2)*	*(3)*	*(4)*	*(5)*	*(6)*	*(7)*	*(8)*	*(9)*	*(10)*
Constant	3.098 (7.609)	3.260 (10.182)	3.359 (9.912)	2.892 (12.840)	3.204 (13.005)	3.404 (12.659)	4.854 (8.699)	4.787 (22.956)	5.187 (19.139)
ln Time	0.159* (3.724)	0.251* (5.966)	0.268* (5.277)	0.087** (2.545)	0.211* (4.892)	0.238* (4.200)	0.24* (6.883)	0.16* (4.073)	0.114** (2.641)
ln LP_t	0.255** (2.724)								
ln LP_{t-1}		0.175** (2.283)							
ln LP_{t-2}			0.147*** (1.772)						
ln $(K/L)_t$				0.328* (5.955)					
ln $(K/L)_{t-1}$					0.206* (3.247)				

ln $(K/L)_{t-2}$						0.154** (2.105)			
ln TFPK							-0.140 (-1.213)		
ln TFPS								-0.113* (-3.109)	
ln TFPT									-0.192* (-3.837)
R^2	0.721	0.829	0.784	0.850	0.855	0.794	0.658	0.739	0.772
$\tilde{R}^2$	0.698	0.814	0.765	0.838	0.843	0.777	0.631	0.718	0.754
S	0.138	0.110	0.115	0.101	0.101	0.112	0.153	0.134	0.125
F	32.27	58.00	41.97	70.99	70.77	44.43	24.05	35.37	42.36
D-W	1.155	0.971	0.742	1.259	1.172	1.203	0.799	1.044	1.115
$\tilde{\rho}$	0.245	0.485	0.593	0.290	0.349	0.357	0.448	0.335	0.324

Notes : 1. Figures in brackets are the respective 't' values.
2. * ** *** Indicates significant at 1%, 5% and 10% levels respectively.

TABLE 10.2.2

Regression Function for Labour Productivity (Assam—All Industries)

Dependent Variable—Partial Labour Productivity

Explanatory Variables	*Model Numbers*									
	X	*XI*	*XII*	*XIII*	*XIV*	*XV*	*XVI*	*XVII*	*XVIII*	*XIX*
(1)	*(2)*	*(3)*	*(4)*	*(5)*	*(6)*	*(7)*	*(8)*	*(9)*	*(10)*	*(11)*
Constant	0.508 (0.365)	0.481 (0.315)	3.123 (1.816)	5.420 (3.032)	4.943 (2.365)	3.973 (2.003)	2.645 (4.678)	2.343 (3.901)	3.453 (5.094)	4.170 (6.198)
ln Time	0.095 (0.971)	0.124 (0.980)	0.367** (2.242)	0.619* (3.324)	0.684* (3.162)	0.745* (3.311)	0.120 (1.395)	0.127 (1.211)	0.348** (2.436)	0.554* (3.359)
ln WR_t	0.899** (2.724)									
ln WR_{t-1}		0.894** (2.390)								
ln WR_{t-2}			0.207 (0.476)							
ln WR_{t-3}				-0.422 (-0.915)						
ln WR_{t-4}					-0.364 (-0.668)					

ln WR_{t-5}						-0.200 (-0.378)				
ln $(K/L)_t$							0.412* (2.981)			
ln $(K/L)_{t-1}$								0.473* (3.057)		
ln $(K/L)_{t-2}$									0.139 (0.758)	
ln $(K/L)_{t-3}$										-0.114 (-0.599)
R^2	0.582	0.577	0.496	0.501	0.536	0.604	0.600	0.623	0.503	0.490
$\tilde{R}^2$	0.548	0.542	0.452	0.456	0.492	0.564	0.568	0.592	0.460	0.444
S	0.259	0.260	0.285	0.282	0.276	0.261	0.254	0.246	0.283	0.285
F	17.38	16.37	11.29	11.04	12.14	15.24	18.73	19.84	11.64	10.57
D-W	0.972	0.738	0.745	0.682	0.893	1.015	1.371	0.734	0.786	0.761
$\tilde{\rho}$	0.494	0.619	0.614	0.588	0.450	0.414	0.274	0.628	0.596	0.566

Notes : 1. Figures in brackets are the respective 't' values.
2. * *** Indicates significant at 1% and 5% levels respectively.

Pre and Post-liberalisation Period

Taking wage rate as dependent upon trend, dummy, labour productivity and product of dummy times labour productivity (Table 10.2.3), Models XX-XXI showed non-significant results, indicating no significant change in relationship between wages and labour productivity during post-liberalisation period.

TABLE 10.2.3
Structural Stability of Regression Functions (Assam—All Industries)

Dependent Variables	*I*		*II*	
	Real Wage Rate		*Labour Productivity*	
Explanatory Variables	*Model Numbers*			
	XX	*XXI*	*XXII*	*XXIII*
Constant	71.547 (7.117)	72.141 (8.597)	-156.502 (-2.821)	-84.86 (-1.245)
Time		2.544* (3.385)		3.814 (1.692)
Dummy	55.262 (1.544)	21.773 (0.692)	318.202* (3.285)	224.933** (2.075)
LP_t	0.217* (3.240)	0.04 (0.525)		
$D . LP_t$	-0.081 (-0.446)	-0.037 (-0.244)		
WR_t			2.906* (5.396)	1.848** (2.274)
$D . WR_t$			-2.647* (-3.569)	-2.03** (-2.53)
R^2	0.782	0.854	0.68	0.716
$\tilde{R}^2$	0.755	0.829	0.64	0.666
S	15.35	12.81	33.699	32.463
F	28.69	33.76	17.02	14.47
D-W	1.44	1.525	1.676	1.361
$\tilde{\rho}$	0.201	0.143	0.134	0.307

Notes : 1. Figures in brackets are the respective 't' values.
2. * ** *** Indicates significant at 1% and 5% levels respectively.

Consider the regression equation in Model XXII, in which labour productivity depends upon dummy, wage rate and product of dummy times wage rate variables. The estimated equation is :

$$LP_t = -156.502 + 318.202\ D + 2.906\ WR_t - 2.647\ D\ .\ WR_t$$

Pre-liberalisation Era I; 1973-74 to 1990-91 and D = 0;

then $LP_t = -156.502 + 2.906\ WR_t$

Post-liberalisation Era II; 1991-92 to 2000-01 and D = 1;

then $LP_t = 161.7 + 0.259\ WR_t$

Coefficients of all variables are significant. The results reveal that in post-liberalisation period though the intercept has increased but, the slope of regression line has become flatter, i.e. the relationship between labour productivity and wage rate in post-liberalisation period has weakened. Thus after liberalisation the labour productivity has become less responsive to wage rate in Assam.

Taking labour productivity as dependent upon trend, dummy, wage rate and product of dummy times wage rate, model XXIII showed non-significant result.

3. BIHAR

Effect of Productivity on Wages

Eight models regarding effect of productivity and capital intensity on wages have been estimated (Table 10.3.1) and the results of selected models with significant effect of explanatory variables are discussed below:

Consider the regression equation in Model I in which wage rate depends upon trend and current period partial labour productivity. Coefficient of time is 0.128 and trend is upward and is significant. The coefficient of LP_t is 0.343 and it shows that 100 percent increase in labour productivity brings about 34.3 percent increase in wage rate in the same year, keeping the effect of time constant. The value of R^2 is 0.774 and of $\tilde{R}^2$ is 0.756 which reveals that about 77.4 percent variations in wage rate were due to trend and current period partial labour productivity. Thus increase in partial labour productivity has benefited the workers in Bihar. The given model fits the data well.

Consider the regression equation in Model III in which real

TABLE 10.3.1
Regression Function for Wages
(Bihar—All Industries)

Dependent Variable—Real Wage Rates

Explanatory Variables	*Model Numbers*							
	I	*II*	*III*	*IV*	*V*	*VI*	*VII*	*VIII*
(1)	*(2)*	*(3)*	*(4)*	*(5)*	*(6)*	*(7)*	*(8)*	*(9)*
Constant	2.931 (7.973)	3.655 (8.183)	2.385 (6.048)	2.847 (5.549)	3.852 (6.680)	3.687 (7.107)	3.557 (6.762)	0.932 (1.909)
ln Time	0.128** (2.503)	0.249* (3.061)	0.143* (3.544)	0.2* (3.070)	0.251* (4.693)	0.254* (5.587)	0.243* (5.160)	0.069*** (1.858)
ln LP_t	0.343* (3.915)							
ln LP_{t-1}		0.144 (1.241)						
ln $(K/L)_t$			0.426* (5.029)					0.48* (6.949)
ln $(K/L)_{t-1}$				0.312** (2.676)				
ln TFPK					0.113 (0.844)			
ln TFPS						0.153 (1.267)		
ln TFPT							0.184 (1.500)	0.286* (3.895)
R^2	0.774	0.680	0.819	0.738	0.645	0.657	0.665	0.889
$\tilde{R}^2$	0.756	0.654	0.804	0.716	0.617	0.630	0.639	0.875
S	0.146	0.171	0.131	0.155	0.183	0.180	0.178	0.104
F	42.78	25.55	56.44	33.81	22.75	23.97	24.86	64.02
D-W	1.640	0.953	1.156	1.464	1.043	1.091	1.129	2.294
$\tilde{\rho}$	0.112	0.388	0.332	0.242	0.337	0.320	0.307	-0.188

Notes : 1. Figures in brackets are the respective 't' values.
2. * ** Indicates significant at 1%, 5% and 10% levels respectively.

wage rate depends upon trend and current period capital intensity. The coefficient of time is 0.143 and trend is upward and is highly significant. The slope coefficient of $(K/L)_t$ is 0.426

and this shows that 100 percent increase in capital intensity, keeping the effect of time constant, brings about 42.6 percent increase in wage rate in the same year. The value of R^2 is 0.819 and of $\tilde{R}^2$ is 0.804 which reveals that about 91.1 percent variations in wage rate were due to trend and current period capital intensity. The given model fits the data well. Thus, capital intensity, which is an index of increased and improved mechanisation, showed that workers have benefited in terms of wages due to increase in the capital intensity.

In Model VIII real wage rate depends upon trend, capital intensity and total factor productivity index (Translog). Coefficient of time is 0.069 and is statistically mildly significant. The slope coefficient of $(K/L)_t$ is 0.48 and this shows that 100 percent increase in $(K/L)_t$ brings about 48.0 percent increase in wage rate, when other variables are held constant. The slope coefficient of TFPT is 0.286 and this shows that 100 percent increase in TFPT brings about 28.6 percent increase in wage rate, when other variables are held constant. The value of R^2 is 0.889 and of R^2 is 0.875 which indicates that about 88.9 percent variations in wage rate were due to time, capital intensity and TFPT. The given model fits the data well.

Effect of Wages on Productivity

Taking labour productivity as dependent upon trend and up to five year lagged wage rate, Models IX-XIV (Table 10.3.2) showed non-significant results.

Taking labour productivity as dependent upon trend and up to three period lagged capital intensity, Models XV-XVIII showed non-significant results.

Taking wage rate as dependent upon time, dummy, labour productivity and product of dummy times labour productivity (Table 10.3.3), Models XIX-XX showed non-significant results, indicating no significant change in relationship between wages and labour productivity during post-liberalisation period.

Taking labour productivity as dependent upon trend, dummy, wage rate and product of dummy times wage rate, Models XXI-XXII showed non-significant results.

TABLE 10.3.2
Regression Function for Labour Productivity (Bihar—All Industries)

Dependent Variable—Partial Labour Productivity

Explanatory Variables	*Model Numbers*									
	IX	*X*	*XI*	*XII*	*XIII*	*XIV*	*XV*	*XVI*	*XVII*	*XVIII*
(1)	*(2)*	*(3)*	*(4)*	*(5)*	*(6)*	*(7)*	*(8)*	*(9)*	*(10)*	*(11)*
Constant	-0.717 (-0.581)	-1.207 (-0.905)	2.347 (1.138)	1.196 (0.633)	3.123 (1.612)	4.220 (2.094)	2.678 (2.780)	2.859 (2.802)	4.213 (3.171)	4.035 (3.464)
ln Time	0.132 (1.333)	0.097 (0.717)	0.489*** (1.892)	0.459 (1.679)	0.804** (2.532)	1.009** (2.789)	0.343* (3.485)	0.448* (3.465)	0.722* (3.536)	0.866* (4.159)
ln WR_t	1.108* (3.915)									
ln WR_{t-1}		1.223* (3.792)								
ln WR_{t-2}			0.314 (0.590)							
ln WR_{t-3}				0.558 (1.098)						
ln WR_{t-4}					-0.012 (-0.022)					

ln WR_{t-5}						-0.347 (-0.592)				
ln $(K/L)_t$							0.306 (1.482)			
ln $(K/L)_{t-1}$								0.220 (0.951)		
ln $(K/L)_{t-2}$									-0.166 (-0.504)	
ln $(K/L)_{t-3}$										-0.209 (-0.695)
R^2	0.736	0.763	0.659	0.722	0.697	0.657	0.609	0.635	0.657	0.713
$\tilde{R}^2$	0.715	0.743	0.629	0.697	0.668	0.623	0.577	0.604	0.628	0.687
S	0.262	0.248	0.296	0.269	0.276	0.280	0.319	0.307	0.297	0.273
F	34.85	38.63	22.20	28.60	24.16	19.18	19.43	20.85	22.07	27.36
D-W	1.570	1.660	1.334	1.270	1.397	1.488	0.863	1.093	1.254	1.390
$\tilde{\rho}$	0.200	0.162	0.186	0.200	0.147	0.105	0.502	0.377	0.211	0.152

Notes : 1. Figures in brackets are the respective 't' values.
2. * ** *** Indicates significant at 1%, 5% and 10% levels respectively.

TABLE 10.3.3
Structural Stability of Regression Functions
(Bihar—All Industries)

Dependent Variables	*I*		*II*	
	Real Wage Rate		*Labour Productivity*	
Explanatory Variables	*Model Numbers*			
	XX	*XXI*	*XXII*	*XXIII*
Constant	60.219 (3.805)	67.149 (3.290)	-35.384 (-0.593)	37.35 (0.419)
Time		1.951 (1.108)		5.63 (1.092)
Dummy	56.786*** (1.740)	4.372 (0.076)	59.701 (0.595)	-162.183 (-0.716)
LP_t	0.53* (4.019)	0.349 (1.661)		
$D . LP_t$	-0.266 (-1.689)	-0.085 (-0.378)		
WR_t			1.305* (3.019)	0.367 (0.382)
$D . WR_t$			0.065 (0.110)	1.09 (0.983)
R^2	0.708	0.722	0.739	0.752
$\tilde{R}^2$	0.671	0.674	0.706	0.708
S	26.347	26.224	55.036	54.81
F	19.35	14.95	22.62	17.40
D-W	1.702	1.511	2.081	2.189
$\tilde{\rho}$	0.112	0.19	-0.053	-0.125

Notes : 1. Figures in brackets are the respective 't' values.
2. * *** Indicates significant at 1% and 10% levels respectively.

4. GUJARAT

Effect of Productivity on Wages

Seven models regarding effect of productivity and capital intensity on wages have been estimated (Table 10.4.1) and the results of selected models with significant effect of explanatory variables are discussed on page no. 370.

TABLE 10.4.1
Regression Function for Wages (Gujarat—All Industries)

Dependent Variable—Real Wage Rate

Explanatory Variables	*Model Numbers*						
	I	*II*	*III*	*IV*	*V*	*VI*	*VII*
(1)	*(2)*	*(3)*	*(4)*	*(5)*	*(6)*	*(7)*	*(8)*
Constant	3.436 (28.873)	3.663 (27.064)	3.744 (45.085)	3.877 (40.544)	3.736 (4.397)	4.808 (7.167)	4.900 (7.605)
ln Time	0.119* (6.666)	0.179* (6.941)	0.097* (4.829)	0.16* (5.291)	0.23* (10.101)	0.237* (11.984)	0.236* (11.845)
ln LP_t	0.242* (8.199)						
ln LP_{t-1}		0.17* (4.696)					
ln $(K/L)_t$			0.176* (8.178)				
ln $(K/L)_{t-1}$				0.126* (4.518)			
ln TFPK					0.143 (0.768)		
ln TFPS						-0.090 (-0.628)	
ln TFPT							-0.110 (-0.797)
R^2	0.960	0.946	0.960	0.944	0.855	0.854	0.855
$\tilde{R}^2$	0.957	0.942	0.956	0.939	0.843	0.842	0.844
S	0.045	0.051	0.046	0.052	0.086	0.087	0.086
F	297.93	210.61	296.82	202.67	73.64	72.98	73.80
D-W	2.573	2.605	2.334	2.553	1.025	1.042	1.063
$\tilde{\rho}$	-0.340	-0.313	-0.192	-0.287	0.335	0.345	0.338

Notes : 1. Figures in brackets are the respective 't' values.
2. * Indicates significant at 1% level.

Consider the regression equation in Model I in which wage rate depends upon trend and current period partial labour productivity. Coefficient of time is 0.119 and trend is upward and is highly significant. The coefficient of LP_t is 0.242 and it shows that 100 percent increase in labour productivity brings about 24.2 percent increase in wage rate in the same year, keeping the effect of time constant. The value of R^2 is 0.960 and of $\tilde{R}^2$ is 0.957 which reveals that about 96.0 percent variations in wage rate were due to trend and current period partial labour productivity. Thus increase in partial labour productivity has benefited the workers in Gujarat. The given model fits the data well.

Consider the regression equation in Model III in which real wage rate depends upon trend and current period capital intensity. The coefficient of time is 0.097 and trend is upward and is highly significant. The slope coefficient of $(K/L)_t$ is 0.176 and this shows that 100 percent increase in capital intensity, keeping the effect of time constant, brings about 17.6 percent increase in wage rate in the same year. The value of R^2 is 0.96 and of $\tilde{R}^2$ is 0.956 which reveals that about 96.0 percent variations in wage rate were due to trend and current period capital intensity. The given model fits the data well. Thus capital intensity, which is an index of increased and improved mechanisation, showed that workers have benefited in terms of wages due to increase in the capital intensity.

Effect of Wages on Productivity

In Model VIII (Table 10.4.2) labour productivity depends upon trend and current period wage rate. Coefficient of time is –0.225 and this is significant. The slope coeffiecient 3.015 shows that 100 percent increase in wage rate results into 301.5 percent increase in labour productivity in the same year, keeping the effect of time constant. Hence, labour productivity is highly responsive to change in wage rate in Gujarat. The value of R^2 is 0.909 and of $\tilde{R}^2$ is 0.901 which indicates that 90.9 percent variations in labour productivity were due to trend and current period wage rate. Hence, wage rate is a highly significant explanatory variable. The model fits the data well.

Taking labour productivity as dependent upon trend and up to three period lagged capital intensity, models X-XIII showed non-significant results.

TABLE 10.4.2
Regression Function for Labour Productivity (Gujarat—All Industries)

Dependent Variable—Partial Labour Productivity

Explanatory Variables	*Model Numbers*					
	VIII	*IX*	*X*	*XI*	*XII*	*XIII*
(1)	*(2)*	*(3)*	*(4)*	*(5)*	*(6)*	*(7)*
Constant	-9.294 (-5.75)	-6.249 (-2.736)	1.402 (8.045)	1.605 (7.298)	1.844 (6.918)	1.863 (6.213)
ln Time	-0.225** (-2.372)	-0.033 (-0.204)	-0.062 (-1.465)	0.023 (0.331)	0.150 (1.443)	0.204 (1.511)
ln WR_t	3.015* (8.199)					
ln WR_{t-1}		2.317* (4.315)				
ln $(K/L)_t$			0.693* (15.331)			
ln $(K/L)_{t-1}$				0.628* (9.781)		
ln $(K/L)_{t-2}$					0.534* (6.197)	
ln $(K/L)_{t-3}$						0.513* (4.848)
R^2	0.909	0.859	0.968	0.950	0.923	0.905
$\tilde{R}^2$	0.901	0.847	0.965	0.946	0.916	0.896
S	0.161	0.199	0.096	0.119	0.146	0.159
F	124.41	73.18	373.57	227.21	138.13	104.64
D-W	1.929	1.676	2.192	1.963	1.331	1.085
$\tilde{\rho}$	0.027	0.150	-0.142	-0.007	0.256	0.386

Notes : 1. Figures in brackets are the respective 't' values.
2. * ** Indicates significant at 1% and 5% levels respectively.

Pre and Post-liberalisation Period

Consider the regression equation in Model XIV, in which wage rate is dependent upon dummy, labour productivity and product of dummy times labour productivity variables in Table 10.4.3. The estimated equation is :

TABLE 10.4.3
Structural Stability of Regression Functions (Bihar—All Industries)

Dependent Variables	*I*		*II*	
	Real Wage Rate		*Labour Productivity*	
Explanatory Variables	*Model Numbers*			
	XIV	*XV*	*XVI*	*XVII*
Constant	59.364 (6.916)	83.717 (10.077)	-67.72 (-1.552)	26.757 (0.295)
Time		2.814* (4.555)		4.116 (1.186)
Dummy	63.84* (3.918)	0.16 (0.009)	-263.689** (-2.281)	-344.385** (-2.583)
LP_t	0.546* (8.303)	0.141 (1.398)		
$D \cdot LP_t$	-0.364* (-4.625)	-0.047 (-0.511)		
WR_t			1.513* (4.502)	0.472 (0.503)
$D \cdot WR_t$			2.066* (3.027)	2.492* (3.252)
R^2	0.923	0.959	0.933	0.936
$\tilde{R}^2$	0.913	0.952	0.924	0.925
S	9.192	6.809	28.233	27.997
F	95.27	135.42	110.60	84.71
D-W	1.745	2.447	1.906	1.701
$\tilde{\rho}$	0.025	-0.227	-0.032	0.031

Notes : 1. Figures in brackets are the respective 't' values.
2. * ** Indicates significant at 1% and 5% levels respectively.

$$WR_t = 59.364 + 63.84\ D + 0.546\ LP_t - 0.364\ D \cdot LP_t$$

Pre-liberalisation Era I—1973 to 1990 and D = 0;

then $WR_t = 59.364 + 0.546\ LP_t$

Post-liberalisation Era II—1991 to 2000 and D = 1;

then $WR_t = 123.204 + 0.182\ LP_t$

The differential intercept and the differential slope

parameter are highly significant. The function has shifted from period I to period II due to significant difference in intercept values and in slope parameters. In post-liberalisation period though the intercept has increased but, the slope of regression line has become flatter, i.e. the relationship between wage and labour productivity during post-reform era has weakened in Gujarat. Since the time period of post-reform era is less, so over long period it has to be seen whether this relationship reverts back or further weakens.

Taking wage rate as dependent upon trend, dummy, labour productivity and product of dummy times labour productivity (Table 10.4.3), models XV showed non-significant result.

Consider the regression equation in Model XVI, in which labour productivity is dependent upon dummy, wage rate and product of dummy times wage rate variables. The estimated equation is :

$$LP_t = -67.72 - 263.689\,D + 1.513\,WR_t + 2.066\,D \cdot WR_t$$

Pre-liberalisation Era I-1973 to 1990 and D = 0;

then $LP_t = -67.72 + 1.513\,WR_t$

Post-liberalisation Era II-1991 to 2000 and D = 1;

then $LP_t = -331.409 + 3.579\,WR_t$

The differential intercept and the differential slope parameter are significant. The function has shifted from period I to period II due to significant difference in intercept values and in slope parameters. In post-liberalisation period though the differential intercept has decreased but the slope of regression line has become steeper, i.e. the relationship between labour productivity and wage rate during post-reform era has strengthened in Gujarat. After liberalisation when market forces have more important role to play, the labour productivity has become more responsive to wage rate.

Consider the regression equation in Model XVII, in which labour productivity is dependent upon time, dummy, wage rate and product of dummy times wage rate variables. The estimated equation is :

$$LP_t = 26.757 + 4.116\,t - 344.385\,D + 0.472\,WR_t + 2.492\,D \cdot WR_t$$

Pre-liberalisation Era I—1973 to 1990 and D = 0;

then $LP_t = 26.757 + 4.116\ t + 0.472\ WR_t$

Post-liberalisation Era II—1991 to 1997 and D = 1;

then $LP_t = -317.628 + 4.116\ t + 2.964\ WR_t$

The differential intercept and the differential slope parameter are significant. The function has shifted from period I to period II due to significant difference in intercept values and in slope parameters. In post-liberalisation period though the differential intercept has decreased but the slope of regression line has become steeper, i.e. the relationship between labour productivity and wage rate during post-reform era has strengthened in Gujarat. After liberalisation when market forces have more important role to play, the labour productivity has become more responsive to wage rate.

5. HARYANA

Effect of Productivity on Wages

Seven models regarding effect of productivity and capital intensity on wages have been estimated (Table 10.5.1) and the results of selected models with significant effect of explanatory variables are discussed below :

Consider the regression equation in Model I in which wage rate depends upon trend and current period partial labour productivity. Coefficient of time is 0.176 and trend is upward and is highly significant. The coefficient of LP_t is 0.383 and it shows that 100 percent increase in labour productivity brings about 38.3 percent increase in wage rate in the same year, keeping the effect of time constant. The value of R^2 is 0.892 and of $\bar{R}^2$ is 0.884 which reveals that about 89.2 percent variations in wage rate were due to trend and current period partial labour productivity. Thus increase in partial labour productivity has benefited the workers in Haryana. The given model fits the data well.

Consider the regression equation in Model III in which real wage rate depends upon trend and current period capital intensity. The coefficient of time is 0.133 and trend is upward and is highly significant. The slope coefficient of $(K/L)_t$ is 0.485 and this shows that 100 percent increase in capital intensity,

Table 10.5.1
Regression Function for Wages (Haryana—All Industries)

Dependent Variable—Real Wage Rate

Explanatory Variables	*Model Numbers*						
	I	*II*	*III*	*IV*	*V*	*VI*	*VII*
(1)	*(2)*	*(3)*	*(4)*	*(5)*	*(6)*	*(7)*	*(8)*
Constant	2.651 (6.423)	3.103 (7.166)	2.271 (6.437)	2.521 (6.496)	2.991 (3.933)	3.223 (4.270)	3.146 (4.263)
ln Time	0.176* (4.816)	0.245* (5.357)	0.133* (4.014)	0.177* (4.058)	0.243* (6.035)	0.268* (7.989)	0.265* (7.844)
ln LP_t	0.383* (4.194)						
ln LP_{t-1}		0.265** (2.668)					
ln $(K/L)_t$			0.485* (5.993)				
ln $(K/L)_{t-1}$				0.418* (4.489)			
ln TFPK					0.294*** (1.815)		
ln TFPS						0.244 (1.522)	
ln TFPT							0.261 (1.660)
R^2	0.892	0.876	0.925	0.913	0.838	0.832	0.835
$\tilde{R}^2$	0.884	0.866	0.919	0.905	0.825	0.819	0.822
S	0.095	0.098	0.080	0.082	0.117	0.119	0.118
F	103.57	84.68	153.52	125.17	64.61	61.94	63.14
D-W	0.888	0.815	1.093	1.073	0.475	0.423	0.444
$\tilde{\rho}$	0.471	0.440	0.421	0.352	0.649	0.674	0.664

Notes : 1. Figures in brackets are the respective 't' values.
2. * Indicates significant at 1%, 5% AND 10% respectively level.

keeping the effect of time constant, brings about 48.5 percent increase in wage rate in the same year. The value of R^2 is 0.925 and of $\tilde{R}^2$ is 0.919 which reveals that about 92.5 percent variations in wage rate were due to trend and current period capital intensity. The given model fits the data well. Thus capital intensity, which is an index of increased and improved mechanisation, showed that workers have benefited in terms of wages due to increase in the capital intensity.

Effect of Wages on Productivity

In Model VIII (Table 10.5.2) labour productivity depends upon trend and two period lagged wage rate. Coefficient of time is –0.271 and this is significant. The slope coeffiecient 1.604 shows that 100 percent increase in wage rate results into 160.4 percent increase in labour productivity in the next second year, keeping the effect of time constant. Hence labour productivity is highly responsive to change in wage rate in Haryana. The value of R^2 is 0.802 and of $\tilde{R}^2$ is 0.785 which indicates that 80.2 percent variations in labour productivity were due to trend and two period lagged wage rate. Hence wage rate is a highly significant explanatory variable. The model fits the data well.

Taking labour productivity as dependent upon trend and up to three period lagged capital intensity, models XII-XV showed non-significant results.

Pre and Post-liberalisation Period

Consider the regression equation in Model XVI, in which wage rate is dependent upon dummy, labour productivity and product of dummy times labour productivity variables in Table 10.5.3. The estimated equation is:

$$WR_t = 35.015 + 107.709\ D + 0.646\ LP_t - 0.367\ D\ .\ LP_t$$

Pre-liberalisation Era I—1973 to 1990 and D = 0;

$$\text{then } WR_t = 35.015 + 0.646\ LP_t$$

Post-liberalisation Era II—1991 to 2000 and D = 1;

$$\text{then } WR_t = 142.724 + 0.279\ LP_t$$

The differential intercept and the differential slope parameter are significant. The function has shifted from period I to period II due to significant difference in intercept values and in slope parameters. In post-liberalisation period though the intercept has increased but, the slope of regression line has become flatter, i.e. the relationship between wage and labour

TABLE 10.5.2
Regression Function for Wages
(Haryana—All Industries)

Dependent Variable—Partial Labour Productivity

Explanatory Variables	*Model Numbers*							
	VIII	*IX*	*X*	*XI*	*XII*	*XIII*	*XIV*	*XV*
(1)	*(2)*	*(3)*	*(4)*	*(5)*	*(6)*	*(7)*	*(8)*	*(9)*
Constant	-0.230 (-0.204)	-1.382 (-1.191)	-2.109 (-1.739)	-1.374 (-0.908)	1.538 (2.171)	1.675 (2.054)	0.789 (1.039)	0.309 (0.488)
ln Time	-0.001 (-0.011)	-0.147 (-1.384)	-0.271** (-2.123)	-0.220 (-1.234)	0.088 (1.330)	0.078 (0.855)	-0.027 (-0.286)	-0.098 (-1.066)
ln WR_t	1.079* (4.194)							
ln WR_{t-1}		1.386* (5.020)						
ln WR_{t-2}			1.604* (5.356)					
ln WR_{t-3}				1.443* (3.735)				
ln $(K/L)_t$					0.681* (4.190)			
ln $(K/L)_{t-1}$						0.665* (3.403)		
ln $(K/L)_{t-2}$							0.898* (4.765)	
ln $(K/L)_{t-3}$								1.035* (6.344)
R^2	0.792	0.803	0.802	0.726	0.792	0.727	0.777	0.842
$\tilde{R}^2$	0.776	0.786	0.785	0.701	0.776	0.704	0.757	0.827
S	0.160	0.147	0.142	0.166	0.160	0.173	0.151	0.127
F	47.71	48.76	46.72	29.09	47.66	31.94	39.98	58.41
D-W	1.175	1.613	1.656	1.657	1.007	1.449	1.442	1.413
$\tilde{\rho}$	0.393	0.177	0.171	0.156	0.491	0.275	0.257	0.267

Notes : 1. Figures in brackets are the respective 't' values.
2. * ** Indicates significant at 1% and 5% levels respectively.

Table 10.5.3
Structural Stability of Regression Functions (Haryana—All Industries)

Dependent Variables	*I*		*II*	
	Real Wage Rate		*Labour Productivity*	
Explanatory Variables	*Model Numbers*			
	XVI	*XVII*	*XVIII*	*XIX*
Constant	35.015 (1.570)	82.486 (6.275)	36.706 (0.877)	110.793 (1.206)
Time		4.513* (7.987)		4.16 (0.907)
Dummy	107.709* (3.340)	-0.869 (-0.04)	-243.332** (-2.367)	-314.641** (-2.419)
LP_t	0.646* (4.780)	0.089 (0.894)		
$D . LP_t$	-0.367** (-2.331)	0.028 (0.293)		
WR_t			0.898* (3.051)	0.085 (0.091)
$D . WR_t$			1.301** (2.531)	1.662** (2.550)
R^2	0.879	0.968	0.836	0.842
$\tilde{R}^2$	0.864	0.962	0.815	0.814
S	17.305	9.1	31.97	32.08
F	58.00	173.27	40.75	30.54
D-W	1.33	1.931	1.944	1.918
$\tilde{\rho}$	0.329	0.026	0.013	0.025

Notes : 1. Figures in brackets are the respective 't' values.
2. * ** Indicates significant at 1% and 5% levels respectively.

productivity during post-reform era has weakened in Haryana.

Taking wage rate as dependent upon trend, dummy, labour productivity and product of dummy times labour productivity (Table 10.5.3), Model XVII showed non-significant result.

Consider the regression equation in Model XVIII, in which labour productivity is dependent upon dummy, wage rate and product of dummy times wage rate variables. The estimated equation is

$$LP_t = 36.706 - 242.332\ D + 0.898\ WR_t + 1.301\ D\ .\ WR_t$$

Pre-liberalisation Era I—1973 to 1990 and D = 0;

$$\text{then } LP_t = 36.706 + 0.898\ WR_t$$

Post-liberalisation Era II—1991 to 2000 and D = 1;

$$\text{then } LP_t = -\ 205.626 + 2.199\ WR_t$$

The differential intercept and the differential slope parameter are significant. The function has shifted from period I to period II due to significant difference in intercept values and in slope parameters. In post-liberalisation period though the differential intercept has decreased but the slope of regression line has become steeper, i.e. the relationship between labour productivity and wage rate during post-reform era has strengthened in Haryana. After liberalisation when market forces have more important role to play, the labour productivity has become more responsive to wage rate.

Consider the regression equation in Model XIX, in which labour productivity is dependent upon time, dummy, wage rate and product of dummy times wage rate variables. The estimated equation is :

$$LP_t = 110.793 + 4.16\ t - 314.641\ D + 0.085\ WR_t + 1.662\ D\ .\ WR_t$$

Pre-liberalisation Era I—1973 to 1990 and D = 0;

$$\text{then } LP_t = 110.793 + 4.16\ t + 0.085\ WR_t$$

Post-liberalisation Era II—1991 to 2000 and D = 1;

$$\text{then } LP_t = -203.848 + 4.16\ t + 1.747\ WR_t$$

The differential intercept and the differential slope parameter are significant. The function has shifted from period I to period II due to significant difference in intercept values and in slope parameters. In post-liberalisation period though the differential intercept has decreased but the slope of regression line has become steeper, i.e. the relationship between labour productivity and wage rate during post-reform era has strengthened in Haryana. After liberalisation when market forces have more important role to play, the labour productivity has become more responsive to wage rate.

6. HIMACHAL PRADESH

Effect of Productivity on Wages

Fourteen models regarding effect of productivity and capital intensity on wages have been estimated (Table 10.6.1) and the results of selected models with significant effect of explanatory variables are discussed below :

Consider the regression equation in Model VI in which wage rate depends upon trend and fifth period partial lagged labour productivity. Coefficient of time is 0.291 and trend is upward and is highly significant. The coefficient of LP_t is 0.098 and it shows that 100 percent increase in labour productivity brings about 9.8 percent increase in wage rate in the fifth year, keeping the effect of time constant. The value of R^2 is 0.855 and of $\tilde{R}^2$ is 0.841 which reveals that about 85.5 percent variations in wage rate were due to trend and fifth period lagged partial labour productivity. Thus increase in partial labour productivity has benefited the workers in Himachal Pradesh. The given model fits the data well.

Taking wage rate as dependent upon trend and up to three period lagged capital intensity, Models VIII-XI showed non-significant results.

Effect of Wages on Productivity

Taking labour productivity as dependent upon trend and up to five year lagged wage rate, Models XV-XX (Table 10.6.2) showed non-significant results.

Taking labour productivity as dependent upon trend and up to three period lagged capital intensity, Models XXI-XXIV showed non-significant results.

Pre and Post-liberalisation Period

Taking wage rate as dependent upon time, dummy, labour productivity and product of dummy times labour productivity (Table 10.6.3), Models XXV-XXVI showed non-significant results.

Taking labour productivity as dependent upon dummy, wage rate and product of dummy times wage rate, Model XXVII showed non-significant result.

TABLE 10.6.1

Regression Function for Wages
(Himachal Pradesh—All Industries)

Dependent Variable—Real Wage Rate

Explanatory Variables	*Model Numbers*													
	I	*II*	*III*	*IV*	*V*	*VI*	*VII*	*VIII*	*IX*	*X*	*XI*	*XII*	*XIII*	*XIV*
(1)	*(2)*	*(3)*	*(4)*	*(5)*	*(6)*	*(7)*	*(8)*	*(9)*	*(10)*	*(11)*	*(12)*	*(13)*	*(14)*	*(15)*
Constant	4.619	4.900	4.859	4.654	4.071	3.709	3.895	4.247	5.159	4.673	4.324	5.080	5.008	5.039
	(14.870)	(20.643)	(20.795)	(20.193)	(18.599)	(19.403)	(18.808)	(11.217)	(20.102)	(16.779)	(16.071)	(12.406)	(13.601)	(13.911)
ln Time	0.272*	0.371*	0.374*	0.384*	0.332*	0.291*	0.345*	0.22*	0.458*	0.373*	0.332*	0.268*	0.241*	0.237*
	(6.148)	(9.124)	(8.151)	(7.621)	(6.083)	(5.625)	(5.445)	(3.444)	(8.276)	(5.127)	(4.155)	(10.318)	(10.783)	(10.520)
ln LP_t	-0.047													
	(-0.696)													
ln LP_{t-1}		-0.139**												
		(-2.589)												
ln LP_{t-2}			-0.135**											
			(-2.477)											
ln LP_{t-3}				-0.107***										
				(-1.943)										
ln LP_{t-4}					0.016									
					(0.299)									
ln LP_{t-5}						0.098**								
						(2.080)								

(*Contd.*)

Table 10.6.1 (Contd.)

(1)	(2)	(3)	(4)	(5)	(6)	(7)	(8)	(9)	(10)	(11)	(12)	(13)	(14)	(15)
ln LP_{t-6}							0.039							
							(0.763)							
ln $(K/L)_t$								0.037						
								(0.427)						
ln $(K/L)_{t-1}$									-0.219*					
									(-3.41)					
ln $(K/L)_{t-2}$										-0.102				
										(-1.365)				
ln $(K/L)_{t-3}$											-0.026			
											(-0.341)			
ln TFPK												-0.140		
												(-1.659)		
ln TFPS													-0.124	
													(-1.652)	
ln TFPT														-0.128***
														(-1.766)
R^2	0.818	0.874	0.835	0.822	0.823	0.855	0.804	0.816	0.891	0.807	0.792	0.833	0.833	0.835
$\tilde{R}^2$	0.804	0.863	0.821	0.806	0.806	0.841	0.783	0.801	0.882	0.790	0.773	0.820	0.820	0.822
S	0.102	0.081	0.084	0.085	0.084	0.074	0.082	0.102	0.076	0.090	0.091	0.097	0.097	0.097
F	56.32	82.93	58.37	50.70	48.72	59.07	38.98	55.50	98.17	48.12	41.94	62.45	62.38	63.43
D-W	1.474	1.584	1.768	1.447	1.634	1.803	1.843	1.212	1.062	1.464	1.352	1.620	1.564	1.566
$\tilde{\rho}$	0.184	0.206	0.090	0.203	0.113	0.043	0.014	0.324	0.461	0.226	0.235	0.129	0.159	0.164

Notes : 1. Figures in brackets are the respective 't' values.

2. * ** *** Indicates significant at 1%, 5% and 10% levels respectively.

TABLE 10.6.2
Regression Function for Labour Productivity (Himachal Pradesh—All Industries)

Dependent Variable—Partial Labour Productivity

Explanatory Variables	*Model Numbers*									
	XV	*XVI*	*XVII*	*XVIII*	*XIX*	*XX*	*XXI*	*XXII*	*XXIII*	*XXIV*
(1)	*(2)*	*(3)*	*(4)*	*(5)*	*(6)*	*(7)*	*(8)*	*(9)*	*(10)*	*(11)*
Constant	6.330 (2.453)	7.212 (2.639)	5.553 (2.131)	5.305 (1.871)	8.408 (2.912)	8.127 (2.746)	0.730 (0.898)	3.087 (3.073)	4.704 (5.743)	5.677 (7.401)
ln Time	0.659* (4.153)	0.762* (3.660)	0.499** (2.082)	0.415 (1.453)	0.733** (2.294)	0.748** (2.070)	-0.046 (-0.336)	0.283 (1.304)	0.398*** (1.859)	0.575** (2.528)
ln WR_t	-0.406 (-0.696)									
ln WR_{t-1}		-0.638 (-0.994)								
ln WR_{t-2}			-0.167 (-0.262)							
ln WR_{t-3}				-0.071 (-0.1)						
ln WR_{t-4}					-0.870 (-1.173)					

(Contd.)

TABLE 10.6.1 (CONTD.)

(1)	(2)	(3)	(4)	(5)	(6)	(7)	(8)	(9)	(10)	(11)	(12)	(13)	(14)	(15)
ln WR_{t-5}								-0.828 (-1.059)						
ln $(K/L)_t$										0.887* (4.746)				
ln $(K/L)_{t-1}$											0.362 (1.444)			
ln $(K/L)_{t-2}$												0.047 (0.214)		
ln $(K/L)_{t-3}$														-0.197 (-0.908)
R^2	0.730		0.667	0.537	0.419		0.391	0.345		0.855	0.681	0.536		0.440
$\tilde{R}^2$	0.708		0.640	0.496	0.366		0.333	0.280		0.844	0.655	0.496		0.389
S	0.300		0.302	0.266	0.265		0.263	0.270		0.220	0.296	0.266		0.260
F	33.80		24.08	13.31	7.93		6.75	5.27		73.84	25.66	13.29		8.63
D-W	1.196		0.872	0.815	0.846		0.867	0.754		1.483	1.017	0.869		0.903
$\tilde{\rho}$	0.369		0.471	0.512	0.507		0.474	0.534		0.210	0.339	0.493		0.488

Notes : 1. Figures in brackets are the respective 't' values.
2. * ** *** Indicates significant at 1%, 5% and 10% levels respectively.

TABLE 10.6.3
Structural Stability of Regression Functions (Himachal Pradesh—All Industries)

Dependent Variables	*I*		*II*	
	Real Wage Rate		*Labour Productivity*	
Explanatory Variables	*Model Numbers*			
	XXV	*XXVI*	*XXVII*	*XXVIII*
Constant	98.714 (6.554)	92.732 (9.802)	-3.26 (-0.018)	598.611 (2.958)
Time		4.692* (6.202)		38.021* (4.060)
Dummy	68.73** (2.447)	3.986 (0.195)	93.77 (0.193)	-1006.321** (-2.163)
LP_t	0.113** (2.583)	-0.006 (-0.194)		
$D . LP_t$	-0.086 (-1.447)	-0.035 (-0.931)		
WR_t			2.409*** (1.877)	-4.713** (-2.334)
$D . WR_t$			0.21 (0.076)	5.175** (2.085)
R^2	0.609	0.854	0.507	0.713
$\tilde{R}^2$	0.56	0.828	0.446	0.663
S	22.114	13.819	140.363	109.438
F	12.47	33.57	8.23	14.27
D-W	0.889	1.905	0.681	1.14
$\tilde{\rho}$	0.545	0.028	0.536	0.388

Notes : 1. Figures in brackets are the respective 't' values.
2. * ** *** Indicates significant at 1% , 5% and 10% levels respectively.

Consider the regression equation in Model XXVIII, in which labour productivity is dependent upon time, dummy, wage rate and product of dummy times wage rate variables. The estimated equation is :

$$LP_t = 598.611 + 38.021\ t - 1006.321\ D - 4.713\ WR_t + 5.175\ D\ .\ WR_t$$

Pre-liberalisation Era I—1973 to 1990 and D = 0;

then $LP_t = 598.611 + 38.021\ t - 4.713\ WR_t$

Post-liberalisation Era II—1991 to 2000 and D = 1;

then $LP_t = -407.71 + 38.021\ t + 0.462\ WR_t$

The differential intercept and the differential slope parameter are significant. The function has shifted from period I to period II due to significant difference in intercept values and in slope parameters. In post-liberalisation period though the differential intercept has decreased but the slope of regression line has become steeper, i.e. the relationship between labour productivity and wage rate during post-reform era has strengthened in Himachal Pradesh. After liberalisation when market forces have more important role to play, the labour productivity has become more responsive to wage rate.

7. KARNATAKA

Effect of Productivity on Wages

Eight models regarding effect of productivity and capital intensity on wages have been estimated (Table 10.7.1) and the results of selected models with significant effect of explanatory variables are discussed below :

Consider the regression equation in Model I in which wage rate depends upon trend and current period partial labour productivity. Coefficient of time is 0.113 and trend is upward and is significant. The coefficient of LP_t is 0.354 and it shows that 100 percent increase in labour productivity brings about 35.4 percent increase in wage rate in the same year, keeping the effect of time constant. The value of R^2 is 0.906 and of $\tilde{R}^2$ is 0.898 which reveals that about 90.6 percent variations in wage rate were due to trend and current period partial labour productivity. Thus increase in partial labour productivity has benefited the workers in Karnataka. The given model fits the data well.

Consider the regression equation in Model III in which real wage rate depends upon trend and current period capital intensity. The coefficient of time is 0.259 and trend is upward and is significant. The slope coefficient of $(K/L)_t$ is 0.151 and this shows that 100 percent increase in capital intensity, keeping

TABLE 10.7.1
Regression Function for Wages (Karnataka—All Industries)

Dependent Variable—Real Wage Rate

Explanatory Variables	*Model Numbers*							
	I	*II*	*III*	*IV*	*V*	*VI*	*VII*	*VIII*
(1)	*(2)*	*(3)*	*(4)*	*(5)*	*(6)*	*(7)*	*(8)*	*(9)*
Constant	2.965 (10.312)	3.335 (9.891)	3.712 (18.759)	3.891 (18.082)	4.009 (6.072)	4.192 (7.678)	4.255 (7.998)	1.903 (3.398)
ln Time	0.113* (3.364)	0.169* (3.439)	0.151* (4.264)	0.212* (4.403)	0.25* (8.930)	0.255* (9.835)	0.256* (9.903)	0.08** (2.198)
ln LP_t	0.354* (5.090)							
ln LP_{t-1}		0.255* (2.939)						
ln $(K/L)_t$			0.181* (3.658)					0.274* (5.499)
ln $(K/L)_{t-1}$				0.12** (2.048)				
ln TFPK					0.087 (0.796)			
ln TFPS						0.047 (0.402)		
ln TFPT							0.033 (0.294)	0.313* (3.384)
R^2	0.906	0.870	0.875	0.849	0.810	0.809	0.808	0.915
$\tilde{R}^2$	0.898	0.859	0.865	0.836	0.795	0.794	0.793	0.905
S	0.077	0.087	0.089	0.093	0.109	0.110	0.110	0.075
F	119.78	80.00	87.23	67.46	53.43	52.88	52.69	86.28
D-W	1.933	1.875	1.357	1.708	1.148	1.124	1.123	1.992
$\tilde{\rho}$	0.033	0.023	0.307	0.081	0.360	0.371	0.372	0.001

Notes : 1. Figures in brackets are the respective 't' values.
2. * ** Indicates significant at 1% and 5% levels respectively.

the effect of time constant, brings about 15.1 percent increase in wage rate in the same year. The value of R^2 is 0.875 and of $\tilde{R}^2$ is 0.865 which reveals that about 87.5 percent variations in wage rate were due to trend and current period capital intensity. The given model fits the data well.

In Model VIII real wage rate depends upon trend, capital intensity and total factor productivity index (Translog). Coefficient of time is 0.08 and is statistically significant. The slope coefficient of $(K/L)_t$ is 0.274 and this shows that 100 percent increase in $(K/L)_t$ brings about 27.4 percent increase in wage rate, when other variables are held constant. The slope coefficient of TFPT is 0.313 and this shows that 100 percent increase in TFPT brings about 31.3 percent increase in wage rate, when other variables are held constant. The value of R^2 is 0.915 and of $\tilde{R}^2$ is 0.905 which indicates that about 91.5 percent variations in wage rate were due to time, capital intensity and TFPT. The given model fits the data well.

Effect of Wages on Productivity

In Model XI (Table 10.7.2) labour productivity depends upon trend and two period lagged wage rate. Coefficient of time is 0.316 and this shows that trend is upward and significant. The slope coeffiecient 0.706 shows that 100 percent increase in wage rate results into 70.6 percent increase in labour productivity in the next second year, keeping the effect of time constant. The value of R^2 is 0.85 and of $\tilde{R}^2$ is 0.837 which indicates that 85.0 percent variations in labour productivity were due to trend and second year lagged wage rate. The model fits the data well.

Consider the regression equation in Model XIII in which labour productivity depends upon trend and current year capital intensity. Coefficient of time is 0.118 and it is upward and highly significant. The slope coefficient shows that 100 percent increase in $(K/L)_t$ brings about 49.5 percent increase in labour productivity in the same year. The value of R^2 is 0.901 and of $\tilde{R}^2$ is 0.893 which reveals that 90.1 percent variations in labour productivity were due to trend and current year capital intensity. The given model fits the data well.

Taking wage rate as dependent upon time, dummy, labour productivity and product of dummy times labour productivity (Table 10.7.3), Models XXV-XXVI showed non-significant results, indicating no significant change in relationship between wages and labour productivity during post-liberalisation period.

TABLE 10.7.2
Regression Function for Labour Productivity (Karnataka—All Industries)

Dependent Variable—Partial Labour Productivity

Explanatory Variables	*Model Numbers*					
	IX	*X*	*XI*	*XII*	*XIII*	*XIV*
(1)	*(2)*	*(3)*	*(4)*	*(5)*	*(6)*	*(7)*
Constant	-2.255 (-1.807)	0.263 (0.188)	0.750 (0.541)	1.514 (1.030)	2.171 (7.350)	2.564 (7.808)
ln Time	0.039 (0.483)	0.251** (2.268)	0.316** (2.422)	0.431** (2.812)	0.118** (2.237)	0.263* (3.585)
ln WR_t	1.436* (5.090)					
ln WR_{t-1}		0.834** (2.551)				
ln WR_{t-2}			0.706** (2.097)			
ln WR_{t-3}				0.496 (1.351)		
ln $(K/L)_t$					0.495* (6.695)	
ln $(K/L)_{t-1}$						0.356* (3.983)
R^2	0.864	0.849	0.850	0.843	0.901	0.884
$\tilde{R}^2$	0.853	0.836	0.837	0.828	0.893	0.875
S	0.156	0.163	0.158	0.157	0.133	0.143
F	79.41	67.46	65.42	58.90	113.57	91.83
D-W	1.388	1.385	1.089	1.284	1.116	1.296
$\tilde{\rho}$	0.250	0.274	0.425	0.335	0.407	0.332

Notes : 1. Figures in brackets are the respective 't' values.
2. * ** Indicates significant at 1% and 5% levels respectively.

Taking labour productivity as dependent upon trend, dummy, wage rate and product of dummy times wage rate, models XXVII-XXVIII showed non-significant results.

TABLE 10.7.3
Structural Stability of Regression Functions
(Karnataka—All Industries)

Dependent Variables	*I*		*II*	
	Real Wage Rate		*Labour Productivity*	
Explanatory Variables	*Model Numbers*			
	XV	*XVI*	*XVII*	*XVIII*
Constant	33.844 (3.020)	50.994 (4.385)	-17.513 (-1.108)	-0.106 (-0.005)
Time		2.235** (2.800)		1.274 (1.016)
Dummy	0.499 (0.011)	-11.168 (-0.273)	89.897*** (1.760)	64.958 (1.147)
LP_t	0.826* (9.663)	0.524* (3.979)		
$D . LP_t$	-0.201 (-1.025)	-0.128 (-0.733)		
WR_t			1.042* (9.340)	0.829* (3.497)
$D . WR_t$			-0.103 (-0.375)	-0.007 (-0.024)
R^2	0.908	0.932	0.964	0.966
$\tilde{R}^2$	0.897	0.92	0.959	0.96
S	11.813	10.42	13.729	13.72
F	79.40	78.49	213.93	160.92
D-W	2.533	2.702	2.399	2.351
$\tilde{\rho}$	-0.308	-0.364	-0.219	-0.206

Notes : 1. Figures in brackets are the respective 't' values.
2. * ** Indicates significant at 1% and 5% levels respectively.

8. KERALA

Effect of Productivity on Wages

Eight models regarding effect of productivity and capital intensity on wages have been estimated (Table 10.8.1) and the results of selected models with significant effect of explanatory variables are discussed on next page.

TABLE 10.8.1
Regression Function for Wages
(Kerala—All Industries)

Dependent Variable—Real Wage Rate

Explanatory Variables	*Model Numbers*							
	I	*II*	*III*	*IV*	*V*	*VI*	*VII*	*VIII*
(1)	*(2)*	*(3)*	*(4)*	*(5)*	*(6)*	*(7)*	*(8)*	*(9)*
Constant	2.393 (7.832)	3.582 (9.018)	2.934 (9.386)	3.645 (11.000)	2.393 (3.436)	2.907 (4.162)	2.965 (4.313)	0.692 (1.388)
ln Time	0.099* (2.992)	0.26* (4.759)	0.166* (5.169)	0.274* (6.326)	0.191* (4.700)	0.243* (7.811)	0.248* (8.231)	0.084* (2.973)
ln LP_t	0.469* (6.436)							
ln LP_{t-1}		0.162 (1.596)						
ln $(K/L)_t$			0.346* (4.560)					0.405* (7.325)
ln $(K/L)_{t-1}$				0.148*** (1.728)				
ln TFPK					0.435* (2.811)			
ln TFPS						0.312** (2.065)		
ln TFPT							0.299** (2.014)	0.433* (5.027)
R^2	0.948	0.915	0.924	0.916	0.895	0.882	0.881	0.963
$\tilde{R}^2$	0.944	0.908	0.918	0.909	0.886	0.872	0.871	0.959
S	0.063	0.077	0.075	0.076	0.089	0.094	0.095	0.054
F	227.08	129.18	152.68	131.51	106.17	93.05	92.30	209.02
D-W	1.198	1.296	1.286	1.114	1.023	0.935	0.925	1.562
$\tilde{\rho}$	0.374	0.310	0.327	0.414	0.364	0.378	0.382	0.187

Notes : 1. Figures in brackets are the respective 't' values.
2. * ** *** Indicates significant at 1%, 5% and 10% levels respectively.

Consider the regression equation in Model I in which wage rate depends upon trend and current period partial labour productivity. Coefficient of time is 0.099 and trend is upward and is significant. The coefficient of LP_t is 0.469 and it shows that 100 percent increase in labour productivity brings about 46.9 percent increase in wage rate in the same year, keeping the effect of time constant. The value of R^2 is 0.948 and of $\tilde{R}^2$ is 0.944 which reveals that about 94.8 percent variations in wage rate were due to trend and current period partial labour productivity. The given model fits the data well.

Consider the regression equation in Model III in which real wage rate depends upon trend and current period capital intensity. The coefficient of time is 0.166 and trend is upward and is significant. The slope coefficient of $(K/L)_t$ is 0.346 and this shows that 100 percent increase in capital intensity, keeping the effect of time constant, brings about 34.6 percent increase in wage rate in the same year. The value of R^2 is 0.924 and of $\tilde{R}^2$ is 0.918 which reveals that about 92.4 percent variations in wage rate were due to trend and current period capital intensity. The given model fits the data well.

In Model V real wage rate depends upon trend and total factor productivity index (Kendrick). Coefficient of time is 0.191 and is statistically significant. The slope coefficient of TFPK is 0.435 and this shows that 100 percent increase in TFPK brings about 43.5 percent increase in wage rate, when the effect of time is held constant. The value of R^2 is 0.895 and of $\tilde{R}^2$ is 0.886 which indicates that about 89.5 percent variations in wage rate were due to time and TFPK. The given model fits the data well.

In Model VI real wage rate depends upon trend and total factor productivity index (Solow). Coefficient of time is 0.243 and is statistically significant. The slope coefficient of TFPS is 0.312 and this shows that 100 percent increase in TFPS brings about 31.2 percent increase in wage rate, when the effect of time is held constant. The value of R^2 is 0.882 and of $\tilde{R}^2$ is 0.872 which indicates that about 88.2 percent variations in wage rate were due to time and TFPS. The given model fits the data well.

In Model VII real wage rate depends upon trend and total factor productivity index (Translog). Coefficient of time is 0.248 and is statistically significant. The slope coefficient of TFPT is 0.299 and this shows that 100 percent increase in TFPT brings about 29.9 percent increase in wage rate, when the effect of time is held constant. The value of R^2 is 0.881 and of $\tilde{R}^2$ is 0.871 which indicates that about 88.1 percent variations in wage rate were due to time and TFPT. The given model fits the data well.

In Model VIII real wage rate depends upon trend, capital intensity and total factor productivity index (Translog). Coefficient of time is 0.084 and is statistically significant. The slope coefficient of $(K/L)_t$ is 0.405 and this shows that 100 percent increase in $(K/L)_t$ brings about 40.5 percent increase in wage rate, when other variables are held constant. The slope coefficient of TFPT is 0.433 and this shows that 100 percent increase in TFPT brings about 43.3 percent increase in wage rate, when other variables are held constant. The value of R^2 is 0.963 and of $\tilde{R}^2$ is 0.959 which indicates that about 96.3 percent variations in wage rate were due to time, capital intensity and TFPT. The given model fits the data well.

Effect of Wages on Productivity

In Model X (Table 10.8.2) labour productivity depends upon trend and one period lagged wage rate. Coefficient of time is 0.281 and this shows that trend is upward and significant. The slope coeffiecient 0.599 shows that 100 percent increase in wage rate results into 59.9 percent increase in labour productivity in the next year, keeping the effect of time constant. The value of R^2 is 0.9 and of $\tilde{R}^2$ is 0.891 which indicates that 90.0 percent variations in labour productivity were due to trend and one year lagged wage rate. The model fits the data well.

Consider the regression equation in Model XIII in which labour productivity depends upon trend and one year lagged capital intensity. Coefficient of time is 0.308 and it is upward and highly significant. The slope coefficient shows that 100 percent increase in $(K/L)_{t-1}$ brings about 41.7 percent increase in labour productivity in the next year. The value of R^2 is 0.918 and of $\tilde{R}^2$ is 0.911 which reveals that 91.8 percent variations in labour productivity were due to trend and one year lagged capital intensity. The given model fits the data well.

Pre and Post-liberalisation Period

Consider the regression equation in Model XV, in which wage rate is dependent upon dummy, labour productivity and product of dummy times labour productivity variables in Table 10.8.3. The estimated equation is :

TABLE 10.8.2
Regression Function for Labour Productivity (Kerala—All Industries)

Dependent Variable—Partial Labour Productivity

Explanatory Variables	*Model Numbers*					
	IX	*X*	*XI*	*XII*	*XIII*	*XIV*
(1)	*(2)*	*(3)*	*(4)*	*(5)*	*(6)*	*(7)*
Constant	-1.614 (-1.795)	1.442 (1.258)	3.874 (3.190)	1.674 (3.318)	2.335 (4.840)	3.394 (6.326)
ln Time	0.022 (0.346)	0.281** (2.735)	0.549* (4.181)	0.19* (3.653)	0.308* (4.881)	0.483* (5.652)
ln WR_t	1.329* (6.436)					
ln WR_{t-1}		0.599** (2.175)				
ln WR_{t-2}			-0.020 (-0.064)			
ln $(K/L)_t$				0.609* (4.973)		
ln $(K/L)_{t-1}$					0.417* (3.350)	
ln $(K/L)_{t-2}$						0.112 (0.764)
R^2	0.929	0.900	0.890	0.906	0.918	0.893
$\tilde{R}^2$	0.924	0.891	0.880	0.898	0.911	0.883
S	0.105	0.123	0.124	0.122	0.111	0.122
F	164.77	107.68	92.86	120.23	134.74	95.490
D-W	1.276	1.786	1.579	1.738	1.793	1.697
$\tilde{\rho}$	0.339	0.086	0.180	0.109	0.093	0.126

Notes : 1. Figures in brackets are the respective 't' values.
2. * ** Indicates significant at 1% and 5% levels respectively.

$$WR_t = 45.596 + 85.107\ D + 0.635\ LP_t - 0.369\ D\ .\ LP_t$$

Pre-liberalisation Era I—1973 to 1990 and D = 0;

then $WR_t = 45.596 + 0.635\ LP_t$

Post-liberalisation Era II—1991 to 2000 and D = 1;

then $WR_t = 130.703 + 0.266\ LP_t$

TABLE 10.8.3
Structural Stability of Regression Functions (Kerala—All Industries)

Dependent Variables	*I*		*II*	
	Real Wage Rate		*Labour Productivity*	
Explanatory Variables	*Model Numbers*			
	XV	*XVI*	*XVII*	*XVIII*
Constant	45.596 (5.213)	51.592 (5.019)	-48.286 (-2.036)	27.138 (0.924)
Time		1.198 (1.098)		6.495* (3.457)
Dummy	85.107* (3.582)	62.968** (2.026)	-88.319 (-0.906)	-294.9* (-2.935)
LP_t	0.635* (11.555)	0.52* (4.397)		
$D . LP_t$	-0.369* (-3.516)	-0.304** (-2.518)		
WR_t			1.408* (8.638)	0.439 (1.411)
$D . WR_t$			0.536 (1.053)	1.396* (2.850)
R^2	0.92	0.924	0.888	0.926
$\tilde{R}^2$	0.91	0.911	0.874	0.914
S	11.756	11.705	23.421	19.408
F	92.52	70.28	63.62	72.48
D-W	1.75	1.525	1.36	1.977
$\tilde{\rho}$	0.108	0.215	0.315	-0.043

Notes : 1. Figures in brackets are the respective 't' values.
2. * ** *** Indicates significant at 1% and 5% levels respectively.

The differential intercept and the differential slope parameter are highly significant. The function has shifted from period I to period II due to significant difference in intercept values and in slope parameters. In post-liberalisation period though the intercept has increased but, the slope of regression line has become flatter, i.e. the relationship between wage and labour productivity during post-reform era has weakened.

In Model XVI wage rate depends upon time, dummy, labour productivity and product of dummy times labour productivity variables. The estimated equation is :

$WR_t = 51.592 + 1.198\ t + 62.968\ D + 0.52\ LP_t - 0.304\ D\ .\ LP_t$
Pre-liberalisation Era I—1973 to 1990 and D = 0;
then $WR_t = 51.592 + 1.198\ t + 0.52\ LP_t$
Post-liberalisation Era II—1991 to 2000 and D = 1;
then $WR_t = 114.56 + 1.198\ t + 0.216\ LP_t$

The trend effect in pre and post-reform period remains the same. The differential intercept and the differential slope parameter are significant. The function has shifted from period I to period II due to significant difference in intercept values and in slope parameters. In post-liberalisation period though the intercept has increased but, the slope of regression line has become flatter, i.e. the relationship between wage and labour productivity during post-reform era has weakened.

Taking labour productivity as dependent upon dummy, wage rate and product of dummy times wage rate, Model XVII showed non-significant result.

Consider the regression equation in Model XVIII, in which labour productivity is dependent upon time, dummy, wage rate and product of dummy times wage rate variables. The estimated equation is :

$LP_t = 27.138 + 6.495\ t - 294.9\ D + 0.439\ WR_t + 1.396\ D\ .\ WR_t$
Pre-liberalisation Era I—1973 to 1990 and D = 0;
then $LP_t = 27.138 + 6.495\ t + 0.439\ WR_t$
Post-liberalisation Era II—91 to 2000 and D = 1;
then $LP_t = -267.762 + 6.495\ t + 1.835\ WR_t$

The trend effect in pre and post-reform period remains the same. The differential intercept and the differential slope parameter are significant. The function has shifted from period I to period II due to significant difference in intercept values and in slope parameters. In post-liberalisation period though the intercept has decreased but, the slope of regression line has become steeper, i.e. the relationship between labour productivity and wage rate during post-reform era has strengthened. After liberalisation when market forces have more important role to play, the labour productivity has become more responsive to wage rate.

9. MADHYA PRADESH

Effect of Productivity on Wages

Nine models regarding effect of productivity and capital intensity on wages have been estimated (Table 10.9.1) and the results of selected models with significant effect of explanatory variables are discussed below:

Consider the regression equation in Model I in which wage rate depends upon trend and current period partial labour productivity. Coefficient of time is 0.046 and trend is upward and is mildly significant. The coefficient of LP_t is 0.261 and it shows that 100 percent increase in labour productivity brings about 26.19 percent increase in wage rate in the same year, keeping the effect of time constant. The value of R^2 is 0.840 and of $\tilde{R}^2$ is 0.827 which reveals that about 84.0 percent variations in wage rate were due to trend and current period partial labour productivity. The given model fits the data well.

Taking wage rate as dependent upon trend and up to three period lagged capital intensity, Models III-VI showed non-significant results.

In Model VII real wage rate depends upon trend and total factor productivity index (Kendrick). Coefficient of time is 0.109 and is statistically highly significant. The slope coefficient of TFPK is 0.342 and this shows that 100 percent increase in TFPK brings about 34.2 percent increase in wage rate, when the effect of time is held constant. The value of R^2 is 0.798 and of $\tilde{R}^2$ is 0.781 which indicates that about 79.8 percent variations in wage rate were due to time and TFPK. The given model fits the data well.

In Model VIII real wage rate depends upon trend and total factor productivity index (Solow). Coefficient of time is 0.139 and is statistically highly significant. The slope coefficient of TFPS is 0.296 and this shows that 100 percent increase in TFPS brings about 29.6 percent increase in wage rate, when the effect of time is held constant. The value of R^2 is 0.740 and of $\tilde{R}^2$ is 0.719 which indicates that about 74.0 percent variations in wage

TABLE 10.9.1
Regression Function for Wages
(Madhya Pradesh—All Industries)

Dependent Variable—Real Wage Rate

Explanatory Variables	*Model Numbers*								
	I	*II*	*III*	*IV*	*V*	*VI*	*VII*	*VIII*	*IX*
(1)	*(2)*	*(3)*	*(4)*	*(5)*	*(6)*	*(7)*	*(8)*	*(9)*	*(10)*
Constant	3.424 (17.560)	3.625 (15.374)	3.681 (12.057)	3.523 (12.087)	3.527 (12.095)	3.416 (12.712)	2.952 (8.191)	3.128 (6.676)	4.347 (16.474)
ln Time	0.046*** (1.766)	0.085** (2.177)	0.049 (1.018)	0.023 (0.385)	0.010 (0.129)	-0.033 (-0.394)	0.109* (5.133)	0.139* (6.551)	0.164* (6.296)
ln LP_t	0.261* (5.364)								
ln LP_{t-1}		0.203* (3.240)							
ln $(K/L)_t$			0.196** (2.549)						
ln $(K/L)_{t-1}$				0.239* (2.952)					
ln $(K/L)_{t-2}$					0.247** (2.789)				

ln $(K/L)_{t-3}$						0.293* (3.287)			
ln TFPK							0.342* (4.183)		
ln TFPS								0.296* (2.834)	
ln TFPT									0.021 (0.391)
R^2	0.840	0.780	0.727	0.768	0.752	0.772	0.798	0.740	0.658
$\tilde{R}^2$	0.827	0.762	0.705	0.749	0.731	0.751	0.781	0.719	0.631
S	0.069	0.080	0.090	0.082	0.082	0.077	0.078	0.088	0.101
F	65.67	42.56	33.29	39.74	34.93	37.22	49.28	35.51	24.06
D-W	1.671	1.638	1.359	1.459	1.870	1.383	1.405	1.150	0.956
$\tilde{\rho}$	0.161	0.173	0.278	0.241	0.051	0.272	0.277	0.391	0.460

Notes : 1. Figures in brackets are the respective 't' values.
2. * ** *** Indicates significant at 1%, 5% and 10% levels respectively.

rate were due to time and TFPS. The given model fits the data well.

Effect of Wages on Productivity

In Model XI (Table 10.9.2) labour productivity depends upon trend and one period lagged wage rate. Coefficient of time is 0.333 and this shows that trend is upward and highly significant. The slope coeffiecient 1.229 shows that 100 percent increase in wage rate results into 122.9 percent increase in labour productivity in the next year, keeping the effect of time constant. The value of R^2 is 0.823 and of $\tilde{R}^2$ is 0.808 which indicates that 82.3 percent variations in labour productivity were due to trend and one year lagged wage rate. The model fits the data well.

Taking labour productivity as dependent upon trend and up to three period lagged capital intensity, models XIII-XVI showed non-significant results.

Pre and Post-liberalisation Period

Taking wage rate as dependent upon time, dummy, labour productivity and product of dummy times labour productivity (Table 10.9.3), models XVII-XVIII showed non-significant results.

Consider the regression equation in Model XIX, in which labour productivity is dependent upon dummy, wage rate and product of dummy times wage rate variables (Tables 10.9.3). The estimated equation is :

$$LP_t = -86.587 - 141.467\ D + 1.721\ WR_t + 1.468\ D\ .\ WR_t$$

Pre-liberalisation Era I—1973 to 1990 and D = 0;

$$\text{then } LP_t = -86.587 + 1.721\ WR_t$$

Post-liberalisation Era II—1991 to 2000 and D = 1;

$$\text{then } LP_t = -228.054 + 3.189\ WR_t$$

The differential intercept is non-significant but the differential slope parameter is significant. In post-liberalisation period the slope of regression line has become steeper, i.e. the relationship between labour productivity and wage rate during post-reform era has strengthened. After liberalisation when market forces have more important role to play, the labour productivity has become more responsive to wage rate.

TABLE 10.9.2
Regression Function for Labour Productivity (Madhya Pradesh—All Industries)

Dependent Variable—Partial Labour Productivity

Explanatory Variables	*Model Numbers*						
	X	*XI*	*XII*	*XIII*	*XIV*	*XV*	*XVI*
(1)	*(2)*	*(3)*	*(4)*	*(5)*	*(6)*	*(7)*	*(8)*
Constant	-5.197 (-3.051)	-1.782 (-0.953)	0.234 (0.126)	0.954 (1.275)	1.069 (1.652)	1.411 (2.280)	1.122 (2.110)
ln Time	0.106 (1.410)	0.333* (3.423)	0.497* (4.418)	0.005 (0.041)	0.071 (0.527)	0.177 (1.105)	0.098 (0.591)
ln WR_t	2.05* (5.364)						
ln WR_{t-1}		1.229* (2.870)					
ln WR_{t-2}			0.723 (1.671)				
ln $(K/L)_t$				0.757* (4.028)			
ln $(K/L)_{t-1}$					0.708* (3.939)		
ln $(K/L)_{t-2}$						0.597* (3.172)	
ln $(K/L)_{t-3}$							0.699* (3.958)
R^2	0.833	0.823	0.827	0.783	0.856	0.865	0.890
$\tilde{R}^2$	0.820	0.808	0.812	0.765	0.844	0.853	0.880
S	0.193	0.201	0.197	0.221	0.181	0.174	0.153
F	62.53	55.87	54.90	45.02	71.19	73.62	89.13
D-W	1.277	1.328	1.032	1.048	1.227	1.646	1.428
$\tilde{\rho}$	0.286	0.257	0.415	0.393	0.353	0.165	0.232

Notes : 1. Figures in brackets are the respective 't' values.
2. * ** *** Indicates significant at 1% level.

Consider the regression equation in Model XX, in which labour productivity is dependent upon time, dummy, wage rate

TABLE 10.9.3

Structural Stability of Regression Functions (Madhya Pradesh—All Industries)

Dependent Variables	*I*		*II*	
	Real Wage Rate		*Labour Productivity*	
Explanatory Variables	*Model Numbers*			
	XVII	*XVIII*	*XIX*	*XX*
Constant	76.178 (9.484)	82.894 (9.092)	-86.587 (-1.809)	46.306 (0.856)
Time		0.970 (1.450)		4.932* (3.565)
Dummy	13.41 (0.892)	-8.396 (-0.399)	-141.467 (-1.596)	-332.3* (-3.682)
LP_t	0.352* (5.133)	0.211*** (1.787)		
$D.\ LP_t$	-0.113 (-1.319)	-0.003 (-0.03)		
WR_t			1.721* (4.200)	0.171 (0.311)
$D.\ WR_t$			1.468** (2.265)	2.626* (4.217)
R^2	0.844	0.857	0.91	0.942
$\tilde{R}^2$	0.824	0.832	0.899	0.932
S	8.973	8.773	24.247	19.879
F	43.17	34.39	81.23	93.82
D-W	1.828	1.66	1.886	2.12
$\tilde{\rho}$	0.052	0.163	0.048	-0.121

Notes : 1. Figures in brackets are the respective 't' values.
2. * ** *** Indicates significant at 1%, 5% and 10% levels respectively.

and product of dummy times wage rate variables. The estimated equation is :

$$LP_t = 46.306 + 4.932\ t - 332.3\ D + 0.171\ WR_t + 2.626\ D\ .\ WR_t$$

Pre-liberalisation Era I—1973 to 1990 and D = 0;

$$\text{then } LP_t = 46.306 + 4.932\ t + 0.171\ WR_t$$

Post-liberalisation Era II—1991 to 2000 and D = 1;

$$\text{then } LP_t = -285.994 + 4.932\ t + 2.797\ WR_t$$

The trend effect in pre and post-reform period remains the same. The differential intercept and the differential slope parameter are highly significant. The function has shifted from period I to period II due to significant difference in intercept values and in slope parameters. In post-liberalisation period though the intercept has decreased but, the slope of regression line has become steeper i.e. the relationship between labour productivity and wage rate during post-reform era has strengthened. After liberalisation when market forces have more important role to play, the labour productivity has become more responsive to wage rate.

10. MAHARASHTRA

Effect of Productivity on Wages

Eight models regarding effect of productivity and capital intensity on wages have been estimated (Table 10.10.1) and the results of selected models with significant effect of explanatory variables are discussed below :

Consider the regression equation in Model I in which wage rate depends upon trend and current period partial labour productivity. Coefficient of time is 0.098 and trend is upward and is highly significant. The coefficient of LP_t is 0.234 and it shows that 100 percent increase in labour productivity brings about 23.4 percent increase in wage rate in the same year, keeping the effect of time constant. The value of R^2 is 0.930 and of $\tilde{R}^2$ is 0.924 which reveals that about 93.0 percent variations in wage rate were due to trend and current period partial labour productivity. The given model fits the data well.

Consider the regression equation in Model IV in which real wage rate depends upon trend and one period lagged capital intensity. The coefficient of time is 0.157 and trend is upward and is highly significant. The slope coefficient of $(K/L)_{t-1}$ is 0.098 and this shows that 100 percent increase in capital intensity, keeping the effect of time constant, brings about 9.8 percent increase in wage rate in the next year. The value of R^2 is 0.927 and of $\tilde{R}^2$ is 0.921 which reveals that about 92.7 percent variations in wage rate were due to trend and one period lagged capital intensity. The given model fits the data well.

In Model VI real wage rate depends upon trend and total

TABLE 10.10.1

Regression Function for Wages (Maharashtra—All Industries)

Dependent Variable—Real Wage Rate

Explanatory Variables	*Model Numbers*							
	I	*II*	*III*	*IV*	*V*	*VI*	*VII*	*VIII*
(1)	*(2)*	*(3)*	*(4)*	*(5)*	*(6)*	*(7)*	*(8)*	*(9)*
Constant	3.459 (20.140)	3.866 (21.072)	3.775 (31.046)	3.974 (33.221)	4.072 (33.356)	1.673 (2.430)	1.791 (2.738)	1.833 (2.704)
ln Time	0.098* (4.398)	0.181* (6.032)	0.081* (3.131)	0.157* (4.619)	0.203* (4.660)	0.141* (6.736)	0.15* (7.857)	0.158* (8.562)
ln LP_t	0.234* (5.550)							
ln LP_{t-1}		0.114** (2.360)						
ln $(K/L)_t$			0.169* (5.284)					
ln $(K/L)_{t-1}$				0.098** (2.763)				
ln $(K/L)_{t-2}$					0.059 (1.459)			
ln TFPK						0.602* (3.960)		
ln TFPS							0.575* (3.991)	
ln TFPT								0.564* (3.787)
R^2	0.930	0.922	0.926	0.927	0.914	0.904	0.904	0.900
$\tilde{R}^2$	0.924	0.916	0.920	0.921	0.906	0.896	0.896	0.892
S	0.052	0.053	0.053	0.051	0.053	0.060	0.060	0.061
F	165.18	142.48	156.01	153.27	121.54	117.03	117.83	112.77
D-W	0.679	0.701	0.847	0.661	0.658	0.808	0.848	0.852
$\tilde{\rho}$	0.580	0.567	0.521	0.604	0.613	0.440	0.409	0.410

Notes : 1. Figures in brackets are the respective 't' values.
2. * ** Indicates significant at 1% and 5% levels respectively.

factor productivity index (Kendrick). Coefficient of time is 0.141 and is statistically highly significant. The slope coefficient of TFPK is 0.602 and this shows that 100 percent increase in TFPK brings about 60.2 percent increase in wage rate, when the effect of time is held constant. The value of R^2 is 0.904 and of $\tilde{R}^2$ is 0.896 which indicates that about 90.4 percent variations in wage rate were due to time and TFPK. The given model fits the data well.

In Model VII real wage rate depends upon trend and total factor productivity index (Solow). Coefficient of time is 0.15 and is statistically highly significant. The slope coefficient of TFPS is 0.575 and this shows that 100 percent increase in TFPS brings about 57.5 percent increase in wage rate, when the effect of time is held constant. The value of R^2 is 0.904 and of $\tilde{R}^2$ is 0.896 which indicates that about 90.4 percent variations in wage rate were due to time and TFPS. The given model fits the data well.

In Model VIII real wage rate depends upon trend and total factor productivity index (Translog). Coefficient of time is 0.158 and is statistically highly significant. The slope coefficient of TFPT is 0.564 and this shows that 100 percent increase in TFPT brings about 56.4 percent increase in wage rate, when the effect of time is held constant. The value of R^2 is 0.900 and of $\tilde{R}^2$ is 0.892 which indicates that about 90.0 percent variations in wage rate were due to time and TFPT. The given model fits the data well.

Effect of Wages on Productivity

Taking labour productivity as dependent upon trend and up to five year lagged wage rate, models IX-XIV (Table 10.10.2) showed non-significant results.

Taking labour productivity as dependent upon trend and up to three period lagged capital intensity, models XV and XVIII showed non-significant results.

Pre and Post-liberalisation Period

Consider the regression equation in Model XIX, in which wage rate is dependent upon dummy, labour productivity and product of dummy times labour productivity variables (Table 10.10.3). The estimated equation is :

$$WR_t = 54.015 + 79.157\ D + 0.532\ LP_t - 0.444\ D\ .\ LP_t$$

TABLE 10.10.2
Regression Function for Labour Productivity (Maharashtra—All Industries)

Dependent Variable—Partial Labour Productivity

Explanatory Variables	*Model Numbers*									
	IX	*X*	*XI*	*XII*	*XIII*	*XIV*	*XV*	*XVI*	*XVII*	*XVIII*
(1)	*(2)*	*(3)*	*(4)*	*(5)*	*(6)*	*(7)*	*(8)*	*(9)*	*(10)*	*(11)*
Constant	-6.359 (-3.4)	-4.308 (-2.168)	-2.284 (-1.053)	-2.404 (-1.17)	-2.391 (-1.247)	-2.547 (-1.483)	1.458 (7.548)	1.787 (8.000)	1.953 (8.585)	2.116 (9.262)
ln Time	-0.030 (-0.318)	0.096 (0.775)	0.239 (1.497)	0.247 (1.429)	0.265 (1.440)	0.273 (1.479)	-0.050 (-1.219)	0.042 (0.665)	0.102 (1.258)	0.158 (1.548)
ln WR_t	2.358* (5.550)									
ln WR_{t-1}		1.88* (4.036)								
ln WR_{t-2}			1.395** (2.662)							
ln WR_{t-3}				1.42** (2.781)						
ln WR_{t-4}					1.412* (2.877)					

ln WR_{t-5}						1.446* (3.194)				
ln $(K/L)_t$							0.692* (13.644)			
ln $(K/L)_{t-1}$								0.596* (8.998)		
ln $(K/L)_{t-2}$									0.544* (7.213)	
ln $(K/L)_{t-3}$										0.493* (5.780)
R^2	0.876	0.890	0.884	0.898	0.912	0.928	0.967	0.958	0.953	0.945
$\tilde{R}^2$	0.866	0.880	0.874	0.889	0.904	0.921	0.965	0.954	0.949	0.941
S	0.163	0.154	0.155	0.141	0.128	0.113	0.084	0.095	0.098	0.103
F	88.07	96.61	87.36	97.28	108.90	128.77	368.07	270.94	235.08	190.77
D-W	0.509	0.839	1.024	0.988	1.283	1.603	1.573	2.185	1.907	1.393
$\tilde{\rho}$	0.693	0.551	0.480	0.497	0.347	0.127	0.206	-0.108	0.033	0.261

Notes : 1. Figures in brackets are the respective 't' values.
2. * ** Indicates significant at 1% and 5% levels respectively.

Table 10.10.3
Structural Stability of Regression Functions (Maharashtra—All Industries)

Dependent Variables	*I*		*II*	
	Real Wage Rate		*Labour Productivity*	
Explanatory Variables	*Model Numbers*			
	XIX	*XX*	*XXI*	*XXII*
Constant	54.015 (11.724)	62.197 (13.024)	-86.438 (-2.733)	8.526 (0.171)
Time		1.265* (3.071)		4.72** (2.351)
Dummy	79.157* (6.306)	58.525* (4.602)	-310.368 (-1.613)	-406.651** (-2.244)
LP_t	0.532* (15.567)	0.376* (6.401)		
$D . LP_t$	-0.444* (-8.138)	-0.352* (-6.303)		
WR_t			1.756* (6.919)	0.618 (1.150)
$D . WR_t$			2.497** (2.024)	2.938** (2.560)
R^2	0.954	0.967	0.93	0.943
$\tilde{R}^2$	0.948	0.962	0.921	0.934
S	5.491	4.724	22.437	20.58
F	165.49	170.08	105.94	95.82
D-W	1.359	1.182	1.935	2.143
$\tilde{\rho}$	0.265	0.306	-0.007	-0.105

Notes : 1. Figures in brackets are the respective 't' values.
2. * ** Indicates significant at 1% and 5% levels respectively.

Pre-liberalisation Era I—1973 to 1990 and D = 0;
then $WR_t = 54.015 + 0.532\ LP_t$
Post-liberalisation Era II—1991 to 2000 and D = 1;
then $WR_t = 133.172 + 0.088\ LP_t$

The differential intercept and the differential slope parameter are highly significant. The function has shifted from period I to period II due to significant difference in intercept values and in slope parameters. In post-liberalisation period though the intercept has increased but, the slope of regression line has become flatter, i.e. the relationship between wage rate and labour productivity during post-reform era has weakened.

In Model XX wage rate depends upon time, dummy, labour productivity and product of dummy times labour productivity variables. The estimated equation is :

$WR_t = 62.197 + 1.265\ t + 58.525\ D + 0.376\ LP_t - 0.352\ D\ .\ LP_t$
Pre-liberalisation Era I—1973 to 1990 and D = 0;
then $WR_t = 62.197 + 1.265\ t + 0.376\ LP_t$
Post-liberalisation Era II—1991 to 2000 and D = 1;
then $WR_t = 120.722 + 1.265\ t + 0.024\ LP_t$

The trend effect in pre and post-reform period remains the same. The differential intercept and the differential slope parameter are highly significant. The function has shifted from period I to period II due to significant difference in intercept values and in slope parameters. In post-liberalisation period though the intercept has increased but, the slope of regression line has become flatter, i.e. the relationship between wage and labour productivity during post-reform era has weakened.

Consider the regression equation in Model XXI, in which labour productivity is dependent upon dummy, wage rate and product of dummy times wage rate variables. The estimated equation is :

$LP_t = -86.438 - 310.368\ D + 1.756\ WR_t + 2.497\ D\ .\ WR_t$
Pre-liberalisation Era I—1973 to 1990 and D = 0;
then $LP_t = -86.438 + 1.756\ WR_t$
Post-liberalisation Era II—1991 to 2000 and D = 1;
then $LP_t = -396.806 + 4.253\ WR_t$

The differential intercept is non-significant but the differential slope parameter is significant. In post-liberalisation period the slope of regression line has become steeper, i.e. the relationship between labour productivity and wage rate during post-reform era has strengthened. After liberalisation when market forces have more important role to play, the labour productivity has become more responsive to wage rate.

Consider the regression equation in Model XXII, in which

labour productivity is dependent upon time, dummy, wage rate and product of dummy times wage rate variables. The estimated equation is :

$$LP_t = 8.526 + 4.72\ t - 406.651\ D + 0.618\ WR_t + 2.938\ D \cdot WR_t$$

Pre-liberalisation Era I—1973 to 1990 and D = 0;

$$\text{then } LP_t = 8.526 + 4.72\ t + 0.618\ WR_t$$

Post-liberalisation Era II—1991 to 2000 and D = 1;

$$\text{then } LP_t = -398.125 + 4.72\ t + 3.556\ WR_t$$

The trend effect in pre and post-reform period remains the same. The differential intercept and the differential slope parameter are significant. The function has shifted from period I to period II due to significant difference in intercept values and in slope parameters. In post-liberalisation period though the intercept has decreased but the slope of regression line has become steeper, i.e. the relationship between labour productivity and wage rate during post-reform era has strengthened. After liberalisation when market forces have more important role to play, the labour productivity has become more responsive to wage rate.

11. ORISSA

Effect of Productivity on Wages

Nine models regarding effect of productivity and capital intensity on wages have been estimated (Table 10.11.1) and the results of selected models with significant effect of explanatory variables are discussed below :

Consider the regression equation in Model II in which wage rate depends upon trend and one period lagged partial labour productivity. Coefficient of time is 0.182 and trend is upward and is highly significant. The coefficient of LP_{t-1} is 0.079 and it shows that 100 percent increase in labour productivity brings about 7.9 percent increase in wage rate in the next year, keeping the effect of time constant. The value of R^2 is 0.895 and of $\bar{R}^2$ is 0.887 which reveals that about 89.5 percent variations in wage rate were due to trend and one period lagged partial labour productivity. The given model fits the data well.

Consider the regression equation in Model V in which real

TABLE 10.11.1
Regression Function for Wages (Orissa—All Industries)

Dependent Variable—Real Wage Rate

Explanatory Variables	Model Numbers								
	I	II	III	IV	V	VI	VII	VIII	IX
(1)	(2)	(3)	(4)	(5)	(6)	(7)	(8)	(9)	(10)
Constant	3.662 (21.178)	3.841 (31.133)	4.008 (28.315)	3.801 (27.777)	3.954 (39.392)	3.923 (41.093)	3.613 (8.759)	3.631 (8.917)	3.807 (8.129)
ln Time	0.1* (4.313)	0.182* (8.926)	0.208* (7.799)	0.072** (2.528)	0.173* (6.354)	0.159* (4.913)	0.146* (6.557)	0.149* (6.810)	0.159* (7.224)
ln LP_t	0.161* (3.789)								
ln LP_{t-1}		0.079** (2.502)							
ln LP_{t-2}			0.031 (0.824)						
ln $(K/L)_t$				0.137* (3.817)					
ln $(K/L)_{t-1}$					0.057*** (1.959)				

(Contd.)

TABLE 10.11.1 (Contd.)

(1)	(2)	(3)	(4)	(5)	(6)	(7)	(8)	(9)	(10)
ln $(K/L)_{t-2}$						0.07** (2.342)			
ln TFPK							0.151 (1.666)		
ln TFPS								0.147 (1.642)	
ln TFPT									0.105 (1.048)
R^2	0.786	0.895	0.844	0.787	0.886	0.870	0.696	0.696	0.677
$\tilde{R}^2$	0.769	0.887	0.830	0.770	0.877	0.859	0.672	0.671	0.651
S	0.078	0.056	0.062	0.078	0.058	0.057	0.093	0.093	0.096
F	45.84	102.73	62.04	46.15	93.54	76.98	28.67	28.56	26.19
D-W	1.397	0.890	0.933	1.161	0.965	0.944	1.232	1.222	1.101
$\tilde{\rho}$	0.123	0.507	0.446	0.262	0.431	0.457	0.142	0.142	0.195

Notes : 1. Figures in brackets are the respective 't' values.
2. * ** *** Indicates significant at 1%, 5% and 10% levels respectively.

wage rate depends upon trend and one period lagged capital intensity. The coefficient of time is 0.173 and trend is upward and is highly significant. The slope coefficient of $(K/L)_{t-1}$ is 0.057 and this shows that 100 percent increase in capital intensity, keeping the effect of time constant, brings about 5.7 percent increase in wage rate in the next year. The value of R^2 is 0.886 and of $\tilde{R}^2$ is 0.877 which reveals that about 88.6 percent variations in wage rate were due to trend and one period lagged capital intensity. The given model fits the data well.

Effect of Wages on Productivity

Taking labour productivity as dependent upon trend and up to five year lagged wage rate, models X-XV (Table 10.11.2) showed non-significant results.

Taking labour productivity as dependent upon trend and up to three period lagged capital intensity, models XVI and XIX showed non-significant results.

Pre and Post-liberalisation Period

Taking wage rate as dependent upon dummy, labour productivity and product of dummy times labour productivity (Table 10.11.3), Model XX showed non-significant result.

Consider the regression equation in Model XXI, in which wage rate is dependent upon time, dummy, labour productivity and product of dummy times labour productivity variables in Table 10.11.3. The estimated equation is :

$$WR_t = 78.009 + 1.947\,t - 27.471\,D + 0.029\,LP_t + 0.118\,D\,.\,LP_t$$

Pre-liberalisation Era I—1973 to 1990 and D = 0;

$$\text{then } WR_t = 78.009 + 1.947\,t + 0.029\,LP_t$$

Post-liberalisation Era II—1991 to 2000 and D = 1;

$$\text{then } WR_t = 50.538 + 1.947\,t + 0.147\,LP_t$$

The trend effect in pre and post-reform period remains the same. The differential intercept and the differential slope parameter are significant. The function has shifted from period I to period II due to significant difference in intercept values and in slope parameters. In post-liberalisation period though the intercept has decreased but, the slope of regression line has become steeper, i.e. the relationship between wage rate and

TABLE 10.11.2

Regression Function for Labour Productivity (Orissa—All Industries)

Dependent Variable—Partial Labour Productivity

Explanatory Variables	*Model Numbers*									
	X	*XI*	*XII*	*XIII*	*XIV*	*XV*	*XVI*	*XVII*	*XVIII*	*XIX*
(1)	*(2)*	*(3)*	*(4)*	*(5)*	*(6)*	*(7)*	*(8)*	*(9)*	*(10)*	*(11)*
Constant	-5.814	-3.581	0.726	-2.492	-0.285	-2.007	1.494	1.447	1.652	1.731
	(-2.255)	(-1.203)	(0.224)	(-0.758)	(-0.08)	(-0.512)	(3.841)	(4.380)	(4.590)	(4.768)
ln Time	-0.004	0.167	0.439**	0.300	0.559**	0.555**	-0.068	-0.036	0.025	0.000
	(-0.036)	(1.083)	(2.259)	(1.402)	(2.320)	(2.084)	(-0.843)	(-0.403)	(0.205)	(0.002)
ln WR_t	2.27*									
	(3.789)									
ln WR_{t-1}		1.705**								
		(2.413)								
ln WR_{t-2}			0.633							
			(0.805)							
ln WR_{t-3}				1.406***						
				(1.737)						
ln WR_{t-4}					0.781					
					(0.879)					

ln WR_{t-5}						1.157 (1.181)				
ln $(K/L)_t$							0.68* (6.647)			
ln $(K/L)_{t-1}$								0.679* (7.112)		
ln $(K/L)_{t-2}$									0.613* (5.406)	
ln $(K/L)_{t-3}$										0.619* (5.070)
R^2	0.626	0.620	0.582	0.603	0.633	0.657	0.787	0.848	0.811	0.792
$\tilde{R}^2$	0.596	0.588	0.545	0.567	0.598	0.623	0.770	0.835	0.794	0.773
S	0.294	0.302	0.319	0.305	0.299	0.289	0.222	0.191	0.214	0.221
F	20.95	19.59	15.98	16.69	18.11	19.16	46.30	67.00	49.19	41.81
D-W	0.960	0.771	0.789	0.666	0.800	1.040	1.379	1.557	1.786	1.294
$\tilde{\rho}$	0.516	0.613	0.605	0.652	0.589	0.446	0.302	0.188	0.057	0.349

Notes : 1. Figures in brackets are the respective 't' values.
2. * ** *** Indicates significant at 1%, 5% and 10% levels respectively.

Table 10.11.3
Structural Stability of Regression Functions (Orissa—All Industries)

Dependent Variables	*I*		*II*	
	Real Wage Rate		*Labour Productivity*	
Explanatory Variables	*Model Numbers*			
	XX	XXI	XXII	XXIII
Constant	81.964 (12.130)	78.009 (18.271)	-75.505 (-1.162)	-42.405 (-0.393)
Time		1.947* (6.204)		1.109 (0.389)
Dummy	-1.786 (-0.112)	-27.471** (-2.547)	-45.983 (-0.396)	-79.484 (-0.543)
LP_t	0.178** (2.737)	0.029 (0.608)		
$D \cdot LP_t$	0.051 (0.526)	0.118*** (1.913)		
WR_t			1.744** (2.683)	1.304 (0.996)
$D \cdot WR_t$			0.797 (0.793)	1.031 (0.868)
R^2	0.714	0.893	0.768	0.769
$\tilde{R}^2$	0.679	0.875	0.739	0.729
S	9.976	6.233	31.881	32.46
F	20.01	48.08	26.42	19.15
D-W	1.138	2.284	1.537	1.477
$\tilde{\rho}$	0.372	-0.348	0.199	0.224

Notes : 1. Figures in brackets are the respective 't' values.
2. * ** *** Indicates significant at 1%, 5% and 10% levels respectively.

labour productivity during post-reform era has strengthened.

Taking labour productivity as dependent upon trend, dummy, wage rate and product of dummy times wage rate, models XXII-XXIII showed non-significant results.

12. PUNJAB

Effect of Productivity on Wages

Ten models regarding effect of productivity and capital intensity on wages have been estimated (Table 10.12.1) and the results of selected models with significant effect of explanatory variables are discussed below :

Consider the regression equation in Model II in which wage rate depends upon trend and one period lagged partial labour productivity. Coefficient of time is 0.277 and trend is upward and is highly significant. The coefficient of LP_{t-1} is 0.227 and it shows that 100 percent increase in labour productivity brings about 22.7 percent increase in wage rate in the next year, keeping the effect of time constant. The value of R^2 is 0.889 and of $\tilde{R}^2$ is 0.880 which reveals that about 88.9 percent variations in wage rate were due to trend and one period lagged partial labour productivity. The given model fits the data well.

Consider the regression equation in Model V in which real wage rate depends upon trend and one period lagged capital intensity. The coefficient of time is 0.26 and trend is upward and is highly significant. The slope coefficient of $(K/L)_{t-1}$ is 0.288 and this shows that 100 percent increase in capital intensity, keeping the effect of time constant, brings about 28.8 percent increase in wage rate in the next year. The value of R^2 is 0.892 and of $\tilde{R}^2$ is 0.883 which reveals that about 89.2 percent variations in wage rate were due to trend and one period lagged capital intensity. The given model fits the data well.

In Model X real wage rate depends upon trend, capital intensity and total factor productivity index (Translog). Coefficient of time is 0.153 and is statistically highly significant. The slope coefficient of $(K/L)_t$ is 0.341 and this shows that 100 percent increase in $(K/L)_t$ brings about 34.1 percent increase in wage rate, when other variables are held constant. The slope coefficient of TFPT is 0.338 and this shows that 100 percent increase in TFPT brings about 33.8 percent increase in wage rate, when other variables are held constant. The value of R^2 is 0.858 and of $\tilde{R}^2$ is 0.841 which indicates that about 85.8 percent variations in wage rate were due to time, capital intensity and TFPT. The given model fits the data well.

TABLE 10.12.1
Regression Function for Wages
(Punjab—All Industries)

Dependent Variable—Real Wage Rate

Explanatory Variables	*Model Numbers*									
	I	*II*	*III*	*IV*	*V*	*VI*	*VII*	*VIII*	*IX*	*X*
(1)	*(2)*	*(3)*	*(4)*	*(5)*	*(6)*	*(7)*	*(8)*	*(9)*	*(10)*	*(11)*
Constant	2.894 (6.278)	3.180 (8.018)	3.972 (8.304)	3.138 (5.862)	2.932 (6.337)	3.137 (6.657)	3.476 (5.747)	3.531 (4.703)	3.298 (4.404)	1.268 (1.307)
ln Time	0.198* (4.655)	0.277* (6.110)	0.389* (6.673)	0.228* (5.169)	0.26* (5.368)	0.297* (4.961)	0.269* (7.184)	0.278* (7.448)	0.267* (6.840)	0.153* (2.910)
ln LP_t	0.322* (3.027)									
ln LP_{t-1}		0.227** (2.365)								
ln LP_{t-2}			0.012 (0.099)							
ln $(K/L)_t$				0.264** (2.141)						0.341* (2.855)
ln $(K/L)_{t-1}$					0.288* (2.560)					

ln $(K/L)_{t-2}$						0.228*** (1.900)				
ln TFPK							0.177 (1.330)			
ln TFPS								0.162 (0.996)		
ln TFPT									0.215 (1.311)	0.338** (2.244)
R^2	0.852	0.889	0.862	0.829	0.892	0.881	0.811	0.805	0.810	0.858
$\tilde{R}^2$	0.840	0.880	0.850	0.815	0.883	0.870	0.796	0.789	0.795	0.841
S	0.114	0.097	0.102	0.122	0.095	0.095	0.129	0.130	0.129	0.113
F	71.76	96.06	71.82	60.46	99.58	84.86	53.52	51.60	53.39	48.49
D-W	1.882	1.589	1.751	1.455	1.759	2.285	1.278	1.227	1.303	2.023
$\tilde{\rho}$	-0.020	0.156	0.081	0.166	0.106	-0.158	0.241	0.261	0.225	-0.109

Notes : 1. Figures in brackets are the respective 't' values.
2. * ** *** Indicates significant at 1%, 5% and 10% levels respectively.

Effect of Wages on Productivity

Taking labour productivity as dependent upon trend and up to five year lagged wage rate, models XI-XVI (Table 10.12.2) showed non-significant results.

Consider the regression equation in Model XVIII in which labour productivity depends upon trend and one year lagged capital intensity. Coefficient of time is 0.221 and it is upward and significant. The slope coefficient shows that 100 percent increase in $(K/L)_{t-1}$ brings about 43.8 percent increase in labour productivity in the next year. The value of R^2 is 0.706 and of $\tilde{R}^2$ is 0.681 which reveals that 70.6 percent variations in labour productivity were due to trend and one year lagged capital intensity. The given model fits the data well.

Pre and Post-liberalisation Period

Consider the regression equation in Model XX, in which wage rate is dependent upon dummy, labour productivity and product of dummy times labour productivity variables in Table 10.12.3. The estimated equation is :

$$WR_t = 36.873 + 117.328\ D + 0.713\ LP_t - 0.519\ D\ .\ LP_t$$

Pre-liberalisation Era I—1973 to 1990 and D = 0;

$$\text{then } WR_t = 36.873 + 0.713\ LP_t$$

Post-liberalisation Era II—1991 to 2000 and D = 1;

$$\text{then } WR_t = 154.201 + 0.194\ LP_t$$

The differential intercept and the differential slope parameter are significant. The function has shifted from period I to period II due to significant difference in intercept values and in slope parameters. In post-liberalisation period though the intercept has increased but the slope of regression line has become flatter, i.e. the relationship between wage rate and labour productivity during post-reform era has weakened in Punjab.

Taking wage rate as dependent upon time, dummy, labour productivity and product of dummy times labour productivity, model XXI showed non-significant result.

Taking labour productivity as dependent upon trend, dummy, wage rate and product of dummy times wage rate, models XXII-XXIII showed non-significant results.

TABLE 10.12.2
Regression Function for Labour Productivity (Punjab—All Industries)

Dependent Variable—Partial Labour Productivity

Explanatory Variables	*Model Numbers*								
	XI	*XII*	*XIII*	*XIV*	*XV*	*XVI*	*XVII*	*XVIII*	*XIX*
(1)	*(2)*	*(3)*	*(4)*	*(5)*	*(6)*	*(7)*	*(8)*	*(9)*	*(10)*
Constant	0.726 (0.616)	0.308 (0.265)	1.218 (0.930)	0.937 (0.723)	0.855 (0.650)	2.918 (1.997)	3.005 (3.342)	2.334 (2.556)	0.963 (1.270)
ln Time	0.067 (0.726)	0.040 (0.353)	0.118 (0.784)	0.108 (0.644)	0.136 (0.721)	0.48** (2.100)	0.235* (3.181)	0.221** (2.312)	0.077 (0.804)
ln WR_t	0.832* (3.027)								
ln WR_{t-1}		0.933* (3.294)							
ln WR_{t-2}			0.716** (2.152)						
ln WR_{t-3}				0.781** (2.290)					
ln WR_{t-4}					0.788** (2.203)				

(Contd.)

TABLE 10.12.2 (CONTD.)

(1)	(2)	(3)	(4)	(5)	(6)	(7)	(8)	(9)	(10)
ln WR_{t-5}						0.182 (0.445)			
ln $(K/L)_t$							0.297 (1.433)		
ln $(K/L)_{t-1}$								0.438*** (1.971)	
ln $(K/L)_{t-2}$									0.789* (4.085)
R^2	0.729	0.764	0.702	0.718	0.729	0.679	0.657	0.706	0.792
$\tilde{R}^2$	0.707	0.745	0.676	0.692	0.703	0.647	0.630	0.681	0.774
S	0.183	0.168	0.184	0.177	0.174	0.188	0.205	0.188	0.153
F	33.59	38.95	27.06	28.02	28.19	21.12	23.99	28.76	43.88
D-W	1.503	1.315	1.496	1.446	1.315	1.207	0.793	1.123	1.122
$\tilde{\rho}$	0.246	0.339	0.247	0.263	0.326	0.345	0.562	0.432	0.428

Notes : 1. Figures in brackets are the respective 't' values.
2. * ** *** Indicates significant at 1%, 5% and 10% levels respectively.

TABLE 10.12.3

Structural Stability of Regression Functions (Punjab—All Industries)

Dependent Variables	*I*		*II*	
	Real Wage Rate		*Labour Productivity*	
Explanatory Variables	*Model Numbers*			
	XX	*XXI*	*XXII*	*XXIII*
Constant	36.873 (1.562)	70.348 (3.801)	17.523 (0.421)	143.984 -2.241
Time		4.77* (4.758)		8.681** (2.438)
Dummy	117.328* (3.030)	15.33 (0.434)	71.899 (0.794)	-156.548 (-1.254)
LP_t	0.713* (4.074)	0.114 (0.636)		
$D . LP_t$	-0.519** (-2.372)	-0.112 (-0.623)		
WR_t			0.873* (2.798)	-0.727 (-1.016)
$D . WR_t$			-0.179 (-0.325)	0.906 (1.410)
R^2	0.763	0.88	0.699	0.761
$\tilde{R}^2$	0.733	0.86	0.662	0.719
S	22.378	16.227	36.051	32.829
F	25.72	42.35	18.59	18.30
D-W	1.813	1.921	1.459	1.641
$\tilde{\rho}$	0.09	-0.005	0.27	0.134

Notes : 1. Figures in brackets are the respective 't' values.
2. * ** *** Indicates significant at 1% and 5% levels respectively.

13. RAJASTHAN

Effect of Productivity on Wages

Nine models regarding effect of productivity and capital intensity on wages have been estimated (Table 10.13.1) and the results of selected models with significant effect of explanatory variables are discussed on next page.

TABLE 10.13.1
Regression Function for Wages (Rajasthan—All Industries)

Dependent Variable—Real Wage Rate

Explanatory Variables	*Model Numbers*								
	I	*II*	*III*	*IV*	*V*	*VI*	*VII*	*VIII*	*IX*
(1)	*(2)*	*(3)*	*(4)*	*(5)*	*(6)*	*(7)*	*(8)*	*(9)*	*(10)*
Constant	3.760 (16.850)	3.808 (25.417)	3.824 (23.436)	3.261 (15.668)	3.803 (24.068)	3.819 (21.320)	3.103 (6.230)	4.146 (6.748)	4.095 (6.801)
ln Time	0.112* (4.218)	0.236* (9.734)	0.242* (8.173)	0.096* (3.484)	0.232* (8.763)	0.239* (7.191)	0.157* (5.451)	0.201* (8.405)	0.202* (8.427)
ln LP_t	0.227* (4.488)								
ln LP_{t-1}		0.072*** (1.798)							
ln LP_{t-2}			0.066 (1.453)						
ln $(K/L)_t$				0.253* (4.870)					
ln $(K/L)_{t-1}$					0.073*** (1.737)				

ln $(K/L)_{t-2}$						0.067 (1.342)			
ln TFPK							0.263** (2.319)		
ln TFPS								0.023 (0.173)	
ln TFPT									0.034 (0.260)
R^2	0.855	0.927	0.906	0.866	0.926	0.905	0.785	0.739	0.740
$\tilde{R}^2$	0.844	0.921	0.898	0.855	0.920	0.896	0.768	0.718	0.719
S	0.078	0.056	0.058	0.075	0.056	0.058	0.095	0.105	0.105
F	73.96	152.47	110.66	80.80	151.17	109.15	45.67	35.43	35.51
D-W	1.539	1.195	1.086	1.871	1.194	1.206	1.399	1.068	1.069
$\tilde{\rho}$	0.077	0.329	0.387	-0.062	0.320	0.320	0.095	0.238	0.238

Notes : 1. Figures in brackets are the respective 't' values.
2. * ** *** Indicates significant at 1%, 5% and 10% levels respectively.

Consider the regression equation in Model II in which wage rate depends upon trend and one period lagged partial labour productivity. Coefficient of time is 0.236 and trend is upward and is highly significant. The coefficient of LP_{t-1} is 0.072 and it shows that 100 percent increase in labour productivity brings about 7.2 percent increase in wage rate in the next year, keeping the effect of time constant. The value of R^2 is 0.927 and of $\tilde{R}^2$ is 0.921 which reveals that about 92.7 percent variations in wage rate were due to trend and one period lagged partial labour productivity. The given model fits the data well.

Consider the regression equation in Model V in which real wage rate depends upon trend and one period lagged capital intensity. The coefficient of time is 0.232 and trend is upward and is highly significant. The slope coefficient of $(K/L)_{t-1}$ is 0.073 and this shows that 100 percent increase in capital intensity, keeping the effect of time constant, brings about 7.3 percent increase in wage rate in the next year. The value of R^2 is 0.926 and of $\tilde{R}^2$ is 0.920 which reveals that about 92.6 percent variations in wage rate were due to trend and one period lagged capital intensity. The given model fits the data well.

In Model VII real wage rate depends upon trend and total factor productivity index (Kendrick). Coefficient of time is 0.157 and is statistically highly significant. The slope coefficient of TFPK is 0.263 and this shows that 100 percent increase in TFPK brings about 26.3 percent increase in wage rate, keeping the effect of time constant. The value of R^2 is 0.785 and of $\tilde{R}^2$ is 0.768 which indicates that about 78.5 percent variations in wage rate were due to time and TFPK. The given model fits the data well.

Effect of Wages on Productivity

In Model XIV (Table 10.13.2) labour productivity depends upon trend and four period lagged wage rate. Coefficient of time is 0.371 and this shows that trend is upward and mildly significant. The slope coeffiecient 1.065 shows that 100 percent increase in wage rate results into 106.5 percent increase in labour productivity in the next fourth year, keeping the effect of time constant. The value of R^2 is 0.786 and of $\tilde{R}^2$ is 0.766 which indicates that 78.6 percent variations in labour productivity were due to trend and fourth year lagged wage rate. The model fits the data well.

TABLE 10.13.2
Regression Function for Labour Productivity (Rajasthan—All Industries)

Dependent Variable—Partial Labour Productivity

Explanatory Variables	*Model Numbers*									
	X	*XI*	*XII*	*XIII*	*XIV*	*XV*	*XVI*	*XVII*	*XVIII*	*XIX*
(1)	*(2)*	*(3)*	*(4)*	*(5)*	*(6)*	*(7)*	*(8)*	*(9)*	*(10)*	*(11)*
Constant	-4.507 (-2.411)	-2.254 (-1.173)	-1.719 (-0.844)	-2.199 (-1.129)	-1.125 (-0.554)	-1.887 (-0.989)	0.572 (1.082)	1.212 (2.286)	0.894 (1.623)	1.425 (2.304)
ln Time	-0.004 (-0.039)	0.187 (1.430)	0.232 (1.414)	0.234 (1.312)	0.371*** (1.784)	0.349 (1.614)	0.043 (0.611)	0.217** (2.442)	0.217** (2.124)	0.366** (2.773)
ln WR_t	1.969* (4.488)									
ln WR_{t-1}		1.396* (2.992)								
ln WR_{t-2}			1.262** (2.474)							
ln WR_{t-3}				1.367** (2.727)						
ln WR_{t-4}					1.065*** (1.986)					

(Contd.)

TABLE 10.13.2 (CONTD.)

(1)	(2)	(3)	(4)	(5)	(6)	(7)	(8)	(9)	(10)	(11)
ln WR_{t-5}						1.244** (2.406)				
ln $(K/L)_t$							0.839* (6.366)			
ln $(K/L)_{t-1}$								0.624* (4.423)		
ln $(K/L)_{t-2}$									0.696* (4.545)	
ln $(K/L)_{t-3}$										0.51* (2.835)
R^2	0.753	0.786	0.774	0.801	0.786	0.812	0.830	0.838	0.849	0.805
$\tilde{R}^2$	0.733	0.769	0.754	0.783	0.766	0.793	0.816	0.825	0.836	0.787
S	0.231	0.218	0.220	0.204	0.209	0.195	0.191	0.189	0.179	0.202
F	38.01	44.15	39.28	44.31	38.62	43.10	60.81	62.23	64.63	45.44
D-W	1.074	1.052	1.347	1.190	1.424	1.715	1.860	1.889	1.611	1.753
$\tilde{\rho}$	0.396	0.420	0.312	0.390	0.281	0.137	0.014	0.052	0.184	0.119

Notes : 1. Figures in brackets are the respective 't' values.
2. * ** *** Indicates significant at 1%, 5% and 10% levels respectively.

Consider the regression equations in Models XVI-XIX in which labour productivity depends upon trend and up to three year lagged capital intensity. The regression coefficient of current year capital intensity was the highest and its level of significance as indicated by 't' value was also the highest. With time lag its level of significance decreased but it remained significant at one percent level. This indicated that capital intensity up to three years lag affected the labour productivity significantly. In case of Model XVIII coefficient of time is 0.217 and it is upward and significant. The slope coefficient shows that 100 percent increase in $(K/L)_{t-2}$ brings about 69.6 percent increase in labour productivity in the next second year. Thus capital intensity, which is an index of intensity of mechanisation, showed that an increase in capital-labour ratio helped in raising the productivity of labour. The value of R^2 is 0.849 and of $\tilde{R}^2$ is 0.836 which reveals that 84.9 percent variations in labour productivity were due to trend and second year lagged capital intensity. The given model fits the data well.

Pre and Post-liberalisation Period

Consider the regression equation in Model XX in which wage rate is dependent upon dummy, labour productivity and product of dummy times labour productivity variables in Table 10.13.3. The estimated equation is :

$$WR_t = 45.469 + 87.243\ D + 0.616\ LP_t - 0.584\ D\ .\ LP_t$$

Pre-liberalisation Era I—1973 to 1990 and D = 0;

then $WR_t = 45.469 + 0.616\ LP_t$

Post-liberalisation Era II—1991 to 2000 and D = 1;

then $WR_t = 132.712 + 0.032\ LP_t$

The differential intercept and the differential slope parameter are highly significant. The function has shifted from period I to period II due to significant difference in intercept values and in slope parameters. In post-liberalisation period though the intercept has increased but, the slope of regression line has become flatter, i.e. the relationship between wage and labour productivity during post-reform era has weakened in Rajasthan.

TABLE 10.13.3
Structural Stability of Regression Functions (Rajasthan—All Industries)

Dependent Variables	*I*		*II*	
	Real Wage Rate		*Labour Productivity*	
Explanatory Variables	*Model Numbers*			
	XX	*XXI*	*XXII*	*XXIII*
Constant	45.469 (4.566)	57.997 (7.337)	-14.844 (-0.305)	100.182 (1.582)
Time		1.815* (4.520)		5.471** (2.522)
Dummy	87.243* (5.258)	50.551* (3.423)	-11.978 (-0.054)	-184.105 (-0.865
LP_t	0.616* (6.002)	0.302* (2.925)		
$D . LP_t$	-0.584* (-4.889)	-0.358* (-3.508)		
WR_t			1.056** (2.282)	-0.552 (-0.724)
$D . WR_t$			0.652 (0.401)	1.748 (1.139)
R^2	0.849	0.92	0.799	0.843
$\tilde{R}^2$	0.83	0.906	0.774	0.816
S	9.071	6.743	31.235	28.24
F	44.89	66.03	31.88	30.84
D-W	1.46	1.517	1.689	2.02
$\tilde{\rho}$	0.243	0.122	0.099	-0.091

Notes : 1. Figures in brackets are the respective 't' values.
2. * ** Indicates significant at 1% and 5% levels respectively.

In Model XXI wage rate depends upon time, dummy, labour productivity and product of dummy times labour productivity variables. The estimated equation is :

$$WR_t = 57.997 + 1.815\ t + 50.551\ D + 0.302\ LP_t - 0.358\ D . LP_t$$

Pre-liberalisation Era I—1973 to 1990 and D = 0;

then $WR_t = 57.997 + 1.815\ t + 0.302\ LP_t$

Post-liberalisation Era II—1991 to 2000 and D = 1;
then $WR_t = 108.548 + 1.815\ t - 0.056\ LP_t$

The trend effect in pre and post-reform period remains the same. The differential intercept and the differential slope parameter are highly significant. The function has shifted from period I to period II due to significant difference in intercept values and in slope parameters. In post-liberalisation period though the intercept has increased but, the slope of regression line has become flatter, i.e. the relationship between wage and labour productivity during post-reform era has weakened in Rajasthan.

Taking labour productivity as dependent upon trend, dummy, wage rate and product of dummy times wage rate, models XXII-XXIII showed non-significant results.

14. TAMIL NADU

Effect of Productivity on Wages

Taking wage rate as dependent upon trend and up to five year lagged labour productivity, models I-VI (Table 10.14.1) showed non-significant results.

Taking wage rate as dependent upon trend and up to three period lagged capital intensity, models VII-X showed non-significant results.

Effect of Wages on Productivity

In Model XIV (Table 10.14.2) labour productivity depends upon trend and current period wage rate. Coefficient of time is 0.148 and this is upward and significant. The slope coeffiecient 1.488 shows that 100 percent increase in wage rate results into 148.8 percent increase in labour productivity in the same year, keeping theœffect of time constant. The value of R^2 is 0.825 and of $\bar{R}^2$ is 0.811 which indicates that 82.5 percent variations in labour productivity were due to trend ana current period wage rate. The model fits the data well.

Consider the regression equation in Model XVII in which labour productivity depends upon trend and one year lagged capital intensity. Coefficient of time is 0.294 and it is upward and highly significant. The slope coefficient shows that 100

TABLE 10.14.1

Regression Function for Wages (Tamil Nadu—All Industries)

Dependent Variable—Real Wage Rate

Explanatory Variables	*Model Numbers*												
	I	*II*	*III*	*IV*	*V*	*VI*	*VII*	*VIII*	*IX*	*X*	*XI*	*XII*	*XIII*
(1)	*(2)*	*(3)*	*(4)*	*(5)*	*(6)*	*(7)*	*(8)*	*(9)*	*(10)*	*(11)*	*(12)*	*(13)*	*(14)*
Constant	3.138 (11.680)	3.821 (15.177)	3.906 (14.734)	4.206 (15.351)	4.229 (15.760)	3.932 (14.161)	3.720 (25.615)	4.037 (30.728)	4.016 (30.386)	4.012 (29.678)	4.476 (6.101)	4.415 (6.652)	4.497 (6.855)
ln Time	0.025 (0.930)	0.138* (4.340)	0.146* (3.697)	0.193* (4.042)	0.218* (4.026)	0.171* (2.809)	0.039 (1.537)	0.148* (4.982)	0.141* (3.912)	0.141* (3.295)	0.129* (5.741)	0.127* (6.079)	0.127* (6.141)
ln LP_t	0.301* (4.506)												
ln LP_{t-1}		0.100 (1.510)											
ln LP_{t-2}			0.078 (1.071)										
ln LP_{t-3}				-0.011 (-0.137)									
ln LP_{t-4}					-0.031 (-0.376)								

ln LP_{t-5}						0.059 (0.685)							
ln $(K/L)_t$							0.171* (4.406)						
ln $(K/L)_{t-1}$								0.049 (1.275)					
ln $(K/L)_{t-2}$									0.057 (1.381)				
ln $(K/L)_{t-3}$										0.059 (1.318)			
ln TFPK											-0.031 (-0.192)		
ln TFPS												-0.017 (-0.121)	
ln TFPT													-0.035 (-0.248)
R^2	0.779	0.830	0.784	0.735	0.722	0.693	0.775	0.826	0.790	0.754	0.601	0.601	0.601
$\tilde{R}^2$	0.762	0.816	0.765	0.711	0.696	0.662	0.757	0.811	0.772	0.732	0.569	0.569	0.569
S	0.068	0.060	0.063	0.066	0.065	0.066	0.068	0.061	0.062	0.063	0.091	0.091	0.091
F	44.18	58.60	41.62	30.46	27.28	22.58	43.07	56.84	43.30	33.70	18.82	18.79	18.85
D-W	1.514	1.292	1.238	1.183	1.229	1.192	1.365	1.292	1.282	1.265	1.172	1.168	1.184
$\tilde{\rho}$	0.201	0.323	0.360	0.369	0.355	0.362	0.269	0.327	0.324	0.339	0.236	0.238	0.229

Notes : 1. Figures in brackets are the respective 't' values.
2. * ** *** Indicates significant at 1%, 5% and 10% levels respectively.

TABLE 10.14.2
Regression Function for Labour Productivity (Tamil Nadu—All Industries)

Dependent Variable—Partial Labour Productivity

Explanatory Variables	*Model Numbers*				
	XIV	*XV*	*XVI*	*XVII*	*XVIII*
(1)	*(2)*	*(3)*	*(4)*	*(5)*	*(6)*
Constant	-2.475	2.119	2.274	2.820	2.920
	(-1.726)	(1.641)	(9.294)	(12.812)	(12.430)
ln Time	0.148**	0.401*	0.094**	0.294*	0.327*
	(2.742)	(6.711)	(2.199)	(5.933)	(5.105)
ln WR_t	1.488*				
	(4.506)				
ln WR_{t-1}		0.361			
		(1.189)			
ln $(K/L)_t$			0.473*		
			(7.232)		
ln $(K/L)_{t-1}$				0.257*	
				(4.005)	
ln $(K/L)_{t-2}$					0.221*
					(2.998)
R^2	0.825	0.875	0.897	0.921	0.897
$\tilde{R}^2$	0.811	0.864	0.889	0.914	0.888
S	0.150	0.129	0.115	0.103	0.110
F	58.76	83.91	109.10	139.12	100.04
D-W	1.341	1.326	2.118	1.835	1.837
$\tilde{\rho}$	0.265	0.328	-0.099	0.068	0.063

Notes : 1. Figures in brackets are the respective 't' values.
2. * ** Indicate significant at 1%, and 5% levels respectively.

percent increase in $(K/L)_{t-1}$ brings about 25.7 percent increase in labour productivity in the next year. The value of R^2 is 0.921 and of $\tilde{R}^2$ is 0.914 which reveals that 92.1 percent variations in labour productivity were due to trend and one year lagged capital intensity. The given model fits the data well.

Pre and Post-liberalisation Period

Consider the regression equation in Model XIX, in which wage rate is dependent upon dummy, labour productivity and product of dummy times labour productivity variables in Table 10.14.3. The estimated equation is :

$$WR_t = 57.239 + 48.869\ D + 0.401\ LP_t - 0.341\ D\ .\ LP_t$$

Pre-liberalisation Era I—1973 to 1990 and D = 0;

then $WR_t = 57.239 + 0.401\ LP_t$

Post-liberalisation Era II—1991 to 2000 and D = 1;

then $WR_t = 106.108 + 0.06\ LP_t$

TABLE 10.14.3
Structural Stability of Regression Functions (Tamil Nadu—All Industries)

Dependent Variables	*I*		*II*	
	Real Wage Rate		*Labour Productivity*	
Explanatory Variables	*Model Numbers*			
	XIX	*XX*	*XXI*	*XXII*
Constant	57.239 (8.538)	63.403 (9.048)	-90.209 (-3.138)	-37.962 (-1.005)
Time		0.95*** (2.022)		2.001*** (1.990)
Dummy	48.869*** (1.932)	37.356 (1.526)	236.326* (3.246)	158.235*** (2.000)
LP_t	0.401* (6.357)	0.253** (2.688)		
$D\ .\ LP_t$	-0.341** (-2.212)	-0.292*** (-1.984)		
WR_t			1.961* (6.768)	1.237** (2.719)
$D\ .\ WR_t$			-1.736** (-2.701)	-1.194*** (-1.796)
R^2	0.767	0.802	0.883	0.9
$\tilde{R}^2$	0.738	0.768	0.868	0.883
S	7.297	6.868	15.16	14.31
F	26.35	23.33	60.29	51.78
D-W	1.754	1.697	1.724	1.813
$\tilde{\rho}$	0.117	0.084	0.124	0.077

Notes : 1. Figures in brackets are the respective 't' values.

2. * ** *** Indicates significant at 1%, 5% and 10% levels respectively.

The differential intercept and the differential slope parameter are significant. The function has shifted from period I to period II due to significant difference in intercept values and in slope parameters. In post-liberalisation period though the intercept has increased but, the slope of regression line has become flatter, i.e. the relationship between wage rate and labour productivity during post-reform era has weakened in Tamil Nadu.

In Model XX wage rate depends upon time, dummy, labour productivity and product of dummy times labour productivity variables. The estimated equation is :

$WR_t = 63.403 + 0.95\ t + 37.356\ D + 0.253\ LP_t - 0.292\ D\ .\ LP_t$

Pre-liberalisation Era I—1973 to 1990 and D = 0;

then $WR_t = 63.403 + 0.95\ t + 0.253\ LP_t$

Post-liberalisation Era II—1991 to 2000 and D = 1;

then $WR_t = 100.759 + 0.95\ t - 0.039\ LP_t$

The trend effect in pre and post-reform period remains the same. The differential intercept is non-significant but the differential slope parameter is mildly significant. In post-liberalisation period the slope of regression line has become flatter, i.e. the relationship between wage and labour productivity during post-reform era has weakened in Tamil Nadu.

Consider the regression equation in Model XXI, in which labour productivity is dependent upon dummy, wage rate and product of dummy times wage rate variables. The estimated equation is :

$LP_t = -90.209 + 236.326\ D + 1.961\ WR_t - 1.736\ D\ .\ WR_t$

Pre-liberalisation Era I—1973 to 1990 and D = 0;

then $LP_t = -90.209 + 1.961\ WR_t$

Post-liberalisation Era II—1991 to 2000 and D = 1;

then $LP_t = 146.117 + 0.225\ WR_t$

The differential intercept and differential slope parameter are significant. The function has shifted from period I to period II due to significant difference in intercept values and in slope parameters. In post-liberalisation period the intercept has increased but the slope of regression line has become flatter, i.e. the relationship between labour productivity and wage rate during post-reform era has weakened in Tamil Nadu. Thus after liberalisation the labour productivity has become less responsive to wage rate.

Consider the regression equation in Model XXII, in which labour productivity is dependent upon time, dummy, wage rate and product of dummy times wage rate variables. The estimated equation is :

$$LP_t = -37.962 + 2.001\ t + 158.235\ D + 1.237\ WR_t - 1.194\ D\ .\ WR_t$$

Pre-liberalisation Era I—1973 to 1990 and D = 0;

$$\text{then } LP_t = -37.962 + 2.001\ t + 1.237\ WR_t$$

Post-liberalisation Era II—1991 to 2000 and D = 1;

$$\text{then } LP_t = 120.273 + 2.001\ t + 0.043\ WR_t$$

The trend effect in pre and post-reform period remains the same. The differential intercept and differential slope parameter are mildly significant. The function has shifted from period I to period II due to significant difference in intercept values and in slope parameters. In post-liberalisation period the intercept has increased but the slope of regression line has become flatter i.e. the relationship between labour productivity and wage rate during post-reform era has weakened in Tamil Nadu. Thus after liberalisation the labour productivity has become less responsive to wage rate.

15. UTTAR PRADESH

Effect of Productivity on Wages

Eleven models regarding effect of productivity and capital intensity on wages have been estimated (Table 10.15.1) and the results of selected models with significant effect of explanatory variables are discussed below :

Consider the regression equation in Model I in which wage rate depends upon trend and current period partial labour productivity. Coefficient of time is 0.17 and trend is upward and is highly significant. The coefficient of LP_t is 0.308 and it shows that 100 percent increase in labour productivity brings about

TABLE 10.15.1
Regression Function for Wages
(Uttar Pradesh—All Industries)

Dependent Variable—Real Wage Rate

Explanatory Variables	*Model Numbers*										
	I	*II*	*III*	*IV*	*V*	*VI*	*VII*	*VIII*	*IX*	*X*	*XI*
(1)	*(2)*	*(3)*	*(4)*	*(5)*	*(6)*	*(7)*	*(8)*	*(9)*	*(10)*	*(11)*	*(12)*
Constant	3.181 (16.124)	3.319 (15.800)	3.601 (20.212)	3.629 (21.468)	3.644 (23.009)	3.643 (23.326)	3.646 (23.912)	2.896 (4.530)	3.045 (8.652)	3.715 (5.245)	2.370 (4.213)
ln Time	0.17* (5.071)	0.217* (4.737)	0.188* (4.617)	0.224* (4.400)	0.274* (4.683)	0.361* (5.564)	0.439* (6.170)	0.275* (7.108)	0.339* (13.104)	0.331* (10.373)	0.169* (4.398)
ln LP_t	0.308* (6.095)										
ln LP_{t-1}		0.26* (4.445)									
ln $(K/L)_t$			0.218* (4.421)								0.24* (5.148)
ln $(K/L)_{t-1}$				0.196* (3.760)							
ln $(K/L)_{t-2}$					0.168* (3.164)						

$\ln (K/L)_{t-3}$						0.123** (2.204)					
$\ln (K/L)_{t-4}$							0.080 (1.392)				
ln TFPK								0.323** (2.273)			
ln TFPS									0.294* (3.744)		
ln TFPT										0.133 (0.888)	0.246** (2.288)
R^2	0.923	0.907	0.893	0.893	0.897	0.905	0.906	0.842	0.878	0.816	0.912
$\tilde{R}^2$	0.917	0.899	0.885	0.885	0.888	0.897	0.897	0.830	0.868	0.801	0.901
S	0.090	0.095	0.106	0.102	0.097	0.092	0.089	0.129	0.113	0.139	0.098
F	150.79	117.28	104.54	100.67	100.30	105.20	100.85	66.76	90.01	55.25	83.25
D-W	1.765	1.821	1.435	1.554	1.582	1.866	1.934	1.173	1.507	0.807	1.697
$\tilde{\rho}$	0.114	0.072	0.282	0.215	0.148	0.026	-0.002	0.354	0.181	0.515	0.151

Notes : 1. Figures in brackets are the respective 't' values.
2. * ** Indicates significant at 1% and 5% levels respectively.

30.8 percent increase in wage rate in the same year, keeping the effect of time constant. The value of R^2 is 0.923 and of $\tilde{R}^2$ is 0.917 which reveals that about 92.3 percent variations in wage rate were due to trend and current period partial labour productivity. The given model fits the data well.

Consider the regression equations in models III-VII in which wage rate depends upon trend and up to four year lagged capital intensity. The regression coefficient of current year capital intensity was the highest and its level of significance as indicated by 't' value was also the highest. With time lag the regression coefficient and its level of significance decreased but it remained significant up to the third lagged year. This indicated that capital intensity up to three years lag affected the labour productivity significantly. In case of Model VI coefficient of time is 0.361 and it is upward and highly significant. The slope coefficient shows that 100 percent increase in $(K/L)_{t-3}$ brings about 12.3 percent increase in labour productivity in the next third year. The value of R^2 is 0.905 and of $\tilde{R}^2$ is 0.897 which reveals that 90.5 percent variations in labour productivity were due to trend and third year lagged capital intensity. The given model fits the data well.

In Model VIII real wage rate depends upon trend and total factor productivity index (Kendrick). Coefficient of time is 0.275 and is statistically highly significant. The slope coefficient of TFPK is 0.323 and this shows that 100 percent increase in TFPK brings about 32.3 percent increase in wage rate, when the effect of time is held constant. The value of R^2 is 0.842 and of $\tilde{R}^2$ is 0.830 which indicates that about 84.2 percent variations in wage rate were due to time and TFPK. The given model fits the data well.

In Model IX real wage rate depends upon trend and total factor productivity index (Solow). Coefficient of time is 0.339 and is statistically highly significant. The slope coefficient of TFPS is 0.294 and this shows that 100 percent increase in TFPS brings about 29.4 percent increase in wage rate, when the effect of time is held constant. The value of R^2 is 0.878 and of $\tilde{R}^2$ is 0.868 which indicates that about 87.8 percent variations in wage rate were due to time and TFPS. The given model fits the data well.

In Model XI real wage rate depends upon trend, capital intensity and total factor productivity index (Translog). Coefficient of time is 0.169 and is statistically highly significant. The slope coefficient of $(K/L)_t$ is 0.24 and this shows that 100 percent increase in $(K/L)_t$ brings about 24.0 percent increase in wage rate, when other variables are held constant. The slope coefficient of TFPT is 0.246 and this shows that 100 percent increase in TFPT brings about 24.6 percent increase in wage rate, when other variables are held constant. The value of R^2 is 0.912 and of $\tilde{R}^2$ is 0.901 which indicates that about 91.2 percent variations in wage rate were due to time, capital intensity and TFPT. The given model fits the data well.

Effect of Wages on Productivity

In Model XV (Table 10.15.2) labour productivity depends upon trend and three period lagged wage rate. Coefficient of time is 0.426 and this shows that trend is upward and mildly significant. The slope coeffiecient 0.946 shows that 100 percent increase in wage rate results into 94.6 percent increase in labour productivity in the next third year, keeping the effect of time constant. The value of R^2 is 0.862 and of $\tilde{R}^2$ is 0.849 which indicates that 86.2 percent variations in labour productivity were due to trend and third year lagged wage rate. The model fits the data well.

Consider the regression equations in models XVII-XXII in which labour productivity depends upon trend and up to five year lagged capital intensity. The regression coefficient of current year capital intensity was the highest and its level of significance as indicated by t value was also the highest. With time lag its level of significance decreased. This indicated that capital intensity up to five years lag affected the labour productivity significantly. In case of Model XXI coefficient of time is 0.623 and it is upward and highly significant. The slope coefficient shows that 100 percent increase in $(K/L)_{t-4}$ brings about 38.6 percent increase in labour productivity in the next fourth year. The value of R^2 is 0.931 and of $\tilde{R}^2$ is 0.924 which reveals that 93.1 percent variations in labour productivity were due to trend and fourth year lagged capital intensity. The given model fits the data well.

TABLE 10.15.2

Regression Function for Labour Productivity (Uttar Pradesh—All Industries)

Dependent Variable—Partial Labour Productivity

Explanatory Variables	*Model Numbers*										
	XII	*XIII*	*XIV*	*XV*	*XVI*	*XVII*	*XVIII*	*XIX*	*XX*	*XXI*	*XXII*
(1)	*(2)*	*(3)*	*(4)*	*(5)*	*(6)*	*(7)*	*(8)*	*(9)*	*(10)*	*(11)*	*(12)*
Constant	-4.659 (-3.357)	-2.434 (-1.591)	-2.511 (-1.856)	-0.843 (-0.551)	0.848 (0.573)	1.594 (4.226)	1.930 (5.163)	1.942 (5.696)	1.680 (5.510)	1.586 (6.091)	1.726 (5.712)
ln Time	-0.119 (-1.007)	0.126 (0.780)	0.148 (0.863)	0.426*** (1.953)	0.809* (3.488)	0.102 (1.183)	0.299** (2.657)	0.411* (3.263)	0.451* (3.561)	0.623* (5.120)	0.831* (5.372)
ln WR_t	1.941* (6.095)										
ln WR_{t-1}		1.397* (3.789)									
ln WR_{t-2}			1.408* (4.113)								
ln WR_{t-3}				0.946** (2.352)							
ln WR_{t-4}					0.414 (1.027)						

ln $(K/L)_t$						0.64* (6.134)					
ln $(K/L)_{t-1}$							0.478* (4.148)				
ln $(K/L)_{t-2}$								0.421* (3.674)			
ln $(K/L)_{t-3}$									0.459* (4.198)		
ln $(K/L)_{t-4}$										0.386* (3.945)	
ln $(K/L)_{t-5}$											0.243** (2.083)
R^2	0.851	0.843	0.883	0.862	0.885	0.852	0.854	0.872	0.904	0.931	0.904
$\tilde{R}^2$	0.839	0.830	0.873	0.849	0.874	0.840	0.842	0.861	0.895	0.924	0.894
S	0.225	0.233	0.200	0.215	0.196	0.225	0.225	0.209	0.179	0.152	0.174
F	71.26	64.57	86.54	68.57	80.70	71.90	70.27	78.14	103.50	140.69	93.68
D-W	1.535	1.750	1.265	1.443	1.463	1.451	1.353	1.398	1.896	1.812	1.590
$\tilde{\rho}$	0.183	0.084	0.311	0.167	0.216	0.271	0.322	0.269	0.016	0.047	0.168

Notes : 1. Figures in brackets are the respective 't' values.
2. * ** *** Indicates significant at 1%, 5% and 10% levels respectively.

Taking wage rate as dependent upon time, dummy, labour productivity and product of dummy times labour productivity (Table 10.15.3), models XXIII-XXIV showed non-significant results.

TABLE 10.15.3

Structural Stability of Regression Functions (Uttar Pradesh—All Industries)

Dependent Variables	*I*		*II*	
	Real Wage Rate		*Labour Productivity*	
Explanatory Variables	*Model Numbers*			
	XXIII	*XXIV*	*XXV*	*XXVI*
Constant	67.54 (4.937)	77.39 (7.324)	-37.641 (-1.343)	-12.675 (-0.284)
Time		4.564* (4.375)		2.127 (0.725)
Dummy	15.825 (0.414)	-56.562 (-1.701)	20.417 (0.300)	-28.349 (-0.295)
LP_t	0.703* (6.347)	0.244*** (1.821)		
$D . LP_t$	-0.186 (-1.144)	0.121 (0.853)		
WR_t			1.031* (5.631)	0.728 (1.593)
$D . WR_t$			0.293 (0.920)	0.485 (1.164)
R^2	0.882	0.936	0.933	0.934
$\tilde{R}^2$	0.868	0.925	0.925	0.923
S	19.951	15.056	27.228	27.501
F	59.93	83.72	111.33	81.98
D-W	1.69	1.929	1.869	1.824
$\tilde{\rho}$	0.08	-0.008	0.032	0.045

Notes : 1. Figures in brackets are the respective 't' values.
2. * ***Indicates significant at 1%, 10% levels respectively.

Taking labour productivity as dependent upon trend, dummy, wage rate and product of dummy times wage rate, models XXV-XXVI showed non-significant results.

16. WEST BENGAL

Effect of Productivity on Wages

Twelve models regarding effect of productivity and capital intensity on wages have been estimated (Table 10.16.1) and the results of selected models with significant effect of explanatory variables are discussed below:

Consider the regression equation in Model II in which wage rate depends upon trend and one period lagged partial labour productivity. Coefficient of time is 0.138 and trend is upward and is highly significant. The coefficient of LP_{t-1} is 0.195 and it shows that 100 percent increase in labour productivity brings about 19.5 percent increase in wage rate in the next year, keeping the effect of time constant. The value of R^2 is 0.940 and of $\tilde{R}^2$ is 0.935 which reveals that about 94.0 percent variations in wage rate were due to trend and one year lagged partial labour productivity. The given model fits the data well.

Consider the regression equations in models IV-IX in which wage rate depends upon trend and up to five year lagged capital intensity. The regression coefficient of current year capital intensity was the highest and it remained significant up to the fifth lagged year. In case of Model VIII coefficient of time is 0.188 and it is upward and highly significant. The slope coefficient shows that 100 percent increase in $(K/L)_{t-4}$ brings about 4.8 percent increase in labour productivity in the next fourth year. The value of R^2 is 0.941 and of $\tilde{R}^2$ is 0.936 which reveals that 94.1 percent variations in labour productivity were due to trend and fourth year lagged capital intensity. The given model fits the data well.

In Model X real wage rate depends upon trend and total factor productivity index (Kendrick). Coefficient of time is 0.137 and is statistically highly significant. The slope coefficient of TFPK is 0.27 and this shows that 100 percent increase in TFPK brings about 27.0 percent increase in wage rate, when the effect of time is held constant. The value of R^2 is 0.855 and of $\tilde{R}^2$ is 0.844 which indicates that about 85.5 percent variations in wage rate were due to time and TFPK. The given model fits the data well.

Table 10.16.1
Regression Function for Wages (West Bengal—All Industries)

Dependent Variable—Real Wage Rate

Explanatory Variables	*Model Numbers*											
	I	*II*	*III*	*IV*	*V*	*VI*	*VII*	*VIII*	*IX*	*X*	*XI*	*XII*
(1)	*(2)*	*(3)*	*(4)*	*(5)*	*(6)*	*(7)*	*(8)*	*(9)*	*(10)*	*(11)*	*(12)*	*(13)*
Constant	3.103 (13.405)	3.519 (16.830)	3.544 (16.789)	4.065 (40.568)	4.090 (56.174)	4.072 (62.666)	4.077 (69.187)	4.089 (75.122)	4.070 (76.635)	3.187 (5.912)	4.731 (7.366)	4.623 (7.135)
ln Time	0.086* (5.090)	0.138* (7.375)	0.144* (6.467)	0.096* (4.382)	0.136* (6.438)	0.132* (5.528)	0.147* (5.146)	0.188* (6.008)	0.177* (5.195)	0.137* (7.758)	0.162* (10.568)	0.163* (10.754)
ln LP_t	0.306* (5.720)											
ln LP_{t-1}		0.195* (3.870)										
ln LP_{t-2}			0.188* (3.569)									
ln $(K/L)_t$				0.096* (3.713)								
ln $(K/L)_{t-1}$					0.072* (3.458)							

$\ln (K/L)_{t-2}$						0.078* (3.812)						
$\ln (K/L)_{t-3}$							0.07* (3.251)					
$\ln (K/L)_{t-4}$								0.048** (2.207)				
$\ln (K/L)_{t-5}$									0.058** (2.617)			
ln TFPK										0.27** (2.289)		
ln TFPS											-0.066 (-0.488)	
ln TFPT												-0.044 (-0.317)
R^2	0.924	0.940	0.932	0.887	0.935	0.936	0.939	0.941	0.938	0.855	0.827	0.826
$\tilde{R}^2$	0.918	0.935	0.926	0.878	0.930	0.930	0.934	0.936	0.932	0.844	0.813	0.812
S	0.043	0.038	0.038	0.053	0.039	0.037	0.034	0.033	0.032	0.060	0.066	0.066
F	152.31	189.10	158.55	98.25	173.52	167.07	170.57	167.81	150.68	73.84	59.57	59.17
D-W	2.026	2.390	2.206	1.713	1.751	2.071	2.510	2.611	2.457	0.980	1.028	0.997
$\tilde{\rho}$	-0.118	-0.198	-0.138	0.056	0.117	-0.109	-0.281	-0.317	-0.277	0.338	0.330	0.341

Notes : 1. Figures in brackets are the respective 't' values.
2. * ** Indicates significant at 1% and 5% levels respectively.

Effect of Wages on Productivity

Taking labour productivity as dependent upon trend and up to five year lagged wage rate, models XIII-XVIII (Table 10.16.2) showed non-significant results.

Taking labour productivity as dependent upon trend and up to three period lagged capital intensity, models XIX-XXII showed non-significant results.

Pre and Post-liberalisation Period

Consider the regression equation in Model XXIII, in which wage rate is dependent upon dummy, labour productivity and product of dummy times labour productivity variables in Table 10.16.3. The estimated equation is :

$$WR_t = 48.175 + 66.448\ D + 0.563\ LP_t - 0.4\ D\ .\ LP_t$$

Pre-liberalisation Era I—1973 to 1990 and D = 0;

then $WR_t = 48.175 + 0.563\ LP_t$

Post-liberalisation Era II—1991 to 2000 and D = 1;

then $WR_t = 114.623 + 0.163\ LP_t$

The differential intercept and the differential slope parameter are significant. The function has shifted from period I to period II due to significant difference in intercept values and in slope parameters. In post-liberalisation period though the intercept has increased but, the slope of regression line has become flatter, i.e. the relationship between wage and labour productivity during post-reform era has weakened in West Bengal.

Taking wage rate as dependent upon time, dummy, labour productivity and product of dummy times labour productivity, model XXIV showed non-significant result.

Taking labour productivity as dependent upon trend, dummy, wage rate and product of dummy times wage rate, models XXV-XXVI showed non-significant results.

17. ALL-INDIA

Effect of Productivity on Wages

Nine models regarding effect of productivity and capital intensity on wages have been estimated (Table 10.17.1) and the

TABLE 10.16.2

Regression Function for Labour Productivity (West Bengal—All Industries)

Dependent Variable—Partial Labour Productivity

Explanatory Variables	*Model Numbers*									
	XIII	*XIV*	*XV*	*XVI*	*XVII*	*XVIII*	*XIX*	*XX*	*XXI*	*XXII*
(1)	*(2)*	*(3)*	*(4)*	*(5)*	*(6)*	*(7)*	*(8)*	*(9)*	*(10)*	*(11)*
Constant	-3.881 (-2.712)	-2.207 (-1.22)	0.131 (0.062)	-2.762 (-1.245)	-0.226 (-0.094)	-1.083 (-0.428)	3.187 (15.989)	3.264 (17.315)	3.217 (20.590)	3.273 (20.694)
ln Time	-0.048 (-0.833)	0.025 (0.284)	0.148 (1.234)	0.015 (0.113)	0.191 (1.185)	0.156 (0.859)	0.042 (0.966)	0.077 (1.406)	0.062 (1.081)	0.064 (0.830)
ln WR_t	1.851* (5.720)									
ln WR_{t-1}		1.47* (3.509)								
ln WR_{t-2}			0.921*** (1.827)							
ln WR_{t-3}				1.602* (3.006)						
ln WR_{t-4}					0.977 (1.662)					

(*Contd.*)

TABLE 10.16.2 (CONTD.)

(1)	(2)	(3)	(4)	(5)	(6)	(7)	(8)	(9)	(10)	(11)
ln WR_{t-5}						1.18*** (1.874)				
ln $(K/L)_t$							0.3* (5.848)			
ln $(K/L)_{t-1}$								0.271* (5.017)		
ln $(K/L)_{t-2}$									0.29* (5.868)	
ln $(K/L)_{t-3}$										0.281* (4.854)
R^2	0.850	0.812	0.765	0.823	0.804	0.811	0.853	0.861	0.892	0.879
$\tilde{R}^2$	0.838	0.796	0.745	0.807	0.786	0.792	0.842	0.849	0.883	0.868
S	0.107	0.119	0.130	0.112	0.117	0.113	0.105	0.102	0.088	0.093
F	70.68	51.76	37.48	51.04	43.16	42.93	72.82	74.35	95.32	80.09
D-W	1,664	1.384	1.237	1.243	1.366	1.624	1.045	1.934	1.904	1.945
$\tilde{\rho}$	0.159	0.305	0.342	0.363	0.274	0.136	0.473	0.033	0.009	0.002

Notes : 1. Figures in brackets are the respective 't' values.
2. * *** Indicates significant at 1% and 10% levels respectively.

TABLE 10.16.3
Structural Stability of Regression Functions (West Bengal—All Industries)

Dependent Variables	*I*		*II*	
	Real Wage Rate		*Labour Productivity*	
Explanatory Variables	*Model Numbers*			
	XXIII	*XXIV*	*XXV*	*XXVI*
Constant	48.175	79.658	-26.249	-9.565
	(4.331)	(9.350)	(-0.797)	(-0.136)
Time	1.813*	0.449		
		(6.286)		(0.269)
Dummy	66.448*	9.33	40.514	30.246
	(2.865)	(0.549)	(0.434)	(0.295)
LP_t	0.563*	0.143		
	(5.943)	(1.611)		
D. LP_t	-0.4**	-0.073		
	(-2.762)	(-0.703)		
WR_t			1.254*	1.07
			(4.347)	(1.433)
D. WR_t			-0.078	-0.011
			(-0.117)	(-0.015)
R^2	0.866	0.951	0.869	0.869
$\tilde{R}^2$	0.849	0.942	0.853	0.847
S	7.245	4.489	14.79	15.084
F	51.79	111.05	53.05	38.27
D-W	1.67	2.711	1.78	1.752
$\tilde{\rho}$	0.142	-0.384	0.085	0.093

Notes : 1. Figures in brackets are the respective 't' values.
2. * ** Indicates significant at 1% and 5% levels respectively.

results of selected models with significant effect of explanatory variables are discussed below :

Consider the regression equation in Model II in which wage rate depends upon trend and one period lagged partial labour productivity. Coefficient of time is 0.196 and trend is upward and is highly significant. The coefficient of LP_{t-1} is 0.106 and it shows that 100 percent increase in labour productivity

TABLE 10.17.1

Regression Function for Wages (All India—All Industries)

Dependent Variable—Real Wage Rate

Explanatory Variables	*Model Numbers*								
	I	*II*	*III*	*IV*	*V*	*VI*	*VII*	*VIII*	*IX*
(1)	*(2)*	*(3)*	*(4)*	*(5)*	*(6)*	*(7)*	*(8)*	*(9)*	*(10)*
Constant	3.604 (18.394)	3.888 (22.207)	4.094 (21.210)	3.713 (25.863)	3.955 (29.297)	3.990 (29.073)	2.965 (4.153)	3.381 (4.737)	3.499 (4.815)
ln Time	0.128* (5.288)	0.196* (7.240)	0.239* (6.823)	0.103* (4.047)	0.18* (5.783)	0.193* (4.972)	0.171* (6.829)	0.189* (8.545)	0.194* (9.039)
ln LP_t	0.196* (4.100)								
ln LP_{t-1}		0.106** (2.326)							
ln LP_{t-2}			0.044 (0.830)						
ln $(K/L)_t$				0.179* (4.864)					
ln $(K/L)_{t-1}$					0.097** (2.540)				

ln $(K/L)_{t-2}$						0.085*** (1.987)			
ln TFPK							0.317*** (2.005)		
ln TFPS								0.223 (1.423)	
ln TFPT									0.197 (1.235)
R^2	0.916	0.935	0.915	0.928	0.937	0.925	0.880	0.871	0.868
$\tilde{R}^2$	0.910	0.929	0.907	0.922	0.932	0.918	0.870	0.860	0.858
S	0.058	0.049	0.052	0.053	0.049	0.049	0.069	0.072	0.072
F	137.09	172.28	123.23	161.59	178.81	141.77	91.34	84.19	82.40
D-W	1.465	1.037	1.172	1.294	1.224	1.196	1.342	1.189	1.140
$\tilde{\rho}$	0.208	0.480	0.390	0.315	0.387	0.397	0.189	0.249	0.268

Notes : 1. Figures in brackets are the respective 't' values.
2. * ** *** Indicates significant at 1%, 5% and 10% levels respectively.

brings about 10.6 percent increase in wage rate in the next year, keeping the effect of time constant. The value of R^2 is 0.935 and of $\tilde{R}^2$ is 0.929 which reveals that about 93.5 percent variations in wage rate were due to trend and one year lagged partial labour productivity. The given model fits the data well.

Consider the regression equation in Model V in which real wage rate depends upon trend and one period lagged capital intensity. The coefficient of time is 0.18 and trend is upward and is highly significant. The slope coefficient of $(K/L)_{t-1}$ is 0.097 and this shows that 100 percent increase in capital intensity, keeping the effect of time constant, brings about 9.7 percent increase in wage rate in the next year. The value of R^2 is 0.937 and of $\tilde{R}^2$ is 0.932 which reveals that about 93.7 percent variations in wage rate were due to trend and one year lagged capital intensity. The given model fits the data well.

In Model VII real wage rate depends upon trend and total factor productivity index (Kendrick). Coefficient of time is 0.171 and is statistically highly significant. The slope coefficient of TFPK is 0.317 and this shows that 100 percent increase in TFPK brings about 31.7 percent increase in wage rate, when the effect of time is held constant. The value of R^2 is 0.880 and of $\tilde{R}^2$ is 0.870 which indicates that about 88.0 percent variations in wage rate were due to time and TFPK. The given model fits the data well.

Effect of Wages on Productivity

In Model XVII (Table 10.17.2) labour productivity depends upon trend and seventh period lagged wage rate. Coefficient of time is 0.501 and this is highly significant. The slope coeffiecient 1.071 shows that 100 percent increase in wage rate results into 107.1 percent increase in labour productivity in the next seventh year, keeping the effect of time constant. The value of R^2 is 0.963 and of $\tilde{R}^2$ is 0.959 which indicates that 96.3 percent variations in labour productivity were due to trend and seventh period lagged wage rate. Hence wage rate is a highly significant explanatory variable. The model fits the data well.

Consider the regression equation in Model XXII in which labour productivity depends upon trend and third year lagged capital intensity. Coefficient of time is 0.179 and it is upward and mildly significant. The slope coefficient shows that 100

TABLE 10.17.2

Regression Function for Labour Productivity (All India—All Industries)

Dependent Variable—Partial Labour Productivity

Explanatory Variables	*Model Numbers*													
	X	*XI*	*XII*	*XIII*	*XIV*	*XV*	*XVI*	*XVII*	*XVIII*	*XIX*	*XX*	*XXI*	*XXII*	*XXIII*
(1)	*(2)*	*(3)*	*(4)*	*(5)*	*(6)*	*(7)*	*(8)*	*(9)*	*(10)*	*(11)*	*(12)*	*(13)*	*(14)*	*(15)*
Constant	-4.967	-4.243	-3.243	-2.760	-1.169	-1.366	-1.549	-1.388	1.265	1.078	1.434	1.731	1.807	1.976
	(-2.261)	(-2.031)	(-1.578)	(-1.283)	(-0.555)	(-0.696)	(-1.019)	(-1.063)	(0.803)	(4.699)	(5.511)	(5.800)	(6.210)	(6.771)
ln Time	-0.008	0.063	0.142	0.178	0.355***	0.377***	0.439**	0.501*	0.832*	-0.045	0.040	0.127	0.179***	0.301**
	(-0.075)	(0.480)	(0.944)	(0.966)	(1.757)	(1.820)	(2.532)	(3.079)	(3.767)	(-1.115)	(0.660)	(1.497)	(1.837)	(2.634)
ln WR_t	2.047*													
	(4.100)													
ln WR_{t-1}		1.869*												
		(3.823)												
ln WR_{t-2}			1.63*											
			(3.294)											
ln WR_{t-3}				1.516*										
				(2.833)										
ln WR_{t-4}					1.097***									
					(2.036)									
ln WR_{t-5}						1.13**								
						(2.195)								

(Contd.)

TABLE 10.17.2 (CONTD.)

(1)	(2)	(3)	(4)	(5)	(6)	(7)	(8)	(9)	(10)	(11)	(12)	(13)	(14)	(15)
ln WR_{t-6}							1.136** (2.780)							
ln WR_{t-7}								1.071* (2.973)						
ln WR_{t-8}									0.330 (0.732)					
ln $(K/L)_t$										0.773* (13.169)				
ln $(K/L)_{t-1}$											0.672* (9.133)			
ln $(K/L)_{t-2}$												0.58* (6.268)		
ln $(K/L)_{t-3}$													0.545* (5.559)	
ln $(K/L)_{t-4}$														0.455* (4.270)
R^2	0.823	0.875	0.888	0.895	0.902	0.916	0.953	0.963	0.938	0.963	0.955	0.939	0.940	0.937
$\tilde{R}^2$	0.809	0.865	0.879	0.886	0.893	0.908	0.948	0.959	0.931	0.960	0.951	0.934	0.935	0.931
S	0.186	0.156	0.145	0.138	0.131	0.119	0.089	0.076	0.093	0.085	0.094	0.107	0.104	0.105
F	58.13	84.01	91.48	93.93	96.60	109.27	191.07	234.73	128.97	322.70	255.11	177.99	173.87	156.61
D-W	0.964	0.774	0.975	1.063	1.130	1.391	2.148	2.248	1.930	1.918	1.578	1.555	1.361	1.403
$\tilde{\rho}$	0.505	0.603	0.478	0.449	0.402	0.197	-0.171	-0.186	-0.040	0.036	0.198	0.189	0.282	0.236

Notes : 1. Figures in brackets are the respective 't' values.
2. * ** *** Indicates significant at 1%, 5% and 10% levels respectively.

percent increase in $(K/L)_{t-3}$ brings about 54.5 percent increase in labour productivity in the next third year. The value of R^2 is 0.940 and of $\tilde{R}^2$ is 0.935 which reveals that 94.0 percent variations in labour productivity were due to trend and third year lagged capital intensity. The given model fits the data well.

Pre and Post-liberalisation Period

Consider the regression equation in Model XXIV, in which wage rate is dependent upon dummy, labour productivity and product of dummy times labour productivity variables in Table 10.17.3. The estimated equation is :

$$WR_t = 46.6 + 83.398\ D + 0.636\ LP_t - 0.515\ D\ .\ LP_t$$

Pre-liberalisation Era I—1973 to 1990 and D = 0;

then $WR_t = 46.6 + 0.636\ LP_t$

Post-liberalisation Era II—1991 to 2000 and D = 1;

then $WR_t = 129.998 + 0.121\ LP_t$

The differential intercept and the differential slope parameter are highly significant. The function has shifted from period I to period II due to significant difference in intercept values and in slope parameters. In post-liberalisation period though the intercept has increased but, the slope of regression line has become flatter, i.e. the relationship between wage and labour productivity during post-reform era has weakened in India.

In Model XXV wage rate depends upon time, dummy, labour productivity and product of dummy times labour productivity variables. The estimated equation is :

$$WR_t = 72.319 + 2.612\ t + 39.287\ D + 0.222\ LP_t - 0.268\ D\ .\ LP_t$$

Pre-liberalisation Era I—1973 to 1990 and D = 0;

then $WR_t = 72.319 + 2.612\ t + 0.222\ LP_t$

Post-liberalisation Era II—1991 to 2000 and D = 1;

then $WR_t = 111.606 + 2.612\ t - 0.046\ LP_t$

The trend effect in pre and post-reform period remains the same. The differential intercept and the differential slope parameter are significant. The function has shifted from period

TABLE 10.17.3
Structural Stability of Regression Functions (All India—All Industries)

Dependent Variables	*I*		*II*	
	Real Wage Rate		*Labour Productivity*	
Explanatory Variables	*Model Numbers*			
	XXIV	*XXV*	*XXVI*	*XXVII*
Constant	46.6 (5.339)	72.319 (8.620)	-49.824 (-1.75)	46.652 (0.883)
Time		2.612* (4.705)		4.434** (2.114)
Dummy	83.398* (3.084)	39.287*** (1.800)	165.67 (1.669)	77.673 (0.764)
LP_t	0.636* (9.153)	0.222** (2.184)		
$D \cdot LP_t$	-0.515* (-4.275)	-0.268** (-2.614)		
WR_t			1.384* (6.116)	0.268 (0.472)
$D \cdot WR_t$			-0.5 (-0.792)	-0.083 (-0.134)
R^2	0.892	0.945	0.937	0.947
$\tilde{R}^2$	0.879	0.936	0.929	0.938
S	8.784	6.405	19.398	18.132
F	66.28	99.03	118.92	103.19
D-W	1.126	1.325	1.328	1.393
$\tilde{\rho}$	0.382	0.332	0.326	0.244

Notes : 1. Figures in brackets are the respective 't' values.
2. * ** *** Indicates significant at 1%, 5% and 10% levels respectively.

I to period II due to significant difference in intercept values and in slope parameters. In post-liberalisation period though the intercept has increased but, the slope of regression line has become flatter, i.e. the relationship between wage and labour productivity during post-reform era has weakened in India.

Taking labour productivity as dependent upon trend, dummy, wage rate and product of dummy times wage rate, models XXVI-XXVII showed non-significant results.

18. INTER-TEMPORAL ANALYSIS OF WAGE-PRODUCTIVITY RELATIONSHIP

An inter-temporal analysis taking wage rate as dependent upon partial labour productivity (Table 10.18.1) in sixteen states revealed that the effect of labour productivity on wage rate increased during 1980-81 to 1990-91, but declined sizably in 2000-01. This corroborates the earlier findings of models XXIV and XXV in table 10.17.3 i.e. the relationship between wages and labour productivity during post-reform era has weakened in India.

TABLE 10.18.1
Wage Productivity Relationship in States : Results of Inter-Temporal Regression Analysis

Dependent Variable—Real Wage Rate

Explanatory Variables	*1980-81*	*1990-91*	*2000-01*
Constant	1.976 (1.586)	1.442 (0.689)	3.136 (3.360)
ln LP	0.568** (2.752)	0.64*** (2.060)	0.383** (2.866)
R^2	0.351	0.233	0.370
$\tilde{R}^2$	0.305	0.178	0.325
S	0.238	0.273	0.188
F	7.570	4.240	8.210
D-W	1.748	1.922	1.549
$\tilde{\rho}$	0.038	-0.052	0.045

Notes : 1. Figures in brackets are the respective 't' values.
2. ** *** Indicates significant at 5% and 10% levels respectively.

An inter-temporal analysis taking partial labour productivity as dependent upon wage rate (Table 10.18.2) in sixteen states showed that the effect of wage rate on labour productivity decreased during 1980-81 to 1990-91 but got strengthened in 2000-01. Thus, after liberalisation when market

TABLE 10.18.2
Wage Productivity Relationship in States : Results of Inter-Temporal Regression Analysis

Dependent Variable—Partial Labour Productivity

Explanatory Variables	*1980-81*	*1990-91*	*2000-01*
Constant	2.691 (2.216)	4.640 (4.568)	1.368 (0.699)
ln WR	0.618** (2.752)	0.363*** (2.060)	0.966** (2.866)
R^2	0.351	0.233	0.370
$\tilde{R}^2$	0.305	0.178	0.325
S	0.248	0.206	0.299
F	7.570	4.240	8.210
D-W	1.264	1.780	2.042
$\tilde{\rho}$	0.318	-0.059	-0.191

Notes : 1. Figures in brackets are the respective 't' values.
2. ** *** Indicates significant at 5% and 10% levels respectively.

forces have more important role to play, the labour productivity has become more responsive to wage rate.

It may be concluded from the discussion that labour productivity has positively and significantly affected the wage rate in all states except in Tamil Nadu. Capital intensity has also significantly affected the wage rate in all states except in Himachal Pradesh, Madhya Pradesh and Tamil Nadu. TFPK has positively and significantly affected the wage rate in Andhra Pradesh, Kerala, Madhya Pradesh, Maharashtra, Rajasthan, Uttar Pradesh, West Bengal. TFPS has also significantly affected the wage rate in Kerala, Madhya Pradesh, Maharashtra, Uttar Pradesh. TFPT has significantly affected the wage rate in Karnataka, Kerala, Maharashtra, Punjab, Uttar Pradesh.

Wage rate has positively and significantly affected labour productivity in all states except Assam, Bihar, Himachal Pradesh, Maharashtra, Orissa, Punjab and West Bengal. Capital intensity has significantly affected labour productivity in all states except Assam, Bihar, Gujarat, Haryana, Himachal

Pradesh, Madhya Pradesh, Maharashtra, Orissa and West Bengal.

It was found that the relationship between wages and labour productivity during post-reform era has weakened. This indicates that proportionate gains from productivity increase were not passed on to the workers in Andhra Pradesh, Gujarat, Haryana, Kerala, Maharashtra, Punjab, Rajasthan, Tamil Nadu, West Bengal and all-India. It was found that the relationship between wage and labour productivity during post-reform era has strengthened in Orissa only.

The relationship between labour productivity and wage rate during post-reform era has weakened in Assam and Tamil Nadu. It was found that the relationship between labour productivity and wage rate during post-reform era has strengthened in Gujarat, Haryana, Himachal Pradesh, Kerala, Madhya Pradesh and Maharashtra. After liberalisation when market forces have more important role to play, the labour productivity has become more responsive to wage rate.

Conclusions

In this chapter main findings of the thesis have been summarized and policy implications have been derived. The study entitled, "Wage Productivity Relationship in India: An Inter-Industry and Inter-State Analysis", examines the wage-productivity relationship in registered manufacturing sector. For inter-industry comparison, fourteen major industry groups of manufacturing sector were taken and for inter-state comparison, all industries in sixteen states along with all-India have been selected.

The major objectives of the study are :

1. To analyse the trends in different economic parameters and productivity indices in major industries at all-India level.
2. To analyse the trends in different economic parameters and productivity indices in all industries of different states and all-India level.
3. To compare the share of labour in GVA at constant prices in different industries at all-India level.
4. To compare the share of labour in GVA at constant prices in industries of major states and at all-India level.

5. To compare wage rate as well as labour productivity in different industries at all-India level and all-industries at state level.
6. To examine the extent of dependence of wage rate on labour productivity, capital intensity and total factor productivity in major industries at all-India level and all-industries at state level.
7. To analyse the dependence of labour productivity on wage rate and capital intensity in major industries at all-India level and all-industries at state level.
8. To examine the inter-temporal wage-productivity relationship in different states of the country.
9. To analyse the effect of liberalisation on relationship between wage rate and labour productivity in major industries at all-India level and all-industries at state level.

Chapter-I is introductory in nature, focusing on the need for linking wages and productivity. The Chapter-II examines the theoretical issues concerning wage-productivity relationship. The Chapter-III reviews the related empirical studies.

Data Base and Analytical Tools

Chapter-IV is devoted to the data base and methodology. The study is based on the Factory Sector data and covers the period 1973-74 to 2000-01. The NIC-1970 was followed to classify factories from 1973-74 to ASI 1988-89. NIC-1987 had then been introduced and followed till ASI 1997-98. From ASI 1998-99, the new series of classification, i.e. NIC-1998 has been introduced. The data have been taken at two digit level of industry and for two years, i.e. 1999-00 to 2000-01, the data of 3 and 4 digit level have been merged at two digit level of industry. However, due to certain conceptual problems (because of changed industrial classification from 1998), the study for inter-industry comparison for three industries namely, (i) cotton textiles; (ii) jute, hemp & mesta textiles, and (iii) textile products, has been restricted to 1973-74 to 1998-99 period.

The time series relating to value-added have been deflated by the wholesale price indices of different industry groups of manufacturing sector for different industries and by the wholesale price index of all commodities for different states and all-India with 1993-94 as base year. The base was shifted from 1970-71 to 1980-81 and then to 1993-94. In case of industries, the time series relating to emoluments have been deflated by the consumer price index (general) for industrial workers (CPI-IW) for different industries. In case of the states, the consumer price indices of the different centres from respective states have been used. The base was shifted from 1960-61 to 1982-83 and then to 1993-94. The time series relating to fixed capital and depreciation were deflated by the wholesale price index of machinery & machine tools for fourteen industry groups of manufacturing sector and for all industries in sixteen states and all-India with 1993-94 as base year. The base was shifted from 1970-71 to 1980-81 and then to 1993-94. Since different variables have different units of measurement, so for bringing uniformity and for better interpretation, the data at constant prices were converted into indices form by taking 1973-74 as the base year.

The data were collected from publications like, (i) Annual Survey of Industries, Central Statistical Organisation (CSO), Ministry of Planning, Government of India, New Delhi; (ii) Handbook of Statistics, Reserve Bank of India; (iii) Handbook of Industrial Policy and Statistics 2001, Office of the Economic Adviser, Ministry of Commerce and Industry; (iv) Handbooks of Indian Labour Statistics; and (v) Reports of Centre for Monitoring Indian Economy.

The tabular analysis has been used. Average annual growth rates, trend and coefficients of variation, etc. have been worked out. Partial and Total Factor Productivity indices have been computed. Various log linear regression equations between wages and productivity have been estimated. By introducing dummy variable and by taking data in indices form, the relation between wages and productivity for pre and post-liberalisation era and total study period was examined. Different linear regression equations using data in indices form were also tried but results were not encouraging. Moreover, the log linear regression equations are better in the sense that the slope coefficient reveals the elasticity of regressand with respect to regressor. To introduce stationarity in the time series, the first difference form using data in indices form was also tried, but the results were found difficult to interpret for long-term policy measures. Finally, time series in level form was obtained by introducing trend as additional explanatory variable in different regressions. Equations with different combinations of variables were tried, keeping in view the problem of multicollinearity. However, the results of only best fit equations were interpreted.

Economic Parameters in Indian Industries

Trends in economic parameters in Indian industries were examined in Chapter-V.

Inter-Industry Comparison of Real Wage Rate

An inter-industry comparison of real wage rate showed that the real wage rate in all industries showed rising trend. The maximum average annual growth rate and variability in real wage rate were observed in Food Products Industry (FPI) followed by Machinery Other Than Transport Industry (MOTI) and minimum growth was in Leather and Fur Products Industry (LFPI) whereas least variability was in Cotton Textiles Industry (CTI). In 1973-74 maximum real wage rate was observed in Chemicals and Chemical Products Industry (CCPI) followed by Basic Metals & Alloys Industry (BMAI). In 1983-84 maximum real wage rate was found in same industry followed by Transport Equipment and Parts Industry (TEPI). Similar result was observed in 1993-94. In 2000-01, the maximum real wage rate was in MOTI followed by BMAI. However, in the above four different years, the least real wage rate was found throughout in Beverages, Tobacco and Tobacco Products (BTTPI).

Inter-Industry Comparison of Share of Labour

An inter-industry comparison of share of labour in real GVA showed a declining trend in all industries but minimum decline was found in CCPI followed by Paper & Paper Products Industry (PPPI) and maximum in Jute, Hemp and Mesta Textiles Industry (JHMTI). The highest variability was observed in Textiles Product Industry (TPI) followed by BTTPI and minimum was in PPPI. In 1973-74 maximum share of labour was observed in JHMTI followed by TPI and least was in CCPI. Similar result was observed in 1983-84. In 1993-94 maximum share of labour was again found in JHMTI followed by CTI and least in Rubber, Petroleum & Coal Products Industry (RPCPI). In 2000-01, the highest value was observed in MOTI followed by TEPI and minimum in RPCPI.

In JHMTI, share of labour in GVA at constant prices was greater than one during 1973-74 to 1990-91 because first, CPI-IW increased steadily from 19.93 in 1973-74 to 141.86 in 1997-98, while Wholesale Price Index (WPI) increased in a fluctuating manner from 59.4 in 1973-74 to 100.87 in 1997-98. Second, in initial years WPI was quite high as compared to CPI-IW, due to which real emoluments were greater than real NVA. Similar was the case in BTTPI, CTI, TPI and MPI. However, share of labour in GVA at current prices was less than one in all industries except in JHMTI in 1985-86 and 1992-93.

Inter-Variable Comparison of Industries

An inter-variable comparison in FPI revealed that the maximum growth rate and variability were observed in Gross Fixed Capital (GFC) followed by Gross Value Added (GVA) and minimum in case of employees. It was found that the growth rates and variability of both the emoluments as well as the wage rate were higher than that of employees. The Index of GVA increased at much higher rate than real emoluments and real wage rate. In BTTPI industry the maximum growth rate and variability were observed in GFC followed by GVA and minimum in case of wage rate. It was found that the growth rate and variability of employees were lesser than emoluments but greater than the wage rate. Index of real emoluments and real wage rate increased at much slower rate than of GVA. In CTI the maximum growth rate and variability were observed in GFC followed by GVA and negative growth rate was in case of employees and least variability was in emoluments. It was found that the growth rates of both the emoluments as well as the wage rate were higher than that of employees. While real emoluments experienced negative growth rate, real wages experienced very low growth rate as compared to growth rate of GVA. In JHMTI the maximum growth rate and variability were observed in GVA followed by GFC and negative growth rate was in case of employees and least variability was in emoluments. It was found that the growth rates of both the emoluments as well as the wage rate were higher than that of employees. In this industry also growth rate of GVA was much higher as compared to that of real emoluments and real wages. In TPI the maximum growth rate and variability were observed in GVA followed by GFC and minimum in wage rate. It was found that the growth rate and variability of employees were lesser than emoluments but greater than the wage rate. In this industry also growth rate of GVA was much higher as compared to that of real emoluments and real wages. In PPPI the maximum growth rate and variability were observed in GFC followed by GVA and minimum in wage rate. It was found that the growth rate and variability of employees were lesser than emoluments but greater than the wage rate. In this industry also growth rate of GVA was higher as compared to that of real emoluments and real wages. In LFPI the maximum growth rate and variability were observed in GFC followed by GVA and minimum in case of employees. It was found that the growth rates and variability of both the emoluments as well as the wage rate were higher than that of employees. However, the growth rates of real emoluments and real wage rate were commensurate with growth rate of GVA in this industry. In CCPI the maximum growth rate and variability were observed in GFC followed by GVA and minimum in case of employees. It was found that the growth rates and variability of both the emoluments as well as the wage rate were higher than that of employees. The growth rates of real emoluments and real wage rate were commensurate with growth rate in GVA in this industry. In RPCPI the maximum growth rate and variability were observed in GFC followed by GVA and minimum in case of employees. It was found that the growth rates and variability of both the emoluments as well as the wage rate were higher than that of employees. Real emoluments and real wage rate in this industry also increased at reasonable rates as compared to GVA. In the Non-Metallic Mineral Products Industry (NMMPI) the maximum growth rate and variability were observed in GFC followed by GVA and minimum in wage rate. It was found that the growth rate and variability of employees were lesser than emoluments but greater than the wage rate. In this industry the increase in real wage rate was not consistent with increase in GVA. In BMAI the maximum growth rate and variability were observed in GFC followed by GVA and minimum in wage rate.

It was found that the growth rate and variability of employees were lesser than emoluments but greater than the wage rate. The increase in wage rate was not commensurate with increase in GVA in this industry. In Metal Products Industry (MPI) the maximum growth rate and variability were observed in GFC followed by GVA and minimum in wage rate. It was found that the growth rate and variability of employees were lesser than emoluments but greater than the wage rate. Increase in wage rate was somewhat on lower side as compared to increase in GVA in this industry. Similar results were found in MOTI and TEPI.

Inter-Industry Comparison

The maximum growth rate and variability in the index of real GVA and real emoluments were found in TPI and minimum in CTI. The highest growth rate and variability in the index of real GFC were observed in TPI and least in JHMTI. The maximum growth rate and variability in the index of real wage rate were found in LFPI and least growth rate was found in PPPI and the minimum variability was in CTI. The maximum growth rate and variability in the index of employees were found in TPI and most negative growth rate was found in CTI and minimum variability was in LFPI.

In FPI, BTTPI, CTI, JHMTI, TPI, PPPI, NMMPI, BMAI, MPI, MOTI, and TEPI, the index of GVA increased at much higher rate than that of wage rate and in LFPI, CCPI and RPCPI, the growth rates of real wage rate were commensurate with those of GVA.

Productivity Indices in Indian Industries

Partial and total factor productivities in Indian industries were worked out in Chapter-VI. An inter-variable comparison in FPI revealed that the maximum growth rate was observed in labour productivity followed by capital intensity and minimum was in capital productivity. The maximum variability was found in capital intensity and minimum was in capital productivity. In BTTPI the maximum growth rate and variability were observed in capital intensity followed by labour productivity and negative growth rate and least variability in capital productivity. In CTI the maximum growth rate and variability were observed in capital intensity followed by labour productivity and negative growth rate and least variability in capital productivity. In JHMTI the maximum growth rate and variability were observed in Total Factor Productivity (Solow) (TFPS) followed by Total Factor Productivity (Translog) (TFPT) and minimum in capital productivity. In TPI the maximum growth rate was observed in labour productivity followed by TFPS and minimum was in capital productivity. It was observed that the maximum variability was in TFPS and minimum was in capital productivity. In PPPI the maximum growth rate and variability were observed in capital intensity followed by labour productivity and most negative growth rate was in capital productivity and least variability was in TFPT. In LFPI the maximum growth rate and variability were observed in capital intensity followed by labour productivity and negative growth rate was in capital productivity and least variability was in Total Factor Productivity (Kendrick) (TFPK). In CCPI the maximum growth rate and variability were observed in capital intensity followed by labour productivity and most negative growth rate was in capital productivity and least variability was in TFPK. In RPCPI the maximum growth rate and variability were observed in capital intensity followed by labour productivity and most negative growth rate was in TFPT and least variability in TFPK. In NMMPI the maximum growth rate and variability were observed in capital intensity followed by labour productivity and most negative growth rate was in capital productivity and least variability in TFPK. In BMAI the maximum growth rate and variability were observed in capital intensity followed by labour productivity and most negative growth rate was in capital productivity and least variability in TFPS. In MPI the maximum growth rate and variability were observed in capital intensity followed by labour productivity and negative growth and least variability in capital productivity. In MOTI the maximum growth rate and variability were observed in capital intensity followed by labour productivity and negative growth and least variability in capital productivity. In TEPI the maximum growth rate and variability were observed in capital intensity followed by labour productivity and negative growth was in capital productivity and least variability in TFPS and TFPT.

Both labour productivity and capital productivity significantly affected the total factor productivity as measured through Kendrick, Solow and Translog indices in all industries except in RPCPI where labour productivity and capital productivity significantly affected the total factor productivity as measured through Kendrick index only.

Inter-Industry Comparison

The maximum growth rate and variability in the index of partial labour productivity was found in the TPI but the minimum growth rate was observed in CCPI and least variability in the PPPI. The highest growth rate in the index of partial capital productivity was found in the TPI and minimum in NMMPI. The maximum variability was in NMMPI and least in FPI. The highest growth rate and variability in the index of real capital intensity were found in NMMPI, but the least growth rate was in CCPI and minimum variability in JHMTI. In case of TFPK, the maximum growth rate and variability were found in the JHMTI and minimum in the CCPI. In case of both TFPS and TFPT, the maximum growth rate was found in the JHMTI and minimum in the RPCPI and the highest variability was observed in TPI and least in CCPI.

It was also perceived that the growth rates of both capital intensity and labour productivity were positive and highly significant in all industries. Except JHMTI and TPI, the growth rates of capital intensity were higher than that of labour productivity in all industries.

Inter-Industry Comparison of Partial Labour Productivity

An inter-industry comparison of partial labour productivity revealed that it showed rising trend in all industries. The maximum average annual growth rate and variability in labour productivity were observed in TPI followed by JHMTI and minimum growth in CCPI and least variability in PPPI. In 1973-74 maximum value of partial labour productivity was observed in CCPI followed by RPCPI and least in JHMTI. In 1983-84 similar results for maximum and minimum values were found in respective industries. In 1993-94 maximum partial labour productivity was found in RPCPI followed by CCPI and least in JHMTI. Similar results for highest and second highest were found in 2000-01.

It was found that the average annual growth rates of labour productivity in all industries were higher than that of wage rate in respective industries. In TPI the difference between average annual growth rates of labour productivity and wage rate was maximum, i.e. average annual growth rate of labour productivity was 8.57 times higher than wage rate and this difference was least in CCPI where average annual growth rate in labour productivity was only 1.88 times higher than wage rate. It means, in comparison to their labour productivity, workers in TPI received the least reward in the form of higher wages and workers in CCPI received the highest reward followed by workers in PPPI. Even in industries like BTTPI, CTI, JHMTI, LFTI, RPCPI, NMMPI, BMAI, MPI, and MOTI the difference between average annual growth rates of labour productivity and wage rate were themselves greater than the average annual growth rates of wage rate in respective industries. This might be because when industries were growing, they went in for more technological innovation which led to increase in labour productivity and therefore higher wages as well.

Economic Parameters of Industries at State Level

Analysis of trends in economic parameters relating to industries in Indian states has been carried out in Chapter-VII.

Inter-State Comparison of Real Wage Rate

An inter-state comparison of real wage rate during 1973-74 to 2000-01 indicated a rising trend in all states. The maximum average annual growth rate in real wage rate was observed in Uttar Pradesh followed by Haryana and minimum growth rate was in Tamil Nadu. The maximum variability was perceived in Uttar Pradesh followed by Bihar and minimum was in Tamil Nadu. In 1973-74 maximum real wage rate was observed in Maharashtra followed by Orissa and least was in Andhra Pradesh. In 1983-84 maximum real wage rate remained in Maharashtra followed by Bihar and Madhya Pradesh jointly and least was in Assam. In 1993-94, the maximum real wage rate was found in Bihar followed by Maharashtra and minimum was in Assam. In 2000-01, the highest real wage rate again was in Maharashtra followed by Orissa and least was in Assam.

Inter-State Comparison of Share of Labour

An inter-state comparison of share of labour in real GVA reported a declining trend in all states, however minimum decline was found in Assam, Haryana and Punjab followed by Kerala and maximum in Madhya Pradesh. The maximum variability was perceived in Himachal Pradesh followed by Orissa and minimum in West Bengal. In 1973-74 maximum value of share of labour was observed in Himachal Pradesh followed by West Bengal and least was in Assam. In 1983-84, maximum value was in West Bengal followed by Orissa and least was in Himachal Pradesh. In 1993-94, the maximum value of share of labour was in West Bengal followed by Haryana and minimum was in Assam. In 2000-01, the highest value was again in West Bengal followed by Bihar and least was in Himachal Pradesh.

Inter-Variable Comparison in States

An inter-variable comparison in Andhra Pradesh revealed that the maximum growth rate and variability were observed in GFC and minimum growth rate was in case of employees and least variability in real wage rate. It was found that the growth rates of both the emoluments as well as the wage rate were higher than that of employees. The Index of GVA increased at a much higher rate than real emoluments and real wage rate. In Assam the maximum growth rate and variability were observed in the Consumer Price Index for Industrial Workers (CPI-IW) and minimum in case of employees. It was found that the growth rates and variability of both the emoluments as well as the wage rate were higher than that of employees. The Index of GVA increased at a higher rate than real emoluments and real wage rate. In Bihar the maximum growth rate and variability were observed in CPI-IW and negative growth and least variability in case of employees. It was perceived that the growth rates and variability of both the emoluments as well as the wage rate were higher than that of employees. Surprisingly index of real wage rate increased at a higher rate than of GVA, emoluments and of employees. In Gujarat the maximum growth rate and variability were observed in GFC and minimum in case of employees. It was found that the growth rates and variability of both the emoluments as well as the wage rate were higher than that of employees. Index of real emoluments and real wage rate increased at much slower rate than GVA. In Haryana the maximum growth rate was observed in GFC and minimum in wage rate. The highest variability was found in GVA and least in wage rate. It was seen that the growth rates and variability of both the emoluments as well as of employees were higher than that of wage rate. However, the growth rates of real emoluments and real wage rate were commensurate with growth rate of GVA. In Himachal Pradesh the maximum growth rate was observed in real GFC and minimum in wage rate. The highest variability was found in CPI-IW and least in wage rate. It was perceived that the growth rates and variability of both the emoluments as well as of employees were higher than that of wage rate. Index of real emoluments and real wage rate increased at a slower rate than of GVA. In Karnataka the maximum growth rate and variability were observed in real GFC and minimum in case of employees. It was found that the growth rates and variability of both the emoluments as well as of wage rate were higher than that of employees. Index of real emoluments and real wage rate increased at a slower rate than of GVA. In Kerala the maximum growth rate and variability were seen in CPI-IW and minimum in case of employees. It was perceived that the growth rates and variability of both the emoluments as well as of wage rate were higher than that of employees. Real emoluments and real wage rate increased at reasonable rates as compared to GVA. In Madhya Pradesh the maximum growth rate and variability were observed in CPI-IW and minimum growth rate in case of employees and least variability in wage rate. It was found that the growth rates of both the emoluments as well as of wage rate were higher than that of employees. The growth of real GVA was much higher as compared to real emoluments and real wages. In Maharashtra the maximum growth rate and variability were observed in CPI-IW and minimum in case of employees. It was perceived that the growth rates and variability of both the emoluments as well as of wage rate were higher than that of employees. In this state also growth of GVA was much higher as compared to of real emoluments and real wages. In Orissa the maximum growth rate and variability were observed in GFC and minimum growth rate was in case of employees and least variability in wage rate. It was found that the growth rates of both the emoluments as well as of wage rate were higher than that of employees. Index of real emoluments and real wage rate increased at a slower rate than of GVA. In Punjab the maximum growth rate was observed in GVA and minimum in wage rate. The highest variability was found in CPI-IW and least in the wage rate. It was perceived that the growth rates and variability of both the emoluments as well as of employees were higher than that of wage rate. The growth rates of real emoluments and real wage rate were commensurate with growth rate in GVA. In Rajasthan the maximum growth rate was observed in CPI-IW and minimum in wage rate. The highest variability was seen in GVA and least in the wage rate. It was found that the growth rates and variability of both the emoluments as well as of employees were higher than that of wage rate. Increase in wage rate was somewhat on lower side as compared to increase in GVA. In Tamil Nadu the maximum growth rate and variability were observed in GFC and minimum in wage rate. It was found that the growth rates and variability of both the emoluments as well as of employees were higher than that of wage rate. Increase in wage rate was somewhat on lower side as compared to increase in GVA. In Uttar Pradesh the maximum growth rate and variability were perceived in GFC and minimum in case of employees. It was found that the growth rates and variability of both the emoluments as well as of wage rate were higher than that of employees. Real emoluments and real wage rate increased at reasonable rates as compared to GVA. In West Bengal the maximum growth rate and variability were observed in CPI-IW and negative growth rate was in case of employees and least variability in emoluments. The growth rate of wage rate was higher than that of employees as well as emoluments, but lesser than the GVA. In case of All-India the maximum growth rate was seen in GFC and minimum in case of employees. The highest variability was found in CPI-IW and least in case of employees. It was perceived that the growth rates and variability of both the emoluments as well as of wage rate were higher than that of employees. Index of real emoluments and real wage rate increased at a slower rate than of GVA.

Inter-State Comparison

The maximum growth rate in the index of real GVA and real GFC were observed in Himachal Pradesh and minimum growth in real GVA and negative growth in real GFC was in Bihar. The highest variability for these variables was seen in Gujarat, but the least for real GVA was found in West Bengal and for real GFC was in Bihar. The highest growth rate in real emoluments was observed in Haryana and least in Bihar, while the maximum variability was found in Himachal Pradesh and minimum in West Bengal. The maximum growth rate and variability in real wage rate were perceived in Uttar Pradesh and minimum in Tamil Nadu. The maximum growth rate in case of employees was observed in Himachal Pradesh and minimum in Bihar. The highest variability was found in Himachal Pradesh and least in Maharashtra.

Generally at different points of time, the value of share of labour in real GVA was highest in West Bengal and this perhaps indicates the policy emphasis at state level. The comparative profile of different economic parameters in states like Andhra Pradesh, Gujarat, Haryana, Himachal Pradesh, Karnataka, Orissa, Punjab, Rajasthan, Tamil Nadu, and Uttar Pradesh with All-India showed that these States were performing better than All-India average, while States like Assam, Bihar, Kerala, Maharashtra, and West Bengal were on lower side as compared to All-India average.

Profile of Productivity Indices at State Level

Partial and total factor productivities in Indian states have been analysed in Chapter-VIII. An inter-variable comparison in Andhra Pradesh revealed that the maximum growth rate and variability were observed in capital intensity followed by labour productivity and negative growth was in capital productivity and least variability was in TFPS. In Assam the maximum growth rate was observed in capital intensity followed by labour productivity and negative was in TFPS. The highest variability was found in TFPT and minimum was in TFPK. In Bihar the maximum growth rate was observed in labour productivity followed by TFPK and minimum was in capital productivity. The maximum variability was found in labour productivity and least was in TFPS. In Gujarat the maximum growth rate and variability were perceived in capital intensity followed by labour productivity and negative growth rate was in capital productivity and least variability was in TFPK. In Haryana the maximum growth rate was seen in capital intensity followed by labour productivity and negative was in capital productivity. The highest variability was found in labour productivity and least was in capital productivity. In Himachal Pradesh the maximum growth rate and variability were observed in capital intensity followed by labour productivity and negative growth rate was in capital productivity and least variability was in TFPK. In Karnataka the maximum growth rate and variability were found in capital intensity followed by labour productivity and negative growth rate was in capital productivity and least variability was in TFPK. In Kerala the maximum growth rate and variability were observed in labour productivity followed by capital intensity and minimum in capital productivity. In Madhya Pradesh the maximum growth rate was perceived in capital intensity followed by labour productivity and negative was in TFPT. The highest variability was found in labour productivity and least was in TFPS. In Maharashtra the maximum growth rate and variability were observed in capital intensity followed by labour productivity and negative growth rate was in capital productivity and least variability was in TFPT. In Orissa the maximum growth rate and variability were found in capital intensity followed by labour productivity and negative growth rate was in capital productivity and least variability was in TFPT. In Punjab the maximum growth rate and variability were perceived in labour productivity followed by capital intensity and minimum growth rate was in capital productivity and least variability was in TFPS. In Rajasthan the maximum growth rate was observed in capital intensity followed by labour productivity and negative was in capital productivity. The highest variability was found in labour productivity and least was in TFPS. In Tamil Nadu the maximum growth rate and variability were seen in capital intensity followed by labour productivity and negative growth rate was in capital productivity and least variability was in TFPK. In Uttar Pradesh the maximum growth rate and variability were observed in capital intensity followed by labour productivity and negative growth rate was in capital productivity and least variability was in TFPT. In West Bengal the maximum growth rate was perceived in capital intensity followed by labour productivity and negative was in capital productivity. The highest variability was found in capital intensity and least was in TFPT. At All-India level the maximum growth rate and variability were seen in capital intensity followed by labour productivity and negative growth rate was in capital productivity and least variability was in TFPT.

Both labour productivity and capital productivity significantly affected the total factor productivity in all states and all-India except in case of Assam where labour productivity and capital productivity significantly affected only TFPK and in Kerala and Madhya Pradesh, labour productivity and capital productivity significantly affected only TFPK and TFPS.

Inter-State Comparison

The maximum growth rate and variability in the index of partial labour productivity have been found in Uttar Pradesh and minimum in West Bengal. The highest growth rate in the index of partial capital productivity was found in Bihar and most negative was in West Bengal. The maximum variability was seen in West Bengal and the least in Kerala. The highest growth rate and variability in the index of real capital intensity were found in Gujarat, but the least growth rate was in Bihar and minimum variability in Punjab. For TFPK, the maximum growth rate and variability were perceived in Bihar but negative growth rate was in Assam and minimum variability in Gujarat. For TFPS and TFPT, the maximum growth rates were found in Bihar but the most negative growth rates and highest variability were in Assam and minimum variability in West Bengal.

Inter-State Comparison of Partial Labour Productivity

An inter-state comparison of partial labour productivity revealed that it showed rising trend in all states. The maximum average annual growth rate in labour productivity was observed in Gujarat followed by Maharashtra and minimum was in West Bengal. The highest variability was found in Uttar Pradesh followed by Gujarat and least was in West Bengal. In 1973-74 maximum partial labour productivity was perceived in Maharashtra followed by Orissa and Rajasthan simultaneously and least was in Himachal Pradesh. In 1983-84 maximum value of labour productivity was in Himachal Pradesh followed by Bihar and least was in Uttar Pradesh. In 1993-94 maximum value was in Bihar followed by Maharashtra and least was in Kerala. In 2000-01 maximum labour productivity was in Himachal Pradesh followed by Maharashtra and least was in West Bengal. In states like Bihar, Gujarat, Himachal Pradesh, Madhya Pradesh, Maharashtra, Rajasthan and Uttar Pradesh, the trends in labour productivity were greater that that of All-India and in states like Andhra Pradesh, Assam, Haryana, Karnataka, Kerala, Orissa, Punjab, Tamil Nadu and West Bengal, the trends in labour productivity were lesser than that of All-India.

It was found that the growth rates of capital intensity and labour productivity were positive and highly significant in all states. Except in three states namely, Bihar, Kerala and Punjab, the growth rates of capital intensity were higher than the labour productivity in all states. It was also observed that the average annual growth rates of labour productivity in all states were higher than that of wage rates in respective states. This might be because when industries in the states were growing, they went in for more technological innovation which increased the labour productivity and therefore higher wages as well. In Madhya Pradesh, the difference between average annual growth rate of labour productivity and wage rate was maximum, i.e. average annual growth rate of labour productivity was 2.96 times higher than that of wage rate and the second highest difference was in Gujarat. The least difference was in Haryana where average annual growth rate of labour productivity was 1.08 times higher than that of wage rate followed by Punjab. Even in states like Gujarat, Himachal Pradesh, Madhya Pradesh, Maharashtra, Orissa, Rajasthan, Tamil Nadu and All-India, the difference between average annual growth rates of labour productivity and wage rate were greater than average annual growth rates of wage rate in respective states.

Thus in comparison to the growth in their labour productivity, workers in Madhya Pradesh received the least reward in the form of higher wages and workers in Haryana received the highest reward followed by workers in Punjab. The average annual growth rate of capital productivity was positive only in Bihar, Kerala and Punjab but was found significant in Bihar only.

Wage-Productivity Relationship in Indian Industries

Chapter IX reports the empirical analysis of wage-productivity relationship in Indian industries. Labour productivity has significantly affected the wage rate in all-industries except in two industries namely, LFPI, and BMAI. Capital intensity has positively and significantly affected the wage rate in all-industries except in five industries namely, CTI, LFPI, RPCPI, NMMPI and BMAI. Total factor productivity (Kendrick, Solow and Translog) has positively and significantly affected the wage rate in FPI, CTI, JHMTI and MPI only.

Wage rate has also significantly affected labour productivity in all industries except CTI, TPI, CCPI, and TEPI. Capital intensity has significantly affected labour productivity in all industries except PPPI.

It was found that the relationship between wages and labour productivity during post-reform era has strengthened in BTTPI, PPPI, NMMPI, BMAI, MPI and TEPI. But the relationship between wages and labour productivity during post-reform era has weakened in FPI, CTI, JHMTI and TPI. This indicates that proportionate gains from productivity increase were not passed on to the workers in these industries.

The relationship between labour productivity and wage rate during post-reform era has strengthened in FPI, JHMTI and MPI. After liberalisation when market forces have more important role to play, the labour productivity has become more responsive to wage rate in these industries. It was found that the relationship between labour productivity and wage rate during post-reform era has weakened in RPCPI, NMMPI, BMAI and MOTI.

Wage-Productivity Relationship at State Level

In Chapter X empirical work on wage-productivity relationship in Indian states was carried out. Labour productivity has positively and significantly affected the wage rate in all states except in Tamil Nadu. Capital intensity has also significantly affected the wage rate in all states except in Himachal Pradesh, Madhya Pradesh and Tamil Nadu. TFPK has significantly affected the wage rate in Andhra Pradesh, Kerala, Madhya Pradesh, Maharashtra, Rajasthan, Uttar Pradesh, West Bengal. TFPS has significantly affected the wage rate in Kerala, Madhya Pradesh, Maharashtra, Uttar Pradesh. TFPT has significantly affected the wage rate in Karnataka, Kerala, Maharashtra, Punjab and Uttar Pradesh.

Wage rate has positively and significantly affected labour productivity in all states except Assam, Bihar, Himachal Pradesh, Maharashtra, Orissa, Punjab and West Bengal. Capital intensity has significantly affected labour productivity in all states except Assam, Bihar, Gujarat, Haryana, Himachal Pradesh, Madhya Pradesh, Maharashtra, Orissa and West Bengal.

It was found that the relationship between wages and labour productivity during post-reform era has weakened, which indicates that proportionate gains from productivity increase were not distributed among the workers in Andhra Pradesh, Gujarat, Haryana, Kerala, Maharashtra, Punjab, Rajasthan, Tamil Nadu, West Bengal and all-India. Since the time period of post-reform era is less, therefore over long period it has to be seen whether this relationship is strengthened or weakened. It was found that the relationship between wage and labour productivity during post-reform era has strengthened in Orissa only.

The relationship between labour productivity and wage rate during post-reform era has weakened in Assam and Tamil Nadu. It was found that the relationship between labour productivity and wage rate during post-reform era has strengthened in Gujarat, Haryana, Himachal Pradesh, Kerala, Madhya Pradesh and Maharashtra. After liberalisation when market forces have more important role to play, the labour productivity has become more responsive to wage rate.

Inter-Temporal Analysis of Wage-Productivity Relationship

An inter-temporal analysis taking wage rate as dependent upon partial labour productivity in sixteen states revealed that the effect of labour productivity on wage rate increased during 1980-81 to 1990-91, but declined sizably in 2000-01. This corroborates the earlier findings that the relationship between wages and labour productivity during post-reform era has weakened in India.

An inter-temporal analysis taking partial labour productivity as dependent upon wage rate in sixteen states showed that the effect of wage rate on labour productivity decreased during 1980-81 to 1990-91 but got strengthened in 2000-01. Thus after liberalisation when market forces have more important role to play, the labour productivity has become more responsive to wage rate.

Policy Implications

The study brings out that the interests of workers and employers are not antithetical and in this context and other findings of the study, following implications can be derived:

1. In view the low rate of growth in real wage rate as compared to labour productivity, there is need to give more incentives to workers.
2. Efforts be made to increase productivity by reducing waste in all forms, by working intelligently and not merely putting in hard work, by convincing workers about the rationale and usefulness of the actions and by positive involvement and commitment of workers.
3. In the light of falling capital productivity and relatively small increase in TFP growth, there is a need to take adequate steps to enhance technical efficiency. The barriers to improving capital productivity need to be investigated at state, industry and enterprise levels and suitable measures be taken to improve productivity.
4. Gain sharing in the form of bonus be encouraged as it is linked to performance and stresses teamwork and cooperation. Gain sharing will prove to be the most effective motivational tool in strengthening wage-productivity relationship.
5. Under the liberalisation policy regime, Government can play important role through subsidized education and training for raising productivity and thus strengthening wage-productivity relationship.
6. As weakening of wage-productivity relationship after liberalisation may largely be due to vast unemployed

labour force, this amounts to exploitation of labour. Government should frame policies for generation of more employment opportunities so that this exploitation is checked.

7. Employees be made to realize through different measures that only increased productivity is the panacea through which they can get higher wages, and achieve and sustain a better standard of life.

Bibliography

Acharya, S. and Nair, N.K. (1978), "Empirical Issues in Total Productivity Measurement : An Experiment with Cement Industry in India", *Productivity*, Oct-Dec., Vol. XIX No. 3.

Agarwal, R. (1972), "Critical Importance of Productivity to Indian's Progress", *Productivity*, National Seminar on Productivity, 24-25 March, 159-62.

Aggarwal, S.C. (1981), "Productivity : A Measure or A Mirage", *Productivity*, Jan.-Mar., Vol. 21, No. 4.

Ahluwalia, I.J. (1990), "Productivity Trends in Indian Industry : Concerns for the Nineties", *Productivity*, Vol. 31, No. 1, April-June.

———, (1991), *Productivity and Growth in Indian Manufacturing*, Oxford University Press, N. Delhi.

———, (1992), "Productivity and Growth in Indian Manufacturing", *RBI Occasional Papers*, Vol. 13, No. 2, June.

———, (1994), "TFPG in Manufacturing Industry", *Economic and Political Weekly*, Oct. 22, p. 2836.

Ahuja, A.K. (1962), "Productivity Analysis of Jute Industry", *Productivity*, Vol. 3, Aug-Nov.

Akerlof, G. and Yeller, J. (1986), *Efficiency Wage Models of Labour Market*, Cambridge : Cambridge University Press.

Akhilesh, K.B., Gupta, S.A. and Mathew, M. (1989), "Productivity Through Personnel Behavioural Information System", *Productivity*, Vol. 30, No. 3, Oct-Dec.

Alagh, Y.K. (1972), *Regional Aspects of Indian Industrialisation*, Bombay University Press.

Arrow, K.J. (1962), "The Economic Implications of Learning by Doing", *Review of Economic Studies,* Vol. 29, June.

Balakrishan, P. and Pushpangadan, K. (1994), "Total Factor Productivity Growth in Manufacturing : A Fresh Look", *Economic and Political Weekly*, July 30, pp. 2028-35.

———, (1995), "Total Factor Productivity Growth in Manufacturing Industry", *Economic and Political Weekly,* March 4, pp. 462-64.

———, (1996), "TFPG in Manufacturing Industry", *Economic and Political Weekly*, Feb. 17, pp. 425-28.

Bande, R., Fernandez, M., and Montuenga, V.M. (2000), "The Role of Productivity in Wage Setting : Differences Across the Spanish Regions", *40th ERSA Congress*, p. 4.

Banerjee, A. (1975), *Capital Intensity and Productivity in Indian Industry*, Macmillan Co., N. Delhi.

Baumal, W.J. and Melennan, K. (1985), *U.S. Productivity Performance and Its Implications*, Oxford University Press, New York.

Benton, W. (1768), Encyclopaedia Britannica, Vol. 23, p. 267.

Benner, A., Montias, J.M. and Neuberger, E. (1993), "Basic Issues in Organizations : A Comparative Perspective", *Journal of Comparative Economics*, Vol. 17, pp. 207-42.

Beri, C.C. (1962), *Measurement of Production and Productivity in Indian Industry*, Asia Publishing House, N. Delhi.

Berndt, E.R. and Khaled, M.S. (1978), "Parametric Productivity Measurement and Choice Among Flexible Functional Forms", *Journal of Political Economy*, Dec.

Bester, H. and Petrakis, E. (2002), "Wages and Productivity Growth in a Competitive Industry", Departmental Working Papers, *WoPEC*.

Bhaduri, R.N. (1971), *Management Accountant*, Vol. XX, Part-II, Sept., p. 244.

Bhandari, M.C. (1973), "Inter-Firm Comparisons : A Fruitful Management Technique", *Productivity*, pp. 176-81.

Bhargava, S. (1995), "Industrial Liberalisation : Policy Issues at State Level", *Economic and Political Weekly*, Aug. 26, M-82-M2-123.

Bhatnagar, S.K. (1983), "Quest for Higher Productivity", *Productivity*, Vol. 24. No. 3 , pp. 231-35.

Bhatnagar, V. (1988), "Wage Productivity Relationship in Indian Industries", *Productivity*, XXVIII, 4, pp. 405-12.

Billimoria, R.P. (1973), "Industrial Peace and Productivity", *APO Symposium on Productivity and Industrial Relations*, Tokyo, 22-26 Oct.

Breman, J. (1995), "Labour, Get Lost : A Late Capitalist Manifesto", *Economic and Political Weekly*, Sept. 16.

Bruce, C. (2002), "The Connection between Labour Productivity and Wages", *Economica Ltd.*, Summer/Autumn, Vol. 7, No. 2.

Bruno, M. (1978), "Duality, International Inputs and Value-added", in Fuss, M. and McFadden, D. (ed), *Production Economics : A Dual Approach to Theory and Application*, Amsterdam North-Holland Publishing Co.

———, (1984), "Raw Materials, Profits and the Productivity Slowdown", *Quarterly Journal of Economics*, Vol. 1, pp. 1-29.

Buch, A.N. (1973), "Participation in Productivity—Worker's Point of View", *Productivity*, National Seminar on Productivity and Trade Union Movement—19-20 Aug. 137-39.

Buckberg, E. and Thomas, A. (1996), "Wage Dispersion in the 1980s : Resurrecting the Role of Trade Through the Effects of Durable Employment Changes", *IMF Staff Paper*, Vol. 43, No. 2, June.

Calvet, J.G. and Jusmet, J.R. (1997), "Wage Trends in Spain Analysed", *European Industrial Relations Observatory*, ES9708217F.

Centre for the Study of Living Standards, (1998), "Productivity: Key to Economic Success", *Atlantic Canada Opportunities Agency*, March.

Chakrabarti, D., "Here is the Need of Productivity Linked Incentives", *Productivity*, pp. 376-79.

Chakrabarti, N. (1997), "Dramatic Change in Labour Conditions", *Yojna*, Jan., pp. 102-3.

Chamber's Encyclopaedia, Vol. 14, p. 363.

Chandrasekhar, C.P. (1996), "Explaining Post-Reform Industrial Growth", *Economic and Political Weekly*, Special Number, Sept., pp. 2537-45.

Chang, H.C. (2003), "International Trade, Productivity Growth, Education and the Wage Differential : A Case Study of

Taiwan", *Journal of Applied Economics*, Vol. VI, No. 1, May, pp. 25-48.

Chatterjee, A. (1994), "Work Culture : A Cognitive Perspective", *Productivity*, Vol. 35, No. 3, Oct.-Dec.

Chatterjee, A.K. (1973), "Productivity in Selected Manufacturing Industries, 1946-65", *Economic and Political Weekly*, M 107-116, Nov. 24.

Chevalier, A., Siebert, S. and Vitanen, T. (2002), "Wage Policy, Employee Turnover and Productivity", April, JEL Classification : J22J3.

Christensen, L.R. and Jorgenson, D.W. (1970), "U.S. Real Product and Real Factor Input, 1929-67", *Review of Income and Wealth*, March.

Christensen, L.R., Jorgenson, D.W. and Lau, L.J. (1973), "Transcendental Logarithmic Production Frontiers", *Review of Economics and Statistics*, Feb., pp. 28-45.

Clark, K. (1957), "Wage Relationship—The Comparative Impact of Market and Power Forces", in Dunlop, J.T. (ed.), *The Theory of Wage Determination*, pp. 176-77, 1957.

CMIE, The Indian Corporate Sector, April 1995.

Coelli, M., Fahrer, J. and Lindsay, H. (1994), "Wage Dispersion and Labour Market Institutions : A Cross Country Study", Research Discussion Paper, 9404, June, Reserve Bank of Australia, Economic Research Department.

Committee on Sharing Gains of Productivity (1967), "Report of the Committee on Sharing Gains of Productivity", *National Productivity Council*, March, pp. 8-9.

CSO (1981), *Wages and Productivity in Selected Industries in Organised Manufacturing Sector, 1960-77*, Bulletin No. ISD/8, Oct., Deptt. of Statistics, Ministry of Planning, N. Delhi.

———, (1982), *Wages and Productivity in Organised Manufacturing Sector, 1960-61 to 1976-77*, Bulletin No. ISD/5, Deptt. of Statistics, Ministry of Planning, N. Delhi.

Dadi, M.M. (1974), "Wage Share in Organized Manufacturing Industries : 1946-65", *Productivity*, 15(1), pp. 88-96.

Dasgupta, A.K. (1976), *A Theory of Wage Policy*, Oxford University Press, Delhi.

Denison, E.F. (1957), "Theoretical Aspects of Quality Change Capital Consumption and New Capital Formation", *Studies in Income and Wealth*, Vol. 19 , pp. 78-84, Princeton : *NBER*

Denison, E.F. (1961), "Measurement of Labour Input : Some Questions of Definition and Adequacy of Data in Output, Input and Productivity Measurement", New York : *NBER*.

———, (1972), "Some Major Issues in Productivity Analysis", *Survey of Current Business*, Vol. 49(5), May, pp. 1-28.

Devaramani, S.C. (1980), "The Growth of Labour Productivity in Organised Industries", *Quarterly Economic Report*, XXV, 1, Jan.-April, pp. 25-37.

Dhalla, R.S., Venkateswarlu, P., Joshi, P.C. (1988), "Labour Productivity Index—Through Sensitivity Analysis", *Productivity*, No. 1, XXIX, pp. 17-22.

Dhawal, M. (1972), "A New Look At Productivity of an Organisation", *Productivity*, National Seminar on Productivity, 24-25 March, 45-48.

Dholakia, B.H., "Measurement of Capital Input and Estimates of Time Series Production Function in Indian Manufacturing", *Indian Economic Journal*, Jan-March, pp. 333-35.

Dholakia, B.H. (1974), *The Sources of Economic Growth in India*, Goods Company, Baroda.

Dholakia, B.H. and Dholakia, R.H. (1994), "Total Factor Productivity Growth in Indian Manufacturing", *Economic and Political Weekly*, Dec. 31, pp. 3342-3334

Diatchenko and Dunlop (1964), *Labour Productivity*, McGraw Hill Publications, New York, p. 220.

Divatia, K.J. (1972), "Linking Wage and Salary Payments to Productivity", *Productivity*, National Seminar on Productivity, 24-25 March, 71-73.

Dowrick, S. (1993), "Wage Bargaining Systems and Productivity Growth in OECD Countries", Economic Planning Advisory Council Background Paper No. 26.

Dunlop, J.T. (1957), *The Theory of Wage Determination*, (ed.) London, MacMillan.

Dunne, T., Foster, L., Haltiwanger, J. and Troske, K. (2002), "Wage and Productivity Dispersion in U.S. Manufacturing : The Role of Computer Investment", Institution for Study of Labour (IZA), *IZA Discussion Paper No. 563*, WoPEC.

Durgesh, C. (1978), "Productivity Dynamics", *Productivity*, April-June, Vol. 19, No. 1.

Edgren, G., Faxen, K.O. and Odhner, C.E. (1973), *Wage Formation and the Economy*, George Allen and Unwin Ltd., London.

Employer's Federation of India (1971), "The Employer's Federation of India Collective Agreement : Trends in the Sixties", *EFI*, Bombay.

Encyclopaedia Britanica, Vol. 23, p. 267.

Erenburg, S.J. (1993), "Productivity, Private and Public Capital and Real Wage in the United States, 1948-1990"', Jerome Levy Economics Institute Working Paper No. 94, May, pp. 1-21.

Fair Wage Committee (1948), *Report of the Committee on Fair Wages*, Government of India.

Fonesca, A.J. (1964), *Wage Determination and Organised Labour in India*, Oxford University Press, Delhi, p. 63.

Frust, G., Raabe, K.H. and Sperling, H. (1962), "Output Per Person Employed in Major Sectors of German Economy, 1950-57", *Productivity Measurement Review*, OECD.

Ghosal, A. (1961), "Productivity in Iron and Steel Industry", *Productivity*, Vol. 3, Nov-Dec.

Ghosh, A. (1984), "Efficiency and Productivity of Indian Manufacturing Industry—A Few Case Studies", *Economic and Political Weekly*, Vol. XIX, No. 31, 32 and 33, Aug. pp. 1397-1423.

Ghosh, A. (1988), "Industrial Productivity : Some Issues Relevant for Policy Making", *Productivity*, Vol. 29, No. 3, Oct.-Dec.

Ghosh, M. (1991), "Productivity, Real Wages and Poverty in Rural India", *Productivity*, Vol. 32, No. 1, April-June.

Ghosh, S. (1989), "Wages Criteria in Collective Agreements in India", *Productivity*, Vol. 29, No. 4, Jan.-Mar.

Gitlow, L.A. (1957), *Labour Economics and Industrial Relations*, Richard D. Irwin, INC, USA, p. 297.

Goel, V.K. (1976), "Linking Bonus to Productivity", *Productivity*, Vol. 17, pp. 329-40.

Goel, V.K. and Nair, N.K. (1979), "Labour Productivity and Output Growth in Indian Mining and Manufacturing Sectors (1951-76)", *Productivity*, July-Sept., (Supplement) Vol. XX, No. 2, pp. S1-S41.

Goldar, B.N. (1986), *Productivity Growth in Indian Industry*, Allied Publishers Pvt. Ltd., New Delhi.

Goldsmith, R.W. (1951), "A Perpetual Inventory of National Wealth", *Studies on Income and Wealth NBER*, Vol. 14, pp. 169-172.

Gollop, F.M. and Jorgenson, D.W. (1980), "U.S. Productivity Growth by Industry, 1947-73", in J.W. Kendrick and B.B. Vaccara (eds.), *New Developments in Productivity Measurements and Analysis*, (London, University of Chicago Press).

Gopal, V.G. (1973), "Productivity and Industrial Relations", *APO Symposium on Productivity and Industrial Relations*, Tokyo, 22-26 Oct.

Gordon, R.J. (1987), "Productivity, Wages and Prices Inside and Outside of Manufacturing in the U.S., Japan and Europe", *European Economic Review*, Vol. 31, pp. 685-739.

Government of India (1981), *Sixth Five Year Plan*, Planning Commission.

———, (1985), *Seventh Five Year Plan*, Planning Commission.

———, (1992), *Eighth Five Year Plan*, Planning Commission.

———, (1997), *Ninth Five Year Plan*, Planning Commission.

———, (2002), *Tenth Five Year Plan*, Planning Commission.

Goyal, R.C. (1974), "Productivity—A Neglected Word in Industrial Relations Policy", *Productivity*, Vol. 15, pp. 345-51.

Griliches, Z. and Ringstad, V. (1971), *Economics of Scale and Production Function*, North-Holland Publishing Co., Amsterdam.

Groot, W. (1995), "The Wage Effects of Investment in Enterprise Related Training", *Empirical Economics*, 20 : 133-47.

Guha, A.B. and Marwaha, (1968), "Productivity in Indian Mines", *Productivity*, Vol. 4, Oct.-Dec.

Gupta, A. (1992), *Wages and Salary Administration in India*, Anmol Publications Pvt. Ltd., New Delhi.

Gupta, D. (1990), "Productivity Trends and Production Function Analysis of Indian Automobile Industry", *PSE Economic Analyst*, Vol. XI, No. 2, pp. 25-44.

Gupta, R.S. (1973), "Models for Sharing the Gains of Productivity", *Productivity*, Feb. 1.

Gupta, R.S. (1986), "Productivity Agreement : An Action Plan", *Productivity*, XXVII, 1, 5-11.

Gupta, S.N. (1985), *Dynamics of Modern Management*, Atlantic Publishers, New Delhi, pp. 155-56.

Hashim, S.R. and Dadi, M.M. (1973), *Capital Output Relations in Indian Manufacturing, 1946-64*, M.S. University of Baroda, Baroda.

Haskel, J. and Pereira, S. (2002), "Skills and Productivity in the UK Using Matched Establishment and Worker Data", *National Statistics : Productivity Workshop 2002*, Nov.

Hellerstein, J.K., Neumark, D. and Troske, K.R. (1996), "Wages, Productivity and Worker Characteristics : Evidence from Plant Level Production Functions and Wage Equations", *NBER Working Papers, 5626*, Jun.

Holzer, H.J. (1990), "The Determinants of Employee Productivity and Earnings", *Industrial Relations*, Vol. 29, No. 3, pp. 403-22.

Hostland, D. (1996), "Real Wages, Labour Productivity and Employment in Canada : A Historical Perspective", Applied Research Branch, Strategy Policy, Human Resources Development, Canada, R-96-5E.

Hulten, C.R. (1979), "On the Importance of Productivity Change", *American Economic Review*, Vol. 69, No. 1, March pp. 126-36.

ILO, (1954), "Higher Productivity in Manufacturing Industries", International Labour Office, Geneva, p. 28.

———, (1956), "Problems of Wage Policy in Asian Countries", International Labour Office, Geneva, p. 44.

———, (1996), *Economic Reforms and Labour Policies in India*, A Report prepared under a project sponsored by UNDP under Technical Support Services-I, ILO, SAAT, New Delhi.

Industrial Wage Committee (1973), *Report of Industrial Wage Committee*, Jammu and Kashmir, Part II, p. 40.

Irland, L.C. and Maxcy, J. (1991), "Maine's Wood Industry : Value-added Relationships, 1982-87", *Forest Products Journal*. 41(9) : 53-56.

Jacob, M.M. (1973), "Distribution of Productivity Gains", *Productivity*, Feb., 1.

James, C.F., Stanislao, J. and Glen, T.M. (1976), "Designing a Wage Incentive Plan : A System Approach", *Productivity*, Vol. 17, pp. 277-85.

Jayadevan, C.M. (1995), "Inter-State Variations in Employment Growth Rates : Evidence from Organised Industry in India", *Indian Journal of Regional Science,* Vol. XXVII, No. 1 and 2, pp. 41-56.

Jha, L.K. (1983), "Strategy for Higher Productivity", *Productivity,* Vol. 24, No. 3, pp. 219-24.

Jorgenson, D.W. and Griliches, Z. (1967), "The Explanation of Productivity Change", *Review of Economic Studies,* Vol. 34(3), July, pp. 249-84.

Kabra, K.N. (1996), "Indian Planning and Liberalisation", *Economic and Political Weekly,* Oct. 5, pp. 2740-45.

Kaiser, H.F. (1971), "Productivity Gains in Forest Products Industries", *Forest Products Journal,* 21(5) : 14-16.

Kendrick, J.W (1977), *Understanding Productivity,* Johns Hopkins Press, Baltimore.

Kennedy, C. and Thirlwall, A.P. (1972), "Surveys in Applied Economics : Technical Progress"., *The Economic Journal,* March, Vol. 82, No. 325, pp. 11-71.

Krishna, K.L. (1970), "Total Factor Productivity : Concept and Measurement", *Productivity,* 10(4) : 701-5.

Krishnamurty, K., Pandit, V., Palanival, T., Saibaba, P. and Pratap, D. (1996), "Indian Economy, 1995-96 to 1997-98- Alternative Scenarios", *Economic and Political Weekly,* March 16, pp. 661-72.

Krishna, R. and Mehra, S.S. (1968), "Productivity Trends in Large Scale Industries", *Economic and Political Weekly,* Oct. 26, Vol. 3 (43), pp. 1655-60.

Krugman, P. (1996), "Estimating the Potential Productivity and Real Wage Effects of Employee Involvement", *Employment Policy Foundation,* U.S.

Kumar, A.V. (1996), "Productivity trends in the Public Sector Steel Industry in India", *The Journal of Institute of Public Enterprises,* Vol. 19 (3 and 4) pp. 135-45.

Labour Bureau (1961), "Industrial Awards in India", Government of India, p. 9.

———, (1971), "Development of Productivity Indices", Efforts Made by Labour Bureau, *Productivity,* Vol. 12, No. 3-4, pp. 359-68.

———, (1974), "Wage Policy in the Five Year Plans : A Review", *Productivity,* Vol. 15(1), pp. 66-79.

Lal, H. (1981), "Increasing Productivity by Defect Elimination – An Organised Approach", *Productivity*, Jan.-Mar., Vol. 21, No. 4.

Lane, P.R. (1998), "Profits and Wages in Ireland, 1987-1996", *Journal of the Statistical and Social Inquiry*, Society of Ireland, XXVII (V), pp. 223-51.

Luther, P.C. (1985), "Productivity in Indian Industry", *Productivity*, Vol. 26, No. 2, 127-30.

Lutz, F.A. (1961), "The Essential of Capital Theory", in FA Lutz and D.C. Hague, *The Theory of Capital*, Macmillan, New York, p. 16.

Mahesh, C. (1976), "Wages and Inflation", *Productivity*, XXVII, pp. 928-38.

Mahindra, H. (1972), "Wages and Productivity Nexus", *Productivity*, National Seminar on Productivity, Special Report, March 24-25, pp. 58-70.

Majumdar, D. (1997), "Labour Markets, Trade Patterns and Worker's Living Standards", *Economic and Political Weekly*, March 1-8, pp. 436-74.

Majumdar, S.K. (1996), "Fall and Rise of Productivity in Indian Industry—Has Economic Liberalisation Had an Impact?", *Economic and Political Weekly*, Nov. 30, pp. M 46-M 53.

Maheshwari, L.N. (1974), "Problems of Productivity : Equipment Replacement", *Productivity*, Vol. 15, pp. 290-304.

Maini, S.K. (1973), "Raising the Productivity and Sharing the Gains", *Productivity*, Feb. 1.

Malgavkar, P.D. (1973), "Creating A New Atmosphere for Productivity", *Productivity*, National Seminar on Productivity and Trade Union Movement—19-20 Aug., 120-24.

Mani, S. (1995), "Economic Liberalisation and the Industrial Sector", *Economic and Political Weekly*, May 27, pp. M 38- M 50.

Mathur, N.D. and Dasot, P. (1980), "Production Analysis : A Case", *Productivity*, Oct.-Dec., Vol. 21, No. 3.

Meher, M.R. (1972), "Productivity Bargaining", *Productivity*, National Seminar on Productivity, 24-25 March, 169-71.

———, (1973), "Some Factors Affecting Labour Productivity", *Productivity*, National Seminar on Productivity and Trade Union Movement, 19-20 Aug., 425-27.

Mehta, P.C. and Bhaduri, S.N. (1973), "Inter-Firm Comparisons", *Productivity*, pp. 172-75.

Melman, S. (1985), *Decision-making and Productivity*, John Wiley and Sons, New York.

Minhas, T.S. (1972), "Rationalization of Wage Scales : A Mathematical Approach", *Productivity*, National Seminar on Productivity, 24-25 March, 74-78

Moghaddam, M.B., Reddy, C. and Rami, S. (1988), "Measurement of Total Factor Productivity Growth in Iranian Industries", *Prajnan*, Vol. XVII. No. 2.

Mohanty, K. (1993), *Wages and Productivity in a Developing Economy*, Discovery Publishing House, New Delhi, p. 2.

Mohapatra, S.B. (1982), "Labour Productivity and Industrial Wages in India", *National Labour Institute Bulletin*, Vol. VIII, No. 182, p. 41.

Monga, M.L. (1979), "Work Stoppage in Indian Industries", *Productivity*, Vol. 20. No. 3, Oct.-Dec.

Mukherjee, K. (1966), "Long Term Trends of Productivity in Jute Industry", *Indian Journal of Industrial Relations*, Vol. 5, Jan., pp. 257-69.

Mukherjee, I.N. (1975), "Productivity Trends in Large Scale Manufacturing Industry—A Comparative Study", *Productivity*, Vol. 16, No. 1-2, pp. 560-74.

Mukhpodhyay, C. (1989), "Work Motivation and Job Involvement", *Productivity*, Vol. 30, No. 2, July-Sept.

Murti and Shastry (1975), "Economies of Scale and Productivity Change in the Indian Manufacturing Industry", *Productivity*, Vol. 16, April-June.

Myrdal, G. (1958), *Economic Theory and Underdeveloped Regions* (Reprint), Vora and Co. Publisher, Bombay.

Nadiri, M.L. (1972), "International Studies of Factor Inputs and Total Factor Productivity : A Brief Survey", *Review of Income and Wealth*, pp. 22-29.

Nandi, K.S. (1972), *Growth in Selected Indian Industries*, The World Press Pvt. Ltd., Calcutta.

Nath, S. (1972), "Productivity Drives : Supervisory and Middle Management Personality", *Productivity*, National Seminar on Productivity, 24-25 March, 34-38.

National Commission on Labour, (1969), *Report of National Commission on Labour,* para 16, p. 238, Government of India.

———, (2002), *Report of Second National Commission on Labour,* Government of India.

NPC (1987), "Labour Productivity Trends in Indian Manufacturing Sectors", *Productivity,* Vol. 28, No. 3, pp. 207-16.

———, (1990a), "Labour and Capital Productivity Estimates for Indian Economy", *Productivity,* Vol. 31, No. 1 April-June.

———, (1990b), "Total Factor Productivity in the Indian Economy During 1950-51-1978-88", *Productivity,* Vol. 31, No. 3, Oct.-Dec.

———, (1992), "Labour Productivity and labour Intensity Ratios in Indian Manufacturing Industries", *Productivity,* Vol. 32, No. 4, Jan.-Mar.

———, (1994), "Labour Productivity Growth in the Indian Economy", *Productivity,* Vol. 35, No. 3, Oct.-Dec.

Nayak, P. and Dey, N.B. (1996), "Productivity in Small Scale Industry in Assam", *Yojana,* Oct. 109.

Neogi, C. and Ghosh (1998), "Impact of Liberalisation on Performance of Indian Industries : A Firm Level Study", *Economic and Political Weekly,* Feb. 28, pp. M-16 to M-24.

Ohanian, L.E. (2002), "Why Did Productivity Fall so Much During the Great Depression?", *Federal Reserve Bank of Minneapolis Quarterly Review,* Vol. 26, No. 2, pp. 12-17.

Oommen, M.A. (1975), "Economic of Scale and Productivity Change in the Indian Manufacturing Industry", *Productivity,* Vol. 16, No. 1, pp. 554-59.

Osoba, A.M. (1982), "Productivity and The Wage System", *Productivity,* Vol. 23, No. 3, pp. 323-30.

Ozmucur, S. (2003), "Wage and Productivity Differentials in Private and Public Manufacturing : The Case of Turkey", Industrial Organization, *Economics Working Paper Archive* at WUSTL.

Papola, T.S. (1970), *Principles of Wage Determination—An Empirical Study,* Somaiya Publications Pvt. Ltd., Mumbai.

———, (1976), "Framework for a National Wage Policy", *Productivity,* Vol. 17, pp. 317-27.

Patibandla, M. (1994), "Defunct Economist and Economic Policy Reforms in India", *Economic and Political Weekly*, Nov. 5-12, pp. 2935-39.

Patibandla, M. and Mallikarjun, M. (1996), "Economic Reforms and Industrial Growth", *Economic and Political Weekly*, May 11, pp. 1118-21.

Peterson, W.C. (1994), *Silent Depression : Twenty-five Years of Wage Squeeze and Middle-Class Decline*, New York : Norton, p. 232.

Poddar, V. (1966), *Cement Industry in India*, Asia Publishing House, Delhi.

Pradhan, G. and Barik, K. (1998), "Fluctuating Total Factor Productivity in India : Evidence from Selected Polluting Industries"', *Economic and Political Weekly*, Feb. 28, , pp. M-25 to M-30.

Raman, M.V.V. (1972), "Quality Strategy for Indian Industries", *Productivity*, National Seminar on Productivity, 24-25 March, 39-44.

Rao, B.P. (1980), "Productivity-Linked Bonus", *Productivity*, July-Sept., Vol. 21, No. 2.

Rao, J.M. (1996a), "Manufacturing Productivity Growth : Method and Measurement" *Economic and Political Weekly*, Nov. 2, pp. 2927-37.

———, (1996b), "Indices of Industrial Productivity Growth Disaggregation and Interpretation", *Economic and Political Weekly*, Dec. 7, pp. 3177-88.

Rao, K.C.S. and Madhavilatha, (1990), "Productivity and Operating Efficiency in Public Enterprises : A Study", *Prajnan*, Vol. XIX, No. 1, pp. 5-29.

Raychaudhiri, B. (1996), "Measurement of Capital Stocks in Indian Industries", *Economic and Political Weekly*, May 25.

Reddy, B.B. (1987), "Capacity Utilisation in Indian Industry", *Productivity*, Vol. 28, No. 2, pp. 133-40.

Reynolds, L.G. (1959), *Labour Economics and Labour Relations*, New Jersey, Prentice Hall.

Reynolds, H. (1957), "The Impact of Collective Bargaining on the Wage Structure in USA, in Dunlop, J.T. (ed.), *ibid.*, p. 208.

Ringstad, V. and Griliches, Z. (1971), *Economies of Scale and the Form of Production Function*, North-Holland Publishing Co., Amsterdam.

Robinson (1970), "Some Problems on Definition and Measurement of Capital", in *Collected Economic Papers*, Vol. II, Basil Blackwell, Oxford, pp. 197-208.

Rogers, M. and Vernon, G., "Wage Inequality and Productivity Growth : Motivating Carrots and Crippling Sticks", *SKOPE Research Paper No. 40*, Spring 2002, pp. 1-37.

Royal Commission on Labour (1969), "Report of the Royal Commission on Labour", Government of India, Ministry of Labour, New Delhi, para 15, p. 10.

Sachindranath, K.P. (1973), "Pre-requisites for Sharing the Gains of Productivity", *Productivity*, Feb. 1.

Saget, C. (2001), "Is the Minimum Wage an Effective Tool to Promote Decent Work and Reduce Poverty? The Experience of Selected Developing Countries", *Employment Paper, 2001/13*, International Labour Office, Geneva.

Saha, A. (1990), "A Multi-Factor Productivity Measurement Model", *Productivity*, Vol. 30 , Nov. 4, Jan.-Mar.

Sahoo, B. (1985), *Wage, Price, Productivity and Industrial Planning*, Ashish Publishing House, Delhi.

Sardana, G.D. and Vrat, P. (1991), "Productivity Management : A Programme for Implementation", *Productivity*, Vol. 32 No. 1, April-June.

Sarma, J.N. and Rao, Y.V.A. (1990), "Indian Cement Industry—A Regional Analysis", *Indian Journal of Regional Science*, Vol. 22, pp. 33-44.

Sekhara, C., Rao, K. and Madhavi Latha, K. (1990), "Productivity and Operating Efficiency in Public Enterprises : A Study", *Prajnan*, Vol. XIX, No. 1, pp. 5-29.

Seth, V.K. (1994), "Labour Marketing Restructuring and Structural Adjustment", *Indian Journal of Labour Economics*, Vol. 37, No. 4, pp. 523-34.

Schreiber, S. (2001), "Will a Productivity Oriented Wage Policy Stabilize the Labour Share?" *CES Economic Studies*, Aufsatze, 1/2001, pp. 25-40.

Shah, P.S. (1981), "Productivity", *Business Standard*, Oct. 22, pp. 7-8.

Shivamaggi, H.B., Rajagopalan, N., Venkatachalam, T.R. (1968), "Wages, Labour Productivity and Cost of Production, 1951-61", *Economic and Political Weekly*, May 4, Vol. III, No. 18, pp. 710-16.

Shram Bureau (1992), *Wage Fixation in Industry and Agriculture in India*, Shram Mantrayala, Bharat Sarkar, Chandigarh.

Singh, L. (1987), "Productivity Trends and Factor Substitutability in Punjab Industry", *Indian Journal of Economics*, Vol. LXVII, No. 266, pp. 399-408, Jan.

Singh, M.M. (1983), "Productivity and Social Changes", *Productivity*, Vol. 24, No. 3, 225-29.

Singh, T. and Ajit, D. (1995), "Production Functions in the Manufacturing Industries in India : 1974-90", *RBI Occasional Papers*, Vol. 16, No. 2, June.

Singh, R.R. (1966), "Productivity Trends and Wages", *Eastern Economist*, April, pp. 216-32.

Singh, S. and Kitchlu, T.N. (1991), "Industrial Relations and Productivity", *Yojana*, Vol. XXXV, Nos. XIV and XV, Aug. 15, p. 71.

Sinha, J.N. and Sawhney, P.K. (1970), *Wages and Productivity in Selected Indian Industries*, New Indian Press, Vikas Publications, N. Delhi.

Skeffington, R. (2002), "Why High Productivity Means More Jobs", *BRW*, Vol. 24, No. 11.

Smith, I.G. (1973), "The Measurement of Productivity", *Productivity*, pp. 38-39.

Solow, R.M. (1957), "Technical Change of Aggregate Production Function", *Review of Economics and Statistics*, Vol. 39(3), August, pp. 312-20.

Somani, G.D. (1961), "A Case Study in Cotton Textile", *Productivity*, Vol. 22, June-July.

Sreenivasan, K. (1964), *Productivity and Social Environment*, Asia Publishing House, N. Delhi.

Srinivas, S. and Sattinger, M. (2003), "The Employment-Productivity Relationship with Employment Criteria", *Report NEP*—LAB—2003-07-13.

Srivastav, J.P. (1982), *Labour Productivity—Socio-Economic Dimensions*, Oxford and IBH Publishing Co., New Delhi, p. 30.

Stanislao, J. and James, C.F. (1976), "Improved Manufacturing Techniques and Productivity", *Productivity*, Vol. 17 (1), pp. 26-36

Stanislao, J. (1977), "Increase Productivity Through Motivation", *Productivity*, Vol. 18, pp. 321-29.

Stonier, A.W. and Hague, D.C. (1957), *A Text Book of Economic Theory*, Longmans Green and Co., London.

Subramanian, K.N. (1970), *Wages in India*, Tata McGraw-Hill Publishers, p. 174.

Suri, G.K. (1976), *Productivity, Wages and Industrial Relations*, N. Delhi : Affiliated East West Press Ltd.

———, (1979), "Training for Productivity in the Industry", *Productivity*, Vol. XX, No. 2, July-Sept.

Szendrovits, A.Z. (1988), "Increasing of Productivity Through Stimulated Decision Making", *Productivity*, Vol. 28, No. 4, 335-44.

Tatom, J.A. (1979), "The Productivity Problem", *Review of Federal Banks of St. Louis*, Sept., pp. 13-16.

Tiwari and Trivedi, (1975), "Production Technique and Its Impact on Labour Productivity in Cotton Textile Industry", *Indian Journal of Economics*, Vol. 17 Oct.

Trivedi, P. and *et. al.* (1999), "Productivity of the Indian Manufacturing Sector : 1973-74 to 1994-95", *Reserve Bank of India Annual Report 1998-99*, p. 51, Development Research Group in Reserve Bank of India, Mumbai.

Tulpule, B. and Datta, R.C. (1988), "Real Wages in Indian Industry", *Economic and Political Weekly*, Oct. 29, pp. 2275-78.

Upender, M. (1996), "Elasticity of Labour Productivity in Indian Manufacturing", *Economic and Political Weekly*, May 25, pp. M-7 to M-10.

Usher, D. (1980), *Measurement of Capital*, Chicago University Press, Chicago.

Verma, P. and Subbayamma, G. (1985), "The Inter-Industry Wage Structure in India : Recent Experience", *Indian Journal of Labour Economics*, Vol. XXVII, Oct.

Verma, P. (1987), *Labour Economics and Industrial Relations*, Tata McGraw Hill Publishing Company Ltd., New Delhi.

Verner, D. (2000), "Wage and Productivity Gaps : Evidence from Ghana", *The World Bank Group, Policy Research Working Paper 2168*, pp. 1-47.

Verter, V. and Eyler, M.A. (1990), "Productivity Measurement, Evaluation and Improvement", *Productivity*, Vol. 31, No. 1, April-June.

Vora, S.M. (1994), "Industrial Productivity Trends : State-wise Analysis", *Productivity*, Vol. 35, No. 1, April-June.

Weiner, H. (1973), "Productivity and Practical Idealism", *Productivity*, National Seminar on Productivity and Trade Union Movement, 19-20, Aug., 113-19.

Wong, S.T. and Heng, O.L. (2001), "First World Per Capita Income But Third World Income Structure? Wage Share and Productivity Improvement in Singapore", Singapore Department of Statistics, *Statistics Singapore Newsletter*, pp. 1-10.

Yotopoulos, P.A. and Nugent, J.B. (1976), *Economics of Development : Empirical Investigations*, New York, Harper and Row Publishers.

Zavodny, M. (1999), "Unions and the Wage-Productivity Gap", Federal Reserve Bank of Atlanta, *Economic Review*, Second Quarter, pp. 44-53.

Index